Archaeology in the Age of the Internet

CAA 97

Computer Applications
and
Quantitative Methods in Archaeology

Proceedings of the 25th Anniversary Conference
University of Birmingham, April 1997

Edited by

Lucie Dingwall, Sally Exon, Vince Gaffney,
Sue Laflin and Martijn van Leusen

BAR International Series 750

1999

Published in 2019 by
BAR Publishing, Oxford

BAR International Series 750

Archaeology in the Age of the Internet - CAA 97

ISBN 9780860549451 paperback
ISBN 9781407350738 e-book
DOI https://doi.org/10.30861/9780860549451

BAR Publishing is the trading name of British Archaeological Reports (Oxford) Ltd. British Archaeological Reports was first incorporated in 1974 to publish the BAR Series, International and British. In 1992 Hadrian Books Ltd became part of the BAR group. This volume was originally published by Archaeopress in conjunction with British Archaeological Reports (Oxford) Ltd / Hadrian Books Ltd, the Series principal publisher, in 1999. This present volume is published by BAR Publishing, 2016.

BAR
PUBLISHING

BAR titles are available from:

BAR Publishing
122 Banbury Rd, Oxford, OX2 7BP, UK
EMAIL info@barpublishing.com
PHONE +44 (0)1865 310431
FAX +44 (0)1865 316916
www.barpublishing.com

Archaeology in the Age of the Internet

CAA 97

Contents

Papers marked *(ABSTRACT)* are found in full on the accompanying CD-Rom.

Section 4: Database Developments

Section 5: Vital Preservation of Great Information

Section 6: Geophysics and Remote Sensing

Section 11: Finds Analysis and Curation

Demonstrations held on the CD-ROM (No longer available)

CAA 97

Archaeology in the Age of the Internet: Proceedings of the 25th Anniversary Conference of CAA University of Birmingham, April 1997

Preface

This volume, and its CD-ROM (which is no longer available), contain the proceedings of the 25th Anniversary Conference on **Computer Applications and Quantitative Methods in Archaeology** (CAA97), held at the University of Birmingham between the 11th and 13th of April 1997.

On its 25th anniversary the CAA conference returned to its birthplace. On the 26th and 27th January, 1973, the first meeting of the Computer Applications in Archaeology group (convened by Sue Laflin) was held at the University of Birmingham, and one of the themes in the current proceedings is to review the history of the conference, not as a nostalgic exercise, but as a means of assessing the progress made by computational and quantitative sciences within archaeology. This is particularly apposite as the organisation and publication of the 1997 conference represents, in a sense, our entry into the "Information Age". Taking as its theme 'Archaeology in the Age of the Internet', it is the first time the conference has been largely prepared, publicised and organized using Internet services such as E-mail and the WWW; it is also the first time that the proceedings have been published digitally on a CD-ROM.

Editing and publishing these proceedings has been a pleasant if, at times, arduous task, and we are grateful to the authors for putting up with our requests for the additional formatting needed to standardise the digital 'look and feel' of the papers. The only items which may, on occasion, have escaped our formatting constraints are the authors' image files, for which we would like to apologise here.

As is usual for CAA publications, the papers have been grouped into themes following the division of the conference into sessions. Of the original 115 papers presented at the conference, 85 are published here.

A Note on the CD-ROM (No longer available)

Whilst the CD-ROM contains the full proceedings, this was not feasible for the accompanying paper volume, which is constrained within limits set by printing costs. Consequently, the Editors decided that the limited space available within the paper publication would be best used by printing those sessions that a) were the shortest and b) contained no extensive colour graphics or interactive features.

The content of the CD-ROM is written in HTML, the public language for WWW text documents. Although the medium of CD-ROM may still be somewhat unfamiliar as a publishing medium to archaeologists, we confidently expect this to be a temporary state of affairs. We can readily anticipate that all future proceedings will be published in a variety of digital formats.

The first or "start" page which you should load to begin using the CAA97 proceedings is *fCAA97.htm*. You can then simply follow desired links or use navigation shortcuts.

The browser interface to this CD-ROM employs frames and colors in order to facilitate navigation between the various types of information contained in the CAA97 proceedings. Most documents, including the table of contents, the papers and abstracts, appear in the 'main' frame. In cases where you click on a link to request further details on, say, a particular reference or author, those details will appear in the lower left hand 'details' frame. The third and smallest frame, in the lower right hand, contains navigation shortcuts to all parts of the CAA97 proceedings except the papers themselves, and displays these in the main frame so you can browse them more easily.

This scheme is supported by color coding. Abstracts and Author details have a light blue background color whereas other documents have an off-white background color. When no information is requested in the bottom frames, these will return to a 'waiting' state indicated by the orange color.

Screen size and the image window

This CD-ROM has been optimised for viewing on an SVGA (800 by 600 pixel) screen, but viewing will improve if you have access to a larger screen, especially with the many large graphics files included in the papers. For images that are too large to fit into the main screen area, we have provided clickable 'thumbnail' images that will open a new full-screen window to display the image itself. By clicking on the Close button of this window you are returned to the main browser screen.

A Note on the Demonstrations held on the CD-Rom (No longer available)

Demonstrations included on the CD.

Detailed Information about how to view individual demonstrations is held within the relevant paper on the CD. Papers with demos have a link to the related demonstration before the bibliography.

VRML, Virtual Reality and Visualisation: The best tool for the job?
G. T. Goodrick

To view the demo worlds provided for this paper you will need to download the VTV Viewer from WARP (www.warp.com). The viewer runs on Win95 and on Win3.1 if you install win32s.

A Computerized Data Base for Lithic Use-Wear Analysis.
E.S. Lohse, D. Sammons

The demonstration will run on Windows95. No viewer is needed.

Mapping the Fourth Dimension: the TimeMap Project
Ian Johnson

Example animations from the TimeMap Project. Included are a quicktime movie and an MPEG movie. The MPEG animation can be run from Netscape Navigator or Internet Explorer. The Quicktime plug-in is included in the latest versions of Netscape Navigator. It can also be downloaded from http://www.apple.com/quicktime/

From The Ground Up: Visualising Ligurian Archaeological Sites
Michael McCullagh, Roberto Maggi, Mark Pearce, Jerry Ratcliffe

An AVI video with sound. This demonstration can be run from recent versions of Netscape Navigator or Internet Explorer.

Acknowledgements

The editors would like to thank the following individuals:

All the volunteers who worked so hard to make the conference a success including; Ernie Jenks, Gerry Richardson, Ian Spears, Vasiliki Vlachodimitropoulou, Anthony Jones, Damien Carr, Mark Hewson, Neville Taylor, Mark Sweeting, Lisa Davis, Paul Hopkins, M. Broadhurst, Ann Aylott, Tikshna Mandal, Anne Hairie, Sue Beighton and Richard Thomas for working so hard before and during the conference. Thanks to the arts faculty computing officers Graham Smith and Costas Physentzides and all staff in Information Services for solving emergency networking problems.
Mavis Sharp for assisted in making the organisation run so smoothly.
Edward Farrar and Julie Zacaroli at the conference office for all their help and patience.
David Dawson, Diana Murray and Jennifer Stewart for loaning us equipment.
Graham Norrie and Richard Pannel for their technical support.
Michael Finney and Sue Bennett in Maths for all their help.
Mark Breedon and Harry Buglass assisted with artwork
Ann Humphries for organising the dinner
Helen Watson for her help with formatting the paper text, Monica Pendavingh for assistance in checking links in the web version and Dr. Roger White for reading the paper text.
Finally we would lke to thank everyone who agreed to chair sessions and contributed papers.

The Editors,

Lucie Dingwall, Sally Exon, Vince Gaffney, Sue Laflin, and Martijn van Leusen

ARCHAEOLOGY
IN THE
AGE OF THE INTERNET

CAA 97

Section 1
25 Years of CAA

CAA 97

Twenty Five Years of Computer Applications in Archaeology

Susan Laflin.

To celebrate twenty-five years of the conference on "Computer Applications and Quantitative Methods in Archaeology", the conference held at Birmingham in the spring of 1997 included a section on this topic. Irwin Scollar was invited to give the keynote address, which is included here: Irwin Scollar "25 Years of Computer Applications in Archaeology". This was followed by a short statement by the founder of the conference: Susan Laflin "Twenty-five Years of CAA: a Personal View" .

The first morning session consisted of four invited speakers on the main application areas featured in the conference throughout the 25 years.

Archaeological prospection has been an important area for over twenty-five years. The School of Archaeological Sciences at the University of Bradford has been active throughout this period and so were invited to give the survey of this area. A. Aspinall and J.G.B. Haigh "Twenty-five years of archaeological prospection" .

Databases and "databanks" have always been recognised as an application where computers could make a valuable contribution, first in America and then elsewhere. They have been used for excavation recording, sites and monuments records in counties and nationally, museum collections and any other application which generates a large collection of data. This aspect is covered in the paper by Jennifer Sewart: Jennifer Stewart "Has 25 Years of Computing Provided Greater Physical and Intellectual Access to Archaeology?"

Coming on to the more mathematical applications, simulation is an important area which has been somewhat neglected by archaeologists. Professor J. Doran from the University of Essex gave an excellent survey at the conference but sadly did not have time to supply a written version for the proceedings. Other statistical techniques have been more widely used and, in the final paper of the morning session Clive Orton from London University gave his paper: Clive Robert Orton "Plus ça Change? - 25 Years of Statistics in Archaeology" .

The afternoon sessions contained a number of other papers. Two speakers also submitted written versions and these are included here. John Wilcock presented his account of statistics over the past 25 years: John Wilcock "Getting the Best Fit? 25 Years of Statistical Techniques in Archaeology" and Morgan Tamplin described the progress in Canada over the same period: Morgan J. Tamplin "Archaeological Computing in Canada: The First (and Last) 25 Years". Three other speakers also attempted to predict future trends in various areas, but none of these wished to have their thoughts recorded in print (and possibly quoted against them in future years).

Contact details

Susan Laflin
University of Birmingham
Edgbaston
Bimingham B152TT
UK
email: S.Laflin@bham.ac.uk

25 Years of Computer Applications in Archaeology

Irwin Scollar

Abstract

Trends in application of computer methods in archaeology were analysed by studying the percentages of 703 CAA papers from 1973 to 1996 devoted to a group of major themes. The result closely mirrors emergent low-cost hard- and pre-packaged software availability. There are some constant areas of interest typified by database management. Recent years show an ever increasing dependence on applications of commercial soft- and hardware with innovation a relative rarity.

1 Trends in application of computer methods

One way to analyse trends in the application of computer methods to archaeology may be to look at the percentages of papers devoted to various subjects at the CAA meetings since their inception. From 1973 to 1997 there were 703 titles published or submitted but not yet published in 1996 and 1997. In this analysis, it will be assumed that the titles of the papers bear a reasonable relationship to their content, and when this can not be determined, a paper was classified as "Other". It is also implicitly assumed that the "supply" of methods or results described by the papers' titles anticipates or reflects "demand" for such methods or services in the archaeological community at or near the time at which they were presented.

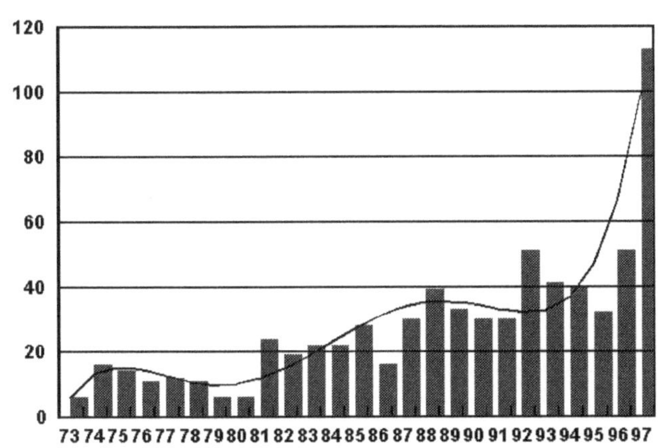

Figure 1: Papers published or submitted by year to CAA

Figure 1 shows a rough four-fold increase in the number of published papers for the first 25 years. The large peak in the submissions to the CAA 97 meeting may not be reflected in the number of papers which will actually be published. A high order polynomial has been fitted to the data to show the trend. The mild peaks in the mid-1970s and late 1980s perhaps represent a more favourable financial situation for travel grants in those years rather than any spectacular technological developments, although these are the years of widespread introduction of PC's. The long-term trend surely reflects both increasing computer awareness in the archaeological community and the availability of ever more reasonably priced hard- and software which can be used or developed to satisfy its needs.

A subjective factor in this analysis is the scheme used for classifying the subjects of the papers. A number of such classifications for this kind of material have been presented in the past as given in the references. These are:

Scollar 1982

1. Statistics
2. Databases & Site Recording
3. Scientific Data

Ryan 1988

1. Quantitative Methods and Simulation
2. Finds Analysis
3. Survey and Excavation Recording
4. Sites and Monuments Records
5. Geophysics
6. Expert Systems & Knowledge Representation
7. Education
8. Publication
9. Scientific Techniques
10. Museums
11. General

Kamermans 1994

1. Statistics
2. Database
3. Graphics and Image Processing
4. GIS
5. Artificial Intelligence
6. Education and Publication

In the current paper the following classes will be used:

1. Statistics

2. Database & Site Recording
3. Graphics, Image Processing, CAD and VR
4. Education, Publication and The Web
5. GIS
6. Prospection & Remote Sensing
7. Simulation and Artificial Intelligence
8. Pattern Recognition
9. Other

This last group differs slightly from Kamermans' classes through the addition of the "Other" category for papers which could not be classified by their titles, and by separating Prospection from Image Processing and Simulation & AI from Pattern Recognition. They are rougher categories than those specified by Ryan. This seems to justified, since many themes fell into two or more of his classes.

Taking all the years together, it can be seen from Figure 2 that Statistics and Database related papers dominate in equal parts to the extent of 46% of the total number of papers. The first was most popular at the beginning and in the middle years, the second has enjoyed fluctuating but continuous popularity throughout the last 25 years.

Graphics, Image Processing, CAD and Virtual Reality techniques are third in the popularity contest at 13% of the papers, with a tendency to increase up to the mid-90's.

Educational papers and especially Web related matters enjoy equal popularity compared to GIS techniques with 9% each, the popularity in both cases rising sharply from the mid-1980s.

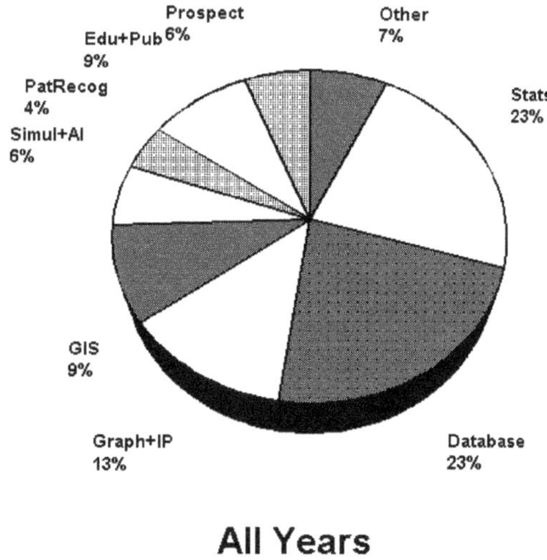

Figure 2: Categories of subjects, all years

Archaeological Prospecting (Remote Sensing) is a small special interest segment of nearly constant proportion, equal over the years in total magnitude to AI and Simulation. Pattern Recognition is the least popular category, and it has practically been abandoned today.

Examining the trends of each item individually, one can see peaks and valleys for which plausible explanations will be offered.

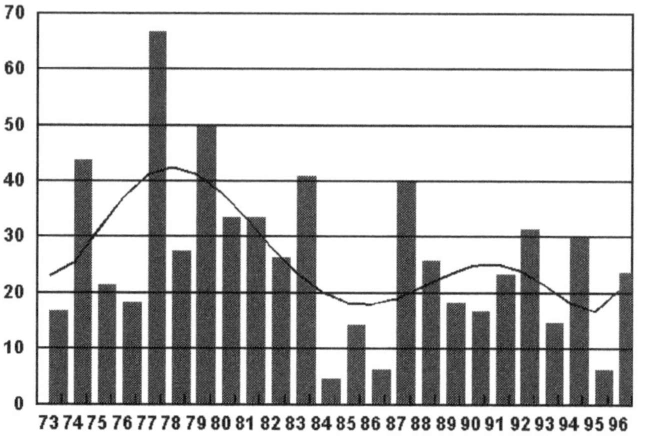

Figure 3: Statistics

In the 1960s statistical methods developed for mainframes, and various computational techniques associated with ancillary sciences, were among the few practical applications of computers in archaeology (Scollar 1982). This reached its peak in the late 1970s after the appearance of seminal publications such as Doran and Hodson (1976) and Hodder and Orton (1976). A few programs, usually in Fortran, were available and widely used. Interest flagged in the 1980's but revived slightly during the early 1990's with the emergence of standard commercial statistical packages having modest graphics for PC's. At the same time the impact of Correspondence Analysis, developed in the 1970s, made itself felt in the archaeological world, both factors probably leading to the second visible peak.

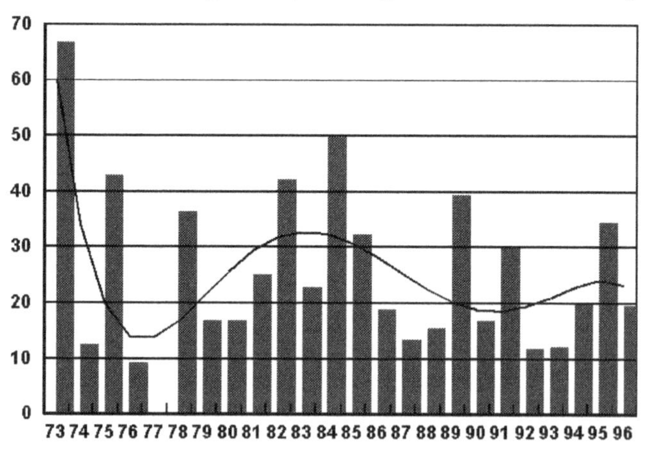

Figure 4: Database

Database methods enjoyed their first boom in the early 1970s, being primarily applied to museum and site inventories on mainframes. Interest flagged until the introduction of Dbase and similar products for microcomputers and the IBM PC in the late 1970s and early 1980s. After that, a roughly constant level of papers continue to deal with database themes. More recent developments in metadatabases in the mid-1990s have revived interest in the general site recording problem which now appears to have been solved. Large networked databases, which achieved some degree of maturity by the early 1990s, also contributed to a recent peak in papers. This has presumably been the consequence of both soft- and hardware availability and the backing of relatively prosperous monuments protection services in several countries.

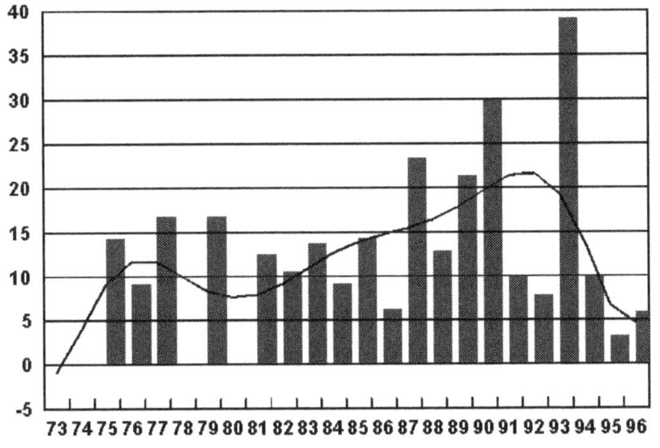

Figure 5: Graphics, Image Processing

The application of graphics, image processing and, more recently, virtual reality techniques was obviously driven by hardware availability at reasonable prices. In 1975, the first semiconductor display originally developed for NASA was bought at a — for archaeology — astronomical price. Scanners and film recorders were similarly expensive. There was only one such installation (at the author's laboratory) in late 1975 (Scollar 1977a; 1977b).

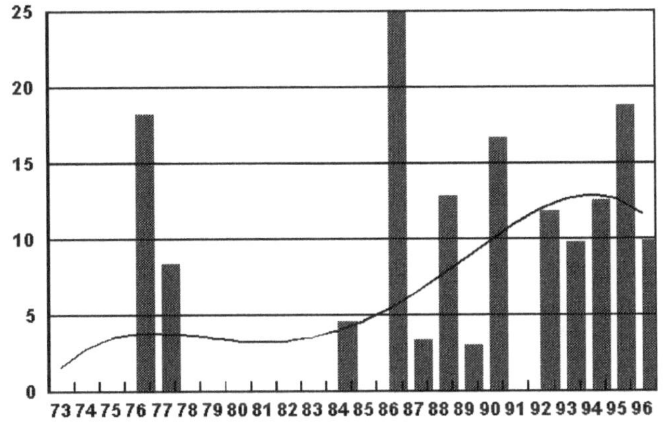

Figure 6: Education, Publication, The Web

When hardware prices dropped throughout the 1980s and 1990s, usage rose to reach a peak in the early 1990s. Today, image processing and high level graphics are on everyone's desk, software has matured, and processors are easily able to handle the computational load which was a challenge for the minicomputers of the mid-1970s. Virtual reality methods are not yet reflected in the diagram, but they will surely contribute to a new peak during the next few years.

A few isolated papers in the mid-1970s reflect the appearance of text editors and primitive text formatting software for minicomputers, and mainframes permitted some simple publication experiments. The spread and acceptance of word processing in the early 1980s, coupled with page-making software, produced the peak which started in the mid-1980s. The introduction of the World Wide Web in the mid-1990s brought publications oriented toward web browsers, probably the most popular new application in this area.

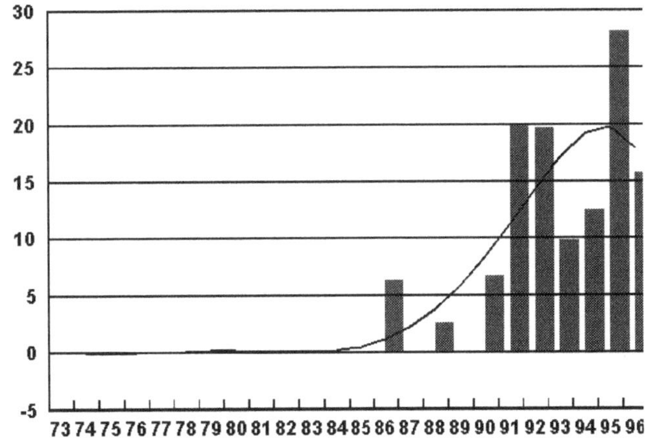

Figure 7: Geographic Information Systems (GIS)

Geographic information systems applied to archaeology emerged as a natural consequence of cheap high level graphic displays, falling hard disk prices facilitating storage of maps and map related data, scanners and related digitising equipment, all of which resulted in an explosion of interest supported by effective commercial software in the early 1990s which continues to this day. Although the novelty is wearing off, it still remains one of the most prominent topics in recent meetings

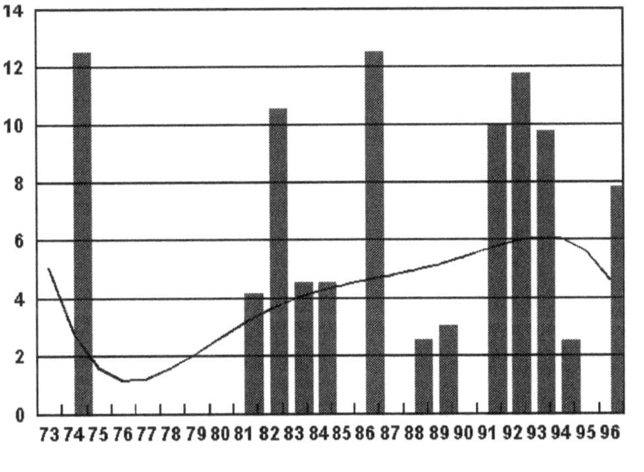

Figure 8: Archaeological Prospection, Remote Sensing

Along with statistics, evaluation of data from geophysical measurements on sites is one of the oldest practical application of computers in archaeology. This began well over a decade before the first CAA meeting in 1973. The moving force was the 'home-grown' development of measuring instruments specialised in digital recording of a large amount of data. It is the only area in this survey where hardware progress was pushed by archaeological requirements up to the 1980s, when commercial equipment replaced early pioneering efforts. At the author's laboratory, resistivity data was evaluated via computer and published as early as 1959. Magnetic data followed in the early 1960s. The work done in the late 70's is classified here under Image Processing, since this was mainly devoted to treatment of aerial photographs and infrared scans.

Activity rose slowly throughout the 1980s and mid-1990s. During the 1980s, work reflects efforts in mapping of oblique aerial photographs and magnetic data. The peak in the 1990s reflects the coming of age of commercial ground penetrating radar with digital recording instruments.

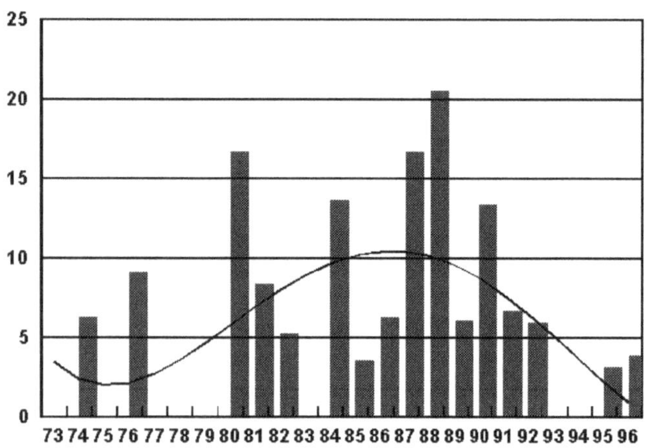

Figure 9: Simulation and Artificial Intelligence

Artificial intelligence methods enjoyed a mild boom during the 1980s, but interest died out almost completely afterward. Simulation techniques have had a low level of interest throughout the CAA period. AI methods have not met with acceptance in the archaeological community as a whole, and this resistance is probably the reason for the abandonment of such techniques.

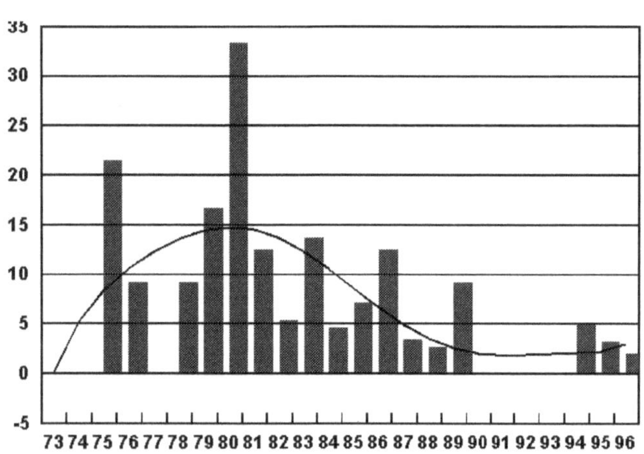

Figure 10: Pattern Recognition

Great hopes too were placed in pattern recognition methods in the 1970s and 1980s, but interest has waned, probably due to resistance in the archaeological community to the replacement of human skill by what is generally considered to be inferior techniques when applied to shapes and appearances of archaeological objects. Like AI, these approaches have never satisfied archaeological requirements, despite the great enthusiasm of their proponents in the early years and the ever-repeated invention of devices for measuring and recording of archaeological objects. Site recording devices for use in the field were also a fertile source of invention, but only commercial digital measuring instruments have achieved wide acceptance.

2 Sources of error

The analysis in this paper has a number of defects, of which the reader should be aware. These are:

Data:

1. The title of a paper may incorrectly reflect its content.
2. Years with few papers have high variance in percentages, and these distort the diagrams.
3. The "Others" category possibly hides meaningful data.
4. Published papers are not equal to papers actually presented, but because of lack of appropriate records it is not known how large this factor is in any given year.

Evaluation:

1. The subjective categories may be too coarse or too fine.
2. The use of a polynomial fit to the data is arbitrary.

Interpretation:

1. The volume of papers may actually fluctuate with available travel money! Papers are given to get a travel grant and do not reflect real work!
2. "Supply" may not be correlated with "demand", i.e. acceptance by the archaeological community of the various techniques may depend on other factors.

Nonetheless, it is felt that even if the data should not be relied upon quantitatively, the curves do correlate well with the subjective impressions of many of those who have witnessed the developments described.

3 Conclusions

The field has been driven by hardware availability at prices which archaeological institutions can afford, and has been limited by available software. Like almost all other disciplines, the field has been financially restricted since its inception. Methods and means derived elsewhere have gone in search of existing archaeological problems to which they can be applied. Archaeological problems do not successfully drive means and methods except in prospecting, because other areas had to profit from the greater Research and Development effort applied elsewhere. Nonetheless, despite this 'hand-me-down' position, archaeological computing has indeed come of age.

If one asks, "Did computer methods make archaeological tasks known prior to computers easier, faster or cheaper", the answer is probably "Yes". If one asks, "Did computer methods reveal or lead to new archaeological knowledge", the answer is probably "Rarely".

4 Survey

An informal survey was conducted by the author on the Archcomp-L listserver. Out of ca. 350 server subscribers, only 8 replied. Nonetheless, the results are interesting.

Considered Acceptable by the respondents:

Statistics:

1. Statistical packages
2. Simple data analysis with explanatory graphics via spreadsheets.
3. Bayesian calibration of 14C dates.
4. Bootstrapped confidence intervals.

Database methods:

1. The development of easy-to-use DBMS
2. Intrasite metadatabases.
3. Museum collection databases.
4. Large scale networked site databases with GIS.

Graphics, Image Processing, CAD

1. Widespread availability of mapping/CAD/image processing software
2. VR as extension of CAD and GIS
3. Electronic imaging

Prospecting

1. Image processing applied to geophysical and air photo data.
2. Publication, The Web
3. The academic Internet
4. Improving communication between scholars around the world.
5. Reducing the costs of publication.
6. Ubiquity of word-processing and desktop publishing software
7. Electronic publishing

GIS

1. The development of GIS for microcomputers

Other positive results:

1. Persuading archaeologists to think quantitatively.
2. Fostering the creation and curation of mass quantities of raw data.
3. The commercial success of microcomputer inexpensive computing
4. True interaction with analytical procedures
5. Experimenting with data

Considered unacceptable by the respondents:

1. Use of statistics software by people who don't know statistics.
2. All of the above when mis-used, especially DBMS.
3. Impermanence of electronic data.
4. Failure of the community to use the systems for sharing information.
5. Fragmentation of efforts to apply technology to the discipline.
6. Application of artificial intelligence.

A dissenting opinion was offered by Torsten Madsen, Aarhus:

"If anybody thinks that computing has become part of archaeology, then they don't know anything of archaeology & computing. The majority are just as illiterate as ever, so apart from everyone who has learned to type ... on the PC instead of the typewriter, little has changed. There is another thing that everyone can do, and that is to use the Internet. If that is progress then yes, indeed something great has happened with computing in archaeology, but personally I consider WWW to be one of the bad things that has happened to archaeology. My annoyance with WWW is not with the media itself but the reaction towards it from the many who have never cared about computers, but now have "realised" that the value of computers are equal to WWW."

Acknowledgements

I wish to thank Hans Kamermans, Leiden, The Netherlands, for generously sending me his spreadsheet data from an unpublished seminar held in London in 1994 which inspired me to analyse the data in this way, and the following members of the Archcomp-l list server for their helpful e-mailed comments: T.Dye, Honolulu, USA, H. Eiteljorg, Bryn Mawr, USA, J.D. Gillespie, Lethbridge, Canada, J.W. Hoopes, Kansas, USA, S. MacEachern, Brunswick, USA, J. Rehmet, Tuebingen, Germany, T. Madsen, Aarhus, Denmark. Susan Laflin most kindly provided photocopies of all the conference proceedings contents for analysis.

Method

The data was entered using the author's Winbasp entry program, with the years treated as units, the categories treated as types, and counts made by raising their frequencies. This was exported as a Dbase file, imported into Excel to compute the totals and percentages, then linked to Stanford Graphics to make the diagrams and fit the high order polynomial curves.

Bibliography

Doran, J E, and Hodson, F R, 1976 *Mathematics and Computers in Archaeology*, Edinburgh

Hodder, I, and Orton, C, 1976 *Spatial Analysis in Archaeology*, Cambridge

Kamermans, H, and Fennema, K (eds), 1996 Future IT for the past., unpublished seminar 'The Problems and Potentials of Electronic Information for Archaeology' held at the British Academy in 1994, summarised in the preface to: *Computer Applications and Quantitative Methods in Archaeology*, Vol.I (Analecta Praehistorica Leidensia 28), Leiden

Ryan, N, 1988 Bibliography of computer applications and quantitative methods, *Computer Applications and Quantitative Methods in Archaeology* (BAR International Series 446(i), ed. S P Q Rahtz), Oxford

Scollar, I, 1977a An installation for interactive transfer of information from oblique aerial photos to maps (with T.S. Huang, B. Weidner, G. Tang), *Computer Applications in Archaeology*, The Computer Centre, University of Birmingham, 105-118

Scollar, I, 1977b L'informatique appliqué á la photographie aérienne, *L'archeologie* 22, 78-87

Scollar, I, 1982 Thirty years of computer archaeology and the future, or looking backwards and forwards at the same time while trying not to twist one's neck. *CAA Conference Proceedings*, 1982, 189-198

Contact details

Irwin Scollar
The Unkelbach Valley Software Works
In der Au 9
D 53424 Remagen
GERMANY
email: al001@rs1.rrz.uni-koeln.de

Twenty five Years of CAA: a Personal View

Susan Laflin.

CAA 97

1 Introduction

It is now twenty-five years since I first organised a meeting on Computer Applications in Archaeology and the situation has changed greatly since that time. That meeting consisted of a small group of pioneers who could see the potential relevance of computers to archaeology and wished to develop these applications. At that time, most archaeologists regarded computers as strange arcane systems, used only by scientists and mathematicians and, being unfamiliar, viewed them with great suspicion and hostility. However the group who gathered then were sufficiently enthusiastic that it seemed reasonable to continue holding such meetings.

2 Motive for starting these Conferences

The next year, in a cold and frosty January, a residential weekend conference was held with participants from America, Canada, and Germany as well as from Britain. The papers were collected and published as a separate book of proceedings and I remember this as the first of a long and successful series of international conferences. In January 1974, the aims of the conference were first formulated:

"To bring together archaeologists and computer scientists, to discuss present achievements in this area, and to suggest ideas for the future."

At that time, the first aim, to bring computer people and archaeologists together and get some sort of discussion going, seemed to me to be the outstanding need - my main motive for organising these conferences at all. From my position as a computer scientist, I could see the potential for using computers to aid in the study of archaeology and I set out on a crusade to explain these possibilities to archaeologists. At first, the progress was slow and the majority of delegates were computer scientists and mathematicians with an interest in archaeology. Gradually, as the idea of using computers in archaeology became more widespread, the proportion of archaeologists has increased and so has the number and variety of the applications. The greatest influence on this has been the spread of personal computers and now the arrival of the internet and world-wide-web. Today, every student starting an archaeology course is aware of the many ways in which computers can speed up and assist their work and there is an expectation that computers will be used by some if not all the members of any archaeological team. Even those most resistant to computers are likely to make use of word-processors. Most of these changes have taken place in society as a whole and are not limited to archaeologists or influenced by the CAA conferences. However I like to think that the news may have spread a little further or a little faster among the archaeological community because of the existence of these conferences as a venue for the exchange of news and ideas.

3 The Future of the Conference

If you compare the original aims with those in the current constitution, you will notice considerable similarity. However this does not mean that conference has outlived its usefulness now that the original need has been satisfied. The relative importance of each aim and the interpretation placed upon them, has changed with the changing situation. Obviously it is necessary to bring together archaeologists and computer scientists as well as mathematicians (including statisticians), if only to provide speakers and audience for the papers. The aim to give a survey of present (or current) work in the field is also fairly obvious for a conference of this nature.

Aims in current constitution:

1. to bring together archaeologists, mathematicians and computer scientists;
2. to encourage communication between these disciplines;
3. to give a survey of present work in the field;
4. to stimulate discussion and future progress.

The methods to be used to encourage communication and stimulate discussion and future progress may need more careful thought and the precise definition of the field to be covered by such a conference will need to be considered from time to time. I can think of a number of ways in which a conference entitled "Computer Applications in Archaeology" could be viewed, and have suggested three possibilities.

1. A meeting of Archaeologists to discuss archeaological results using computer software.
2. A meeting of writers of software for archaeologists to discuss relevant computing techniques and algorithms.
3. A marketplace where those selling software designed for archaeologists can meet and display their wares.

I hope the conference will be extended to include aspects of all these, as well as others I have not yet considered. I think it would be sad if any one of these became the sole aim of the conference, because I feel that the past success has depended on the breadth of its coverage and I hope the future will be equally successful. These have all been covered to some extent in the present and recent conferences, although they could be given greater emphasis and encouragement.

The first function has been met here in this conference, especially for the landscape archaeology practitioners and I hope this will continue to expand and develop. The third one is to some extent covered by the demonstrations, but it could become a little more obvious. If future organisers wish to invite traders to come and sell software at the conference, this would need to be stated more clearly in the documentation. I think it could be a very useful service included in the conference, but this for others to decide in the future.

The second function is again covered to some extent in this and other recent conferences, but could also become more explicit and deliberate. It would need a deliberate attempt to look at the underlying principles of particular methods - for example some of the ray-tracing techniques published in the SIGGRAPH proceedings could provide a very efficient viewshed analysis in GIS software. Are they used in the present systems? If not, how much advantage in speed would they produce? This would require a workshop-style session which could be held within the conference and might lead to noticeable improvements in the efficiency of the software generally available.

To conclude, we have come a long way in the past twenty-five years. I hope we shall do equally well in the next twenty-five.

Contact details

Susan Laflin
University of Birmingham
Edgbaston
Bimingham B152TT
UK
email: S.Laflin@bham.ac.uk

Twenty five years of archaeological prospection

A. Aspinall and J.G.B. Haigh

CAA 97

Abstract

Much of the basic instrumentation in current use in archaeological geophysics had already been developed by 1972. The next fifteen years were a period of consolidation and adaptation for general use. The last ten years, up to 1997, have seen the introduction of new methods of field investigation, such as ground-penetrating radar and other electromagnetic methods. In Britain, partly as a result of legislation on land utilisation, there has been an explosion of archaeological interest in geophysical survey. The improvements in instrumentation have been paralleled by developments in data handling, presentation and interpretation. The problems of the 1970s were mainly concerned with the visualisation of data, allowing only minimal interpretation. In the 1980s, as increasing computer power became available, methods of data enhancement were introduced. In recent years attention has been focused on reconstructing the physical objects which give rise to the observed data, only a short step from direct archaeological interpretation.The future prospects are towards the interlinked development of instrumentation and interpretative methodology.

1 Introduction - the state of development twenty-five years ago

To discuss what has happened in geophysical prospection for archaeology over the last twenty-five years, we must first look back to the "state of the art" in 1972, at the start of the period. At that time the only journal devoted exclusively to the subject was *Prospezioni Archeologiche*, which had been founded in 1966 under the motivation of Richard Linington for the Lerici Foundation in Rome. Since it ceased publication in 1984, it is opportune to look at the contents of the issue for 1972-73, where we discover that many of the articles still look reasonably up-to-date! The paper by Linington (1972) himself, for instance, still remains the classic mathematical description of the magnetic field observed in archaeological prospection. Clark and Haddon-Reece (1972) set out their design for an automatic recording system based on fluxgate magnetometers, well ahead of the time when similar systems would be adopted by the majority of workers.

Indeed, most of the basic developments in hardware had already been made, and have been well documented by Clark (1990). In 1946 Richard Atkinson carried out the first significant earth resistance survey, using a "Megger" Earth Tester and a Wenner array (Atkinson, 1963). Tony Clark followed in 1956 with a dedicated instrument, the Martin-Clark meter, which became the standard instrument for use with a switched Wenner array; essentially it used a potentiometric backing-off procedure to give a "null" balance and was, therefore, slow in use. In 1958 Martin Aitken and Teddy Hall developed the first proton magnetometer (or gradiometer) for archaeological use; with a sensitivity down to 1 nT (nanoTesla), it was again slow in operation, taking up to one minute for verified readings.

The success of these prototype instruments led to developments which were effectively completed by 1972. The "direct-reading" earth resistance meter gave an analogue output proportional to earth resistance in all but the most exacting soil conditions. The prototype alkali-vapour magnetometer was in place, giving a potential sensitivity 100 times better than the proton magnetometer, but with depressing handling problems. At Oxford John Aldred had developed the first fluxgate gradiometer, which rapidly led to more convenient forms from Frank Philpott at Plessey and Geoff Bartington at Littlemore.

The possibility of simultaneous measurement of magnetic and conductive properties, well established in geology, entered the province of archaeology through the use of the metal detector principle and the development of phase-sensitive amplifiers. The SCM (soil conductivity meter, better known as the Banjo) became the SSM when it was realised that, at its operational frequency, it was measuring soil susceptibility! The PIM (pulsed induction meter) also came into use without a full understanding of its operational principles, which involve quadrature susceptibility or magnetic viscosity. Ground-penetrating radar (GPR) and seismic methods were in the wings and developments in Japan and the USA were reported around 1972, but as yet there were no significant contributions to archaeology.

Innovation in hardware was lively. The spiked wheel resistance system and continuous analogue recording from both resistance and magnetic surveys with potentiometric distance transducers led to the prolific production of *x-y* plots as linear records. Otherwise data were mainly recorded by hand for later processing, usually in a grid format. It is useful to examine what techniques for data processing were available in the early 1970s. As in other aspects of archaeological prospection, Irwin Scollar led the way by using the computer facility at Bonn to present magnetometer data in a dot-density format, the preferred style for most data for years afterwards (Scollar, 1966). Others, with more modest means, devised simple semi-conductor matrix image displays to produce intensity plots proportional to the magnitude of the data, photographed them, and pieced them together appropriately, with variable results .

The computing facilities available to the majority of workers were fairly primitive. Some were employing mini-computers, usually designated primarily for other purposes, with miscellaneous display and printer facilities, to produce plots of large-scale surveys. Others were using limited central computing resources to simulate patterns of intensity on line printers. Data treatment was at an elementary level, usually in terms of simple spatial filters, but Scollar was already utilising the Bonn computer to investigate more sophisticated procedures (Scollar, 1966). It is in the recording and treatment of data that the most obvious and far-reaching advances have been made over the last quarter century, enabled by the steadily increasing power of micro-computers.

2 Advances in field instrumentation

What has changed over the last twenty-five years? In terms of hardware, perhaps the most significant development was the fitting of digital logging systems to existing equipment. Thus the early "Bradphys" resistance meter in 1985 evolved into the Geoscan RM4 with a DL110 data logger, capable of logging 1000 readings before it becomes necessary to download the data into a more permanent store (Clark, 1990, p45). There have been corresponding developments with magnetometers; for instance, the Geoscan FM18 fluxgate gradiometer has a built-in logger with a capacity of 3000 readings (Clark, 1990, p17). Alternative data-logging systems appeared, originally developed as hand-held organisers. Transfer of readings to portable computers in the field rapidly became the norm, allowing raw data to be turned into visible results within minutes of recording.

Nowadays field-based systems are capable of processing vast quantities of data; the Geoscan RM15 resistance meter can store 30000 readings, and the FM36 magnetometer 16000 readings. These large capacities are the result of the rapid developments in micro-electronics and mass storage over the last few years. They both represent more data than field teams could produce in a working day, when the instrumentation still relied on the manual intervention of the operator to allow each reading to be recorded. The rapid turn-round of data has led to calls for more rapid acquisition of readings. The improved recording rate could be used simply to extend the area of survey, an important consideration in Britain, where there is a statutory requirement to examine all archaeologically sensitive land prior to its development. Otherwise it may be used to reduce the sampling interval, thereby increasing the survey intensity and improving the detail visible in the results. To satisfy these requirements, various mobile systems for earth resistance survey have appeared (Hesse *et al.*, 1986).

Another important development is the switched system of many electrical probes, slaved to the logger through a multiplexer, allowing the rapid assessment of thirty or more data values, with a variety of inter-probe spacings and array configurations (Griffiths and Turnbull, 1985). The resulting data-bank offers a new potential for interpretative procedures (Szymanski and Tsourlos, 1993). Of course, there are logistical problems in transferring the whole multi-probe assembly to a new location ready for the next scan, but their solution is a matter of efficiency in field procedure.

The current range of fluxgate and caesium-vapour magnetometers permits reliable sampling to take place within a fraction of second (Becker, 1996). When allowance is made for the movement of instruments and survey markers, it is feasible to acquire around 40000 readings in the course of a day's work of 10 to 12 hours. Using very close sampling (0.5 m or 0.25 m), it is possible to obtain detailed views of magnetic anomalies which are amenable to more sophisticated techniques of interpretation.

What alternative hardware techniques have been developed? Low frequency (up to 50 kHz) electromagnetic systems have shown limited innovation in the past 10 years. In France, however, Alain Tabbagh has developed the so-called Slingram (twin coil and boom) instrument (Hesse *et al.*, 1986). There is growing appreciation of the significance of the phase of the returned signal as a means of distinguishing between the conducting and magnetic features, although the complications of the viscous component in the magnetic response remain a problem.

There is also the question of depth of survey, a problem which has persisted over many years and which may ultimately prove to be insoluble, in terms of desired accuracy and reliability. Wider coil separation gives greater depth of penetration but poorer resolution. In Britain, the Bartington electromagnetic system, reminiscent of a metal detector, but with the facility for dual frequency operation, is now used extensively for studies of top-soil magnetic susceptibility (Clark, 1990).

The study of vertical sections, leading to the possibility of 3-dimensional examination of a site, has perhaps found its most significant stimulation in the past twenty years through developments in GPR (Malagodi *et al.*, 1996). By selective use of central frequencies from 100 MHz to 1 GHz, it is now feasible to penetrate to depths of many metres of soil and to make detailed studies behind solid walls. To the non-specialist, however, visualisation of anything but the simplest of features presents considerable difficulties. The complex manner in which heterogeneous media and their interfaces influence the velocity of propagation and reflection characteristics of electromagnetic waves leads to processing problems which have still not been solved. The most attractive visual presentation has been realised through the use of close-spaced vertical scans from which "horizontal" sections (time slices) have been produced. Such techniques, however, do not solve the problems of complex raw data and their resolution into discrete features.

Other vertical sections have been produced following the use of multi-probe systems in earth resistance survey; they are often presented as simple or tomographic "pseudo-sections". They are normally of limited resolution and reflect the complexity of resistance anomalies resulting from 3-dimensional buried features. In principle, it should also be possible to ascertain some information about the depth of features by using multi-sensor magnetometers, with an array of sensors set at different heights. In practice, the sheer complexity of features at the majority of archaeological sites has so far prevented anything more than the most rudimentary three-dimensional information being obtained.

3 Advances in data processing

In terms of data processing and presentation, the past quarter century can be divided roughly into three overlapping decades, corresponding to three recognised levels of image processing. This is the case for the majority of people, but there were always some workers with access to advanced equipment who were able to make pioneering developments well ahead of the rest of the field.

During the 1970s surveyors were mainly concerned with the *visualisation* of data, or visual presentation, to give a visible form to its essential features with whatever computing equipment was available. As computer power became more affordable through the 1980s, effort was concentrated on the *enhancement* of the visible image, to make the significant features stand out more clearly and to separate different classes of feature. In the 1990s, as constraints on computer resources steadily disappear, people are able to concentrate on the *reconstruction* of the physical objects which give rise to the measured signals, and which they hope correspond to the archaeological features of interest.

4 Data visualisation

The importance of *dot-density* patterns in the development of area survey has already been mentioned; they were among the most successful of the techniques of data presentation during the early part of this period (Aspinall and Haigh, 1988). Their importance still continues to the present day, although in a somewhat changed context; when a printer is used to obtain a hard copy of a grey-scale image, the printing software interprets the different intensities as patterns of dots. The procedure is partly hidden from the user, but it may still be necessary to make an informed selection from various "dithering" techniques. An incidental advantage is that the images are effectively "screened" and ready for publication. True solid shades of grey can be produced only by the very latest laser printers, the most expensive in terms of capital and running costs.

When images are displayed on a computer monitor, it is usually more attractive to represent intensities in terms of a *grey-scale*. The appearance of the results greatly depends on the quality of the graphics card, particularly on the number of grey levels available (2, 4, 16, 64, or 256). In the early days workers had to be satisfied with fairly coarse results, but most modern computers, including the "lap tops" likely to be used during field surveys, are available with graphics cards of high quality.

Contour diagrams were popular around 1980, as pen plotters became available on the majority of central computer systems (Haigh and Kelly, 1987). They provide a very accurate way to display data, but they can be rather confusing for the non-specialist and have largely been displaced by other techniques. It is easy to see the regions of rapid change, reflected in the density of the contour curves, but it is harder to distinguish "peaks" from "troughs", unless some form of colour coding is introduced.

Colour displays became generally available on micro-computers from the mid-1980s onwards. The discreet use of colour can be a useful way of emphasising the contrast in specific regions of the plan, but gaudy presentations are liable to distract attention from the underlying data. There are some situations in which the use of colour can be particularly recommended, for instance, in distinguishing between positive and negative readings in a magnetometer survey. It is worth noting that a coloured plan is equivalent to a contour diagram, since the emphasised boundary between adjacent regions of contrasting colours constitutes a contour curve.

There is some enthusiastic support for viewing data by a *3-dimensional construction* of the plotted surface. This can be achieved quite simply through a fishnet or wire-frame diagram, but the availability of 3D graphics on the more powerful modern computers allows it to be shown more realistically as a lit surface. Although the latter results can be very impressive, especially in their ability to distinguish between peaks and troughs, they can sometimes be confusing, and the present authors generally prefer a good, clear 2-dimensional plan (grey-scale, linear contour, or colour map) as an accurate method to represent the data (Aspinall and Haigh, 1988).

A great incentive for improved methods of data visualisation has come from the advent of *automatic data loggers*, allowing large quantities of data to be transferred quickly and accurately to a computer system. The provision of reliable, high-resolution data enables a reliable picture of the results to be obtained. Furthermore, using the power of modern portable computers, the surveyors can assess the success of their work, even as the survey is proceeding.

5 Image enhancement

It is natural to apply the standard techniques of image processing in an attempt to improve the desired features of the visualisation and to suppress those which seem less desirable. *Contrast stretching* and *histogram manipulation* are the most fundamental of such techniques, enabling the best use to be made of whatever range of grey or colour levels is available. It should be ensured that the top level matches the maximum reading, and the bottom level the minimum, and that there is a good balance of readings over the intermediate levels.

Spatial filtering, which was very popular in the late 1970s and early 1980s, involves overlapping the data with a suitable mask in order to emphasise certain aspects of the image. Simple examples include sharpening filters to emphasise the edges of features, and smoothing filters to suppress noise and small features. More sophisticated low-pass filters can emphasise extended features at the expense of smaller ones; similarly high-pass filters emphasise compact (possibly archaeological) features at the expense of more extended (geological) ones (Cheetham et al., 1991). Closely related to sharpening filters are a more specialised group for *edge detection*, often used as a first step towards automatic interpretation of images.

One particularly important concern is *noise suppression*. This can be achieved by means of smoothing filters, as described in the last paragraph, but may result in the blurring of edges. Geophysical data often suffer from "salt and pepper" noise where, for a variety of reasons, the instrument is liable to give occasional anomalous readings at random intervals. It is preferable to isolate such readings on the basis of a statistical comparison with their neighbours, and to replace them with suitable interpolated values.

Once the image has been cleaned up, attention can be directed to the details of the display. It is common to represent each reading as a grey square of appropriate intensity at the relevant position on the plan. An assemblage of *grey squares* often has a "blocky" appearance, through which it is not easy to discern the underlying shape of a feature. Some method of interpolation is desirable, to give smoother edges to the features. *Bilinear interpolation* is an obvious answer, and has long been used, particularly in the construction of fishnet diagrams and contour maps. It has a number of disadvantages, especially in its tendency to reduce contrast in the highlights, and a more sophisticated technique may be called for. *Bicubic interpolation* is more difficult to implement reliably, but has proved to be a practical technique for modern computers and to be capable of overcoming many of the disadvantages of bilinear interpolation.

Although an assemblage of survey readings has a general appearance which is superficially similar to a digital image, some essential differences have to be taken into account. The physical processes underlying geophysical survey are usually more complicated than those involved in the formation of a photographic image; the error distribution is of a different nature; whereas a digital image normally consists of a complete rectangular array of values, with at most a small number of missing pixels, geophysical results are restricted by the shape of the accessible region of survey, and may have large numbers of missing values. For all these reasons, standard imaging procedures should not be applied uncritically to survey data.

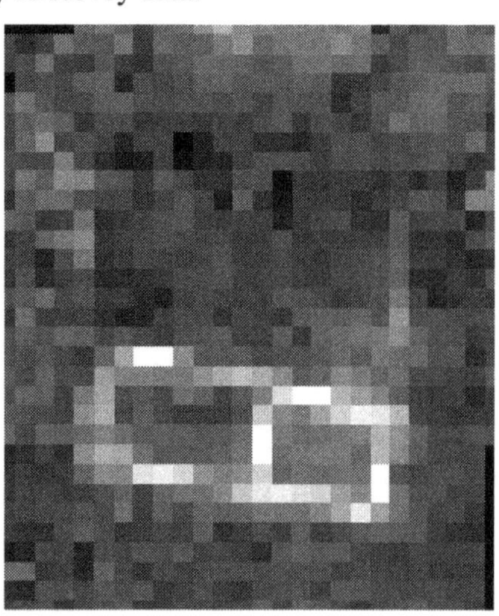

Figure 1: The foundations of a small chapel revealed by twin-probe resistance survey. The interval between readings is 1 m; regions of high resistance are shown as light squares.

One particular problem with geophysical survey concerns "aliasing", which occurs when a detected feature has a horizontal dimension smaller than the sampling interval. The feature may then appear as a series of disjointed items, several sampling intervals apart. Figure 1 is a grey-scale representation of a twin-probe resistance survey, revealing the foundations of a small chapel; the readings are at intervals of 1 m. The walls are obviously continuous features running at a small angle to the direction of survey, but have been revealed as disconnected horizontal strips. In Figure 2 the data have been enhanced by bicubic interpolation; this gives a better impression of the continuous nature of the walls, but still presents them as series of connected horizontal segments, rather than truly linear features.

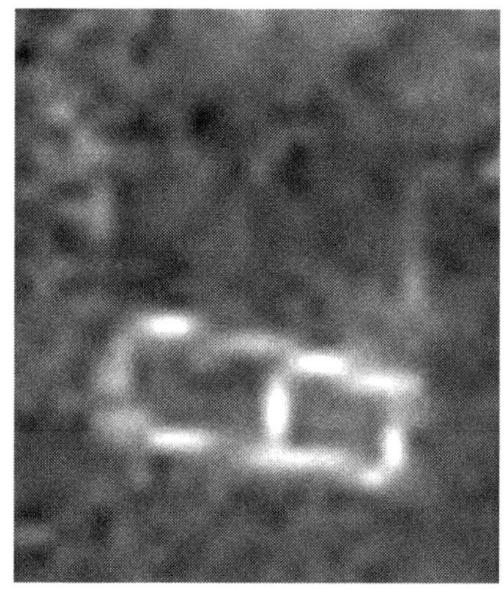

Figure 2: The data of Figure 1, displayed with bicubic interpolation.

The only certain way to avoid aliasing is to ensure that the sampling interval is smaller than the dimensions of the smallest feature that can be detected by the equipment. Unfortunately it is difficult to make an accurate frequency analysis of the response of most geophysical instruments, and hence to predict the optimal sampling interval. This provides a sound reason for the use of modern fast data loggers, since they permit sampling intervals to be set at values smaller than the resolution of the instruments.

6 Physical reconstruction using inverse data methods

Back in the early 1980s numerical procedures based on the fast *Fourier transform* were regarded with some awe. Any realistic calculation required a large amount of computer time, even on powerful machines, and you were often recommended to buy specialist processors costing thousands of pounds. Nowadays it takes only a few seconds to run the same calculation on a modern personal computer and, when an intensive application demands results in a fraction of a second, specialist processors can be purchased for a few hundred pounds each.

At a basic level, Fourier transforms provide alternative filters in frequency space to the spatial filters described in the last section; whether it is preferable to use a spatial filter or its equivalent in frequency space depends upon the size and nature of the filter (Cheetham *et al.*, 1991). At a deeper level, they can be used to construct an inverse for any linear process which is believed to have degraded the quality of the perceived image. The inverse filter may be applied to the observed image in the hope of *restoring* it to its original quality, or of *reconstructing* the ideal image. For instance, the signal (or spread function) from a small subsurface magnetic source, effectively a dipole induced by the earth's field, has the general appearance shown in Fig. 3, with an intense positive lobe to the south of the source and a diffuse negative lobe to the north (Linington, 1972). The precise form of the spread function depends on geographical location on the earth's surface; the form shown in Figure 3 is typical of British latitudes. The superposition of spread functions from a collection of such sources gives rise to the characteristic positive and negative pattern of magnetometer readings. In order to reconstruct the archaeological sources of the observed signals, we might attempt to calculate a frequency filter which inverts the effect of the spread function.

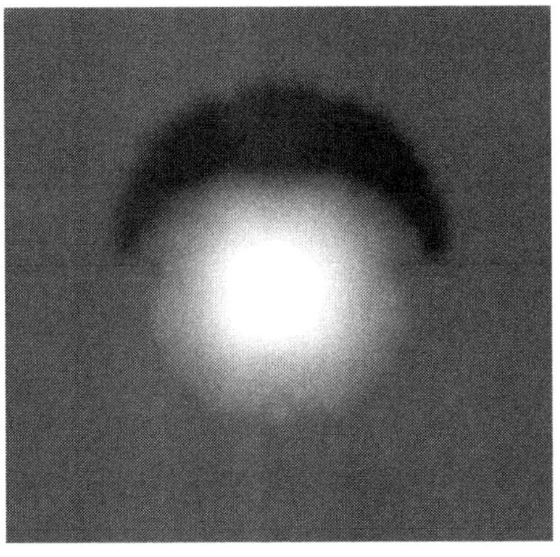

Figure 3: The spread of gradiometer readings over a small induced magnetic dipole in British latitudes. Positive anomalies are shown as light regions, negative anomalies as dark. The diagram represents an area about 10 m square.

Now that sufficient computing power is readily available to apply Fourier methods to reconstruction problems in archaeological magnetometry, it is found that they do not generally work. The major difficulties are that Fourier methods require a complete rectangular image to be available, not often the case in archaeological geophysics, and that they tend to amplify any noise within the data. The distribution of errors in magnetometer data is of such a nature that a reconstruction based on an inverse spread function is entirely dominated by noise, without any discernible pattern of features. Although there are some techniques, notably the Wiener filter, which are designed to reduce the problem of noise, they do not give very useful results in this instance.

In order to overcome these difficulties, it is necessary to turn to more complicated inverse data methods. Here the physical situation is modelled for features of specified shape and the parameters defining the features are adjusted, until an optimum fit to the observed data is achieved. In order to obtain sensible results, it is generally necessary to make some *a priori* assumptions about the nature of the underlying features, so that *constrained inversion* is achieved, taking the defined prerequisites into account. Statisticians prefer to describe the prerequisites as a *prior* distribution for the model, and the constrained optimisation as leading to a *posterior* distribution, when the procedure is known as a Bayesian method. These techniques have been successful in reconstructing physical features (Allum *et al.*, 1995 and 1996), although they have yet to be adapted to a form suitable for the majority of magnetometer surveys.

A crucial advantage of inverse data methods (or Bayesian methods) is that they are not confined to any particular shape of data set; the data need not conform to a rectangular array, as they must for Fourier techniques. The points in the reconstruction set need not match the locations of those in the data set. Provided that the prior distribution is defined appropriately, for instance, it is possible to calculate many more reconstructed points than data points, so providing an automatic form of interpolation. This is particular useful when features are expected to have smoothly curving boundaries.

There have been similar theoretical advances in connection with multi-probe resistance surveys (Szymanski and Tsourlos, 1993). The calculations tend to be much heavier than those for magnetometry, since it necessary to estimate the flow of electric current through all the surrounding soil, rather than use a standard spread function for each reconstructed point. In order to limit the calculation to a realistic size, the reconstruction has to be restricted to a "pseudo-section" through the features of interest, rather than fully extended into three dimensions. Nevertheless Szymanski and Tsourlos have had considerable success in accurately locating a variety of features within the cross-section, using any of the standard probe arrangements. Furthermore, they have issued a practical computer code which is capable of analysing results as quickly as a competent field team should be able to collect them.

7 Future prospects

Clearly the most conspicuous development over the last few years has been in GPR, and it is likely that such systems will continue to develop. At high frequencies the use of "one-shot" and frequency-modulated radar systems is attractive. It is also important that more attention should be paid to electromagnetic systems at low frequencies, in order to exploit the simultaneous measurement of conductive and magnetic properties without the need to use probes.

These modern instruments tend to be expensive to purchase and to require high technical competence for their operation. They produce huge amounts of data; even by modern standards, sophisticated software and massive computing resources are required to obtain the best results from them. More conventional instruments are likely to provide the basis for the majority of archaeological survey for some time to come. Their performance will be improved by the multi-plexing of simultaneous readings, and by analytical software which can be supported on the modern range of portable "lap-top" computers.

We have discussed how multi-probe resistance surveys can be used, not only to indicate the horizontal location of features, but also to give an accurate estimate of their depth below the ground surface. There can be little doubt that these techniques will be improved and refined over the next few years. Magnetometry will continue to develop through the increasing portability of stable, sensitive instruments; again the use of multiple sampling, probably through an array of sensors at different heights, will broaden the data base. In the longer term the development of high-temperature superconductors should lead to a new range of more sensitive and more versatile magnetometers.

The last few years have been marked by concurrent developments in both the field instrumentation and in the data processing necessary to analyse the readings. It is important that this situation should continue. There is now a great opportunity to produce new instruments which are designed not merely to record more data more rapidly, but to provide results which can be analysed in response to specific tasks. The multi-probe resistance systems and the multi-sensor magnetometer arrays make some initial steps along this path.

The question then arises as to how archaeologists intend to take into account these new sources of more precise and more reliable information. It cannot be satisfactory simply to say that they will provide a better starting point for traditional excavation techniques. Archaeological methodology as a whole must be updated to accommodate the improved sources of geophysical data in a wider and more versatile information system.

During the period when they were preparing this paper, the authors were saddened by news of the untimely death of Tony Clark. The earlier references to his work are a clear indication of the signal contribution he has made to the development of archaeological geophysics. The authors wish to take this opportunity to record their appreciation of his life and work.

Bibliography

Allum, G T, Aykroyd, R G, and Haigh, J G B, 1995 A new statistical approach to reconstruction from area magnetometry data, *Archaeological Prospection* 2, 197-205.

Allum, G T, Aykroyd, R G, and Haigh, J G B, 1996, Restoration of magnetometry data using inverse-data methods, in Kammermans, H. and Fennema, K. (eds.) *Interfacing the Past: Computer Applications and Quantitative Methods in Archaeology 1995* (Analecta Praehistorica Leidensia 28), 111-119.

Aspinall, A, and Haigh, J G B, 1988. A review of techniques for the graphical display of geophysical data, in Rahtz, S.P.Q. (ed.) *Computer and Quantitative Methods in Archaeology 1988* (British Archaeological Reports, International Series 446 (ii)), 295-307.

Atkinson, R J C, 1963. Resistivity surveying in archaeology, in Pyddoke, E. (ed.) *The Scientist and Archaeology* (Phoenix House, London) 1-30.

Becker, H, 1996, *Archaeologische Prospektion*, Bayerisches Landesamt fuer Denkmalpflege, Munich.

Cheetham, P N, Haigh, J G B, and Ipson, S S, 1991 The archaeological perception of geophysical data in P. Budd *et al.* (eds.) *Archaeological Sciences 1989* (Oxbow Monograph 9), Oxbow Books, Oxford, 273-287.

Clark, A J, 1990. *Seeing Beneath the Soil*, Batsford, London.

Clark, A J, and Haddon-Reece, D, 1972. An automatic recording system using a Plessey fluxgate gradiometer, *Prospezioni Archeologiche* 7, 107-114.

Griffiths, D H, and Turnbull, J, 1985 A multi-electrode array for resistivity surveying, *First Break* 3(7), 16-20.

Haigh, J G B, and Kelly, M A, 1987 Contouring Techniques for archaeological distributions, *Journal of Archaeological Science* 14, 231-241.

Hesse, A, Jolivet, A, and Tabbagh, A, 1986 New prospects in shallow depth electrical surveying for archaeological and pedological applications, *Geophysics* 51, 585-594.

Linington, R E, 1972 A summary of simple theory applicable to magnetic prospecting in archaeology, *Prospezioni Archeologiche* 7, 9-59.

Malagoli, S, Orlando, L, Pivo, S, and Rosso, F, 1996 Location of archaeological structures using GPR method: three-dimensional radar acquisition, *Archaeological Prospection* 3(1) 13-23.

Scollar, I, 1966 Computer treatment of magnetic measurements from archaeological sites, *Archaeometry* 9, 61-71.

Szymanski, J E, and Tsourlos, P, 1993. The resistance tomography technique for archaeology, *Archaeologia Polona* 31, 5-32.

Contact details

Department of Archaeological Sciences
University of Bradford
Bradford
A. Aspinall
West Yorkshire BD7 1DP
UK

Department of Mathematics
University of Bradford
Bradford
J.G.B. Haigh
West Yorkshire BD7 1DP
UK
J.G.B.Haigh@bradford.ac.uk

Has 25 Years of Computing Provided Greater Physical and Intellectual Access to Archaeology?

CAA 97

Jennifer Stewart

Abstract

This paper reviews the last quarter century of data collection, management and curation in archaeological computing, and briefly notes the main developments from the 1970s use of 'off-site' University mainframes through to more recent usage of networked microcomputers and integrated software packages. The main achievements of the last 25 years are outlined: the development of data standards and terminology control, cooperation and collaborative ventures by national bodies such as the MDA, RCHME and EH, as well the growing realisation of the strategic importance of information and the need to secure its intellectual property rights. Areas for further work aredentified: the impermanence of digital data, and the need to avoid excavation-to-museum duplication in data management systems. Longer term issues such as the bipolarity of increasing public access versus the need for copyright and site/monument security and other such issues relating to power and control are briefly addressed, as well as the central issue as to whether 25 years of computing now provide greater physical and intellectual access to archaeology.

1 Introduction

As noted by Peres de Cuellar (1997, 10), anniversaries are always privileged moments: celebrations such as this 25th Anniversary Conference can stimulate thought on the ground which has been covered, as well as pointing out possible new directions. This paper will briefly survey the last quarter century of archaeological data collection and management as represented by the conference proceedings of CAA ('Computer Applications in Archaeology' and its younger sister, 'Computer Applications and Quantitative Methods in Archaeology'), and then highlight some achievements as well as identifying areas for further work.

It has been common to define a sequential pathway, a form of the Great Chain of Being in archaeological computing, moving inexorably in logical stages from data collection, through to data management, leading to data manipulation and analysis, finally arriving at dissemination (often paralleled with the possibly arcane distinction of raw data into meaningful information leading to (shared) knowledge). However archaeological use of IT and information systems (IS) is now more of a complex, converging, multistranded web (or Web), rather than a linear feature on the computing landscape. Despite this complexity and interrelatedness, some areas of computing endeavour have had to be excluded in this brief survey: quantitative methods, statistics and classification, archaeometry, visualisation (including imaging, CAD, multimedia, and virtual reality), expert systems and artificial intelligence. Geographic Information Systems (GIS) as a combination of database management, graphic applications and statistical analysis have not been covered here (but see for example, Kamermans and Fennema's preface to the CAA 1995 conference and the fifteen articles devoted to GIS at that conference (Kamermans and Fennema 1996). Education and publication through computerised means will be touched on briefly, where appropriate to the central theme.

2 History

The history and development of archaeological computing, both IT and IS, have been well documented in CAA (Booth 1995a; Hansen 1993; Lock 1995; Webb 1986). Reilly and Rahtz (1992) provide a comprehensive and world-wide perspective of archaeological IT and IS. In the early days of 'off-site' processing of data on large University mainframes in the 1970s, a favourite phrase to describe this activity was 'information retrieval': an interesting connotation as the activity was neither information nor retrieval (in 1990s' parlance): it would now be termed data analysis.

In 1978 John Wilcock, in one of the earliest articles of its kind, was to consider the application of personal computing and microcomputers to site recording and the retrieval, analysis and publication of excavation material (Wilcock 1978). By the early 1980s, the first articles describing the use of microcomputers and the new relational database management systems for excavation material were being published (Booth 1982; Stewart 1980a). The term 'databanks' with all its mainframe connotations had been superseded by 'databases' with several units running BBC or Amstrad home computers (for example, Moffett 1986). By this date there were also the first references in CAA to Sites and Monuments Records (Moffett 1984) and their databases, the issues of which have been comprehensively covered by various authors (Lang 1992; Clubb and Lang 1996; Lang this volume).

By 1989, the youngish discipline of archaeological computing felt it had come of age and marked this transition by codifying its activities, as seen in Ryan's bibliography of publications on computer applications in CAA and in other sources (Ryan 1988). Ryan classified over 700 articles into 11 categories: data collection and curation (including SMRs, education, publication and museums) numbered less than 200.

By the early 1990s, the shift away from large scale, text-based, off-site data processing was complete, with a wider diversity of articles on the issues concerning the management of data: SMRs and cultural resource management, GIS, metadata, imaging via videodiscs and visualisation, electronic journals, as well as the first reference in CAA to condition surveys of museum collections (Keene and Orton 1992). Few articles, though, considered the bigger picture, or reflected on the wider issues of computer archaeology. This was left to publications such as Ucko's thought-provoking article on the impact of IT on archaeology (Ucko 1992). However articles such as Cheetham and Haigh (1992) were beginning to question the purpose of all this computerisation activity. While accepting that archaeological database systems were poor contenders to bridge the gap from data into information, they voiced the common concern that the discipline could be tarred as '...[the] manipulation of ambiguous data by means of dubious methods to solve a problem that has not been identified' (Cheetham and Haigh 1992, 13). Hansen's amusing article with cartoons was a timely paper to describe and map out the state of European archaeological databases and SMRs, and especially the problems in the exchange of data (Hansen 1993). In recent years the trend has been to use industry standard relational database management systems (RDBMS) and standard office applications for excavation material, such as the use of Microsoft Access for the IDEA project (Andersen and Madsen 1996).

This period also saw several government organisations beginning to assess the wider, strategic implications of data management and collation (Booth 1995b; Clubb and Startin 1995; Clubb and Lang 1996; Murray 1995), although in fact the strategic issues had already been discussed ten years earlier by Cooper (1985). In the same period, a change in emphasis shift was discernible, away from data collection to increasing public access to the results of archaeological computing (Booth 1996).

3 Achievements

After 25 years of endeavour in archaeological computing what are the main achievements? The major development in data management has been the development of standards: whether as the Royal Commission on the Historical Monuments of England (RCHME) data standards (1993) or controlled vocabulary such as the RCHME Thesaurus of Archaeological Terms (RCHME 1986), or in partnership with English Heritage for the Thesaurus on Architectural Terms (RCHME and EH 1989), the Thesaurus of Archaeological Site Types (RCHME and EH 1992) or the Thesaurus on Monument Types (RCHME and EH 1995). The real issue for the coming years will be how to ensure standards such as these continue to work as the metaphorical glue, rather than becoming the concrete in the systems.

Collaboration on a national scale has been both a challenge and a lasting achievement: SPECTRUM, the product of museum cooperation organised by the Museum Documentation Association has provided the first ever national (if not international) documentation standard (Grant 1994). The LASSI (Larger Scale Systems Initiative) consortium of the Museums and Galleries Commission and eight museums now has a standardised database system for the management of collections, as well as electronic access and exchange of information (Grant et al 1996). SCRAN (Scottish Cultural Resources Access Network) project in Scotland (Royan 1997) is building up a networked multimedia resource for the study of history and material culture in Scotland and may well act as a catalyst for other such public access ventures.

Cooper (1985) was one of the first to identify information as a resource, to be managed strategically to deliver the business needs of the organisation, and with this realisation came the need to secure this resource through the establishment of intellectual property rights (Beagrie this volume). With increasing dissemination via electronic means, this will continue to make this an important factor to address in the coming years.

The maturity of archaeological computing, if not of data management and dissemination, has been demonstrated by Lock in his cogent description of contextualisation, (Lock 1995) making sense of the complexity of the subject by showing the linked development of the technology and the archaeological theory 'drivers'. He highlights and contrasts the current trend towards data-enriching environments with the emphasis on visualisation, multimedia, integrated software and increased access, compared with the 'data minimising' systems of the 1970s which concentrated on reductionist quantification, and limited access and exchange of information on mainframes which provided little scope for creative theorising.

4 'Could do better'

However, identification and addressing other key issues has not been so rapid in other areas: the impermanence of the results of all this data management, the digital archives, is only now being considered at a national level (for example, with the work of the Archaeological Data Service).

The need to avoid the duplication of excavation and museum recording so that excavation generated records should be absorbed and utilised in the museum's documentation system was identified as an issue at least 15 years ago (Stewart 1980b), but still requires realisation in the late 1990s. Ryan's suggestions on the excavation archive as a hyperdocument may assist here (Ryan 1995).

5 Future issues

One senses for the future a bipolarity of several issues, such as the provision of democratic access versus the interests of copyright, security and the protection of sites and monuments, and individuals. The slow increase in user-centric approaches to access may be constrained by issues of power and control in electronic dissemination (see Section

5), if not threats of what the media have called the 'dumbing down' of information. The degradation of what information scientists call 'disintermediation' or the use of intermediaries is eroding the rise of the archaeological knowledge worker. Murray notes the increasing demand for access to archaeological data without the intervention and interpretation by professional archaeologists (Murray 1995). And finally, the rise of the World Wide Web, (see, for example, the European Archaeological Heritage Web (van Leusen et al 1996)) while increasing potential access to archaeological collections via on-line imaging and electronic catalogues, and via electronic journals (Heywood *et al* 1996), may also make us question the quality of disseminated data. As Murray has noted, systems such as GIS, based on selections of data, may give a false sense of uniformity as the means to assess the quality or accuracy of data, such as source data, have been removed (Murray 1995).

6 Conclusion

The central issue has been whether more than a quarter of a century of computing now provides greater physical and intellectual access to archaeology (landscapes as well as artifactual and information collections). Improved access to archaeological sites, monuments and landscapes requires to be addressed elsewhere, but access to museum and information collections has already been briefly assessed. Despite 25 years of endeavour have we really moved museums from 'junkyards to Aladdin's caves' as the Museums Association itself termed it (Museums Association 1994)? While there have been some success stories (Museums Association 1994; Stewart 1984, 1995), the backlog and curation problems so familiar from the past still seem to haunt us in the digital age, and this impression requires further research and analysis. Virtual, or surrogate access, to archaeological information collections has dramatically increased (Stewart 1996), as have all the caveats surrounding its access, as noted in section 5.

It may not be possible for us to address the issue as to whether we now have greater access to archaeology, because although information is the answer, we are still unclear on the question. And that question reinvents itself according to the tenets of the time: the 'Audit Culture' of the eighties pushed the emphasis in archaeological computing, at least in museums, into collections management, data standards and automated inventory (Roberts 1985, 1988). A parallel development can be seen in the government organisations charged with cultural resource or cultural information management (Clubb and Startin 1995). In the nineties, the mantra of egalitarian access and dissemination is repeated, perhaps a little too often, without the intellectual rigour of questioning what is required and how can we provide it (but see for example the Catechism project at the National Museums of Scotland (McCorry and Morrison 1995), as well as Booth's analysis of access requirements for visitors to the Science Museum (Booth 1996)).

And as for archaeology at the eve of the twenty first century, computing may well help redefine our values and beliefs, who we are and our role in the Information Age and in the global information society. At the 1995 G7 Ministerial Conference on the Information Society, the group identified the acceleration of the multimedia digitisation of museum collections and their accessibility to the public and as a learning resource as a prime requirement to aid the realisation of the global information society (National Computing Centre 1995).

However, in the era of democratising archaeological knowledge (as noted by Reilly and Rahtz 1992; Huggett 1995) we also need to address the issues of power and control when disseminating information (Ucko 1992) and thus avoid Burke's early realisation (1978) of a world divided into information 'haves' and 'have-nots', or Reilly and Rahtz's concerns about 'intellectual colonialism' (Reilly and Rahtz 1992). Will, for example, access to virtual museum collections dissolve away the intractable problems in the restitution of cultural property – I think not.

Web References

Archaeological Data Service (ADS), http://ads.ahds.ac.uk/ahds/

Royal Commission on the Historical Monuments of England (RCHME), http://www.rchme.gov.uk

Scottish Cultural Resources Access Network (SCRAN) http://www.scran.ac.uk/

Bibliography

Andersen, J, and Madsen, T, 1996 IDEA – the Integrated Database for Excavation Analysis, in *Interfacing the Past. Computer Applications and Quantitative Methods in Archaeology CAA95* (eds H Kamermans and K Fennema), 3-14

Booth, B K W, 1982 Some projects to store and process data from survey and excavation with the aid of a computer, in *Computer Applications in Archaeology 1981* (eds I Graham and E Webb), 20-25

Booth, B K W, 1995a Has archaeology remained aloof from the information age?, in *Computer Applications and Quantitative Methods in Archaeology 1994* (eds J Huggett and N Ryan), BAR International Series, 600, 1-12

Booth, B K W, 1995b Strategic Planning Issues: Preface, in *Computer Applications and Quantitative Methods in Archaeology 1993* (eds J Wilcock and K Lockyear), BAR International Series, 598, 65

Booth, B K W, 1996 *An investigation of museum data storage and access technologies including case studies on archaeological records at the National Maritime Museum and visitor information at the Science Museum,* Unpublished PhD thesis, UCL Institute of Archaeology

Burke, J, 1978 *Connections,* London:BBC

Cheetham, P N, and Haigh, J G B, 1992 The archaeological database - new relations?, in *Computer Applications and Quantitative Methods in Archaeology* (eds G Lock and J Moffett), BAR International Series, S 577, 7-14

Clubb, N D, and Startin, W D, 1995 Information systems strategies in national organisations and the identification, legal protection and management of the most important sites in England, in *Computer Applications and Quantitative Methods in Archaeology 1993* (eds J Wilcock and K Lockyear), BAR International Series, 598, 67-73

Clubb, N D, and Lang, N A R, 1996 A strategic appraisal of Information Systems for archaeology and architecture in England – past, present and future, in *Interfacing the past. Computer Applications and Quantitative Methods in Archaeology* (eds H Kamermans and K Fennema), *CAA95,* 51- 72

Cooper, M, 1985 Computers in British Archaeology: the need for a national strategy, in *Current Issues in archaeological computing* (eds M A Cooper and J D Richards), BAR International Series, 271, 79-91

Grant, A, 1994 *SPECTRUM. The UK Museum Documentation Standard,* Cambridge: MDA.

Grant, A, Keener, S, and Warren, J, 1996 Multi-talented, *Museums Journal*, 1996 (Aug.), 26-27.

Hansen, H J, 1993 European archaeological databases: problems and prospects, in *Computing the past. Computer Applications and Quantitative Methods in Archaeology CAA92* (eds J Andersen, T Madsen and I Scollar), 229-237

Heywood, M, Ross, S, and Richards, J, 1996 Internet archaeology: an international electronic journal for archaeology, in *Interfacing the past. Computer Applications and Quantitative Methods in Archaeology CAA95* (eds H Kamermans and K Fennema), 517-523

Huggett, J, 1995 Democracy, data and archaeological knowledge, in .). *Computer Applications and Quantitative Methods in Archaeology 1994* (eds J Huggett and N Ryan), 23-26

Kamermans, H, and Fennema, K (eds), 1996 *Interfacing the past. Computer Applications and Quantitative Methods in Archaeology. CAA95*

Keene, S, and Orton, C, 1992 Measuring the condition of museum collections, in *Computer Applications and Quantitative Methods in Archaeology* (eds G Lock and J Moffett), BAR International Series, S577, 163-166,

Lang, N A R, 1992 Sites and Monuments Records in Great Britain, in *Sites and monuments. National Archaeological Records* (ed C U Larsen), 171-183, Copenhagen: National Museum of Denmark

Lock, G, 1995 Archaeological computing, archaeological theory, and moves towards contextualism, in *Computer Applications and Quantitative Methods in Archaeology 1994* (eds J Huggett and N Ryan), 13-18

Moffett, J, 1984 The Bedfordshire County Sites and Monuments Record Database Management System, in *Computer Applications in Archaeology 1984* (ed S Laflin), 101-109

Moffett, J, 1986 Archaeology, databases and microcomputers, in *Computer Applications in Archaeology CAA 1985* (ed E Webb), 109-113

Murray, D M, 1995 The management of archaeological information – a strategy, in *Computer Applications and Quantitative Methods in Archaeology 1993* (eds J D Wilcock and K Lockyear), BAR International Series, 589, 83-87

Museums Association, 1994 Junkyard to Aladdin's Cave: transforming access to collections, *Museums Journal*, 1994 (Nov.), various articles

McCorry, H, and Morrison, I O, 1995 *Report on the Catechism Project.* Edinburgh: National Museums of Scotland

National Computing Centre, 1995 The G7 Ministerial Conference on the Information Society – conclusions and actions, *NCC Briefing*

Perez de Cuellar, 1997 Culture, development and museums on the eve of the 21st century, *ICOM News* Special Issue, 10-12

RCHME, 1986 *Thesaurus of Archaeological Terms,* 1st edition, London: Royal Commission on the Historical Monuments of England

RCHME, 1993 *Recording England's past: a data standard for the extended national archaeological record,* London: Royal Commission on the Historical Monuments of England

RCHME and EH, 1989 *Revised Thesaurus of Architectural Terms,* London: Royal Commission on the Historical Monuments of England

RCHME and EH, 1992 *Thesaurus of Archaeological Site Types,* 2nd edition, London: Royal Commission on the Historical Monuments of England

RCHME and EH, 1995 *Thesaurus of Monument Types: A Standard for use in Archaeological and Architectural Records,* Swindon: Royal Commission on the Historical Monuments of England

Reilly, P, and Rahtz, S, 1992 Introduction: archaeology and the information age, in *Archaeology and the Information Age: a global perspective* (eds P Reilly and S Rahtz), One World Archaeology, 1-28, London: Routledge

Roberts, D A, 1985 *Planning the Documentation of Museum Collections*, 8-15, Duxford: MDA.

Roberts, D A, 1988 Collections Management for Museums, in *Collections Management for Museums* (ed D A Roberts), 1-4, Cambridge: MDA.

Royan, B, 1997 On-line in the North, *Museums Journal*, 1997 (Feb), 23

Ryan, N S, 1988 A bibliography of computer applications and quantitative methods in archaeology, in *Computer and Quantitative Methods in Archaeology 1988* (ed S P Q Rahtz), BAR International Series, 446, I, 1-27

Ryan, N, 1995 The excavation archive as hyperdocument?, in *Computer Applications and Quantitative Methods in Archaeology 1994* (eds J Huggett and N Ryan), BAR International Series, 600, 211-220

Stewart, J D (ed), 1980a *Microcomputers in archaeology,* MDA Occasional Paper 4, Duxford: MDA

Stewart, J D, 1980b Integrated excavation and museum recording systems: methods, theories and problems, *Museum Archaeology*, 5, 11-27

Stewart, J, 1984 Museums – 'cabinets of curiosities' or centres of information?, in *Information Systems in Archaeology* (ed R Martlew), 77-89, Gloucester: Alan Sutton.

Stewart, J, 1995 Transforming the management and access of museum collections with IT, in *The Future for Europe's Past* (eds T Stevens and V James), Proceedings of COMETT Workshops, 3.37-3.40, Swansea: Swansea Institute of Higher Education on behalf of the EU COMETT Programme

Stewart, J, 1996 Where is the knowledge we have lost in information?, in *Information: the hidden resource, museums and the Internet* (eds A Fahy and W Sudbury), Proceedings of the Seventh International Conference of the MDA, 419-423, Cambridge: MDA

Ucko, P, 1992 Foreword, in *Archaeology and the Information Age: a global perspective* (eds P Reilly and S Rahtz), One World Archaeology, v1ii-xi, London: Routledge

Van Leusen, M, Champion, S, Lizee, J, and Plunkett, T, 1996 Towards a European Archaeological Heritage Web, in *Interfacing the past. Computer Applications and Quantitative Methods in Archaeology. CAA95* (eds H Kamermans and K Fennema), 507-514

Webb, E, 1986 Introduction, in *Computer Applications in Archaeology 1985* (ed E Webb), iii

Wilcock, J D, 1978 The automated archaeologist. A review of new personal computing and office automation methods of relevance to site recording, retrieval, analysis and publication, in *Computer Applications in Archaeology 1978* (ed S Laflin), 48-52

Contact details

Jennifer Stewart
Director of Information Services and Development
Royal Commission on the Historical Monuments of England
National Monuments Record Centre
Great Western Village
Kemble Drive
Swindon SN2 2GZ
UK
email: swncsd@rchme.gov.uk

CAA 97

Plus ça Change? - 25 Years of Statistics in Archaeology

Clive Robert Orton

Abstract

Taking as its starting point the seminal Mamaia conference of 1970 and the first CAA conference (both attended by the author), this paper examines the changing role of statistics in archaeology, as perceived by archaeologists, statisticians, and the author himself. It concentrates on how and why archaeologists have used statistics, rather than on the particular techniques they have used, although there is of course an interaction between the two. It discusses the questions: do archaeologists understand what statistics is about? do they really want to? do modern computer packages help or hinder? what (if anything) has changed?

1 CAA and the history of statistics in archaeology

The start of the series of CAA conferences did not mark a particularly significant point in the history of the use of statistics in archaeology. Indeed, statistics was not on the agenda at the first conference, which dealt entirely with 'Information Retrieval', only appearing on the agenda for the second conference in 1974. The 'Quantitative Methods' sub-title did not appear until the 1981 London conference (the first to be held outside Birmingham), although statistics had featured strongly in some of the intervening years. So before looking at the period 1973-1997, I shall try to set the activities of CAA in the field of statistics in a wider context, both historically and geographically.

CAA started shortly after the seminal conference *Mathematics in the Archaeological and Historical Sciences* which was held in Mamaia, Romania, in 1970 (Hodson *et al* 1971), and which can be seen as a formal international recognition of the status of quantitative methods in archaeology, or as a rite of passage from a phase of experimentation to one of acceptance and optimism. Participation was mainly from Romania and the UK, but ten other European countries, Canada, India, and the USA were also represented. This conference followed the international conference *Archéologie et Calculateurs*, held by the CNRS in Marseille in 1969 (Gardin 1970), with mainly French participation, but eleven other European countries, Canada, Turkey, the USA, and Venezuela were also represented. The first CAAs were neatly sandwiched between two conferences on the related subject of sampling: *Sampling in Archaeology* in the USA in 1973 (Mueller 1975) and *The Role of Sampling in Contemporary British Archaeology* in 1977 (Cherry *et al* 1978).

The picture given by the Marseille and Mamaia conferences is of widespread but mainly uncoordinated experimentation and development across Europe, the USA and Canada, and a need to bring researchers together to share ideas and experiences. They followed about twenty years of relatively small-scale and isolated research, the start of which I shall mark by some sampling experiments undertaken by Treganza and Cook (1948) and the little-known work of Myers (1950). The 1950s saw statistics impinging on debates about typology (e.g. Spaulding 1953), and attempts to formalise the previously intuitive technique of seriation (Robinson 1951), both in the USA. The first review paper came in the mid-'50s (Heizer and Cook 1956), followed at the end of the decade by what appears to have been the first quantitative methods conference in archaeology, held in 1959 at Burg Wartenstein, Austria, under the auspices of the Wenner-Gren Foundation for Anthropological Research (Heizer and Cook 1960); many of the contributions would now be recognised as archaeometry.

The papers that really put quantitative methods 'on the map' in the USA and the UK included Binford's study of Mousterian variation (Binford and Binford 1966), Cowgill's overview of techniques (Cowgill 1968), Clarke's study of beaker pottery (Clarke 1962; 1970), and Hodson's work on Iron Age cemeteries and artefacts (Hodson 1969; 1970).

By the early 1970s there was a feeling of 'spring-time' in the air, with green shoots appearing and bringing the promise of a bountiful harvest. Ideas as well as people seemed to be coming together and pointing the way forward. Outright opposition was rare (e.g. Hawkes 1968) and could be dismissed as a Luddite reaction by people who did not really understand what was going on. CAA seemed well placed to be part of this movement. A quotation from Spaulding (1960, 83) sums up this feeling that surrounded the birth of CAA:

". . . archaeologists are universally users of quantitative methods in the broadly descriptive and comparative sense and that they frequently resort to more explicit statistical techniques for treating special problems. I . . . predict that applications of the latter type will become increasing common . . . . The failure of our predecessors to employ elaborate quantitative techniques was not the result of either ignorance or stupidity; they were properly and understandably preoccupied with the gross description and ordering of the grand cultural types, one does not need regression analysis or chi-square to grasp and describe the essential difference between an Acheulian and a Magdalenian assemblage. Similarly, the current trend towards utilization of more elaborate and theoretically sophisticated quantitative methods is not dilettantism or a naive attempt to appropriate some of the current prestige of the physical sciences by aping their methods. It is rather an effort to discover and communicate subtle differences between closely related assemblages, so that details can be inserted into the broad outline. It is not an exaggeration . . . to predict that the future of archaeology is in large measure bound up with the success or failure of this effort."

2 Where are we now?

We can contrast this confidence with a range of recent views:

". . . there seems to be as yet little assimilation amongst archaeologists of the basic notions of experimental design which . . . plays an essential part in all applications of statistics. Perhaps . . . archaeostatistics can be said to be immature, and not yet of the same status as its better-known companion subjects." (Fieller 1993, 280).

"In certain respects the development of quantitative methodology in archaeology can be . . . seen as imitating developments in other areas such as geography or taxonomy. Such imitation has been decried, with one major concern being the fear that methodologies thus imported embody assumptions inappropriate to archaeological data and problems. This . . . has led to calls for the development of methodology that is 'congruent' or 'concordant' with archaeological problems (e.g. Carr, 1985; Aldenderfer, 1987a).

. . . there is an attendant danger that can be highlighted by analogy with the development of the 'quantitative revolution' in geography. There, quantitative methods were associated with a particular theoretical standpoint -- positivism -- that engendered unrealistic expectations about what such methods might achieve. The inevitable disappointment with, and backlash against, this approach encompassed (in some quarters) quantitative methods with the result that methodologically useful babies were unfairly thrown out with the theoretical bathwater." (Baxter 1994, 7)

"There has been some decline in popularity in recent years because statistical methods are less popular with 'real world' archaeologists than twenty years ago. Statistical approaches were very much part of the 'new archaeology', now called processual archaeology, and post-processualists seem to feel less at ease with this subject. But there are signs that in the near future the pendulum will swing again in the other direction. The application of 'hard science' in archaeology is on its way back. The main reason for this is that much of the funding for scientific archaeological research is by way of 'hard science' projects linked to the environment. We are not sure whether statistical applications in archaeology are part of 'hard science' but they will certainly benefit from this development." (Kamermans and Fenema 1996)

"Although simple quantitative and statistical procedures have had a long history of use in archaeology, the decades of the 1960s and 1970s witnessed the "Great Borrowing", in which archaeologists searched through all sorts of sciences, ranging from physics to ecology, in an effort to find methods to help make sense of archaeological data (Clark and Stafford 1982). . . .there has been much misuse of methods and a fragmentation of effort. There have been frequent expressions of dissatisfaction with the use of quantitative methods in archaeological research; . . . quantitative methods have yet to fulfil the promise we thought they offered." (Aldenderfer 1987a, 90)

"How archaeologists present the evidence they collect, the hypotheses they make . . ., and the interpretations they construct is about to change. Technological, sociological, and economic forces outside archaeology along with shifts in popular expectations of archaeological presentation are fostering a situation in which the image is soon to become the major component of archaeological argument." (Ross 1996)

I would add to these my personal observations that most archaeologists are still afraid of statistics, regarding the subject as third, after death and taxes, in a list of inevitables to be avoided for as long as possible. The thought that one day they will have to "do some statistics" on the data they have collected is pushed to the back of their mind until it can be avoided no longer, at which point the answer to their plea of "what can I do?" is probably the apocryphal one to the lost traveller: "if that's where you want to go, I wouldn't start from here".

3 How did we get here?

So how did we get from the optimism of 25 years ago to the fragmented situation of the 1990s, with feelings about quantitative methods that range from at best disappointment to at worst irrelevance? Like true (if old-fashioned) archaeologists, we can try to answer this question by breaking the 25-year period into phases. Aldenderfer (1987b, 12) explored the idea that "topics in a scientific discipline follow a predictable course of four stages: early exploration, discovery, consolidation and accommodation', suggesting that the late 1970s/early 1980s might mark the transition of quantitative methods from the discovery phase to the consolidation phase. However, he also pointed out that "quantitative methods have penetrated archaeology at different rates in different subject areas" (*ibid.*: 13), and that a more detailed model was therefore needed. We can add that a simple chronological model does not explain the fragmentation of opinion in which we now find ourselves. For both reasons, it seems more useful to look at the past 25 years in terms of the tensions within a series of themes, which lie on a spectrum from the purely statistical to the purely archaeological, for example:

Statistical

Exploratory statistics	<-->	Confirmatory statistics
Statistical analysis	<-->	Statistical design
Classical statistics	<-->	Bayesian statistics
Numerical presentation	<-->	Graphical presentation
Commercial packages	<-->	Home-grown' packages

Sources of techniques; archaeology, other disciplines, 'all-purpose'sampling metaphor as a basis for interpretation
<--> Taphonomy

Achaeological

New Archaeology' <--> post-processual archaeology.

Although these themes are inter-related, it is worth looking at each to see how it may have contributed to our present situation.The first three themes can cause problems because archaeologists perceive statistics as a monolithic discipline. It may come as a shock to discover that statisticians disagree with one another, and there are different schools of thought and different emphases within the discipline; this shock can quickly lead to confusion in the face of conflicting advice

.Find type	Context date by latest century							
	to 11th	11th	12th	13th	14th	15th	16th	later	Totals
beads	1	2	1	-	4	2	8	19	**37**
belt-fittings	5	8	5	12	17	27	4	13	**91**
buckles	4	14	17	57	55	44	34	33	**258**
building ironwork	25	20	24	58	39	21	19	24	**230**
combs	9	12	6	2	2	-	4	10	**45**
furniture	16	10	6	20	8	4	8	8	**80**
gaming equipment	8	6	9	10	7	5	4	8	**57**
hones	17	28	7	42	29	23	5	9	**170**
horse furniture	5	8	6	26	12	5	4	11	**77**
horseshoes	23	36	52	104	63	17	19	33	**347**
jewelry	24	17	13	25	21	10	8	22	**140**
keys	12	32	23	38	21	15	10	19	**170**
kitchen equipment	11	6	13	13	9	6	12	10	**80**
knives	38	56	42	66	48	22	34	44	**350**
lighting equipment	5	20	35	50	19	7	2	6	**144**
locks	7	9	6	12	10	5	5	3	**57**
mortars	-	-	-	7	14	14	4	8	**47**
points	-	-	6	3	3	13	43	77	**145**
querns	7	18	7	10	6	-	1	1	**50**
reliquary fittings	8	21	25	24	15	17	6	6	**122**
sewing equipment	2	-	4	2	8	1	3	21	**41**
sewing pins	1	1	1	16	15	39	64	242	**379**
shoes	60	27	6	13	-	-		-	**107**
tacks	19	16	20	21	7	13	5	13	**114**
tenter-hooks	2	3	9	43	18	5	-	2	**82**
textile tools	16	34	30	36	19	5	1	9	**150**
toggles	2	2	2	5	-	1	-	1	**13**
tools	26	52	11	20	16	10	7	12	**154**
weapons	5	2	5	25	6	5	5	11	**64**
weights	1	5	4	3	5	3	6	6	**33**
Totals	**359**	**465**	**405**	**763**	**496**	**339**	**326**	**681**	**3834**

Figure 1: Numbers of finds from medieval Winchester by type and context date (from Biddle, Barclay and Orton 1990)

3.1 Explore or confirm?

The first theme covers the thorny issue of hypothesis tests, which are much mis-understood by archaeologists, and which generate much discussion among statisticians as to when and whether they should be used. What a hypothesis test does is to construct a very simple hypothesis (the 'null' hypothesis), usually representing 'no change' (e.g. when a new treatment is applied to a material), 'no difference' (e.g. between two C14 dates), 'no association/correlation' (e.g. between two variables) or 'randomness' (e.g. of a spatial pattern). The 'test' itself then ascertains whether it is reasonable to believe this null hypothesis in the light of data which are subsequently collected. Two inherent problems are:

1. it is a conservative procedure, i.e. it favours the null hypothesis since the data have to be strong enough to force us to change our mind about the null hypothesis,
2. it is heavily dependent on sample size: if we take a big enough sample, we are likely to be able to 'reject' a null hypothesis as implausible, even though the observed difference or pattern in the data is so small as to be of no practical importance.

When used in archaeology, I see hypothesis testing as a necessary precaution that precedes analysis and interpretation. For example, if there is no statistical evidence that the dates of two 'events' are not the same, it would be unwise to build an interpretation on the observed difference between the two C14 determinations that represent them. We hope that the null hypothesis will be rejected, so that we can proceed to interpret our data with our backs covered.

Unfortunately, this statistical procedure has sometimes been linked with a rigid 'hypothetico-deductive' approach to archaeology (Shennan 1988: 4) which may require the testing of complicated hypotheses that are quite beyond the procedure's scope. This has led to two equally erroneous and contrasting perceptions:

1. it may be fine in theory, but it doesn't work in practice,
2. it's only for people who believe in the 'hypothetico-deductive' approach.

A balanced view is lost.

The opposite approach, of exploratory data analysis, also has its dangers. Its objective is to make apparent patterns that may be present in the data, but are not immediately obvious (this is especially true of multivariate data). This is valuable, e.g. when using a correspondence analysis plot to expose the patterns hidden in a contingency table. As an example, contrast Figs. 1 and 2: the chronological pattern of the artefact types is present in the table (Fig. 1), but is very hard to see. The plot (Fig. 2) contains less information than the table (only 64%), but several chronological patterns are immediately apparent, for example the contrast between querns, which are 'early' at the bottom of the plot, and mortars, which fulfil the same function and are 'late' (at the top of the plot).

The danger is that the human eye is good at seeing patterns, *even when they are not there*, leading to the risk of over-interpretation. A quick check of the statistical significance of the overall pattern could remove this risk. What one may not do is to detect a possible pattern, e.g. in the value of a correlation coefficient, and then test the null hypothesis that it takes that value, *on the same data*. To take this route, one needs to explore half the dataset for a possible pattern, and then test it on the other half.

Archaeological criticism of the 'hypothetico-deductive' approach, combined with statistical warnings about the dangers discussed above, can create feelings of confusion which can deter archaeologists from using statistics at all.

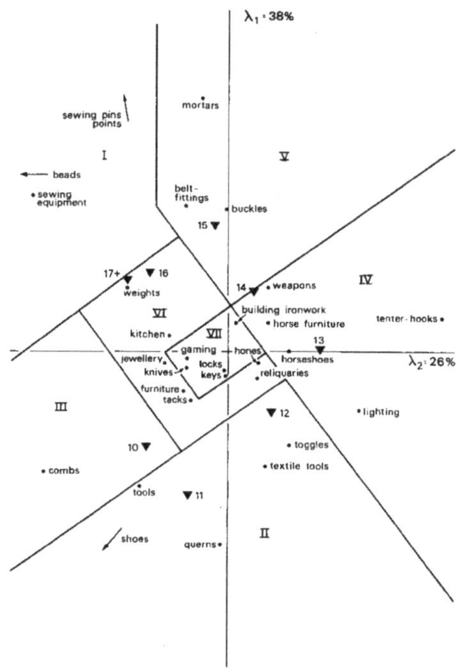

Figure 2: Correspondence analysis of numbers of finds from medieval Winchester by find type and context date. (from Biddle, Barclay and Orton 1990)

3.2 Analysis by design

Most archaeologists see statistics simply as an analytical tool: you collect your data, you analyse them, and you interpret the results. The idea that statistics has anything to do with the collection of data, or of the preceding stage of research design, is alien to them. Given the wish to postpone involvement with statistics for as long as possible, this is hardly surprising, but it has unfortunate consequences. It is very galling for an archaeologist to be told by a statistician that they have collected "the wrong data" or "not enough data" or, most puzzling of all, "too many data". "What's it to do with them?" they ask, "all I wanted was an analysis."

As an illustration, suppose an archaeologist wants to distinguish between different pottery fabrics on the basis of the statistical distribution of the sizes of the inclusions in the clay that are visible in a cross-section, and suppose that the differences lie in the relative proportions of the larger inclusions. There is a choice of method for describing the distributions: (s)he can either (a) count the numbers of inclusions in each of a series of size ranges, or (b) count the numbers of inclusions of each size range that are 'hit' by a sample of points in the cross-section. In either case, the data can be (correctly) compared by use of the Kolmogorov-Smirnov test. But if method (a) is chosen, it may well suggest that fabrics that are visually quite distinct are statistically "not significantly different". A few minutes statistical thought would suggest that method (b), with its greater emphasis on the larger inclusions (because, being larger, they have a higher probability of being 'hit' by the sampling points), is more likely to result in such differences being assessed as "significantly different". This actually happened, resulting in much extra work for the archaeologist (who here remains nameless to avoid embarrassment). The point is that, by not bringing in statistical considerations until the analysis stage, the archaeologist chose the 'wrong data' (for this particular problem) and created much unnecessary work. Choice of the correct analytical technique for the data in hand was not enough.

Further, each statistical technique carries its assumptions, and if a dataset does not fit in with those assumptions, the technique should not be used. Conversely, if a certain technique is to be used, the data must be chosen to fit its assumptions. Also, statistical input at the design stage can offer useful advice on the quantity of data needed to answer a certain question to a certain level of confidence: too few data and the results are inconclusive, too many and resources are wasted.

Resistance to statistical input at any stage other than "analysis" thus hamstrings the archaeologist's endeavour, causing inefficiency in the use of both time and money, and leads to disappointment with their results and disenchantment with statistics as a whole (see Fieller, quoted above).

3.3 Bayes rules ok?

There are some things that conventional ('Classical') statistical theory does not do very well. To appreciate the sort of problem that can arise, try working out the effect on two C14 dates of being told that one is stratigraphically earlier than the other. Suddenly, along came a new type of statistician, the Bayesians, who say that this sort of problem is grist to their mill, and start talking about "prior knowledge" and the like. They have a view of statistics that is in many ways closer to the archaeologists': that probability is subjective, and that statistics is about "the orderly influencing of opinions by data". Just when the archaeologist is getting excited, they let slip that the mathematics is hideously complicated, the software is not user-friendly and anyway you need at least a Sun workstation to run it. Feelings of let-down, almost of betrayal, can result. Statistics was bad enough, but two rival versions of the discipline are just too much.

Fortunately, areas where this approach is likely to yield pronounced benefits are beginning to be identified (e.g. interpretation of scientific dating techniques). Software is now available to perform the more routine tasks (e.g. OxCal, see Ramsey 1995), and ways of providing help for the more difficult problems are being developed (Buck and Christen, this volume).

3.4 How graphic are graphics?

"One picture is worth a thousand words", they say, but how many numbers is it worth? On of the developments in statistics in the past 25 years has been the growth of visual approaches to data, initially focused on the 'exploratory data analysis' (eda) school (Tukey 1977), and more recently under the name of 'data visualisation'. This is all to the good; we have already seen (section 3.1) how much easier it is to spot a pattern in (for example) a scatter plot than a table of figures. But we have also seen that the plot cannot, by itself, tell us whether it actually means anything: for that, we need some serious number-crunching. We need to remember what numbers are good at and what graphics are good at. At its simplest, numbers give information and graphics convey ideas or impressions. If I want to catch a train, I look up a timetable, not a timegraph, but if I want to show the relationship between the rows and columns of a table I use a scatter plot, not the table itself (compare Figs. 1 and 2 again). The reader of the graphic has to take on trust that there are enough data behind it to give it credibility.

Archaeologists can miss out in two ways here: they may have discovered analytically a very interesting pattern, but be unable to display it visually in a way that 'grabs' their reader, or they may plot a very pretty picture that means absolutely nothing because it is based on a handful of sherds (or coins, or flints, . . .). Once again, there may be a feeling that statistics has let them down.

3.5 Off the shelf or out of your head?

A very strong external trend over our period has been the increasing availability of commercial computer packages for data analysis and visualisation. At the start of our period, commercial software for data analysis was almost non-existent, and researchers had to write their own. Indeed, this was often a major part of a research project, and archaeologists required a proficiency in Basic, Pascal, C, etc. Today, there is a wide choice of software available for statistical analysis, from simple spreadsheet bolt-ons (like the Analysis Toolpak in Excel), through serious analytical packages like SPSS and BMDP, to very serious ones like Statistica, S-plus, GLIM and Genstat. Specialised archaeological software is now only needed for techniques that are unique to archaeology, such as seriation (e.g. Winbasp, iagraves, etc.), analysis of dating evidence (e.g. OxCal) and 'fragmentary data' (e.g. Pie-slice).

What have we gained, and what have we lost? We have gained freedom from an endless re-inventing of the wheel, and the need to acquire low-level programming skills. We have not acquired a sense of discrimination: even in Excel, dozens of techniques are available at the click of a button. The problem is -- which to choose? Here archaeologists are still on their own, and easy availability does not make their choice any easier. We have freed them from the need to know how to do the calculations (though I would claim there are still benefits in knowing), but not from knowing which calculations. Some have tried to avoid the decision by hitting the 'all options' button (e.g. in cluster analysis) and have drowned in their print-out. Ideas that this aspect could be handed over to an expert system have quietly disappeared.

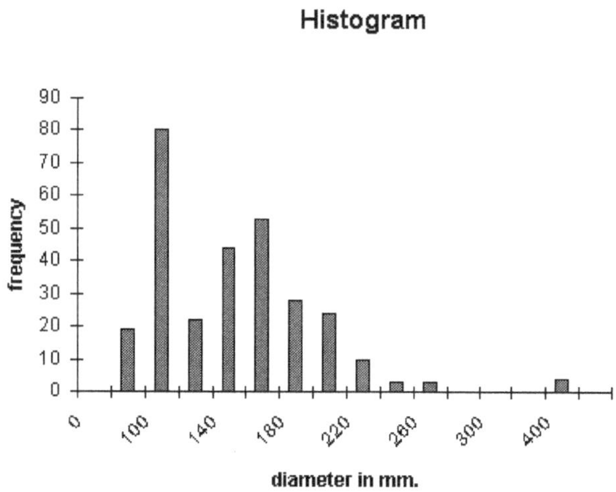

Figure 3: Example of so-called histogram produced by the use of Excel.

Also, I think we have lost quality. As graphical output has become widely available, it has often become worse in a communicative sense. For example, Excel cannot produce true histograms; it produces bar charts with a label saying "histogram" (Fig. 3). This can be seen as simple innumeracy, or as an example of our Alice in Wonderland world, where people believe that by attaching labels to things they make them become what the label says. Another bug-bear is the use of 3-dimensional graphics for 2-dimensional datasets; they obscure rather than illuminate, and can even mislead (Fig. 4) (see also Lockyear 1994). The comments of Tufte (1983) should be compulsory reading for all archaeologists.

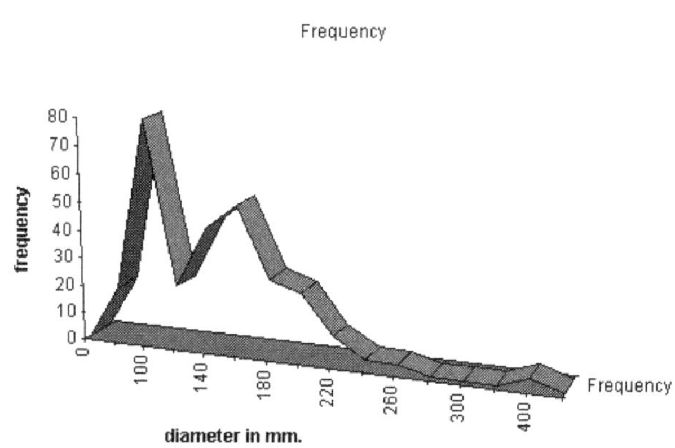

Figure 4: Example of three-dimensional line chart produced by the use of Excel.

Thus the undoubted technological and commercial advances have not made life easier for the user or for the reader, although they made have made it faster to obtain results. The clarity that could come from well-displayed data is still too often missing.

3.6 The Borrowers

Many statistical techniques have arisen in a particular field of application, and have later been transferred, more-or-less satisfactorily, to other disciplines. One of the beauties of mathematics (of which statistics is just part) is the ability of abstract systems to simultaneously represent widely differing physical realities. For example, the same mathematical model can be used to represent the condition of objects in a museum store, and the fate of heart-transplant patients (Orton 1996). This means that many of the 'problems' of analysis that archaeologists encounter may have already been met, and overcome, by someone working in a quite different discipline, and that a literature search may therefore save months or even years of work. Archaeologists have been well aware of this, and are in fact notorious 'borrowers' from other disciplines, as the quotation in section 2 from Aldenderfer (1987a, 90) suggests.

The start of our period saw Aldenderfer's "Great Borrowing" in full swing, with geography and ecology as favoured source disciplines, but the net stretching far wider, into areas as unlikely as astronomy. Some spectacular failures, for example the prediction by trend-surface analysis that North Oxfordshire pottery was probably made in South Wales or the North Sea led to a reappraisal (Hodder and Orton 1976: 166), and to a recognition that there had to be a measure of 'concordance' in the underlying models.

Inevitably the pendulum swung, in this case to the NIH (not invented here) syndrome, which argued that techniques should only be used in the discipline for which they were originally designed. This led to some bizarre 'home-grown' applications being used in situations where perfectly acceptable 'all-purpose' statistical techniques were available.

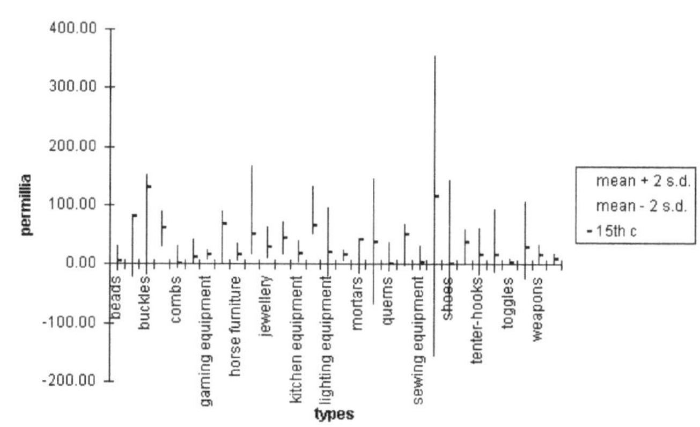

Figure 5: Example of a 'permillia' plot. The column of figure 1 representing the 15th century is plotted against the other columns across the range of artefact types. The bars show the ranges of ± 2 s.d. about the overall mean values. To display all of figure 1 would require a separate plot for each column.

A good example comes from the study of coin hoards, which usually involve simple datasets consisting of the counts of different types of coins in different hoards. The data can therefore be studied by techniques appropriate for contingency tables, such as the chi-squared test, log-linear analysis and correspondence analysis (e.g. Lockyear 1996). Dissatisfaction with existing techniques led Reece (1981) to devise his own technique, which he called "permillia". It first expresses the composition of each hoard as a series of "permillia" (i.e. per thousands, instead of the more usual percentages) of coins of each type. The permillia of the types are plotted, and compared to the mean value of the permillia of each type across all hoards, together with a range, usually the mean ± two standard deviations. An example of this approach, applied to the data of Figs. 1 and 2, is shown as Fig. 5. Values that lie outside their range are taken as evidence of divergence from the underlying pattern. This approach has three statistical flaws:

1. the permillia values from which each standard deviation is calculated do not have the same statistical distribution. Even under the implicit null hypothesis that all the hoards have the same pattern (and hence all hoards have the same mean permillia for any chosen coin type), the values all have different standard deviations because they are based on hoards of different sizes. The calculation of the standard deviation in this way (i.e. on percentages or permillia), and its use in constructing a hypothesis, is invalid.
2. probability arguments based on "± 2 s.ds" are implicitly based on normal distributions. The extent to which permillia tend not to be normal is demonstrated by the high proportion of ranges that include negative values,
3. the use of multiple significance tests (which is implicit in this approach) alters the significance levels of such tests. For example, in a small dataset of ten types in ten hoards, there would be 100 such tests. Even in purely random (artificial) data, the chance of at least one difference appearing to be statistically significant at the 5% level is very high (99.4%), and even at the 1% level it is better than 'evens' (63.4%).

Reece withdrew this technique under statistical pressure (Reece 1988, 22-3), but it has recently re-appeared (van Arsdell 1996) and the argument must be repeated (Orton 1997a). Re-inventing square wheels is a peculiarly futile pursuit.

Thus archaeologists must tread a path between two dangers -- the inappropriate use of borrowed techniques on one side and the unnecessary recreation or parodying of existing techniques on the other. Unless they are skilled in modelling, it may not be obvious to them why a technique is inappropriate, and if they do not familiarise themselves with a wide literature, they may be surprised to find "it's been done before". Small wonder if they feel "damned if they do, and damned if they don't", and confused about the whole business.

3.7 What's in a sample?

Sampling, as a means of learning about the characteristics of a population by studying some of its members, is a well-established statistical approach to many practical problems, from opinion polls to industrial quality control. Its *raison d'être* is that it is simply not necessary, and sometimes impossible, to examine all of a population to find out what we need to know about it. There is no point in devoting more resources to a problem than are needed to resolve it -- the result is just a waste of time and/or money.

Archaeologists have always been samplers *par excellence*, in a practical sense. Problems of resources require sampling to be employed on excavations, in scientific dating, and in many forms of non-intrusive fieldwork. Traditionally, it has been done on an intuitive basis, using 'professional judgement', although there were some suprisingly early attempts to examine the effects of sampling on data collection (e.g. Treganza and Cook 1948). Around the start of our period, the 'New Archaeology', with its emphasis on research design, led to this process becoming more explicit and statistical, as evidenced by the two conferences mentioned in section 1 (Mueller 1975; Cherry *et al* 1978). The over-rigid use of formal schemes caused some absurdities (Hole 1980), but it became generally accepted that this was an area where statistics had much to offer. The question of professional judgement remained, and under the influence of PPG 16 (DoE 1990) many archaeologists have sought the Holy Grail of a 'minimum percentage' for field evaluations (English Heritage 1997, 57) and have been upset when statisticians tell them that it does not exist. A more fruitful approach would be to agree a level of probability that a site contains no significant archaeological remains, that would entitle one to declare it 'clean', and design fieldwork projects to achieve this level. Bayesian statistics can help here too, by allowing archaeologists to incorporate their 'prior knowledge' (the closest to professional judgement it can get) into the calculations, thus reducing sample size (Orton 1997b). The price is a distinct step up in complexity, which would require specialised software and training.

But there is another, more controversial, way in which archaeology is sometimes thought of as sampling. Even if we excavate a complete site (supposing we could define what that meant), we would not discover all the artefacts and ecofacts that once existed on that site. One of the more perceptive questions that visitors ask is "where did all the missing bits [pottery, bone, etc.] go?" The answer is that we don't really know, but we haven't got them. This creates a very different sort of sample, since it is neither designed nor purposively selected: it just happened. Do the same rules of inference apply? Almost certainly not. But it is easy to unthinkingly behave as if they did. For example, if we compare the proportions of a certain type of pottery at several sites in a region, we implicitly assume that those proportions reflect in some way the proportions in some 'parent' populations from the sites. Why else would we compare them? Ideally, we want our estimates of the 'parent' proportions to be free of the effects of the post-depositional histories of the assemblages. This may mean attempting to model those effects (e.g. by recursive sampling, see Orton 1982) or by looking for 'invariants' -- parameters which are likely to survive the post-depositional histories (Orton 1993). Either way, the outcome is likely to be a set of statistical criteria on (for example) how pottery should be quantified, which may be welcomed by the archaeologist, or may be seen as an unwarranted interference. The tendency of statistics to get in the way of archaeologists' wish to "do their own thing" may cause resentment.

3.8 Newer than 'New'

It was a great misfortune for archaeology that the use of statistical techniques became associated in the popular mind with the school of thought known as the 'New

Archaeology' (aka processual archaeology). The link was claimed by the New Archaeologists as part of their bid for academic respectability, although statistical techniques were in use in archaeology well before the rise of New Archaeology, and some of their most cogent advocates were very scathing about New Archaeology: "we find its claims greatly exaggerated and therefore dangerous. . . . a bizarre mixture of naiveté and dogmatism" (Doran and Hodson 1975, 5). When processual archaeology came under criticism from the post-processual school, statistics tended to be found guilty by association. This is regrettable, and is perhaps an example of what has been called "The curse of originality". For a new approach to make itself appear distinctive, it may be necessary to reject certain aspects of an older paradigm with which it has really no quarrel (just as politicians tend to dismiss *all* their opponents' policies, even the ones with which they secretly agree). There may also be an element of genuine misunderstanding, based on the over-stated claims for statistics made by the New Archaeologists.

So what does statistics still have to offer archaeology in a post-processual era? Above all, it offers method. Even post-processual archaeologists use statistical techniques (e.g. Shanks and Tilley 1992: 137-240), but it seems to me that they have a problem with method. Archaeological analysis is primarily about *data* -- we may argue about which data, and how to collect or measure them, or from which theoretical perspective we view them, but ultimately they are data like any other. The view that archaeologists create data is an attack of *hubris*: the data are there, and our role is to select and record. If you create your data and I create mine, then we are in the position of the witnesses to a traffic accident that consisted of a collision between two stationary vehicles.

Conversely, what statistics does not do is to impinge directly on archaeological theory, although theory can impinge on statistics by creating a need for new forms of analysis, such as social status analysis (socistat), devised by Hodson for his analysis of the Hallstatt cemetery (Duncan *et al.* 1988). The role of statistical method is to mediate between data and theory; the creation of that theory is entirely the archaeologist's responsibility. But the acid test for any theory is whether is stands up to the data (i.e. whether the data support it or not), and this is where statistical method can have its say, not only in the analysis but also in the selection and collection of data.

4. Conclusion

What can we say now, in the late 1990s, about this long but uneasy relationship between archaeology and statistics? It has gone through various phases; some represent the usual oscillations that accompany the adoption of a new methodology, while some were caused by the vagaries of archaeological fashion, in which schools of thought have over- or under-played the role of statistics to suit their own agendas. It has also seen the introduction of many new techniques, most notably correspondence analysis in the 1980s (Bølviken *et al.* 1982) and kernel density estimation in the 1990s (Baxter and Beardah 1996); this aspect will be dealt with in more detail by Wilcock (this volume).

But other things, I suggest, have not changed. Many archaeologists still approach statistics with the air of a soldier about to enter a minefield. They sense rewards on the far side, but also sense traps for the unwary en route. Even when they are trying very hard, something may blow up in their face (see van Arsdell 1996; Orton 1997a). I think this is to some extent a self-fulfilling prophecy. Archaeologists are, as a rule, independent people who like to "do their own thing" and do not like the imposition of external constraints. To them, statistics should be "on tap, but not on top" (an old Civil Service saying, referring to the role of specialists in government, but equally applicable here). This means that while they are happy to borrow tools from the statistical bag, they are not keen to adopt the statistical ethos of data, for example as portrayed in the Statistical Cycle (Fig. 6). To do so would be to submit themselves to an outside authority, and the attitude of "it's my data and I'll do what I like with it" is very strong. It follows that although they may know how to perform techniques, they do not fully understand the implications of their data, and thus lay themselves open to the very sorts of errors that they fear they will make.

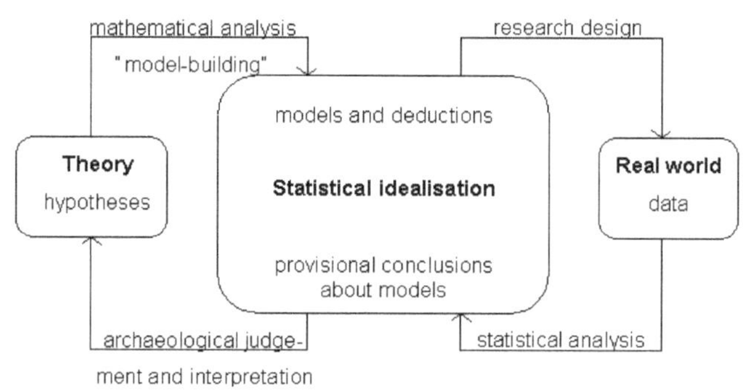

Figure 6: The Statistical Cycle.

What can be done? At the risk of sounding like a 'data fascist', I think that if archaeologists want the benefits of statistical techniques, they must submit to the disciplines that the use of such techniques inevitably bring. Once acquired, such disciplines can actually be liberating rather than constricting, since they free the archaeologist from a wide range of inappropriate decisions and actions, and from the need to try to think things out from first principles. Archaeological data are not uniquely difficult (whatever archaeological pride may say), and many of their features crop up in other subjects (where, of course, they may be handled just as badly). Recognition that statistics is not just a bag of techniques, but encompasses issues like the appropriateness of models, the quality and survival of data, and efficient design, can open up a wide range of relevant experience to archaeologists.

This will not come about overnight; some archaeologists may be too 'old' to change, others may cling to their philosophical uniqueness and purity, while others may clothe their fear in posturing. Perhaps only the real education of the next generation of archaeologists will put this rocky relationship on a proper footing.

Acknowledgements

I am grateful to Sue Laflin for suggesting this topic, to John Wilcock for agreeing to share it, and to Kris Lockyear for commenting on a draft of this paper.

Bibliography

Aldenderfer, M S, 1987a On the structure of archaeological data in Aldenderfer M. S. (ed.). *Quantitative Research in Archaeology*, 89-113. Newbury Park Sage Publications.

Aldenderfer, M S, 1987b Assessing the impact of quantitative thinking on archaeological research: historical and evolutionary insights in Aldenderfer M. S. (ed.). *Quantitative Research in Archaeology* 9-29. Newbury Park Sage Publications.

Baxter, M J, 1994, *Exploratory Multivariate Analysis in Archaeology*. Edinburgh Edinburgh University Press.

Baxter, M J, and Beardah, C C, 1996 MATLAB routines for Kernel Density Estimation and the Graphical Representation of Archaeological Data in Kamermans H. and Fenema K. (eds*.). Interfacing the Past Computer Applications and Quantitative Methods in Archaeology CAA95* (Analecta Praehistorica Leidensia 28), 179-184.

Biddle, M. Barclay K, and Orton, C, 1990 The chronological and spatial distribution of the objects in Biddle M. *Object and Economy in Medieval Winchester* (Winchester Studies 7ii), 42-73. Oxford Clarendon Press.

Binford, L R, and Binford, S R, 1966 A preliminary analysis of functional variability in the Mousterian of Levallois facies *American Anthropology* 68, 238-95.

Bølviken, E E, Helskog K, Helskog K, Holm-Olsen I M, Solheim, L, and Bertelsen, R, 1982 Correspondence analysis: an alternative to principal components *World Archaeology* 14, 41-60.

Carr, C, (ed.) 1985 *For Concordance in Archaeological Analysis*. Kansas City: Westport Publishers.

Cherry, J F, Gamble, C, and Shennan, S, 1978 *Sampling in Contemporary British Archaeology*. (British Archaeological Reports British Series 50).

Clark, G, and Stafford, R, 1982 Quantification in American Archaeology *World Archaeology* 14, 98-119.

Clarke, D L, 1962 Matrix analysis and archaeology with particular reference to British Beaker pottery *Proceedings of the Prehistoric Society* 28, 371-82.

Clarke, D L, 1970 *Beaker Pottery of Great Britain and Ireland*. Cambridge Cambridge University Press.

Cowgill, G L, 1968 Archaeological applications of factor cluster and proximity analysis *American Antiquity* 33, 367-75.

DoE 1990 *Planning Policy Guidance: Archaeology and Planning*. London Department of the Environment.

Doran, J E, and Hodson F R, 1975 *Mathematics and Computers in Archaeology*. Edinburgh Edinburgh University Press.

Duncan, R, Hodson, F R, Orton, C R, Tyers P A, and Vekaria A, 1988 *Data analysis for archaeologists: the Institute of Archaeology programs*. London Institute of Archaeology.

English Heritage 1997 *English Heritage Archaeology Division Research Agenda* [draft April 1997]. London English Heritage.

Fieller, N R J, 1993 Archaeostatistics: old statistics in ancient contexts *Journal of the Royal Statistical Society series D* 42, 279-95.

Gardin, J-C, (ed.) 1970 Archeologie et Calculateurs. Paris CNRS.

Hawkes, J, 1968 The proper study of mankind *Antiquity* 42, 255.

Heizer, R F, and Cook S F, 1956 Some aspects of the quantitative approach in archaeology *Southwestern Journal of Anthropology* 12, 229-248.

Heizer, R F, and Cook S F, (eds.) 1960 *The Application of Quantitative Methods in Archaeology* (Viking Fund Publications in Anthropology 28).

Hodder, I, and Orton C, 1976 *Spatial Analysis in Archaeology*. Cambridge Cambridge University Press.

Hodson, F R, 1969 Searching for structure within multivariate archaeological data *World Archaeology* 1, 90-105.

Hodson, F R, 1970 Cluster analysis and archaeology: some new developments and applications *World Archaeology* 1, 299-320.

Hodson, F R, Kendall D G, and Tautu P, (eds.) 1971 *Mathematics in the Archaeological and Historical Sciences*. Edinburgh Edinburgh University Press.

Hole, B L, 1980 Sampling in archaeology: a critique *Annual Review of Anthropology* 9, 217-34.

Kamermans, H, and Fenema K, 1996 Preface in Kamermans H and Fenema K (eds*.). Interfacing the Past Computer Applications and Quantitative Methods in Archaeology CAA95* (Analecta Praehistorica Leidensia 28) xi-xiii.

Lockyear, K, 1994 Ranters corner -- PUPs *Archaeological Computing Newsletter* 41, 1-2.

Lockyear, K, 1996 Dmax based cluster analysis and the supply of coinage to Iron Age Dacia in Kamermans H, and Fenema K, (eds.). *Interfacing the Past Computer Applications and Quantitative Methods in Archaeology CAA95* (Analecta Praehistorica Leidensia 28), 165-178.

Mueller, J W, (ed.) 1975 *Sampling in Archaeology*. Tucson University of Arizona Press.

Myers, O H, 1950 *Some Applications of Statistics to Archaeology*. Service des antiquities de l Egypte Cairo Government Press.

Orton, C R, 1982 Computer simulation experiments to assess the performance of measures of quantity of pottery *World Archaeology* 14, 1-20.

Orton, C R, 1993 How many pots make five? - an historical review of pottery quantification *Archaeometry* 35 , 169-184.

Orton, C R, 1996 Markov models for museums in Kamermans H. and Fenema K (eds.). *Interfacing the Past Computer Applications and Quantitative Methods in Archaeology CAA95* (Analecta Praehistorica Leidensia 28), 149-153.

Orton, C R, 1997a Testing significance or testing credulity? *Oxford Journal of Archaeology* 16, 219-225.

Orton, C R, 1997b A bayesian approach to a problem of archaeological site evaluation in Lockyear K. Sly T J T and Mihailescu-Bîrliba V (eds.). *Computer Applications and Quantitative Methods in Archaeology. CAA96* (Edîtura Demiurg Iasi).
Ramsey, C B, 1995 *OxCal. A radiocarbon calibration and analysis program.* Oxford Research Laboratory for Archaeology University of Oxford.
Reece, R, 1981 The “Normal” Hoard in Carcassonne C. and Hackens T. (eds.). *Numismatique et Statistique* (Strasbourg PACT 5), 299-308.
Reece, R, 1988 *My Roman Britain.* Cotswold Studies 3. Cirencester Cotswold Press.
Robinson W S 1951 A method for chronologically ordering archaeological deposits *American Antiquity* 16 293-301.
Ross S 1996 Archaeology s new language: multimedia in Higgins A Main P and Lang J (eds.). *Imaging the Past* (British Museum Occasional Paper 114) 286-7.
Shanks M and C Tilley 1992 *Re-constructing Archaeology* (2nd edn). London Routledge.
Shennan S 1988 *Quantifying Archaeology.* Edinburgh Edinburgh University Press.
Spaulding A C 1953 Statistical techniques for the discovery of artifact types *American Antiquity* 18, 305-13
Spaulding A C 1960 Statistical description and comparison of archaeological assemblages in Heizer R F and Cook S F (eds.) *The Application of Quantitative Methods in Archaeology* (Viking Fund Publications in Anthropology 28) 60-83.
Treganza A E and Cook S F 1948 The Quantitative Investigation of Aboriginal Sites: Complete Excavation with Physical and Archaeological Analysis of a Single Mound *American Antiquity* 13 207-297.
Tufte E R 1983 *The Visual Display of Quantitative Information.* Cheshire Conn. Graphics Press.
Tukey J W 1977 *Exploratory Data Analysis.* Reading MA Addison-Wesley.
Van Arsdell R 1996 A statistical analysis of Icenian coin hoards *Oxford Journal of Archaeology* 15 235-242.

Contact details

Clive Robert Orton
UCL Institute of Archaeology
31-34 Gordon Square
London WC1H 0PY
UK
email: c.orton@ucl.ac.uk

Getting the Best Fit? 25 Years of Statistical Techniques in Archaeology

John D. Wilcock

CAA 97

Abstract

The paper catalogues the first 25 years of CAA contributions, from diverse authors, institutions and countries, to statistical techniques in archaeology, including data analysis, Numerical Taxonomy, Similarity Studies, Factor Analysis, Principal Components Analysis, Correspondence Analysis, Multivariate Statistics, Matrix analysis, Regression, Pottery Quantification, Shape Coding, Cluster Analysis, Seriation, Multidimensional Scaling, Correlation of dating measurements, Simulation, Computer Modelling and archaeological theory, Expert Systems, Artificial Intelligence, Stratigraphical Analysis, Spatial Analysis and Geographical Information Systems. The introduction briefly covers seminal achievements to the discipline of computing archaeology before the advent of CAA in 1973.

1 Introduction

1.1 Early days

Irwin Scollar (1982) in his address entitled "Thirty years of computer archaeology and the future" started out by saying that the title was wrong, and that it should really read something like "25 or so years", and yet in 1997 CAA97 celebrated 25 years of Computer Applications and Quantitative Methods in Archaeology in the meetings of CAA since 1973. Obviously this points out that all was not darkness on the face of the earth before CAA, so we should begin by exploring the seminal work which was undertaken in archaeological applications of computers since the machines became available for such research in the late 1940s and early 1950s.

1.2 Late 1950s, 1960s

These were the days of mainframe computers, electronic valves and early transistor machines, regarded primarily as calculating engines. Much of the work concerned mathematical and statistical techniques applied to archaeological data. Techniques had however been developed in a pencil-and-paper fashion before the advent of computers, examples being the "Sequence Dating" (matrix ordering, seriation) of Flinders Petrie (1899) involving the ordering of Egyptian pre-Dynastic pottery records written on slips of paper, which was later adopted for Zuñi pottery classification in the USA (Kroeber 1916), and various matrix ordering and minimum spanning tree derivation methods.

1.3 Main strands in computing archaeology

There have been in general three different categories of problem, with three different corresponding groups of workers involved in computing archaeology from the beginning. The first group was mathematicians and statisticians. In the late 1950s and early 1960s the first and second generation computers were regarded primarily as calculating engines. Much of the work concerned mathematical and statistical techniques applied to archaeological data. The paper on seriation by Robinson (1951) can be regarded as the beginning of the seriation class of numerical methods in archaeology. In this we have the first example of "hunting in pairs", where Brainerd and Robinson each contributed their expertise to a joint project. In the UK, data analysis methods became popular in archaeology from about 1966, following the availability of a standard work by Sokal and Sneath (1963). Numerical taxonomy was likewise encouraged by papers by Hodson, Sneath and Doran (1966) and Doran and Hodson (1966), and factor analysis by Binford and Binford (1966). Cultural pattern studies employed factor analysis (Binford & Binford 1966), Multidimensional Scaling (Doran and Hodson 1966), Principal Components Analysis (Hodson 1969), Canonical Analysis (Graham 1970), and Constellation Analysis (Azoury & Hodson 1973). In France, at the laboratory for mathematical statistics at the University of Paris VI, Escofier (1969) developed Correspondence Analysis.

The second group of people consisted of scientists and engineers concerned with scientific data from prospection measurements (resistivity meter, proton gradiometer) made on archaeological sites, and from chemical and emission analyses made on artefacts for composition or dating. It is not surprising that scientists, engineers, mathematicians and statisticians were first in the field, for they had early access to first and second generation computers.

The third group of people were museum people who may or may not have been archaeologists. According to Cowgill (1967a; 1967b; 1968) site data was first put into a computer in about 1959 by Ihm (1961) and Gardin. Gardin claims that this 1959 work, on the Euratom IBM 650 at Ispra, Italy, on a collection of Eurasian Bronze Age axes, was the first use of statistical techniques in archaeology using a computer. Early computers had little memory, so the first implementations of databanks are heavily concerned with data coding and compression. Early databanks were also set up in the early 1960s for excavation and museum catalogues.

Archaeologists really got involved much later (late 1970s, early 1980s) when they could afford personal microcomputers. This review paper will be confined to comments on the quantitative methods of data analysis used for processing data about archaeological entities: Numerical Taxonomy, Similarity Studies, Factor Analysis, Principal Components Analysis, Correspondence Analysis, Multivariate Statistics, Matrix analysis, Regression, Pottery Quantification, Shape Coding, Cluster Analysis, Seriation, Multidimensional Scaling, Correlation of dating measurements, Simulation, Computer Modelling and archaeological theory, Expert Systems, Artificial Intelligence, Stratigraphical Analysis, Spatial Analysis and Geographical Information Systems. Developments in all areas have been hardware and software driven by progress in computers and computing (processor speed, memory size, operating systems and high-level languages) outside the archaeological field.

1.4 Early conferences

Conferences with some content of mathematics and statistics applied to archaeology before the inception of CAA included:

1. 1950 New York (Brainerd 1951)
2. 1959 Burg Wartenstein (Spaulding 1960)
3. 1963 Moscow (Koltchin 1965)
4. 1966 Rome (Centre National de la Recherche Scientifique 1968)
5. 1968 New York (Metropolitan Museum of Art 1968)
6. 1969 Marseilles (Gardin and Richaud (eds.) 1970)
7. 1970 Mamaia (Hodson, Kendall and Tautu 1971; Wilcock 1970; Hodson and Kendall 1971)
8. 1971 Sheffield (Renfrew 1973)
9. 1971 Marseilles (Kendall 1974)

The 1970 Mamaia conference covered the subject areas Typology & Taxonomy, Seriation — including Petrifaction, Kendall's HORSHU and *Operation Speckled Band* (an unbending of the "horseshoe" configuration common in seriations shown on multidimensional scaling scalograms, being a literary reference to Conan Doyle's Sherlock Holmes novel *The Speckled Band*), Population Genetics & Historical Demography, "Unusual Applications" — Mosaic analysis, databases, geophysics, graphics, and excavation data capture, showing that these last topics were in their infancy, Linkage and Multidimensional Scaling, and "New Techniques" — glottochronology, comparison of multivariate analyses, cemetery analysis, and pottery shape analysis. Around this time Principal Components Analysis replaced Factor Analysis, which was really never applied in archaeology, and Multidimensional Scaling appeared, only to go out of favour in modern computing archaeology.

In particular the Mamaia conference provided a gathering ground for young computer archaeologists, some of whom decided to set up the Computer Applications in Archaeology Association for the running of annual conferences, which were held initially in Britain from 1973.

In the following bibliographies, seminal works, both books and papers, are given up to 1973. Although there are many books on computing archaeological topics and papers published outside CAA, dated 1974 or later, these are not given below, since the purpose of this paper is to review the achievements of CAA only, against the background of earlier work. The coverage is up to and including CAA95.

2 Data analysis, numerical taxonomy, similarity studies, factor analysis, principal components analysis, correspondence analysis, multivariate statistics, matrix analysis, regression, pottery quantification, shape coding and cluster analysis

Numerical taxonomy as applied to archaeology concerns the attachment of numerical quantities to certain attributes of archaeological materials, whereby the description of the materials may be made more objective. By calculating suitable similarity coefficients between pairs of objects based on these numerical quantities a typology may be constructed which is based solely on the population.

The subject stands on the broad-based theory of statistics developed over the past 75 years. An important early paper by Mahalanobis (1936) gives the definition of the generalised distance coefficient between species and sub-species, based on pooled variance and covariance. The increasing availability of computers made numerical taxonomy more popular, and this increased interest was reflected in papers by Sneath and Sokal (1962) and Sokal and Sneath (1963). These works defined taxonomic terms, with reference to biological data. The most important techniques for archaeologists are seriation, phenon diagrams (dendrograms), similarity coefficients and taxonomic distance. A research seminar on statistics and archaeology held at the Institute of Archaeology, London on 30 May 1964 reflected the increasing interest among archaeologists, and a relevant paper was that by Roe on the metrical and statistical analysis of hand-axe groups, published in more detail in 1968.

In the USA Brown and Freeman (1964) used regression in the study of sherd frequencies from the Carter Ranch Pueblo, using a UNIVAC computer, Binford and Binford (1966) carried out an analysis of Mousterian artefacts, and Cowgill (1968) investigated the advantages and limitations of multidimensional scaling, factor analysis and cluster analysis, discussing his own work and the results of Hodson, Binford, and Brown and Freeman.

There has been a lively debate over the validity of polythetic agglomerative, monothetic divisive, single-link, multiple-link and average-link clustering methodologies. In 1965 there appeared the first of a series of papers concerning clustering methods, which aroused a controversy which has continued to the present. The protagonists were a Cambridge group (Jardine, Jardine and Sibson) and a group from Australia (Lance, Williams, Clifford and Dale); the controversy concerned clustering methods, automatic classification, taxonomic hierarchies and the rigour of the associated mathematics, or lack of it. Much of the controversy can be attributed to different linguistic usage, but in the remaining differences probably both schools had something to offer. It seems pointless to adhere blindly to rigorous mathematical arguments about single-link clustering being the only valid procedure, when average-link clustering gives sensible and useful results in many archaeological applications. On the other hand, the proliferation of methods without adequate theoretical background leaves the archaeologist in some doubt as to which to use, and perhaps leads to a subjective choice of algorithm which the automatic classification methods were originally constructed to avoid.

Most of the methods are based on storage of the data in matrix or half-matrix form, the items vs. properties incidence matrix leading to the Q-type item vs. item square matrix comparing items, and the R-type property vs. property square matrix comparing the performance of properties. The incidence and square matrices may be manipulated by re-ordering columns and rows to give linear seriations, and minimum spanning trees may also be derived. The property vs. property square matrix is also the starting point for Principal Components Analysis.

One of the earliest applications of matrix ordering in Britain (to British Beaker pottery) was by Clarke (1963), the first of many books and papers produced by this author before his untimely death.

The Cumulative Percentage Graph and its application was described by Doran and Hodson (1966), Kerrich and Clarke (1967) and Whallon (1972).

Several manual methods have been developed, whereby small sets of data may be analysed without the use of a computer. The methods re-order matrices to produce linear seriations (Gelfand 1971), or take the two highest links from each column, followed by deletion of the weakest links in each loop, to produce the minimum spanning tree (Renfrew and Sterud 1969).

Data analysis has received the largest coverage in the literature, perhaps because of its theoretical appeal, and because it is less labour-intensive than data recording from instruments or creating databases. The simplest applications in this field for computers are the generation of descriptive statistics and the manipulation of quantities of data too large to be managed by hand. The routine production of basic descriptive statistics, diagrams and charts is now commonplace, providing the starting point for more complex analytical studies.

Data analysis is the dominant activity in archaeology, and classification comes a close second. Their extension into computing has led to a variety of methods largely developed from the biological sciences. Cluster Analysis is the core of the computerised classification procedures, but the methods are linked to many other areas such as Factor Analysis, Principal Components Analysis and Correspondence Analysis. These methods have become possible only through use of the computer.

The early applications of data analysis were often tackled by archaeologists and statisticians "hunting in pairs", problems of type coding being left to the archaeologists to do by hand, and the statisticians calculating similarity values and re-ordering matrices in order to seriate or classify the data.

In data analysis most attention has been paid to procedures for classifying, ordering (in terms of time or evolution) and grouping artefacts, assemblages or sites (Similarity Coefficients, Shape Analysis, Cluster Analysis, Seriation), procedures for discovering "factors" or dominant characteristics (Principal Components, Multidimensional Scaling, Multidimensional matrix ordering), and procedures for discovering geographical or spatial relationships (Curve Fitting, Pattern Recognition, Nearest Neighbour Analysis, Chi-Squared, Pearson's Contingency Coefficient, Local Density Analysis, Trend Surface Analysis, etc.).

Thus it was that the mathematical clustering algorithms which appeared in the 1950s and 1960s for biology and biometrics were readily adapted for use in archaeology (Hodson, Sneath & Doran 1966; Doran 1967). Since the early 1970s well-known and reliable packages such as CLUSTAN and SPSS have reduced the problems of data analysis for the archaeologist. The use of well-tested packages is to be encouraged, since this reduces the need for programming, but archaeologists should not use the algorithms uncritically and should understand the statistical limitations of the methods and when they should or should not be used. The "results" will depend very much on the algorithm used, and this is not well understood by some archaeologists — there will always be an "answer" but is it the correct answer? In the early days the algorithms were severely restricted in matrix size by the amount of memory available, and outputs were restricted to line printer. The improved memory space and cheap colour graphics available in modern desk-top computers has revolutionised the presentation of clustering and classification results. The use of well-tested packages is to be encouraged, since users may then concentrate on matters of data selection, entry and validation rather than on programming. However, what may then be supposed to be an objective procedure because a computer is being used, is subjective in the sense that different results are obtained from different algorithms, a point little understood by some archaeologists.

English language workers often ignore the significant contributions which have been made by the French (summarised by Djindjian 1989). Several statistics laboratories in France contributed to a quantitative movement known as 'the French School of Data Analysis'. The chief contributions were numerous multivariate analysis methods, Correspondence Analysis, and cluster analysis algorithms (Typological Analysis, Morphological Analysis, culture pattern studies, provenance studies).

3 Seriation, multidimensional scaling, correlation of dating measurements

Seriation received attention first because there were in existence well-known manual methods for matrix ordering and minimum spanning tree linkage long before computers became generally available. The first notable "hunting in pairs" team was Brainerd and Robinson (Brainerd 1951). Belous (1953) applied the new seriation ideas to the Central California chronological sequence, while Ascher (1959) used a three-pole plot to illustrate seriation. Ascher and Ascher (1963) developed the first computer program for the ordering of matrices after the method of Brainerd and Robinson, and Dempsey and Baumhoff (1963) extended the seriation method to presence/absence data.

The first computer program for Multidimensional Scaling was designed by Shepard (1962), with the support of Kruskal (1964a; 1964b), and the method was further developed by Kendall (1963; 1969a; 1969b ;1970; 1971a; 1971b) from the work of Flinders Petrie (1899). Kendall's 1971a paper introduced a multidimensional scaling algorithm modified by a circular product transformation, the HORSHU method (see above in the description of the 1970 Mamaia conference) developed by Wilkinson (the "circle-up" method of unbending the horseshoe).

One of the simplest and fastest algorithms for seriation was developed by Goldmann, an archaeologist and Kammerer, a programmer (Goldmann 1968; 1972). Interest in seriation increased through the early and mid 1970s, since when little new has appeared.

Hodson (1968; 1969) worked on a collection of La Tène brooches from a linear cemetery at Münsingen-Rain, using average-link cluster analysis, principal components analysis and multidimensional scaling. Hodson, Sneath and Doran (1966) particularly discussed the Münsingen-Rain application. Hodson (1970) later developed the k-means cluster analysis method.

Seriation is one of the extremely few quantitative analytical methods which can be said to have been developed by archaeologists strictly for archaeological application. In importance in the field of archaeological problems it can probably be said to be third (with data analysis first and classification second). In the late 1960s, however, there was an explosion of methodology which was not led by archaeologists, but rather by mathematicians and statisticians. The problem of seriation was attacked theoretically, leading to a variety of methods which archaeologists must now choose between. Multidimensional Scaling, very popular in the late 1960s and early 1970s, has links with seriation if one reads around the 'horseshoe' on a scalogram, but the method has gone out of favour in the 1990s.

4 Simulation, computer modelling and archaeological theory

Ideas and approaches derived from the world of computers have had a significant impact on archaeological thought and method. The introduction of computer processing has influenced the analysis of archaeological data by enabling more complex manipulations and statistical calculations to be done than could have been achieved in any other way. More importantly, the need for clarity and logical precision in computing has forced archaeologists into more precise ways of thinking, leading in turn to new ideas for analysis or even to reconsideration of theory. The process is cumulative, and use of a computer inevitably leads to further applications for that computer.

Simulation is one of the newer and less important computer applications in archaeology. The approach offers an attractive approach to model building, linked to systems theory. An archaeological explanation becomes a matter of defining the variables and actors in a population or culture, and of defining the relationships and interactions between these variables and actors. The main obstacles have been the difficulty of estimating the size of parameters for a hypothetical system from the available archaeological data, and thereafter the difficulty of checking the validity of the results of the simulation against what actually happened in archaeological time.

Chenhall (1966; 1968) discussed the logic of models, and Cowgill (1967a; 1967b: 1968) was instrumental in introducing the SYMAP software for mapping, using it to interpret the urbanisation of Teotihuacan, Mexico, on the basis of detailed mapping, surface reconnaissance and selected excavations.

The first of many papers by Doran (1967a), formerly a member of the Department of Machine Intelligence and Perception, Edinburgh, put forward a computer scientist's viewpoint on the use of computers in archaeology. Further papers (1967b; 1970; 1971a; 1972) described the development of general machine intelligence concepts applied to archaeology. The papers explore systems theory and computer simulations applied to archaeology, evaluating attempts by Clarke and others to make use of concepts drawn from systems theory and cybernetics, and also comparing archaeological reasoning and machine reasoning. The 1971 paper described the computer analysis of the linear cemetery at Münsingen-Rain. The fibulae data consists of measurements and motifs, and the results were presented in distribution map and histogram form.

5 Expert systems and artificial intelligence

Attempts to use Expert System methodology in archaeology have largely failed because of the extremely diffuse nature of the archaeological situation. Where a modicum of success has been achieved, such as in the classification of teeth (Brough and Parfitt 1984), the data fields and measurements are already precisely defined in a scientific sense.

6 Stratigraphical analysis

A number of techniques for ordering archaeological contexts based on context relationships have been developed. These all sprang from the Harris Matrix type of definition of context relationships (Harris, E.C. 1975. 'The stratigraphic sequence: a question of time', *World Archaeology*), and the methods now provide routine tools for analysis of the relationships between excavated contexts on an archaeological site.

7 Spatial analysis and geographical information systems

Spatial analysis began with the central place theory of Christaller (1933), but geographers in general were slow to adopt quantitative methods and the use of computers.

In plant studies spatial analysis using quadrats was employed in the late 1950s and early 1960s, but the introduction of geographical co-ordinates came much later in computing archaeology, archaeological spatial analysis techniques not appearing until the late 1960s and early 1970s. The simple archaeological area plots of the mid-1960s have given way to standard mapping and contouring packages such as SYMAP, and more recently to sophisticated GIS packages. Trend Surface Analysis was applied by Sneath (1967) to distributions of various skull types.

For successful use in archaeology, spatial analysis techniques will be needed beyond those described by Hodder and Orton (Hodder, I. and C. Orton 1976. *Spatial analysis in archaeology*, Cambridge University Press, Cambridge). With the availability of larger memories, larger data sets have been manipulated through the 1980s and 1990s using Geographical Information Systems. However, although many pretty overlay pictures have been obtained by logical conjunctions of the improved data sets, there has been insufficient development in spatial simulation techniques to influence archaeological theory.

8 Commentary and conclusions

With respect to the importance of statistics and quantitative methods in computing archaeology, a study has been made of the developments reported in the published papers of the Computer Applications and Quantitative Methods in Archaeology Conferences since 1973. The further developments in computing archaeological techniques attributable to CAA are listed in the bibliographies below, and the coverage of the CAA conferences between 1973 and 1995 is comprehensive for statistical methods. The selection of seminal books and papers up to 1973 is mine alone, and no work outside CAA is listed from 1974 onwards, since the brief is to examine the contribution of CAA to the subject, within the context of earlier work.

A raw count of the number of pages published in various CAA years is shown in Fig. 1, with peaks in the two-volume publications of 1988 and 1995.

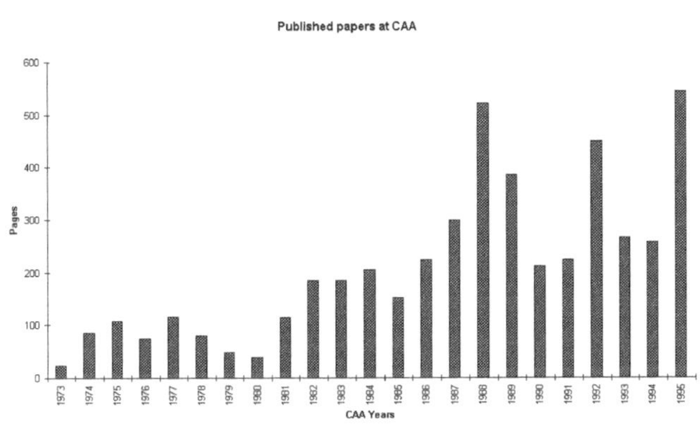

Figure 1: A graph of the raw page counts of papers published in the CAA years 1973–1995, showing peaks in the two-volume publications of 1988 and 1995.

A more enlightening summary is shown by the graph of Fig. 2, which shows the percentage importance of quantitative methods at CAA. Databases and statistics were the earlier and most important applications. Starting with a 65% emphasis on databases in 1973, a cyclic effect is detectable, databases being more important in 1973, 1982–1985 and 1989–1991, and statistics being more important in 1974–1980, 1987 and 1992. The lower statistics peaks from 1987 onwards are a consequence of more diverse areas of application being developed in later years.

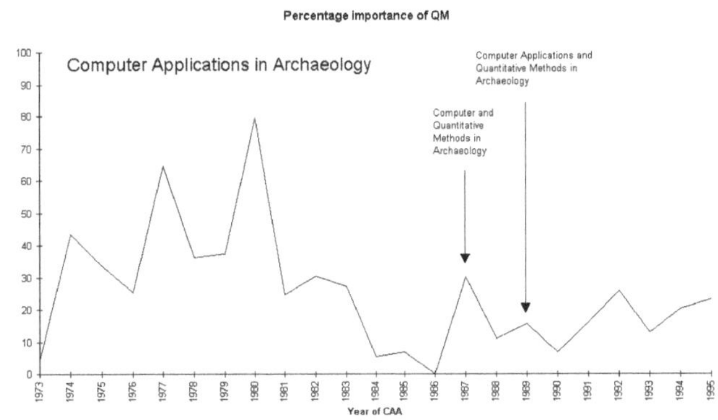

Figure 2: A graph of the percentage importance of quantitative methods (QM) at CAA for the years 1973–1995, with the titles of the conferences. Statistics and QM were better represented in 1974–1980, 1987 and 1992. The lower statistics peaks from 1987 onwards are a consequence of more diverse areas of application being developed in later years. An apparent decline in popularity of QM papers in 1986 prompted QM workers to make representations, and the original "Computer Applications in Archaeology" title was changed in 1987 to "Computer and Quantitative Methods in Archaeology" to encourage more QM papers. In 1989 the title was changed again to "Computer Applications and Quantitative Methods in Archaeology" which it has remained ever since.

The original title of the conferences was "Computer Applications in Archaeology" (CAA). However, the apparent decline in quantitative methods evident at the 1986 CAA Conference prompted quantitative methods workers, and particularly Bob Laxton, to propose a change in title of the Conferences to "Computer and Quantitative Methods in Archaeology", and this was accepted in 1987. In 1989 the title was changed again to "Computer Applications and Quantitative Methods in Archaeology" which it has remained ever since.

Finally, what is the health of quantitative methods in Computing Archaeology generally? 1995 shows a rising limb, and the indications are that a relative importance for quantitative methods of about 25% of all papers at CAA will be maintained. We shall see!

Bibliography

Seminal Books and Papers before CAA

General

Binford, L R, 1964 A consideration of archaeological research design, *American Antiquity,* 29(4), 425–441

Binford, L R, 1965 Archaeological systematics and the study of culture process, *American Antiquity,* 31(2), 203–210

Brainerd, G W, 1951 In Griffin, J B (ed), Essays on archaeological methods, *Anthropological Papers* 8, Museum of Anthropology, University of Michigan

Burton, V, Bonin, A, Lourie, J and Spiselman T, 1970 The computer and archaeology, *American Journal of Archaeology,* 74, 221–223

Centre National de la Recherche Scientifique 1968 *Calcul et formalisation dans les sciences de lhomme*, Paris

Chenhall, R G, 1965 et seq. *Newsletter of computer archaeology*, Department of Anthropology, Arizona State University, Tempe, Arizona

Chenhall, R G, 1966 The description of archaeological data in computer language, *American Antiquity,* 32(2), 161–167

Chenhall, R G, 1971 *Computers in anthropology and archeology*, IBM Data Processing Application GE20-0384-0, International Business Machines

Cole, A J (ed) 1969 *Numerical taxonomy*, Academic Press, London & New York

Cowgill, G L, 1967a Computer applications in archaeology, *Computers and the Humanities,* 2(1), 17–23

Cowgill, G L, 1967b Computer applications in archaeology, Fall Joint Computer Conference, *AFIPS* 31, 331–337

Doran, J E, 1971b An evaluation of statistical applications, *Newsletter of Computer Archaeology,* 7(2), 1–2

Gardin, J-C, 1958 Four codes for the description of artifacts: an essay in archaeological technique and theory, *American Anthropologist,* 60, 335–357

Gardin, J-C, 1965 On a possible interpretation of componential analysis in archaeology, *American Anthropologist,* 67(5 part 2), 9–23

Gardin, J-C, 1967 Methods for the descriptive analysis of archaeological material, *American Antiquity,* 32(1), 13–30

Gardin, J-C, 1971 Archaeology and computers: new perspectives, *Int. Soc. Sci. J.,* XXIII(2), 189–203

Gardin, J-C and Richaud, A M (eds) 1970, *Archéologie et calculateurs, Problèmes sémiologiques et mathématiques*, Editions du CNRS, Centre National de la Recherche Scientifique, Paris

Hodson, F R and Kendall, D G, 1971 Mathematics in archaeology and history, *Antiquity,* 45, 55–56

Hodson, F R, Kendall, D G and Tautu, P, 1971 *Mathematics in the archaeological and historical sciences*, University of Edinburgh Press, Edinburgh

Kendall, D G, 1974 Archaeology and mathematics, *Antiquity,* XLVIII, 40–45

Koltchin, B A (ed) 1965 *Archeologija I estestvennye nauki*, Institut Archeologii, Akademia nauk SSSR, Nauka, Moskva

Metropolitan Museum of Art, 1968 *Computers and their potential applications in museums*, Arno Press, New York

Petrie, W M Flinders, 1899 Sequences in prehistoric remains, *J. Royal Anthrop. Inst.,* 29, 295–301

Renfrew, C, 1973 *Before civilization. The radiocarbon revolution and Prehistoric Europe*, Jonathan Cape, London

Renfrew, C (ed) 1973 *The explanation of culture change: Models in prehistory*, Gerald Duckworth & Co Ltd, London

Sneath, P H A, 1957 The application of computers to taxonomy, *Journal of General Microbiology,* 17, 201–226

Sneath, P H A and Sokal, R R, 1962 Numerical taxonomy, *Nature,* 193(4818), 855–860

Sneath, P H A and Sokal, R R, 1973 *Numerical taxonomy. The principles and practice of numerical classification*, W.H. Freeman and Company, San Francisco

Sokal, R R and Sneath, P H A, 1963 *Principles of numerical taxonomy*, W.H. Freeman and Company, San Francisco

Sokal, R R and Rohlf, F J, 1962 The comparison of dendrograms by objective methods, *Taxon,* XI(2), 33–40

Tugby, D J, 1965 Archaeological objectives and statistical methods: a frontier in archaeology, *American Antiquity,* 31(1), 1–16

Watson, R A, 1972 The new archaeology of the 1960s, Antiquity, XLVI, 210–215

Whallon, R, Jr. 1972 The computer in archaeology: a critical survey, *Computers and the Humanities,* 7 (1), 29–45

Wilcock, J D, 1969 Computer applications in archaeology, *Datafair 69, Abstracts of the British Computer Society Symposium Papers*, The British Computer Society, London

Wilcock, J D, 1970 Our man in Mamaia, *Science and Archaeology,* 2/3, 12–16

Factor analysis, principal components analysis, correspondence analysis

Binford, L R, 1972 *An archaeological perspective*, Academic Press Inc. (London) Ltd, London

Binford, L R and Binford, S R, 1966 A preliminary analysis of functional variability in the Mousterian of Levallois facies, *American Anthropologist,* 68, 238–295

Escofier, B, 1969 Lanalyse factorielle, *Les cahiers du Buro 13*

Gower, J C, 1966 A Q-technique for the calculation of canonical variates, *Biometrika,* 53, 588–589

Graham, J M, 1970 Discrimination of British Lower and Middle Palaeolithic handaxe groups using canonical variates, *World Archaeology*, 1, 321–342

Hotelling, H, 1936 Simplified calculation of principal components, Psychometrika, 1(1), 27–35

Seriation and multidimensional scaling

Ascher, M, 1959 A mathematical rationale for graphical seriation, *American Antiquity*, 25(2), 212–214

Ascher, M and Ascher, R, 1963 Chronological ordering by computer, *American Anthropologist*, 65, 1045–1052

Belous, R E, 1953 The Central California chronological sequence re-examined, *American Antiquity*, 18(4), 341–353

Brainerd, G W, 1951 The place of chronological ordering in archaeological analysis, *American Antiquity*, 16(4), 301–313

Dempsey, P and Baumhoff, M, 1963 The statistical use of artifact distributions to establish chronological sequence, *American Antiquity*, 28(4), 496–509

Doran, J E, 1967a Electronic computers and archaeology: a computer scientists viewpoint, Research Seminar on archaeology and related subjects, Institute of Archaeology, London, 23 January 1967

Doran, J E, 1971a Computer analysis of data from the La Téne cemetery at Münsingen-Rain, in Hodson, F R, Kendall, D G and Tautu, P, 1971 *Mathematics in the archaeological and historical sciences*, 422–431, University of Edinburgh Press, Edinburgh

Doran, J E and Hodson, F R, 1966 A digital computer analysis of Palaeolithic flint assemblages, *Nature*, 210(5037), 688–689

Gelfand, A E, 1971 Seriation methods for archaeological materials, *American Antiquity*, 36(3), 263–274

Goldmann, K, 1968 Zur Auswertung archäologischer Funde mit Hilfe von Computern, *Die Kunde*, 19, 1–8

Goldmann, K, 1972 Zwei Methoden chronologischer Gruppierung, *Acta Praehistorica et Archaeologica*, 3, 1–34

Hodson, F R, 1968 *The La Tène cemetery at Münsingen-Rain. Catalogue and relative chronology*, Verlag Stämpfli and CIE AG Bern

Hole, F and Shaw, M, 1967 *Computer analysis of chronological seriation*, Rice University Studies, 53(3), 1–166

Kendall, D G, 1963 A statistical approach to Flinders Petries sequence dating, *Bulletin of the International Statistics Institute*, 40, 657–680

Kendall, D G, 1969a Incidence matrices, interval graphs and seriation in archaeology, *Pacific Journal of Mathematics*, 28, 565–570

Kendall, D G, 1969b Some problems and methods in statistical archaeology, *World Archaeology*, 1, 68–76

Kendall, D G, 1970 A mathematical approach to seriation, *Phil. Trans. Roy. Soc. London*, A269, 125–135

Kendall, D G, 1971a Seriation from abundance matrices, in Hodson, F R, Kendall, D G and Tautu, P, 1971 *Mathematics in the archaeological and historical sciences*, 215–222, University of Edinburgh Press, Edinburgh

Kendall, D G, 1971b Abundance matrices and seriation in archaeology, *Zeitschrift für Wahrscheinlichkeitstheorie*, 17, 104–112

Kroeber, A L, 1916 Zuñi potsherds, *Anthropological Papers of the American Museum of Natural History*, New York, 18(1), 1–37

Kruskal, J B, 1964a Multidimensional scaling by optimizing goodness-of-fit to a nonmetric hypothesis, *Psychometrika*, 29(1), 1–27

Kruskal, J B, 1964b Nonmetric multidimensional scaling: A numerical method, *Psychometrika*, 29(2), 115–129

Kruskal, J B, 1971 Multidimensional scaling in archaeology: time is not the only dimension, in Hodson, F R, Kendall, D G and Tautu, P, 1971 *Mathematics in the archaeological and historical sciences*, 119–132, University of Edinburgh Press, Edinburgh

Kuzara, R S, Mead, G R and Dixon, K A, 1966 Seriation of anthropological data: A computer program for matrix ordering, *American Anthropologist*, 68(6), 1442–1455

Robinson, W S, 1951 A method for chronologically ordering archaeological deposits, *American Antiquity*, 16(4), 293–301

Robinson, W S and Brainerd, G W, 1952 Robinsons coefficient of agreement — a rejoinder, *American Antiquity* 18(1), 60–61

Shepard, R N, 1962 The analysis of proximities: multidimensional scaling with an unknown distance function. I., *Psychometrika*, 27(2), 125–140

Torgerson, W S, 1965 Multidimensional scaling of similarity, *Psychometrika*, 30(4), 379–393

Wilkinson, E M, 1971 Archaeological seriation and the travelling salesman problem, in Hodson, F R, Kendall, D G and Tautu, P, 1971 *Mathematics in the archaeological and historical sciences*, 276–283, University of Edinburgh Press, Edinburgh

Similarity studies, classification, shape coding and cluster analysis

Azoury, I and Hodson, F R, 1973 Comparing Palaeolithic assemblages: Ksar Akil, a case study, *World Archaeology*, 4(3), 292–306

Ball, G H, 1965 Data analysis in the social sciences: what about the details?, *American Federation of Information Processing Societies Fall Joint Computer Conference*, 27(1), 533–559, Macmillan, London

Ball, G H and Hall, D J, 1967 A clustering technique for summarizing multivariate data, *Behavioral Science*, 12(2), 153–155

Clarke, D L, 1962 Matrix analysis and archaeology with particular reference to British Beaker pottery, *Proceedings of the Prehistoric Society* N.S., XXVIII, 371–382

Clarke, D L, 1963 Matrix analysis and archaeology, *Nature*, 199(4895), 790–792

Clarke, D L, 1968 *Analytical Archaeology*, Methuen & Co Ltd, London

Clarke, D L, 1970 *Beaker pottery of Great Britain and Ireland*, 2 volumes, Cambridge University Press, London
Clarke, D L (ed) 1972 *Models in archaeology*, Methuen & Co Ltd, London
Clarke, D L, 1973 Archaeology: the loss of innocence, *Antiquity,* XLVII, 6–18
Cole, A J and Wishart, D, 1970 An improved algorithm for the Jardine-Sibson method of generating overlapping clusters, Computer Journal, 13(2), 156–163
Cormack, R M, 1971 A review of classification, *J. R. Statist. Soc.* B., 33(3), 321–367
Cowgill, G L, 1968 Archaeological applications of factor, cluster and proximity analysis, *American Antiquity,* 33(3), 367–375
Crawford, R M M and Wishart, D, 1967 A rapid multivariate method for the detection and classification of groups of ecologically related species, *J. Ecol.,* 55, 505–524
Doran, J E and Hodson, F R, 1966 A digital computer analysis of palaeolithic flint assemblages, *Nature,* 210, 688–689
Doran, J E, 1967b Computers in archaeology, 72nd ordinary meeting of the British Region of the Biometric Society, 7 December 1967, London
Edwards, A W F and Cavalli-Sforza, L L, 1964 Reconstruction of evolutionary trees, *Phenetic and Phylogenetic Classification,* 6, 67–76, The Systematics Association, London
Edwards, A W F and Cavalli-Sforza, L L, 1965 A method for cluster analysis, *Biometrics,* 21(2), 362–375
Freeman, H, 1961 On the encoding of arbitrary geometric configurations, *IRE Transactions on Electronic Computers* June 1961, 260–268
Friedman, H P and Rubin, J, 1967 On some invariant criteria for grouping data, *J. American Statistical Association,* 62(320), 1159–1178
Gardin, J-C, 1956 *Le fichier méchanograhique de loutillage*, Inst. Française dArchéologie de Beyrouth, 1–20
Gardin, J-C, 1958 Four codes for description of artifacts, an essay in archaeological technique and theory, *American Anthropologist,* 60(2), 335–357
Gardin, J-C, 1971 *Étude dun système integré dacquisition et dexploitation automatiques de données scientifiques*, Rapport CNRS 36/1971/CRI-IRIA Projet III-43
Gower, J C, 1966 Some distance properties of latent root and vector methods used in multivariate analysis, *Biometrika,* 53(3 and 4), 325–338
Gower, J C, 1967 A comparison of some methods of cluster analysis, *Biometrics,* 23(4), 623–638
Gower, J C and Ross, G J S, 1969 Minimum spanning trees and single link cluster analysis, *Applied Statistics,* 18(1), 54–64
Hartigan, J A, 1967 Representation of similarity matrices by trees, Jour. Am. Statist. Ass., 62(320), 1140–1158
Hodson, F R, 1969 Searching for structure within multivariate archaeological data, *World Archaeology,* 1, 90–105
Hodson, F R, 1970 Cluster analysis and archaeology, some new developments and applications, *World Archaeology,* 1, 299–320
Hodson, F R, Sneath, P H A and Doran, J E, 1966 Some experiments in the numerical analysis of archaeological data, *Biometrika,* 53(3 and 4), 311–324
Ihm, P, 1961 Classification automatique des objets de lâge du bronze, *Compte-rendus du séminaire sur les modèles mathématiques dans les sciences sociales,* 1960-1(3), 28–33, École Pratique des Hautes Études, 6e Section, Paris
Jardine, C J, 1970 Algorithms, methods and models in the simplification of complex data, *Computer Journal,* 13(1), 116–117
Jardine, C J, Jardine, N and Sibson, R, 1967 The structure and construction of taxonomic hierarchies, *Mathematical Biosciences,* 1, 173–179
Jardine, N and Sibson, R, 1968 The construction of hierarchic and non-hierarchic classifications, *Computer Journal,* 11(2), 177–184
Jardine, N and Sibson, R, 1971 Choice of methods for automatic classification, *Computer Journal,* 14(4), 404–406
Kerrich, J E and Clarke, D L, 1967 Notes on the possible misuse and errors of cumulative percentage frequency graphs for the comparison of prehistoric artefact assemblages, *Proceedings of the Prehistoric Society* N.S., XXXIII, 57–69
Krumbein, W C, 1959 Trend surface analysis of contour-type maps with irregular control-point spacing, *Journal of Geophysical Research,* 64(7), 823–834
Kruskal, J B, 1956 On the shortest spanning subtree of a graph and the travelling salesman problem, *Proc. Amer. Math. Soc.,* 7, 48–50
Lance, G N and Williams, W T, 1965 Computer programs for monothetic classification ("association analysis"), *Computer Journal,* 8(3), 246–249
Lance, G N and Williams, W T, 1966 Computer programs for polythetic classification ("similarity analyses"), *Computer Journal,* 9(1), 60–64
Lance, G N and Williams, W T, 1967a A general theory of classificatory sorting strategies I. Hierarchical systems, *Computer Journal,* 9(4), 373–380
Lance, G N and Williams, W T, 1967b A general theory of classificatory sorting strategies II. Clustering systems, *Computer Journal,* 10(3), 271–277
Mahalanobis, P C, 1936 On the generalised distance in statistics, *Proc. Nat. Inst. Sci. India,* 12, 49–55
Matthews, J, 1963 Application of matrix analysis to archaeological problems, *Nature,* 198, 930–934
Orton, C R, 1970 The production of pottery from a Roman-British kiln site: a statistical investigation, World Archaeology, 1(3), 343–358
Renfrew, C and Sterud, G, 1969 Close-proximity analysis: a rapid method for the ordering of archaeological materials, *American Antiquity,* 34(3), 265–277

Roe, D A, 1964 Metrical and statistical analysis of handaxe groups in the British Lower Palaeolithic, Research Seminar on Statistics and Archaeology, Institute of Archaeology, London, 30 May 1964

Rogers, D J and Tanimoto, T T, 1960 A computer program for classifying plants, *Science,* 132(3434), 1115–1118

Rohlf, F J, 1970 Adaptive hierarchical clustering schemes, *Syst. Zool.*, 18, 58

Rubin, J, 1967 Optimal classification into groups: an approach for solving the taxonomy problem, *J. Theoret. Biol.,* 15(1), 103–144

Sackett, J R, 1966 Quantitative analysis of Upper Palaeolithic stone tools, *American Anthropologist,* 68, 356–394

Sibson, R, 1971 Some observations on a paper by Lance and Williams, Computer Journal, 14(2), 156–157

Sneath, P H A, 1966 A comparison of different clustering methods as applied to randomly-spaced points, *The Classification Society Bulletin* 1

Spaulding, A C, 1953 Statistical techniques for the discovery of artifact types, *American Antiquity,* 18(4), 305–313

Spaulding, A C, 1960 Statistical description and comparison of artifact assemblages, in Cook, S F and Heizer, R F (eds), The application of quantitative methods in archaeology, 60–92, *Viking Fund Publications in Archaeology* 28, Quadrangle Books, Chicago

Thomas, D H, 1971 On the use of cumulative curves and numerical taxonomy, *American Antiquity,* 36(2), 206–209

Tugby, D J, 1958 A typological analysis of axes and choppers from Southwest Australia, *American Antiquity,* 24(1), 24–33

Voss, O, 1966 Dokumentationsproblemer Indenfor Arkaeologien, *Kuml*, 97–134

Wagner, N E, 1971a Computer studies of Ontario Iroquois, The Canadian Archaeological Association, 26 February 1971

Wagner, N E, 1971b *Coding and clustering pottery by computer*, Waterloo Lutheran University, Waterloo, Ontario

Ward, J H, 1963 Hierarchical grouping to optimise an objective function, *J. Am. Statist. Ass.*, 58, 236–244

Whallon, R Jr, 1971 A computer program for monothetic subdivisive classification in archaeology, University of Michigan Museum of Anthropology, *Technical Reports* 1, *Contributions in Computer Applications to Archaeology* 1

Whallon, R Jr, 1972 A new approach to pottery typology, American Antiquity, 37(1), 13–33

Williams, W T, Clifford, H T and Lance, G N, 1971 Group-size dependence: a rationale for choice between numerical classifications, Computer Journal, 14(2), 157–162

Williams, W T, Lance, G N, Dale, M B and Clifford, H T, 1971 Controversy concerning the criteria for taxonomic strategies, Computer Journal, 14(2), 162–165

Wishart, D, 1969 An algorithm for hierarchical classifications, *Biometrics,* 25, 165–170

Simulation and archaeological theory

Binford, S R and Binford, L R (eds), 1968 *New perspectives in archaeology*, Aldine Publishing Co., Chicago

Borillo, M, 1971 Formal procedures and the use of computers in archaeology, *Norwegian Archaeological Review,* 4 (1), 2-27

Bourelly, L, 1972 Quelques aspects de la notion moderne de simulation, in *Les Méthodes Mathématiques de lArchéologie,* 186–189, C.N.R.S. Centre dAnalyse Documentaire pour lArchéologie, Marseille

Chenhall, R G, 1968 The impact of computers on archaeological theory: an appraisal an projection, *Computers and the Humanities,* 3(1), 15–24

Clarke, D L, 1968 *Analytical archaeology*, Methuen, London

Doran, J E, 1970 Systems theory, computer simulations and archaeology, *World Archaeology,* 1(3), 289–298

Doran, J E, 1972 Automatic generation and evaluation of explanatory hypotheses, , in *Les Méthodes Mathématiques de lArchéologie*, 200–211, C.N.R.S. Centre dAnalyse Documentaire pour lArchéologie, Marseille

Gardin, J-C, 1971 Archaeology and computers: new perspectives, *Int. Soc. Sci. J.,* 23(2), 189–203

Heizer, R F and Cook, S F (eds), 1960 *The applications of quantitative methods in archaeology*, Viking Fund Publications in Archaeology 28, Quadrangle Books, Chicago

Spatial analysis (curve fitting, pattern recognition, nearest neighbour analysis, chi-squared, pearsons contingency coefficient, local density analysis, trend surface analysis, etc.)

Brown, J A and Freeman, L G Jr, 1964 A UNIVAC analysis of sherd frequencies from the Carter Ranch Pueblo, Eastern Arizona, *American Antiquity,* 30(2), 162–167

Christaller, W, 1933 *Die zentralen Orte in Suddeutschland*, Jena

Freeman, L G Jr and Brown, J A, 1964 Statistical analysis of Carter Ranch pottery, *Fieldiana: Anthropology* 15, Chicago Natural History Museum

Greig-Smith, P, 1952 The use of random and contiguous quadrats in the study of the structure of plant communities, *Annals of Botany* N.S., 16(62), 293–316

Greig-Smith, P, 1961 Data on pattern within plant communities I. The analysis of pattern, *Journal of Ecology,* 49, 695–702

Kershaw, K A, 1957 The use of cover and frequency in the detection of pattern in plant communities, *Ecology,* 38(2), 291–299

Sneath, P H A, 1967 Trend surface analysis of transformation grids, *J. Zool. Lond.,* 151, 65–122

Thompson, H R, 1958 The statistical study of plant distribution patterns using a grid of quadrats, *Australian J. Botany,* 6, 322–342

CAA

General

Scollar, I, 1982 Thirty years of computer archaeology and the future, *Computer Applications in Archaeology 1982*, 189–198, University of Birmingham

Wilcock, J D, 1973 A general survey of computer applications in archaeology, Proceedings of the First Annual Conference on Computer Applications in Archaeology, University of Birmingham, *Science and Archaeology*, 9, 17–21

Data analysis, similarity studies, multivariate statistics, matrix analysis, regression, pottery quantification, shape coding and cluster analysis

Allsworth-Jones, P, 1975 The Early Upper Palaeolithic in Central Europe: A cluster analysis of some Aurignacian and some Szeletian assemblages, *Computer Applications in Archaeology 1975*, 81–92, University of Birmingham

Allsworth-Jones, P and Wilcock, J D, 1974 Palaeolithic "leafpoints" — an experiment in taxonomy, *Computer Applications in Archaeology 1974*, 36–46, University of Birmingham

Barcelo, J A, 1993 Back-propagation algorithms to compute similarity relationships among archaeological artefacts, *Computer Applications and Quantitative Methods in Archaeology 1993*, 165–176, Staffordshire University

Barcelo, J A, 1995 Heuristic classification and fuzzy sets. New tools for archaeological typologies, *Interfacing the Past. Computer Applications and Quantitative Methods in Archaeology CAA95*, 155–164, *Analecta Praehistorica Leidensia* 28, University of Leiden

Baxter, M J, 1991 Archaeological uses of the biplot — a neglected technique?, *Computer Applications and Quantitative Methods in Archaeology 1991*, 141–148, University of Oxford

Baxter, M J and Cool, H E M, 1990 An approach to quantifying window glass, *Computer Applications and Quantitative Methods in Archaeology 1990*, 127–131, University of Southampton

Baxter, M J, Cool, H E M and Heyworth, M P, 1995 Detecting unusual data: an archaeometric example, *Interfacing the Past. Computer Applications and Quantitative Methods in Archaeology CAA95*, 95–101, *Analecta Praehistorica Leidensia* 28, University of Leiden

Beardah, C C and Baxter, M J, 1995 MATLAB routines for Kernel Density Estimation and the graphical representation of archaeological data, *Interfacing the Past. Computer Applications and Quantitative Methods in Archaeology CAA95*, 179–184, *Analecta Praehistorica Leidensia* 28, University of Leiden

Biro, K T, 1992 Good or bad? Raw material procurement criteria in the Carpathian Basin. A diachronic approach, *Computing the Past. Computer Applications and Quantitative Methods in Archaeology CAA92*, 405–413, Aarhus University Press, Aarhus University

Buck, C E, 1992 The provenancing of archaeological ceramics: a Bayesian approach, *Computing the Past. Computer Applications and Quantitative Methods in Archaeology CAA92*, 293–301, Aarhus University Press, Aarhus University

Bullas, S G, 1994 Identifying your local slag... the use of quantitative methods and microstructure analysis in determining the provenance of British bloomery slags from the late Iron Age to the end of the Roman occupation, *Computer Applications and Quantitative Methods in Archaeology 1994*, 95–99, University of Glasgow

Callow, P, 1981 Have computer, will classify? A Stone Age problem, *Computer Applications in Archaeology 1981*, 26–35, University of London, Institute of Archaeology ISBN 0 905853 12 1

Callow, P and Webb, R E, 1974 Cluster analysis of French Mousterian industries, *Computer Applications in Archaeology 1974*, 16, University of Birmingham

Caseau, B and Caseau, Y, 1994 A method for the analysis of incomplete data and its application to monastic settlements in Italy (4th-6th century), *Computer Applications and Quantitative Methods in Archaeology 1994*, 113–121, University of Glasgow

Clark, G A, 1974 On the analysis of multidimensional contingency table data using log linear models, *Computer Applications in Archaeology 1974*, 47–58, University of Birmingham

Dallas, C, 1991 Relational description, similarity and classification of complex archaeological entities, *Computer Applications and Quantitative Methods in Archaeology 1991*, 167–178, University of Oxford

Daniels, S G H, 1980 Two software packages for archaeological quantitative data analysis, *Computer Applications in Archaeology 1980*, 3–8, University of Birmingham

Djindjian, F, 1989 Fifteen years of contributions of the French school of data analysis to quantitative archaeology, *Computer Applications and Quantitative Methods in Archaeology 1989*, 193–204, University of York

Durham, P, Lewis, P and Shennan, S J, 1995 Image processing strategies for artefact classification, *Interfacing the Past. Computer Applications and Quantitative Methods in Archaeology CAA95*, 235–239, *Analecta Praehistorica Leidensia* 28, University of Leiden

Fieller, N and Flenley, E, 1987 Statistical analysis of particle sizes and sediments, *Computer and Quantitative Methods in Archaeology 1987*, 79–94, University of Leicester

Fleming, S J, Bedal, L-A and Swann, C P, 1993 Glassmaking at Geoy Tepe (Azerbaijan) during the early 2nd millennium BC: a study of blue colourants using PIXE spectrometry, *Computer Applications and Quantitative Methods in Archaeology 1993*, 199–204, Staffordshire University

Galloway, P, 1976 Cluster analysis using fragmentary data, *Computer Applications in Archaeology 1976*, 41–47, University of Birmingham

Gao, L, Luo, H and Wilcock, J D, 1989 The analysis of ancient Chinese pottery and porcelain shapes: a study of classical profiles from the Yangshao culture to the Qing dynasty using computerised profile data reduction, cluster analysis and fuzzy boundary discrimination, *Computer Applications and Quantitative Methods in Archaeology 1989*, 363–374, University of York

Goodson, K J, 1989 Shape information in an artefact database, *Computer Applications and Quantitative Methods in Archaeology 1989*, 349–361, University of York

Green, D F, 1975 Testing a traditional typology using cluster analysis, *Computer Applications in Archaeology 1975*, 25–32, University of Birmingham

De Guio, A and Secco, G, 1988 Archaeological applications of the Percolation Method for data analysis and pattern recognition, *Computer and Quantitative Methods in Archaeology 1988*, 63–93, University of Birmingham

Hall, N S and Laflin, S, 1984 A computer aided design technique for pottery profiles, *Computer Applications in Archaeology 1984*, 178–188, University of Birmingham

Hodson, F R and Tyers, P A, 1988 Data analysis for archaeologists: the Institute of Archaeology packages, *Computer and Quantitative Methods in Archaeology 1988*, 31–41, University of Birmingham

Huggett, J W, 1993 Numerical techniques for burial analysis, *Computer Applications and Quantitative Methods in Archaeology 1993*, 183–190, Staffordshire University

Jones, L D, 1987 Some computer applications to petrological analysis of pottery, *Computer and Quantitative Methods in Archaeology 1987*, 253–261, University of Leicester

Keene, S and Orton, C, 1991 Measuring the condition of museum collections, *Computer Applications and Quantitative Methods in Archaeology 1991*, 163–166, University of Oxford

Kobylinski, Z and Buko, A, 1992 Computer clustering in the analysis of non-morphological attributes of pottery sherds: two examples from Poland, *Computing the Past. Computer Applications and Quantitative Methods in Archaeology CAA92*, 349–356, Aarhus University Press, Aarhus University

Laflin, S, 1978 A study of similarity coefficients, *Computer Applications in Archaeology 1978*, 69–76, University of Birmingham

Laflin, S, 1979 A density function for cluster analysis, *Computer Applications in Archaeology 1979*, 36–38, University of Birmingham

Laflin, S, 1985 Input and analysis of profiles using a microcomputer, *Computer Applications in Archaeology 1985*, 91–94, Institute of Archaeology, London

Laflin, S, 1986 Use of a Sinclair Spectrum for shape analysis, *Computer Applications in Archaeology 1986*, 83–90, University of Birmingham

Laflin, S, Roper, A, Symonds, R P and White, R H, 1992 Analysis of pottery from Wroxeter Roman city, *Computing the Past. Computer Applications and Quantitative Methods in Archaeology CAA92*, 389–404, Aarhus University Press, Aarhus University

Leese, M N, 1979 A statistical study of Welsh Bronze Age metal artifacts, *Computer Applications in Archaeology 1979*, 45–52, University of Birmingham

Leese, M N and Bradley, S M, 1994 Conservation condition surveys at the British Museum, *Computer Applications and Quantitative Methods in Archaeology 1994*, 81–86, University of Glasgow

Leese, M N, Hughes, M J and Stopford, J, 1989 The chemical composition of tiles from Bordesley: a case study in data treatment, *Computer Applications and Quantitative Methods in Archaeology 1989*, 241–249, University of York

Leese, M N and Main, P L, 1983 An approach to the assessment of artefact dimensions as descriptors of shape, *Proceedings of the Conference on Computer Applications and Quantitative Methods in Archaeology CAA83*, 171–180, University of Bradford

Lloyd-Jones, J, 1994 Measuring biological affinity among populations: a case study of Romano-British and Anglo-Saxon populations, *Computer Applications and Quantitative Methods in Archaeology 1994*, 69–73, University of Glasgow

Lockyear, K, 1995 Dmax based cluster analysis and the supply of coinage to Iron Age Dacia, *Interfacing the Past. Computer Applications and Quantitative Methods in Archaeology CAA95*, 165–178, *Analecta Praehistorica Leidensia* 28, University of Leiden

Main, P L, 1978 The storage, retrieval and classification of artefact shapes, *Computer Applications in Archaeology 1978*, 39–48, University of Birmingham

Main, P L, 1981 SHU — An interactive graphics program for the storage, retrieval and analysis of artefact shapes, *Computer Applications in Archaeology 1981*, 75–82, University of London, Institute of Archaeology ISBN 0 905853 12 1

Main, P L, 1986 Accessing outline shape information efficiently within a large database, *Computer Applications in Archaeology 1986*, 73–82, University of Birmingham

Main, P L, 1987 Accessing outline shape information efficiently within a large database II: database compaction techniques, *Computer and Quantitative Methods in Archaeology 1987*, 243–251, University of Leicester

Menard, C and Sablatnig, R, 1995 Pictorial, three-dimensional acquisition of archaeological finds as basis for an automatic classification, *Interfacing the Past. Computer Applications and Quantitative Methods in Archaeology CAA95*, 415–428, *Analecta Praehistorica Leidensia* 28, University of Leiden

Morris, G and Scarre, C J, 1981 Computerised analysis of the shapes of a class of Prehistoric stone tools from West-Central France, *Computer Applications in Archaeology 1981*, 83–94, University of London, Institute of Archaeology ISBN 0 905853 12 1

Moscati, P, 1994 Quantitative analysis of Etruscan cinerary urns, *Computer Applications and Quantitative Methods in Archaeology 1994*, 101–104, University of Glasgow

Orton, C, 1991 Quantitative methods in the 1990s, *Computer Applications and Quantitative Methods in Archaeology 1991*, 137–140, University of Oxford

Orton, C, 1992 What lies behind the quantification debate?, *Computing the Past. Computer Applications and Quantitative Methods in Archaeology CAA92*, 273–278, Aarhus University Press, Aarhus University

Orton, C and Tyers, P, 1989 Error structures of ceramic assemblies, *Computer Applications and Quantitative Methods in Archaeology 1989*, 275–285, University of York

Orton, C and Tyers, P, 1990 A technique for reducing the size of sparse contingency tables, *Computer Applications and Quantitative Methods in Archaeology 1990*, 121–126, University of Southampton

Perry, D W, 1982 Cluster analysis: An aid to environmental interpretation?, *Computer Applications in Archaeology 1982*, 150–161, University of Birmingham

Pike, H, 1980 Cluster analysis of Greek pottery from Carthage, *Computer Applications in Archaeology 1980*, 17–27, University of Birmingham

Rees, D, Wilkinson, G G, Orton, C R and Grace, R, 1988 Fractal analysis of digital images of flint microwear, *Computer and Quantitative Methods in Archaeology 1988*, 177–183, University of Birmingham

Richards, J D, 1982 Profile analysis of Early Anglo Saxon pottery, *Computer Applications in Archaeology 1982*, 105–113, University of Birmingham

Ringrose, T J, 1992 Diversity Indices and archaeology, *Computing the Past. Computer Applications and Quantitative Methods in Archaeology CAA92*, 279–285, Aarhus University Press, Aarhus University

Rulf, J, 1992 Pre-processing of archaeological data, *Computing the Past. Computer Applications and Quantitative Methods in Archaeology CAA92*, 329–332, Aarhus University Press, Aarhus University

Scaife, B, Fleming, S J and Hancock, R G V, 1993 Clay resources at early Chinese kiln sites: The search for a reliable INAA, *Computer Applications and Quantitative Methods in Archaeology 1993*, 205–210, Staffordshire University

Scott, A, Whittaker, J, Green, M and Hillson, S, 1990 Graphical modelling of archaeological data, *Computer Applications and Quantitative Methods in Archaeology 1990*, 111–116, University of Southampton

Scott, W A, 1988 An application of the EM algorithm to archaeological data analysis, *Computer and Quantitative Methods in Archaeology 1988*, 43–52, University of Birmingham

Smith, L D, 1974 Cluster analysis of twenty-nine Epipalaeolithic sites in Israel, *Computer Applications in Archaeology 1974*, 3–15, University of Birmingham

Sneath, P H A, 1982 Classification and identification with incomplete data, *Computer Applications in Archaeology 1982*, 182–187, University of Birmingham

Stark, B L and Hepworth, J T, 1982 A Diversity Index approach to analysis of standardization in Prehistoric pottery, *Computer Applications in Archaeology 1982*, 87–104, University of Birmingham

Tirpakova, A and Vlkolinska, I, 1991 The application of some mathematical-statistical methods for the analysis of Slavic pottery, *Computer Applications and Quantitative Methods in Archaeology 1991*, 183–186, University of Oxford

Tomber, R, 1987 Multivariate statistics and assemblage comparison, *Computer and Quantitative Methods in Archaeology 1987*,29–38, University of Leicester

Townsend, M E, 1977 A cluster analysis of weapon heads, *Computer Applications in Archaeology 1977*, 99–104, University of Birmingham

Tyers, P and Orton, C, 1990 Statistical analysis of ceramic assemblies — a years progress, *Computer Applications and Quantitative Methods in Archaeology 1990*, 117–120, University of Southampton

Tyldesley, J B, Hardy, E A, and Williamson, M H, 1983 Estimating missing measurements on animal bone, *Proceedings of the Conference on Computer Applications and Quantitative Methods in Archaeology CAA83*, 151–160, University of Bradford

Vach, W and Alt, K W, 1992 Detection of kinship structures in prehistoric burial sites based on odontological traits, *Computing the Past. Computer Applications and Quantitative Methods in Archaeology CAA92*, 287–292, Aarhus University Press, Aarhus University

Weber, T, 1994 Multivariate methods for the classification of Lower and Middle Palaeolithic stone inventories, *Computer Applications and Quantitative Methods in Archaeology 1994*, 105–112, University of Glasgow

Wilcock, J D, 1974 The PLUTARCH System, *Computer Applications in Archaeology 1974*, 64–68, University of Birmingham

Wilcock, J D, 1977 A comparison of monothetic divisive and polythetic agglomerative classifications of archaeological data, *Computer Applications in Archaeology 1977*, 55–60, University of Birmingham

Wilcock, J D, 1993 Analysis of multidimensional matrices for archaeological data, *Computer Applications and Quantitative Methods in Archaeology 1993*, 191–197, Staffordshire University

Wilcock, J D, 1994 The incorporation of cluster analysis into multidimensional matrix analysis, *Computer Applications and Quantitative Methods in Archaeology 1994*, 55–62, University of Glasgow

Wilcock, J D and Coombes, T, 1985 Some further developments in hardware and software for the automatic capture of artefact shapes by television camera, *Computer Applications in Archaeology 1985*, 145–151, Institute of Archaeology, London

Wilcock, J D and Shennan, S J, 1975 The computer analysis of pottery shapes with applications to Bell Beaker pottery, *Computer Applications in Archaeology 1975*, 98–106, University of Birmingham

Principal components analysis, correspondence analysis

Axboe, M, 1992 Gold bracteates and correspondence analysis, *Computing the Past. Computer Applications and Quantitative Methods in Archaeology CAA92*, 333–342, Aarhus University Press, Aarhus University

Baxter, M J and Beardah, C C, 1994 Graphical presentation of results from principal components analysis, *Computer Applications and Quantitative Methods in Archaeology 1994*, 63–67, University of Glasgow

Baxter, M J and Heyworth, M P, 1989 Principal components analysis of compositional data in archaeology, *Computer Applications and Quantitative Methods in Archaeology 1989*, 227–240, University of York

Bertelson, R, 1987 The finds pattern of archaeological excavations: Correspondence Analysis as explorative tool, *Computer and Quantitative Methods in Archaeology 1987*,25–28, University of Leicester

Callow, P, 1976 British and French handaxe series, *Computer Applications in Archaeology 1976*, 33–40, University of Birmingham

Callow, P and Webb, R E, 1977 Structure in the S.W. French Mousterian, *Computer Applications in Archaeology 1977*, 69–76, University of Birmingham

Cool, H E M and Baxter, M J, 1993 Finds from the fortress: artefacts, buildings and correspondence analysis, *Computer Applications and Quantitative Methods in Archaeology 1993*, 177–182, Staffordshire University

Gob, A, 1987 Multivariate analysis of lithic industries: the influence of typology, *Computer and Quantitative Methods in Archaeology 1987*, 15–23, University of Leicester

Müller, J, 1995 The use of correspondence analysis for different kinds of data categories: Domestic and ritual global amphorae sites in Central Germany, *Interfacing the Past. Computer Applications and Quantitative Methods in Archaeology CAA95*, 217–222, *Analecta Praehistorica Leidensia* 28, University of Leiden

Ringrose, T, 1987 Correspondence analysis as an exploratory technique for stratigraphic abundance analysis, *Computer and Quantitative Methods in Archaeology 1987*, 3–14, University of Leicester

Ryan, N S, 1982 Micro-computer analysis of Romano-British coin loss, *Computer Applications in Archaeology 1982*, 162–171, University of Birmingham

Scollar, I, Herzog, I and Greenacre, M J, 1992 Colour and graphic display aids for correspondence analysis, *Computing the Past. Computer Applications and Quantitative Methods in Archaeology CAA92*, 325–327, Aarhus University Press, Aarhus University

Seriation, correlation of dating measurements

Avery, M, 1987 DATRAN: analysing radiocarbon dates, *Computer and Quantitative Methods in Archaeology 1987*, 75–78, University of Leicester

Bayliss, A and Orton, C, 1988 Seriation with parallel series — an historical example, *Computer and Quantitative Methods in Archaeology 1988*, 161–176, University of Birmingham

Buck, C E and Litton, C D, 1990 A computational Bayes approach to some common archaeological problems, *Computer Applications and Quantitative Methods in Archaeology 1990*, 93–99, University of Southampton

Graham, I, 1974 Seriation of graves and pits, *Computer Applications in Archaeology 1974*, 16, University of Birmingham

Graham, I, Galloway,P and Scollar, I, 1975 Model studies in seriation techniques, *Computer Applications in Archaeology 1975*, 18–24, University of Birmingham

De Guio, A and Secco, G, 1984 A new computer seriation algorithm, *Computer Applications in Archaeology 1984*, 199–209, University of Birmingham

Herzog, I and Scollar, I, 1988 A mathematical basis for simulation of seriatable data, *Computer and Quantitative Methods in Archaeology 1988*, 53–62, University of Birmingham

Laxton, R R, 1987 Some results on mathematical seriation with applications, *Computer and Quantitative Methods in Archaeology 1987*,39–44, University of Leicester

Laxton, R R and Litton, C D, 1983 Information theory and dendrochronology: the effect of pre-whitening, *Proceedings of the Conference on Computer Applications and Quantitative Methods in Archaeology CAA83*, 137–149, University of Bradford

Laxton, R R and Restorick, J, 1989 Seriation by similarity and consistency, *Computer Applications and Quantitative Methods in Archaeology 1989*, 215–225, University of York

Leese, M N, 1987 Methods for finding calendar date bands from multiple-valued radiocarbon calibration curves, *Computer and Quantitative Methods in Archaeology 1987*, 147–151, University of Leicester

Litton, C D, 1981 Dendrochronological analysis of timbers from Lincoln Cathedral, *Computer Applications in Archaeology 1981*, 70–74, University of London, Institute of Archaeology ISBN 0 905853 12 1

Litton, C D and Leese, M N, 1990 Some statistical problems arising in radiocarbon calibration, *Computer Applications and Quantitative Methods in Archaeology 1990*, 101–109, University of Southampton

Loving, S H, 1995 Estimating the age of stone artifacts using probabilities, *Interfacing the Past. Computer Applications and Quantitative Methods in Archaeology CAA95*, 251–261, *Analecta Praehistorica Leidensia* 28, University of Leiden

Madsen, T, 1989 Seriation and multivariate statistics, *Computer Applications and Quantitative Methods in Archaeology 1989*, 205–214, University of York

Orton, C, 1983 A statistical techniques for integrating C-14 dates with other forms of dating evidence, *Proceedings of the Conference on Computer Applications and Quantitative Methods in Archaeology CAA83*, 115–124, University of Bradford

Pike, H H H M and Bradley, R, 1974 Note on the analysis of lithic assemblages, *Computer Applications in Archaeology 1974*, 27–29, University of Birmingham

Reinhold, S, 1995 Time versus ritual — Typological structures and mortuary practices in Late Bronze/Early Iron Age cemeteries of North-East Caucasia (Koban Culture), *Interfacing the Past. Computer Applications and Quantitative Methods in Archaeology CAA95*, 195–202, *Analecta Praehistorica Leidensia* 28, University of Leiden

Rozoy, J-G, Bennink, J, Newell, R R and Constandse-Westermann, T S, 1991 The Rozoy Numerical Ordination and Seriation program package for the analysis of nominal data matrices with MS-DOS Personal Computers, *Computer Applications and Quantitative Methods in Archaeology 1991*, 187–190, University of Oxford

Salac, V, 1992 Seriation of Iron Age settlement sites in NW Bohemia — system of databases, CAAF program, *Computing the Past. Computer Applications and Quantitative Methods in Archaeology CAA92*, 343–348, Aarhus University Press, Aarhus University

Scott, A, 1992 A parametric approach to seriation, *Computing the Past. Computer Applications and Quantitative Methods in Archaeology CAA92*, 317–324, Aarhus University Press, Aarhus University

Multidimensional scaling

Bonsall, C and Leach, C, 1974 A multidimensional scaling analysis of British microlithic assemblages, *Computer Applications in Archaeology 1974*, 16, University of Birmingham

Spatial analysis (curve fitting, pattern recognition, nearest neighbour analysis, chi-squared, pearsons contingency coefficient, local density analysis, trend surface analysis, etc.)

Boekschoten, G R and Stapert, D, 1995 A new tool for spatial analysis: Rings and sectors plus density analysis and trace lines, *Interfacing the Past. Computer Applications and Quantitative Methods in Archaeology CAA95*, 241–250, *Analecta Praehistorica Leidensia* 28, University of Leiden

Buck, C E, Cavanagh, W G and Litton, C D, 1988 The spatial analysis of site phosphate data, *Computer and Quantitative Methods in Archaeology 1988*, 151–160, University of Birmingham

Clark, G A, Effland, R W, and Johnstone, J C, 1977 Quantitative spatial analysis: computer applications of nearest neighbor and related approaches to the analysis of objects distributed across two-dimensional space, *Computer Applications in Archaeology 1977*, 27–40, University of Birmingham

Cogbill, S, 1980 Computer post-hole analysis with reference to the British Bronze Age, *Computer Applications in Archaeology 1980*, 35–38, University of Birmingham

Constantine, A G, Gower, J C, and Zielman, B, 1992 A Cappadocian tablet problem, *Computing the Past. Computer Applications and Quantitative Methods in Archaeology CAA92*, 303–315, Aarhus University Press, Aarhus University

Djindjian, F, 1988 Improvements in intra-site spatial analysis techniques, *Computer and Quantitative Methods in Archaeology 1988*, 95–106, University of Birmingham

Eisler, J, Pejsa, J and Preuss, K, 1988 A digital model of archaeological excavations as the starting point of a database of primary information in Egyptology: method — procedure — experience, *Computer and Quantitative Methods in Archaeology 1988*, 109–132, University of Birmingham

Fieller, N and Oneill, S, 1982 Orientations of Bronze Age houses: Statistical analysis of directional data, *Computer Applications in Archaeology 1982*, 172–181, University of Birmingham

Fieller, N, Nolan, R and Robson, D, 1983 Spatial analysis in irregular regions, *Proceedings of the Conference on Computer Applications and Quantitative Methods in Archaeology CAA83*, 161–170, University of Bradford

Fletcher, M and Attwell, M, 1987 How many tombs make a site?, *Computer and Quantitative Methods in Archaeology 1987*, 61–74, University of Leicester

Fletcher, M and Lock, G, 1980 Computer assisted pattern perception within post hole distributions, *Computer Applications in Archaeology 1980*, 39–48, University of Birmingham

Fletcher, M and Reilly, P, 1987 Viking settlers and the Isle of Man: some simulation experiments *Computer and Quantitative Methods in Archaeology 1987*, 95–117, University of Leicester

Galanidou, N, 1992 Quantitative methods for spatial analysis at rockshelters: the case of Klithi, *Computing the Past. Computer Applications and Quantitative Methods in Archaeology CAA92*, 357–366, Aarhus University Press, Aarhus University

Goodier, A J, 1983 The formation of boundaries in the pagan Anglo-Saxon period: a statistical study, *Proceedings of the Conference on Computer Applications and Quantitative Methods in Archaeology CAA83*, 93–101, University of Bradford

Haigh, J G B, 1981 Procedures for the surface sampling of archaeological sites, *Computer Applications in Archaeology 1981*, 61–69, University of London, Institute of Archaeology ISBN 0 905853 12 1

Haigh, J G B, 1991 Radial basis functions and archaeological surfaces, *Computer Applications and Quantitative Methods in Archaeology 1991*, 157–161, University of Oxford

Haigh, J G B and Kelly, M A, 1986 Interactive spatial analysis on a micro, *Computer Applications in Archaeology 1986*, 162–170, University of Birmingham

Johnson, I, 1977 Local density analysis: A new method for quantitative spatial analysis, *Computer Applications in Archaeology 1977*, 90–98, University of Birmingham

Johnstone, J C, Effland, R W and Clark, G A, 1977 The Arizona State University nearest neighbor program: Documentation and discussion, *Computer Applications in Archaeology 1977*, 45–54, University of Birmingham

Jonkers, A R T, 1993 A different perspective: spatial analysis of Hazendonk unit C by layer reconstruction based dimension reduction, *Computer Applications and Quantitative Methods in Archaeology 1993*, 115–125, Staffordshire University

Kelly, M A and Haigh, J G B, 1983 Determination of archaeological structure by spatial analysis and association, *Proceedings of the Conference on Computer Applications and Quantitative Methods in Archaeology CAA83*, 181–188, University of Bradford

Litton, C D and Restorick, J, 1983 Computer analysis of post hole distributions, *Proceedings of the Conference on Computer Applications and Quantitative Methods in Archaeology CAA83*, 85–92, University of Bradford

Peterson, J, 1991 Fourier analysis of field boundaries, *Computer Applications and Quantitative Methods in Archaeology 1991*, 149–156, University of Oxford

Peterson, J W M, 1988 Information systems and the interpretation of Roman cadastres, *Computer and Quantitative Methods in Archaeology 1988*, 133–149, University of Birmingham

Peterson, J W M, 1994 Flavian fort sites in South Wales: a spreadsheet analysis, *Computer Applications and Quantitative Methods in Archaeology 1994*, 87–93, University of Glasgow

Peterson, J W M, 1995 A computer model of Roman landscape in South Limburg, *Interfacing the Past. Computer Applications and Quantitative Methods in Archaeology CAA95,* 185–194, *Analecta Praehistorica Leidensia* 28, University of Leiden

Rodgers, P, 1987 Multi-response permutation procedures, *Computer and Quantitative Methods in Archaeology 1987*,45–54, University of Leicester

Scollar, I, 1989 Geodetic and cartographic problems in archaeological data bases at and within the boundaries of some countries, *Computer Applications and Quantitative Methods in Archaeology 1989*, 251–273, University of York

Sneath, P H A, 1986 Some experiments in fitting pairs of diagrams that lack defined reference points, *Computer Applications in Archaeology 1986*, 179–196, University of Birmingham

Williams, W and Pike, H, 1984 The layout of Woodhenge *Computer Applications in Archaeology 1984*, 189–198, University of Birmingham

Wünsch, G, 1994 Spatial interrelationships analysis and its simple statistical tools, *Computer Applications and Quantitative Methods in Archaeology 1994*, 75–80, University of Glasgow

Simulation and computer modelling

Doran, J E, 1981 A computational model of early state collapse, *Computer Applications in Archaeology 1981*, 115, University of London, Institute of Archaeology ISBN 0 905853 12 1

Doran, J E, 1986 A contract-structure model of sociocultural change, *Computer Applications in Archaeology 1986*, 171–178, University of Birmingham

Freeman, P, 1987 How to simulate if you must, *Computer and Quantitative Methods in Archaeology 1987*, 139–146, University of Leicester

Iliff, N, 1980 The use of simulation in the understanding of patterning in cemeteries — Its potentials, problems and limitations, *Computer Applications in Archaeology 1980*, 28–34, University of Birmingham

Kamermans, H, 1994 Survey sampling, right or wrong?, *Computer Applications and Quantitative Methods in Archaeology 1994*, 123–126, University of Glasgow

Lockyear, K, 1990 Simulating coin hoard formation, *Computer Applications and Quantitative Methods in Archaeology 1990*, 195–206, University of Southampton

Lockyear, K, 1992 Coin hoard formation revisited..., *Computing the Past. Computer Applications and Quantitative Methods in Archaeology CAA92*, 367–376, Aarhus University Press, Aarhus University

Miller, A P, 1993 The York archaeological assessment: computer modelling of urban deposits in the City of York, *Computer Applications and Quantitative Methods in Archaeology 1993*, 149–154, Staffordshire University

Mithen, S J, 1987 Simulation as a methodological tool: inferring hunting goals from faunal assemblages, *Computer and Quantitative Methods in Archaeology 1987*, 119–137, University of Leicester

OFlaherty, B, 1988 The Southampton-York archaeological simulation system, *Computer and Quantitative Methods in Archaeology 1988*, 491–497, University of Birmingham

Orton, C, 1985 Two useful parameters for pottery research, *Computer Applications in Archaeology 1985*, 114–120, Institute of Archaeology, London

Orton, C, 1995 Markov models for museums, *Interfacing the Past. Computer Applications and Quantitative Methods in Archaeology CAA95,* 149–153, *Analecta Praehistorica Leidensia* 28, University of Leiden

Rahtz, S, 1988 A resource-based archaeological simulation, *Computer and Quantitative Methods in Archaeology 1988*, 473–490, University of Birmingham

Reynolds, P J, 1988 Sherd movement in the ploughzone — physical data base into computer simulation, *Computer and Quantitative Methods in Archaeology 1988*, 201–219, University of Birmingham

Sanjuan, L G and Lopez, J R, 1995 Predicting the ritual? A suggested solution in archaeological forecasting through qualitative response models, *Interfacing the Past. Computer Applications and Quantitative Methods in Archaeology CAA95*, 203–216, *Analecta Praehistorica Leidensia* 28, University of Leiden

Scott, R B, 1988 Simulating ancient strategic warfare, *Computer and Quantitative Methods in Archaeology 1988*, 505–521, University of Birmingham

Steele, J, Sluckin, T J, Denholm, D R and Gamble, C S, 1995 Simulating hunter-gatherer colonization of the Americas, *Interfacing the Past. Computer Applications and Quantitative Methods in Archaeology CAA95*, 223–227, *Analecta Praehistorica Leidensia* 28, University of Leiden

Sumner, A, 1988 A Monte Carlo analysis of the Merrivale stone rows, *Computer and Quantitative Methods in Archaeology 1988*, 185–190, University of Birmingham

Wainwright, J and Thornes, J B, 1990 Computer and hardware modelling of archaeological sediment transport on hillslopes, *Computer Applications and Quantitative Methods in Archaeology 1990*, 183–194, University of Southampton

Weber, T, 1992 Mathematical models for the reconstruction of prehistoric settlement patterns: Central German examples, *Computing the Past. Computer Applications and Quantitative Methods in Archaeology CAA92*, 377–388, Aarhus University Press, Aarhus University

Wise, A L and Thorne, T, 1994 Global palaeoclimate modelling approaches: some considerations for archaeologists, *Computer Applications and Quantitative Methods in Archaeology 1994*, 127–132, University of Glasgow

Expert systems and artificial intelligence

Baker, K G, 1987 Towards an archaeological methodology for expert systems, *Computer and Quantitative Methods in Archaeology 1987*, 229–236, University of Leicester

Barcelo, J A, 1992 Computer-based techniques for the representation of automatic problem-solving in archaeology, *Computing the Past. Computer Applications and Quantitative Methods in Archaeology CAA92*, 239–249, Aarhus University Press, Aarhus University

Bishop, M C and Thomas, J, 1984 BEAKER — An expert system for the BBC Micro, *Computer Applications in Archaeology 1984*, 56–62, University of Birmingham

Brough, D R and Parfitt, N, 1984 An expert system for the ageing of a domestic animal, *Computer Applications in Archaeology 1984*, 49–55, University of Birmingham

Bullas, S G, 1994 ID-MARGARY: an Inference Database for the MApping Recognition and Generation of Ancient Roads and trackwaYs, *Computer Applications and Quantitative Methods in Archaeology 1994*, 133–136, University of Glasgow

Doran, J, 1987 Expert systems and archaeology: what lies ahead?, *Computer and Quantitative Methods in Archaeology 1987*, 237–241, University of Leicester

Ennals, R and Brough, D, 1982 Representing the knowledge of the expert archaeologist, *Computer Applications in Archaeology 1982*, 56–62, University of Birmingham

Francfort, H P, 1990 Palamede — application of expert systems to the archaeology of prehistoric urban civilisations, *Computer Applications and Quantitative Methods in Archaeology 1990*, 211–214, University of Southampton

Gibson, P M, 1992 The potentials of hybrid neural network models for archaeofaunal ageing and interpretation, *Computing the Past. Computer Applications and Quantitative Methods in Archaeology CAA92*, 263–271, Aarhus University Press, Aarhus University

Gibson, P M, 1995 An archaeofaunal ageing comparative study into the performance of human analysis versus hybrid neural network analysis, *Interfacing the Past. Computer Applications and Quantitative Methods in Archaeology CAA95*, 229–233, *Analecta Praehistorica Leidensia* 28, University of Leiden

Ozawa, K, 1989 Rule-based dating of artefacts, *Computer Applications and Quantitative Methods in Archaeology 1989*, 375–386, University of York

Palmer, M and Doran, J, 1992 Contrasting models of Upper Palaeolithic social dynamics: a distributed artificial intelligence approach, *Computing the Past. Computer Applications and Quantitative Methods in Archaeology CAA92*, 251–262, Aarhus University Press, Aarhus University

Patel, J and Stutt, S, 1989 Beyond classification: the use of artificial intelligence techniques for the interpretation of archaeological data, *Computer Applications and Quantitative Methods in Archaeology 1989*, 339–347, University of York

Sermon, R, 1994 The use of computers in the decipherment of the Hackness Cross cryptic inscriptions, *Computer Applications and Quantitative Methods in Archaeology 1994*, 253–257, University of Glasgow

Stutt, A, 1988 Second generation expert systems, explanations, arguments and archaeology, *Computer and Quantitative Methods in Archaeology 1988*, 353–367, University of Birmingham

Vitali, V, 1990 Formal methods for the analysis of archaeological data: data analysis vs expert systems, *Computer Applications and Quantitative Methods in Archaeology 1990*, 207–209, University of Southampton

Vitali, V and Lagrange, M-S, 1988 VANDAL: an expert system for the provenance determination of archaeological ceramics based on INAA material, *Computer and Quantitative Methods in Archaeology 1988*, 369–375, University of Birmingham

Wilcock, J D, 1985 A review of expert systems: their shortcomings and possible applications in archaeology, *Computer Applications in Archaeology 1985*, 139–144, Institute of Archaeology, London

Stratigraphical analysis

Agresti, E, Maggiolo-Schettini, A, Saccoccio, R, Pierobon, M and Pierobon-Benoit, R, 1995 Handling excavation maps in SYSAND, *Interfacing the Past. Computer Applications and Quantitative Methods in Archaeology CAA95*, 31–36, *Analecta Praehistorica Leidensia* 28, University of Leiden

Boast, R and Chapman, D, 1990 SQL and hypertext generation of stratigraphic adjacency matrices, *Computer Applications and Quantitative Methods in Archaeology 1990*, 43–51, University of Southampton

Desachy, B and Djindjian, F, 1990 Matrix processing of stratigraphic graphs: a new method, *Computer Applications and Quantitative Methods in Archaeology 1990*, 29–37, University of Southampton

Djindjian, F, 1991 Reconstructing stratigraphy: a discrete sampling approach, *Computer Applications and Quantitative Methods in Archaeology 1991*, 179–181, University of Oxford

Haigh, J G B, 1985 The Harris Matrix as a partially ordered set, *Computer Applications in Archaeology 1985*, 81–90, Institute of Archaeology, London

Herzog, I, 1993 Combining stratigraphic information and finds, *Computer Applications and Quantitative Methods in Archaeology 1993*, 109–114, Staffordshire University

Herzog, I and Scollar, I, 1990 A new graph theoretic oriented program for Harris Matrix analysis, *Computer Applications and Quantitative Methods in Archaeology 1990*, 53–59, University of Southampton

Huggett, J W and Cooper, M A, 1990 The computer representation of space in urban archaeology, *Computer Applications and Quantitative Methods in Archaeology 1990*, 39–42, University of Southampton

Maggiolo-Schettini, A, Seccacini, P, Serratore, C D, Pierobon-Benoit, R and Soricelli, G, 1994 SYSAND: a system for the archaeological excavations of Anderitum (Javols, Lozère, France), *Computer Applications and Quantitative Methods in Archaeology 1994*, 229–233, University of Glasgow

Ryan, N S, 1988 Browsing through the stratigraphic record, *Computer and Quantitative Methods in Archaeology 1988*, 327–334, University of Birmingham

Ryan, N S, 1994 The excavation archive as hyperdocument?, *Computer Applications and Quantitative Methods in Archaeology 1994*, 211–220, University of Glasgow

Wilcock, J D, 1975 Archaeological context sorting by computer, *Computer Applications in Archaeology 1975*, 93–97, University of Birmingham

Wilcock, J D, 1981 STRATA — The microcomputer version, *Computer Applications in Archaeology 1981*, 112–114, University of London, Institute of Archaeology ISBN 0 905853 12 1

Wilcock, J D, 1983 Some further developments of the STRATA System, *Proceedings of the Conference on Computer Applications and Quantitative Methods in Archaeology CAA83*, 189–190, University of Bradford

Wünsch, G, Arasa, E and Perez, M, 1995 Dissecting the palimpsest: an easy computer-graphic approach to the stratigraphic sequence of Túnel VII site (Tierra del Fuego, Argentina), *Interfacing the Past. Computer Applications and Quantitative Methods in Archaeology CAA95*, 453–456, *Analecta Praehistorica Leidensia* 28, University of Leiden

Contact details

Dr John Denis Wilcock
Computing Archaeology Research Group
School of Computing
Staffordshire University
P.O. Box 334
Stafford ST18 0DG
UK
email: j.d.wilcock@soc.staffs.ac.uk

Archaeological Computing in Canada: The First (and Last) 25 Years

Morgan J. Tamplin

CAA 97

Abstract

The use of computers by archaeologists in Canada is best understood in relation to the general history of computing and the recent history of Canadian archaeology. We use computers to solve research problems which are similar to those in other countries but regional, cultural, linguistic and historical differences have produced a unique pattern of research dispersed through a variety of jurisdictions and institutions. I review this situation and summarize a history of computer use by archaeologists from the last three decades of Canadian Archaeological Association meeting programs and abstracts.

1 Introduction

I presented a history of Canadian archaeological computing at CAA97 in the session, "25 Years of CAA ", as a contrast to archaeological computing in Britain and Europe. Research on the topic is by no means straightforward and this short note is only a "work in progress". As in my original presentation I first introduce the problems of geography and politics within which Canadian archaeologists must work, with or without computers. Rather than summarizing current research, I present a preliminary history of computer applications from the annual meeting programs of the Canadian Archaeological Association. Although still incomplete, this summary provides a better context for the development of archaeological computing in Canada better than an overview of the current situation.

2 The Context of Canadian Archaeology

To understand Canadian archaeology, one must first review the problems posed by our unique geography and cultures. Consider the problem of scale. The land spans about 5300 km from East to West (St John's, Newfoundland is closer to the UK than Victoria, British Columbia) and 4300 km north to south. In this 10 million square kilometres is a population of only 30 million people, most of whom are unevenly distributed in widely dispersed urban centres within 300 km of our southern border with the United States.

The government of Canada directs federal activities across the entire country from the capital in Ottawa. There are ten provinces and three northern territories and within many provinces there are regional jurisdictions. Below that level are municipal governments of various sizes, most of them small compared to Europe.

Federal archaeology is dircted by two ministries: The Secretary of State and Canadian Heritage. The former oversees the Canadian Museum of Civilization (CMC) including the Archaeological Survey of Canada (ASC), which was traditionally responsible for investigating prehistoric aboriginal sites across the country. More recently its activities have been drastically cut back and most field activities restricted to federal lands other than national parks, some First Nations and northern territories.

The Social Sciences and Humanities Research Council (SSHRC) also falls within this Secretariat. It funds university-based research, including archaeology, across Canada and outside our borders. In the North American anthropological tradition, archaeology is viewed as a social science and in Canada at least, it receives little support from science ministries. As a national learned society, the Canadian Archaeological Association, (also called CAA!), receives SSHRC support for meetings and publications.

The other ministry, Canadian Heritage, directs Parks Canada and the Canadian Heritage Information Network (CHIN). The former is responsible for the archaeology of marine sites and national parks in both the provinces and northern territories. It previously concentrated on historic European sites but increased its prehistoric research activity as new 'wilderness parks' were established in the far north. CHIN developed and maintains national site and collections databases but its future responsibility for them is being phased out. Archaeological collections and site databases will soon become a provincial responsibility.

Except for clearly-defined federal lands, cultural resources in Canada are a provincial or territorial responsibility. Most regional or municipal governments provide little or no support to archaeological research Archaeological sites, designated or not, are administered by a variety of provincial ministries, usually tourism, culture or natural resources. Some provincial archaeologists do active field and laboratory research but many simply control or monitor the work conducted by academic, avocational and commercial practitioners. .

Provinces fund some non-government research on a modest scale. Provincial societies mainly run by avocational archaeologists get small grants for operations, education and research. Contract archaeologists provide their services to developers and government agencies, to fulfil the reporting requirements of provincial heritage and environmental impact legislation. Provincial governments support both museums and universities and most academic research is conducted by the archaeologists employed by those institutions.

3 Archaeological Computing in Canada

I have found no published record of computer use by Canadian archaeologists in the 1960s. Reviews of Canadian archaeology published in the 1970's (Noble 1972, 1973; Trigger 1976) do not mention computers and there are few references in the literature until the mid 1980s. Only one paper appears in the journal of the Canadian Archaeological Association, *The Canadian Journal of Archaeology* (CJA) with the word computer (ordinateur, actually) in the title (Marois 1983). It reports on a survey of computer use in archaeology and ethnology by 18 member institutions of the Pan American Institute of History and Geography.

The Canadian Archaeological Association was formed in 1967 and held its first meeting in 1968. As the Archaeological Survey of Alberta archives in Edmonton has the only complete set of Canadian CAA programs and abstracts, the following is a summary of the computer-related meeting papers available to me. Length restrictions prevent giving a comprehensive bibliography of all relevant meeting abstracts and as these are not easily accessible even in Canada, I shall summarize session themes and cite only a few landmark papers.

There is no mention of computer use at the first two meetings in 1968 and 1969. I could find no programs or abstracts from 1970 to 1974 but computers do not appear in the association bulletins do not mention computers either. Thus, Michael Kelly may have delivered the first Canadian archaeological computing paper in 1975, "Cataloging in COBUL" [sic]. The unfortunate typo suggests that meeting organizers were not yet familiar with computer terms. In 1977, Jack Nance chaired a session on "Quantitative Methods in Archaeology" with six other contributors, most of whom used computers in their research. This may be the first Canadian CAA "computer session".

In 1980, there were only two papers on quantitative topics, with Ball and Bobrowsky (1980) and Howes (1980) reporting on computer-based research. Terrance Gibson (1982) may have presented the first report on Canadian computer use in the field, illustrated by a dramatic slide depicting data entry into a wind-powered Apple, on a barren ridge in the high Arctic twilight!

In 1983, using an Osborne II, I demonstrated a Basic program which converted Canadian site coordinates to their four letter Federal designation (Tamplin 1983) and this may have been the first computer demonstration during a meeting session. In 1984, Gibson, Finnigan and Klimko first reported on a Saskatchewan archaeological database which has been maintained to this day.

At the mid-decade 1985 Winnipeg meeting, computer applications dominated the program, with three sessions on these and related topics. Federal Data Co-ordinator Judy Marsh (1985a, b), organized a session, presented two papers on Data Recording Standards and Databases and chaired a panel discussion on the CHIN database. Gibson and Finnigan (1985) updated their Saskatchewan site database project.

Arnold (1986) may have presented the first Canadian CAA paper on Cluster Analysis in a lithic analysis session and in 1987, Stanley van Dyke organized the first Archaeology Microcomputer Workshop, with 10 participants demonstrating various software applications, at the University of Calgary's new microcomputer lab. Papers on computerized artifact databases, faunal analysis, and micro-mainframe statistical analysis were presented in a more formal session specifically called, for the first time, "Computer Applications" (Finnigan 1987; Tamplin 1987; Watson 1987). Gibson's 1988 paper may be the first report on visual database use in Canadian archaeology.

At the 1990 and 1991 meetings, Luke Dalla Bona organized symposia on Database Management GIS and Predictive Modelling. Gibson (1992) proposed integrating Canadian archaeological databases, continuing this ongoing theme from previous meetings. In 1993, Luke Dalla Bona and Pierre Desrochers combined databases and GIS in a bilingual session: "Archaeology at 1:125,000" with 10 participants including Kenneth Kvamme (1993) who is already familiar to participants at the "other" CAA meetings. Fiset (1993) and Innes (1993) reported two computer applications in a Cultural Resource Management session. In 1994, Dalla Bona organized a session, "Advances in Computer Applications in Archaeology" where Gibson and Tremayne (1994) also presented an application for cultural resource management.

In 1996, the annual meeting program first appeared on the Association's new web site, started and maintained by Dalla Bona. Only three computing-related papers appear: Lundrigen (1996), Summa (1996) and Turnbull and Keenlyside (1996). The latter may be the first report of a CD-ROM application, produced on Maliseet/Micmac Culture including ethnography and archaeology.

A month after Birmingham's computer CAA97, the 1997 Canadian CAA held two computer-related sessions at the annual meetings in Saskatoon. Gibson organized a discussion on, "The Forest Industry and Archaeological Resource Management", combining site potential mapping, predictive modelling and archaeological resource management. A general session on, "Computer Applications in Archaeology", organized by Nathan Frison, Michael Magee and Brad Himour addressed GIS, database and educational applications.

4 Conclusion

Certain people such as Gibson, Finnigan, Marsh, and Dalla Bona stand out both as pioneers and continuing contributors to Canadian archaeological computing but I cannot yet report the work of professionals and talented amateurs from proceedings of regional meetings, including francophone organizations. Unpublished reports and interviews with participants - the oral traditions - are another potentially rich, untapped resource. The search for these and other sources continues.

Bibliography

Arnold, T, 1986 Cluster Analysis on Several Paleo-Indian Complexes and its Cultural Implications, *Canadian Archaeological Association 19th Annual Meeting Abstracts*,4

Ball, B F and Bobrowsky, B T, 1980 Application of Trend Surface Analysis to Archaeological Site Assessment: Advances in Merlin's Projections, *Canadian Archaeological Association, 13th Annual Meeting Abstracts, 5*

Finnigan, J, 1987 When Trees Equal Artifacts: Computing Beyond the Information Explosion, *Canadian Archaeological Association 20th Annual Meeting Abstracts, 59*

Fiset, B, 1993 Un systèm d'information urbaine à référence spatiale appliqué à l'archéologie, *Canadian Archaeological Association 26th Annual Meeting Abstracts, 41*

Gibson, T H, 1982 Alternative Approaches to Collecting and Interpreting Archaeological Data from Arctic Surface Sites, *Canadian Archaeological Association 15th Annual Meeting Abstracts*

Gibson, T H, Finnigan, J and Klimko, O, 1984 Archaeological Data Management and the Nipawin Reservoir Heritage Study, *Canadian Archaeological Association 17th Annual Meeting Abstracts*

Gibson, T and Finnigan, J, 1985. Developing Standards and Maintaining Consistency within a Multi-Site Data Base: the Nipawin Example, *Canadian Archaeological Association 18th Annual Meeting* Abstracts, 16

Gibson, T H, 1988 Disseminating Archaeological Data Using a Visual Electronic Data Base, *Canadian Archaeological Association 20th Annual Meeting Abstracts,* 66

Gibson, T H, 1992 A Proposal for the Integration of Canada's Archaeological Databases, *Canadian Archaeological Association 25th Annual Meeting Abstracts*

Gibson, T H and Tremayne, A, 1994 Cultural Resource Management: Métis Loss of a Land Base, *Canadian Archaeological Association 27th Annual Meeting Abstracts,* 78

Howes, D, 1980 A Predictive Model for Foothills Site Location, *Canadian Archaeological Association 13th Annual Meeting Abstracts, 21*

Innes, R, 1993 Archèmuse, un systèm de gestion des collections archéologiques, 45

Kvamme, K L, 1993 The History and Practice of Predictive Modelling in Archaeology, *Canadian Archaeological Association 26th Annual Meeting Abstracts, 48*

Kelly, M E, 1975 Cataloguing in COBUL [sic], *Canadian Archaeological Association 8th Annual Meeting Abstracts,* 16

Lundrigen, N, 1996 A Computer-Generated Lab for the Introduction of Forensic Anthropology at a Pre-College, *Canadian Archaeological Association 27th Annual Meeting Program*

Marois, R, 1983 Ordinateurs et Archéologie/Ethnologie, *Canadian Journal of Archaeology,* 7:2, 239-243

Marsh, J, 1985a An Experimental Multi-record Type Database for Collections Management, *Canadian Archaeological Association 18th Annual Meeting Abstracts, 32*

Marsh, J, 1985b The Viability of a National Sites Database: The Results of a User Workshop, *Canadian Archaeological Association 18th Annual Meeting Abstracts, 33*

Noble, W C, 1972 One hundred and twenty-five years of archaeology in the Canadian provinces *Canadian Archaeological Association Bulletin,* No. 4, 1-78

Noble, W C, 1973 Canada, in Fitting, J E. (ed.), *The Development of North American Archaeology,* Anchor Books, Doubleday, New York, 49-83

Summa Informatics Inc., 1996 A Heritage Resource Database with Microtext Import, *Canadian Archaeological Association 27th Annual Meeting Program*

Tamplin, M, 1983 Micro Computers and Site Location: The Case for Thinking Small, *Canadian Archaeological Association 16th Annual Meeting. Abstracts*, 30-31

Tamplin, M J, 1987 Computerized Carcass Reconstruction: Beyond MNI and NISP, *Canadian Archaeological Association 20th Annual Meeting Abstracts, 106*

Trigger, B, 1976 The Archaeological Base in Canada: Training, Facilities, Opportunities, in McKay, A G (ed.), *New Perspectives in Canadian Archaeology,* Royal Society of Canada, 185-195

Turnbull, C and Keenlyside, D, 1996 CD-ROM on Maliseet/Micmac Culture, *Canadian Archaeological Association 27th Annual Meeting Program*

Watson, G D, 1987 Archaeological Research Aided by a Micro Computer - Mainframe Connection, *Canadian Archaeological Association 20th Annual Meeting Abstracts,* 109

Contact details

Morgan J. Tamplin
Trent University
Department of Anthropology
Computer Studies Programme
Peterborough
Ontario
CANADA K9J 7B8
email: mtamplin@trentu.ca

ARCHAEOLOGY
IN THE
AGE OF THE INTERNET

CAA 97

Section 2
Landscape Archaeology and GIS

How Archaeological Sites co-exist with Fast-paced, Intense Army Training Activities

Cheryl L. Huckerby, Christine M. Poulsen

CAA 97

Abstract

GIS conversion of management information into easy-to-read spatial representations is the keystone to successful integration of cultural resource management at a fast paced Army training facility in the USA. It enables incorporation of cultural resource management issues into training plans and their implementation. An easy-to-use graphical user interface accesses data in a variety of formats such as high-altitude photography, archived documents and 35mm photographs. The system was designed with novice-level GIS end-users in mind: training officers and cultural resource managers and allows spatially based information from other sources to be used more efficiently in cultural resource management decisions. Inclusion of cultural resource issues in GIS-based Army planning and training products enables training officers to settle compliance issues early in the planning process.

1 Introduction

As a federal facility, Fort Lewis (WA, USA) is required to identify, protect, and nominate cultural resources potentially eligible for the National Register of Historic Places. Primary legislation directing these activities are the National Historic Preservation Act (NHPA), the Archaeological Resource Protection Act (ARPA), and the Native American Graves Protection and Repatriation Act (NAGPRA). A detailed and dynamic database linked with geographic information system (GIS) capabilities facilitates cultural resource monitoring and condition assessment under these laws, accompanying regulations, and Executive Orders from the President.

GIS is a keystone to successful integration of cultural resource management with training plans at Fort Lewis. GIS converts diverse data into easy-to-read and -access maps trainers and field personnel incorporate in their training activities. The cultural resource manager in cooperation with other environmental managers is able to identify areas sensitive to different training activities. For example, one area may not be sensitive to vehicles driving over it whereas another area is. GIS maps meet the diverse protection requirements of each cultural resource site.

2 Fort Lewis description and history

Fort Lewis covers approximately 87,000 acres (360 Km2) in Washington state (USA) (See Fig. 1). Training is the installation's primary purpose. Training areas encompass 75,573 acres (306 Km2) of deciduous Evergreen forest interspersed with open grassland prairies. Fort Lewis was established in 1917 when the county purchased approximately 69,000 acres (279 Km2) from homesteaders and allotment holders to induce the Army to establish a permanent facility in the Northwest. Another 18,000 acres (73 Km2) was added to the installation during World War II. The Nisqually River bisects the installation. Additional smaller water sources run through or dot the installation.

Native American Salish speakers of several tribes (i.e., Nisqually and Puyallup) inhabited the region relying heavily on the shores of Puget Sound and the large rivers (i.e., Nisqually) for food resources. The grasslands provided deer and smaller game to supplement water resources. After the region became a US territory in 1849 with the signing of a treaty with Great Britain, US Government officials arranged a treaty with Puget Sound Native Americans producing several reservations. The existing Nisqually reservation is the southern half of the original reservation. The northern half lies within Fort Lewis Boundaries. This land was attained by Pierce county through the reallocation of allotments that had been granted to Native Americans who then sold or forfeited them by not paying taxes.

Figure 1: Location of Fort Lewis Military Installation.

The Hudson Bay Company established trading posts in the region. Fort Nisqually was one trading post located near present day Fort Lewis. In addition to the trading post, stations such as Tlithlow were built to supply traders and settlers moving to the region. A subsidiary holding of the Hudson Bay Company was the Puget Sound Agricultural Company. Stations of this subsidiary focused on producing agricultural goods for the trading posts.

3 Cultural resource management

Fort Lewis' cultural resource management program includes three major regulatory compliance and coordination areas: Native American Issues, Prehistoric and Historic Archaeology, and Historic Structures. Compliance and coordination in these areas is driven by Federal laws and regulations on resource identification, evaluation and management. Cultural resources are defined as any prehistoric, historic, or traditional place, and related items, both important and not important. Currently we have an aggressive program of known-resource record verification, new resource inventory, evaluation of importance, and development of long-term management plans. Specific resource types include, historic buildings, historic districts, historic (pioneer and Native American) archaeological sites, prehistoric archaeological sites, and traditional cultural places.

Information, historical and graphic, on cultural resources has been traditionally gathered in a variety of formats: photographs (aerial and 35mm), site forms (according to state and federal guidelines), field sketch maps, and other archival documents. While these formats are descriptive and useful, every-day upkeep and quick retrieval of information can be burdensome and space-intensive. Modern day technology enables these traditional formats to be combined with non-traditional formats and computer analytical capabilities.

Data needed for cultural resource management overlaps other management programs on the installation: forestry, fish and wildlife, and environmental engineering. Due to the large storage requirement for geographical electronic data, each program must access a shared data repository instead of maintaining individual databases.

4 Decision support system components

The system was based on an analysis of two groups of end users: cultural resource managers and training officers. Both groups are decision-makers that require immediate access to spatially distributed information yet they have purposes that appear to contradict. The system developed from a need to examine and evaluate the impact of installation activities, both training and general operations, on cultural resources in an expedient manner yet comprehendible to non-Cultural Resource Management (CRM) personnel. The system is based on CRM needs and manual procedures in addition to the needs of integration with existing computer systems within Public Works and particularly, other environmentally related programs.

Descriptions of the major system components are as follows:

Geographic Information System (GIS): A GIS is an organized collection of computer hardware, software, geographic data, and personnel designed to efficiently capture, store, update, manipulate, analyze, and display all forms of geographically referenced information. The GIS will answer a basic set of questions that other types of software systems can not answer or answer collectively: what exists at a particular location, what changes have occurred at a particular location over time, what spatial patterns exist, where are certain conditions satisfied, and what impacts will occur as a result of a specific activity. This translates to functionality such as watershed identification, drainage patterns, proximity analysis, planning and zoning, and land/property assessment.

Relational Database Management System (RDBMS): A RDBMS integrates files in a database for multi-facet access and manipulation. Compared to conventional file systems, data redundancy is reduced while integrity and management is improved. Many GIS link with database management systems or RDBMS. This allows non-spatial data to be queried with geographic data thus enlarging the analytical capabilities and flexibility of the cultural resource management system.

Field Computers/software: Portable computers equipped with database software reduces transcription errors and eliminates a time-intensive step in getting the data into the end user system. Data is quickly and easily downloaded into the RDBMS and can be utilized soon after.

Global Positioning System (GPS): Portable GPS field units have substantially improved the accuracy of geographic coordinate data at Fort Lewis. After error correction, the data is downloaded directly into the GIS so the maps can be updated accordingly.

To facilitate use of a sophisticated and complex type of GIS by novice-level end users, a graphical user interface (GUI) simplifies access by incorporating task-descriptive text instead of computer jargon. The GUI is an integral part of the project since a computer system is beneficial only if it gets the information to the intended recipients in a relatively smooth and timely manner. For example, Standard Query Language (SQL) queries are presented behind button options and multiple commonly used names are linked to unique spatial boundaries. In addition to GIS spatial data and a relational database management system, the interface access data stored in a variety of formats allowing full integration with a simple point and click process.

The main system is run on a SUN™ Microsystems UNIX workstation platform. PC access extends usage through additional ARCVIEW™ licenses linked through a network. Data access is controlled through monitored access privileges within the programs and the computer network. Input of data is supervised by the cultural resource manager and all other users will have read-only access to designated files based on access requests submitted to the cultural resource manager. For example, training officers only access non-descriptive buffered areas that are designated as environmentally sensitive to training activities. No other information is supplied or accessible. Yet the field trainers have the information needed to identify landscape strengths and weaknesses relative to training objectives and equipment capabilities while meeting environmental compliance requirements.

Cultural resource locations spatially link to other geographically represented information such as topography, wetlands, elevations and vegetation diversity. Additional environmental concerns such as threatened and endangered species, wildlife distributions, timber harvesting and water quality, use and enhance these other information sources.

Spatial qualities of these diverse data types facilitate their analysis with ARC/INFO™ (ESRI, Inc.) to produce integrated maps.

5 Conclusions

The benefit of this program is the integration of cultural resource information into GIS products (see Figures 2 and 3). This enables spatially based information from other sources to be employed in cultural resource management decisions. Analysis and queries are performed in minutes rather than hours and the results can be presented in the short time it takes to print out the hardcopy map. Report generation in other formats is delivered with equal time efficiency.

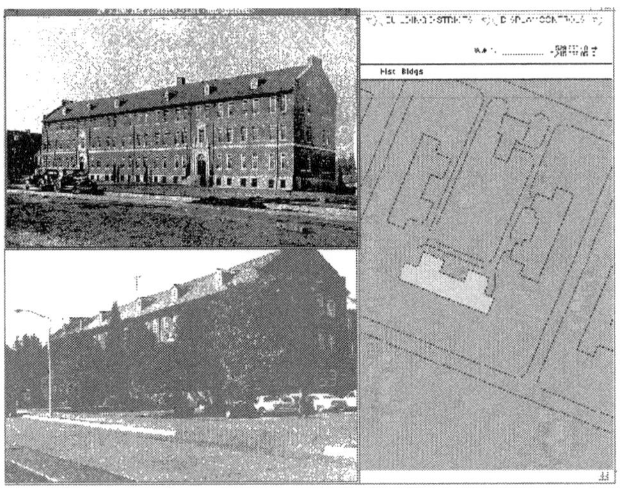

Figure 2: Clicking on the corresponding building on the map accesses historical and / or present day photographs (as well as architectural drawings) of buildings.

Inclusion of cultural resource issues in GIS based Army planning and training products enables training officers to settle compliance issues early in the planning process before they can affect finalized training plans This avoids delays in project and exercise commencement dates and assures the protection of sensitive and unique cultural resources for future generations.

The natural progression of this project is to enhance the interface and product capabilities such that they are compatible with many technologies employed by personnel at a training facility. In addition, such enhancements will expedite planning inquiries and environmental compliance clearance for a variety of activities. Future inclusion of additional environmental areas of concern such as endangered species, wetland habitat preservation, stream preservation, etc., will make environmental compliance a more accessible and efficient part of training planning.

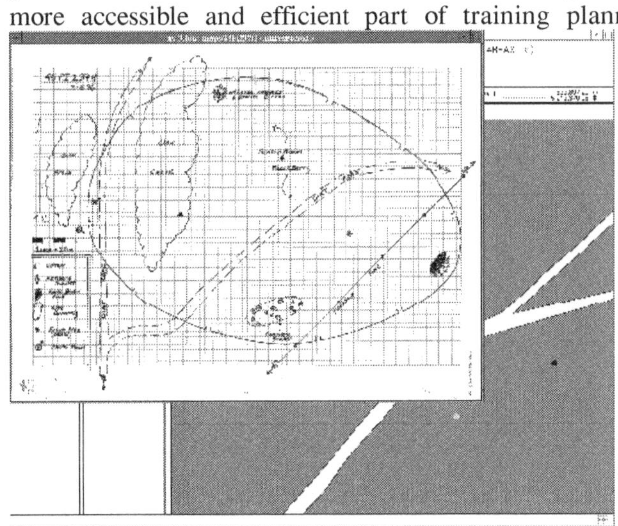

Figure 3: Simply clicking on the corresponding archaeological/historical site on the map, accesses field sketch maps. Photographs of the site are accessed in the same manner. Access to this type of sensitive data is limited only to designated users.

Acknowledgements

This project is made possible through Department of Defense funding. Development of the graphical user interface is funded in part by a Department of Defense Legacy grant. Participation by the first author is supported in part by an appointment to the Environmental Management Participation Program for the U.S. Army Environmental Center (USAEC) administered by the Oak Ridge Institute for Science and Education through an agreement between the U.S. Department of Energy and USAEC. Participation by the second author is through the Anteon Corporation.

Contact details

Cheryl L. Huckerby[1], Christine M. Poulsen[2]
[1]Oak Ridge Institute for Science and Education
[2]Anteon Corporation
Department of the Army, Public Works
ATTN: AFZH-DEQ MS17, Box 339500
Fort Lewis, Washington
USA, 98433-9500
email: [1]cheryl.huckerby@lewis-deh2.army.mil
email: [2]poulsen@lewis-deh2.army.mil

CAA 97

The Use of Monte-Carlo Techniques for the Estimation of Visibility

K. Nackaerts, G. Govers, L. Loots

Abstract

In archaeological research, visibility analysis is usually based on binary viewshed maps. However, Digital Elevation Models inherently contain errors due to inaccuracies in the original topographic data and the data structure used. Therefore the binary classification will be subject to an unknown amount of error. It would be more appropriate to use a method for visibility calculation which allows us to take the uncertainty on the elevation data into account. In this paper a further development of a method to calculate fuzzy viewsheds is proposed. The method is based on Monte-Carlo simulation of the DEM-error. From a large number of simulations, the visibility probability of a given cell can then be calculated. First experiments with this new methodology for our study area indicate that the hidden error in classical binary viewsheds is considerable. The deterministic use of such binary viewsheds for visibility analysis may therefore lead to erroneous conclusions. Furthermore, binary viewshed calculations appear to be rather sensitive to the algorithms used for DEM construction and visibility calculation. Fuzzy viewsheds appear to be much more robust. The application of fuzzy viewsheds requires information on the mean elevation error as well as an estimation of the number of Monte Carlo simulations needed. The first can be obtained by comparing interpolated elevation data with manually measured values. For the estimation of the required number of simulations two methodologies are proposed.

1 Introduction

Many commercial GIS packages offer easy to use raster-DEM based viewshed algorithms which calculate the visibility of each cell of the study area in a deterministic way: a cell is either classified as visible or invisible. By this, the analysis of visual relationships between elements in a landscape (e.g. ancient watchtowers) might look simple and will result in deterministic information.

However, one must not forget that DEMs are inherently liable to a wide range of inaccuracies due to the map-making process, digitalisation of analogue maps, interpolation, vector to raster conversion errors, etc . Limitations in the algorithms that analyse the visibility between cells in a raster-DEM -referred to as data structure induced errors (Sorensen and Lanter 1993)- can also have a major impact on the result. All these errors can sum up and may interact with each other, resulting in inaccuracies of unknown extent in the binary viewshed (Sorensen and Lanter 1993, 1158; Fisher 1991, 1327) and the observed visual relationships.

To solve this problem, Fisher (1991, 1322; 1992, 345; 1993, 344) proposed a method for calculating fuzzy viewsheds. In these viewsheds, the probability of a cell lying in the viewshed area is calculated by means of a Monte Carlo simulation of the DEM error. Sorensen and Lanter (1993, 1150-1158) presented other algorithms to deal with DEM inaccuracies in the visibility determination, but they only take data structure induced errors into account. Because their algorithms neglect all other sources of inaccuracies (see above) an approach as proposed by Fisher seemed the most appropriate for this study.

In this paper, we focus on the estimation of a minimum number of simulations needed for the calculation of fuzzy viewsheds. Two new methodologies are proposed. First, an exploratory method is described, resulting in qualitative information. Second, a quantitative method is proposed, based on the binomial distribution function, by which it is possible to calculate confidence intervals for the calculated fuzzy visibilities. The results clearly show that the use of too few simulations will lead to unreliable documents.

2 Fuzzy visibility

To account for the problem of inaccuracies in the DEM, a Monte Carlo simulation of the DEM (Fisher 1992, 345) was performed, in which a simulated random error-matrix was added to the original DEM resulting in new DEMs. These new simulated DEMs represent samples of a population that describes the real DEM. A classic visibility determination (as described above) is then performed using each of these simulated DEMs, resulting in different binary viewshed maps. As such, the visibility values (0 or 1) of a raster cell in each simulated viewshed map can be seen as Bernoulli trials out of a binomial distributed population. The probability that a cell lies within or without the real viewshed (i.e. fuzzy visibility) can then be estimated by dividing the sum of all these values by the total number of simulations for each cell. This results in a fuzzy viewshed map that takes the inaccuracy of the DEM into account.

For the simulation process, information about the distribution of the DEM error (interpolation and data-structure related elevation error) and an estimation of the number of simulations is necessary. Too many simulations will cause excessive computation times while too few simulations lead to inaccurate results (see below). The first is achieved by sampling the DEM error. This was done by comparing the interpolated elevation value with the manually measured elevation in the same sample point. No spatial autocorrelation in the DEM errors and an equal distribution of the DEM error over the study area are assumed. However, these elements are not extensively researched and a discussion of them would lead too far from the subject of this study (Fisher 1991, 1322).

3 Number of simulations

3.1 Exploratory approach

The estimation of the number of simulations was accomplished by an examination of the evolution of the fuzzy visibility values in 100 uniform randomly spread sampling points. This evolution can be visualised by plotting the fuzzy visibility against the total number of simulations. A visual interpretation of the behaviour of the fuzzy visibility values showed a stabilisation of these values after approximately 50 simulations for the study area.

3.2 Quantitative approach

The simulation process can also be compared with Bernoulli trials (Sachs 1982):

1. The result of each simulation is either a success (a cell is visible) or a failure (a cell is invisible).
2. A result is independent of the result of a previous simulation.
3. The probability of success is a constant as can be derived from the asymptotic behaviour of the fuzzy visibilities as described above.

The cumulative visibility of a given cell (Y) is called a binomial random variable. This variable follows a binomial distribution. This characteristic enables the calculation of confidence intervals using the statistics specifically developed for binomial distributions.

If n is greater than 20, the normal approximation may be used (Conover 1971):

$$L = \frac{Y}{n} - x_{(1-\alpha/2)}\sqrt{Y(n-Y)/n^3} \qquad [1]$$

$$U = \frac{Y}{n} + x_{(1-\alpha/2)}\sqrt{Y(n-Y)/n^3} \qquad [2]$$

where $x_{1-\alpha/2}$ is the quantile of a normally distributed random variable.

4 Results

Idrisi for Windows (Eastman 1995) was used for this study. The simulation process was automated by the Idrisi Macro Language (IML).

4.1 Number of simulations

Using the exploratory method, performing more than 50 simulations seemed not to result in a decrease of the variance of the fuzzy visibility values. These results were compared for observation points located in different positions in the landscape of the study area. Since the results of this comparison were positive, it was decided to use at least 50 simulations for the determination of the different fuzzy viewsheds.

Confidence intervals can be calculated using functions [1] and [2] for a given level of significance, number of simulations and a given fuzzy visibility. A steep increase of accuracy is visible during the first simulations. After 100 simulations, the confidence interval for a fuzzy visibility of 0.5 (this corresponds to the widest confidence interval) is approximately equal to 0.5 +/- 0.1 (α=0.05). If, for example, 25 simulations result in a fuzzy visibility of 0.5, the real value lies between 0.3 (rather invisible) and 0.7 (rather visible) with a significance level of 5%. Out of this information we decided to use 100 simulations, delivering an acceptable accuracy against acceptable calculation times.

4.2 Fuzzy viewsheds

A comparison of a Boolean and a fuzzy viewshed map from the same observation point clearly demonstrates the deceptive accuracy of a binary viewshed map. In our test case, important areas are Boolean classified as visible although the fuzzy viewshed map indicates fuzzy visibilities of less than 0.5. The probability that a cell lies within the viewshed is smaller in these areas than the probability that the cell lies outside the viewshed. The mean fuzzy visibility of the Boolean viewshed of our testcase equalled 0.5. This means that a cell indicated as visible in the Boolean viewshed has an equal probability of being visible as being invisible, given the inaccuracies in the DEM. Binary viewsheds should therefore be used with the necessary care.

The fuzzy viewsheds make shaded decisions possible and give important information about the accuracy of possible decisions. These fuzzy documents are used in the study of the function of some fortifications around the ancient city of Sagalassos (SW-Turkey) as described by L. Loots et al. (this volume).

Acknowledgements

This text presents the results of the Belgian Programme on Interuniversity Poles of Attraction initiated by the Belgian State, Prime Minister's Office, Science Policy Programming. The text also presents the results of the Conserted Action of the Flemish Government (GOA 97/2) and the Fund for Scientific Research-Flanders (Belgium) (FWO) (G.0215.96). Scientific responsibility is assumed by its authors.

Bibliography

Conover, W J, (ed), 1971 *Practical Nonparametric Statistics*, John Wiley & Sons Inc., New York

Eastman, J R, 1995 *Idrisi for Windows User's Guide*, Clark Labs for Cartographic Technology and Geographic Analysis, Clark University, Worcester, USA

Fisher, P, 1991 First experiments in viewshed uncertainty: the accuracy of the viewshed area, *Photogrammetric Engineering & Remote Sensing*, 57(10), 1321-1327

Fisher, P, 1992 First experiments in viewshed uncertainty: simulating fuzzy viewsheds, *Photogrammetric Engineering & Remote Sensing* 58(3), 345-352

Fisher, P, 1993 Algorithm and implementation uncertainty in viewshed analysis, *International Journal of GIS*, 7(4), 331-347

Sachs, L, 1982 *Applied statistics, a Handbook of Techniques*, Springer-Verlag, New York Inc.

Sorensen, P and Lanter, D, 1993 Two algorithms for determining partial visibility and reducing data structure induced error in viewshed analysis, *Photogrammetric Engineering & Remote Sensing*, 59(7), 1149-1160

Contact details

K. Nackaerts
Sagalassos Archaeological Research Project
Laboratory for Experimental Geomorphology
Catholic University of Leuven
Redingenstraat 16
B-3000 Leuven
BELGIUM
email: kris.nackaerts@agr.kuleuven.ac.be

G. Govers
Fund for Scientific Research
Laboratory for Experimental Geomorphology
Catholic University of Leuven
Redingenstraat 16
B-3000 Leuven
BELGIUM

L. Loots
Sagalassos Archaeological Research Project
Catholic University of Leuven
Faculteit Letteren
Blijde Inkomstraat 21
B-3000 Leuven
BELGIUM
email: lieven.loots@arts.kuleuven.ac.be

Modelling Human Range Expansion Across a Heterogeneous Cost Surface

Celia Glass, James Steele, David Wheatley

CAA 97

Abstract

Understanding the first human colonization of South America depends on accurate dating of early sites, and on realistic models of the effects of habitat variation on dispersal rates. In this study, we report application of regression models to analysis of the spatial structure of the early radiocarbon record of human occupation in that continent. Our method allows for the differing levels of precision in radiocarbon dates from different early sites. Cost distance analysis was used to explore the effects of habitat variability on rates of spread. Our analysis suggests that humans coming into South America in the late glacial dispersed most rapidly through the more productive open habitats, including the open montane habitat of the Andean mountain chain.

1 Introduction

This paper reports work done by our group on the first human colonization of South America. Most archaeologists will know that there is continuing debate on the timing of this colonization: everyone agrees that humans were leaving their mark in the archaeological record by about 12,000 years b.p., but new sites are regularly reported with dates that suggest an *earlier* human presence there. The problem is that these dates are usually marred by unreliable associations with cultural material, while the absence of convincing evidence of equally early (pre-12,000 b.p.) human occupation of *North* America makes it hard to see where the putative pre-Clovis South American population could have come from. What *is* clear is that the 'ice-free' corridor between the two North American ice sheets, which is usually thought to have given humans access south from Beringia, only opened up after about 13,000 b.p. (e.g. Lundqvist and Saarnisto 1995). It is also clear that radiocarbon-dated sites from that period of the late glacial are extremely sparse in both North and South America:

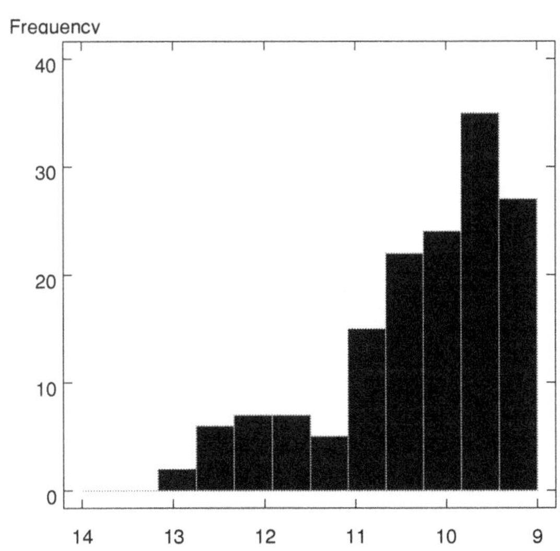

Figure 1. Early South American sites by age (data from Borrero 1996).

Figure 1 graphs the increasing frequency of archaeological radiocarbon dates from southern South America from 13,000 to 8,000 b.p., suggesting that in the earliest phase human occupation of that continent was very sparse (Borrero 1996). If we break down these events into sites by region, we see that there is also some suggestion of regional differences (Figure 2): the greatest expansion of site numbers in the late glacial occurs in Brazil and in northern Chile/northwest Argentina, whereas the early but sparse occupation of Peru and Patagonia seems to establish a pattern for those regions which characterized the rest of the late glacial. The increase in dated events post-12,000 b.p. must indicate either the expansion from a glacial refugium of a pre-existing South American population, or the spread of a colonizing population coming into the continent — presumably from the north.

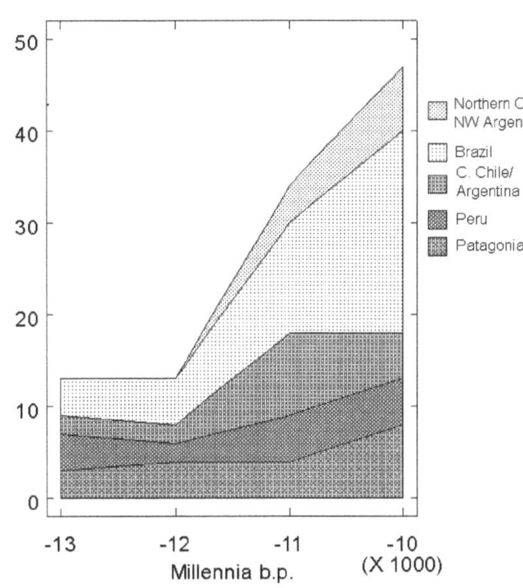

Figure 2. Early South American sites by age and region (data from Borrero 1996).

The work which we report in this paper examines the *spatial* structure of first clear human occupation of South America in the late glacial. We explicitly address only one question relevant to these wider archaeological debates. Do the earlier sites with clear signs of human presence tend to be closer to the farthest northwestern part of the continent (suggesting a pattern of late glacial first colonization), or are they scattered more randomly across the landscape (suggesting a pre-existing population reaching archaeological visibility)? In order to address this question, we have taken a small sample of early South American sites which are accepted by the majority of archaeologists, and which excludes a number of highly controversial sites and phases (Figure 3; Table 1). This is not our own sample: we have taken it, subject to minor amendments and two additions, from a paper published in *American Antiquity* in 1993 by David Whitley and Ronald Dorn. Whitley and Dorn's own analyses led them to argue that people must have reached South America well before the time of the North American Clovis culture. But were they right?

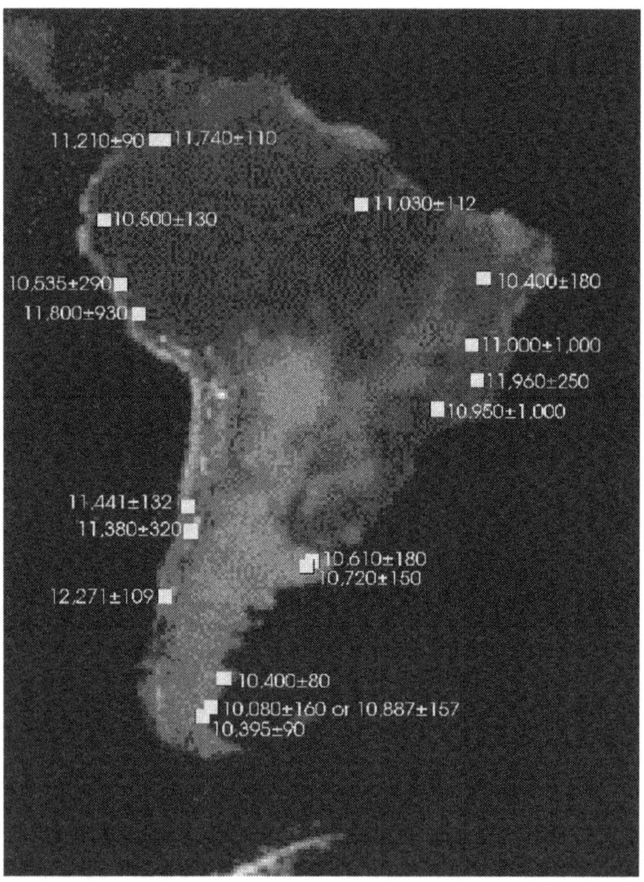

Fi

Figure 3. The locations of the sites used in this analysis, with their radiocarbon dates.

2 Methodology

To examine the spatial structure of this sample of early sites we have used weighted linear regression techniques. We take as our two variables *distance* to a site from the north-western-most point of South America at the junction with the Central American isthmus, and the *date* of the site. Our hypothesis is that dates should become progressively younger with increasing distance. If this hypothesis is not supported, then we will have to reconsider the model of a late glacial colonization event.

Because a radiocarbon date is a probability distribution and regression techniques require point values, we have taken the modal value of the calibrated probability distribution as our point value, and weighted it inversely to the square of half the one-sigma range. For normally distributed radiocarbon dates, this method would be adequate. Recently, however, the radiocarbon calibration curve has been extended back into the late glacial (Stuiver and Reimer 1993): clearly we must calibrate our dates before entering them into the regression, but the irregular shape of calibrated probability distributions for radiocarbon dates makes our statistical treatment problematic. In practice the early part of the calibration curve is sufficiently smooth for this to present no major problems: we are, however, currently examining ways of treating calibrated dates statistically which take account of such irregularities.

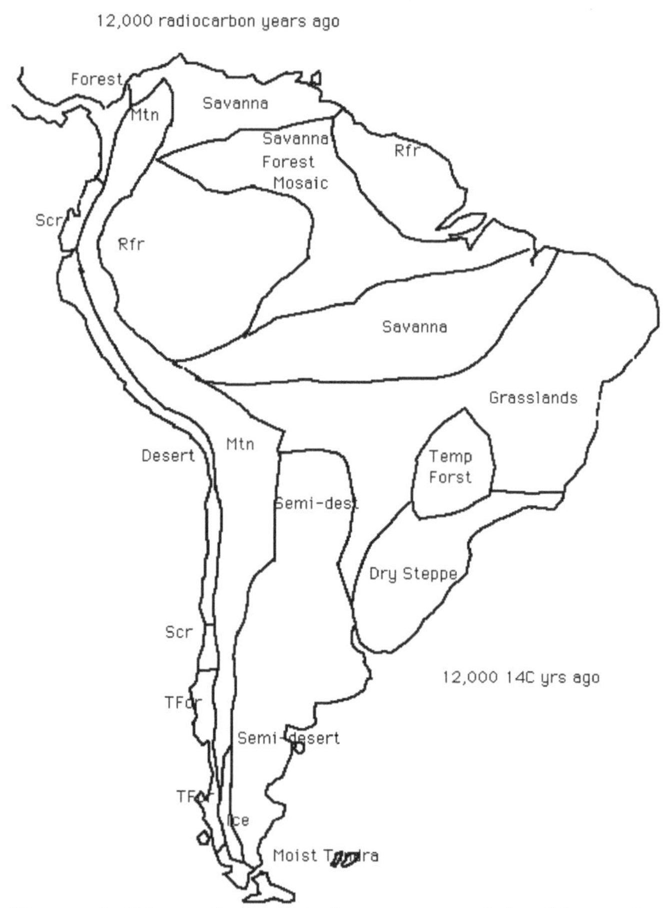

Figure 4. The paleovegetation map used in this analysis (from Adams 1995).

In an earlier analysis of this sample using weighted linear regression (there, of date against distance), two contrasting distance measures were used (Steele *et al.* in press). These were the geodesic distance, and the distance as measured on a road atlas from El Paso (a point at the south-western boundary of the U.S. Clovis culture area) to each of the early South American archaeological sites in Whitley and Dorn's sample. Results were discouraging (Table 2). Although in all cases the best-fit model showed a trend for sites to get younger with increasing distance, this was only statistically significant when Monte Verde 2 – the famously early site in southern Chile, dated to about 12,300 ^{14}C years b.p. – was omitted. Since a panel of leading sceptics has now visited that site and declared it to be both reliably dated and reliably associated with human artefacts, we cannot accept results which leave Monte Verde 2 out of the picture. On the face of it, therefore, we must reject our hypothesis that the spatial structure of early South American sites indicates an expansion from the north-west.

But how should we measure distance to these sites in ways which take adequate account of habitat variation and its effects on human expansion? Whitley and Dorn argued that distances measured from road atlases represented "reasonable and conservative surrogate measures for shortest and most feasible routes, assuming foreknowledge of the local environment on the part of the migrating population" (1993: 647). But while this measure takes account of topography, it takes little or no account of differences in the accessibility of the different vegetation zones of late glacial South America to a hunter-gatherer population, differences which we would expect to have had large effects on human dispersals. We propose that a better measure of effective distance for a colonizing population would be cost distance – a function of the relative frictions on expansion presented by different vegetation types.

For our new analyses, we have therefore taken a preliminary reconstruction of the vegetation zones of South America for the period 12,000 – 11,000 b.p. (Figure 4, from Adams, n.d.), and imported it into a raster GIS system (GRASS). We have then calculated cost distances from the north-western-most part of South America to each of the sites in our sample under varying assumptions about the frictions which different vegetation types would have presented to a colonizing population. We wanted to explore the space of possible friction weightings for each of these vegetation types, without prejudging the issue of which ones would have been most accessible to a colonizing population. To reduce computer time, we first assimilated each of the fourteen habitat types in our original reconstruction to one of four broad categories (Table 3).

One was for the more *Productive Open Habitats*, one was for *Closed Forest Habitats*, and one category contains a more heterogeneous mix of *Intermediate/Mixed* vegetation types. *Sea and Ice* were assumed to constitute a fourth category with essentially infinite friction value: in other words, we assumed that the colonization process took place by land. We then independently varied the frictions of each of the first three categories systematically, using eight possible friction values in a logarithmic series [1, 3, 9, 27, 81, 243, 729, 2187]. We were interested in discovering which combinations of friction values gave cost distances to each of our archaeological sites which best approximated the order seen in their radiocarbon dates. Figure 5 gives some examples of such cost surfaces, with the locations of the archaeological sites plotted on them.

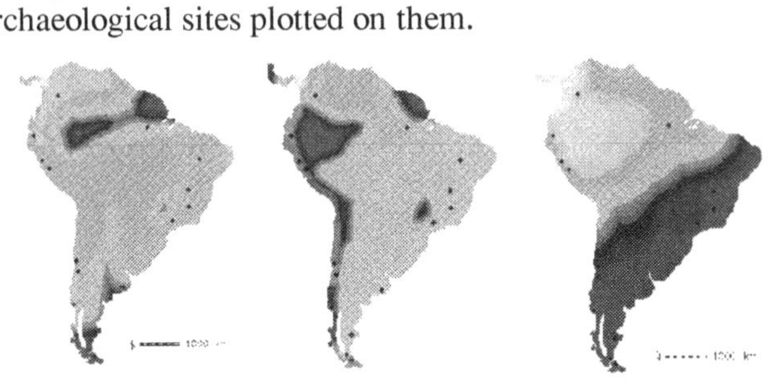

Figure 5. The cost surfaces – examples.

Since weighted linear regression is affected only by changes in the *relative* cost distances to each site, we were interested only in the effects of varying the *relative* frictions of our three main vegetation categories. We were thus able to further reduce the number of analyses required by varying friction values independently for only two vegetation categories at a time, in each case holding the third one constant with a value of 1. Our analysis therefore has the potential to tell us about the *relative* accessibility of different habitats to a colonizing population, but not to tell us the *absolute* rates of expansion across this or that habitat type, though this is a subject of further investigation.

To measure goodness of fit, we used the coefficient of determination (r^2) for the weighted linear regression of date against distance. This gives us an estimate of the proportion of the variation in calibrated dates for our sample which is accounted for by variation in cost distance to each site from a common point of origin. In looking at the effects of changing the cost distance variable on r^2, this exercise should ultimately enable us to rank habitat types in terms of their accessibility to an expanding human population, using empirical archaeological data. Our expectations are modest: as Table 2 shows, adjusted values for r^2 in the initial analyses using road map and geodesic distance were, respectively, 0.01 and 0.08!

3 Results

The main finding of our new regression analyses, done using cost distance as our spatial measure, is that the best weighted r^2 which we are able to achieve with our given dataset is 0.42. In other words, we can still explain less than half of the variation in calibrated dates using the best cost distance measure. While this figure seems low, it is nonetheless an improvement of more than threefold on the same measure of fit for a homogeneous surface. Moreover, we cannot expect a very good fit of the regression model given the uncertainties in the dates of the eighteen sites we are using.

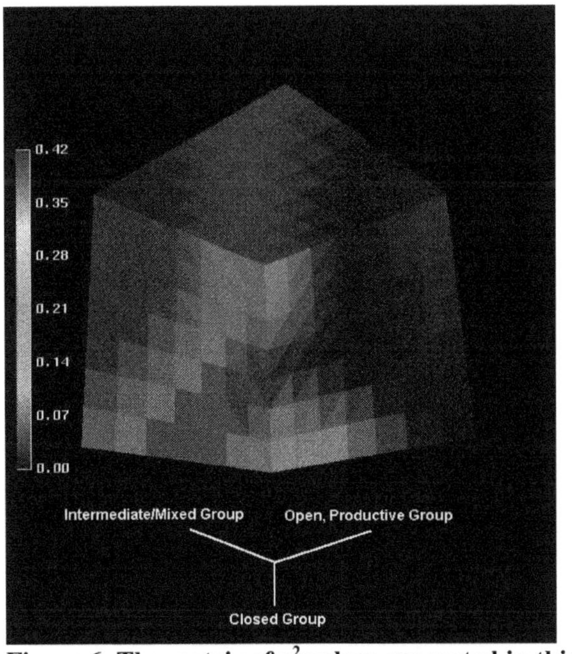

Figure 6. The matrix of r^2 values generated in this analysis, using the earlier date for Fell's Cave.

Another very encouraging finding is the consistent way in which r^2 varies with varying friction values for the three broad vegetation groups (Figure 6). The highest correlations between cost distance and calibrated dates were found when the parts of the vegetation surface which belong to the intermediate or heterogeneous vegetation group were given the highest friction values – and these *last* values must be very substantially greater than those for the open, productive habitat group. The majority of the highest correlations were also associated with classifications of the surface in which the open, productive habitat group were given the lowest friction values, and the closed forest parts of the surface were given intermediate friction values. For example, the highest value for r^2 was achieved when the friction ratios were 1 : 2187 : 243 (for the vegetation groups open : heterogenous mixed : closed).

There were some exceptions to this pattern: in some cases, a high r^2 was achieved when the closed habitat group was given lower friction weight than the open group, although in such cases the intermediate/mixed group always maintained a relatively high friction weight. Further numerical details may be found in our forthcoming Working Paper (Glass *et al.* 1997).

Finally, we were uncertain which to use of two possible dates for Fell's Cave, the early site in Patagonia – although the probability was that the earlier date was the more reliable. We therefore repeated the analysis using the later date. There was a remarkable consistency in the weighted r^2 results for the two sets of data. Those in which the earlier date for Fell's Cave was used gave consistently higher values for that measure.

4 Discussion

More than thirty years ago, Bennett and Bird (1965) argued that the earliest humans to colonize South America would most probably have come via the isthmus of Panama, migrating up into the Andean highlands via the Cauca and Magdalena rivers (which both flow south to north). The Andean environment would (they proposed) have offered little subsequent obstacle to southward migration, with expansion into the Pampas and Patagonia once Argentina had been reached, and entry into the eastern Brazilian highlands from northern Argentina. Lynch (1983) endorsed that view, and also proposed that '"openness" ranked high on the Paleo-Indian list of desirable habitat characteristics' (*ibid.*: 111): he thus argued that the observed predominance of early sites in open habitats was not due solely to archaeological survey bias. The recently reported site of Monte Alegre in central Amazonia (Roosevelt *et al.* 1996) complicates this picture, and we have included that site in our sample: but it nonetheless remains our impression that the spatial patterning in these dated early South American sites can best be explained as a result of preferential dispersal into the more productive open habitats. Further work needs to be done both to improve the accuracy and precision of the dates for a number of these sites, and to enlarge the existing sample of generally accepted late glacial occupation events, before we can use these results either as predictors of undiscovered site locations, or as a control on simulation models of demic expansion (e.g. Steele, Sluckin, Denholm and Gamble 1996). Nonetheless, we believe that our results both vindicate our spatial methodology, and tend to support the conventional model of a late glacial colonization of South America.

A number of further tasks have come to light as a result of this phase of our work. The first involves developing more reliable ways of including calibrated radiocarbon dates in spatial analyses which require the dates to be assigned point values. While we believe our approach – using the modal value weighted inversely to the square of half the one-sigma range – is reasonable, it becomes increasingly inaccurate with increasing irregularity and skew in the calibrated probability distribution. We are developing a bootstrapping approach to this problem, as a companion project to that reported in this paper.

The second task we need to address concerns the classification of habitat into broad groups for cost distance analysis. There are many reasons why we should try to assimilate the fine vegetation distinctions of our original paleohabitat map to as few coarse grained categories as we can: but in the analyses reported here, we may have pared down our broad categories to at least one too few. Interpretation of this first set of results requires us to review the criteria for including habitat types in that broad category of intermediate or heterogeneous types which needs to have a high friction weight (Table 3). In addition to a series of less productive open habitats (moist tundra, desert, semi-desert, and scrub), that group contains one anomaly – the tract of savanna/forest cover reconstructed for a drier northwest-southeast transect across the Amazon basin (Figure 4). We were uncertain whether to treat this as an open or as a closed vegetation type, not least because the paleoenvironmental literature records continuing debate over the extent to which last glacial cooling led to the division of the equatorial forest into patches separated by extensive tracts of savanna grassland or of savanna/woodland mix. Inspection of the sites and the paleovegetation map suggests that the reason we need to give a high friction weight to the broad class of vegetation types which include this reconstructed Amazonian savanna-forest tract, is that we need to make that tract relatively inaccessible if we are to match the observed dates of first human occupation immediately to its south and east. This needs to be confirmed by future analyses of the effects of independently varying friction values of the savanna/forest region alone.

The remaining tasks relate to the quality of the archaeological and paleoecological data which we have used. It is clear not only that many of the sites in our given sample would benefit from more precise and accurate dating, but also that the sample is too small and potentially systematically biased to contemporary habitats which are accessible to survey. It is also likely that the paleoecological reconstructions are based on too few pollen core control points to be wholly reliable – an additional source of uncertainty which can also only be remedied by further field work (Adams 1995). Nonetheless, we believe that these kinds of analyses of the existing data can, and indeed should, guide research designs for future fieldwork.

Site	Lat/Long[a]	Paleoeconomic indicators	Cultural materials	^{14}Cdates[d, e]	S.D.	Cal. yrs B.P.	Range to one- and two-sigma, Cal. yrs B.P.	Dist. (geodesic)[b]	Dist. (road map)[c]
1. El Abra, Columbia	[5º1' N, 73º57' W]		Unifacial percussion-flake tools including scrapers, knives and spoke-shaves.	11210	90	13117	13225-13018 13346-12918	4498	6,470
2. Tibito, Columbia	[4º58' N, 73º59' W]	Mastodon, horse and deer remains.	Unifacial assemblage of cores and flake tools.	11740	110	13685	13853-13534 14031-13396	4513	6,470
3. Cubilan, Ecuador	[3º37' S, 79º 14' W]		Leaf-shaped and tanged points.	10500	130	12373	12539-12168 12686-11870	4882	7,320
4. Guitarrero, Peru	9º12' S, 77º43' W	Deer, camelid, birds, other animals.	Bifacial projectile points, scrapers, perforators, blades, cores, hammerstones.	10535	290	12414	12722-11954 13003-11005	5493	8,480
5. Pachamachay, Peru	11º7' S, 76º11' W	Unidentified large mammals (fragmentary remains).	Straight-edged and curved-edge unifaces, unstemmed projectile points.	11800	930	13708	14947-12755 16330-11004	5763	8,990
6. Monte Alegre, Brazil	1° 60' S, 54° 4' W	Fish, mollusks, reptiles, birds, large mammals. Plant remains including tree fruits.	Triangular stemmed bifacial points, limaces, flakes and blades; red pigment rock.	11030	112	12944	13065-12828 13189-12708	6679	[N/A]
7. Quereo, Chile	[31º50' S, 71º18' W]	Mastodon, horse, deer, camelid and other animal remains.	Crude stone flakes and possible simple tools.	11441	132	13353	13520-13205 13708-13067	7990	11,720
8. Pedra Furada, Brazil	8º50' S, 42º33' W		Unifacially retouched '*limaces*', choppers, pebble hammerstones, and flakes.	10400	180	12243	12481-11880 12677-11087	8153	11,994
9. Tagua-Tagua, Chile	[34º18' S, 71º2' W]	Mastodon, horse, aquatic birds, camelid and other animal remains; some with possible butchery marks.	Flakes, hammer stones, flakers, cores; a few miscellaneous bone tools.	11380	320	13248	13610-12930 14008-12616	8239	12,020
10. Lapa do Boquete, Brazil	[15º29' S, 44º22' W]		Unifacial tools.	11000	1000	12879	13950-11046 15387-9965	8455	12,440
11. Alice Boer, Bed III, Brazil	[22º24' S, 47º33' W]		Unifacial flake scrapers, knives; bifacial pressure-flaked tools including contracting stemmed (tanged) points.	10970	1020	10940	11960-9920	8702	12,880
12. Abrigo de Santana, Brazil	[19º0' S, 43º53' W]		Two small quartz flakes, fragments of red ochre.	11960	250	13895	14231-13589 14607-13309	8744	12,440
13. Monte Verde II, Chile	41º30' S, 73º15' W	Plant remains indicating an economy focused primarily on plant gathering.	Edge-used flakes; unifacial and bifacial edge-trimmed tools, including bifacial, projectile points; pecked and ground bola and grinding stones. Organic material artefacts.	12271	109	14332	14540-14146 14760-13972	8840	12,900
14. Cerro La China II, Argentina	37º57' S, 58º37' W		Bifacial tools, including fishtail projectile points.	10610	180	12497	12689-12270 12867-11939	9213	13,480
15. Cerro La China I, Argentina	37º57' S, 58º37' W	Armadillo remains.	Fishtail projectile points.	10720	150	12611	12767-12440 12916-12234	9213	13,480
16. Piedra Museo, Argentina	47º54' S, 67º52' W	50 m. from a paleolagoon. Fauna include ostrich (cf. *Rhea americana*), camelid (*Lama (Vicugna) gracilis*), and horse (*Hippidion saldiasi*).	Fishtail projectile points, unifacially-worked scrapers and knives (some heat-treated).	10400	80	12243	12376-12079 12489-11862	9669	[N/A]
17. Fell's Cave, Argentina	52º4' S, 70º0' W	Mylodon, horse, guanaco, bird and other remains.	Fishtail projectile points, utilized flakes, cores, ground and pecked discs.	10080 or 10887	160 157	11321 12810	11999-11001 12291-10954 12972-12647 13133-12470	9987	14,320
18. Tres Arroyos, Argentina	53º21' S, 68º15' W	Guanaco, fox, horse, camelid, bird and rodent remains.	Edge-trimmed flake tools.	10395	90	12291	12425-12128 12541-11910	10170	14,420

GENERAL NOTES:

[a] Lat/Long is approximate, and estimated, in cases enclosed in square brackets. Otherwise, exact as extracted from the literature.

[b] Great circle distance (kms) from El Paso, located at 31º 46' N, 106º 29' W.

[c] Shortest roadway distances (kms) from El Paso as calculated from road maps by Whitley and Dorn (1993:647), who "take these as reasonable and conservative surrogate measures for the shortest and most-feasible routes, assuming foreknowledge of the local environment on the part of the migrating population."

[d] Uncalibrated radiocarbon dates.

e A southern hemisphere correction of -40 radiocarbon years was applied to sites south of the equator (Stuiver and Reimer 1993). This, of course, takes no account of variation through time in the effect of hemispheric circulation patterns on atmospheric carbon ratios: it is possible that this correction should only be applied to southern-hemisphere sites south of the tropics.

Table 1. List of dates used in this analysis, and associated information.

	X	a (s.e.)	b (s.e.)	p	r^2 (adj.)
All sites					
Cal. BP	geodesic	13666 $\pm$484	-0.10 $\pm$0.06	0.13 n.s.	0.08
Cal. BP	road map	13543 $\pm$530	-0.05 $\pm$0.05	0.30 n.s.	0.01
Excluding MV 2:					
Cal. BP	geodesic	13799 $\pm$368	-0.13 $\pm$0.05	0.02*	0.28
Cal. BP	road map	13721 $\pm$408	-0.08 $\pm$0.04	0.05 n.s.	0.20

Table 2. Results of weighted least-squares regression analysis of the relationships between dates and distance from El Paso. Equations are of the form Y = a + bX. Weights used were the square of half the one-sigma range. The Table shows two sets of results, with Monte Verde 2 – the principal outlier – either included or excluded. * = model significant at 95% level. From Steele, Gamble and Sluckin (in press).

Open Productive Habitat Category	Intermediate/Mixed Types
Includes:	Includes:
Savanna	Savanna/Forest Mosaic
Grassland	Moist Tundra
Dry Steppe	Desert
Mountain	Semi-Desert
	Scrub
Closed Forest Habitat Category	
Includes:	Sea and Ice
Forest	Includes:
Tropical Rainforest	Sea
Temperate Forest	Ice

Table 3. Broad paleovegetation categories into which the original types were assimilated for this analysis.

Bibliography

Adams, J M, 1995 *Preliminary Vegetation Maps of North and South America, 15,000-9,000 b.p.* (Project report for NERC.)

Bennett, W C and Bird J B, 1965 *Andean Culture History* (2nd edition), London

Borrero, L A, 1996 The Pleistocene-Holocene transition in southern South America, in Straus, L G, Eriksen, B V, Erlandson, J M and Yesner, D R (eds.), *Humans at the End of the Ice Age: the Archaeology of the Pleistocene-Holocene Transition*, 339-354, New York, Plenum Press

Glass, C A, Steele, J and Wheatley, D W, 1997 *Human colonization of South America: Regression Models*, Department of Mathematics, OR Preprint Series No. OR89 (in prep.)

Lundqvist, J and Saarnisto M, 1995 Summary of Project IGCP-253, *Quaternary International*, 28, 9-18

Lynch, T F, 1983 The Paleo-Indians, in Jennings, J (ed.), *Ancient South America*, 87-137, San Francisco, W.H. Freeman and Co.

Roosevelt, A C, Lima da Costa, M, Lopes Machado, C, Michab, M, Mercier, N, Valladas, N, Feathers, J, Barnett, W, Imazio da Silveira, M, Henderson, A, Sliva, J, Chernoff, B, Reese, D S, Holman, J A , Toth, N and Schick K, 1996 Paleoindian cave dwellers in the Amazon: the peopling of the Americas, *Science*, 272, 373-384

Steele, J, Gamble C and Sluckin T, in press Estimating the rate of Paleo-Indian expansion into South America, in Nicholson, R and O'Connor, T (eds.), *Proceedings of the 1995 AEA*, Oxford, Oxbow Books

Steele, J, Sluckin, T, Denholm, D and Gamble C, 1996 Simulating hunter-gatherer colonization of the Americas, Analecta *Praehistorica Leidensia*, 28, 223-227

Stuiver, M. and Reimer, P J, 1993 Extended ^{14}C data base and revised CALIB 3.0 ^{14}C age calibration program, *Radiocarbon*, 35, 215-230

Whitley, D S and Dorn R I, 1993 New perspectives on the Clovis vs. Pre-Clovis controversy, *American Antiquity*, 58, 626-647

Contact details

Celia Glass[1], James Steele[2*], David Wheatley[2]
[1]Department of Mathematics,[2]Department of Archaeology
University of Southampton
Highfield, Southampton SO17 1BJ UK
[*]email: tjms@soton.ac.uk

Deconstructing the Land: the Archaeology of Sacred Geographies

César Parcero-Oubiña

CAA 97

Abstract

This paper illustrates new potential for the application of GIS in archaeological research. The aim of this text is to show how, by means of the application of a structured and detailed methodological procedure, it is possible to apply GIS analysis to the study of some spatial features that lie usually far from the interaction between archaeology and computing. We will illustrate the potential of this strategy with a brief summary of a case study in Galicia. Within our analysis, the role of GIS in archaeology is reviewed, in order to re-evaluate its actual importance. In this way, we direct our interest into the crucial distinction between description (analysis) and interpretation (meaning).

1 Introduction[1]

The enormous analytical power which new technologies (in this case, computers) offer to archaeological study has lead, on many occasions, to a progressive move away from the objectives of archaeological study. These are being undermined by the strong attraction offered by these new instruments for data analysis, and which have become an end in themselves. In other less extreme, but more frequent cases, the application of a particular tool (GIS) to the archaeological record -- particularly in landscape and spatial applications -- has lead to an overvaluing, and even a monopolisation, of the most obvious aspects of the record: those which refer to the use of the environment, whether for productive or socio-political ends. In contrast, the possibility of applying this technology to the study of less obvious aspects, such as the symbolic concept of the space, has been systematically ignored.

We believe that this problem is mainly derived from the excessive importance given to the tools of analysis themselves (GIS), due to their obvious novelty and the wide range of possibilities they offer. Consequently, crucial questions relating to archaeological analysis are being pushed into the background.

In this paper we intend to show how, without having to discover new frontiers in using GIS as a tool, it is possible to obtain more benefits using well-known information analysis techniques. This allows the possibility of applying current methods to the study of non-immediate aspects in archaeological landscapes, enhancing the potential of gaining access to the symbolic concepts of the archaeological landscape.

2 General approach

The following suggestions are not intended as a final product of our investigation, nor do we even wish to offer a theoretical discussion as a foundations for further work. We do, however, consider it necessary to detail the initial concepts which direct our investigation, and the rules which underlie its development -- something comparable to the rules of play. These principles also correspond to the general guidelines of the work carried out by the Landscape Archaeology Research Group in the University of Santiago de Compostela (Spain), of which we form a part. This development may be consulted, for example, in Criado 1995.

2.1 Regarding the use of GIS in archaeology

We do not intend to enter into a wide-ranging process of compiling and criticising the habitual use of GIS in archaeological investigation. Firstly, this is not the aim of this work. Secondly, it is an overly specific task for this study, and thirdly, because readers of this text, situated as it is in a volume which is dedicated specifically to computer applications in archaeology, will already have sufficient understanding of the subject.

What we do intend to do is to clarify what is our position in this area. A position which is not original, and does not intend to be original. The use of GIS in archaeology, as with any other instrument or information analysis technique which may be available, cannot be disconnected from the essence and logic of archaeological investigation. Landscape Archaeology (our line of work) like any other manifestation of archaeological investigation, cannot be dedicated only to the collection and systemisation of data, nor to the processing of this information through more or less sophisticated technologies, such as GIS. The final objective should always be to *generate social significance* from archaeological data and to produce interpretations based on the material under study. In our opinion, archaeology does not differ from other areas which study historical dimensions (Bermejo 1990, Neustupný 1995), although in other aspects it is distinct.

2.2 About landscape

It has already been said that our line of work is Landscape Archaeology (as defined in Criado 1995). This assumption basically incorporates two concepts regarding landscape:

1. We try to analyse those elements which compose the archaeological record, whatever its scale -- from sites (Méndez 1994), to material cultural objects (Prieto and Cobas 1995). These are all treated as objects which are involved in the landscape and are participants within it.

This decision is not gratuitous or random: the landscape appears to us as the most valid *contextual element* in order to fully understand the archaeological record, and the way that this is constituted within a spatial matrix.

2. The landscape is not only a contextual framework but is also susceptible to being converted into another element of the archaeological record. It is possible to understand the landscape as an object in itself, along with certain formal features, which means that it may be analysed and interpreted using archaeological methodology. *The landscape is not only a context, but may also be an object under study*, as it is not just space, but a social product.

2.3 Regarding the archaeological analysis of the landscape

The perspectives from which Landscape Archaeology can be made are very varied and non-exclusive. In fact, it is possible to combine several of them into a single study (Parcero 1995). One of the critical factors which brings about this diversity of approximations is the treatment of *time*.

With respect to this, in this study we propose an analytical approximation which may be able to deal with more than the static analysis of the landscape conceptualised as space. We believe that the potential of incorporating the temporal component will help to enrich this area, primarily through the *diachronic study of different types of landscape superimposed on the same physical space*. This approach conceives the landscape according to the double perspective proposed in section 2.2 and should lead (see section 2.1) to the construction of interpretations concerning correlations or differences detected in different types of landscape.

2.4 The methodology of analysis

As suggested above it is also intended to conceptually distinguish between the fundamental phases of the archaeological study of landscape (analysis and interpretation). Here we can illustrate how this distinction takes shape within the actual process of investigation. The *analysis* of the objects under study should allow for the transformation of a group of physical realities (objects from the real world) which are generally dispersed, unconnected or genetically unequal, into a structured group of recognisable evidence, with perfectly defined formal features, and accordingly without the subjective weight of interpretation.

Interpretation will only be possible if the objects under interpretation have been previously analysed through their non-subjective formal features. We therefore consider it necessary to reconstruct study objects based on *description*, through the *analysis of their formal components*, according to their own rules, and without introducing meanings during the analytical process.

3 The objects of study

Having explained the principles upon which our work is based, we will present the documentation (objects) used for analysis. It is not difficult to guess that, as we are exploring the applications of GIS in the archaeological record, these objects are classified into two groups or classes:

1. Firstly we need a physical, orographical or environmental matrix, which reveals human activity in any historical or prehistoric context. The first object of analysis will accordingly be *space*, understood from an ahistoric or, more exactly, deculturised point of view: space as surroundings, as a simple physical support, characterised by a series of features (forms, relief, geology etc.) which pre-exist human activity and are situated over it (or, more precisely, beneath it). Space, understood in this way, is a passive object (not a subject), and is thus susceptible to objective analysis.
2. Secondly, we define the anthropic component, resulting from the *archaeological record*. In principle, any sub group from the archaeological record is susceptible to this second object of study. However, the more evident and direct that the spatial implications of this record are, then the easier it is to put them in context with the first object under study. The easiest realities to analyse will be, for example, the models of placement and the patterns of site distribution, etc. We propose a non-restrictive vision of the archaeological record, which fits not only the 'ancient' (prehistoric) elements but also the historic and traditional record, including land use in the rural world to juridical, political or symbolic aspects of the socio-cultural landscape in different historical moments.

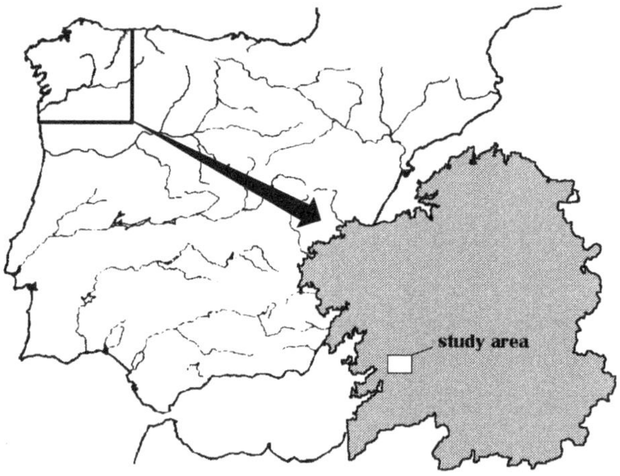

Figure 1: Location of the study area in the Iberian peninsula.

In the following example, the intention is to carry out a diachronic analysis of different types of landscape superimposed in a specific area of Galicia, in the North-western Iberian peninsula (see Fig. 1). This is an area of around 130 km^2 on the western flank of Galicia, near the coast. There are a large number of archaeological elements within this physical matrix, corresponding to different cultural contexts, with the most outstanding being rock carvings from the Bronze age (Bradley et al. 1996) which have recently been integrated into another study (Parcero *et al* forthcoming) We will not consider these now, but instead will deal with the analysis of the following elements of the record:

1. The distribution of fortified settlements (castros) in the Iron Age (ca. 8th Century B.C. – 2nd Century A.D.). There are 11 sites in the area (see Fig. 2) whose exact periods of occupation are unknown (note 2) although they respond to the same type of socio-cultural rationality, which is essentially related to the fact that they are fortified (note 3).
2. The situation of two indigenous-Roman stone inscriptions (see Fig. 2) presumably of a religious nature (parcero *et al* forthcoming)
3. The distribution of the traditional rural population (from the Middle Ages) (see Fig. 3). We have data which allow us to offer a global distribution of population in the area up to the middle of the 19th century (note 4).
4. The traditional judicial boundaries (parishes) (see Fig. 3). At this time it is not clear where the origin of these limits lies. Those which we offer come from at least the start of the 17th century (note 5).

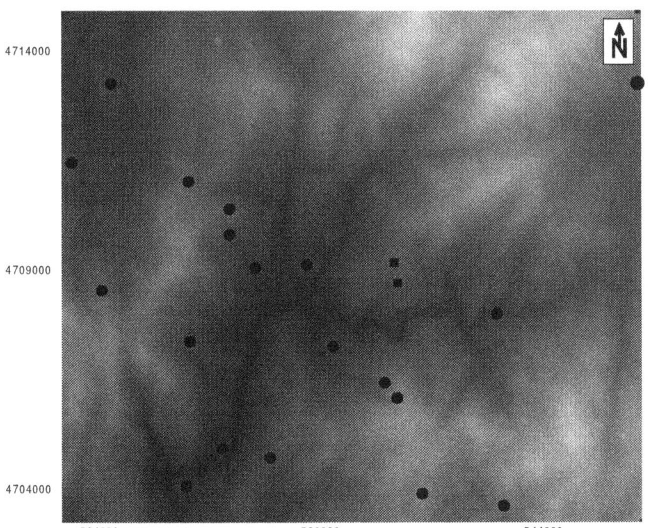

Figure 2: Distribution of Iron Age hillforts (round dots) and inscriptions (square dots) over a DEM of the study area.

4 The procedures of information analysis

We already have a group of data susceptible to analysis. We have briefly indicated what method of analysis we believe to be the most convincing: description. There are various ways of describing objects. Our proposal may be expressed through the opposition between *deconstruction and reconstruction*. Thus, the analytical procedure which we follow is based on breaking down the study objects (physical space and the elements selected from the archaeological record) into their component parts and analysing the formal relationships between them.

The deconstructive process may therefore be understood as breaking down and extracting the minimal formal features which comprise each of the elements under study. For example, the physical medium may be broken down into elements such as slopes, height, hydrological network, plant cover, etc. From this maximum breakdown one may then begin to analyse the relationships between each element, looking for significant correlations between them and enabling the construction of new elements, formed by the combination of the initial elements, etcetera.

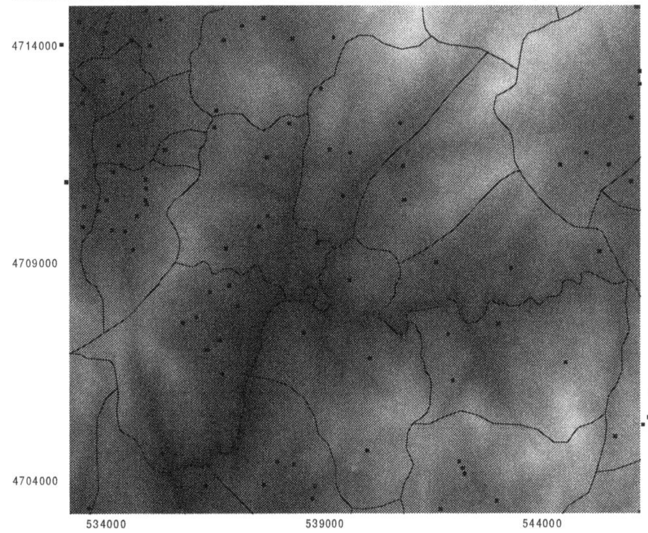

Figure 3: Distribution of traditional villages and parish boundaries over a DEM of the study area.

Each of the study objects previously presented must be broken down in this way and independently analysed. It is only in a second stage when the correlation between the different objects analysed in this way has been provided that meaning and interpretation will emerge.

The role and utility of GIS in each of the stages of analysis is quite clear. GIS becomes an extremely interesting tool for the analysis of data, in the manner suggested here, particularly given their ability to process large amounts of data and the ability to use this facility for the process of deconstructing the objects under study (above all relief). GIS allow for a much more neutral and 'objective' analysis than any other traditional instrument used for this work, as a resultof their ability to obtain statistical indices which support the perceptions and impressions obtained from analysis.

Their use does not end with the first stage of analysis. The ability of GIS packages to connect different types of data is well known (in fact this is one of their essential functions), along with their capability for determining significant correlations and for obtaining differential indices of significance. This use is particularly important as, without access to a GIS, it is unthinkable to check all of the possible correlations between numerous types of data.

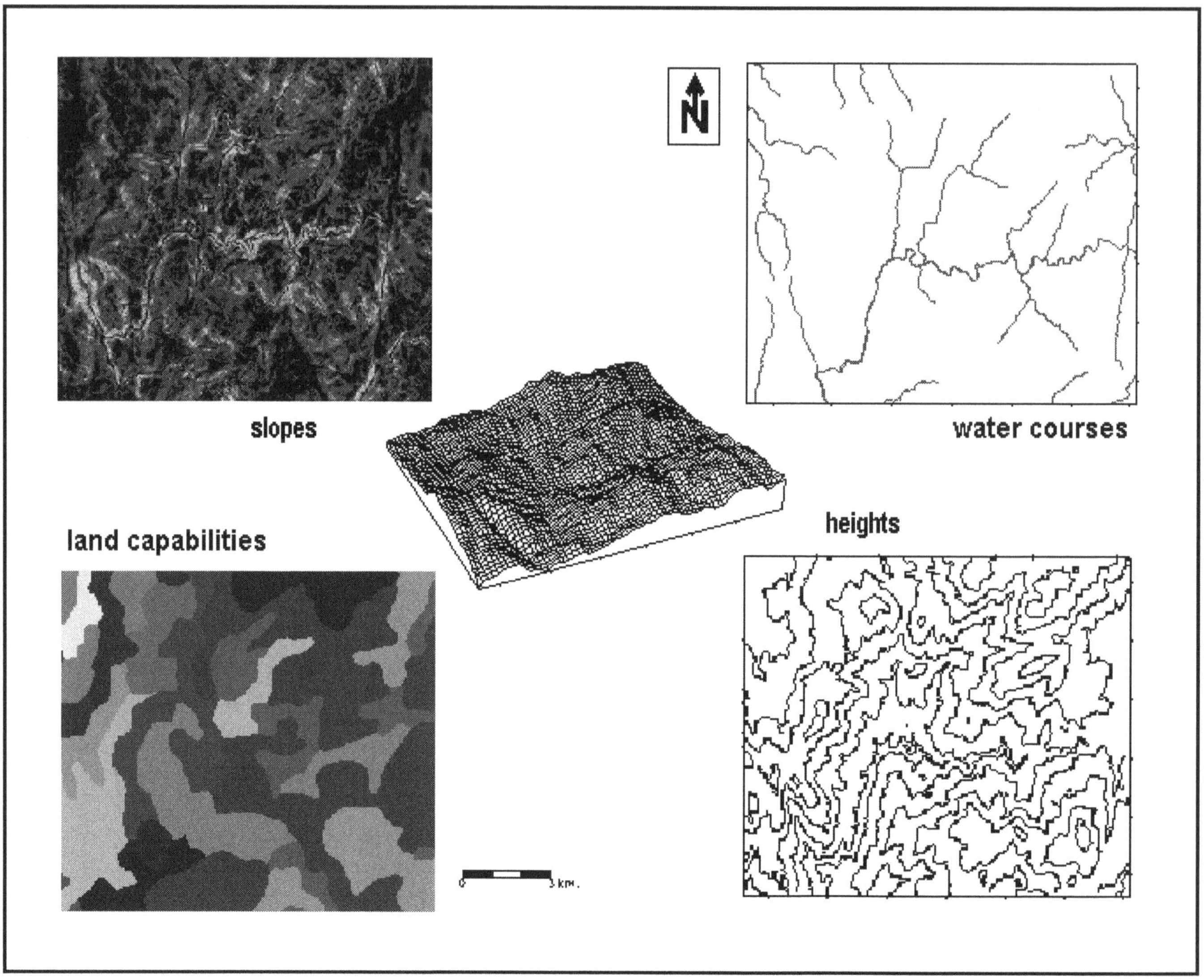

Figure 4: The physical matrix deconstructed into some of its basic elements.

Entering into more detail, the steps which we will follow in the analysis are the following:

1. Independent formal (deconstructive) analysis of the study objects – relief and archaeological documentation. Some elements which may be isolated are:
   - 1.1 elemental forms
   - 1.2 conditions of visibility
   - 1.3 lines of sight
   - 1.4 significant elements and places
   - 1.5 occupation basins
   - 1.6 elements relating to movement
   - 1.7 the hierarchy of elements
2. Investigation of connections between the different types of elements isolated within each group of study objects in order to find significant correlations and groupings. Including, for example, connections between slope maps, the presence of water courses and the nature of terrain order to obtain a new working object in the form of a map of accessibility.
3. The establishment of correlations between objects within both spheres and the determination of the most characteristic elements. Significant correlations can be the relationship between a type of settlement and soil,or with present day land use.
4. From description to interpretation 1: a proposal of hypothetical models which explain these correlations, starting with the most basic models and arriving at general models for each category within the archaeological record. The intention is not to explain the previous correlations through purely causal arguments such as: if A shows a positive correlation with B, then one of them is the cause of the other. The intention is, on the contrary, to produce coherent readings which, paying attention to the contexts from which the data arises (the context of A and the context of B), generate new interpretative factors: if A and B show a positive correlation, then maybe there is a C which relates to both of them. Statistical models are thus created for each of the cultural sequences analysed.
5. From description to interpretation 2: a comparison between the models established in 4, and with correspondences and disconnections being established between them. The product of 4 should be the emergence of a new group of objects for analysis which need not correspond to physical realities but may relate to non-material products, with interpretative models. Now, with

respect to the possibility of analysing superimposed landscapes in the same space, the intention is to find common ground between these models and landscapes, and to bring about new dynamic models in which time is incorporated.

6. The interpretation of models produced in this manner, from the possible existence of principles of organisation and the conceptualisation of the landscape which is similar or different for each of the contexts analysed. The final result is an interpretative discourse capable of explaining the different patterns of construction and conception of a particular space throughout the chosen temporal sequence.

The first three steps are susceptible to the use of GIS. It is clear from this scheme that their use is not the finality of the study (which is incomplete without having arrived to at least the fourth point), nor as an interpretative instrument as such (as they are absent as of the fourth point), but instead they are viewed as :

1. Useful for the management and analysis of large sets of data (an instrument in the truest sense of the word).
2. tools used to objectify the results of the analysis and to reaffirm observations which were apparently subjective.
3. Instruments for contrasting hypotheses derived from using other analytical methodologies.

5 Analysis

Given that the objective of this text is simply to illustrate a procedure in archaeological investigation, we are not going to offer a detailed analysis (this may be consulted in Parcero *et al* forthcoming, where the range of data used is larger). We will offer some brief notes which will give an example of the analytical procedure which was presented in the previous section (note 6).

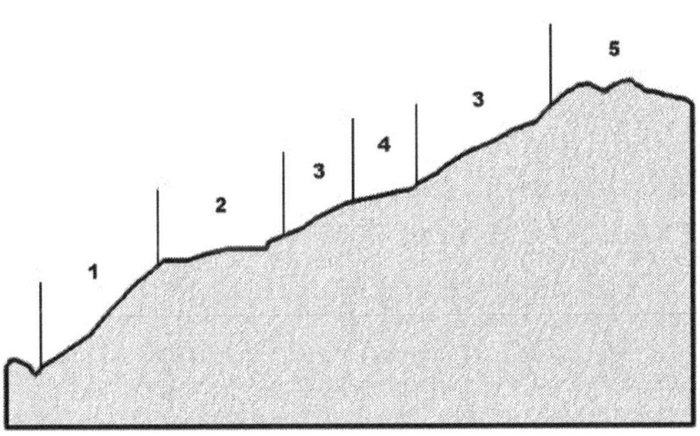

Figure 5: Ideal profile of the study area with the Units of Relief.

The *breaking down* of objects under study is best seen in the treatment of the physical environment. We have basically worked with the following components (see Fig. 4): relative altitude, slopes, type of terrain, distribution of water courses, traditional land use and actual use. From the combination of this series of data, we have defined a new study object and called it *Units of Relief* (in Fig. 5 an ideal topographical profile of the area is shown, and the distribution of each of these units is indicated). Five units were isolated:

1. Slopes above rivers covered with forest.
2. Low and open land, valleys. These are infrequent and are very localised. There is a concentration of intensively used land and of population within these areas.
3. Lateral mountain sides, land with extensive use, today mainly reforested.
4. Flat interfluvial surfaces producing wetlands or marshes.
5. Rocky hilltops with light or non-existent soil cover, used either extensively or not at all.

Moving up one stage in the analytical process, the combination of these elements enables us to obtain new objects of study: these we have called *Relief Sectors*. There are three of these: (see Fig. 6)

1. Central area, with open shapes and clear areas of occupation, with a wide surface occupied by Unit 2 type land.
2. An area, to the East, associated with steep hillsides (Units 1 and 3).
3. An area which repeats, to a lesser degree, the previous characteristics.

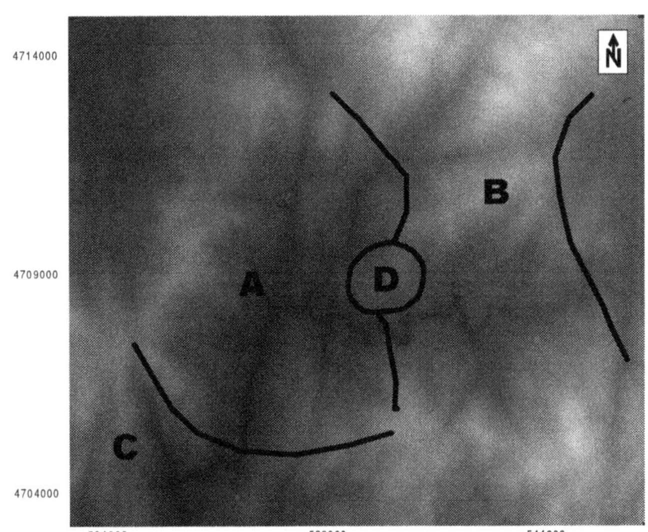

Figure 6: Relief Sectors over a DEM of the study area.

Once the essential forms of the physical space of the working area have been broken down, we are in position to move to a new phase of analysis, incorporating the correlation of the two types of study objects: the physical matrix and archaeological record. We will not go into detail about this analysis, which must basically include the following types of correlation and seek significant similarities or differences:

1. Hill forts-units-sectors
2. Inscriptions-units-sectors
3. Villages-units-sectors
4. Parish limits-units-sectors

6 Results

The results derived from this analytical process may be classified into two main categories, the first preceding the second: description (static hypothetical models) and interpretation (dynamic significant models).

6.1 Description

The first stage in the analytical process is simply to observe the most significant results from the analysis through a simple succession of descriptions which, at this stage of the analytical process, gives rise to hypothetical models for the different contexts which have been analysed:

1. For the oldest of the cultural contexts studied -- the Iron Age -- two different types of landscape exist together: the occupied landscape, revealed by the presence of hill forts, and the non-occupied landscape, far from settlements, where inscriptions are found (see Fig. 2). Each of these spatial forms is marked not only by different elements of the record, but also because it related to different physical forms (Units of Relief). The second also coincides with the point where differentiated physical formations meet (Relief Sectors).
2. The next cultural context analysed -- the traditional rural world -- provided a new model of spatial occupation. This model, in general terms, is quite similar to the occupation space in the Iron Age. For this period we also know something about the system of judicial boundaries. These follow a certain rationality (connected with water courses and Unit 3 and 5 – type lands). This rationality, however, is clearly and strangely broken in a single point, where the parish limits go beyond the barrier imposed by the river Lérez (note7).
3. The comparison between the two previous points allows us to highlight the similarity between the settlement spaces in both periods, the similarity of patterns of occupation, and the use of the environment in inhabited areas. Logically, important differences also appear, some of degree (an increase in the density of occupation, and an increase in pressure upon the environment) associated with others which are structural and basic and can be used to distinguish between socio-cultural contexts: passing from a fortified model of settlement to another, open, model.
4. Another important point for the comparison of these models is that a singular and significant point in the landscape is marked in both, and this is based on particular physical features, these are cultured in different ways at each moment (inscriptions vs. parish limits), but clearly significant for both periods. This new correlation thus offers a degree of coincidence and difference which is similar to that presented in the previous point for the space of the settlement.

6.2 Interpretation

The final stage consists of giving significance to the previous models, producing an interpretation which allows a wide-ranging understanding of the relationships between the different elements which are superimposed in a precise physical space and which leads, through the sum of various landscapes, to a new landscape to which we have access today. In our case we may offer two types of interpretation:

1. The coincidences we have shown between the two models of landscape analysed should not lead us to think directly in a linear continuity of cultural contents throughout different stages, but that the differences between them should also be considered. In this way one sees the answer to organisational and relative patterns with the environment which are *similar* (in both cases we are dealing with complex rural societies, with similar ways of exploiting their surroundings) but neither of these situations is identical or evolutionary (hill forts compared to villages, inscriptions compared to limits without artificial reference).
2. Concurrences may also indicate the possibility of the recognition of a *sacred landscape* in the area, renewed in the Iron Age and reinterpreted in the traditional rural world. This recognition is possible not only through the reading of two inscriptions of a votive nature (precise objects and not landscape), but above all through their contextualisation with the rest of the objects analysed: space and archaeological record belonging to different contexts.

This is, broadly speaking, where we must finish. Obviously there are many other possibilities of interpretation, and we could drive our lecture to many different ends. But if we are trying to be as close to data as possible, interpretations should stop where data begin to be blurred.

Notes

1 This text is a specific development of part of a larger paper (Parcero *et al* forthcoming). For this reason I am not the single author of the text, but must acknowledge my colleagues Manuel Santos and Felipe Criado. Obviously I am greatly indebted to both

2 Only one of the hillforts has been excavated, demonstrating an early period of occupation and abandonment, within the first Iron Age (8th-6th centuries B.C.) (Álvarez 1986).

3 Compared to other parts of Europe (Hogg 1975, Bewley 1994, Collis 1984), the Iron Age in the north-western Iberian peninsula is characterised by the fact that only fortified settlements exist (hill forts). Also, fortification is a feature almost exclusive to the Iron Age and is only repeated, with notable differences, in the Middle Ages.

4 In this way the changes which occurred in the rural environment from the 1950's and 1960's may be avoided. In any case, it should be remembered that Galicia is a region with an urban and industrial development that has been limited until quite recently. Therefore the survival of traditional ways of life until the middle of this century, and in some areas until even more recently, is noteworthy. The study area also lacks significant nuclei of population. We may therefore consider that this distribution of population until the middle of the 19th century is quite similar to that which existed in the Middle Ages.

5 The parish boundaries may be traced back to, at least, the Middle Ages (XI-XII centuries).

6 We have used IDRISI for Windows 2.0 package developed by Clark University, MA, U.S.A. For the production of the DEM of the study area we used Surfer for Windows 32 v.6.04 from Golden Software Inc.

7 This point is not simply a parish boundary, it is also an episcopal boundary (from at least the XVII century) and for municipalities (from their origin in the XIX century).

Bibliography

Bermejo Barrera, J C, 1990 From the archaeology of religion to the archaeology of simbolic forms: theoretical and methodological foundations. *Dialogues dHistoire Anciene* 16-2, 211-230.

Bewley, R, 1994 *Prehistoric Settlements*. London, Batsford-English Heritage.

Bradley, R, Criado, F, Fábregas, R, 1996 Rock art and the Prehistoric Landscape of Galicia: the results of field survey 1992-4. *Proceedings of the Prehistoric Society* 61, 347-70.

Collis, J, 1984 *The European Iron Age*. London, Batsford.

Criado, F, 1995 The visibility of the archaeological record and the interpretation of social reality, in Hodder, I. et alii (eds.). *Interpreting Archaeology*. London, Routledge, 194-204.

Hogg, A H A, 1975. *Hillforts of Britain*. London, Hart-Davis, Mac Gibbon.

Méndez Fernández, F, 1994 La domesticación del paisaje durante la Edad del Bronce gallego. *Trabajos de Prehistoria* 51-1, 77-94.

Neustupný, E, 1995. The significance of facts. *Journal of European Archaeology*, 3-1, 189-212.

Parcero Oubiña, C, 1995 Elementos para el estudio de los paisajes castreños del Noroeste peninsular. *Trabajos de Prehistoria*, 52-1, 127-144.

Parcero, C, Criado, F, and Santos, M, Forthcoming Rewriting Landscape: incorporating sacred landscapes into cultural traditions, *World Archaeology,* 1998

Prieto, P, Cobas, I, 1995 From landscape to pottery: spatial regularities on Material Culture. Paper presented at the First Annual Meeting of the European Association of Archaeologists (Santiago de Compostela, 1995).

Contact details

César Parcero-Oubiña
Grupo de Trabajo en Arqueología del Paisaje
Departamento de Historia I
Universidade de Santiago de Compostela
15703 Santiago de Compostela
SPAIN
email: phcpar@usc.es

Landscape Archaeology and GIS
Abstracts of papers held on CD-ROM

CAA 97

Reconstructing Archaeology from the Landscape: GIS, CAD and The Roman Signal Station at Whitby
Tyler Bell

This paper is a concise presentation of the ACAD and GIS methodology by which the probable height and location of a Roman signal station at Whitby can be determined, and is intended to complement a separate paper which discusses in full the archaeological evidence for such a station (Bell forthcoming). Here a CAD-based schematic of the topography between Whitby and the neighbouring station at Ravenscar is used to determine a height for the signal stations to have been intervisible (50 metres). This finding is tested using a GIS viewshed function to determine the minimum height (45 metres) and probable location of the structure on the Whitby coast. Without aiming to prove conclusively that a Roman signal station existed at Whitby, this paper introduces a methodology by which further information about the missing signal station may gleaned from the landscape in which these structures existed.

A GIS Study on the Spatial Development of Coastal Catalunya
Federica Massagrande

GIS and multivariate statistical analysis were used to study the development of the Roman settlement pattern in the region of Tarragona and the Maresme in Spain. Though these two areas are geographically similar and almost neighbouring, the Roman settlement pattern varied considerably between the two throughout the time in which Spain was under Roman rule. The data clearly shows the effect the foundation of the town of Tarraco (Tarragona) had on the Roman rural settlement, while the lack of a strong centre in the Maresme caused the rural organisation of the area not to change significantly after the rural settlement was first established. The influence of the pre-existing Iberian settlement on the Roman settlement pattern was also investigated. Correspondence Analysis was also used to study the distribution of different pottery types in the two areas and assess which pottery types were associated with sites with certain characteristics and with the main communication routes. The GIS and CA study clearly shows that despite the geographical proximity of the two areas, the rural settlement pattern was shaped by different factors at play in the two territories.

GIS in Palaeolithic Archaeology. A Case Study from the Southern Netherlands.
Hans Kamermans and Eelco Rensink

This paper examines locational features of Palaeolithic and Mesolithic findspots in the loess region of the southern Netherlands, using a Geographic Information System (GIS). GIS applications in hunter-gatherer archaeology have so far been rather rare, although (as is true for later periods) GIS could be a useful tool for the locational analysis of hunter-gatherer stone artefact distributions. This paper deals with the methodological problems encountered when trying to extract environmental variables from a GIS and using them for analysis. The accuracy of digital maps, the statistical tests to investigate the relationship between artefact distribution and environmental variables and the use of predictive modelling are discussed using the south of Dutch Limburg as the study area. It will be concluded that, in our study, GIS has proven to be a valuable tool as a first step of research, dealing with the representativeness and interpretation of Palaeolithic and Mesolithic lithic scatters documented from a geologically dynamic loess landscape. However, due to a number of methodological flaws, GIS is as yet not the analytical tool we can use to answer our research questions.

An Analysis of the Structure and Function of Prehistoric Maori Pa Sites
Claire Reeler

Maori pa sites are fortified settlements built in the prehistoric period in New Zealand, usually situated on an elevated position. A sample of sites has been mapped using a total station theodolite in order to provide data for the 3D modelling of these sites. GIS analysis in ARC/INFO of the 3D models of pa is used to answer questions about the structure of the these sites, their relationship with the landscape and aspects of their function within prehistoric society. The relationship between the internal organisation of these sites and the landform on which they are situated is particularly important. The use of GIS allows several types of analysis of these features, such as slope and aspect, area and arrangement of features, line of sight between parts of the site and immediate surroundings and movement of sunshine across different parts of the site at different times of the year. These types of analysis can add to our understanding of how and why pa sites were built where they were.

Fuzzy Viewshed Analysis of the Hellenistic City Defence System at Sagalassos, Turkey
L. Loots, K. Nackaerts and M. Waelkens

This paper presents the results of the interdisciplinary study of the Hellenistic outer defences at the site of Sagalassos. The aim of this study was to analyse the reciprocal relation and intervisibility of a small part of the Hellenistic outer defences, i.e. a fortress and two watchtowers on the mountain tops immediately north and southwest of the city, and the main north and south approaches to the city. This analysis uses a GIS, thus combining archaeology, computer science and geography. Because of the deceptive accuracy of binary viewshed maps, fuzzy viewsheds were calculated. Two types of viewsheds, projective and reflective, were produced. Because of the sensitivity to the positioning of the observation points of the projective viewsheds, it was decided to also calculate reflective viewsheds. Both projective and reflective viewsheds show that the different towers guard a well defined part of the main north and south approaches to the city. It also became clear that the visibility of the different watchtowers interact, and that they can be integrated into a single system, thus indicating a contemporaneous date for all elements of this system of outer defences. The results of the method used in this study, seems promising enough to further develop and apply it. Also the drawbacks of both projective and reflective viewsheds become clear, leading to the conclusion that a combination of these two types of viewshed often offers the best view on the visibility in the study area.

Modelling Prehistoric Land Use Distribution in the Rio Aguas Valley (SE Spain)
Philip Verhagen, Sylvia Gili, Rafa Micó and Roberto Risch

The Rio Aguas Project has been aiming to better understand the long-term ecological consequences of different economic and social strategies in the lower Rio Aguas valley (province of Almería, SE Spain). The area has a long history of human occupation, during which several periods of strong pressure on the environment have occurred. This pressure has however not always been generated by the same economic or social structures. Part of the work for the project was undertaken as a GIS modelling of the agricultural production landscape. The purpose of this modelling was two-fold: firstly, to gain insight into the potential of the Rio Aguas valley for different agricultural strategies. And secondly, to start reconstructing the possible production zones in the past, using palaeo-ecological and archaeological evidence on diet and population. The paper will discuss the methodology applied and the implications for the interpretation of the prehistory of the Rio Aguas valley.

Mapping the Fourth Dimension: the TimeMap Project
Ian Johnson

This paper outlines the need for an explicit methodology for recording and managing spatio-temporal data in archaeology and related disciplines. It describes the essential components of a methodology being developed by the University of Sydney TimeMap(tm) project, viz: a model for recording spatio-temporal data; provision for recording fuzziness in spatial and temporal limits; temporal interpolation between known information; display and animation of data through a time-enabled GIS interface; and a metadata standard allowing access to remote datasets across the Internet without restructuring. Examples of the user interface and animation products are included.

The Enhancement of the South Etruria Survey: GIS in the Study of the Research History of the Southern Faliscan Area
U. M. Rajala, A. R. Harrison, and S. K. F. Stoddart

The enhancement of the south Etruria survey is one of the projects connected to the Tiber Valley project launched by the British School at Rome. The purpose of the enhancement project is to use new methods to analyse material collected by the British School at Rome during the south Etruria project between the 1950s and 1970s. The idea is to bring together researchers in Britain and Italy to process the material using modern research procedures. As an example of the potential of GIS in the enhancement, a study using Arc/Info to analyse the relationship of the Roman road network to the results of surveys carried out in the area of the southern Ager Faliscus is presented. It is a preliminary investigation into the effect of different research strategies. As a result of this work, the influence of ancient transport networks on the results of pre-1960s surveys is proven

GIS and Prehistoric Mammal Acquisition Patterns
Cheryl L. Huckerby

Geographic information system (GIS) analyses of mammal species' landscape distributions produces species assemblage lists that are comparable with archaeological species assemblage lists. Using digitised environmental maps and associated information entered into attribute tables, GIS analyses identified three (3) species assemblages possibly reflective of prehistoric Aboriginal people's emphases. These were 1) preference for specific landscapes, 2) preference for specific species, and 3) restrictions on time available to travel from an occupation site. Comparisons with an archaeological assemblage from Cathedral Cave in Carnarvon Gorge, (Queensland, Australia) identified differences in the listed species. For example, a dominant species determined from the GIS analyses, the Common Ringtail Possum (Pseudocheirus peregrinus, Thomson and Owen, 1904, 27), was ranked 10th in the archaeological species list.

ARCHAEOLOGY
IN THE
AGE OF THE INTERNET

CAA 97

Section 3
Numerical Methods

CAA 97

Coins, Copies and Kernels - a Note on the Potential of Kernel Density Estimates

Kris Lockyear

Abstract

One of the more remarkable aspects of the distribution of Roman Republican coinage is the vast quantities of these coins recovered from the territory of Romania, roughly ancient Dacia. Yet more remarkable is the evidence for the contemporary copying of these coins in a manner which makes the identification of them as copies extremely difficult. Obviously, some estimation of the date of these copies, and the proportion of the Dacian assemblage which are copies, is essential in any attempt to interpret their significance in social and economic terms. In order to provide some answers to these questions, an archaeometallurgical project was organised by the author. The project sampled some 200 coins from Romania, and UK museums, which were then analysed using atomic absorption spectrometry. The statistical analysis of this data, after some initial success, proved a difficult task. This paper reviews the analyses, problems and solutions, with particular emphasis on the use of kernel density estimates in the examination and interpretation of bivariate scattergrams and maps from principal components analysis.

1 Introduction

The analysis and graphical representation of large complex data sets is a problem that has been addressed in many ways with varying degrees of success. Data reduction methods, such as Principal Components Analysis (PCA) or Correspondence Analysis (CA) are often very successful but can still suffer from crowded plots. Use of colour helps to discern structure in the data, such as groups, (Scollar *et al* 1993) but is not a perfect solution. Plotting boundaries on scatter plots or maps, perhaps derived from the results of a PCA or CA, has also been used (e.g., Goldberg and Iglewicz 1992), along with two-dimensional variations on the box-plot (Becketti and Gould 1987). Many of these methods suffer, however, from a prior assumption that the underlying distribution is regular, e.g., elliptical. In many cases, this assumption is false. An alternative is the use of Kernel Density Estimates (KDEs) which can be used to plot two dimensional 'contour plots' on bivariate maps (e.g., Bowman and Foster 1993). The application of KDEs to archaeological problems was first suggested by Baxter and Beardah (1995) who have also developed routines in matlab to perform these analyses (Beardah and Baxter 1996b), and published a number of papers on their application in archaeology (Baxter and Beardah 1996; Beardah and Baxter 1996a; Baxter *et al* 1997; see also Baxter, this volume and Beardah, this volume).

The aim of this short paper is to present an example of the use of these routines in the analysis of a complex data set, and to suggest some desiderata for the future. A fuller publication of all aspects of the statistical methodology employed and the lessons learnt will be published elsewhere. The final report on the project is to be submitted to the Romanian journal Dacia. This paper will not consider the statistical theory behind the method for which the reader is referred to the excellent book by Wand and Jones (1995).

2 The problem

One of the many remarkable aspects of the numismatic history of the late Iron Age in Romania is the evidence for the copying of Roman Republican coins by the native population. Evidence for this, in the form of coin dies, cast coins and die links, indicate the presence of these copies, but the scale of the copying has been disputed. This is because the copies are so exact that normal methods of identification cannot supply an answer (see Lockyear 1996b for a full discussion of the problem).

Obviously, the significance of these copies in the development of late Iron Age society in the region is largely dependent on what proportion of the coin assemblage are genuine Roman coins, and what proportion are locally made copies. The main influx of Roman *denarii* into the region was between c. 75 and c. 65 BC. A logical context for these copies would therefore be immediately after that date (Lockyear 1996a).

In order to estimate the proportion of copies in the total assemblage, a programme of archaeometallurgical analysis was instigated by the author in collaboration with Mathew Ponting, Clive Orton, and Gheorghe Poenaru-Bordea. In May 1992, 178 samples were obtained from *denarii*, tetradrachms of Thasos, and from two silver bars found with the Stăncuţa hoard (STN[1]; Preda 1958). Amongst the *denarii* sampled were known imitations, cast and struck copies[2]. Details of the hoards and samples are given in Table 1. Subsequently, comparative material from the Ashmolean and the British Museum was sampled. The samples were analysed by Matthew Ponting using atomic absorption spectrometry and the data passed to myself for statistical analysis. A preliminary batch of 30 coins was analysed in 1992 (Lockyear and Ponting 1993), and the remaining coins in 1994-5.

The first batch of samples were analysed using a single solution method which proved to be problematic; the second batch, therefore, was analysed using a two solution method. Three samples from the first batch were re-analysed in the second batch.

Hoard	No.	Sample	Reference	Reason
Zătreni	41	6	ZAT; Chiţescu 1981, no. 215	early hoard in Muntenia
Poiana	152	20	IPO; Chiţescu 1981, no. 148	hoard from major settlement in Moldavia
imitations	--	6	Chiţescu 1981, nos. 11, 28, 84, 67, 165, 239	unprovenanced, for comparison to hoard material
Popeşti	?	3	in preparation	3 tetradrachms of Thasos, by request of Poenaru-Bordea
Breaza	122†	19	BRZ; Poenaru Bordea & Ştirbu 1971; Chiţescu 1981, no. 29	contains cast copies
Stăncuţa	34	9	STN; Preda 1958; Chiţescu 1981, no. 188	mixed hoard of tetradrachms, *denarii* and silver bars
Voineşti‡	94	3	VOI; Ştirbu 1978, p. 90, no. 4	by request of C. Ştirbu
Poroschia	552	66	PRS; Chiţescu 1980; Chiţescu 1981, no. 154	contained possible copies
Şeica Mică	348	44	SEI; Floca 1956; Chiţescu 1981, no. 193	hoard from Transylvania, used by Crawford in RRC

Table 1. Romanian hoards sampled May 1992. †Bucureşti lot. ‡Not published in detail and therefore contents not listed in the CHRR database.

3 Analysis

The data analysis had a number of stages:

1. Data cleaning;
2. Univariate analysis using dot-plots and summary statistics;
3. Comparison of elements to the date of minting;
4. Bivariate analysis using scattergrams and KDE 'contour' plots;
5. Multivariate analysis using PCA, the results of which were plotted on a map along with contours derived from KDE;
6. Estimation of the number of copies per hoard using the results from 5.

This paper will concentrate on stages 4 and 5, but will first summarise briefly the other stages.

3.1 Stages 1-3

The data initially required some checking and cleaning to remove erroneous data points and measurements, to identify analyses undertaken on very small samples, etc. To do this the data were converted from a series of excel spreadsheets to a relational database structure. To account for variable sample size a dual method of estimating missing data values was used (Lockyear 1996b, 410-15).

One of the major problems with the data set is that the silver alloy used is extremely pure. This meant that although some 13 elements were looked for, very few were detectable in the majority of cases. The univariate analyses used both summary statistics (Lockyear 1996b, Table 14.9), and dot-plots (Lockyear 1996b, Figs. 14.9-14.17) to examine each element individually, and specific coins which appeared unusual on this basis were noted. These analyses identified one of the coins from the Ashmolean Museum as being a copy! This was a timely reminder that simply because a coin comes from a UK museum does not mean it is necessarily genuine.

Of the elements looked for, only five had sufficient measurements above the detection limit for further analysis. Of these, silver formed over 93% of 75% of the coins. In order to avoid problems of closure (Aitchison 1986)--that is the fact that the all the percentages sum, obviously, to 100--this element was dropped from all subsequent analyses[3]. This left four elements: copper (Cu), lead (Pb), gold (Au) and bismuth (Bi). Each of these elements were plotted against the date of the coins (Lockyear 1996b, 421-24) to test for possible temporal trends in the data. There was the slightest hint that copper levels may have increased from 157 to 50 BC, but otherwise no temporal patterning was detected.

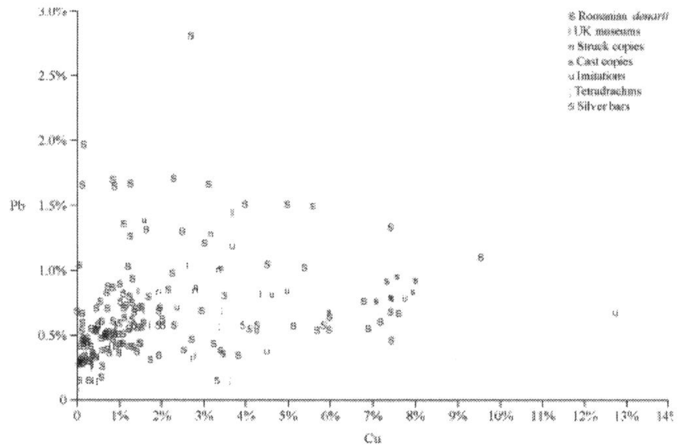

Figure 1. Scattergram of Cu v. Pb for all samples (except 191 which was omitted due to poor data)

3.2 Stage 4 - bivariate analysis

Two bivariate scattergrams were constructed; one of the two major elements (Cu v. Pb) and one of the two minor elements (Au v. Bi). The use of multiple symbols allowed some grouping to be seen in the plots, e.g., the cast coins from Breaza (BRZ) fall into a small group, but the pattern is far from clear (Fig. 1). It would seem that the copies generally have higher levels of copper and/or lead, and that most UK museum coins have low levels of these elements, but the separation is not clear cut.

In order to make the division between known copies, UK museum coins (assumed to be mainly genuine) and the remainder of the *denarii* clearer, a number of KDE contour plots were created -- see Figure 2 for an example. These plots were created with the kdedemo2 set of macros for matlab which will be discussed in section 4.1. The package offers four different kernel functions and a variety of methods for estimating the value of the bandwidth h; this procedure is analogous to selecting the bin-width when constructing a histogram (Beardah and Baxter 1996b). These different options were tried, but the 'best' results, judged solely on visual criteria, were obtained by using the recommended options of the normal kernel and using the Sheather-Jones method of selecting h (called 'solve-the-equation 2' in the kdedemo2 package).

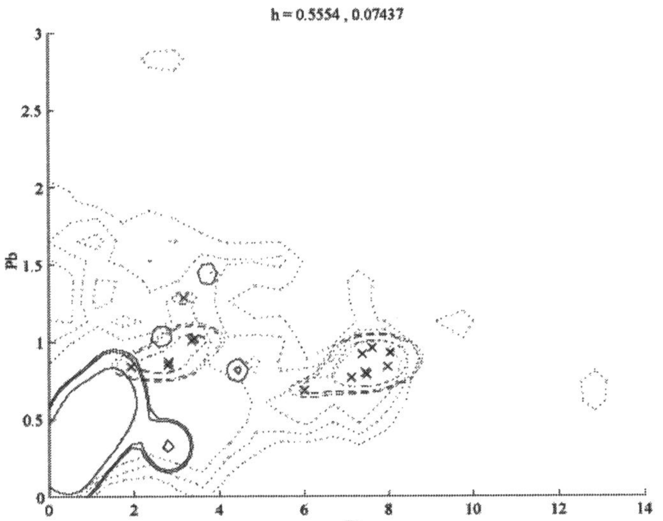

Figure 2. Kernel density estimate percentage contour plot, 85, 95 and 100% contour lines for: all samples (dotted), UK museums (solid) and cast/struck copies (dashed). Sample 191 omitted. Cu v. Pb. Crosses mark location of cast/struck copies.

Figure 2 plots the 85%, 95% and 100% contour levels for the three groups of coins. In lay terms, the 85% 'contour' line for copies contains 85% of the data points for those copies whilst maximising the density of data points within that line. This principle obviously applies to each line/group. It can be clearly seen from the figure that there is good separation between the UK museum coins (bottom left) and two groups of copies. These two groups represent the cast coins from Breaza (the right- hand group) and the struck copies from Poroschia (left-hand group). There is a slight overlap with one copy lying on the edge of the main group of UK coins, and three UK coins lying away from that main group. It is important to note that there are many other 'unknown' *denarii* that lie outside the main UK group, interspersed and surrounding the copies. Similar patterning was observed with the two minor elements.

3.3 Stage 5 - the multivariate analysis

Success with the bivariate plots suggested that a multivariate analysis might increase the separation between groups. PCA was performed on the data set using the same four elements. The analysis was performed using a correlation matrix and the first two axes 'explained' 59.1% of the variation in the data.

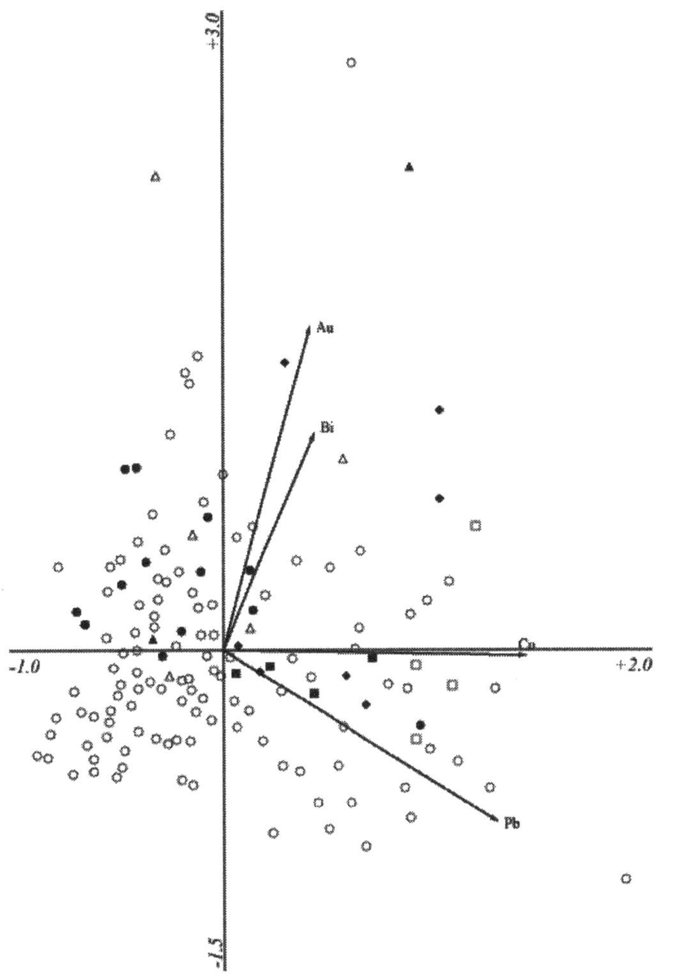

Figure 3. Biplot from PCA of full metallurgical data set omitting sample 191. 1st and 2nd axes of inertia. Open circles: *denarii* from Romania; filled circles UK museum *denarii*; open squares: cast copies from Breaza; filled squares: struck copies from Poroschia; open triangles: tetradrachms; filled triangles: silver bars; diamonds: imitations.

Figure 3 presents the biplot from this analysis. As can be seen, there is a correlation between copper and lead, and a second correlation between gold and bismuth. The first principal axis mainly represents variation in the copper levels, and to a lesser extent the lead values; the second axis represents the gold and bismuth values which appear to be moderately negatively correlated with lead. As can be seen from the plot, the majority of the UK museum samples occur in the top left quadrant of the plot, i.e., they are associated with low levels of all four elements. This of course means that they are actually associated with high levels of silver and thus the problem of closure has not been completely avoided by dropping that element.

Again, however, the patterning is not completely obvious. Some points are clear, for example the three data points that lie at the top extreme of the second axis are all from the Stăncuța (STN) hoard, and all have high levels of gold. What makes this

even more fascinating is that these points represent three different types of object: a tetradrachm of Thasos, a Republican *denarius*, and a silver bar.

To make the pattern clearer a further set of KDE contour plots were produced using the normal kernel function and the Sheather-Jones method of selecting h of which Figure 4 is an example. In this plot only *denarii* were included in the calculations, and the separation of the UK museum coins and the copies can be clearly seen. There is still a little overlap, but it is minimal[4].

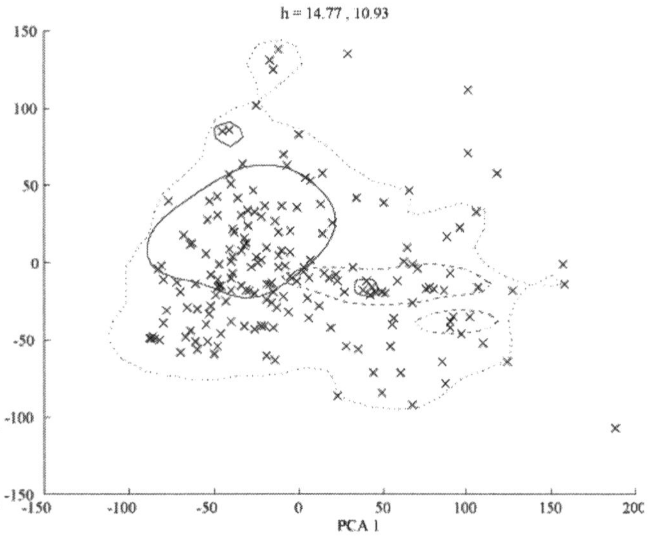

Figure 4. Kernel density estimate percentage contour plot of PCA 1 v. PCA 2. 95% contour lines marked: all *denarii* (dotted), UK museums (solid) and cast/struck copies (dashed). Individual points also marked. Samples 58 & 191 omitted.

The difficulty now was to divide the unclassified *denarii* from Romania into two classes: those which are probably copies and those which are probably genuine. To do this the *denarii* were divided into four groups. These groups were labelled 'core', 'penumbra', 'outside' and 'far-out'. The first group, the core coins, consisted of all coins which lay within the main 95% contour line for the UK museum material in Figure 4. The far-out group consisted of all coins which had a score of >0.5 on the first principal axis and >1.15 or <-0.35 on the second. These limits excluded all UK museum coins. The three coins analysed twice (see section 2) showed a 0.25-0.31 difference in their co-ordinates, mainly on the first principal axis. The coins that were left were therefore divided into the penumbra category which included all coins within 0.31 of the main 95% UK coin contour, and the outside group which were all coins that lay outside that band but within the limits set for the far-out category. A number of observations can be made about the composition of these four groups. Firstly, only a single UK museum coin lies in the far-out category, and a further coin in the out-side category. In the case of the former (coin no. 181) this is the copy identified as such by the univariate analyses discussed above. Of the cast coins from Breaza, all lie in the far-out category, but the struck coins from Poroschia mainly lie in the penumbra or outside categories. The imitations occur in most groups including the core group.

3.4 Stage 6 - estimating totals of copies

The final stage was to estimate the number of copies per hoard. To do this I decided to use the number of coins in the far-out category as the number of copies. No doubt some of the coins in this group are in fact genuine, but there is also a likelihood that some of the coins in the core category are copies as shown by the fact that some of the imitations have the same metallurgical composition as the main mass of points.

Estimates and confidence intervals were obtained using the method outlined by Shennan (1988) for those hoards where enough samples were taken. For the remainder the confidence limits were obtained from Table P of Rohlf and Sokal (1995). For the Şeica Mică (SEI) hoard 16 coins from the 44 sampled fell in the far-out category giving an estimate of 36.3% with 95% confidence limits of ± 12.4%. This seems remarkably high. Taking an ultra-conservative view and only accepting coins with very high copper levels we still get six copies, giving us 13.6% ± 8.8%. For Poroschia (PRS) 30 coins from 62 were in the far-out category giving us a figure of 48% ± 11%, or 16% ± 8% if we take the ultra-conservative line. Similar figures were obtained from the other hoards.

From this it can be seen that although the precise level of copying is still very unclear, and will become the subject of a further project, it can no longer be sustained that the level of copying in the region was minimal and insignificant (cf. Crawford 1980; Crawford 1985). This phenomenon appears to be a major part of the numismatic history of the region, and certainly reflects important political and social developments at that time.

4 Discussion

4.1 The kdedemo2 package

The kdedemo2 set of macros for matlab were written by Beardah (Beardah and Baxter 1996a; Beardah and Baxter 1996b). These macros were downloaded from Nottingham Trent University in April 1996 and were run on a UNIX workstation although they would work equally well on a Windows-based PC. They are available via Internet Archaeology.

A few comments about matlab and these macros are appropriate here. Firstly, the PostScript produced by matlab is not true encapsulated PostScript and required some manual editing by the author before the plots were usable by other packages. Secondly, the differences between line types were sometimes poorly rendered on the printed plots. As regards the kdedemo2 macros, these were easy to use and very powerful. One facility which the author would have liked was the ability to calculate/plot the contours for one group, and then list the data-points which lay outside that contour from a second group; facilities were provided to list outliers from a single group. It is possible, however, to obtain this information direct from matlab (Beardah *pers comm*). Also, a check box to force matlab to create true maps where $x = y$, essential in the plotting of the results of CA, would be useful.

The division of the coins into the four categories was undertaken manually from the plots and other data. The additional features suggested for the kdedemo2 macros would have made this task easier, and it is hoped that they might be implemented at a later date. A more experienced user of matlab would have been able to use the full potential of the package to speed-up this task.

4.2 Final comments

From the above it can be seen that KDEs are a powerful exploratory tool, particularly when used with PCA or CA of complex data sets. The method enabled the successful investigation of the problem. In terms of the current example, it would be useful if some more formal method could be developed which would integrate the metallurgical data along with other information, such as the date of the coin, the weight and the diameter, to provide a estimate of the probability for each coin being a copy. It has been challenging and I hope useful to investigate the different methods, in particular the use of KDEs, by which this very complex data set can be analysed. Nevertheless, the most challenging and interesting question remains to be answered. Why did the Dacians copy Roman Republican *denarii*?

Acknowledgements

I would like to thank my close collaborators on this project, Matthew Ponting and Clive Orton. Matthew took and analysed all the samples used in this analysis for which I am very grateful, as well as patiently answering my innumerable questions about the technique and the data. I would also like to thank John Merkel for allowing the first 30 samples to be analysed. Grants were generously awarded by the Fund for Applied Science in Archaeology, the Royal Numismatic Society and the UK Numismatic Trust, which enabled the completion of the AAS analyses. I would also like to thank my colleagues in Romania, Gh. Poenaru-Bordea, Adrian Popescu and his family, Radu Ocheşeanu, Constanţa Ştirbu, Catalin and Geta Borţun, Ecaterina Ţinţăreanu, Aniko Mitruly, Lili Ardea, Doina Comşa and Virgil Mihăilescu-Bîrliba and family. Without their help and support this project would have been impossible. I would also like to thank the British Museum, particularly Roger Bland and Andrew Burnett, and the Heberdean Coin Room, Ashmolean Museum, particularly Chris Howgego and Cathy King, for allowing us to sample coins from their collections. Mike Baxter and Christian Beardah are to be thanked firstly for bringing KDEs to my attention, but also for their help and encouragement. I have also had many long and fruitful discussions on this problem with Richard Reece, to whom I am grateful. Finally, Clive Orton, Mike Baxter, Christian Beardah and Dale Serjeantson kindly read drafts of this paper. Any errors which remain are, as always, my own.

Notes

1 All hoards mentioned in this text are accompanied by a three letter code in small capitals. This is a unique identifier used in the author's Coin Hoards of the Roman Republic CHRR database, and in other publications and allows the precise identification of individual hoards.

2 The cast copies from the Breaza (BRZ) hoard were deliberately selected and therefore have to be left out of any estimation; some coins in the Poroschia (PRS) hoard were suggested by Chiţescu to be copies, but were not deliberately selected for. In 1993, subsequent to sampling but prior to analysis, these coins were positively identified as struck copies by the author on the basis of die-linkage.

3 This method has been called naïve but in practice is a robust option and does not suffer from the problems which often occur with the alternatives (see Tangri and Wright 1993 and the reply by Baxter 1993).

4 Note that this plot has been `clipped' to exclude sample 58 which although included in the calculation of the contour lines, was so extreme it caused the plot to be very compressed.

Bibliography

Aitchison, J A, 1986 The Statistical Analysis of Compositional Data. Chapman and Hall, London

Baxter, M J, 1993 Comment on D. Tangri and R. V. S. Wright, 'Multivariate analysis of compositional data..., Archaeometry, 35 (1)(1993)', Archaeometry 35(1), 112-115

Baxter, M J and Beardah, C C 1995 Graphical presentation of results from Principal Components Analysis, In Huggett, J and Ryan, N S (eds.), Computer Applications and Quantitative Methods in Archaeology 1994, 63-67, British Archaeological Reports International Series No. 600, Oxford

Baxter, M J and Beardah, C C, 1996 Beyond the histogram: improved approaches to simple data display in archaeology using Kernel Density Estimates, Archeologia e Calcolatori, 7(1), 397-408

Baxter, M J, Beardah, C C and Wright, R V S, 1997 Some archaeological applications of Kernel Density Estimates, Journal of Archaeological Science, 24(4), 347-354

Beardah, C C and Baxter, M J, 1996a The archaeological application of Kernel Density Estimates, Internet Archaeology 1, http://intarch.ac.uk/journal/issue1/beardah index.html

Beardah, C C and Baxter, M J, 1996b MATLAB routines for Kernel Density Estimation and the graphical representation of archaeological data, In Kamermans and Fennema (1996), 179-184

Becketti, S and Gould, W, 1987 Rangefinder box plots. a note, The American Statistician, 41(2), 149

Bowman, A and Foster, P 1993 Density based exploration of bivariate data, Statistics and Computing, 3, 171-177

Chiţescu, M, 1980 Tezaurul de la Poroschia (jud. Teleorman) şi unele probleme privind monedele geto-dacice de tip roman republican, Studii şi Cercetări de Numismatică 7, 53-70

Chiţescu, M, 1981 Numismatic Aspects of the Dacian State. British Archaeological Reports, Oxford, International Series 112

Crawford, M H, 1980 Imitation of Roman Republican denarii in Dacia, Studii şi Cercetări de Numismatică 7, 51-2

Crawford, M H, 1985 Coinage and Money under the Roman Republic, Methuen, London

Floca, O, 1956 Contribuţii la cunoaşterea tezaurelor de argint dacice: tezaurul de la Sărăcsău şi Şeica Mică Editura Academiei Republicii Populare Romîne, Bucureşti

Goldberg, K M and Iglewicz B, 1992 Bivariate extensions of the boxplot, Technometrics, 34(3), 307-320

Kamermans, H and Fennema, K (eds.) 1996 Computer Applications and Quantitative Methods in Archaeology CAA95, Institute of Prehistory, University of Leiden, Leiden, Analecta Praehistorica Leidensia 28

Lockyear, K, 1996a Dmax based cluster analysis and the supply of coinage to Iron Age Dacia, In Kamermans and Fennema (1996), 165-178

Lockyear, K, 1996b Multivariate Money. A statistical analysis of Roman Republican coin hoards with special reference to material from Romania, Ph.D. thesis, Institute of Archaeology, University College London

Lockyear, K and Ponting, M J, 1993 Metallurgical Analysis of Roman Republican denarii in Romania -- Interim Report, Unpublished

Poenaru Bordea, Gh and Ştirbu, C, 1971 Tezaurul de denari romani republicani şi de la începutul principatului descoperit la Breaza, comuna Lisa (jud. Braşov), Studii şi Cercetări de Numismatică 5, 265-282

Preda, C, 1958 Asupra descoperirii monetare de la Stăncuţa (Reg. Galaţi), Studii şi Cercetări de Numismatică 2, 239-251

Rohlf, F J and Sokal, R R, 1995 Statistical Tables W. H. Freeman and Company, New York, third edition

Scollar, I, Herzog, I and Greenacre M J, 1993 Colour and graphic display aids for correspondence analysis, In J. Andresen, T. Madsen and I. Scollar (eds.), Computer Applications and Quantitative Methods in Archaeology 1992, 325-327, Aarhus University Press, Aarhus

Shennan, S J, 1988 Quantifying Archaeology, Edinburgh University Press, Edinburgh

Sţirbu, C, 1978 Noi tezaure monetare intrate în patrimoniul Muzeului de Istorie al R. S. România, Cercetări Numismatice, 1, 89-92

Tangri, D and Wright, R V S, 1993 Multivariate analysis of compositional data: applied comparisons favour standard principal components analysis over Aitchison's loglinear contrast method, Archaeometry 35(1), 103-115, (Pages 112-115, a reply by M. J. Baxter)

Wand, M P and Jones, M C, 1995 Kernel Smoothing. Monographs on Statistics and Applied Probability 60, Chapman and Hall, London

Contact details

Kris Lockyear
University College London
The Institute of Archaeology
31-34 Gordon Square
London
WC1H 0PY
email: tcfacll@ucl.ac.uk

Time Series and Neural Networks in Archaeological Seriation. An example on early pottery from the Near East

CAA 97

Juan A. Barceló, Josep Miquel Faura

Abstract

Archaeological Seriation has been a current topic in Quantitative Archaeology. Nowadays, most scholars use Multidimensional Methods (Correspondence Analysis) in order to reduce the dimensionality in a set of data and obtain a uni-dimensional view that is related to chronological ordering. This paper criticizes this view, and proposes a new model based on bi-dimensional statistics (a generalization of hypothesis testing), using Neural Networks to calculate non-linear fittings among a series of observations. A case study on the first pottery evidence from the Near Eastern Late Neolithic (the Tell Halula sequence) will be presented.

1 Defining the problem: early pottery in the Near East

The First Pottery in the Near East appears, once production economy has been consolidated, in totally sedentary societies. Chronologically, the earliest pottery remains should be dated to the period ranging from the 9th. Millennium BP to the beginning of the 8th. They have been identified in sites in Anatolia (Mellaart 1975), the Syrian-Cilician region (Garstang 1953, Braidwood 1960, Contenson 1992), the Balikh Valley (Cauvin 1974, Le Mière 1979, Akkermans 1990, Le Mière & Nieuwenhuisse 1996), Northern Mesopotamia (Le Mière 1986, Campbell 1992) and the Zagros Region (Mortensen 1963). Along the Euphrates valley, however, there are only a very few sites with early pottery production.

Early pottery is a scarce material in all those sites, with little typological diversity, and of coarse manufacture. There are small to middle sized vases, made with non-purified fabrics and great quantity of vegetal inclusions. They are of simple shape such as bowls or hole-mouth jars. The finish is also very simple, mainly coarse pottery but including a few burnished items. Nevertheless in a very short period of time pottery manufacture develops and typological diversity increases, producing regional differences such as the *dark-faced burnished wares* in the Syrian-Cilician Region (Braidwood 1960) or the *Archaic Painted Ware* in the Zagros Region (Mortensen 1963).

In most cases, Early Pottery is analysed as a chronological indicator, and not as a consequence of historical processes. Many archaeologists seem only interested in describing the change in quantities of different kinds of pottery as an indication of time. Sentences like "If there are less than 5 fragments of Type A in this archaeological layer, then the chronology is *XX* " appear in many publications.

Our approach is completely different. We think that the frequencies of different kinds of pottery may or may not be correlated with time. The abundance of pottery is a consequence of some social and economic processes, and some of these processes are positively correlated with time. For instance: the total amount of pottery, the amount of "luxury" (well manufactured) pottery and the degree of typological diversity increases through time. Nevertheless, this correlation is not obvious, because the archaeological record is disturbed. Early pottery remains in the Near East have not been discovered in primary contexts, but as apparently random spreads of discarded material . The archaeological record of early pottery in the Near East consists mainly of sherds. They are not the result of *in situ* fragmentation, that is, we do not have broken vessels, but accumulations of unconnected sherds. The most obvious explanation for the formation process of those accumulations of sherds is cleaning and rubbish. Consequently, we cannot propose a correlation about pottery production/consumption and time, but we should limit ourselves to correlate time with rubbish formation. Rubbish is the result of some social actions, which are indirectly linked with production and consumption. Therefore we can assume that any change in the nature of rubbish is related with changes in consumption (there is an increase of refuse material from most commonly used pottery), which are also related with changes in productive systems (technology) and social demand.

As a result, any inference about correlation between frequency and time should take into account the influence of depositional, post-depositional and archaeological sampling.

We have developed some methods, although not entirely new, to deal with this problem. Our objective is not to offer an explanation of how pottery was invented, but to discover the *degree* of correlation between time and frequency, and inconsistencies derived from the nature of the archaeological data and the sampling procedure used. We do not pretend to obtain "definitive" solutions, but to consider some of the factors that may prevent archaeologists from making "simple" correlations between time and the archaeological record.

In this paper we offer a methodological approach to the reliability of correlations between time and the quantity of pottery. The data analysed come from the Tell Halula Site.

This archaeological site, located at the middle Euphrates valley, is being excavated by the Syrian Spanish Archaeological Expedition (Molist et al., 1996). This site provides continuous occupation from the Middle Pre-Pottery Neolithic B Phase (PPNB) until the end of historical phases on the first half of 7th. Millennium BP (8700 BP and 7400 BP). Detailed analyses of each archaeological and historical phase have been carried out. They allow the observation of a continuous cultural evolution, and of the origins of significant transformations, like animal domestication, the first pottery production, changes in raw material exploitation and distribution, and the even more complex structuring and use of space and the associated architectural structures.

In this site early pottery appears from Late Neolithic levels. Chronologically, those pottery remains are among the oldest in the Euphrates valley. We have only processed information from the layers with pottery.

There is not a General Typological Framework to describe Near Eastern early pottery production. Consequently, we have adapted the descriptive-morphological features used by other archaeologists (Braidwood 1960, Akkermans & Le Mière 1992, Campbell 1992) to describe the same type of early pottery in the sites excavated by them:

T1: THICK COARSE SIMPLE WARE (with vegetal inclusions)

T3: BURNISHED THICK COARSE WARE (with vegetal inclusions)

T5: PATTERN BURNISHED COARSE WARE (with vegetal inclusions)

T6: SLIPPED COARSE WARE (with vegetal inclusions)

T7: SLIPPED BURNISHED COARSE WARE (with vegetal inclusions)

T8: COARSE IMPRESSED AND INCISED WARE (with vegetal inclusions)

T9: EARLY COARSE PAINTED WARE (with vegetal inclusions)

T11: UNBURNISHED FINE WARE (with mineral inclusions)

T12: BURNISHED FINE WARE (with mineral inclusions)

T13: PATTERN BURNISHED FINE WARE (with mineral inclusions)

T14: SLIPPED FINE WARE (with mineral inclusions)

T15: SLIPPED BURNISHED FINE WARE (with mineral inclusions)

T16: DARK-FACED BURNISHED WARE (with mineral inclusions)

T19: GREY BLACK WARE (with mineral inclusions)

T20: BLACK WARE (with thick mineral inclusions)

T23: FINE PAINTED WARE (with mineral inclusions)

T24: UNBURNISHED FINE-COARSE WARE (with mineral inclusions)

T27: FINE IMPRESSED AND INCISED WARE (with mineral inclusions)

2 A seriation analysis of depositional units with pottery.

We have begun our analysis by ordering the quantity of different kinds of pottery in stratigraphical order. The main goal is to study whether changes in the quantity of different kinds of pottery are correlated with changes in the stratigraphic order. There were 161 depositional units and more than 7000 pottery sherds in all these units. A depositional unit is exactly the same as an occupation floor. In Tell Halula pottery *always* appears outside occupation floors. We do not have information about primary deposition, but accumulations of rubbish material (sherds) as a result of cleaning practices carried out in the neolithic houses. The materials do not appear concentrated in rubbish pits, but as random spread in areas without walls or architectural structures.

The initial assumption was that quantity of unconnected sherds in a depositional unit was a consequence of the number, and the nature and diversity of cleaning practices performed at this occupation floor. We are not interested in studying each deposition isolated, but in determining the general tendency of rubbish accumulation spread over the site. That is, to determine whether there were changes in the quantity of accumulated material through time, and if those changes were related with transformation in social practices and economy

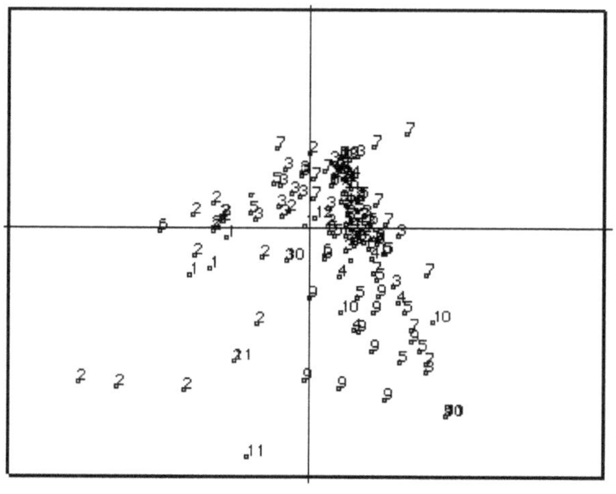

Figure 1. Correspondence Analysis of occupation floors in Tell Halula

Correspondence Analysis (fig. 1) showed that there was no Seriation Structure in the data. This seemed at first sight a contradictory result in view of the archaeologists' assumptions that the most recent depositional units had more sherds than the oldest ones. Global inertia is low (0.2778 the first component, 0.1382 the second one, 0.0961 the third, 0.0837 the fourth, etc.).However this result was expected. In standard seriation studies, the assumption is made that the total number of objects found is assumed to be a function of the total number of people who used them at any given time.

However, the frequency of the observed objects reflects the frequency of production, *only if enough objects have been found.*

It is evident that the main assumption of seriation analysis does not apply in this case, for two reasons:

1. depositional units have very different sizes and shapes, and most of them have not been recorded in the same way. The excavation of some of them was incomplete.
2. frequencies have been estimated using sherd count, and not vessel count. The number of sherds is hardly an adequate estimation of the original quantities. However, we are not interested in estimating the quantity of whole vessels in each occupation floor, but the quantity of rubbish, and it may be estimated using the number of sherds.

These problems in the nature of the data do not prevent the existence of a correlation between time and quantity of pottery, only the interpretation of Correspondence Analysis. The difficulty is that there are many sources of variation in the data series (not only "time"). *Sampling* may be one source, but the social and economic process that caused the accumulation of rubbish are another. There are differences among deposition units, but these differences are not related with the amount of pottery they originally had. They are a consequence of the process that broke pottery and created a variable accumulation of sherds. It is important to realize that the socio-economic process of rubbish formation is temporally very slow. Rubbish accumulations are not formed in a single moment as a consequence of a single action, but they grow with time, as a result of an accumulation of depositional actions.

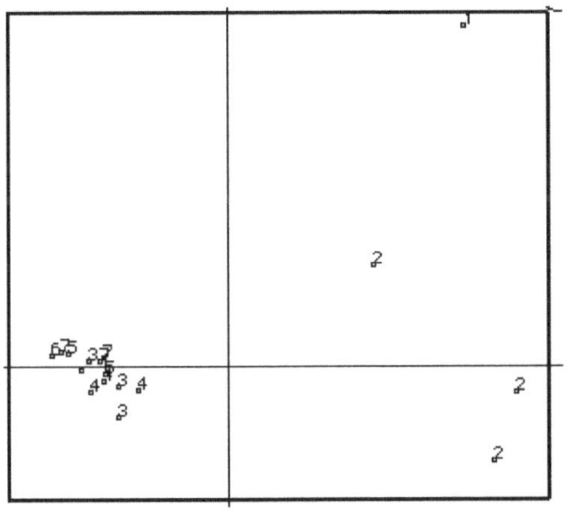

Figure 2. Correspondence Analysis of occupation floors with more than 30 sherds of pottery (numbers in the figure represent the stratigraphic order of each deposition unit in the sequence)

The effects of sampling in the seriation are clearly seen if we select from the original 161 depositional units with pottery, those with more than 30 sherds. The original distribution of 161 depositional units is significantly non normal, but if we reduce the data to units with more than 30 sherds and select the most frequent type of pottery *-Thick Coarse Simple Ware-* the resulting distribution is significantly normal (Lillicfors probability = 0.247). Selections of units with more than 15 sherds produced non-normal distributions, too. A Correspondence Analysis of those 18 deposition units with more than 30 sherds (Fig. 2) shows more sound results.

Global inertia is higher than in the other case (0.54 for the first component, 0.13 for the second one, 0.12 for the third,...). It is easy to see that there is a strong correlation (although characteristically non linear) between the seriation of frequencies and the stratigraphic order.

In other words, there is some kind of regularity in the changing pattern of rubbish accumulation along the period.

This "regularity" or serial structure was hidden when we considered all depositional units, that is, the pattern cannot be seen when we include occupation floors in which sherds have been accumulated randomly. A few sherds may have been spread by an enormous quantity of processes. "Random" means here "indeterminate". Nevertheless, when more than 30 sherds appear in an occupation floor, the "indeterminacy" decreases, and it is easier to determine which socio-economic process produced that accumulation. A comparison of those socio-economic processes is only possible in cases with a low degree of indeterminacy.

3 Statistical analysis of stratigraphic sequence

3.1. Finding order in the stratigraphic sequence of depositional units

Our data are a typical example of *longitudinal investigation*, that is a repeated measurement of a given phenomenon ("the quantity and diversity of pottery rubbish") over time (Frederiksen and Rotondo 1979, Mccleary and Welsh 1992, Mcdowell et al.1980). In our case *time* is represented by *stratigraphic order.* We will deal further with problems derived from this fact.

If we consider that the system we are studying is the formation of pottery accumulations (the social formation of rubbish), it is obvious that this process is not completely static or unchanging. The possible kinds of change can range from cyclical or periodic change in which the quantity and diversity of rubbish accumulations return to prior states of accumulation, or formation processes that develop, grow, decline, or in other ways exhibit changes that permanently alter the characteristics of the accumulation. Consequently, an important problem in our study is to demonstrate that there is some correlation between the quantity of pottery and time (or stratigraphic order in this case); the quantity of different kinds of pottery should exhibit a periodic pattern of change, growth and development. This problem involves investigating the *stationarity* of the stratigraphic series, that is, the existence of linear or non-linear trends in the sequence.

However, the stationarity, lack of stationarity or discontinuities associated with this pattern of change are not only a consequence of a social process correlated with time, but the result of sampling or the specificity of some depositional units. For instance, a discontinuity in any point, may be explained as a "temporal" change in the social process that produced rubbish, or as an individual property of that depositional unit, where rubbish was accumulated differentially due to a different function, a different post-depositional process (preservation) or a different sampling procedure.

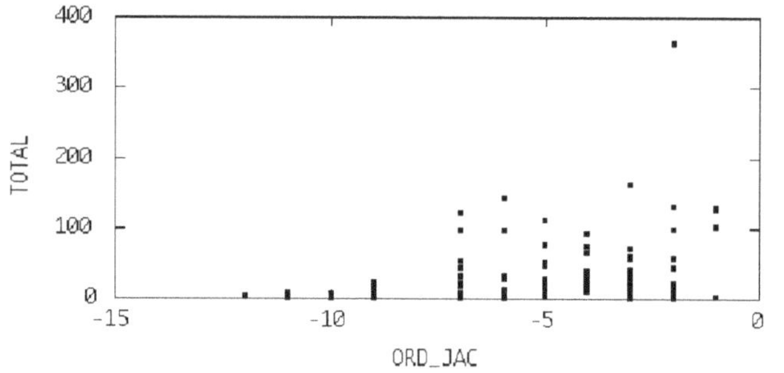

Figure 3. A dot plot of stratigraphic sequence quantity of pottery

These plots allow the study of a social action (deposition of rubbish) whose behaviour at any point in the stratigraphic sequence is governed by possibly non-deterministic rules. However, archaeological data are not homogeneous. In each time phase there are a number of different occupation floors with pottery, and it appears that the quantity of pottery in contemporaneous occupation floors is different. In spite of the these differences, it may be possible to calculate a general tendency (pattern) in the data: it seems that the quantity of pottery grows through time. This tendency is not linear, however. Although at the beginning of the series all occupational floors have very few sherds of pottery or nothing at all, at the end of the series (late phases), there are occupation floors with pottery and others without pottery. The better explanation for this fact is that the nature of accumulation (and not only *quantity*) changes with time. Not only frequency increases, but also the variability of depositional process. At the beginning (the origins of pottery), pottery is scarce and rubbish is spread randomly; at the end of the sequence (once pottery manufacture and use is consolidated), there are a lot of vessels in circulation; rubbish is not produced by a series of random actions of discard, but as a result of specific processes that are different in different occupational floors. Rubbish accumulation becomes specialised and spatialized.

If we need to analyse the correlation between quantity of pottery and time, then we should take into account, that the process of rubbish accumulation is not homogeneous during the whole period, and that rubbish formation processes at the beginning of the sequence are not comparable to formation processes at the end of the series. Nevertheless, we may interpolate a line that *resumes* only that part of the variability that is correlated with time. This line is what we call its *path* or *trajectory*.

Using the classical distinction between population and sample, each point in the plot (the frequency of pottery *X* in depositional unit *Y*) represents a statistical population, and each depositional unit is a sample produced by a stochastic process. The analysis pretends to build a model of the stochastic process that produced the observed series. Following Wold's theorem, this process may be represented by the following expression:

DATA = DETERMINISTIC COMP. + STOCHASTIC COMP. + RANDOM COMP.

The theorem states that a temporal process may be modelled as the sum of two independent processes: the first is totally *deterministic* and the other is characteristically *non deterministic* (also called *stochastic* or *probabilistic*). The objective of the analysis will be to decompose the series variance in deterministic components and stochastic ones. The deterministic component reflects consistent effects through time, and it includes other kinds of systematic variation:

1. SECULAR VARIATION or *trend*, which represents the general orientation followed by the series of samples through time
2. SEASONAL VARIATION *or cycles*, which represents fluctuations of trend at periodic intervals

The stochastic component reflects the effects of *serial dependency*. In a time series it is not evident that the value of a variable in a specific time point is independent of the values this variable has had before or will have thereafter. We call *serial dependency* this property of temporal series: the degree of dependence between contiguous points in a sequence (Mcdowall et al., 1980, Uriel 1985).

In our case, the *deterministic* component is the part of total variance explained only by time; the *stochastic* component is the part of total variance explained by sampling and individual properties (depositional, post-depositional) of depositional units.

Trend (the deterministic component) may be detected investigating non-stationarity of mean and variance in the series, that is, whether both indexes increase (or decrease) through time. In our case it is easy to see that the mean and variance of pottery in different occupation floors is not constant, but changes are not uniform. We may be forced to think that there is no *linear trend* in the series, but stochastic or random variation among the quantity of pottery rubbish accumulated in different places through time.

In order to eliminate the disturbing effects of sampling differences, we have added all depositional units belonging to a same archaeological layer. A layer has been defined by the Tell Halula archaeologists as a relevant change in architecture, a new building or a modification in a former building. Depositional units (pits, occupation floors, activity areas, hearth, outside courts, etc.) are always related with houses, consequently, the rebuilding of the house, or the construction of a new one constitutes a significant change in the temporal sequence. Addition of depositional units in archaeological layers allows the elimination of effects due to the different nature of the depositional process - rubbish accumulated in a hearth is not the same as the material dispersed on an outside court.

The period in which pottery appears has been divided in Tell Halula into 19 building/rebuilding levels; therefore, the 161 depositional units have been grouped into 19 occupation phases. This transformation of data changes slightly our working hypothesis. We are not comparing rubbish accumulated in occupation floors, but the total amount of rubbish accumulated in a time period of undetermined duration (stratigraphic layer). We want to discover whether the quantity and diversity of pottery rubbish is correlated with time. The spatialisation of rubbish formation process during the later phases prevents a deeper correlation. We know already that rubbish is accumulated differently in early phases than in later ones, and that difference is based on spatial differences. But, are there other differences to add to this one? Is the *quantity* and *diversity* of pottery different in early phases than in later ones? When did this difference begin ?

3.2 A seriation analysis of archaeological layers

As in previous cases, a Correspondence Analysis of archaeological layers (Fig. 4) shows no serial structure, although inertia is relatively high (0.52 the first component, 0.15 the second one, 0.12 the third,...). The only thing we may say is that the last period (No. 12) is significantly different from the rest.

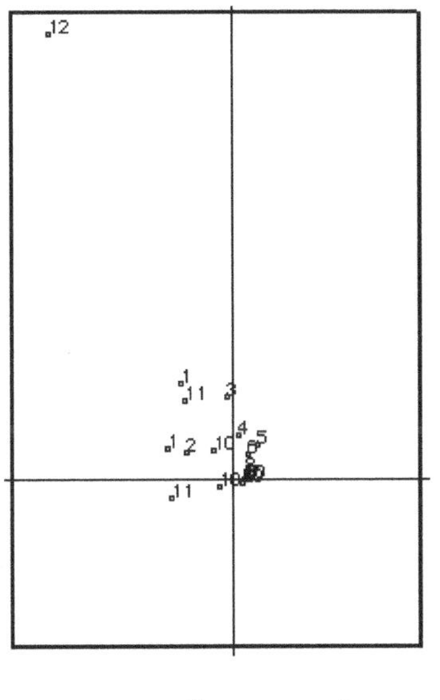

Figure 4. Correspondence Analysis of Archaeological layers. Numbers represent the stratigraphic order of each layer. Although there are 19 layers, they come from 3 different sectors, and there are temporal simultenities between them. Two contemporaneous layers from different excavation sectors have been represented using the same order number.

Why does the archaeological layer seriation lack any serial structure? The frequency of different pottery types in each layer is a result of the quantity of pottery accumulated in all contemporaneous occupation floors, and probably not all depositional units belonging to a single layer have been recovered. *Sampling* is again a source of variation. Another source of irregular variation may be the inclusion of three different, non-contiguous, sectors of the site: Sector 1, Sector 7 and Sector 14, separated by approximately 350 meters. The formation process of rubbish accumulation and spread may have been different in each one.

According to the theory of Serial Analysis, what we call in archaeology *seriation* is in fact a *deterministic trend.* And there is nearly always some degree of deterministic trend. Our case is not an exception, but we cannot observe it, because it is hidden by sampling differences in the data. Our purpose will be, then to *extract* this deterministic component, as if *sampling* differences and error introduced by spatial differences among sectors were the source of random noise.

Furthermore, if the trend shows an increase through time, and the most recent layers have been excavated with more detail and extension that the oldest, then this trend would be the result of differential excavation. But this is not the case. A previous study on the extension of depositional units (Saña 1997) has demonstrated that their size is not correlated with stratigraphic order. Therefore, we are sure that the quantity of pottery is not related to the size of depositional units or the excavated area.

3.3 Discovering "trend" in the stratigraphic sequence.

The analysis of trends and cycles is a descriptive enterprise at its best. The problem with many such analysis, however, is that even basic questions about trend are assumed rather than proven, and that such interpretations seem too readily accepted as a fact. We cannot assume trends by visually examining peaks and valleys in the data. Only statistical analysis can answer whether observed trends are significant or not (Mccleary and Welsh 1992), and the presence of outliers in these data make any visual interpretation questionable.

Smoothing techniques are a simple approach to uncover patterns in data with a minimum of preconceptions and assumptions as to what hidden patterns may be (Goodall 1990, Freixa et al., 1992. Without any assumption at all, the possibilities are too broad. The user of smoothing techniques assumes that the most useful relationships between the variables are smooth: an almost continuous curve or surface that does not jiggle too rapidly and may include a small number of steps or transitions.

The goal of smoothing is to separate the data into a smooth component and a rough component:

$$\text{DATA} = \text{SMOOTH} + \text{ROUGH}$$

The *Rough* should contain as little structure as possible. In our case, the percentage of total variance explained by the rough component is greater that the percentage explained by the smooth component, but the latter is a real model of deterministic temporal variation in the stratigraphic order. Its relevance as a source of variation was originally greater, but it has been reduced because we are not analysing primary data, but samples ordered stratigraphically.

This is not the proper place to elaborate a theory of smoothing in statistics (See Goodall 1990, Cleveland 1993, among others, or the more technical works by Kitagawa and Gersch 1996, Györfi et al., 1989, Müller 1988). There are many different techniques for smoothing a data series, and each one has its advantages and disadvantages. Fig. 5a,b,c compares some different smoothing functions on different types of pottery from Sector 7.

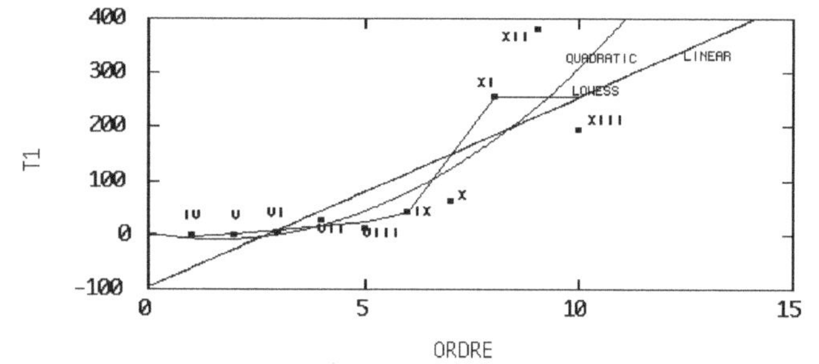

Figure 5a. Thick Coarse Simple Ware. Roman numerals represent stratigraphic order. Lines represent three different smoothing techniques (linear, non-linear quadratic, non-linear Loess coefficient).

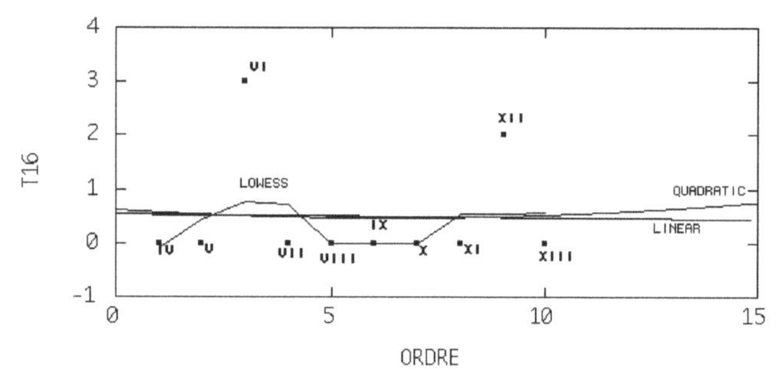

Figure 5b. Dark-faced Burnished Ware. Roman numerals represent stratigraphic order. Lines represent three different smoothing techniques (linear, non-linear quadratic, non-linear Loess coefficient).

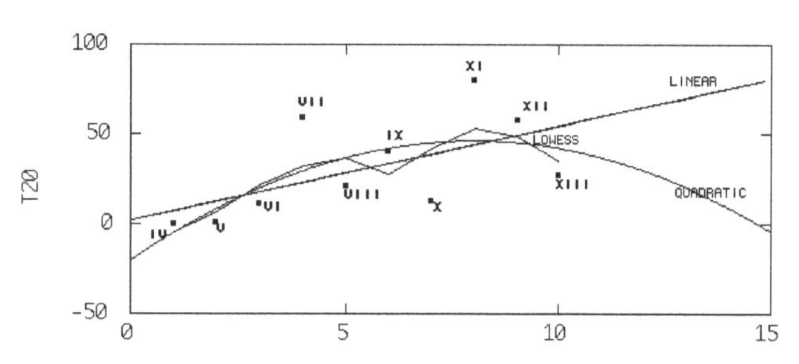

Figure 5c. Black series with thick mineral inclusions. Roman numerals represent stratigraphic order. Lines represent three different smoothing techniques (linear, non-linear quadratic, non-linear Loess coefficient).

The main distinction is between non-linear smoothing and linear interpolation. Smoothing is also a technique of curve fitting, but whereas linear interpolation calculates a *global* trend, *smoothing* makes a revision at each point, based on observations in the neighbourhood of this point. As a result, we obtain a calculation of *local* trends.

Cleveland and McGill (Cleveland & Mcgill 1984) advocated the smoothing of scatterplots to assist in detecting the shape of the point cloud in situations where the error in the data is substantial, or where the density of points changes along the abscissa. However, other authors have stressed doubts on the benefits of the technique (Spence and Lewandowsky 1990), because it is unclear what is being estimated when these smoothing functions are fitted. No well-defined parametric function is employed, and the use of different, arbitrary fitting procedures could easily yield markedly dissimilar functions. This criticism is especially relevant in our case. If we determine the existence of a trend in our data, should we conclude that we have discovered a *source of variation related to time*? First of all, smoothing does not *always* discover a trend. In some cases, we have obtained a horizontal line as the smoothing result (Fig. 5b), showing an absence of correlation between the variable under question and time.

What are the results we have obtained so far? First of all it is clear that parametric interpolation (linear and non linear - quadratic) do not produce reliable information, that is to say, the regression line does not properly *represent* the data points. The *loess* function produces far better results. If the underlying pattern in the seriation of archaeological layers with pottery were simple, parametric fitting would be enough (in terms of fitting to raw data). But this is not the case, because of sampling differences and the use of an incorrect frequency estimator. There is a pattern underlying the data, but it is too complex to be represented by a parametric function. The *loess* function follows the original data more precisely.

The name *loess* is short for *local regression* (see a more detailed presentation of this method in Cleveland 1993). Two parameters need to be chosen to fit a loess curve. the first parameter, a, is a smoothing parameter; it can be any positive number (in our case it is 0.5). As a increases, the curve becomes smoother. The second parameter, l, is the degree of certain polynomials that are fitted by the method. In our case, l = 2.

The observations are assigned *neighbourhood weights* using a weight function, calculated as the normal distribution around a centroid (number of observations multiplied by the parameter a). The weight function has a maximum at the centroid, decreases (normally) as we move away from this value, and becomes zero. The observations whose x_i lie closest to the centroid receive the largest weight, and observations further away receive less. A line is fitted to the data using weighted least-squares with weight $w_i(x)$ at (x_i, y_i). The $w_i(x)$ determine the influence that each (x_i, y_i) has on the fitting of the line. The influence decreases as x_i increases in distance from x, and finally becomes zero. The loess fit is the value of the line at x. A loess fit is displayed by evaluating it a grid of equally spaced values from the minimum value of the x_i to the maximum, and then connecting these evaluated points by line segments.

Of course, loess fitting does not explain all the variation in the data, but only the proportion of variance correlated with stratigraphic order, and this proportion is very low. Fig. 6a,b shows the residuals of some fittings, that is, the difference between original data and smoothed data (loess function).

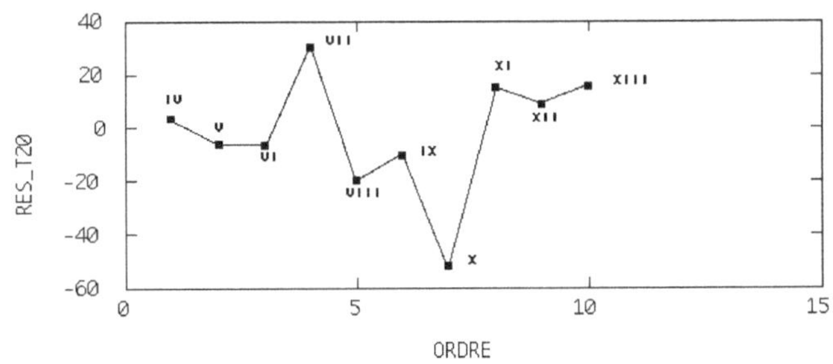

Figure 6b. Residuals for variable: Black Series with Thick Mineral Inclusions

These two plots show that there is a considerable amount of regularity in the residuals, meaning that smoothing has not deleted all existing trend. What is worst, there is already some regularity correlated with stratigraphic order. The difference between original and smoothed data increases until the 10th layer, which coincides with the increasing of quantity in original data. In other words, residuals grow as the quantity in pottery in each layer grows. This fact may be explained in historical terms, since as pottery becomes more frequent, rubbish accumulation becomes more spatialised, and variability in a single archaeological layer increases. Given that the smoothing function is an estimation of the central tendency of the series, any increase in variability or any reduction in serial dependence causes an increase in the residuals.

In other words, the smoothed function does not provide a good fit to the data, except in some parts of the series. Fig. 6a shows a linear ordering of residuals around zero for the first 6 phases. This fact coincides with the archaeological interpretation (Faura 1996) that during the first centuries early pottery is accumulated in very low quantities, and this is specially the case for the "Thick Coarse Simple Wares" Series. However, in other cases ("Black Wares with Thick Mineral Inclusions" Series) non-random irregularities in residual distributions occur, even for the first (ancient) part of the series. According to the archaeological analysis (Faura 1996) this is produced because the Black series is a chronologically fixed production, that begins production very early in the historical sequence, reaches a climax during phase 7th., and decreases in popularity thereafter, disappearing at the end of the sequence.

An analysis of Sector 7 is not enough to discover trend, because later occupation floors do not appear there, but in Sector 14 and Sector 1. Fig. 7 shows the existence of a general linear trend for the three layers from S14, and a great heterogeneity for layers from Sector 1.

In this case we have a good example of bad fitting, or lack of correlation between the quantity of pottery and the stratigraphic sequence. The smoothed function is very well fitted to Sector 7 data (points without label in the plot), and relatively well to data from sector 1; but the function is not able to integrate information from sector 14. But even when the function does not fit, there is a lot of archaeological information that allows a partial testing of the archaeological hypothesis (cf. Faura 1996). We are not saying that there was more pottery in certain phases of Tell Halula site than in the others, but that rubbish was accumulated differentially in time and space. There is an increase in rubbish accumulation of Thick Coarse Simple Wares at the end of Sector 7 sequence, and this increase coincides with the linear increase of sherds accumulated in Sector 14. The quantities are different, but the trend is the same

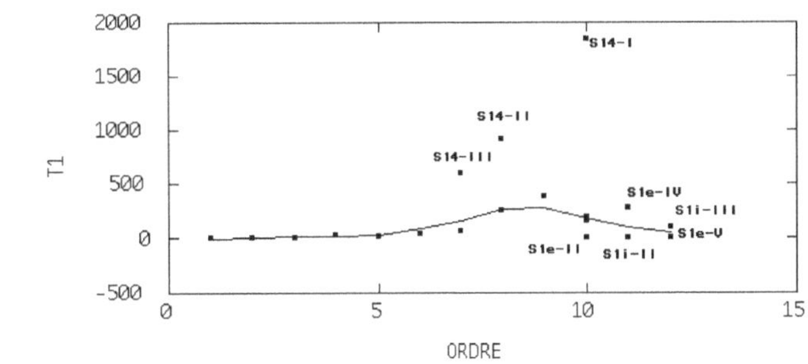

Figure 7. Thick Coarse Simple Ware Series. Smoothed function of all layers from Sector 1, Sector 7 (see the number of layers in previous figures), and Sector 14. Ordering of layers follow archaeological information about simultaneities among different sectors

Burnished Thick Coarse wares evolve in a different way. There is not a bell-shaped smoothed function, but an asymmetric increase, showing that there is more rubbish accumulated at the end of the sequence that at the beginning. (Fig. 8).

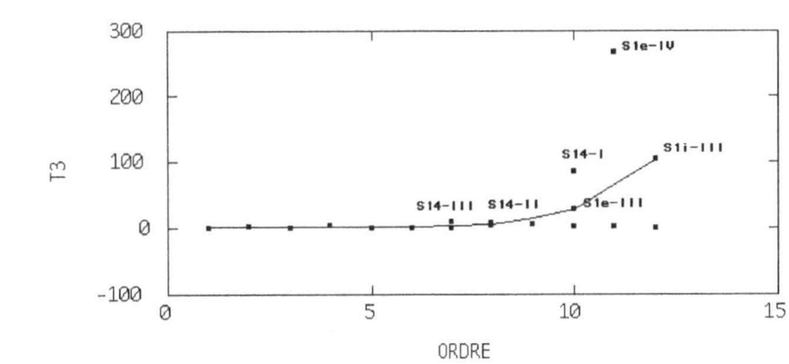

Figure 8. Burnished Thick Coarse Ware Series. Smoothed function of all layers from Sector 1, Sector 7 (see the number of layers in previous figures), and Sector 14. Ordering of layers follow archaeological information about simultaneities among different sectors

Fitting is better than in previous case, but it is not very good for data from sector 1. The smoothed function follows exactly the stratigraphic evolution for sector 1 and 14, and tests again the archaeological hypothesis (Faura 1996), but it neglects some layers from sector 1, those without pottery. This is a very good example of the ability of the method to find the best possible solution. The Smoothed function allows the discovery of an increase of rubbish of this kind of pottery accumulated at the end of the sequence, although this rubbish was concentrated spatially. The same fitting has been discovered for the Coarse Impressed, Incised and Painted Wares, and for the *Dark-faced Burnished Ware* (Fig. 9). In this latter case, the smoothed function has a lack of fit in a point at the beginning of the sequence (Sector 7th Phase VI). The function ignores the fact that during this phase a sudden increase in rubbish from this kind of pottery was produced.

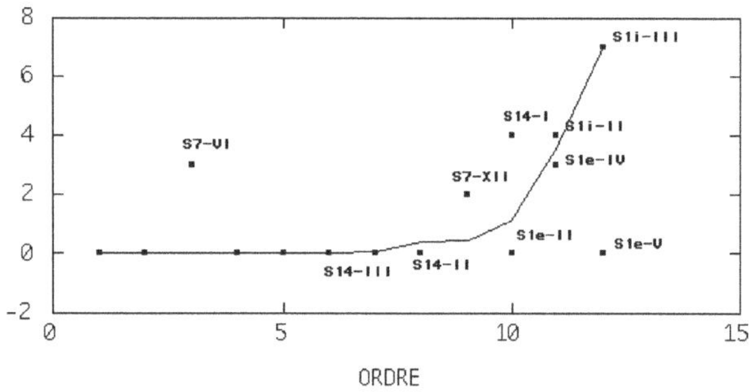

Figure 9. Dark-faced Burnished Ware. Smoothed function of all layers from Sector 1, Sector 7 (see the number of layers in previous figures), and Sector 14. Ordering of layers follow archaeological information about simultaneities among different sectors

In the following case (Fig. 10), the explanation is the same - an increase in rubbish accumulation at the end of the sequence, but the smoothed function makes a great mistake, calculating erroneously a decrease in quantity (belly-shaped curve). Spatialisation is here more accentuated than in the other case, and this fact produces the lack of fitting.

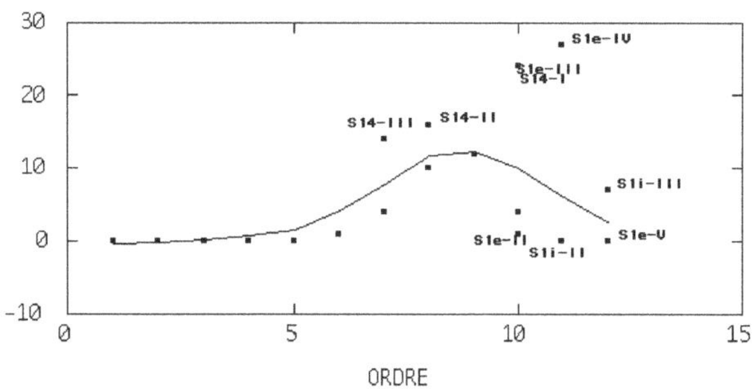

F

Figure 10. Slipped Coarse Ware. Smoothed function of all layers from Sector 1, Sector 7 (see the number of layers in previous figures), and Sector 14. Ordering of layers follow archaeological information about simultaneities among different sectors

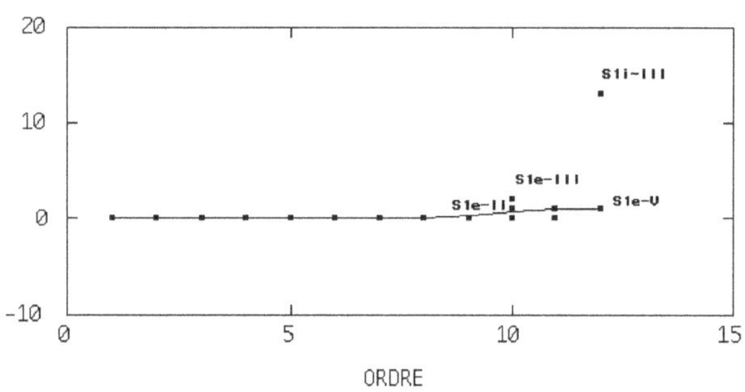

Figure 11. Grey Black Ware. Smoothed function of all layers from Sector 1, Sector 7 (see the number of layers in previous figures), and Sector 14. Ordering of layers follow archaeological information about simultaneities among different sectors

The Fine Impressed, Incised and Painted ware Series and the Grey Black Ware Series are another example of bad fitting (Fig. 11). Here smoothed function shows an absolute lack of correlation quantity/stratigraphic ordering, even when there is an statistically significant increase of quantity at the end of the sequence (Phase III at Sector 1i).The Series for Black Wares with Thick Mineral Inclusions is much more intriguing (Fig. 12). At first sight, it seems to show a typical lack of fit between the smoothed function and the raw data, as if the function was not able to calculate the degree of spatialisation at the end of the sequence. Nevertheless, a closer inspection of the plot, shows a better coincidence with the archaeological hypotheses (this ware is characteristic of the early part of the sequence, and its quantity decrease at the end, cf. Faura 1996). The function fits very well with the data from Sector 7 and Sector 1, showing that there is no change in the spatial accumulation of rubbish during late phases. The problem is the same as we saw with the Thick Coarse Simple Ware Series: the accumulation of this kind of rubbish is different in Sector 14. In this case, not only the quantity of sherds accumulated, but also the trend, because the linear cumulative trend in Sector 14 is completely different to the belly-shaped (and in this case it is not a bad fitting) curve fitted to Sector 7 and Sector 1.

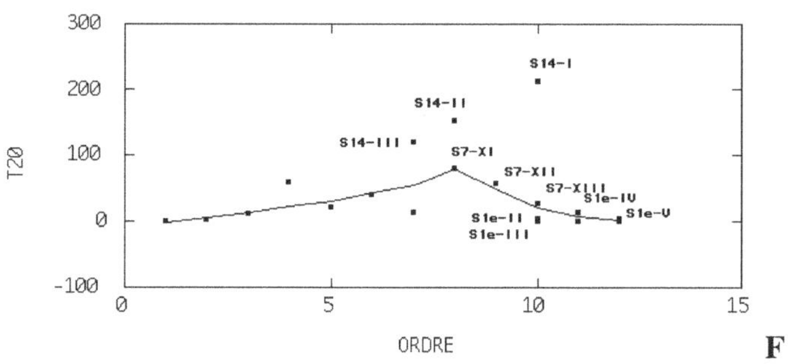

F

Figure 12. Black Wares with Thick Mineral Inclusions. Smoothed function of all layers from Sector 1, Sector 7 (see the number of layers in previous figures), and Sector 14. Ordering of layers follow archaeological information about simultaneities among different sectors

The series for Unburnished Fine-Coarse Ware (Fig. 13) shows a much better fit. In this type of pottery, rubbish accumulation in Sector 14 is not statistically different from that in the other Sectors of the site.

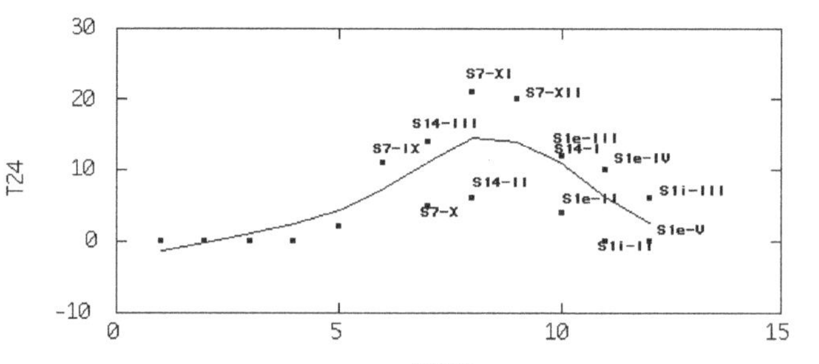

Figure 13. Unburnished Fine-Coarse Ware. Smoothed

function of all layers from Sector 1, Sector 7 (see the number of layers in previous figures), and Sector 14. Ordering of layers follow archaeological information about simultaneities among different sectors

To sum up, what appears as a result is an increasing of variability in rubbish spread at the end of the sequence. For the majority of pottery types we may infer three different "historical" stages: a *formation* period, where pottery is scarce and rubbish spread seems random (until S7-IX/S7-X); a second period (S7-XI, S7-XII, S7-XIII, S14-IIII, S14-II) where the quantity of pottery increases, but rubbish formation do not change (linear increase of frequencies), and finally, a third period (S14-I, S1 all layers) where frequencies increase and rubbish formation changes from a random to a non-random pattern, beginning a spatialisation of the social actions producing rubbish. These statistical results coincide with archaeological hypotheses (Faura 1996).

Nevertheless if this is the general trend for the *majority* of pottery types, it is not the trend for *all* types. *Thick Coarse, Unburnished Fine and Coarse, and Black Wares* have a distinctive trend, characterised by a decline in frequency during the third period, and reaching a peak during the second one. Variability of rubbish spread maintains the same tendency throughout the sequence; there are two peaks at S7-VI and S7-VII that are ignored by the smoothing function, because there is no serial dependency with values in neighbouring time-points.

An historical explanation would be that during the third period, the moment of consolidation of pottery manufacture and use, new types appear that substitute the older ones. Old vessels are being broken due to their use, and they become slowly part of rubbish. As the old types are substituted by new types, better manufactured or more suitable for their new uses, their circulation decreases and their proportion in rubbish accumulations (directly related with the quantity of vessels in use) decreases too, until they disappear.

4 The reliability of the chrono-stratigraphic sequence

Up to now we have been analysing stratigraphic order *as if* it were an analogue of temporal order. However, this assumption is mostly wrong. Although seriation order is the same, stratigraphic order assumes the same longitude for all time intervals; for instance, archaeological layer 1 should have the same duration than archaeological layer 2. Sometimes archaeologists introduce correction factors, such as the depth of the archaeological layer, assuming that deeper layers take more time to accumulate.

Fig. 14 shows a seriation by Correspondence Analysis of smoothed values for S7 layers. Here, the distance between contiguous layers is not homogeneous. Some authors have used this pattern to infer the existence of temporal intervals of different duration between archaeological layers. Using this assumption, the period of time from S7-IV to S7-VII would be much longer than the period of time between S7-VII and S7-XII, or the period between S7-XII and S7-XIII.

These results are exactly compatible with those obtained through chronological analysis (Faura 1996). The distance between S7-IV and S7-V should be of ca. 300 years, between S7-V and S7-VI 200, between S7-VI and S7-VII 200, between S7-VII and S7-XII 200. There is no statistically significant difference between S7-VII, S7-VIII, S7-IX, S7-X, S7-XI, S7-XII, because differences less than 100 years are hardly noticeable in the archaeological record, and they cannot be measured using calibrated C14. The distance between S7-XII and S7-XIII is, again, ca. 200 years. What does it mean in historical terms? That the few rubbish sherds accumulated in earlier phases take more time to accumulate than the greater quantities of rubbish of later phases. At the end of the sequence (from 6250 BC and later) more quantities of pottery were broken, and their sherds accumulated in less time than in earlier times.

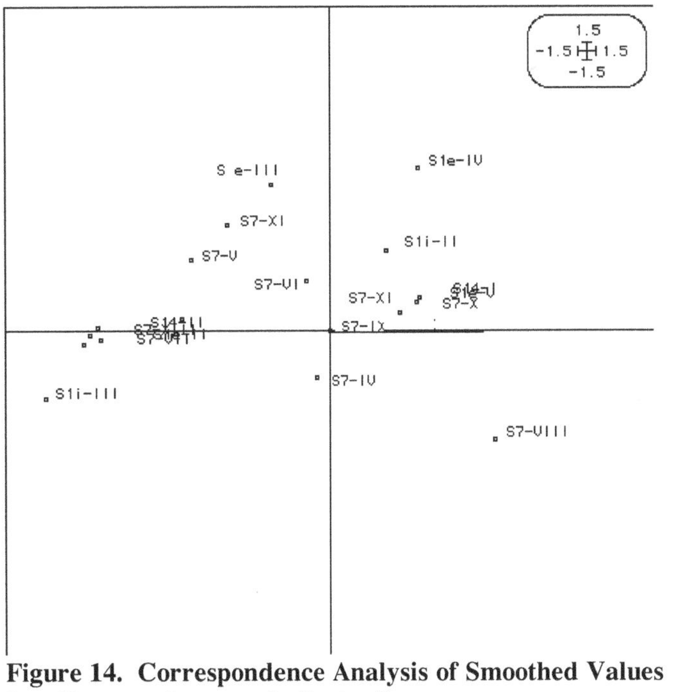

Figure 14. Correspondence Analysis of Smoothed Values for all types of pottery in Sector 7

In other words, seriation analysis of stratigraphic order provides consistent results with temporal scale (as far as we know it). It is important to realise that this correlation quantity of accumulated pottery/temporal order exists only for the Sector 7 sequence and with smoothed values. Remember that the loess function fitted Sector 7 data better than Sector 1 and Sector 14 data. Seriation analysis has also proved that rubbish was accumulated in Sector 14 in a different way, because occupation floors in the sectors were different, and different social actions were performed on them. The same is true for Sector 1 (1e and 1i), where *spatialisation* is more evident as a source of variation, and where the time of layer formation was much shorter than in other sectors (depositional history is also different).

We have tried to test this chronological and historical hypothesis using radiocarbon dates. Six radiocarbon dates are available for the early pottery series in Tell Halula (see Faura 1996, Molist et al. 1996, Saña 1997) (Fig. 15).

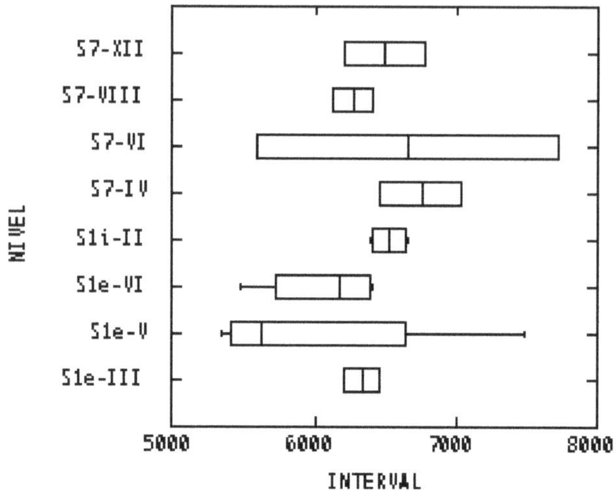

Fi

Figure 15. Calibration intervals for C14 dates from Tell-Halula (using CALIB 3.0)

Radiocarbon dates are bad candidates for temporal seriation, because they cannot be represented as fixed points, but as intervals. We have used CALIB 3.0 to compute the 2sigma intervals. These dates produce some inconsistencies with archaeological results, especially in S1, whose radiocarbon chronology seems much older than the date expected by archaeologists. Even in the simpler S7 seriation, there are some problems, as the uncertainty of S7-VI (a layer that produced more than a surprise in the frequencies of pottery), and the inverse values for S7-VIII (stratigraphically older) and S7-XII (stratigraphically one of the most recent in this sector).

We have tried to extract some pattern from these overlappings, trying to eliminate intervals that are statistically two long or with less relevance. These calculations have been carried out using a neural network with the following data:

LEVEL	DATE	Total Quantity of Pottery
S7-iv	7034	5
S7-iv	6465	5
S7-vi	7727	25
S7-vi	5596	25
S7-viii	6415	35
S7-viii	6119	35
S7-xii	6779	539
S7-xii	6200	539

This table has been processed through the Neural Network, following this input-output schema:

INPUT VECTOR	MIDDLE LAYER	OUTPUT VECTOR
Year	Hidden Unit 1	Quantity of Pottery
	Hidden Unit 2	

The input unit contains "time" values (transformed into a 0/1 scale, that is, 6200 is represented as 0.6200) and the output unit contains frequencies (also transformed). We have used back-propagation to learn this network (cf. Barcelo 1993, Caudill and Butler 1992, Rogers and Vemuri 1994, Zirili 1997, Masters 1995).

Seriation results for the total quantity of pottery, after 15000 iterations, are very bad. The Neural Network has learnt correctly the negative correlation between time (negative values because we are in BC years) and quantity of pottery, but it has not been able to learn the correct values. The beginning of the series (5 sherds at -7034) is totally different according to the model generalised by the network. It is obviously wrong to place a quantity of 140 sherds of pottery at the 9000 BC!

Although the method is sound, and it has been used with success in other domains (see Rogers and Vemuri 1994, Zirili 1997, Masters 1995), in our case, predicted values are too bad, and contradictions too important. The neural network can never learn correct values if the input contains contradictory information like: in the year 6200 BC there can be 25, 35 or 539 sherds. There is nothing wrong in using neural networks with C14 intervals, but not in this case, because we do not have enough data to eliminate contradictions. If we had more than 30 calibrated dates, calculations would be more significant.

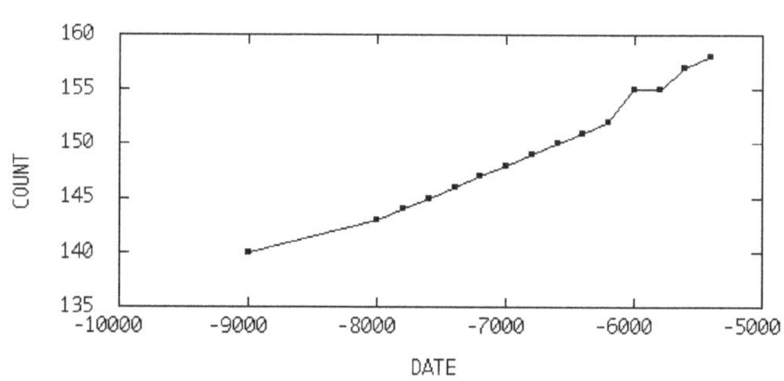

Figure 16. Function fitted to neural network estimates. Inputs are total quantity pottery per layer in Sector 7.

Even in those circumstances (too few data, overlapping intervals), a Neural Network algorithm has been proved to be suitable for this kind of analysis. In our example, it has not calculated a well fitted curve to the quantity/chronology correlation because we have not enough data. Some essays using simulated data (30 radiocarbon intervals, that is around 60 inputs) show that a neural network is the best method to calculate a trend not affected by the overlapping intervals. In the Tell Halula case, the neural network has been able to delete the influence of S7-VI interval (7727-5596). Although estimations are wrong, the general trend (there is more rubbish accumulated at 5596 BC, than at 7727 BC) has been correctly calculated.

If neural network estimates were correct, then we could

compare the stratigraphic seriation (each layer has the same duration) with the c-14 calibrated intervals seriation. A better chronology of archaeological layers would be possible, and a better interpretation of the correlation between *quantity* and *time*.

5 Conclusions.

In this paper we have introduced some techniques to extract the maximum quantity of information from stratigraphic order. This has not been a classical example of *seriation*, as developed by other authors (Marquardt 1978, Herzog & Scollar 1988, Laxton 1987, 1990, Laxton & Restorick 1989, Andresen 1993, Wilcock 1995), because we were not interested in obtaining a *serial order* from "similarity" among archaeological units, but in describing and analysing the correlation between *quantity* and *time* as represented by stratigraphic order.

The methodology we have introduced is not new, but we think it is the most appropriate when data are intrinsically noisy and unequally sampled. We have applied some techniques in the worst imaginable scene. Of course our research continues and we are now analysing *diversity* between archaeological units, as represented by differences in pottery percentages.

The low frequencies are also a cause of noise in the data. We have processed archaeological layers and not depositional units because we have tried to increase the original frequencies. Nevertheless, earliest layers have too few sherds to be considered significant samples. Of course we cannot do without, because historically when pottery appears there were only a few items. Once the critical analysis of post-depositional disturbance is finished we will process depositional units instead of adding then in archaeological layers.

Even in these "bad" but "real" circumstances, non-parametric smoothing is able to produce some results. Unequal samples and the use of bad estimators of quantity do not prevent the existence of a hidden trend in the data: a non-linear increase in the quantity of pottery, associated with changes in the ways rubbish is produced and accumulated. At the moment of consolidation of pottery manufacture and use, new types appear that substitute for the older ones. Old vessels are being broken due to their use, and they become slowly part of rubbish. As far as these old types are substituted by new types, better manufactured or more apt to new uses, their circulation decreases and their proportion in rubbish accumulations (directly related with the quantity of vessels in use) decreases too, until their disappearance.

A Neural Network has been programmed to deal with this problem. Although this technique seems very useful in this context, the scarce quantity of radiocarbon dates has prevent a more correct model of the correlation between quantity (of pottery) and (absolute) time. More work in this domain is needed.

Acknowledgments.

Specials thanks to all members of the Syrian Spanish Archaeological Expedition for their help in field work, processing the material and ideas and encouragement throughout this research. Funds have been made available by the Spanish ministry of Science and Culture (DGYCIT, PB093-0903).

Bibliography

Akkermans, P M M G, 1990 Villages in the Steppe. Later Neolithic Settlement and Subsistence in the Balikh Valley, Northern Syria, University of Amsterdam Press

Akkermans, P M M G, and Le Mière, M, 1992 The 1988 Excavations at Tell Sabi Abyad, a Later Neolithic Village in Northern Syria, American journal of archaeology 96

Andresen, J, 1993 Archaeological Chronology And Information Science, in Actes du XIIième Congrès International des Sciences Préhistoriques et Protohistoriques, Vol I, Bratislava: Institut Archéologique dL'académie Slovaque des Sciences.

Barcelo, J A, 1993 Back-propogation algorithms to compute similarity relationships among archaeological artifacts, in Computer Applications And Quantitative Methods In Archaeology, 1993 (eds D Whateley And K Lockyear), Bar International Series, Oxford

Braidwood R J, and Braidwood, L, 1960 Excavations in the Plain Of Antioch, I.O.I.P. Nº 56, The Oriental Institute of the University Of Chicago, Chicago

Campbell, S, 1992 Culture, Chronology and Change in the Later Neolithic of North Mesopotamia, Phd. Dissertetation, University of Edinburgh

Caudill, M, and Butler, C, 1992 Understanding Neural Networks. Computer Explorations, 2 vols, The MIT Press, Cambridge (MA)

Cauvin, J, 1974 Les Débuts de la céramique sur le Moyen Euphrate: noveaux documents, Paleorient, 2

Cleveland, W S, 1993 Visualizing data, Summit (NJ), Hobart Press

Cleveland, W S, and McGill, R, 1984 The many faces of a scatterplot, Journal of the American Statistical Association, 79, 531-553

Contenson, H, 1992 Préhistoire de Ras Shamra. Les sondages stratigraphiques de 1955 à 1976, Éditions Recherche sur les Civilisations, Paris

Faura, J M, 1996 Un conjunt ceramic del VIII milleni BP a la vall de lEeufrates: Les produccions de Tell Halula (Síria), Masters Thesis, Universitat Autónoma de Barcelona

Frederiksen, C H and Rotondo, J A, 1979 Time-series and the Study of Longitudinal Change, in Longitudinal Research in the Study of Behaviour and Development, (eds J R Nesselroade and P R Baltes), New York: Academic Press,

Freixa, M, Salafranca, L, Guardia, J, Ferrer, R, and Turbany, J, 1992 Análisis Exploratorio de Datos: Nuevas Técnicas Estadísticas,: Barcelona: Promocipiones y Publicaciones Universitarias,

Garstang, J, 1953 Prehistoric Mersin. Yümük Tepe in Southern Turkey, Oxford: Clarendon Press

Goodall,C, 1990 A Survey of Smoothing Techniques, in Modern Methods of Data Analysis (ed J Fox and J Scott Long), Newbury Park: Sage Publications

Györfi, L, Härdle, W, Sarda, P, and Vieu, P, 1989 Nonparametric Curve Estimation from Time Series, New York: Springer-Verlag

Herzog, I, and Scollar, I, 1988 A Mathematical Basis for Simulation of Seriable Data, in Computer Applications in Archaeology 1988, BAR (Int. Series, 446), 53-62, Oxford

Kitagawa, G, and Gersch, W, 1996 Smoothness Priors Analysis of Time Series, New York: Springer-Verlag

Laxton, R R, Restorick, J, 1989 Seriation by similarity and consistency, in Computer Applications in Archaeology 1989, BAR (Int. Series s548), 215-225, Oxford

Laxton, R R, 1987 Some results on mathematical seriation with applications, in Computer Applications and Quantitative Methods in Archaeology 1987 (eds C L N Ruggles and S P Q Rahtz), BAR International Series, Oxford

Laxton, R R, 1990, Methods of chronological ordering, in New Tools from Mathematical Archaeology. (Ed A Voorrips and B S Ottaway), Warsaw

Le Mière, M, 1979 La céramique préhistorique de Tell Assouad, Djezireh, Syrie, Cahiers de l'Euprhrate, nº 2, Editions du CNRS

Le Mière, M, 1986 Les premières céramiques du Moyen Euphrate, These de Doctorat, Université Lyon-2

Le Mière, M, and Nieuwenhuyse, O, 1996 The Prehistoric Pottery, in Tell Sabi Abyat. The Late Neolithic Settlement (ed P M M G Akkermans), Netherlands Historisch-Archeologisches Institut, Istanbul

Marquardt, W, 1978, Advances in archaeological seriation, in Advances in archaeological method and theory, vol. I, (ed M Schiffer), Academic press, New York

Masters, T, 1995 Neural Networks and Hybrid Algorithms for Time Series Prediction, London: John Wiley

Mccleary,R, Welsh,W N, 1992 Philosophical and Statistical Foundations of Time Series Experiments, in Single-Case Research Design and Analysis (Ed T R Kratochwill and J R Levin), Hillsdale (NJ): Lawrence Erlbaum Associates

Mcdowell, D, McCleary, R, Meidinger, E E, and Hay, R A, 1980 Interrupted Time Series Analysis, Newbury Park: Sage Publ.

Mellaart, J, 1975 The Neolithic of the Near East, London: Thames and Hudson

Molist, M (ed), 1996 Tell Halula (Siria). Un yacimiento neolítico del Valle medio del Eufrates. Campañas de 1991 y 1992, Ministerio de Cultura, Madrid

Mortensen, P, 1963 Early village farming occupation, Tepe Guran, Luristan, Acta Archaeologica, 34

Müller, H G, 1988 Nonparametric Regression Analysis of Longitudinal Data, New York: Springer-Verlag

Rogers, J, and Vemuri, D, 1994 Artificial Neural Networks Forecasting time series. IEEE Computer Society Press

Saña, M, 1997, Recursos animals i societat del 8800 BP al 7000 BP a la vall mitjana de l'Eufrates, Phd. Dissertation, Universitat Autònoma de Barcelona

Spence, Y, and Lewandowsky, S, 1990 Graphical Perception, in Modern Methods of Data Analysis (Ed J Fox and J Scott Long), Newbury Park: Sage Publications

Uriel, E, 1985 Análisis de Series Temporales, Madrid: Paraninfo

Wilcock, J, 1995 Analysis of multidimensional matrices for archaeological data, Computer Applications in Archaeology 1993, BAR (Int. Series, 598), Oxford, 191-197

Zirili, J S, 1997 *Financial Prediction using Neural Networks,* London: Thompson Computer Press

Contact details

Juan A. Barcelo
Laboratori Arqueologia Quantitativa
Dept. de Prehistòria
Facultat de Lletres. Edifici B
Universitat Autonoma de Barcelona
08193 Bellaterra
SPAIN
e-mail: ilphd@blues.uab.es

Josep Miquel Faura
Missión Arqueológica Española en Siria
Facultat de Lletres. Edifici B
Universitat Autonoma de Barcelona
08193 Bellaterra
SPAIN

CAA 97

Making Complex Radiocarbon Calibration Software More Accessible: a New Approach?

C. E. Buck, J. Andrés Christen

Abstract

The present authors have spent many years developing a Bayesian framework for the calibration of radiocarbon determinations in the light of a range of archaeological information. In the process we have written thousands of lines of robust C code which is, in general, very well tested. The code is complex and the statistical theory behind what it does is far beyond the comprehension of most members of the archaeological community. As a result only a handful of researchers world-wide have access to and can utilise our software. Surely there must be a way to give other researchers access while at the same time not devoting all our research time to rewriting the code and developing `pretty' front ends for a range of different hardware types! In this paper we report on our efforts to develop an Internet-based Bayesian radiocarbon calibration facility (BCal). This facility will allow archaeologists to issue instructions in terms of the archaeological and radiocarbon concepts that they already understand rather than using the C programming language directly. We hope that BCal will be a user-friendly graphical interface (perhaps in HTML or JAVA) to allow the user to submit archaeological information and radiocarbon determinations for calibration without any need for programming knowledge at all. The calibrations would be undertaken remotely on our UNIX workstations regardless of the operating system and processor type available on their local machines and the results made available for use locally in a range of graphical and text formats.

1 Introduction

For several decades many researchers interested in the application of statistics to archaeological data interpretation have decried the use of 'off the peg' statistical methodologies developed primarily for use in other disciplines. Nonetheless those same researchers (including the present authors) have for various reasons made only a small proportion of their purpose built software available to the wider archaeological community. This means that, even if the feasibility of the statistical approaches is demonstrated and the results are well received, very few other researchers ever adopt the methodologies.

The present authors have spent many years (along with other workers) developing a Bayesian framework for the calibration of radiocarbon determinations in the light of a range of archaeological information. In the process we have written thousands of lines of robust C code which is, in general, very well tested. The code is complex and the statistical theory behind what it does is far beyond the comprehension of most members of the archaeological community. As a result only a handful of researchers world-wide have access to and can utilise our software. This paper reports on attempts to remedy the situation.

2 Bayesian radiocarbon calibration

Since the amount of atmospheric ^{14}C has not been constant over time, radiocarbon determinations as supplied by the professional laboratories must be calibrated onto the calendar scale before they are a really useful aid in dating past human activity. The need for such calibration has been known for some time, but it is only recently that statisticians have developed Bayesian radiocarbon calibration techniques that take into account the very special nature of archaeological dating evidence.

Bayesian radiocarbon calibration allows us to combine information from a range of different sources to arrive at a coherent interpretation of all the available dating evidence. In formal terms we combine: *a priori* chronological information with radiocarbon data and the calibration curve via a statistical model to arrive at posterior probability distributions for the calendar dates of interest.

There are now published Bayesian methodologies for tackling a wide range of radiocarbon dating problems. These include:

1. Calibrating single determinations with or without *termini*.
2. Calibrating groups of related determinations with simple or complex stratigraphic relationships.
3. Probabilistic assessment of the chronological location of samples of unknown stratigraphic origin within a radiocarbon sequence that is well understood.
4. Inferring the dates of chronological events (such as phase boundaries) whose relative chronological location is known, but for which we have no direct dating evidence.
5. Identification of outliers in a collection of radiocarbon determinations.
6. Selection of samples from a currently available pool of organic materials in order to optimise our chances of answering the chronological questions posed.

With the appropriate prior information and relative chronological sequence modelled into the calibration process, users of this framework obtain posterior probability distributions for each calendar date in which they are interested (including those for which they do not have direct dating evidence). These can be summarised using either graphical methods or summary statistics and a range of these are now well documented and demonstrated elsewhere.

3 What are the problems?

The archaeological information can be modelled and there is a Bayesian framework in place for tackling a wide range of chronological issues, so what's stopping the majority of the archaeological community from adopting these techniques? There are two main problems.

1. Each archaeological project has unique prior information, unique data and requires different statistical models from other projects we've tackled. This means that each project requires its own computer code via which the posteriors are calculated.
2. The techniques used to calculate the posteriors are based on Markov chain Monte Carlo simulation and are commonly extremely CPU intensive.

There are a number of approaches we could take to solving these problems:

1. Simplify the procedures using 'reasonable' assumptions so that the same models and similar priors can be used for a large number of projects and calculations can be done on standard desktop PCs.
2. Assume that statisticians will always have to help in the process and set up consultancies to provide archaeologists with the advice they need.
3. Find a way to standardise the code we use without compromising on the quality and range of statistical models available.
4. Make our code available to others for use on their own machines if they have sufficiently powerful ones.
5. Make CPU on our machines available to others who do not have the necessary power on their own desktop.

In deciding which approach to take, there were a number of achievements upon which we could build:

1. A huge library of robust and well tested C routines for tackling a large number of radiocarbon calibration problems within the carefully developed Bayesian framework.
2. A large number of case studies which make use of the library and from which we have gained the experience to begin to standardise the software without compromising on the quality of the statistical modelling available.

There were, however, a number of things that we still needed to develop:

1. An interpreter that sits between the C code and the user, preventing them from having to learn a programming language, but at the same time allowing them to provide explicit and coherent information from which posterior probabilities will be calculated.
2. A graphical user interface to the interpreter with built in checking mechanisms for internal consistency.
3. The CPU time needed to undertake the calculations.
4. Access to the results in a range of formats suitable for presentation both on-line and for publications.

We have already developed much of what is needed and we have a clear structure in which our new calibration environment will operate (Figure 1). It is time now to decide what form the graphical user interface should take and how best to make use of available CPU.

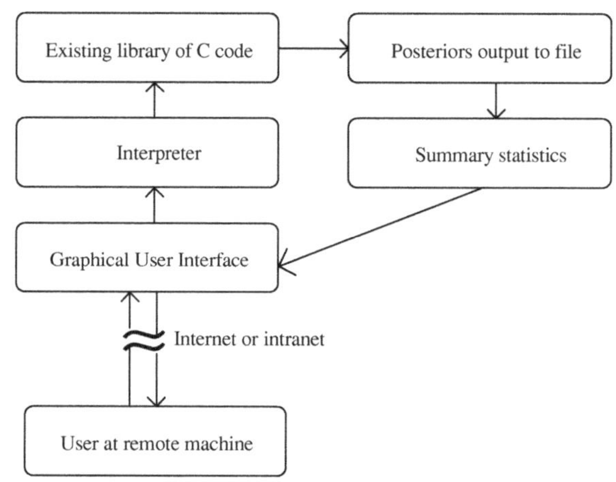

Figure 1: The structure of the proposed Internet-based Bayesian radiocarbon calibration facility (BCal).

4 The interpreter - *mexcal*

This part of the software is written in C++. It takes lines from a text-based input file (in which all the objects needed for the current calibration are declared), interprets them and makes calls to the necessary calibration routines. A *mexcal* input file is text-based and contains one line for each piece of modelling information and data, given in a standard form. Since the standard format relates directly to the archaeological problem and the data available it is a good deal easier to program in *mexcal* than in C++. For those of us who have worked in this area for sometime, the saving achieved by using the interpreter rather writing new C code is several days work. Typically one can define a new problem in a matter of minutes or hours rather than hours or days.

5 The graphical user interface - *BCal*

This part of the software is still at the design stage and our ideas about it are evolving all the time as access to the Internet becomes more wide spread and the bottle necks get worse. Nonetheless, the interface will need to have the capability

1. for user-friendly submission of information ready for calibration, and
2. presentation of results to the user when they are complete.

We already have the necessary code to provide all of the input and output. What we still require is the mechanism for interfacing with the user. We are planning:

1. a WWW server on which the software will sit,
2. HTML (or JAVA) interface screens with associated CGI scripts to check the consistency of the input information.
3. submission of the checked information to *mexcal*.

The mexcal program will then be submitted to run on an appropriate server.Upon completion of the calibration the user will be e-mailed with information about the success or failure of the job and a URL at which the output can be viewed.

6 Questions on which we are still working and would appreciate comments

1. Are HTML and JAVA the best way to provide the platform independent interface or are there better ways?
2. Are there any useful tricks for providing server security in situations where one is providing users with access to CPU in this way?
3. How much post processing of the output data should our software do and how much should we leave to the user?
4. How should we undertake the consistency checking of user input?

7 Obtaining further information

Since this paper was presented, the authors have obtained funding for the Bcal project from the University of Wales, Cardiff. Readers interested in the latest progress should visit http://bcal.cf.ac.uk.

Contact details

Caitlin E. Buck
School of History and Archaeology
University of Wales
Cardiff
WALES

J. Andrés Christen
Instituto de Matemáticas
Unidad Morelia
UNAM
MÉXICO

CAA 97

Numerical Methods
Abstracts of papers held on CD-ROM

Testing Multivariate Normality, with Applications to Lead Isotope Data Analysis in Archaeology
M. J. Baxter

Applications of multivariate analysis in archaeology often either assume that the data have a multivariate normal distribution, or work better if this is the case. The assumption is rarely tested. In this paper a test of multivariate normality based on a multivariate kernel density estimate, developed independently by Bowman and Foster (1993) and Henze and Zirkler (1990), is applied to trivariate lead isotope ratio data. There is clear evidence of non-normality, violating an assumption that is common in the statistical analysis of such data. The paper both illustrates the utility of kernel density estimates in a manner not previously demonstrated in the archaeological literature, and challenges an assumption that is prevalent in the field of lead isotope ratio analysis.

Uses of Multivariate Kernel Density Estimates in Archaeology
Christian C. Beardah

Though the technique of Kernel Density Estimation is now well established, it is still under-employed by archaeologists. For multivariate data this may be because the methodology is less well developed than in the case of univariate data. In this paper we aim to illustrate through archaeological examples some uses of multivariate Kernel Density Estimates (KDEs). In particular we shall examine the important issue of smoothing parameter selection in the bivariate case. Recent developments in the automatic data-based selection of smoothing parameters will be reviewed and particular emphasis will be placed on an illustration of the role of the so-called orientation parameter. Methods for the automatic selection of this parameter are in their infancy. We shall illustrate the effect it can have on the appearance of the KDE and therefore the archaeological conclusions drawn from it.

Bayesian Seriation as a Tool in Archaeology
Ulrich Halekoh and Werner Vach

The seriation of objects based on findings or traits accompanying them is a major task in archaeological research. An example is the chronological ordering of graves based on the gravegoods found therein. Correspondence analysis is a well established tool to solve this task but has only limited capability to show the accuracy of the provided seriation. We introduce a new approach based on a stochastic model and a Bayesian analysis which allows for a given dataset not only to determine an estimate for the underlying order, but also to asses its variability. This hints to subgroups of graves that are nearly exchangeable with respect to their relative chronological position and hence contributes to prevent over-interpretation. We also provide means to characterize traits that carry substantial chronological information and may be useful for the classification of new graves. Additionally, our approach may enable the archaeologist to incorporate prior information as sex-specific classifications of graves or their stratigraphic relationships.

Some Aspects Of The Evolution Of The Gravettian Culture In The Eastern Balkans
Tsoni Tsonev

Recent archaeological excavations in northern Bulgaria have revealed one of the longest Gravettian sequences known so far. It has been established that there are significant shifts of raw materials supply within various occupation levels. There seems to be no coherent methodology for interpretation of such data. A formal approach is suggested for fitting and modelling these data and their possible archaeological interpretation.

Neural Networks and Fuzzy Logic Analysis in Archaeology
Claire Reeler

Neural networks are designed to simulate the way a human brain learns and interprets patterns. Fuzzy logic is a way of quantifying classifications that are not easily restricted to opposites. These are both techniques borrowed from the field of artificial intelligence. Used together these two techniques can give us a different perspective on archaeological analysis and can allow us to model the world in a way that is closer to the way that humans think and behave. This process allows us to attempt to understand the processes of human cognition that lie behind the archaeological evidence with which we work. By building human cognition into the analysis, we make the data easier to work with for ourselves, and potentially get closer to the people whom we are trying to understand through the archaeological record. Both techniques can be applied to almost any kind of archaeological analysis, but provide a particularly useful adjunct to conventional statistical methods and GIS. This paper uses an example from New Zealand to show the potential of these forms of analysis in archaeology.

Multivariate Statistic Analysis of the Relationship between Archaeological Sites and the Geographical Data of their Surroundings. A Quantitative Model
José A Esquivel, José A Peña, M. Oliva Rodríguez-Ariza

In the last years, the analysis of settlement patterns has been accomplished from different quantitative points of view, including statistic analysis, GIS, etc. This work is focused on obtaining a quantitative model of index parameters based in the UTM coordinates, using a 1:10.000 scale map. The set of indexes is studied by means of statistical analysis (Kruskal-Wallis, principal components analysis, cluster analysis and Voronoi tesselations), providing the chronocultural settlement patterns and the relationships between the archaeological site, the surrounding area and the chronological period of the site.

ARCHAEOLOGY
IN THE
AGE OF THE INTERNET

CAA 97

Section 4
Database Developments

Database Developments
Abstracts of papers held on CD-ROM

CAA 97

ImageFinder Cultura: An Image Database System for Classical Archaeology
Barbara Kopf

The Institute of Classical Archaeology of the University of Vienna (IKAWIEN) owns an extensive photographic archive. Due to a number of administrative and conservatory aspects the Viennese Institute of Classical Archaeology decided to install a flexible image reference database which is able to link images with complex text information. The objective of this project is to create easy access to large stocks of images. After a detailed definition phase the database system ImageFinder Cultura was designed in close cooperation with the company Docuphot AG, Switzerland. In the development of the database considerable emphasis was placed upon userfriendliness and high image quality, as well as adherence to scientific and scholarly criteria. Although the current prototype was optimized for the workflow and needs of the photographic archives at the IKAWIEN, it is versatile enough to offer attractive features and functionalities that can be put to advantageous use in a variety of other areas of art and research.

Equus Data Management System (SGDE): a Research Tool for the Study of the Horse in the Iberian Iron Age
Fernando Quesada Sanz, Mar Gabaldón and P. Pablo Herrero

A set of six files (all of them complete Databases in their own right) on the role of the horse in the Iberian Iron Age (including horse trappings, literary sources, iconography, faunal remains, coins and bibliography) have been integrated into SGDE (Sistema de Gestión Documental Equus). The system is an attempt to reconcile the conflicting research requirements of an interdisciplinary team with different needs, experience, and responsibilities; and the implementation of a coherent and user-friendly system capable of managing data of different kinds. The files include texts, original Latin and Greek sources, image fields, preliminary statistical treatment of numeric data, graphics, etc., all within the same graphic environment, using colour codes and button links to navigate within the system.

Databases - Research Tools and Communication Aids
Hans-Dieter Bader

Any research model which claims to be testable by fellow researchers depends on explicit categories, explicit methods and interpretations based on these categories and methods. Some archaeological research still fails in this respect resulting in unproductive controversial interpretations. Database management systems usually force the researcher to apply systematic categories and criteria in a consistent way to the research subject. By expressing these categories in an explicit way, they are open to communication and discussion. The transformation of the criteria in each category in the progression from data capture to data analysis shows clearly how research methods are applied to the data. As a result of this process the research method is made explicit and open for discussion. Archaeological research looks at material objects in three dimensional space. The material objects are experienced and communicated via categories fitting the chosen research method. Any database application working with a two or three dimensional visualisation tool like a GIS should enable any archaeological research to be transparent and therefore open for communication. Database management systems can be shown to play a vital role in a systematic research approach and the following discussion of the research.

ARCHAEOLOGY IN THE AGE OF THE INTERNET

CAA 97

Section 5 Vital Preservation of Great Information

Vital Preservation of Great Information: The Archaeology Data Service and Digital Archiving in Archaeology

CAA 97

Alicia Wise

Papers in the following section of these CAA Proceedings were originally presented in a session entitled "The Archaeology Data Service and Digital Archiving in Archaeology". The purpose of this session was to bring together international contributions on the three themes that run through preservation of computer resources in archaeology:

1. great resources that need to be preserved
2. documentation standards
3. digital archiving

Harrison Eiteljorg sets the scene in "*Archiving Archaeological Data*" where he argues that archiving is a professional responsibility we each have to future archaeologists. His paper provides a good introduction to the concept of digital data migration, with excellent examples ranging from the migration of deeply-structured databases to AutoCAD files. One important point he makes is that even in applications where standard export formats exist, for example CAD packages, migration may not be a simple thing for digital archives. In all cases migration requires professional archaeological knowledge, and a thoroughly documented dataset. He also convincingly argues that the sooner data are archived, the better for all concerned: no segment of the archaeological population can be complacent about this. He sums up with a 6-point list of ways the archaeological discipline can promote proper digital archiving.

Henrik Jarl Hansen describes a very interesting web-based resource in Denmark called Guder & Grave in "*Digital Danish Archaeology: Gods and Graves - an Internet publication on the Bronze Age*." This impressive website is a product of the national museum of Denmark and is designed to give the public access to state-supported institutions and their collections. Contents are drawn from the stores of the Danish National Museum, the National Archaeological Record database, and the Object Register of the Department of Prehistory and Early History. Guder & Grave is well worth a visit at http://www.natmus.dk/ Have this paper close at hand if you do visit, or if you're interested in technical solutions for serving the contents of large databases over the web.

The third paper is entitled "*Museums on-line: Access to Museum Information*" and is written by *David Dawson* of the Museums Documentation Association. This is the first paper in the group that begins to address the issues of documentation standards in digital presentation and preservation. As an archaeologist turned museum-documentation-and-computer-specialist, Dr Dawson is in a particularly good position to summarise efforts within the museum community to network international resources. Projects discussed include the Scottish Cultural Resources Access Network (SCRAN), CIMI, and Aquarelle. The museum community has made considerable effort in networking information, and this has largely been possible due to their widespread attention to documentation standards.

The theme of documentation standards is developed in *Gillian Quine's "The Role of Data Standards in Digital Access and Interchange*." She provides an overview of the excellent standards work of the Royal Commission on the Historical Monuments of England (RCHME) Data Standards Unit. Data standards are simply and neatly defined as rules for recording information to increase compatibility, consistency, accessibility and retrievability. This paper is especially important in advocating a new and more positive philosophy held by standards organisations: advocating standards developed within the archaeological community (or some other community) rather than those imposed by outside organisations. The resulting new generation of standards is flexible, stream-lined, and multi-faceted rather than monolithic. Useful standards for British archaeologists mentioned herein include the NMR data standard, MIDAS, the SMR software standard, and metadata. Regarding metadata specifically, Dr. Quine makes the very welcome point that metadata must be used in conjunction with other standards to be helpful.

"*The importance of metadata to archaeology: one view from within the Archaeology Data Service*" by *Paul Miller* develops this metadata theme. Metadata is defined as a means of turning data into information and as a tool for facilitating the location of web-based resources in this increasingly complex world. Paul's paper provides a helpful guide through the jargon-ridden world of metadata. Here you can discover what 'elements', 'schemes', 'types', and the 'Dublin Core' really are. The author concludes that metadata will "increase the reuse value of all those kilometres of rotting paper, wrinkling mylar, and de-magnetising magnetic media in rarely visited archives around the world."

This neat ending leads nicely into the final paper, "*Digital Preservation in Archaeology*" by *Alicia Wise and Julian Richards*. As CAA delegates and Proceeding readers will be aware, a huge quantity of vital archaeological information is stored each year in machine-readable formats. This paper is about the importance of preserving archaeological information, and deals specifically with digital archiving efforts underway at the Archaeology Data Service in Britain. This work is facilitated by an outpouring of support within archaeology and academia generally: sister-services in other disciplines, funding agencies which require digital archiving from grant recipients, and pilot projects in all sectors of archaeology. Awareness of the need for digital archives offering one-stop access to digital records has arrived in archaeology.

Contact details

Alicia Wise
Archaeology Data Service
Department of Archaeology
University of York
King's Manor
York YO1 2EP
UK
email: info@ads.ahds.ac.uk
http://ads.ahds.ac.uk/ahds/

Archiving Archaeological Data

Harrison Eiteljorg, II

CAA 97

Abstract

Archiving archaeological data is a crucial task for the next decade and beyond. As we are all obliged to rely more upon studying materials already found and less on the excavation of new sites, we will find ourselves dependent as well on the excavation records that should accompany the artifacts. Those records must be available to us in useful forms if we are to continue working with the artifacts. The Archaeological Data Archive Project is concerned with preserving those records that are in computer form, and making them available as required. There is an erroneous assumption that computer records from field projects are properly looked after, but this is not necessarily so; archival storage of machine-readable documents is more complex than normally appreciated. The requirements are not onerous, but they are very different from the requirements for archiving paper-based information. The misunderstanding of the depth of the problem and the casual treatment of machine-readable data should concern us all. Personnel from the Archaeological Data Archive Project advise those preparing data for archival storage, archive data when required or help others to do so, provide information about data in the archive, and make those data available to scholars in useful forms. Problems with this seemingly simple process have included misunderstanding of the perils involved, reluctance to share information, and institutional pressures against public access. These and other problems will not disappear, but progress is being made.

The Archaeological Data Archive Project was conceived at a meeting of the computer committee of the Archaeological Institute of America in December of 1992. Over the following months of gestation the idea was discussed and refined until the final form of the project emerged - an attempt to provide a safe, secure home for archaeological data in machine readable form. Directing the project fell to the Center for the Study of Architecture and to me personally; the Archaeological Institute of America did not consider this to be an appropriate project for the Institute despite its involvement in the development of the archive.

We on the committee assumed the value of archiving archaeological data without argument or discussion, but we have learned that the importance of archival storage must be made explicit. It is, we believe, a clear professional responsibility, not simply from some pious sense of preserving all information, but because, as archaeologists are so fond of saying, we destroy much of our evidence as we work. Despite this, few of us would claim to have understood so well what we dug as to preclude the possibility of someone else learning more - if and only if that person has access to the excavation information that should be available in our data files. So we need to preserve the information about excavations as well as the artifacts so that others may learn from both.

I would also argue that archaeologists of the future will find fewer and fewer chances to excavate and, as a consequence, need to mine our data for new clues to the questions of the day. As we dig less in the ground and more in museum storerooms, we will need the data from old excavations as well as the artifacts, the excavation records that should accompany the artifacts and make them meaningful. Of course, those of us who are working in the field will be equally beholden to the records of past excavations for our raw data, since those records are crucial for dating and *comparanda*. Thus, the records from old excavations must be available to us in useful forms if we are to continue working with the artifacts we find in the field or the ones we find in museum cases and storage rooms.

"Useful forms" has several meanings. At its simplest, it means that the data files should be in the forms used by the creators and susceptible to the same kinds of analyses in the distant future as when they were created. Thus, database files should be able to generate the same tables, respond identically to the same queries, and create the same statistics for a user in the future as for their creator yesterday.

That seems to be a simple requirement, but we must recognize that it is more difficult than it may seem, because computer data files are linked inextricably to the programs designed to use them and the operating systems of the computers on which they live. A database file or a CAD file requires a program that can use the file if it is to be useful and a platform on which that program can run. What is obvious to some, as a corollary, is that data files we use today must be different if they are to be equally useful tomorrow. That is, the data in the files must be put into new and different formats if those data are to accessed and manipulated in the future as they can be today.

An archive for computer data, then, requires that data files be changed to retain their utility, not kept the same. Of course, we are talking about careful, controlled change here. We must change the format of the computer files so that the data remain as nearly unchanged as possible. This is, of course, commonly called data migration.

Data migration is not technically demanding in most cases. It does require familiarity with both the donor and the recipient data formats; it also requires familiarity with the data to be migrated. In some cases, when the data are very complex and include important multiple relationships, familiarity with the data must be intimate. The best example I've encountered of the complexity we're likely to find is the conversion of a set of data tables from the database management system called Advanced Revelation to Microsoft's database management system *du jour*, Access. As many scholars doubtless know, Advanced Revelation permits the use of repeating fields - fields that allow multiple entries - and a single record may have several such repeating fields, each related to the other so that the first entry in one field goes with the first entry in another. It is possible to build an extremely rich and complex data set with such a system, but, of course, the files are far from standard. This is about as far from a normalized database as one can get, but it does, for instance, provide an easy way to record all figures on a pot without regard for how many there may be and without creating separate data tables.

Translating the Advanced Revelation data into an Access system has been extremely time-consuming. Whereas one might hope that data could simply be dumped from one system to another, that could not be done here. Not only were there intermediate steps, there was an entirely new file structure required. Many individual data tables were required where there might have been only one before. The job is still in progress, and, while the outcome is in sight, the cost will have been substantial.

Advanced Revelation is not alone in providing such potential problems for data transfer. Repeating fields are also permitted in File Maker Pro, and a similar feature is available in Fourth Dimension; so seemingly mainstream choices may leave an excavator with data requiring substantial work if they are to be useful to anyone beyond the excavation team.

One more example, this one from the world of CAD, computer-aided design. AutoCAD is so dominant in the PC world that its native file structure is often used as the standard. Autodesk, the parent company, even sells software to read and write the AutoCAD format - DWG files - so that other software developers can add that feature to their programs. What Autodesk does not tell consumers is rather startling, though. The specifications for DWG files are not simply a specific and restricted set of drawings entities (lines, circles, surfaces, and so on). Instead, the specifications provide for a set of supported entities and any new entity the programmer chooses to add, provided only that the new entity be identified according to certain rules. So long as the new entities are added correctly, the file is considered a proper DWG file. Note, however, that a new entity though included in a DWG file need not be known to Autodesk or to any standards body. Indeed, only the programmer needs to know of the existence of such an entity. As a result, no program can certainly read a file fully just because it is a DWG file. Indeed, even AutoCAD itself will not be able to read a proper DWG file if that file contains new entities unknown to the programmers or of no concern to them. (I should be clear about this. AutoCAD - or another CAD program that accepts DWG files - will read the file, but the unknown entities may be ignored, in which case the user will have no way to know of their presence. In other cases, the presence of certain entities may be known, but the system will be unable to use them, and the user will not be able to edit or query them.)

The entities in question are not arcane ones. It is true that many are design entities that permit parametric modeling, but some are simply better, more complex surface representations such as those we might use to define a column or a complex molding.

Imagine an archive with one of these non-standard DWG files. (An interesting bit of language there - a non-standard standard! - sometimes the electronic world seems even stranger than that of Hal). How does the archive treat such a file so that the user in the future can see and understand all entities in the file? Obviously, the archive must have information and personnel to a) understand the files received and b) understand how to translate the items into some more universal and useful form. Such facilities are neither easily obtained nor inexpensive.

I have sketched out a rather bleak picture; databases that must be completely reorganized to be moved from one system to another; CAD files that require substantial expertise to be useful even today, much less years in the future. Any archive, whether it be the Archaeology Data Service at York University or the Archaeological Data Archive Project I represent, must be concerned with these problems.

Up to this time, we at the Archaeological Data Archive have actually experienced few migration problems. AutoCAD files have not been migrated to Release 13 format, but release 12 files can be used by either Release 12 or Release 13; so there is no urgency. (As I write this, Release 14 is arriving; I do not know what that will bring.) We have moved some files to release 13 for internal use, and the process was automatic. An interesting and unexpected problem has been encountered, though. If we were to move the CAD files in the archive to Release 13, users of Release 12 would be unable to use the files; they are not backward-compatible. Since there is not a good generic format for CAD files (equivalent to DBF for data tables), this is a significant problem, and it may be necessary for the archive to maintain CAD files in multiple iterations. This is a good reason to seek generic, non-proprietary formats for data.

We have also been obliged to convert files that were provided in inappropriate or less useful formats. Both spreadsheet and ASCII files have been converted to DBF format and comma-delimited ASCII. Neither process was difficult, but I would not have wanted to entrust either job to someone not conversant with archaeological material. Furthermore, only when I tried to use one of the data sets myself did I realize that the simple translation had been inadequate and some reorganizing of the data was required.

If the reasons for preservation and migration of data are clear, is it also clear why there should be external archives? After all, we have for decades kept data from old excavations in the offices or archives of sponsoring institutions. Why do we now need an external organization to take care of excavation records?

The first reason is simple. Universities and other research organizations often do an excellent job of archiving records, but some do no job. The archival care is especially weak when materials stay in the hands of excavators for years after the completion of the project and are, by the time of his/her death or retirement, more or less out of sight and out of mind. The need for maintaining data in perpetuity also stresses the good intentions of research organizations.

A more important problem exists for electronic data that are likely to be rather rarely used. Most university computing centers are prepared to backup data but not really to archive them - at least not in a routinized, scheduled-migration fashion. If files are in use and a user takes responsibility, those files may be properly cared for, but there is unlikely to be anyone with the specific responsibility to care for data files from long-forgotten excavations. Furthermore, if general technical personnel, not people trained in archaeology, are charged with the responsibility of caring for archaeological files, how well will those files be treated when they must be migrated? Will such personnel understand the requirements of the translation process for the data under consideration? In order to understand, they will need specific information about the files (current format, relationships, data types, and so on); will that information have been collected at the outset?

If, on the other hand, computer files are to be archived by traditional archival personnel, those experts must attend to an entirely new set of problems, since the standard archival processes for objects do not apply.

A colleague recently suggested, in a meeting at which we both spoke, that data stability should not be a problem with standards such as SGML. That is certainly possible for the text world, though it would require us to use SGML for material where that is not particularly suitable - or to migrate the files at the very beginning of the process. In any case, standards like that do not exist for databases or CAD models, and even good standards in the computer world, such as SGML, have a short, brutish life.

Data archives should deal with these problems with relative ease. Monitoring of data file types and needs for migration will be one of the prime jobs of the archive. Another will be maintaining accurate and complete information about the processes required for a wide variety of file types. (Note that these archives will probably be virtual ones - not located in a single place on a single machine. As a result, the data migration services, for instance, may be developed in different places for different data types but made available to all parts of the archive.) None of this is, as the current saying has it, rocket science. In fact, much is quite simple intellectually. But it must be done in a self-conscious, routine way.

An archaeological data archive will also have the advantage that its personnel will understand the nature and meaning of the data. That will be necessary for proper migration, as has been brought home to us already.

The one problem for an archive that may be more severe than for an excavation sponsor is money. Large institutions with long lists of supporters have an easier time raising money than do small, specialized ones. Hence, the ADS in Britain is a consortium, with funding widely spread among its members, which are themselves institutions. The Archaeological Data Archive Project expects to put together a consortium in the U.S. along roughly similar lines.

I have said things here that, by and large, have been said before - by myself and others, but the difficulties here are not well understood in the academic community at large. They have often been downplayed, lest the fear of impermanence frighten away those who are already uneasy about computers. So these things must be said again and again, but with a realistic appraisal of the remedies.

One other problem should be mentioned. Many of our colleagues equate putting material on the Web or on a CD with archiving that material. When pushed, they understand the difference, but they do not consider archival storage to be a need separate and distinct from putting material into electronic form. This distinction must be made clear to all, since archiving represents a crucial step beyond putting material into digital form.

Having concluded that archives are necessary and possible, I must turn to what they are not yet - real. Archives without data are not valuable. An empty archive is not, in fact, an archive. It may be an archive-in-waiting or an archive of the future, but it is not yet an archive.

We now have, in the Archaeological Data Archive a handful of files; this service has not been recognized by our colleagues as either necessary or desirable enough to encourage many to take advantage of it. Furthermore, we archaeologists have, generally speaking, a less than stellar record when it comes to handling our information. We often fail to systematize the material for others; we don't generally expect others to use our raw data but only the predigested parts that we put into publications. Yet we, of all scholars, should be among those most scrupulous about making our raw information available to others. We all know that, our own individual genius aside, little that we say about the ancient world today will be incontrovertible tomorrow. We all understand that we are obliged to destroy much of our primary evidence to obtain more.

Yet we sometimes treat our data as if they were our private possessions, to be shown to selected others when, if, and as we please. When we do make material available, we rarely consider it part of our responsibility to provide easy, indexed access.

Our institutions are often helpful only after the fact. They will archive material, but they don't regularly help scholars prepare their own records for archival storage. Certainly they do not give credit for the time and effort required to do that until it's too late and someone else must prepare material for archival preservation after the creator has gone.

I am not concerned here about the reasons for our sometimes unscientific handling of basic information; nor do I want to seem to be straining for a pulpit from which to preach. Rather, I want simply to make it clear that archival storage of our records requires that the creators of the records take the time and the responsibility to prepare them for the archive and then actually turn them over. Institutions must also recognize the importance of this work.

Such time and effort can, of course, be mandated. Sooner or later, it surely will be, as is already happening in Britain and the U.S. However, I would like to see us as scholars, as the liberators and guardians of the most basic information about the material culture of humankind, take pains to treat our knowledge with the respect it requires before we are forced to by governments that will, in many cases, muddle the process beyond redemption. When the responsible bureaucrats are not archaeologists, they will rarely understand our problems or our needs. They will just make rules that are tidy but may not be appropriate. We need to preempt them, to create good, sensible rules about data archiving, and we need to start actually archiving our files to show our good intentions.

Permit me, please, to suggest a few rules we should use to head off the ones governments might impose.

First, we need to stop playing the waiting game. I'll publish when I'm ready, and the data will remain mine until then. I am not suggesting that data be made public immediately upon recording, but I am suggesting that data files be archived immediately. Those files can be kept private, but, were there a time limit on the privacy, there would be a simple spur to more prompt publication as well as the proper care of the data in the meantime.

Second, we need specifications about how data will be transmitted. That is, we need to know that certain file types are acceptable and what information (metadata) must accompany the files (see Miller, this volume). If we wait too long to agree about these kinds of things, we will, I fear, be presented with fixed systems for recording our information by host governments - our own or others - and the results will be catastrophic. Can you imagine a commissioner looking over your shoulder to tell you how to structure your data file? How to make your CAD model?

Third, we need to work on some of the common issues of vocabulary and authority lists that will help us all to work more efficiently and to make our data more easily understood. The people at the Getty have given us examples of this, some of which have been well received.

Fourth, scholars need to spend some of their time - as they now spend time on other professional duties such as reviewing articles and manuscripts - helping archives evaluate data files that have been offered for storage. An archive cannot and should not accept all things offered and must be sure that material stored meets certain standards. Scholars must be willing to treat reviewing potential archival material with the same seriousness they treat reviewing articles.

Fifth, we have to decide how to handle new information that is clearly related to information already in the archive. We need to be sure that two-way links are maintained to connect new information to old - and old to new. The individual data files must retain their integrity, but they must also be receptive to inclusion into a larger whole.

Sixth, it is very difficult now to obtain information from a variety of sources and to make all the information somehow compatible so that all can be seen and analyzed together. There is a strong temptation to try to fix that problem by creating data coordination schemes that will allow disparate data to be combined. Here I believe that we must resist temptation, because this problem will be solved by the commercial marketplace and I think, as a result, we are best served by spending our time on the other pieces of our puzzle. Microsoft and Oracle and the other players in this arena will worry about data incompatibility. (Indeed, this is already happening.) They must find a solution, and we will have to use it, whether we've already developed our own or not, because what they develop will be the standard. I do not believe that we belong in the software business.

If, as I have said here, archives are essential, and if, as I have also argued, independent archaeological archives are required for archaeological data, and if, as I have just pointed out, we will soon be required to provide archival data files to host governments, then, I say again, let us not wait and risk being forced into poor systems. Instead, let us begin to archive our records now, and let us cooperate in such ways that the archives can provide to us all the full and complete access to critical information that we need for our work.

Contact details

Harrison Eiteljorg, II
Archaeological Data Archive Project
Bryn Mawr University
PO Box 60
Bryn Mawr, PA 19010
USA
email: neiteljo@brynmawr.edu

Digital Danish Archaeology. Gods and Graves - an Internet Publication on the Bronze Age

Henrik Jarl Hansen

CAA 97

Abstract

Publications on the Internet are still in their infancy and with Gods & Graves we have taken our first steps at the National Museum in Denmark. Gods & Graves is a presentation of spectacular finds from the Danish Bronze Age based on two large archaeological databases. It allows the Internet visitor to go behind the scenes in the National Museum's Bronze Age exhibition and gain access to pictures of objects which are normally kept in the Museum's stores, and to see photographs and drawings from the archives as well as reading original textual information. Gods & Graves is a pilot project to CultureNet Denmark.

1 Introduction

In 1996 the International Documentation Committee "CIDOC" met for the first time outside the north-western hemisphere in Nairobi, Kenya (CIDOC 1996). This gave the delegates a welcome opportunity to discuss the conditions for information technology (IT) within museum communities in different parts of the world. The attitudes were very different. Some regarded the emergence of the Internet as a revolution for the possibilities of communication and instant access to knowledge for people in Africa. Others regarded the Internet as a tool for the upper class to keep information away from the others. Is this also true if we substitute the words "people in Africa" with "smaller museums in Europe"? Is IT only for the rich? In Africa a computer costs the same as employing a museum professional for one year. In the Nordic countries the equivalent is less than a month. Despite this, a lot of museums in our part of the world are at the same level as the African ones, they cannot find the money to invest in information technology.

On the other hand many efforts have been made in the field of digital archaeology in Denmark during the last 20 years, as in our neighbouring countries. More presentations at CAA clearly demonstrate this (Hansen 1993; Andresen and Madsen 1996). But despite the progress there is still a long way to go, and as time passes it is getting more obvious that conditions for digital archaeology are much better in the centre(s) than in the periphery. We have to change peoples way of thinking before we can get much further at the local level. I would argue that the result is that access to relevant information is problematic if you are located outside the sphere of the attractive digital centres and it could still get worse, if we are not taking this dilemma seriously. It is not enough to digitise the information, it must also be widely accessible. This problem must be addressed for instance via free access in public places like libraries, schools and museums.

In 1994 the Danish government (the Ministry of Research) published the report "The Info-society year 2000" and based upon that a policy document in 1995 "From vision to action - Info-society 2000". The Ministry of Culture's contribution to the IT policy was the establishment of a "CultureNet Denmark" and in order to speed the process eight pilot projects were supported by the Ministry in 1996 and in 1997 a further nine received funding. The CultureNet's aim is to use information technology to give the public better access to the many state and state-supported institutions, their collections, services and events. The pilot projects are very wide-reaching from this years "Danish Operas 1900-1996" to last years archaeologically "Gods & Graves".

The paper will focus on the Gods & Graves project, as it is a breakthrough in making scientific and administrative information available both to the general public and to the researcher using the good old "new technology". Gods & Graves is a publication on the Internet and it allows the visitor to go behind the scenes in the National Museum's Bronze Age exhibition and gain access to pictures of objects which are normally kept in the Museum's stores, and to see drawings and photographs from the archives as well as reading original textual information. The Internet publication contains descriptions of 219 graves and sacrificial sites from Denmark's early Bronze Age with pictures of most of the objects, including many close-ups, in addition to drawings, sketches and photographs from the excavation reports. Introductory chapters give a general introduction to the Bronze Age, to the project and to the databases from which the material is taken. The publication also includes a comprehensive glossary and a chronology which can be called up on the screen at any time.

2 Background

The Gods & Graves publication is based on material from two large databases located at the National Museum in Copenhagen: The National Archaeological Record (DKC) and the Object Register of the Department of Prehistory and Early History (GENREG).

The National Archaeological Record (DKC) is a database of archaeological sites and monuments. DKC has the task of registering all cultural-historical remains from the past to the present from the land and on the sea-bed. For practical reasons efforts have until now been concentrated on prehistoric finds and monuments. The central registration of the cultural history of more recent times will be started in the course of 1998. The record is primarily a tool intended for use by museums, universities and related institutions. As the database contains sensitive information it is not freely accessible. However, we are giving the public access to selected information in the register, while the professionals have full access to texts, maps etc. regulated by the use of passwords. The database contains information on almost 140,000 locations, which also can be viewed on digital maps using the Record's interactive mapping-system.

The other major database behind Gods & Graves is the object register GENREG. This holds information about The National Museum's collections which contain well over a million items, mainly from Denmark's prehistory and history, but also including a large ethnographic collection. In 1987 the Museum began electronic registration of this enormous amount of material, and now, 10 years later, the task is almost complete. The result is a database containing information in text form relating to about 1 million museum numbers and with about 200,000 pictures.

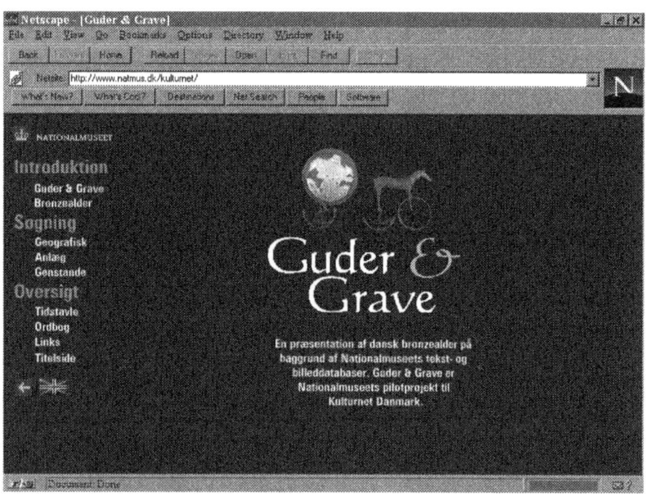

Figure 1. The welcome screen to Gods & Graves - the National Museums pilot project to CultureNet Denmark.

The main purpose behind the Gods & Graves pilot project was to test and develop techniques which in the future will let us use the computer to combine information automatically from the two databases. We also wanted to test the Internet technology to link and present information from the databases on-line. This will allow the public or the researcher to query the databases from many different angles and retrieve relevant information on the archaeological site, its geographical location, the recorded structures on the site and finally to view pictures of the objects and read a variety of related descriptions.

A good part of the Gods & Graves project could be done automatically, but we ended up with a substantial material that could only be solved manually. Anyway the exercise gave us the opportunity to view and work with the data from a new perspective. The experiences from the pilot project will be used in the future development of the museums' databases.

3 Presentation of the system

Gods & Graves is designed in such a way that the user can always orientate him- or herself in the system with the help of a navigation column at left side of the screen. This means that even from the title page one has an idea of what information and search facilities the publication offers (see Figure 1). Access to the data is through three main chapters; "Introduktion" (Introduction), "Søgning" (Search) and "Oversigt" (General information). Each chapter is subdivided so that with a single click one can move on to the desired information.

The chapter "Introduktion" gives access to a description of the Gods & Graves project including a short guide to the use of the system and also a general introduction to the Bronze Age. Both texts contain references (hyperlinks) to more information.

Figure 2. Geographical searches. From the map of

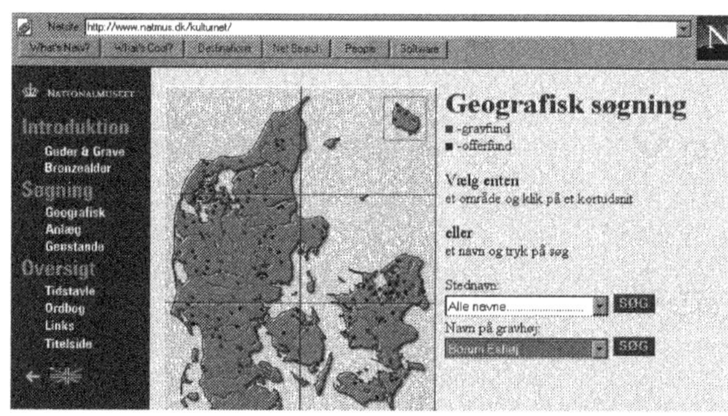

Denmark the user can either choose a name from one of the boxes on the right (like here: "Borum Eshøj"), or "click" on one of the six regions on the map. From the regional map it is possible to choose a particular site by "clicking" on it. The red dots are graves. The blue dots are sacrificial sites.

Similarly the chapter "Oversigt" contains a glossary, a time chart, references to other relevant Internet pages in addition to the project description, an interim report and the final report. The glossary and the time chart can be called up onto the screen at any time. The search possibilities are of course the system's most important facility. Text and pictures from the two databases DKC and GENREG can be accessed from three angles. The user can search by geographic position, monument type or artefact type. These queries should be considered as different avenues to the same information.

Using the geographic querying it is possible to search via a "clickable" map of Denmark, a technique, which in simplified form derives from DKC's mapping system. Alternatively, via comboboxes one can give a placename or the name of a hoard or a burial mound, for example "Borum Eshøj" (see Figure 2). Which ever way is used, the locality is presented with a detailed map (see Figure 3) showing the precise geographic location of the find along with topographic details. In addition detailed information on the antiquarian and archaeological activity at the site over the years is given. It is normally information on excavation, preservation and perhaps on the legend associated with the site. For instance the story about how the chamber in a mound was found, when a wounded hare hopped into a hole in the mound and the farmer's wife followed after. The texts are illustrated with both recent and contemporary photographs, water-colours and drawings (see Figure 4). The texts alone are a gold mine, so even though Gods & Graves is very visually orientated, the texts are not just there for decoration.

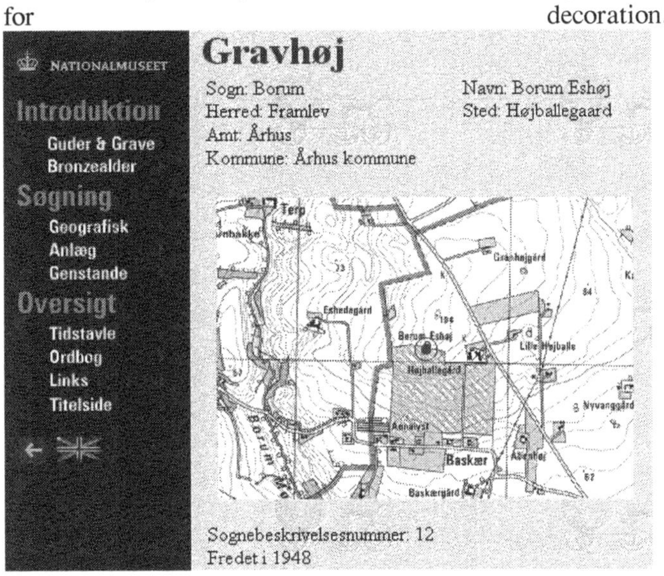

Figure 3. For each of the Bronze Age sites included in Gods & Graves there is geographic information and a modern map with the archaeological site marked. It is also possible to read about the finds and excavations and see related photographs and drawings.

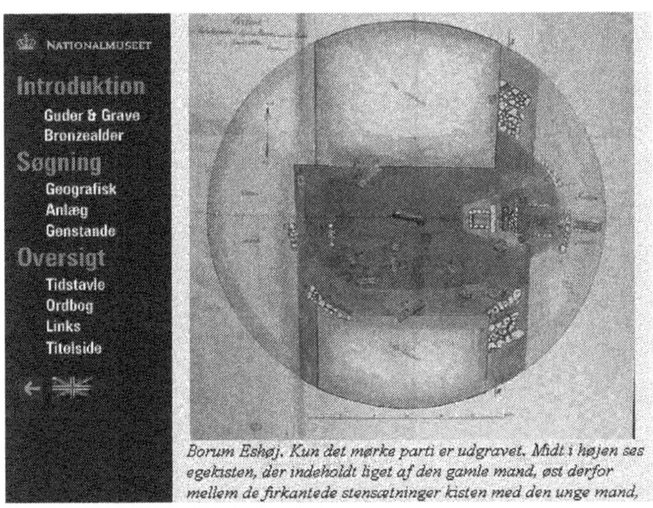

Figure 4. Borum Eshøj. Plan of excavation 1875.

In addition to the text, each query on a locality results also in a series of standardised "Facts about the site", for example what features or constructions are registered at the particular site as well as dimensions of burial mounds and graves. There is also a hyperlink from this part of the publication so that one can see pictures of the artefacts which have been found at the site or find an elaborate explanation in the glossary.

If the user only wants to access pictures of artefacts and is not interested in the archaeological information this can be done direct by querying by "Genstande" (Artefacts) from the navigation column. This query on the other hand, leads through a hierarchically built list of the accessible artefact types, so that one can see depictions of all bronze swords, oak coffins or beltboxes for instance (see Figure 5). The pictures are at first fairly small (thumbnails) but they can always be enlarged, whereby decorative and technical details become fully visible (Figures 6 and 7). Just as it is possible to jump from a locality to the associated artefacts, one can of course also get from a given artefact to information on the site it comes from.

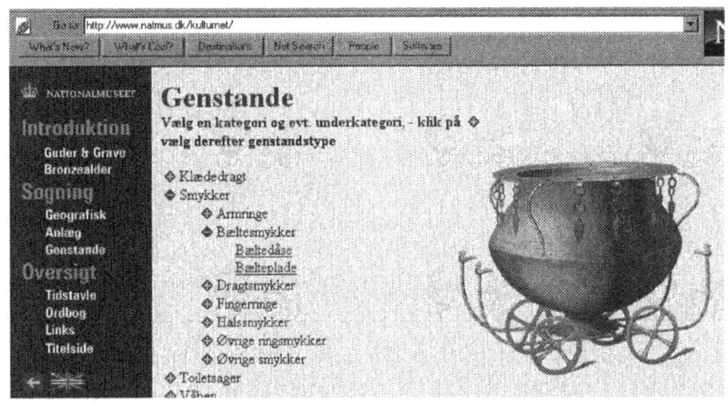

Figure 5. Example of a "Search by object" (bæltedåse) via main- and sub-categories.

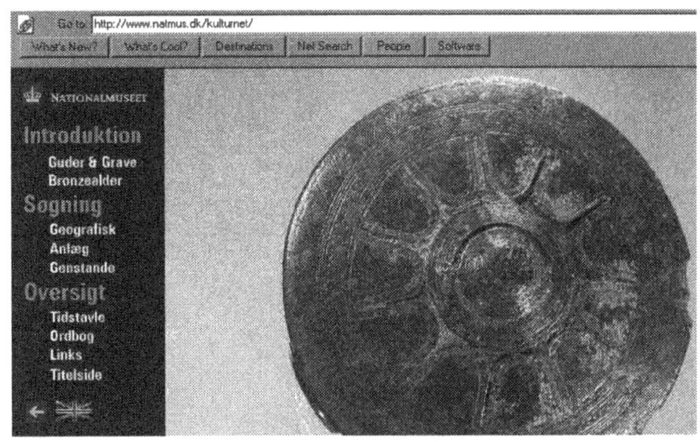

Figure 6. The result of the query in Figure 5 is eight beltboxes. One of them is from "Maglehøi" in Norh Sealand.

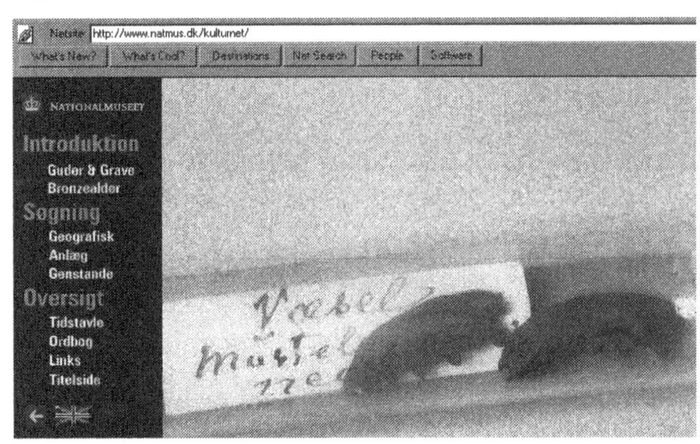

Figure 7. Among the "magic" content in the beltbox from Maglehøi are two jaws from a Weasel.

The last query type is through "Anlæg" (Monuments / Structures). Here the user can choose via a list of for example all burial mounds, cremation graves or hoards. The results are, as described above, the same set of details in the form of text and illustrations associated with the particular locality.

It is always possible to call up the time chart or the glossary on screen just as the information can be reached via the many hyperlinks. The glossary contains a little over 100 references on Bronze Age artefacts and monument types as well as more general subjects like burial customs, bronze casting and dendrochronology. Many entries contain reference to named localities. In this way one can for example go direct from a description of "snoreskørt" (skirt made of cords) to Gods & Graves information on the Egtved girl's grave, where one can also see the conservator Gustav Rosenberg's reconstruction sketch from 1924 (see Figure 8).

Figure 8. One of the features in Gods & Graves is a glossary. The example shows the explanation in Danish of "snoreskørt" (skirt made of cords), the activated hyperlink to Egtved with Gustav Rosenberg's sketch of the Egtved Girl from 1924.

4 The technology

Gods & Graves is developed from, as explained above, the two un-connected databases DKC and GENREG. A new database was designed for the project, which joined the two big databases together, and which, amongst other things, solved the problem of the different ways of recording inventory numbers. The CultureNet database, which was implemented in Access 7.0, is in its structure much more simplified in comparison with the original databases. Amongst other things many one-to-many relationships are reduced to a many-value-text field, where the text is pre-formatted to HTML-code (with the formatting as lineshift, hyperlinks etc.) This solution was chosen to reduce the time it takes to generate HTML-text.

Gods & Graves consists of both static HTML-pages and of HTML-pages which are dynamically generated. For the most part a "cgi"-program (common gateway interface) is used while fewer pages are generated with java-script. A cgi program or cgi script is a program which runs on the web server and returns information (in HTML-code) to the client who queries. A cgi program can be written in many different languages. For Gods & Graves it has been done in Visual Basic 4.0.

With a query to the database the following happens. From a computer (the client) a query is sent via the Internet to the National Museum's web server. Here a cgi program starts, which first makes a query in the Gods & Graves database and then generates a HTML-file which is finally returned to the client. Here the client's browser generates the final presentation of the page which can incidentally have a surprising result. At any rate the client's browser is a source of great uncertainty in connection with designing an Internet publication.

In Gods & Graves there is access to text and illustrations on 219 localities encompassing 1550 inventory numbers. For comparison it might be mentioned that registered in the museum's collections from this period are circa 9500 numbers. The number of artefacts is bigger than the quantity of inventory numbers because groups of artefacts can be registered under one number. The majority of the artefact pictures accessible in the Gods & Graves database are digital photos (around 2000 items). Where it has not been possible to take new photos, for example of the oak coffins, older ones have been used which have been thus digitised. The pictures of the artefacts which are presented in Gods & Graves are in JPEG format compressed to circa 25-50 Kb, though they are recorded in a considerably better resolution (10 Mb) and are saved after lossless compressing as 2 Mb pictures. It will be possible to show them in a considerably better quality when technology allows without having to take new photos.

5 Conclusion

There can be no doubt that publications on the Internet still are in their infancy. But the work with Gods & Graves has been enormously informative for those involved. As a direct result we have now opened on-line access to DKC - The National Archaeological record, with the use of more or less the same techniques. Differentiated access to the data is controlled by password, so that there is access for local museums, administrators, researchers and interested public without compromising data security. In other words the database cannot be misused as a treasure map for metal-detector armed antiquity hunters, but it can be used to give the public an interest and respect for antiquities and an understanding of the amount of work behind archaeological collecting and registration.

Bibliography

Andresen, J and Madsen T, 1996 IDEA - the Integrated Database for Excvation Analysis, In Kammermans H and Fennema K (eds.), *Interfacing the Past. Computer Applications and Quantitative Methods in Archaeology, CAA 95,* Analecta Praehistorica Leidensia,18,3-14

CIDOC, 1996 *ICOM Study Series 3, Committee for Documentation (CIDOC),* Paris, 25-28

Forskningsministeriet, 1994 Info-samfundet år 2000

Forskningsministeriet, 1995 Fra vision til handling. Info-samfundet år 2000

Hansen, H J, 1993 European archaeological databases: problems and prospects. In: Andresen J, Madsen T and Scollar I (eds.). *Computing the Past. Computer Applications and Quantitative Methods in Archaeology, CAA 92,* 229-237

Internet references

CultureNet Denmark: http//www.kulturnet.dk/

Gods & Graves: http//www.natmus.dk/kulturnet/

The Danish National Archaeological Record: http//www.dkc.natmus.dk/

Contact details

Henrik Jarl Hansen
The National Archaeological Record
The National Museum of Denmark
Ny Vestergade 11
DK-1471 Copenhagen K
DENMARK
e-mail: jarl@natmus.dk

Museums On-line: Access to Museum Information

David Dawson

"It is proposed to call a meeting of the Curators of a few provincial Museums... to discuss the possibility of obtaining... A compendious index of the contents of all provincial Museums and collections..."
H.M. Platneur, 1888

"The Department will draw up a strategy for improving access to cultural assets through information technology."
Department of National Heritage , Treasures in Trust, 1996

The idea of enabling access to museum collections is over 100 years old. The museum profession is closer than ever before as a result of three major factors:- the use of computers for museum documentation, the focus on collections information given by the Museums and Galleries Commission Registration scheme, and new funds from the National Lottery

The wide-spread adoption of SPECTRUM, the UK Museum Documentation Standard, has provided a framework for museums and software suppliers to clearly establish museum requirements and to deliver collections management systems. Existing software, such as MODES or Micromusee has been upgraded to meet SPECTRUM requirements, and SPECTRUM has been used to design new collections management systems, such as Admuse. The largest development has been LASSI - the Larger Scale Systems Initiative - a group of large museums which has established common requirements, and selected Multi Mimsy as their preferred system. The suppliers of these systems are now beginning to develop Public Access and Web interfaces to the data held on the systems. However, the first UK museum archaeological data to be available on the Web was created by Hampshire Museums exporting data as HTML pages from their MODES databases and using reports to create linked index pages.

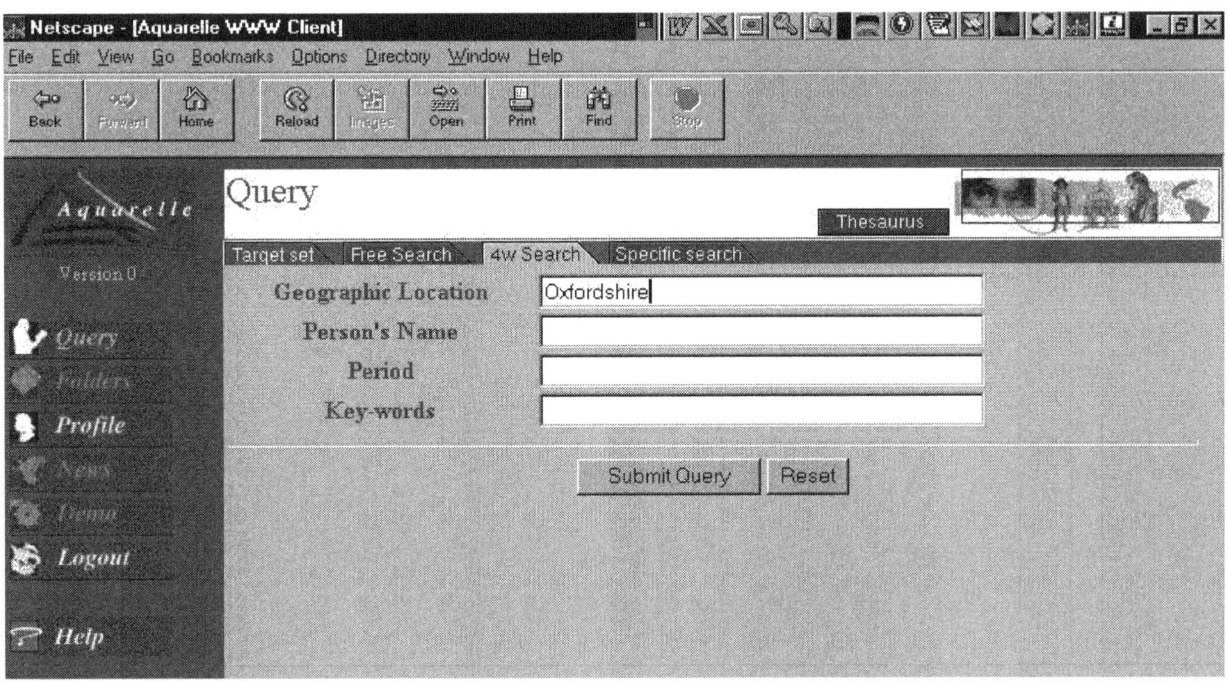

Figure 1: Aquarelle Project

In 1992 Museums and Galleries Commission Registration Scheme was launched, establishing minimum standards for museums. The scheme included a requirement for museums to document their collections and has resulted in a new emphasis of the use of computers for recording collections. The 1997 MDA Survey of IT in Museums shows that over 10 million records having been entered by the 250 museums surveyed, a 40% increase in just 2 years. Increasingly documentation and computers are seen as the vehicle for enhancing public access to information about collections, a theme emphasised by Treasures in Trust, the 1996 Review of Museums by the then Department of National Heritage.

The progress on cataloguing collections has been achieved almost entirely within existing resources, but grants from the Heritage Lottery Fund is enabling a range of county-wide and regional schemes to get off the ground. Examples include surveys of Geological collections in Dorset and Surrey museums, and a scheme in its early stages to enable access to information held in and about Cornwall, with archaeology forming a major component. The most wide-ranging IT based project is SCRAN - the Scottish Cultural Resources Network. SCRAN is a £7million Millennium Project to build a networked multimedia resource base of object records from Scottish museums, site information from RCHMS and specially commissioned multimedia essays. These will be used for the study, teaching and appreciation of history and material culture in Scotland. At the time of writing, the SCRAN on-line database has just gone live with 60,000 text records of objects from over 30 museums, galleries and archives. A few hundred of these records are attached to images. By the Millennium this is planned to grow to 1.5 million text records and 100,000 multimedia objects, including movies, sound clips and VR.

At the same time, two international projects are looking at enabling access to information held in different databases across the Internet. The Consortium for the Computer Interchange of Museum Information (CIMI) has a project that demonstrates solutions to the difficulties in achieving on-line access to cultural heritage information held in multiple databases independent of the hardware and software used to store the data or search for it. The project is using Z39.50 protocols to access multiple databases, and SGML to deliver object records, bibliographic records and catalogue essays to the end user.

This approach is being further enhanced by the Aquarelle Project (see Figure 1). Funded by the EU, this aims to enable access to Cultural Heritage information, and includes MDA, RCHME and the Culture Ministries of France, Italy and Greece. It will be using a similar technical approach to CIMI but with the added elements of multi-lingual searching and the ability to create SGML digital folders, for publishing on the Internet. A driving force behind the project is the need to digitise the paper files and photographs of archaeological sites and historic buildings, and to relate them to museum collections. The project is nearing the completion of the first prototype, and is already demonstrating what can be achieved. UK museums are becoming increasingly interested in Aquarelle as it is starting to demonstrate that Z39.50 can offer the opportunity to integrate data from museums, SMR's, Record Offices and Libraries.

CIMI, Aquarelle and a range of museum collections management system suppliers are beginning an Interoperability Testbed project which will further expand the range of systems which can implement Z39.50.

For the first time, the mix of new technology, a new commitment to collections information in the museum profession and new sources of funding are making the goal of public access to museum collections seem achievable.

Web addresses

SCRAN - http://www.scran.ac.uk/

CIMI - http://www.cimi.org/cimi/

Aquarelle - http://aqua.inria.fr/

MDA - http://www.open.gov.uk/mdocassn/

Contact details

David Dawson
Outreach Manager
Museum Documentation Association
67 Spring Street
Chipping Norton
Oxfordshire, OX7 5NN
UK
email: david@mdaserv.demon.co.uk

The Role of Data Standards in Digital Access and Interchange

Gillian Quine

CAA 97

Abstract

This presentation will explore recent initiatives within the RCHME to improve access to and exchange of digital information and demonstrate how they conform with national and international standards for recording both the archaeological and architectural heritage. RCHME has played a key role in the development of these standards, which recognise and define shared concepts, use common protocols for recording data and, thus, facilitate both exchange of and access to information. It is hoped that the crucial role which standards must play in sharing cultural heritage information will have been demonstrated and that methods for encouraging their widespread adoption and use will have been explored.

1 Introduction

Since 1984, the Royal Commission on the Historical Monuments of England (RCHME) has played a key role in the development of national and international data standards for the recording of information about archaeology and the built heritage. Recent examples include the 1993 Recording England's Past standard (RCHME 1993), the standard for Urban Archaeology Databases (RCHME and English Heritage 1993), the Thesaurus of Monument Types (RCHME and English Heritage 1995), the Council of Europe's core data standard for architectural records (Council of Europe 1995) and the Comité International pour la Documentacion's (CIDOC, the documentation committee of the International Council of Museums) international core data standard for archaeological sites and monuments (CIDOC 1995). Last year the RCHME established its own Data Standards Unit within the National Monuments Record (NMR), recognising the importance of data standards and the need to apply them rigorously internally, as well as the value of outreach and continuing involvement in national and international initiatives.

This paper concentrates on the role of data standards in heritage inventories and their importance in access to and the exchange of digital information, and looks specifically at three recent initiatives in which the RCHME has been involved.

Data standards, within this paper, are defined as rules or protocols for recording information, including vocabulary control. The key words in relation to data standards are compatibility, consistency, accessibility and retrievability.

2 RCHME'S data standards unit

The Data Standards Unit was established in May 1996 and has the following responsibilities:

1. establishing and maintaining data standards;
2. disseminating information about data standards and vocabulary control;
3. training staff in the importance and use of data standards;
4. ensuring consistency in the recording of information across the organisation; and
5. ensuring that the quality of data is maintained.

The Unit also has an outreach role. It can offer advice and information on data standards and vocabulary control, and provide training in these areas. It also provides specific advice and recommendations on data standards and terminology control as part of reference data audits for Sites and Monuments Records (SMRs) maintained by local authorities in England.

3 The role of data standards in heritage inventories

The purpose of heritage inventories is to compile, present and provide access to information required to understand and interpret the historic environment for the purposes of management, conservation, preservation, education and enjoyment. Data standards ensure that compilation occurs consistently, through the use of common units of information and vocabulary control, and that information is presented in a consistent and meaningful way, through the use of a combination of controlled index fields and free text. Access to information, by making data retrievable, and dissemination are enhanced with users able to search on, retrieve and make sense of relevant information.

The application of organisational data standards leads to internal consistency: the application of national and international standards provides opportunities for communication and the sharing of information between organisations. Compatibility, shared access and the ability to exchange data sits at the heart of recent heritage standards.

Standards have also been developed to assist organisations at an early stage in planning and developing new information systems for their inventories. Adopting a common format, which can be developed and tailored to meet specific requirements, ensuring that information can be accessed and retrieved effectively through a consistent approach, and employing terminology control mechanisms, helps inventories to meet their objectives and fulfil the requirements of their users. For existing inventories, the use of a common and well-defined format can also ease the process of migrating data from one information system to another.

The RCHME regards data standards and terminology control as a key element of its lead role and participates in both national and international initiatives on the recording and dissemination of heritage data, with the aim of providing access to a common store of inventory information.

4 How effective are data standards?

The development of data standards is not without difficulties. Concerns have been raised within the archaeological community about the relevance and applicability of particular data standards and whether standardisation is actually achievable or desirable. Typical criticisms of, and concerns about standards, include the following:

1. they are sets of rules which inhibit creativity and flexibility;
2. they do not cover the needs of individual organisations in sufficient detail;
3. those developed to cater for specialist needs become too complex and unwieldy;
4. international data standards should not be imposed at a local level;
5. they should not be dominated by the needs of larger, national organisations;
6. they are principally designed for classification rather than as tools to aid retrieval;
7. they must contain full definitions of the fields and explain how to use them, and
8. they must be responsive to suggestions from users.

Many of the criticisms can be overcome by the adoption of a more pro-active approach to standard development, with user consultation, feedback and education being essential elements of the process. Data standards which have clearly defined aims, can be linked with other standards, have sufficient flexibility to allow users to comply with a core but retain their individuality beyond this, and can be developed as requirements change, are now considered more effective.

The positive aspects of data standards continue to outweigh possible disadvantages. Besides maximising consistency, compatibility and retrieval, they provide a means by which to update information efficiently, facilitate the transfer and exchange of data from one information system to another, and, through the use of fields or concepts for recording information, encourage greater analysis of data and its structuring into a more logical form. This serves to enhance both the manipulation and presentation of information.

Data standards also require the use of terminology control. Strict control of vocabulary, through the use of simple word-lists and more complex thesauri, not only ensures that the data is recorded in a consistent fashion and is of a high quality (achieved through the validation of inputted data against authority files), but also that users are provided with a simple means of accessing all of the information which is relevant to a particular enquiry.

5 Core data

Recent initiatives involving the RCHME have ensured that core data lies at the heart of new data standards. Core data is defined as the "*minimum amount of information required in indexing, ordering and classifying material independently of the form in which it is held*" (Council of Europe 1995). Consistent core data also ensures that information is retrievable. The core data record is not intended to be comprehensive but to act as an index to additional information required for the full understanding and interpretation of a record, held within the information system, the heritage organisation and elsewhere. In the context of both recording and the exchange of information, the value of core data lies in the fact that the fewer fields of data which are used the greater the degree of control on the consistency and quality of the information.

The RCHME is implementing core data within the NMR Inventory (see 6.1 below) and encouraging SMRs to exchange data at core level.

6 Recent data standard's initiatives

Recent English data standards have drawn heavily on the European and CIDOC core data standards, and include an internal standard for the National Monuments Record (NMR), the MIDAS standard and a data standard for SMRs.

6.1 The NMR data standard

RCHME staff have played a major role in the development of European and international core data standards for archaeological and architectural records over the last few years (see Appendix 1). Internally, although data standards were recognised as important, they were only applied in an *ad hoc* way, and a standard for recording monuments did not exist. Following extensive internal consultation and in the light of international developments, a core data standard for the NMR Inventory was ratified by Commissioners in December (RCHME 1996). The standard consists of four parts. These detail core data for NMR monument records to be compiled or edited to a consistent standard in all cases where the information is available, additional fields to be compiled by RCHME archaeological and architectural survey teams, additional fields appropriate to Maritime records, and non-core fields to be used when justified in the context of particular projects. The standard has been implemented within the NMR. Validation and enhancement projects ensure that core data requirements are met and quality assurance procedures check that the quality and consistency of data is maintained.

6.2. MIDAS

MIDAS, the Monument Inventory Data Standard (RCHME forthcoming), has its origins in a revision of Recording

England's Past (RCHME 1993) by the Data Standards Working Party. This group comprises representatives from the RCHME, English Heritage, the Association of Local Government Archaeological Officers (ALGAO), British and Irish Bibliography and The National Trust. The aim of this standard and manual is to enhance retrieval of information from monument related inventories, to provide a common format in order to ensure that important information is recorded, to promote consistency within a given inventory and between inventories, to facilitate the exchange of information, to assist the migration of records from old information systems to new ones, and to enhance the opportunities for evolution of inventories.

MIDAS has been influenced by Recording England's Past, the Council of Europe and CIDOC standards, the NMR Core Data Standard, and the museum documentation standard *SPECTRUM* (MDA 1994). Its development has been a collaborative process, based on the shared experiences of the working party members and feedback from a large group of peer reviewers. MIDAS is very clear about its aims and its audience, and not only sets out the standard but also provides practical advice and guidance for the holders of existing monument inventories and the creators of new ones. Compatibility with existing heritage standards, and the ability to fit these together, was regarded as a priority.

6.3 The SMR software standard

The SMR Software Standard (RCHME forthcoming) has been produced by the Data Standards Unit, supported by a group with representatives from ALGAO. The work was undertaken in the context of the RCHME lead role for the co-ordination of Sites and Monuments Records. Steve Stead was engaged as a consultant to the Unit and the Suffolk, West Yorkshire, South Yorkshire, Northamptonshire and Lincolnshire SMRs acted as reference sites.

The purpose of the data standard is to bring together the best elements from the standards which underlie a number of heritage databases, including English Heritage's Record of Scheduled Monuments (RSM), RCHME's National Monuments Record database (MONARCH), the Urban Archaeological Databases, and local authority Sites and Monuments Records, in order to inform the development of new software for SMRs. MIDAS lies at the core of the data standard, to ensure compatibility between the new national standard for monument inventories and a standard which caters for the specific needs of SMRs. The data standard has also been heavily influenced by a revised version of the CIDOC standard (unpublished, Nairobi 1996) and the Council of Europe's architectural standard. Although designed primarily in the context of a text database, it does take into account the need to link to Geographical Information Systems (GIS) and other spatial tools.

The data standard is being used as a design document by exeGeSIs Spatial Data Management, which has been commissioned to produce an SMR database and GIS software. Design and testing of the software will take place over the summer and it will be launched in the Autumn. The standard, and technical documentation, will be released after the software is made available.

7 Metadata

The RCHME has contributed to discussions on metadata with the Archaeology Data Service and in the context of the AQUARELLE Project, a European project which aims to provide an information network on the cultural heritage using the Internet as a delivery mechanism. The value of metadata in aiding the identification (resource discovery) and linking of relevant entries in various inventories is recognised by the RCHME. MIDAS discusses the role of metadata and includes a form for recording a metadata entry for an inventory, and the SMR Software will have the capability of generating metadata records. Although metadata is a flexible and effective resource discovery tool, it is not a substitute for consistently applied data standards and terminology control. Efficient and effective access to and retrieval of information can only be achieved through a combination of both these tools.

8 Conclusion

The aim of this paper was to emphasise the importance of data standards in the context of heritage inventories and to focus on some of the recent initiatives in which the RCHME has been involved. The format of data standards and the way in which they are being developed is changing. It is recognised that there is a need to produce standards that have clear aims and objectives, that cover the requirements of the target audience, that concentrate on core data rather than trying to be prescriptive on all fields of information, and that can adapt to changing needs. The effectiveness of standards is often questioned. However, the advantages of standards in terms of consistency, retrievability and compatibility, as well as in terms of facilitating access to and the sharing of heritage information, continue to outweigh any potential disadvantages.

Bibliography

CIDOC, 1995 *Draft International Core Data Standard for Archaeological Sites and Monuments,* Paris: International Council of Museums

Council of Europe, 1995 *Core data index to historic buildings and monuments of the architectural heritage,* Council of Europe

Council of Europe, forthcoming *Core data standard for archaeological sites and monuments*, Council of Europe

Museums Documentation Association, 1994 *SPECTRUM: The Museum Documentation Standard*, Cambridge: Museums Documentation Association

Royal Commission on the Historical Monuments of England, 1993 *Recording England's Past: A Data Standard for the Extended National Archaeological Record,* London, RCHME and ACAO

Royal Commission on the Historical Monuments of England forthcoming *MIDAS: A Manual and Data Standard for Monument Inventories*
Royal Commission on the Historical Monuments of England, forthcoming SMR '97: *A Data Standard for England's Sites and Monuments Records*
Royal Commission on the Historical Monuments of England, 1996 *The NMR Core Data Standard*, Unpublished standard, ratified by Commissioners in December 1996
Royal Commission on the Historical Monuments of England and English Heritage, 1993 *Urban Archaeology Databases Data Standards and Compilers Manual,* Unpublished consultation draft
Royal Commission on the Historical Monuments of England and English Heritage, 1995 *Thesaurus of Monument Types: A Standard for Use in Archaeological and Architectural Records*, Swindon, RCHME

Appendix 1 Heritage data standards with RCHME input

Data Standards

RCHME and ACAO Recording England's Past *A Data Standard for the Extended National Archaeological Record* (1993)

RCHME and English Heritage Urban Archaeology Databases Data Standards and Compilers Manual (1993)

Council of Europe Core Data Index to Historic Buildings and Monuments of the Architectural Heritage (1993)

CIDOC Draft International Core Data Standard for Archaeological Sites and Monuments (1995)

Council of Europe Core Data Standard for Archaeological Sites and Monuments (forthcoming)

RCHME National Monuments Record Core Data Standard (unpublished 1996)

RCHME MIDAS *A Data Standard and Manual for Monument Inventories* (forthcoming 1997)

RCHME and ALGAO Data Standard for SMRs (forthcoming 1997)

MDA *SPECTRUM* Archaeological Guide (forthcoming 1997)

Vocabulary Control

RCHME and EH Thesaurus of Monument Types (1995)

MDA Archaeology Object Name Thesaurus (forthcoming 1997)

Council of Europe European Bronze Age Monuments *A multilingual glossary of archaeological terminology* (draft 1995)

RCHME Thesaurus of Building Materials (unpublished 1996)

RCHME authority lists and thesauri used in NMR databases (unpublished)

Contact details

Dr Gillian Quine
Data Standards Manager
RCHME
National Monuments Record Centre
Kemble Drive
Swindon SN2 2HZ
UK
email: datastd@rchme.gov.uk

CAA 97

The Importance of Metadata to Archaeology: One View from within the Archaeology Data Service

Paul Miller

Abstract

The provision of valuable archaeological data across a medium such as the Internet is all very well, but it is becoming increasingly difficult for potential users of your data to actually find it. The current unstructured indexing of the World Wide Web by search engines such as Alta Vista is insufficient for the needs of the Archaeology Data Service (ADS), but it also appears that many of the more complex indexing schemes available are also unsuitable, largely due to their very complexity. The ADS has undertaken to explore means by which disparate archaeological resources may be coherently yet simply described, and this paper will report upon a number of the issues addressed in developing a suitably encompassing yet streamlined metadata system, before providing a flavour of the manner in which the completed scheme will operate.

1 Introduction

Metadata. This word is increasingly to be seen bandied about by information professionals from a range of disciplines -- including archaeology -- but its meaning remains unclear to many, and the potential benefits are rarely elucidated in such a way as to make sense to the uninitiated (Miller forthcoming).

This paper introduces the concept of metadata for an archaeological audience, and discusses some of the ways in which metadata is -- and might be -- an aid to archaeological endeavour.

An important point to bear in mind with current metadata research is that this international cross-disciplinary effort is proceeding extremely rapidly, such that the content of this paper -- composed whilst sat in the sun on a summer's day in August of 1997 -- runs the risk of being superseded by developments between now and its publication in the -- doubtless wet and horrible -- northern hemisphere Spring of 1998. In an attempt to maintain currency, metadata issues are outlined in general -- and hopefully timeless -- terms, with more detailed issues being referred to by means of pointers to external resources, primarily on the World Wide Web which is itself the main driving force behind much current metadata research.

2 What is metadata?

Metadata is commonly defined simply as 'data about data'. Whilst undeniably correct, this definition is perhaps less helpful than it might be in introducing a potentially confusing topic to readers.

More helpfully, the Archaeology Data Service considers metadata as 'a means of turning *data* into *information* [intelligible and of value to those other than the creator of a resource]'. Metadata, then, may be seen as the extra information associated with any object or resource which allows a viewer to place it in context and make sense of it.

In a traditional paradigm such as paper publication, the metadata for a publication might include the author's name, the title of the publication, the publisher, *etc*. It can be seen, therefore, that the metadata for a book is actually much the same as the cataloguing information that might be recorded for that book by a librarian constructing a library catalogue. Here, as elsewhere, metadata often serves as a generic term for procedures that have been established over many years, rather than being something wholly new. Indeed, some of the initiatives currently thought of as metadata standards have been evolving for many years. The MAchine Readable Cataloging (Library of Congress 1997) system used in libraries all around the world, for example, was originally developed to define the manner in which catalogues should be described for storage on computer tape for transfer between different libraries.

3 Metadata for resource discovery

Metadata is a generic term, used to span all aspects of resource (or data) management and manipulation from discovery to storage and reuse. Each of these -- and other -- areas is extremely important in archaeology and elsewhere, and deserving of greater exploration, but the aspect of metadata attracting greatest interest at present is that of *resource discovery*.

Resource Discovery is the process by which a potential user searches for and locates information of use to them. The process may well also include some means of evaluating the resource's fitness for purpose before it is actually retrieved. With the phenomenal growth of resources on the Internet's World Wide Web, and the need for some means by which those searching on-line might avoid the ever-present danger of information overload (Miller 1996), much of the current research into resource discovery is being directed towards the Web community. Many of the lessons learned on the Web are of equal value off-line and apply as much to searching for books in a library or excavation records in an archive as they do to locating electronic resources in cyberspace.

Whereas many of the best known metadata schemes exist to provide subject-specific descriptions of particular resource types for tightly delimited purposes (MARC to describe the contents of library catalogues or the *Content Standards for Digital Geospatial Metadata* (Federal Geographic Data Committee 1997) to describe digital map data, for example), an important aspiration of those defining the metadata appropriate for resource discovery is to develop a scheme of cross-disciplinary value. It is one thing to develop a means of describing a map, a library book, or an archaeological excavation, and quite another to devise a single system for describing all three. This task is rendered yet more difficult when it is considered that the resulting system must describe resources in a manner which appears intuitive to spatial scientists (looking for a map), librarians (managing their books) and an archaeologist (after the records from an excavation) whilst remaining compact enough as not to prove too daunting to those tasked with entering data into it or retrieving material from it.

4 Dublin Core and the Archaeology Data Service

Given the role of the Archaeology Data Service (Wise and Richards, this volume), and its reliance upon electronic delivery of data, developments in resource discovery are being watched extremely closely (Miller and Wise 1997, Miller and Greenstein 1997), and great hope is being placed in one particular resource discovery initiative; the Dublin Core.

The Dublin Core (Weibel *et al* 1997) arose from an international cross-domain effort to define a means primarily of providing author-generated metadata for small-scale resources on the World Wide Web. This effort has been driven by a programme of four workshops in North America, Europe and Oceania (Miller and Gill 1997), pilot implementation by a number of extremely enthusiastic groups in Europe and elsewhere, and an active electronic mailing list upon which issues are debated between workshops. A fifth workshop is due to be held in the Finnish capital, Helsinki, in October 1997, where attention will be devoted to some of the many ways in which the scope of Dublin Core has been redefined in order to enable its adoption within large resource discovery projects such as the Nordic Metadata Project (1997) and the Arts & Humanities Data Service (Miller and Greenstein 1997).

The definition of the Dublin Core has evolved somewhat since the first workshop in Ohio in 1995 (Weibel *et al* 1995), but is felt to have stabilised - for now - with fifteen elements, each of which is importantly both optional and repeatable, and potentially refinable by means of optional qualification with 'SCHEME', 'SUBELEMENT' or 'LANGUAGE' information.

The fifteen elements are Title, Creator, Subject, Description, Publisher, Contributors, Date, Type, Format, Identifier, Source, Language, Relation, Coverage and Rights, with the official definition of each element available from the Dublin Core's World Wide Web site (Weibel and Miller 1997). An interpretation of these definitions intended specifically for a (UK) Humanities audience is available from the Arts & Humanities Data Service (Miller 1997).

The three optional qualifiers are available in order to allow clarification both of the way in which an element is being used and of the context from which the element value is drawn.

SCHEME is used to identify a controlled terminology or coding scheme from which any value is drawn, allowing the recorder, for example, to identify that dates are drawn from International Standard 8601 and that 1997-06-05 therefore must refer to June rather than May. This qualifier might also be used to identify various specialist thesauri, allowing users to determine the context from within which a particular term was selected.

SUBELEMENT allows the recorder to specify which particular aspect of each of the fifteen elements is being recorded at any given time. The Dublin Core's Coverage element, for example, deals with both spatial and temporal coverage, and allows the entry of text (place names, archaeological periods, *etc.*) as well as various forms of number. Whilst an entry of 'North Lanark' is perfectly acceptable as a coverage, this value becomes more meaningful when qualified with the SUBELEMENT 'placeName' (telling the searcher that 'North Lanark' is the name of a place) or even 'placeName.authority.unitary' (telling the searcher -- and the computer's search engine -- that 'North Lanark' is the name of an administrative Unitary Authority). Further examples of the manner in which SCHEMEs and SUBELEMENTs can be used are available from the Arts & Humanities Data Service (Miller and Greenstein 1997).

Finally, LANG allows the recorder to specify the language in which the *metadata* is expressed. This differs from the Dublin Core's Language element, which defines the language of the *resource*. A copy of Shakespeare's *Hamlet* in the French national library in Paris, for example, may well still be in English (so the Dublin Core Language element will record 'English'), but the cataloguing information -- the metadata -- will most logically be in French, so each Dublin Core element would therefore be qualified by a LANG qualifier recording the value 'fr', the code for French in ISO 639.

5 Resource Discovery versus Content Detail

Although potentially an extremely powerful resource discovery tool, the Dublin Core is by no means capable of replacing entrenched standards such as MARC, CSDGM, or the plethora of smaller standards relevant to archaeology (see Miller and Wise 1997 for a partial list of these), *and nor was it ever intended to*. The Dublin Core -- and any related initiative which follows, arising from the World Wide Web Consortium's work on resource discovery -- is intended *solely* as a resource discovery tool, and the very simplicity which makes it so powerful in this arena renders it almost useless at the more detailed level served by these other standards.

The almost ridiculously obvious, yet architecturally elegant, solution proposed to solve the potential problem of combining subject detail with discipline-neutral generalisation is the Warwick Framework's notion of a metadata 'package' (Lagoze *et al* 1996). Proposed at the second Dublin Core workshop, and developed further by Carl Lagoze and others, the Warwick Framework makes it possible for a 'package' of generalised Dublin Core metadata (tailored for resource discovery in an interdisciplinary environment) to be associated with a 'package' of extremely detailed discipline-specific metadata in any suitable format (tailored directly to the needs of the host discipline). The user thus interacts with the broadly intelligible Dublin Core description until he/she has found the resource and decided it is what they want, at which point they may view far more detailed information relating to such arcana as book binding types or aerial photographic camera apertures. It is thus potentially possible for archaeological data to be recorded in a wide variety of formats, described using any number of metadata syntaxes, and still uniformly searched by means of a single Dublin Core-based distributed catalogue.

This is the premise upon which the Archaeology Data Service is constructing its catalogue, a prototype version of which should be available from http://ads.ahds.ac.uk/ahds/ on the World Wide Web by the time this paper is published.

6 Conclusion

Deployment of metadata throughout archaeology is by no means a panacea for all of the profession's failings but -- especially as the potential for reuse of data within archaeology and beyond continues to grow -- documented adoption of resource description and discovery standards cannot help but increase the reuse value of all those kilometres of rotting paper, wrinkling mylar, and demagnetising magnetic media in rarely visited archives around the world.

For far too long, the archaeological community has demonstrated a depressing degree of insularism in insisting upon barely adequate home-grown solutions to problems rather than adopting and adapting more generic solutions from the world outside our trenches, and our documentation procedures are no exception.

A large number of initiatives in disciplines other than our own have much to offer -- and we, too, have much to offer them. An integrated approach to the recording of metadata about their -- and our -- work is an important step towards closer integration in the future. Let's not throw this opportunity away by adopting a home-grown solution to metadata recording, but rather take part in the ongoing international efforts and shape these emerging standards in such a way that they meet *our* needs, as well as the needs of others.

Bibliography

ISO 639 - "Code for the representation of names of languages", Geneva: International Organisation for Standardisation

ISO 8601 -- "Data elements and interchange formats -- Information interchange -- Representation of dates and times", Geneva: International Organisation for Standardisation

Federal Geographic Data Committee, 1997 Content Standards for Digital Geospatial Metadata April 1997 Draft , http://www.mews.org/nsdi/revis497.pdf

Lagoze, C, Lynch C A and Daniel R, 1996 The Warwick Framework: a container architecture for aggregating sets of metadata , http://cs-tr.cs.cornell.edu:80/Dienst/UI/2.0/Describe/ncstrl.cornell%2fTR96-1593?abstract=warwick

Library of Congress, 1997 MARC home page , http://www.loc.gov/marc/

Miller, P, 1996 Metadata for the Masses, Ariadne, 5 , http://www.ukoln.ac.uk/ariadne/issue5/metadata-masses/

Miller, P, forthcoming *Metadata: an aid to interdisciplinary resource discovery*?, Computers and the Humanities

Miller, P, 1997 Unifying Resource Discovery Metadata for the Humanities: an application based upon the Dublin Core, in Miller, P, Greenstein D (eds), *Discovering Online Resources across the Humanities: a Practical Implementation of the Dublin Core,* Bath, United Kingdom Office for Library and Information Networking, 34-55

Miller, P and Gill T, 1997 Down Under with the Dublin Core, Ariadne, 8 , http://www.ariadne.ac.uk/issue8/canberra-metadata/

Miller, P and Wise A, 1997 Resource Discovery Workshops: Final report from the Archaeology Data Service , http://ads.ahds.ac.uk/ahds/project/metadata/workshop1_final_report.html

Miller, P, Greenstein D (eds), *Discovering Online Resources across the Humanities: a Practical Implementation of the Dublin Core,* Bath, United Kingdom Office for Library and Information Networking

Nordic Metadata Project, 1997 The Nordic Metadata Project home page , http://linnea.helsinki.fi/meta/index.html

Weibel, S, Godby J, Miller E and Daniel R, 1995 OCLC/NCSA Metadata Workshop Report , http://www.oclc.org:5047/oclc/research/publications/weibel/metadata/dublin_core_report.html

Weibel, S and Miller E, 1997 Dublin Core Metadata Element Set: Reference Description . http://purl.org/metadata/dublin_core_elements

Weibel, S, Iannella R and Cathro W, 1997 The 4th Dublin Core Metadata Workshop Report, D-Lib Magazine, June 1997 , http://hosted.ukoln.ac.uk/mirrored/lis-journals/dlib/dlib/dlib/june97/metadata/06weibel.html

Contact details

Paul Miller
Collections Manager
Archaeology Data Service
King's Manor
York YO1 2EP
UK
email: collections@ads.ahds.ac.uk
www: http://ads.ahds.ac.uk/ahds/

Digital Preservation in Archaeology

Alicia Wise and Julian Richards

CAA 97

Abstract

Archaeology is in a special position in that much of the creation of its data results from destruction of primary evidence, making access to data all the more critical in order to test, assess, and subsequently reanalyze and reinterpret both the data and the hypotheses arising from them. Over the years, archaeologists have amassed a vast collection of fieldwork and post-excavation data archives, a significant proportion of which remain unpublished. Access to data, even those which are published, is often difficult or inconvenient at best. The Archaeology Data Service (ADS), established October 1st 1996, is working towards provision of digital data over the Internet through an integrated on-line catalogue to its collections and the collections of partner organisations. The work of the ADS thus proceeds along two tracks: digital preservation and facilitating access to digital information.

1 Archaeological data

Initiatives around the globe are exploring access to and preservation of digital information. Archaeologists in many countries are participating in this research largely because computer technology is becoming more and more common for the recording of and the creation of primary data in our discipline, and in related disciplines. Significant international attention is focused on the use of relational and object-oriented databases to manage and retrieve large amounts of archaeological information and the World Wide Web as a vehicle for the wide dissemination of information about archaeology. Though in recent years CD-based multimedia applications have been gaining popularity among archaeologists, the Internet seems poised to subsume most of these projects.

While it is not possible to describe in detail the myriad number of digital resources which exist, not even the most extensive Web gateways can do that, a sample of international projects is offered below.

Information technology is developing rapidly down under. The Australian National University sponsors a WWW gateway called Archaeology World (Australian National University 1997) and sites accessible through this gateway offer on-line access to databases, images, and texts. As digital preservation is a pressing topic at places such as Australia's National Preservation Office (National Preservation Office 1997), the infrastructure to accommodate widespread archiving in archaeology is developing rapidly.

Canadian archaeologists are well served by CHIN (Canadian Heritage Information Network 1997). Information on this extensive website include an inventory of archaeological artifacts and other objects in Canadian museums, and extensive information about a variety of resources of interest to archaeologists and museums professionals.

Europe is producing a number of promising information technology projects, largely through funding programmes of the European Commission and the European Union. One such project is Aquarelle , a partnership of cultural heritage organisations and software developers in England, France, Greece, and Italy (Aquarelle 1997). The goal of this project is to develop software to allow the international transfer of multimedia folders between museums and cultural resource managers (Dawson, this volume). Another project has resulted in Guder Grave, an impressively designed website containing information about all aspects of the European Bronze Age (Jarl Hansen, this volume and National Museum of Denmark 1997). Currently this resource is available only in Danish, but translations of the web material should make this valuable resource more accessible in countries where Dutch, English, and French are spoken. Europe is also well-served by an extensive web-based gateway, the Archaeological Resource Guide to Europe (Champion and van Leusen 1997).

The Israel Antiquities Authority has developed a centralized database for recording information about all archaeological excavations in the country. Upkeep of this database has been facilitated by the development of a bilingual thesaurus to control terminology entered by excavators, and by a database template distributed to excavators for guiding the construction of recording systems for their projects (Cohen 1996).

In the United Kingdom a variety of resources exist from the relational databases underpinning the National Monuments Records in England, Northern Ireland, Scotland, and Wales to the diverse county-level Sites and Monuments Records. The Council for British Archaeology (CBA) is involved with projects designed to integrate these varied digital resources and others including the British and Irish Archaeological Bibliography (British and Irish Archaeological Bibliography 1997) and an extensive gateway to British Archaeology (Heyworth 1997). CBA projects also include an electronic journal (Internet Archaeology 1997) and a digital archive (Archaeology Data Service 1997).

In the United States there are a wide-variety of good digital resources available over the World Wide Web. One that is frequently used is ArchNet, a virtual library for archaeology maintained by staff at the University of Connecticut's library

(Plunkett and Lizee 1997). ARGOS is a collection of peer-reviewed websites covering classical archaeology which are accessible through a searchable front-end (Beavers and Sonpal 1997). Other projects in the United States include the National Archaeological Database (NADB) which was created by the National Park Service to manage its enormous collection of archaeological survey and excavation data. Recently the Centre for Advanced Spatial Technologies at the University of Arkansas has taken on the challenge of integrating the information in the NADB with a GIS interface (National Park Service and CAST 1997). Additionally, a variety of State Historic Preservation Offices are investing in the creation of large relational databases to maintain their large records of archaeological interventions. Some of these databases have been created with GIS front ends, others are not quite so technically involved, but all are extremely useful resources. Last, but certainly not least, is the Archaeological Data Archive Project at Bryn Mawr University (see Eiteljorg this volume and Eiteljorg 1997).

Worrying is the infrequency with which the long term preservation of these, and other, valuable digital resources is discussed. Two organisations provide notable exceptions. One is the Archaeological Data Archive Project just mentioned. The other is the Archaeology Data Service in the United Kingdom. These two projects share a common interest in *digital archiving and facilitating access to digital information*.

2 The Archaeology Data Service

The idea for a digital archiving service for archaeology in Britain was stimulated in early 1996 by a call for proposals from the Arts and Humanities Data Service (AHDS). The AHDS was then a newly established service of the body responsible for funding all information technology programs in Britain's universities, the Joint Information Systems Committee, and consisted of an Executive at King's College London and one service provider. This first service provider, the History Data Service, is a digital archive for historians residing at the University of Essex Data Archive.

A bid to provide a similar digital archiving service for archaeology was discussed in an informal lunchtime meeting at the Computer Applications in Archaeology UK meeting in York in February 1996 and subsequently developed into a consortium proposal by the Universities of Birmingham, Bradford, Glasgow, Kent at Canterbury, Leicester, Newcastle, Oxford, and York, with the Council for British Archaeology (Richards 1996). An announcement that this bid was successful was made later that spring, the first member of staff was appointed in July, and the Archaeology Data Service began life on October 1st, 1996.

The success of this bid focused on the consortium management approach. Each contributor to the original proposal nominated a representative or representatives to sit on the ADS management committee, in order to guide the service through its development phases. The membership of this management committee has subsequently been broadened to reflect a greater number of perspectives in archaeology. For this reason, a committee member represents the Royal Commissions for Ancient and Historical Monuments in England, Scotland, and Wales. Another member represents the Association of Local Government Archaeological Officers, the body which advocates needs of archaeologists in England and Wales involved in the curation and protection of archaeology during and after the development control process.

The consortium organisation of the ADS offers other strengths as well. Each member of the management committee brings a different range of archaeological and technological skills a different range of hardware and software. This diversity of resources, uniquely possible in a service primarily based in the university sector, means the ADS is in a position to offer a broader range of services than its 2 full-time and 2 part-time funded posts would otherwise allow.

The ADS is hosted by the Archaeology Department at the University of York, but the consortium structure focuses direct attention on the fact that archaeological data archives are dispersed. From the beginning, it has been assumed that the holdings of the ADS would be dispersed among consortium members and would be linked to digital archives held by other organisations. The Internet, existing initiatives to standardise the contents and descriptions of archaeological data, and new standards for metadata (Miller 1996, Wise and Miller 1997) and international communications standard Z39.50 mean that these data do not need to be brought together in one single physical location in order to make them available to the wider community.

There is also a fractal nature to the ADS. Managed by a consortium of experts, the service is also advised by a diverse 40-member advisory committee and is part of the inter-disciplinary and distributed Arts and Humanities Data Service.

The advisory committee consists of British archaeologists from all sub-fields in the discipline: artifact specialists, computer archaeologists, contracting unit staff, cultural resource managers, environmental archaeologists, government-mandated regulatory bodies, independent or avocational archaeologists, museum curators and archivists, scientific archaeologists, underwater archaeologists, university-based researchers and teachers, and others.

The Arts and Humanities Data Service has developed into a cohesive, integrated, yet distributed whole (Burnard and Short 1994, Greenstein 1996, Greenstein and Trant 1996, Ross 1995). Service providers have been appointed to address the digital archiving needs of a variety of disciplines in addition to archaeology and history. These include ancient and modern texts and linguistic corpora at the Oxford Text Archive; broadcasting, music, and theatre at the University of Glasgow's Performing Arts Data Service; and architecture, art history, museum studies and all other aspects of imaging in the arts and humanities at the Surrey Institute of Art and Design's Visual Arts Data Service.

The aims of the ADS are:

1. to collect, describe, catalogue, preserve, and provide user support for digital resources that are created as a product of archaeological research.

2. to take an AHDS-wide responsibility for promoting standards and guidelines for best practice in the creation, description, preservation and use of spatially referenced information.
3. to take, in collaboration with existing agencies, a major role within the UK archaeological community in promoting standards and guidelines for best practice in the creation, description, preservation, and use of digital archaeological research data.

The brief of the ADS is to provide for data generated in the course of archaeological research by British archaeologists, wherever they are working. In theory, therefore, there are no geographical limits on collections but in practice the focus is expected to be on the archaeology of the British Isles. As digital archives for archaeology develop, like the Archaeological Data Archive Project in the United States, it is intended to develop reciprocal archiving policies.

For those classes of archaeological data where there are existing archival bodies the role of the ADS is to collaborate with the appropriate national and local agencies to promote greater use of existing services. In cases where no existing agency has an obvious responsibility, the ADS will act to accession data directly.

The collections policy of the ADS is therefore developing on two fronts to:

1. archiving and preservation of digital data
2. facilitating access to distributed digital information

3 Digital preservation

Archaeology is in a special position in that much of the creation of its data results from the destruction of primary evidence. Increasingly, the digital record may be the only record of precious research materials. With the ever-increasing pace of change in computer hardware and software, in a few years' time that data may be lost forever.

The ADS is trying to ensure that orphaned data sets are not lost and is developing agreements with those organisations that fund archaeological research to ensure that archaeological data sets are offered for deposit and preservation. A range of funding bodies already recognize the importance of digital preservation and either recommend or require that digital data sets be offered to the ADS or other appropriate service providers within the AHDS:

1. British Academy
2. Carnegie Trust
3. Council for British Archaeology
4. Economic and Social Research Council
5. Leverhulme Trust
6. Natural Environment Research Council
7. Wellcome Trust Institute for the History of Medicine

Data sets offered to the ADS or other service providers in the AHDS will be subject to an evaluation procedure before acceptance. This is because timely deposit of digital information is not enough to ensure that it can be preserved and re-used in the future. Thorough documentation of the dataset, the purpose for which it was collected, the ways in which it was recorded and transformed, and the ways in which it is structured are essential for digital archiving. This is because data must be migrated to new software, operating systems, and hardware platforms as technology changes. Without thorough documentation the information necessary for accurate data migration is missing.

There is another reason that data sets offered to the ADS will be evaluated before acceptance. Computers have been used to create and record archaeological data for more than three decades. There is therefore an enormous backlog of digital data which could be preserved. More and more data are appearing, however, that can only be archived in digital formats The ADS must prioritize its collections procedures. It will not be possible to hold all computerised archaeological data: instead those data which have secondary use value and are documented thoroughly to facilitate reuse must come first.

At present there is very little information about either the cost of digital archiving, or the level of demand for re-use from an accessible archaeological archive. To inform its collections policy, the ADS is collecting information about these issues by implementing a number of archiving pilot studies.

3.1 Pilot studies in digital preservation

In order to develop appropriate procedures for handing digital archaeological data, a series of pilot projects are being organised. These pilots project explore two main aspects of digital archiving:

1. Archiving specific data types (e.g. texts, CAD, GIS, databases, geophysics, text)
2. Archiving data derived from a variety of sources (e.g. excavation, buildings recording, museum archives)

Pilot projects in development or currently underway by the ADS include:

CAD Archiving , The RCHME has proposed developing a CAD pilot project with the ADS. We will be looking to the established expertise of the Archaeological Data Archive Project at Bryn Mawr University for collaboration on this project.

Electronic Publishing , Internet Archaeology, a fully electronic journal, and the ADS are currently identifying a project or projects which are ready for both publication and archiving. The aim of this pilot would be to explore the issues related to a synthetic article published electronically and based on a fully functional database archived with the ADS.

Fieldwork Archiving , The ADS is working with English Heritage, a government CRM body, and contracting units, such as the Oxford Archaeological Unit, to identify and develop one or more fieldwork archiving pilots. The objectives of these pilot projects will be to determine the costs of digital archiving; the types of archaeological data which should be digitally archived; the types of digital data which have commercial value, the types of documentation necessary to inter-connect artifact, paper, and digital archives; and the information/training necessary to ensure archaeologists can reuse the digital archive.

Text Archiving , With the backing of the ADS, the Council for British Archaeology has applied successfully to the Fast Track Digitisation programme for funding to digitise its occasional and research report series. This will involve over 105 volumes of text and images saved in PDF format, and the aim of this pilot is to examine strategies for the delivery of electronic texts.

3.2 Guides to good practice in digital archiving

In its role of promulgating standards the ADS is also developing a series of Guides to Good Practice. These are primarily aimed at the creators and depositors of digital data and will provide advice on appropriate archive file formats as well as covering the generation of metadata. There are four explicitly archaeological guides covering:

1. Excavation and fieldwork archives
2. Geographical Information Systems
3. Geophysics
4. Satellite imagery and aerial photographs

Guides produced by other service providers will cover related areas, such as databases, sound and video images (Wissenburg 1997).

4 Facilitating access to digital information

Widespread access to digital information serves two important functions: it improves communication about archaeology and it aids the preservation of digital data. 'Improving communication' happens in a variety of ways: researchers gain access to primary data too expensive to print conventionally or that were never printed at all, anyone with Internet access gains access to archaeological information even if they have no access to a specialist library, spatially distributed archaeological resources can be discovered without costly trips to the numerous archives, museums, SMRs, and NMRs which have developed, and archaeological synthesis across regional and national boundaries generally becomes easier. 'Preservation of digital data' is aided when digital datasets are downloaded and used in different computing environments thus increasing the number of formats and operating systems datasets are migrated into.

It is necessary to develop national and international strategies for digital archiving in archaeology. The ADS is working closely with national and local agencies in the UK to develop a coherent policy for the preservation of digital fieldwork archives and other datasets. Any digital archiving strategy must recognize that not all digital information can be preserved, and that clear definitions of those categories of digital data which have a secondary usage value, and thus need to be preserved, are available. It is also necessary to distinguish between data which is to be made available for open public access and that which is to be stored and maintained but not yet released. Wherever possible it is desirable to negotiate research access to such data, whilst recognising that there may be cases (for example, copyright restrictions pending full publication of a project, or developer funding) where the data depositor still has a financial interest in the data set and will wish to maintain a degree of control over it. Finally, developing methods to inter-connect the growing numbers of digital datasets held in different archaeological organisations, and making these as easily accessible as possible, is an important goal for digital archiving strategies.

4.1 Case studies

Two examples clearly illustrate the importance of facilitating access to archaeological information: the first is the experience of an undergraduate archaeologist in Britain and the other is the experience of a professional archaeological consultant.

Gigi Signorelli, a recent graduate of the University of York Archaeology Department, did an undergraduate dissertation entitled "Agricultural Strategies in North East Scotland: Barley Production from the Prehistoric to the Medieval Period". Part of this research required him to assemble a thorough record of all archaeological sites in which evidence for any kind of cereal crop was collected in this region and for this time period. A thorough literature search in the library revealed the few sources as evidence for cereal production were often buried within texts instead of being included as main features of the title or subject keywords (a common frustration in archaeology). His next line of attack was to contact the National Monuments Record of Scotland in Edinburgh. He paid a visit to Edinburgh on his limited student budget, and arrived to discover that the kind of information he needed was not instantly available from the NMRS and that it would be better for him to contact or visit the various SMRs in his region of interest. Out of money, and quickly running out of time, he considered changing his research topic. In consulting with staff in his department, he was told about a computerised database of archaeological plant remains created by Philippa Tomlinson and Allan Hall (Tomlinson and Hall 1996) which he could access over the World Wide Web. In Gigi's own words "Searching through the ABCD gave me a very good starting point for my research and it actually provided me with the main material I needed for the entire project." (Signorelli 1997).

A second case study also highlights the importance of making information in existing archaeological archives more accessible to potentia-- important for both the staff and the users of those archives. A professional archaeological consultant, Dr. Catherine Mortimer, is completing a study of cruciform brooches from Anglian contexts in England, and is faced with the challenge of making sure she has identified all known examples of this artifact class. No newcomer to her research topic, Dr. Mortimer worked with several hundred British examples of cruciform brooches for her PhD research and only needs to fill in any gaps in her database. To accomplish this straight-forward task, however, has been anything but easy. She has been forced to write to the National Monuments Record in England and 43 county Sites and Monuments Records. Luckily, most of her queries have met with polite and informed responses from helpful SMR staff members. Think of the time, though, that has been required to process the same query 44 different times and the effort that will be involved in making sense of responses formatted in 44 different ways.

4.2 Pilot studies

Just as the ADS is developing pilot studies to examine issues of digital preservation, so to is it collaborating with outside organisations to examine issues of connecting distributed digital resources. Again, there are two major areas of research:

1. Building digital connections between existing archives
2. Re-use of digital datasets

Accessing Scotland's Past , Foremost among these pilots is Accessing Scotland's Past (ASP) which aims to build digital connections between existing archives, in this case the National Monuments Record (NMR) of Scotland and the Sites and Monuments Records (SMRs) of the Shetland Isles and the West of Scotland.

Accessing Scotland's Past is a pilot project between the ADS, Royal Commission on the Ancient and Historical Monuments of Scotland (RCAHMS), the Shetland Amenity Trust, and the West of Scotland Archaeology Service. Funding for the pilot comes from the Scottish Cultural Resources Access Network (SCRAN) and the Joint Information Systems Committee (JISC).

The goal is to interconnect data held in a NMR, two SMRs, and the ADS. A key research aim of this pilot is to prototype the ADS metadata cataloguing system. International communication standards such as ISO 23950 (better known as Z39.50) and cataloguing standards such as Dublin Core metadata are the linchpins for this pilot.

Museums Pilot , A possible pilot study demonstrating the integration of archives distributed across museums and the ADS is under development. Partners for this project are currently being sought. Museums in Britain are the official repositories for all artifact and paper-based archives resulting from archaeological fieldwork. Many museums are facing two crises: one a lack of space as the quantity of recovered artifacts grows and the second a lack of resources for digital archiving as archaeologists begin to deposit computer diskettes.

University Teaching and Learning , A pilot is under development between the ADS and the Association for Environmental Archaeology. The idea is to develop a suite of web-based teaching materials about environmental archaeology which will be used to facilitate access to and reuse of digital datasets mounted at the ADS.

4.3 Workshops

Given that the point of preservation is to enable re-use, the ADS is also developing a range of end user services. The ADS takes responsibility, in collaboration with the AHDS, for the education of researchers and accordingly organizes appropriate training courses for both data providers (e.g. methods of documentation), and data users (e.g. network access tools). The ADS publicises its activities, not only through the central work of the AHDS Executive, but also through its own Web pages, conference presentations, and through a bi-annual hardcopy newsletter circulated widely throughout the archaeological community.

5 Conclusion

In summary, a variety of initiatives are underway at the Archaeology Data Service in collaboration with UK and international partners. The aim of these initiatives is to enable the collection, description, cataloguing preservation and re-use of all forms of digital data in archaeology. It is recognized that without widespread input from all stakeholders within and outside of the archaeological community, it will be impossible to develop workable solutions that address all of our very real needs.

In 1997 one millennium is drawing to a close and the digital age has already begun in archaeology. Now is the time to tackle the difficult issues surrounding preservation of the digital data we are actively creating before such a back-log develops that irreplaceable archaeological information is lost forever.

Bibliography

Aquarelle, 1997 Aquarelle, http://aqua.inria.fr

Archaeology Data Service, 1997 Archaeology Data Service, http://ads.ahds.ac.uk/

Australian National University, 1997 Archaeology World, http://artalpha.anu.edu.au/web/arc/arcworld.htm

Beavers, A F, and Sonpal, H, 1997. ARGOS, http://argos.evansville.edu/

British and Irish Archaeological Bibliography, 1997 British and Irish Archaeological_Bibliography, http://britac3.britac.ac.uk/cba/bab.html

Burnard, L, and Short, H, 1994 An Arts and Humanities Data Service, report of a Feasibility Study commissioned by the Information Systems Sub-Committee of the Joint Information Systems Committee of the Higher Education Funding Councils.

Canadian Heritage Information Network, 1997 Canadian Heritage Information Network, http://www.chin.gc.ca/

Champion, S, and van Leusen, M, 1997 Archaeological Resource Guide to Europe, http://www.bham.ac.uk/ARGE/

Cohen, R, 1996 Integration of Distributed Databases, *Archeologia E Calcolatori,* 7, 831-835.

Eiteljorg, H, 1997 Archaeological Data Archive Project, http://csaws.brynmawr.edu:443/web1/adaparchive.html

Greenstein, D, 1996 Humanities Computing in the Digital Age: Present Perspectives and Future Trends, *Times Higher Education Supplement,* April.

Greenstein, D, and Trant, J, 1996 The Arts and Humanities Data Service: Collecting digital research data; building a framework for digital resource preservation and interchange, *Ariadne,* 4, http://ukoln.bath.ac.uk/ariadne/issue4/
Heyworth, M, 1997 Council for British Archaeology, http://britac3.britac.ac.uk/cba/
Internet Archaeology 1997, http://intarch.ac.uk/
Miller, A P, 1996 Metadata for the Masses, *Ariadne,* 5, http://www.ukoln.ac.uk/ariadne/issue5/metadata-masses/
National Museum of Denmark, 1997 Guder & Grave, http://www.natmus.min.dk/kulturnet/
National Park Service and CAST, 1997 National Archaeology Database, http://www.cast.uark.edu/other/nps/nadb/
National Preservation Office, 1997 Preservation and Digital Information, http://www.nla.gov.au/dnc/tf2001/padi/padi.html
Plunkett, T, and Lizee, J, 1997 ArchNet, http://spirit.lib.uconn.edu/ArchNet/ArchNet.html
Richards, J D, 1996 The Archaeology Data Service, *Archaeological Computing Newsletter,* 46, 19-23.
Ross, S, 1995 Preserving and maintaining electronic resources in the visual arts for the next century?, *Information Services and Use,* 15,373-384.
Signorelli, G, 1997 My first approach to and use of the Archaeobotanical Computer Database (ABCD), *Arts and Humanities Data Service Newsletter,* 2, http://www.kcl.ac.uk/projects/ahds/public/newslet/newsl1_2.htm
Tomlinson, P, and Hall, A, 1996 A review of the archaeological evidence for food plants from the British Isles: an example of the use of the Archaeobotanical Computer Database (ABCD), *Internet Archaeology,* 1, http://intarch.ac.uk/journal/issue1/tomlinson_index.html
Wise, A L, and Miller, P, 1997 Why metadata matters in archaeology, *Internet Archaeology,* 2, http://intarch.ac.uk/issue2/wise_index.html
Wissenburg, A, 1997 Guides to Good Practice of the Arts and Humanities Data Service, http://www/kcl.ac.uk/projects/ahds/public/guides.htm#create

Contact details

Alicia Wise and Julian Richards
Archaeology Data Service
Department of Archaeology
University of York
King's Manor
York YO1 2EP
UK
email: info@ads.ahds.ac.uk
http://ads.ahds.ac.uk/

ARCHAEOLOGY
IN THE
AGE OF THE INTERNET

CAA 97

Section 6
Geophysics and Remote Sensing

CAA 97

The Use of Ground-Penetrating Radar on Small Prehistoric Sites in the Upper Midwestern United States

Clark A. Dobbs, David L. Maki, Drew M. Forsberg

Abstract

The use of ground-penetrating radar on prehistoric sites in the United States remains relatively uncommon because of its perceived expense and the assumption that radar works well only on large, complex sites. Recent studies at sites in the Upper Midwest indicate that these concerns are no longer completely valid. One such site is 21AN106, a 2,000 year old prehistoric camp located north of Minneapolis, Minnesota. In 1996, IMA Consulting conducted a radar study at this site as part of data recovery before disturbance of the site by a pipeline expansion project. Initial testing of the site suggested that it consisted of a series of thin loci of artifacts scattered across a relatively large area at the base of a sand dune. The radar study used a 450 MHz antenna over a 10 metre by 85 metre corridor across the site and successfully identified a series of very small clusters of artifacts. This information allowed excavation at the site to be tightly focused, reducing overall project costs. Further, residues from ceramics within the artifact clusters provided evidence that corn was used at the site between AD 200-300, seven centuries earlier than had been previously documented in the Upper Midwest.

1 Introduction

Geophysical survey methods — particularly ground-penetrating radar — are still only episodically used on archaeological projects in the Midwestern United States. These methods are sometimes viewed with scepticism by regulators and clients because of the perceived expense of such studies and the notion that such methods 'don't work' on many of the archaeological properties found in this portion of the world. Our experience in recent years, however, suggests that the expense of geophysical surveys is often far outweighed by the fine-scale data they provide for the analysis, interpretation, and excavation of archaeological sites.

Geophysical survey data becomes particularly important when sites are to be disturbed by construction projects and require data recovery ('rescue archaeology') before construction may begin. The costs of archaeological data recovery may be quite high and project sponsors are justifiably concerned about containing costs. However, when construction is delayed because archaeological sites were inadequately evaluated or characterised, the *total* costs to the project in down time, delayed schedules, or missed delivery dates can rapidly become quite large. The actual costs of geophysical survey, when considered in this context, are relatively small.

During the last several years, IMA Consulting (IMAC) staff have been integrating geophysical methods into our cultural resource management tool-kit. Although our primary focus has been to develop practical systems and applications for geophysical studies within the context of cultural resource management, an equally important concern has been to integrate geophysical studies into broader theoretical issues in archaeology, particularly intra-site analysis and interpretation.

In this paper, we review one example of this approach: the integration of ground-penetrating radar into a data recovery project at site 21AN106 in the north-central United States.

2 21AN106: site and project description

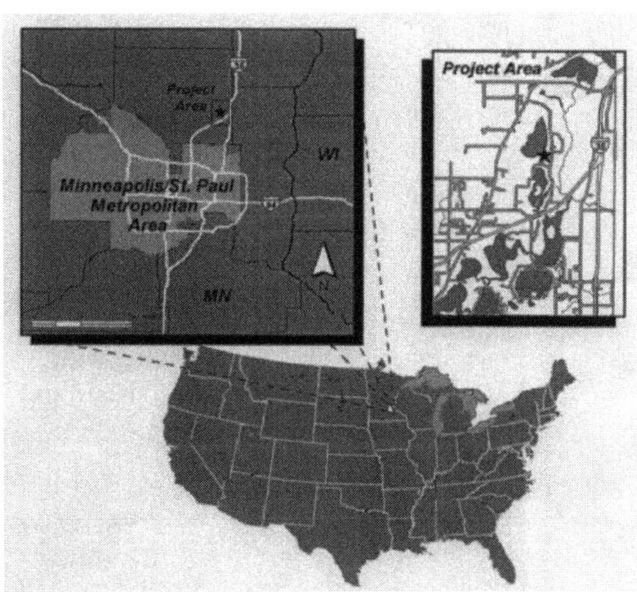

Figure 1. Map of the study area

21AN106 is small archaeological site situated on a small dune between Crossways and Rondeau lakes in the Anoka Sand Plain a few tens of miles north of the cities of Minneapolis and St. Paul, Minnesota (see Fig. 1). Initial testing of the site in 1995 indicated it contained a series of thin artifact and rock concentrations scattered discontinuously both horizontally and vertically across the dune. Ceramics from the site suggested that it fell broadly within the Middle and Late-Middle Woodland periods, ca. 1,500 to 2,200 years ago. Ploughing, erosion, and animal burrowing had substantially disturbed the upper 50 centimetres of the site.

2.1 Physical setting

The Anoka Sand Plain is a particularly distinctive geomorphic region within Minnesota. The Sand Plain was initially formed by glacial outwash at the end of the last Wisconsin glaciation and covers an area of approximately 2,200 km^2 in east-central Minnesota (Wright 1972:535-536). Since glaciation, the topography of the Anoka Sand Plain has been modified by a number of processes. Ice-block depressions have filled with water to form small kettle lakes and wetlands. Streams have formed shallow valleys and terraces. Finally, aeolian activity during warm and dry climatic episodes when vegetation was sparse formed numerous sand dunes that are still prominent on the landscape.

The age of the aeolian activity is uncertain. Keen and Shane (1990:863) suggest that the main period of dune formation was during the mid-Holocene dry period about 7,500-6,000 years BP. However, other studies suggest both earlier and later periods of aeolian activity occurred as well. A peat deposit, buried by some 24 feet of dune sand, at a nearby location yielded a radiocarbon date of 9,210 +/- 90 years BP (Donohue and Associates 1990). A recent investigation (Ketz et al. 1996) at a site located to the southwest of 21AN106 encountered a buried soil beneath about 2 metres of aeolian sand. A radiocarbon date of ~2,500 years BP was obtained on disseminated organic carbon associated with the A-horizon of the buried soil. Moreover, historic accounts of dune activity exist (Winchell and Upham 1888:418), and this geomorphic process can be observed in specific locations even today (Keen 1985:8). It is likely therefore that the aeolian history is complicated, and that several periods of landscape instability are recorded in the aeolian sediments and landforms.

The lakes along the Rice Creek drainage are predominantly shallow. A topographic map (United States Geological Survey 1993[1967]) of the area indicates that most of the lakes—including Crossways and Rondeau lakes—are no deeper than 5 feet. Only Peltier and Centreville lakes, located 2 to 5 miles to the south, are deeper than 15 feet. Shallower lakes in this region would have been particularly sensitive to changes in the amounts of precipitation, surface runoff, and groundwater. Lake levels may have fluctuated frequently, and area lakes may have dried completely. Changes in available water would have affected communities of plant and animals living in and around the lakes, thereby influencing the subsistence and settlement practices of human inhabitants relying upon those resources as well.

A model of Holocene vegetation and climate history for the Anoka Sand Plain has been constructed based on pollen analysis of lake sediment cores taken at Lake Ann in Sherburne County, Minnesota (Keen and Shane 1990). The patterns observed at Lake Ann compare favourably with other regional vegetation and climate histories (Bradbury et al. 1993; Webb III et al. 1993), with allowances made for local variations.

During the Holocene, the Anoka Sand Plain experienced a succession of changes in climate and vegetation (Keen and Shane 1990). In the Early Holocene, immediately following deglaciation, pollen records at Lake Ann indicate that spruce parkland became dominant by about 11,000 years BP. Between 10,000-9,100 years BP, a warming trend is indicated. Spruce parkland was replaced by a mixed conifer-hardwood forest.

The Mid-Holocene (9,100-4,000 years BP) brought severe changes in climate, which Keen and Shane (1990) divide into three major episodes: 9,100-6,500; 6,500-5,100; and 5,100-4,000 years BP. Each of these episodes is characterised by a sequence of drought and reduced vegetation cover, increased flux of aeolian sediment, a return to higher precipitation and greater vegetation cover, and a slow decline in aeolian flux (Keen and Shane 1990,1653).

Decreases in precipitation and increases in temperature led to the development of prairie vegetation. Lake levels were substantially lower during these periods of lower precipitation and higher evapotranspiration (Bradbury et al. 1993; Keen and Shane 1990). The combination of open vegetation conditions and lower water tables allowed the sediments of the Anoka Sand Plain to be eroded, transported, and redeposited by strong northwesterly winds, resulting in significant dune formation (Keen 1985). The pollen record reflects these episodes of dune formation by an increase in sage and ragweed pollen, plant types that colonise disturbed ground. Increases in precipitation and decreases in temperature produced increases in forest vegetation. Aeolian activity decreased correspondingly.

The Late Holocene (4,000 years BP to present) is characterised by a general trend toward modern climatic conditions (Bradbury et al. 1993; Keen and Shane 1990). In the Anoka Sand Plain, prairie vegetation decreased while forest vegetation (pine and oak) increased. Lake levels appear to have reached their maximum extent between 3,500 and 4,000 years ago (cf. Bradbury et. al. 1993; Abbott, Binford, Brenner, and Kelts 1997). Although evidence for short term fluctuations in climate during historic times (e.g. the Medieval Warm Period and the Little Ice Age) has been found elsewhere (Bradbury et al. 1993; Grimm 1981), no evidence was observed at Lake Ann (Keen and Shane 1990). Nevertheless, development of hardwood vegetation in the Big Woods south of the Anoka Sand Plain about 300 years BP corresponds to the cooler climate of the Little Ice Age (Grimm 1981).

At the time of initial Euro-American settlement, areas of good drainage in the Anoka Sand Plain were dominated by open oak groves interspersed with tall grass prairie, whereas areas of poor drainage were marked by mixed hardwoods, sedges, marsh grass, and tamarack (Agricultural Experimental Station 1980). In 1847, the earliest land surveyors characterised the Rice Creek drainage as an area of "tamarac [sic] swamp and floating marses [sic] with spots of timbered highland" (United States Bureau of Land Management 1850-1963?). The shallow lakes and drainage ways along Rice Creek may have fostered stands of wild rice (Jenks 1901:1122-1123). Where urbanisation has not altered the landscape, this basic vegetation pattern still remains today.

In summary, the Sand Plain is a complex network of small streams, lakes, and wetlands interspersed with dunes, small stream terraces, and small upland areas composed of glacial till. Each of these features contains distinctive suites of plant and animal resources ranging from fish, turtles, small mammals and wild rice along the streams and lakes to patches of mixed forest containing maple and oak in the uplands. This mosaic of seasonally available resources made the Sand Plain a particularly attractive location for prehistoric people during certain periods in the past. At the same time, the landforms and vegetation of the Sand Plain are particularly susceptible to relatively minor shifts in temperature and precipitation. Thus, the Sand Plain is an ideal venue for fine-scale analysis of the interaction between culture and environment.

2.2 Cultural setting

There is evidence that all of the major cultural traditions in Minnesota were present on the Anoka Sand Plain at one time or another during the last 11,000 years. However, a dramatic increase in human activity occurred approximately 500 BC, with the beginning of the Woodland period, and continued until about AD 700-800. The most striking aspect of this period is the presence of numerous sites containing Middle Woodland materials related to the Havana Hopewell complex of Illinois, some 500 miles to the south.

The term 'Middle Woodland' subsumes the complex cultures that developed along the Ohio, Illinois, and Mississippi River valley's between roughly 2,200 and 1,800 years ago. These cultures are distinctive and are best known for the appearance of complex and sophisticated mound and mortuary centres, long-distance trade in exotic raw materials (e.g. copper, marine shell, obsidian), increased population density, and the first use of corn as a cultigen in eastern North America. The major Middle Woodland centres are in Ohio and Illinois, although Middle Woodland influence is seen at many sites throughout the midcontinental region. Although the appropriate interpretation of Middle Woodland culture and interaction remains a matter of debate, it is clear the this culture represents a major florescence of Native American culture some 2,000 years ago.

The Anoka Sand Plain contains the most northerly Middle Woodland centre, which is represented by the Howard Lake phase. Although there are no radiocarbon dates from Howard Lake sites, the chronological position of this phase is estimated to be 800 BC to AD 200 (Johnson 1971). The large number of Middle Woodland sites in the Anoka Sand Plain indicate that it was an important population centre (Dobbs et al. 1990; Harrison 1978; Wendt 1986, 1987a, 1987b, 1988) and several large conical Middle Woodland mounds are present in the area. Howard Lake ceramics are quite similar to the Havana Hopewell materials of Illinois and artifacts made of exotic raw materials, particularly copper, have been found in this area.

The Howard Lake Phase appears to parallel the rise and subsequent decline of Middle Woodland farther to the south. There are several subsequent Woodland phases on the Sand Plain, and sporadic use of the region continued until the time of European contact. However, the most intense period of Woodland use of the region appears to encompass about eight centuries from ca. 2,200 years ago until around 1,400 years ago and is documented by over 300 sites within several miles of 21AN106.

There appears to be a distinct site hierarchy within the Middle and later Woodland sites in this region. Several large sites, most commonly associated with mounds, appear to have been used over extended periods of time. Many other sites are smaller in scale and may or may not be associated with mounds. Finally, there are a number of small sites that appear to have been used on an occasional basis for specific tasks. Although these sites tend to have low artifact density and few, if any, cultural features, analysis of their function and position within the landscape may provide important clues to the natural and/or cultural aspects of the Middle and Middle-to-Late Woodland florescence on the Anoka Sand Plain. 21AN106 is of one these small, ephemeral sites and research at the site was directed toward determining its function and role within the larger Woodland settlement system.

2.3 21AN106 project description

Northern Natural Gas Company (Northern) owns and operates an interstate natural gas pipeline system that transports gas throughout the midwestern United States. As part of an expansion project of its system in 1996, Northern proposed to construct an additional pipeline segment (known as a loopline) 25 feet north of its existing natural gas pipeline in Anoka County, Minnesota. To comply with federal environmental regulations, Northern commissioned a number of studies to evaluate the effect that its proposed project would have on the environment. One of these studies was designed to locate and evaluate any cultural properties that would be affected by the project.

A file search and Phase I cultural resource survey of the pipeline route revealed that the proposed loopline would cross archaeological site 21AN106 (Breakey 1995). Subsequent evaluation of this site (Dobbs and Breakey 1995) demonstrated that the site contained clusters of fire-cracked rock (FCR), ceramics, and other artifacts scattered within the dune from the ground surface to roughly 80 centimetres below surface. The ceramics appeared to be Middle and/or Middle-Late Woodland in age. The physical setting of the site adjacent to two lakes and within a larger cluster of archaeological sites suggested that a careful study of both the artifacts from the site and its internal settlement pattern could provide important information about the evolution of Middle Woodland settlement patterns and systems within the Anoka Sand Plain. Based on this information, regulatory agencies concluded the site was eligible for listing on the National Register of Historic Places and that excavation of the portion of the site to be affected by pipeline construction would be required if the site could not be avoided. An analysis of the pipeline route and the various environmental constraints at this particular site demonstrated that the site could not be avoided, and data recovery was selected as the most suitable treatment option for the site.

Developing an excavation plan for the site posed several key problems. Some of the most important information that the site might yield was in the structure and patterning of the deposits within the site itself. However, the area to be disturbed by construction was roughly 3 metres wide, extended 85 metres across the length of the site, and cultural materials were buried to a depth of up to 80 centimetres. A complete excavation of this large area was well outside both the scope of the budget for the entire project and beyond what could be justified by the information present at the site. Mechanical stripping of the entire area was also considered. However, the sandy soils of the dune were prone to collapse, and damage to the site surface in these types of conditions would have been very difficult to prevent. Moreover, the concentrations of materials at the site were relatively small and subtle to identify. Mechanical stripping could have easily destroyed such concentrations before the were recognised.

Various sampling approaches to the site were also considered but were rejected for several reasons. A systematic sampling design had been used during initial testing of the site and this approach had provided a reasonable picture of the variability of materials within the site. However, what was particularly important was an understanding of the *patterning* of cultural debris across the site, the internal consistency of this patterning, and its relationship to the immediately adjacent lake and wetland margins. While only a sample of artifact concentrations within the site were to be excavated, it was essential that the totality of the patterning of these concentrations and any other features present be understood. Finally, both Northern and the regulatory agencies were concerned that the sandy soils of the area might create conditions that could require a larger working area during construction than would be excavated by the archaeologists.

3 Radar study at 21AN106

Geophysical survey of the entire construction corridor seemed a reasonable way to identify patterning of cultural materials, and several different geophysical methods were evaluated. Soil resistance was immediately eliminated since it could not identify the types of subtle patterning present at the site. Magnetic survey using a fluxgate gradiometer was considered but quickly eliminated when it became clear that the background signal from the existing buried pipeline would overwhelm any magnetic signals created by cultural material.

Finally, ground-penetrating radar (GPR) was evaluated. Our evaluation concluded that radar would not be affected by the proximity of the existing pipeline and could provide information on both the depth and horizontal distribution of cultural materials. The sandy sediments at the site provided an ideal medium for radar survey and, because the site was within a dune, the only natural sediments present should be wind-blown sands. Any rock within the site would therefore have to be of cultural origin. Finally, individual pieces of FCR and concentrations of FCR and artifacts identified during the initial testing were six inches or greater in diameter. Initial calculations demonstrated that targets of this size could be resolved and identified by radar using a 450 MHz antenna.

Based on these considerations, we concluded that the use of GPR at 21AN106 had a reasonable chance of identifying the types of cultural information we wanted to recover, and a radar survey was included as the first step in the excavation process (Maki and Forsberg 1996).

3.1 Basic principals of GPR

GPR sends high frequency radio waves into the ground with a transmitter antenna. Some of these waves are reflected back to the surface, while of the rest of this wave energy either continues to penetrate the soil or is scattered and/or absorbed (called attenuation). The energy that is reflected back to the surface is picked up by a receiver antenna. The time it takes the wave to travel from the transmitter to the subsurface feature and back to the receiver, is the *two way travel time*. The transmitter and receiver are dragged across the ground surface at a fixed interval (see Fig. 2), creating a two dimensional plot of distance versus travel time.

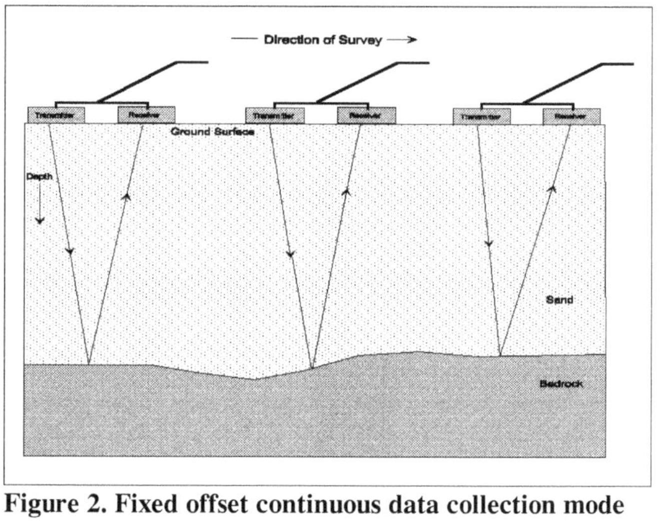

Figure 2. Fixed offset continuous data collection mode

The response plotted is dependent upon the geometry of the subsurface target. A planar feature beneath the surface (such as a change in soil stratigraphy or water content) will appear as a planar anomaly, roughly proportional to the actual subsurface feature. A subsurface object will appear as an inverted hyperbolic shape. This is due to the cone shaped geometry of the radar pulse as it travels beneath the surface (see Fig. 3). The forward edge of the cone encounters the object first and a two way travel time is plotted. As the cone moves over the object this travel time approaches a minimum. The top of the hyperbola corresponds to the true horizontal location and estimated depth of the object.

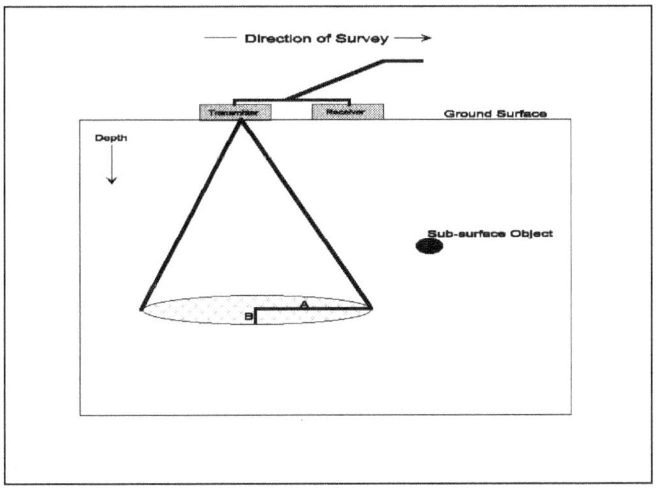

Figure 3. Geometry of the electromagnetic pulse beneath the ground surface

The velocity which the wave travels through the soil varies with soil type. Knowing the soil type at a particular site allows one to *estimate* this velocity. Knowing the travel time and estimated velocity of the wave, a depth to the subsurface reflector can be *estimated* by the following equation:

depth = velocity * (time/2)

The depth to which GPR can penetrate varies with soil type. The attenuation and dielectric properties of the soil change as a function of moisture content and density. Generally, depth of penetration is greater in dry sandy soils and is reduced in moist clayey soils.

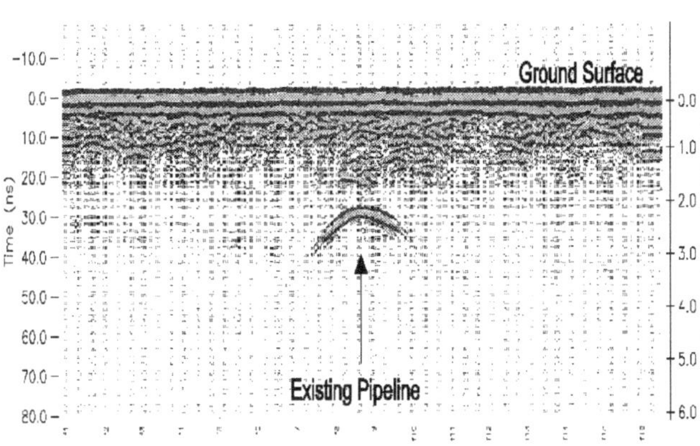

Figure 4. A typical GPR response from a subsurface target. The left axis is the two way travel time. The right axis is the estimated depth. The markers along the bottom of the plot indicate distance along the transect in meters.

The resolution of the radar data varies with the frequency of the wave. Higher frequencies have greater resolution but less depth of penetration. For example, a 450 MHz antenna penetrates from zero to four metres into the soil with the ability to detect objects on the order of centimetres. A 20 MHz antenna penetrates tens of metres into the earth with a resolution on the order of metres.

The aeolian dune topography at 21AN106 is nearly ideal for high resolution GPR data collection. The homogenous sands permit sufficient depth of penetration to allow the use of a high frequency antenna. For this reason the decision was made to use a high resolution 450 MHz antenna. The performance of this antenna was tested by collecting data over a known subsurface object (the existing Northern pipeline) at the onset of the survey (see Fig. 4). This test confirmed the depth of penetration and resolution of the antenna was sufficient for this soil type.

3.2 Radar survey design

Complete areal coverage of the loopline corridor at a depth of one metre below surface was the objective of the survey design process. The loopline corridor extended 6 metres to the north of the proposed pipeline and 4 metres to the south of the proposed line. The length of the project area was 85 metres.

GPR data was collected in 20 metre long transects. The spacing of these transects was based upon the GPR illumination equation. The equation is as follows (Annan and Cosway 1994):

$A = (\lambda / 4) + (depth / (k-1)^{0.5})$

where λ = wavelength = velocity/frequency

k = relative permittivity

B = A / 2

The following parameters were used in the above equation to arrive at the illumination radius given below:

At 450 MHz and an estimated velocity of 0.15 m/ns: λ = .333 metres, k was estimated at a value 4, depth used was one metre. The dimensions are.

A = 0.66 metres

B = 0.33 metres

These dimensions resulted in a choice of 0.5 metres as the transect interval for the survey. At a 0.5 metre transect interval there is an overlap of 0.16 metres between each transect, resulting in complete areal coverage of the corridor.

Calculations were next made to determine whether targets would be visible to the radar, and if so, what was the size of the smallest detectable target. There are two conservative rules of thumb to predict whether the target will be visible. First, a contrast in electrical properties of the surrounding soil matrix (host) and the target material is required. The power reflectivity expression (Annan and Cosway 1992) is a measure of this contrast. The expression is as follows:

$P_r = | (k_{host} - k_{target}) / (k_{host} + k_{target}) |^2$

A value greater than 0.01 for P_r indicates the target will be visible. Assuming a host material of dry sand (k = 4) and a target of FCR/ceramic (k = 6) results in a power reflectivity of 0.0102 which is greater than 0.01. Therefore the power reflectivity should be sufficient to make targets visible to GPR. The second rule of thumb is a ratio of target depth to smallest target dimension of less than or equal to 10:1. This implies that at one metre below surface a target size of 10 centimetres should be visible.

The size of targets visible to the radar was estimated using the following equation (Annan and Cosway 1992):

frequency used = 150 / (x * K_{host}) where x = resolution required

At 450 MHz and in dry sand, solving for x results in a minimum target size of 8.3 centimetres.

In short, FCR/ceramic clusters should be visible to the GPR. The diameter of these detectable clusters should be on the order of 10 centimetres.

3.3 System settings

Data were collected using the pulseEKKO 1000 GPR in fixed offset reflection mode. The frequency used was 450 MHz with an antenna separation of 0.25 metres and a 100 ns time window. A stepsize of 0.05 metres with a stacks setting of 32 and a sampling interval of 200 ps was used (32 readings were taken every 5 centimetres and the result was averaged).

3.4 Field methods

The centrelines of the existing pipeline and proposed loopline were surveyed and marked by Northern Natural surveyors. The loopline right-of-way was surveyed by IMAC at the onset of the project. A grid system was then established over the site for later use during the excavation phase of the project (see Fig. 5).

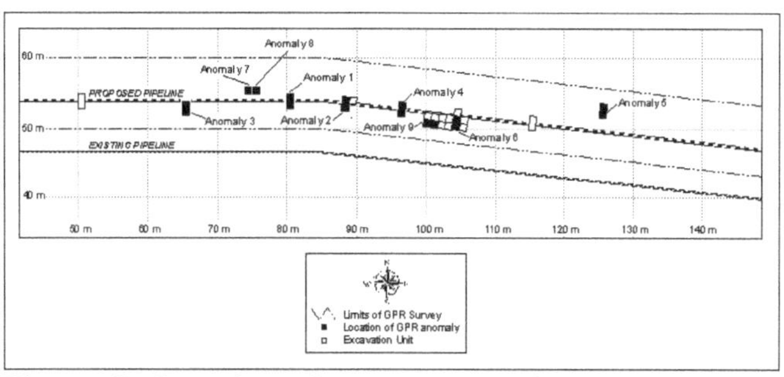

Figure 5. Location of radar anomalies and excavation units at site 21AN106

GPR data was then collected in 20 metre transects spaced at 0.5 metre intervals throughout the 85 metre construction corridor. Each 20 metre segment of GPR data was saved as a computer file to be processed and analysed in the lab at a later date.

3.5 Data processing and analysis

The analysis of the GPR data was carried out by processing the data using different gains and filtering techniques. *Gain* is a scalar with which the raw data is multiplied to enhance the presentation of the data. *Filtering* is the use of mathematical averaging techniques to "clean" noise from the data and/or enhance certain characteristics of the data.

Constant gain and SEC (Spreading and Exponential Compensation) gain were used. *Constant gain* is simply a constant by which the raw data is multiplied. *SEC gain* is a function by which the raw data is multiplied. The function is as follows:

$$SEC = C + (1 + \tau / \tau_w) * e \wedge (\beta * \tau)$$

where: C = constant

$\tau = (t - (\tau_w + t_o))$

τ_w = pulse width

t_o = time zero

β = attenuation * velocity / 8.69

velocity = 0.1 m/ns

attenuation = 0.5 dB/m

This gain function was selected in the hope of preserving stratigraphic detail near the ground surface where the reflection strength is high, while enhancing details at depth (the exponential part of the function).

The filtering used was down-the-trace (temporal) averaging and trace-to-trace (spatial low pass filtering) averaging. Down-the-trace averaging was used to reduce the random noise in the data. Trace-to-trace averaging was used to enhance stratigraphic detail in the data.

Each transect of data from 21AN106 was processed and plotted using the following three processing options.

1. Constant Gain = 150 , no filter.
2. SEC Gain with Attenuation = 1 and Constant = 150, down-the-trace averaging with a window of 3 points.
3. SEC Gain with Attenuation = 1 and Constant = 150, down-the-trace averaging with a window of 3 points and trace-to-trace averaging with a window of five points.

All data was initially processed using an estimated wave propagation velocity of 0.15 m/ns. This estimated velocity was later recalibrated after excavation revealed the true depth of subsurface objects. The recalibrated velocity was calculated by solving the depth equation (see GPR Basics) for velocity, using known values for depth and travel time. Recalibration revealed the true velocity to be closer to 0.10 m/ns. The data files were then plotted again using this new velocity estimate. However, it should be noted that this value is still an approximation. An absolute value could be calculated only if the soil were *completely* homogenous.

3.6 Results

Processing and analysis of the GPR data from 21AN106 revealed three main types of radar signatures. These were:

1. A planar response, due to changes in soil stratigraphy and moisture content. This signature was present in nearly all radar profiles at 0.8 - 0.9. metres below surface and again at 1.5 - 2.0 metres below surface. Examination of soil profiles indicates that the upper planar response is due to a change in moisture content whereas the lower planar response marks a change from loosely-packed fine aeolian sand to dense clayey lacustrine deposits.
2. A point target or object response, exhibiting an inverted hyperbolic shape. These anomalies were likely due to subsurface objects (possible artifacts).
3. Vertical and horizontal areas of disturbed soil. These anomalies are were likely due to areas of disturbed soil,

possibly of a cultural origin (post-holes, fence-posts storage pits).

A total of nine GPR anomalies were excavated. For the location of excavation units which were placed to investigate these anomalies see figure 5. A description of cach anomaly and the results of excavation follow.

Anomaly 1: A vertical soil disturbance.

Associated Excavation Units: 1 and 2.

Description: Anomaly 1 appeared as a vertical disturbance at a depth of 30-180 centimetres below surface (see Fig. 6). The anomaly was interpreted as a possible fence-post-hole, rodent burrow, or shovel test from the Phase II site evaluation. During excavation, cultural material was recovered from 50 to 150 centimetres below surface, however, no features were discovered that suggested a cultural origin for the anomaly. An extensive (both vertical and horizontal) system of rodent burrows were mapped. These burrows are the probable cause of the GPR anomaly. The burrows were easily distinguished because the soil which had filled them was darker (10YR3/2), texturally different (loamy fine sand), and richer in organic material than the surrounding matrix (10YR5/3 fine sand). Presumably, this material represents topsoil that filled the rodent burrows subsequent to their abandonment. The difference in the dielectric properties between the burrow fill and surrounding matrix likely produced the reflection in the radar profile.

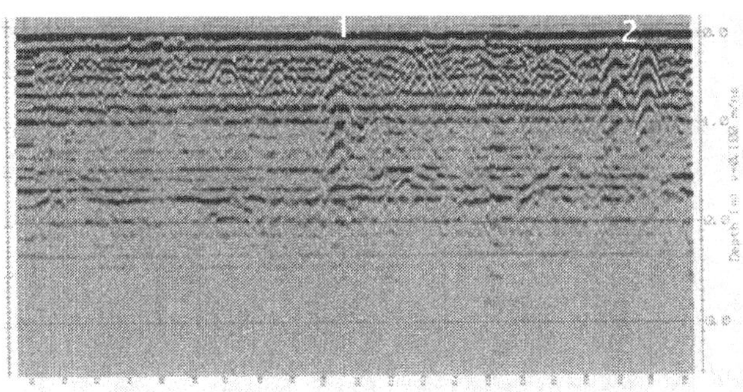

Figure 6. Anomaly 1: Vertical disturbance at f10.5. Anomaly 2: Two vertical disturbances at f19 anf f20. Note planar responses at 0.8 to 0.9 meters and 1.5 to 2.0 meters. The upper response results from changes in soil moisture content due to capillary action from the water table below. The lower response marks a change from loose fine sand to dense clayey sand observed at about 1.5 meters below surface in excavation profiles.

Anomaly 2: A vertical soil disturbance.

Associated Excavation Units: 3 and 4.

Description: Anomaly 2 registered as two adjacent vertical disturbances between 20-100 centimetres below surface (see Fig. 6). The anomaly was interpreted as possible fence-post-holes, rodent burrows, or shovel tests from the Phase II site evaluation. During excavation, cultural material was recovered from 50 to 150 centimetres below surface, however, no cultural features were discovered that suggested a cultural origin for the anomaly. An extensive (both vertical and horizontal) system of rodent burrows were mapped. These burrows are the probable cause of the GPR anomaly. The burrows were easily distinguished because the soil which had filled them was darker (10YR3/2), texturally different (loamy fine sand), and richer in organic material than the surrounding matrix (10YR5/3 fine sand). Presumably, this material represents topsoil that filled in the rodent burrows subsequent to their abandonment. The difference in the dielectric properties between the burrow fill and surrounding matrix likely produced the reflection in the radar profile.

Anomaly 3: Point target.

Associated Excavation Units: 5 and 6.

Description: Anomaly 3 registered as a point target reflection at 60-80 centimetres below surface (see Fig. 7). During excavation, a small cluster (~10 centimetres in diameter) of cultural material (3 pieces of FCR and 2 ceramic sherds) was encountered between 73-75 centimetres below surface. Although other cultural material was recovered, no other clusters or large objects were encountered, suggesting that the cluster at 73-75 centimetres below surface was the cause of the reflection.

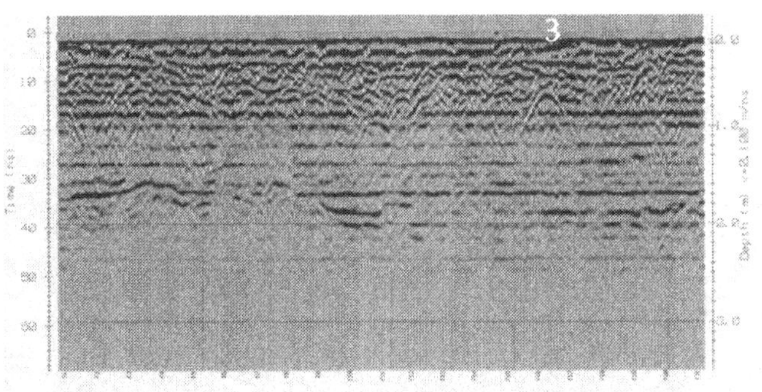

Figure 7. Anomaly 3: Point target response at f16.

Anomaly 4: Point target.

Associated Excavation Units: 9 and 10.

Description: Anomaly 4 registered as a point target 30-50 centimetres below surface. Several small (5-10 centimetres in diameter) clusters of FCR were identified between 40 and 90 centimetres below surface during excavation in unit 10. It is uncertain which of these clusters, if any, was the cause of the anomaly.

Anomaly 5: Point target.

Associated Excavation Units: 11 and 12.

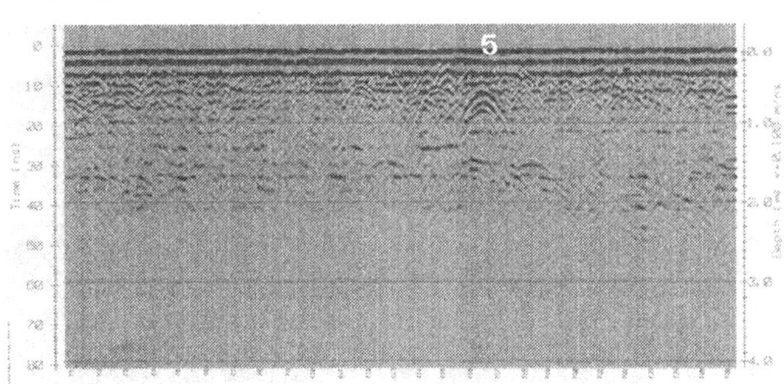

Figure 8. Anomaly 5: Strong point target response at f17

Description: Anomaly 5 registered as a very strong point target reflection 60 centimetres below surface (see Fig. 8). During excavation, a thin oblong piece of iron (later identified as a tine from a harrow rake dating to the 1940's) was recovered from between 60-64 centimetres below surface in unit 12. The depth at which this strong metal reflector was recovered was used in the recalibration of the radar data.

Anomaly 6: Point target.

Associated Excavation Units: 13 and 14.

Description: Anomaly 6 registered as a point target at a depth of 30-40 centimetres below surface. Several small (5-10 centimetre diameter) clusters or single cobble sized pieces of FCR were recovered between 40 and 90 centimetres below surface during excavation in unit 10. It is uncertain which of these features, if any, was the cause of the anomaly.

Anomalies 7 and 8: Point target and horizontal disturbance.

Associated Excavation Units: 15 and 16.

Description: These excavation units were placed to sample two adjoining anomalies. Anomaly 7 registered as a point target 60-70 centimetres below surface. Excavation revealed two clusters of FCR near the unit's centre at 55 centimetres below surface. One of these clusters may have produced the reflection.

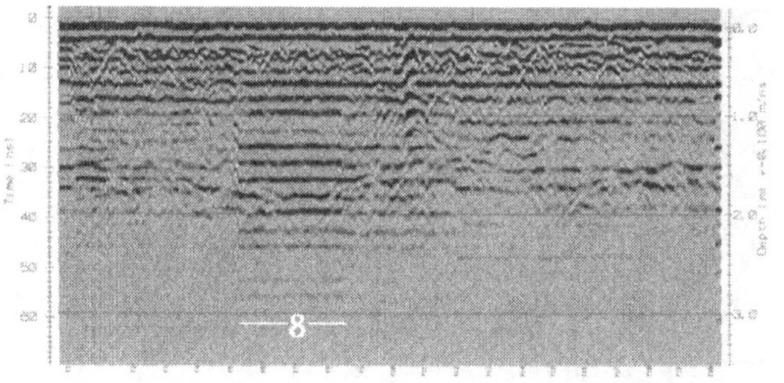

Figure 9 Anomaly 8: Unusual horizontal disturbances at f5-f8.5

Anomaly 8 consisted of a section of unusual horizontal disturbance of unknown origin present at 0.60 - 2.5 metres below surface (see Fig. 9). Excavation revealed a linear rodent burrow (5-10 centimetres in diameter) running approximately parallel to the centreline from the centre of unit 15 through unit 16 and continuing on to the east. The burrow was easily distinguished because the soil which had filled it was darker (10YR3/2), texturally different (loamy fine sand), and richer in organic material than the surrounding matrix (10YR4/3 fine sand). Presumably, this material represents topsoil that filled in the rodent burrow subsequent to its abandonment. The difference in dielectric properties between the burrow fill and the surrounding matrix may have produced the GPR anomaly. The orientation of the burrow (approximately parallel to the radar transect at 1.5 metres north of the centreline) may also have contributed to the unusual response seen in the radar profile.

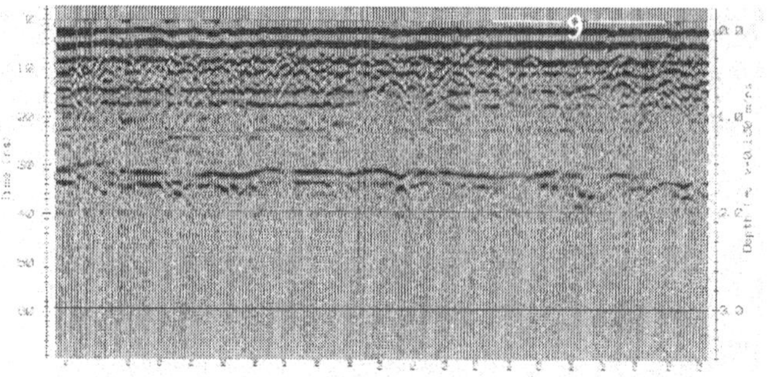

Figure 10 Anomaly 9: Area of weak scattered response at f10-f13

Anomaly 9: Area of scattered weak disturbance.

Associated Excavation Units: 20 and 21.

Description: Anomaly 9 was not particularly prominent in the radar profile. However, there was a subtle area of scattered response at 0.5 - 1.0 metres below surface, which, it was hoped, was caused by scattering due to a high concentration of small artifacts. While excavation revealed no single discrete feature which could account for the anomaly, a relatively high density of FCR was concentrated between 50-110 centimetres below surface in both units 20 and 21. The presence of these artifacts may have caused the scattering observed in the radar profile.

4 Discussion

Data recovery at 21AN106 consisted of two phases: first, a geophysical survey of the construction corridor using GPR to identify cultural materials or features (Maki and Forsberg 1996); second, the excavation of 30 1-x-1-m test units within the construction area (Forsberg and Dobbs 1997). The entire proposed pipeline corridor to be impacted by construction was surveyed using GPR, and a number of radar anomalies were identified. The anomalies thought most likely to have been created by cultural features were chosen for further investigation. Several other areas within the site were also excavated based on the results of the earlier testing.

The radar survey provided high resolution data on the presence/absence and location of subsurface features that proved to be accurate when tested by excavation. A total of nine GPR anomalies were investigated: two vertical soil disturbances, one horizontal soil disturbance, five point targets, and one area of scattered response. All of the disturbed soil anomalies investigated were the result of bioturbation (rodent burrows). Three of the five point targets investigated yielded objects which were the likely reflectors. Numerous objects were discovered associated with the remaining two point targets. It was unclear which if any of these objects were the source of the GPR anomaly. Finally, the area of scattered response did prove to have a higher concentration of artifacts than the surrounding soil matrix.

Controlled excavation resulted in the recovery of 2,456 artifacts. Major prehistoric artifact classes included chipped stone tools and chipping debris, ceramics (all grit tempered), and FCR. In addition, a single conical spear point fashioned from native copper was found. Small numbers of historic artifacts were recovered at depth. Finally, small quantities of charcoal, unidentifiable bone fragments, and other material of uncertain cultural origin were recovered.

Phytolith analysis of food residues from seven ceramic sherds provide direct evidence for use of wild rice and corn and possible use of an unidentified grass and cucurbits (gourd/squash) (Thompson 1996). Accelerator mass spectrometry (AMS) dating of these same residues yielded six radiocarbon dates [Beta-98075 (2030±60 BP); Beta-98076 (2040±50 BP); Beta-98077 (1700±60 BP); Beta-98078 (1680±50 BP); Beta-98079 (2040±50 BP); Beta-98080 (2130±50 BP)] which provide an age range for plant use (and occupation) at the site. AMS dates indicate that wild rice use occurred between 200 BC - AD 75, whereas use of corn occurred AD 200-500. This date for corn use is the earliest yet obtained in this northerly portion of the upper Midwest and the wild rice dates are also the earliest yet obtained along the southern margin of wild rice usage.

Evidence for a wide range of subsistence activities at the site (e.g. hunting, fishing) were lacking. Rather, 21AN106 appears to have functioned as a limited activity or resource extraction site. Its location overlooking Rondeau Lake, where extensive wild rice beds exist, suggests that wild rice attracted prehistoric humans to the area. The artifact assemblage suggests that 21AN106 was a processing site, with FCR and ceramics dominating the assemblage. The presence of FCR (associated with stone boiling) and certain ceramic types (e.g. St. Croix/Onamia at 21AN106) often associated with intensified wild rice use has been interpreted as evidence for wild rice processing at other sites (e.g. Mooers and Dobbs 1993). Direct evidence for wild rice use is provided by wild rice chaff phytoliths identified in food residues from three ceramic sherds. AMS dating of the food residues indicates that wild rice use occurred between ca. 200 BC - AD 75. Phytolith analysis indicates that use of an unidentified wild grass and possibly cucurbit (squash or gourd) co-occurs with wild rice use. Phytolith analysis also provides direct evidence for corn use between AD 200 - 500. While the use of corn by Middle Woodland groups to the south is reasonably well documented, these dates represent a significantly earlier use of corn along the northern frontier of the Middle Woodland world than might be expected.

5 Conclusions

The radar survey provides us with a reasonably clear picture of the internal site plan of 21AN106. This information, when coupled with the excavated data and other paleoecological information, makes it possible to develop a hypothesis which may explain the florescence of Middle and Middle-to-Late Woodland culture on the Anoka Sand Plain.

At least two dynamic geomorphic processes influenced the evolution of the Sand Plain landscape and, therefore, prehistoric settlement activity upon this landscape. These forces are the creation and modification of sand dunes by wind, and changes in lake levels.

Models for dune activity on the Anoka Sand Plain indicate that major episodes of dune formation occurred in the Mid-Holocene between 9,100-4,000 years BP (Keen 1985; Keen and Shane 1990). These episodes correspond to periods of lower precipitation, higher temperatures, reduced vegetation cover, and lower lake and groundwater levels. The shallow lakes along Rice Creek—including Crossways and Rondeau lakes—would have been particularly responsive to decreases in precipitation and groundwater and probably dried up altogether. Thus, sediment in these lakes and the surrounding shallow marshes was exposed to erosion and transport by wind.

Direct evidence for changes in lakes levels in the Rice Creek area is not yet available. However, given regional models (Webb III et al. 1993; Winkler et al. 1986) for lake level fluctuations it is likely that lake levels dropped substantially during the Mid-Holocene, rose during the early Late Holocene to levels higher than at present, and subsequently dropped to about modern levels. There is increasing evidence that this phenomenon occurred throughout the western hemisphere (Abbott et al. 1997).

During the warm and dry Mid-Holocene, when lake levels were low, vegetation cover reduced, and sand dune activity widespread on the Anoka Sand Plain, the area must have been relatively inhospitable. However, as climatic conditions ameliorated after 4,000 years BP, lake levels rose and the landscape stabilised. Thus, although conditions for human settlement were poor throughout most of the Archaic Period, by Late Archaic times, roughly 4,000 years ago, the Rice Creek area would have offered a relative wealth of resources such as wild rice, waterfowl, and fish.

We hypothesise that the expanded use of the Anoka Sand Plain by Middle Woodland groups — and the specific location of 21AN106 — is the result of complex interaction between changes in the physical environment of the Sand Plain, the emergence of the Woodland Tradition throughout the upper Midwestern United States, and interaction with sophisticated Middle Woodland groups farther to the south, similar to other situations documented in both Minnesota and other parts of the New World (e.g. Mooers and Dobbs 1993; Binford et al. 1997). As lake levels dropped from their maximum levels, a variety of new areas appeared that were optimal for wild rice growth. Almost simultaneously, around 2,500 years ago, new ideas about how to process and use 'wild' grains — most notably wild rice and corn — emerged. Whether these ideas and their associated technology are local developments or were adopted from more southerly groups remains unclear. However, it is apparent that the relationship between changes in the Sand Plain landscape which were conducive to wild rice production and procurement, and the Woodland florescence in this same area, are more than coincidental.

By roughly 1,500 years ago, the Sand Plain was no longer the focus of intensive Woodland settlement and use. While several different factors may have contributed to this change, certainly the continued drop in lake levels may have been a key factor. At 21AN106, even modest changes in lake levels of a few feet would have significantly changed the relationship of the nearby rice beds to the site itself. Such minor fluctuations in lake levels would have had little effect on the larger, central sites in the Woodland settlement system which were adjacent to deeper lakes. However, they seemingly had a very significant effect on the location and character of smaller, processing and procurement sites like 21AN106.

Obviously, ground-penetrating radar was only one in a variety of tools used in the investigation and interpretation of 21AN106. However, radar facilitated a comprehensive examination of the entire portion of the site and provided important information on the patterning of cultural materials within the site itself. This information allowed us to structure the site excavation in a way that maximised the information we recovered while maintaining careful control over archaeological costs. While the same information could have been recovered without the radar survey, a significantly larger area would have had to have been dug — and we would have been left with continued nagging doubts about what we might have missed and what really lay in the unexplored areas between our excavation units.

Acknowledgements

The authors wish to thank Northern Natural Gas Company for sponsoring this project. The kind assistance of Ron Beidelman, Mike Underwood, and other Northern personnel was essential to this undertaking. In addition, we would like to thank Natural Resource Group, Inc. — particularly Julie Myhre and Ted Lofstrom — for co-ordinating efforts at 21AN106.

Bibliography

Abbott, M R, Binford, M W, Brenner M, and Kelts K R, 1997. A 3500 14C High-Resolution Record of Water-Level Changes in Lake Titicaca, Bolivia/Peru. *Quaternary Research* 47(2) 169-180.

Agricultural Experiment Station 1980. *Minnesota Soil Atlas: Stillwater Sheet.* Miscellaneous Report 171-1980. University of Minnesota, St. Paul.

Annan, A P, and Cosway S W, 1992 *Ground Penetrating Radar Survey Design.* Paper prepared for the Annual Meeting of SAGEEP Chicago, April 26-29, 1992.

Annan, A P, and Cosway, S W, 1994 *GPR Frequency Selection.* GPR'94: Proceedings of the Fifth International Conference on Ground Penetrating Radar. Kitchener, Ontario, Canada

Binford, M W, Kolata, A L, Brenner, M, Janusek, J W, Seddon, M T, Abbott, M, and Curtis J, H.1997. Climate Variation and the Rise and Fall of an Andean Civilization. *Quaternary Research* 47(2), 235-248.

Bradbury, J P, Dean, W E, and Anderson R Y, 1993 Holocene Climatic and Limnologic History of the North-Central United States as Recorded in the Varved Sediments of Elk Lake, Minnesota: A Synthesis, in Bradbury, J P, and Dean W E, (eds.). *Elk Lake, Minnesota: Evidence for Rapid Climate Change in the North-Central United States* (Geological Society of America Special Paper 276), 309-328.

Breakey, K, 1995 *A Phase I Archaeological Survey of a Segment of the Northern Natural Pipeline Corridor, The Elk River Looping Project in Anoka County, Minnesota.* Reports of Investigation Number 321. IMA Consulting, Minneapolis, Minnesota.

Dobbs, C A, and Breakey, K, 1995 *An Evaluation of 21AN106 on the Northern Natural Gas Company Pipeline, Anoka County, Minnesota.* Reports of Investigation Number 329. IMA Consulting, Minneapolis, Minnesota.

Dobbs, C A, Wendt, D, and Johnson, C M, 1990 *Testing and Phase II Evaluation of the Forsham Lake Site (21AN20), Anoka County, Minnesota.* Reports of Investigation Number 71. Institute for Minnesota Archaeology, Minneapolis, Minnesota.

Donohue and Associates 1990 *EIS Hydrogeologic Site Investigation, Volume I, Anoka County: Landfill Inventory Site EIS, Sites D, P, and Q.* Maple Grove, Minnesota.

Forsberg, D M, and Dobbs, C A, 1996 *Archaeological Data Recovery at Site 21AN106, Anoka County, Minnesota.* IMA Consulting, Inc. Reports of Investigations Number 395

Grimm, E C, 1981 *An Ecological and Paleoecological Study of the Vegetation in the Big Woods Region of Minnesota.* Unpublished Ph.D. dissertation, University of Minnesota, Minneapolis.

Harrison, C, 1978 Archaeological Survey of Anoka and Isanti Counties (draft). Statewide Archaeological Survey, Minnesota Historical Society.

Jenks, A E, 1901 The Wild Rice Gatherers of the Upper Great Lakes. *Annual Report of the Bureau of Ethnology*, 19(2), 1013-1137.

Johnson, E J, 1971 Excavations at the Gull Lake Dam (21CA27). *Minnesota Archaeologist* 31(2), 44-69.

Keen, K L, 1985 *Sand Dunes on the Anoka Sand Plain.* Unpublished Master's thesis, Department of Geology, University of Minnesota, Minneapolis.

Keen, K L, and Shane, C K, 1990 A Continuous Record of Holocene Activity and Vegetation Change at Lake Ann, East-Central Minnesota. *Geological Society of America Bulletin* 102, 1646-1657.

Ketz, K A, Dolence, T, Roberts, T, Anderson, J, and Tennedine, J, 1996 *Phase III Data Recovery for Site 21AN75, Lino Lakes, Anoka County, Minnesota.* 106 Group Ltd., St. Paul, Minnesota.

Maki, D, and Forsberg D M, 1997 *Ground Penetrating Radar Survey of Archaeological Site 21AN106, Anoka County, Minnesota.* Reports of Investigation 415. IMA Consulting, Minneapolis, Minnesota.

Mooers, H D, and Dobbs C. A. 1993 Holocene Landscape Evolution and the Development of Models for Human Interaction with the Environment: An Example from the Mississippi Headwaters Region. *Geoarchaeology* 8(6), 475-492.

Thompson, R G, 1996. *Phytolith Analysis of Selected Sherds from 21AN106, Anoka County, Minnesota*. Reports of Investigation 417. IMA Consulting, Minneapolis, Minnesota.
United States Bureau of Land Management 1850-1963 Minnesota Survey Plats. United States Department of the Interior, Washington, D.C. Available on microfilm at Wilson Library, University of Minnesota, Minneapolis.
Unites States Geological Survey 1993[1967]. *Centreville Quadrangle, Minnesota*. Revised 1993. 7.5 Minute Series (Topographic). Washington, DC.
Webb III, T, Bartlein, P J, Harrison, S P, and Anderson K H, 1993 Vegetation, Lake Levels, and Climate in Eastern North America for the Past 18,000 Years, in Wright, Jr., H. E., Kutzbach, J E. Webb III, T, Ruddiman, W F, Street-Perrott, F A, and Bartlein P. J, (eds.). *Global Climates Since the Last Glacial Maximum*, (University of Minnesota Press, Minneapolis, Minnesota), 415-467.
Wendt, D, 1988 Application of Shovel Testing and Spatial Analysis to a Disturbed Limited Woodland Site in Anoka County, Minnesota. *Minnesota Archaeologist* 47(1), 3-33.
Winchell, N H, and Upham W, 1888 *The Geology of Minnesota: Final Report*. Geological and Natural History of Minnesota, (2),399-444.
Winkler, M G, Swain, A M, and Kutzbach J E, 1986. Middle Holocene Dry Period in the North Midwestern United States: Lake Levels and Pollen Stratigraphy. *Quaternary Research* 25, 235-250.
Wright, H E, Jr. 1972 Quaternary History of Minnesota, in Sims, P. K. and Morey G B, *Geology of Minnesota: A Centennial Volume* (Minnesota Geological Survey, St. Paul), 515-547.

Contact details

Clark A. Dobbs
IMA Consulting, Inc.
2635 Fourth Street SE
Minneapolis
Minnesota 55414
USA
email: cdobbs@bitstream.net

CAA 97

GPR Analysis and Modelling with GIS Applications, Empúries, Spain

Margaret S. Watters

Abstract

GIS and statistical analyses of raw, scanned ground-penetrating radar data serve to assist in the computer determination / identification of sub-surface features. Time slice interpolation and the interpolation of standard deviation activity maps have successfully imaged prominent repeating anomalies across several parallel profiles reflecting man-made features. Thorough analysis of the 95 surveyed radar transects the nature of sub-surface features will be revealed and subsequently assigned an ethnic identity. Terms: ground-penetrating radar, time slice, standard deviation "activity maps"

1 Introduction

During June of 1996 Boston University conducted a student field school at Empúries, Spain. Empuries is an important archaeological site spanning from the 6th century BC to the second century AD. Located on the northeastern coast of Spain in the area of Catalunyia, Empuries boasts a combined occupation of indigenous and Greek residents with later Roman settlement. Around 575 BC, Phocaean Greeks branching out from Masallia, modern day Marseille, settled at Palaeopolis, on a small island at the mouth of the river Fluvia. After developing into a major port and exchange centre, the Greek population of Paleopolis expanded to the mainland across from their island city to a settlement called Neopolis. Roman occupation began to the west of Neopolis in 278 BC with the establishment of a military garrison. The first and second centuries BC saw development of a more civic nature, and which expanded to enclose Neopolis within defensive walls. During this period the site took on the Latinised name of Emporiae, or market. Late first century AD saw the silting of the Fluvia river course and the decline and abandonment of Empúries. (Harrison 1988)

According to first century AD authors Livy and Strabo, Greek colonists lived side by side with the indigenous population of this area, the Indicans. (Livy: 34.9.4 - 9.4, Strabo: Geography 3.4.5 - 9). The modern-day parking lot of the site was targeted in the early 1980's in an attempt to locate the reported Indican village of Indica. Excavation revealed 4th and 3rd century BC burials with mixed Greek and Iberian amphorae, a 2nd century unidentified structure, and two subsequent phases of Roman metal working structures. No positive identification of indigenous occupation was discovered during this work, and no positively identified Indican structures were found elsewhere on the site. (Sanmarti et al. 1983-1984)

As part of a larger study investigating the interaction of the indigenous and colonial populations at the site of Empúries, the parking-lot of Neopolis was selected for geophysical survey in an attempt to establish the presence or absence of an indigenous settlement. Ground-penetrating radar was selected as the most suitable geophysical method for investigation. Ever present cars, fences and ferrous debris, and a lack of ground moisture ruled out magnetic and resistance survey.

The ground-penetrating radar survey was conducted as part of a student field school run through Boston University. A GSSI Sir System 3 radar unit with 300 and 500 MHz antennae were used. Data was recorded on paper scrolls. Grids surveyed in the parking lot bordered the previous excavation of the 1980s. 20 to 40 m transects, with 1 m spacing, were oriented on a north-south axis with east-west intersections at points of interest. This paper presents an attempt at interpretation of seven, 20 m transects on the eastern edge of grid 3.

The basic premise of radar interpretation is the recognition and identification of repeating anomalies across profiles which are interpreted as reflecting man-made or geological features. Through detailed manual interpretation or computer processing these repeating anomalies can be identified and imaged in horizontal site plans. Different methods of analysis were applied in the investigation of the contents of our data. Initial in-field viewing and traditional box grid construction of paper profiles revealed significant repeating anomalies. Recent research however, allowed the interpretation of these data using a more up-to-date methodology. Consequently, all paper profiles were digitally scanned and converted into digital imagery.

2 Data interpretation and GIS

The developing field of computer applications and quantitative methods in archaeology directly contributes to the processing of radar data. The nature of the data presented here forces one to look beyond simple visual and manual analysis of black and white profiles for the identification of prominent anomalies. In order to remove the data from an interpretative process based on experience, preconceived ideas, and prejudices and toward more objective results, a series of visual and statistical processes were applied to the data in order to provide feature identifications with a more substantial basis. In order to accomplish this, several Geographic Information Systems (GIS) tools and simple variance statistics were employed, and the initial results are presented here.

3 Rectification

As everyone who has used radar in the field knows, different people pull antennae at different rates. Radar profiles were collected by a number of students, thus the profiles vary in drag rate and spacing between meter marks. Along with intermittent use of the 300 and 500 MHz profiles, the data is quite irregular.

In order to rectify spatially each profile so they can be submitted to further analysis, scanned profiles were processed within Idrisi. This GIS allowed for cropping of profiles at designated row and column co-ordinates and stretching each cropped image in order to create final images of each designated radar profile of the same size and resolution. Once resampled, the temporal axis of the profiles was converted to depth. As the survey area surrounded an open excavation, transects were run along exposed balks which permitted measurement of the depth and nature of subsurface features. (Fig. 1)

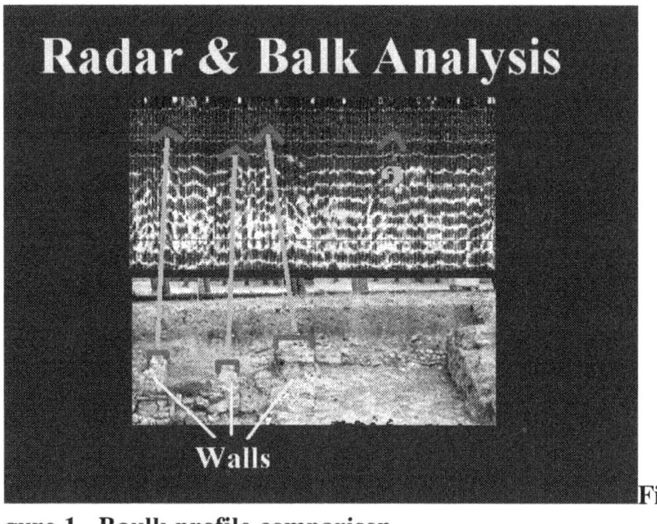

Figure 1. Baulk profile comparison

4 Image enhancement

GIS operations assist in the further investigation of geophysical data through the enhancement of imagery via contrast enhancement, false colour display, data interpolation, and filtering. These processes tend to emphasise trends running throughout the data.

5 Time slice analysis

Profile stacking is an initial step in the process for the recognition of repeating anomalies. Following the idea of Goodman, Nishimura, and Rogers (1995), isolation and concatenation of time slices in parallel profiles provides continuous data for a specific time and, later, a calculated depth for the survey area. A designated number of rows of data are isolated from each radar profile at a specified time (or depth). These rows are kept in the same order and pasted together in an image. (Fig. 2)

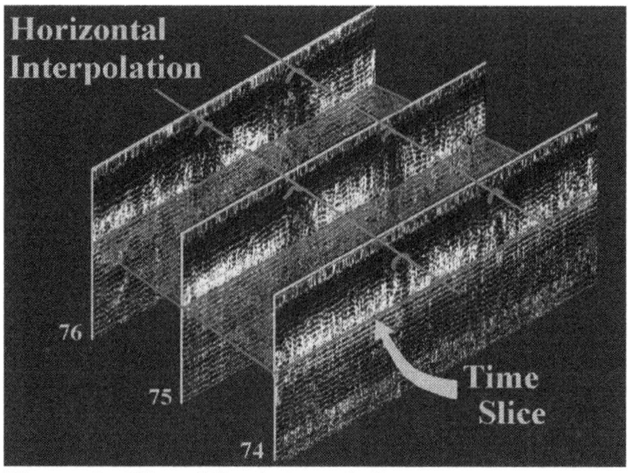

Figure 2. Time Slice interpolation

This image can be viewed orthographically (Fig. 3), which graphs the values of each column in its respective isolated row. Orthographic display of isolated time slices assists in manual identification of repeating trends in parallel profiles.

Another step, away from manual interpretation, is through interpolation of the isolated rows of information. Interpolation through GIS normally performs a two dimensional search for surrounding values in order to determine connecting surfaces. This process cannot be applied to the present data as it consists of parallel rows of information, making only a one-dimensional search possible. Initial interpolation of raw data appears extremely striped but can be smoothed through repeated filtering. This process produces a horizontal plan of the survey area.

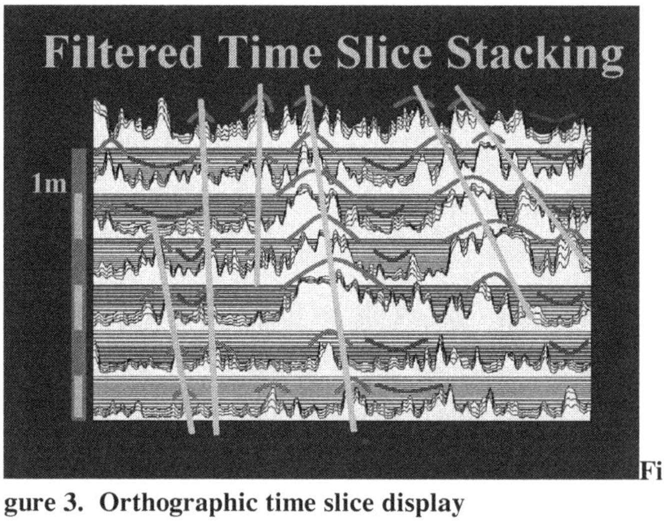

Figure 3. Orthographic time slice display

6 Variance statistics

As utilised by Fletcher and Bradley (1995), application of variance statistics to radar profiles also assists in anomaly and feature identification. Variance statistics show particularly active or rapidly changing areas in radar profiles which tend to correlate with significant anomalies. A special purpose program was written to determine the standard deviation and mean values of each profile in our study area. Calculations were performed on groups of 5 image columns, representing intervals of 20 cm on the ground, within the image representing 500 columns, or 20 m transects. The final file is reduced to a single row of 100 columns representing activity, obtained through the calculation of standard deviations, for each 20 m transect.

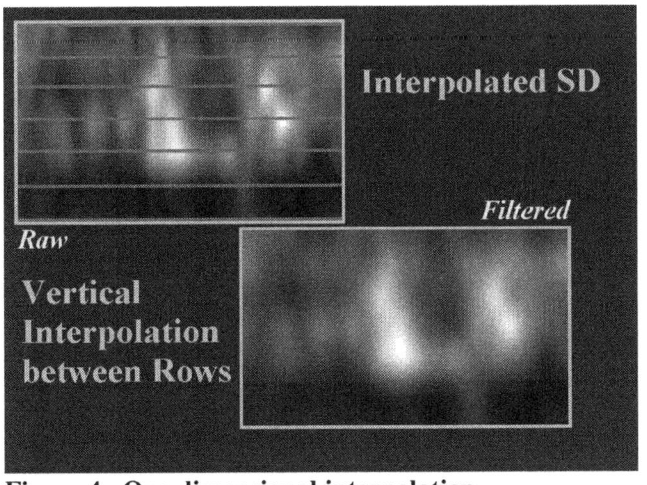

Figure 4. One dimensional interpolation

The resulting transects, pasted in order, can be viewed orthographically as with the time slice analysis. One dimensional interpolation (Fig. 4) can also be performed to generate a horizontal image of profile activity.

7 Conclusions

Despite the fact time slice analysis and calculated variance "activity maps" represent different data, they both reflect the same prominent trend which runs through each radar transect. Thus, we can conclude that, aided by GIS operations of image rectification and enhancement, both time slice interpolation and "activity analysis" in radar transects can be used to create horizontal plan views for given data. (Fig. 5) Through this process we are able to investigate, not only the presence of significant anomalies, but are able to trace their depth and changes in the site.

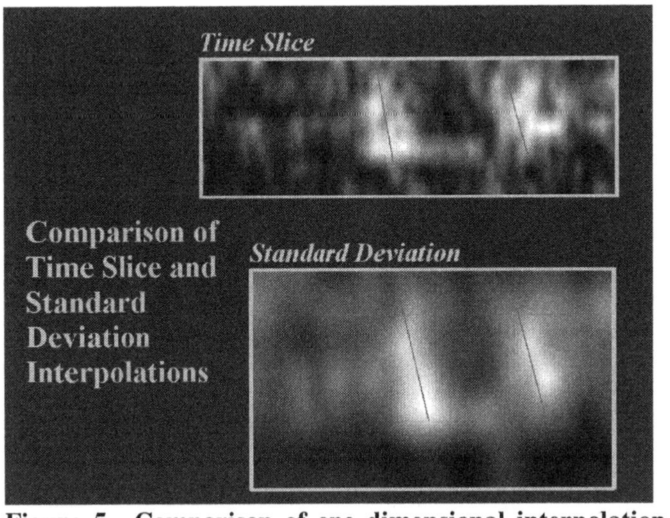

Figure 5. Comparison of one dimensional interpolation of time slice and standard deviation analyses

The application of GIS functions and statistical analyses in this case clearly reveals a substantial sub-surface feature which was identified as two parallel walls running for 5m in an east west orientation. Based on excavation baulks, these walls are probably 50 cm in width and situated at a depth of 1 to 1.5 m below the surface. These results suggest a continuation of the complex of Roman metal working installations, revealed during the parking lot excavation of 1982.

Acknowledgements

I would like to thank Dr. Kenneth Kvamme for his input to this paper in the form of good advice as well as allowing me to use his programs Colvar I, Colvar II, and Terrpac.

Bibliography

Bradley, J and Fletcher, M, 1996 Extraction and visualisation of information from ground penetrating radar surveys, *Computer Applications and Quantitative Methods in Archaeology*, Vol. 1, 103-110

Goodman, D, Nishimura, Y, and Rogers, J D, 1995 GPR Time slices in Archaeological Prospection, *Archaeological Prospection*, Vol. 2, 85-89

Harrison, R J, 1988 *Spain at the Dawn of History. Iberians, Phoenicians and Greeks,* London, Thames and Hudson

Sanmarti, G E, Brufau J M N, and Abadias X A, 1983-1984 Les excavacions a l'area del parking al sud de la Neapolis d'empuries (informe preliminar), *Empuries,* 45-6

Contact details

Margaret S. Watters
Department of Archaeology
Boston University
675 Commonwealth Avenue
Boston MA
ZIP 02115
USA
Megg@acs.bu.edu

Geophysics and Remote Sensing Abstracts of papers held on CD-ROM

CAA 97

GPR Surveys in Three Estonian Medieval Towns
R. Vissak

No Abstract Supplied

The Application of Geophysical Techniques at Wroxeter Roman City
Christopher F. Gaffney and Paul K. Linford

This paper provides an overview of the geophysical research that has been carried out at the Roman city of Wroxeter (Viroconium) in Shropshire over the past three years, stimulated by the Wroxeter Hinterland Project directed by Birmingham University Field Archaeology Unit (BUFAU). A major part of this geophysical work has been the completion of a fluxgate gradiometer survey over the entire 75 hectare area within the city defences, to build up a complete magnetic map of the remains. The results of this survey are presented and some of the key features identified during initial analysis are discussed. Further investigations, on a smaller scale, have also been undertaken with a range of other geophysical techniques; these are summarised and, where possible, initial results are presented. A strategy for the archaeological interpretation of such a large geophysical dataset is outlined and the research agenda for the geophysics is reviewed and some suggestions made concerning the analytical strength of each technique.

Digital Mapping and Remote Sensing at Merv (Digital Data Integration in a Field Context)
G. Barratt, S. Bullas and S. Doyle

The paper falls into four main sections; section 1 is a brief introduction to the geographical and historic context of the Merv cities, the historical context content is based on work published by Georgina Herrmann, director of the International Merv Project. Section 2 gives an overview of the work carried out as part of the mapping programme in the period of 1992 to 1996. Section 3 describes field work carried out as part of the programme in 1996 and shows principally the use of digital survey and GIS technology to integrate ground based geophysical data with more distant aerial remote sensing in an attempt to approach a particular problem. Section 4 deals largely with the creation of a GIS system designed as a map integration and CRM tool for the area of the cities. The main text of the paper is written by Barratt with contributions in the areas of ground based geophysical remote sensing by Bullas and in the Merv GIS by Doyle. Any omissions and mistakes are attributed to the former.

Mud and Old Bullets: Geophysical and Behavioural Anomalies in Adverse Environmental and Climatic Conditions. A case study in the Use of Stratified Systematic Unaligned Sampling at Merv, Türkmenistan
Stephen Bullas

Although successfully pioneered some 20 years ago in the research of geographic settlement patterns, Stratified Systematic Unaligned Sampling (SSUS) has proved slow to be adopted as a sampling methodology in archaeological prospection. The 1996 season at Merv, Türkmenistan, presented a planned opportunity to realise the technique under controlled conditions in the intra-site comparison of industrial debris resulting from Early Islamic metalworking. The primary aim of the survey was to confirm or deny the hypothesis of a specialised industrial site and, if confirmed, to ascertain its approximate extent. A secondary aim of the survey was to conduct research into whether or not unfired mud bricks (in sufficient quantities) - lying shallow beneath the surface on beds of the alluvial clay from which they were made - could be detected by magnetic means. The views of a number of archaeological geophysicists working in Central Asia, North Africa, the United States and Europe were sought before the season started and the results of the various surveys undertaken using susceptibility and gradiometry are presented in this paper. Finally, a comparison of this year's results is made with previous years' resistivity and remote sensing (SPOT) surveys.

Archaeological Prospection with GPR Approaches: Case Studies in Xian and Shangqiu, China
Libing Gao

During 1995 and 1996, three ground-penetrating radar surveys were carried out in conjunction with field archaeological investigations in China. The first survey was a detailed, high-resolution radar survey at the site of Hanyuan Hall, a ninth century palace. The latter two radar surveys were rapid, low-resolution reconnaissance surveys undertaken using the magnetic method and RS images as part of the Shangqiu Project. Geoarchaeological and geophysical teams worked jointly during the spring and fall of 1996. This paper will discuss several radar profiles with different patterns of anomalies and geological interpretation and compare them with the core profiles. The survey design, data acquisition and processing are also discussed. Ongoing work involves continuing to perform GPR and other geophysical surveys in the area surrounding and within the Eastern Zhou city to locate building structures, graves and ancient riverbeds.

Remote Sensing into the Study of Ancient Beiting City in North-Western China
Jianguo Liu

This paper presents an aerial-photographic study of ancient Beiting city, situated in the northern part of Tianshan Mountain in Xinjiang, north-western China. Ancient Beiting city was an important urban settlement on the ancient Silk Road (see figure 1). It is composed of exterior and interior walls, and bounded by moats. Several canals in the interior of the city are connected to outside moats. In this study three types of aerial photograph were examined. The analysis of these aerial photos revealed a palatial wall and some street remains, which were confirmed by subsequent field work.

A PC-Based System for Computer Assisted Archaeological Interpretation of Aerial Photographs
Sam Redfern

Medium altitude aerial survey photographs are a useful source of information for archaeologists, particularly in the identification, measurement and classification of monuments. However these photographs contain far more information than can be extracted by the human eye. Measurements of shape and size can be crudely ascertained by manually studying aerial photographs. Digital image processing on a computer can be used to extract more accurate measurements. Digital Elevation Models (DEMs) are becoming an essential data product for computer literate landscape archaeologists. Using DEMs, measures of location can also be computed for monuments identified in aerial photographs. However the generation of DEMs continues to be an expensive and labour-intensive process, requiring either ground survey, interpolation from existing contour maps, or the application of expensive photogrammetric equipment. This paper describes how a standard desktop personal computer has been used to:

1. Analyse stereo pairs of aerial photographs and automatically generate DEMs for their overlapping region, by measuring the parallax values of the points visible in both photographs.
2. Accurately trace the boundaries of circular and sub-circular monuments visible in the photographs.
3. Generate integrated and accurate measurements of shape, size, and location for these monuments. These measurements are then used to produce monument classification.

Export the DEMs and monument information to a Geographical Information System (GIS), for integration with other spatial data.

ARCHAEOLOGY
IN THE
AGE OF THE INTERNET

CAA 97

Section 7
Museums, Education and the Internet

The Virtual Museum - who needs it?

Sue Gordon

CAA 97

Abstract

Electronic public access to museums has become a reality - not as a result of a national, centrally controlled, network of museum collections but as a by-product of the growing popularity and availability of the Internet. This paper examines the growth of electronic access to museums and their collections by the specialist, the general public and by schools and asks some pertinent questions. Can such a serendipitous beast as the World Wide Web really deliver the "virtual museum"? What about "virtual objects"? Who will visit the "virtual museum" and what will they get from it? What can educational groups get out of the "virtual museum"? Is this the end of school visits to "real" museums? Are these "real" questions or are we driving up a "virtual blind alley"?

1 A 'compendious index'

Electronic public access to museums has become a reality - not as a result of a national, centrally controlled, network of museum collections but as a by-product of the growing popularity and availability of the Internet. Before the advent of the World Wide Web, electronic access to museum collections was envisaged by the museum world as being made possible by a national centralised catalogue, although no such catalogue was ever set up.

National and local authority museums have always been under pressure to make collections more accessible, both to governments for inventory purposes and to the public who, through central and local taxation have paid for many of the objects in care and, it can be argued, have a right to be able to share in and enjoy as much of their material heritage as can be made available.

The idea of sharing museum information had been around a long time. In 1888 one of the newly established Museums Association's primary objectives was the establishment of a "compendious index of the contents of all provincial museums" (Platnauer and Howarth (eds.) 1890). In the 1960s the Information Retrieval Group of the Museums Association was established (Roberts and Light 1986). This group, and later the Museums Documentation Association, was concerned with data standards and terminology control, both fundamental to the establishment of a national index and to the dissemination of collections' information over national networks.

In the UK the use of communications networks by museums has, until recently, been restricted to those who have close links to university departments with access to the UK Joint Academic Network (JANET). The Ashmolean Museum in Oxford has made the Beazley Archive available over JANET to selected researchers using JANET since the early 1980s (Delouis, D. 1993) and the Science Museum and the Natural History Museum have had access to JANET through Imperial College also since the 1980s. But examples like this are few. Lack of national standards in museum computer systems and, perhaps more fundamentally, lack of computer systems in museums at all has meant that the opportunity to create an electronically accessible national catalogue of museum objects simply has not been there however much the will might have been.

2 Object records and the World Wide Web

The Museums Association estimates that there are approximately 2,500 museums and galleries in the UK (MA Museums Briefing number 15, March 1997). An estimate in 1985 (Roberts, 1985) proposed a figure of over 100 million objects in the care of the nation's museums. In a recent survey 257 UK museums reported a total of 9 million records on computer (Gill, T. and Dawson, D. 1996). If each museum were to make its object catalogue available as a searchable database on the Web it could be argued that, with appropriate hyperlinks, this would form one, large, national database.

Today the Internet, or more precisely, the World Wide Web presents an opportunity to create a national catalogue of sorts. A brief look at each of the UK museum web sites (130 in March 1997) listed on the Virtual Library Museum pages (note 1) revealed twelve museums (four of these have archaeological collections) with inventory or catalogue records available on-line. It is likely that in total these records amount to no more than 100,000. Put simply, the number of object records available on the World Wide Web from UK museums is probably less than point one percent (.1%) of the total number of objects cared for by UK museums.

The fact is that of those UK museums with their own Web site, most have no object records available on the Web and those that do, with very few exceptions, make only a few selected records available. Why, after more than two years of Internet activity and 'hype' has so little apparent progress been made towards on-line collections? Putting aside the problems of entering large backlogs of data, and for many museums this is still a major problem, there are other obstacles. Firstly there are problems with the data itself. Few museums, if any, have 'clean' data in their computerised catalogues and curators are understandably reluctant to put erroneous or sketchy data on public display. Secondly, although tools that can link large relational databases to Web pages are available and relatively easy to use current licensing policies tend to make these tools expensive. Copying the data to an inexpensive, Web compatible database, may be cheaper but will require the services of technical staff who understand both the native database and the Web software. The cost of repeating this process periodically to keep the Web version current should not be forgotten. Thirdly, security across the Internet is a real problem -- no museum wants to risk having their collections catalogue compromised deliberately or by accident.

None of these problems are insurmountable as a visit to the Hampshire County Council Museums Service Web site will demonstrate (note 2). This site has 80,000 object records from its MODES database available for searching on the Web -- so it can be done, providing a museum has the necessary technical resources on hand and the courage to risk criticism from its peers. Another exceptional, and one might even say heroic, effort is the SCRAN project in Scotland which aims to have 1.5 million records on-line by the year 2001 (note 3).

Although the majority of UK museums may not be able, or willing, to make complete object databases available on the Internet for some time to come, they can add contextual information to selected inventory or catalogue records and create 'virtual exhibits' on-line as the Science Museum has done (note 4) with its on-line Flight exhibition and Treasures of the Science Museum (Gordon, S. 1995, 1996).

3 Virtual Objects and exhibits

The 'virtual exhibit' (both on CD-ROM and on the World Wide Web) and its surrounding 'hypermedia cloud' of information runs parallel to the way in which museums present their collections to the public in the real world. Gone are the rows of objects in glass cases with labels that might only be understood or appreciated by the specialist. Fewer objects, with more supporting information presented in different ways, cater for a wider range of visitors in terms of age, background and learning preference. Electronic object labels now include video and sound clips, simulations or animation to provide a rich supporting programme for the objects on display.

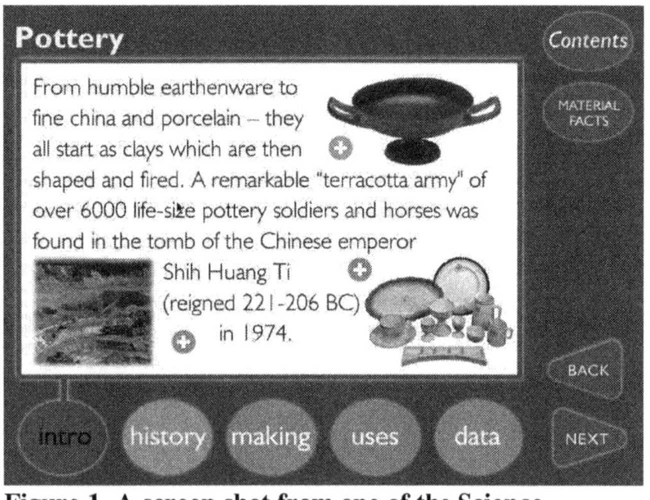

Figure 1. A screen shot from one of the Science Museum's Challenge of Materials gallery Information Stations. (copyright The Trustees of the Science Museum).

In contrast with a more traditional approach to exhibition development many museums now provide their visitors with a far wider range of information about objects on display than that contained in the average inventory or catalogue record. For example, the Science Museum's Challenge of Materials gallery includes multimedia Information Stations with screens like the one shown in Figure 1.

The visitor to the Challenge of Materials gallery can choose to go into as little or as much depth about the subject as they wish by navigation through the Information Station screens. The multimedia nature of the interface encourages the visitor to explore and find out more about the material on display in the gallery than they might have otherwise been inclined to do. The addition of a quiz further encourages the younger visitor or those who are a little reluctant to use a computer. In a gallery setting, this kind of information provision is just one of the many ways in which the visitor can start to be drawn into the subject of the exhibit. On the other hand, viewed in isolation on the World Wide Web or on CD-ROM and without the real objects for reference there is a danger that this kind of high-tech interface becomes the focus of attention rather than the content that it is meant to deliver.

With that caveat in mind there are some good examples of virtual exhibits on the World Wide Web. The Natural History Museum's Science Casebook presents factual information about a small number of objects and invites visitors to play detective and solve a mystery (note 5). On the way the 'virtual' visitor gathers background information about the real object, learns about discoveries made by real scientists and about the way in which the museum works behind the scenes.

A different kind of virtual exhibit is illustrated in Figure 2. This Quicktime VR Movie (note 6) allows you to pan through 360 degrees and zoom in on the astronaut's controls of the Apollo 10 Command Module. The inside of the capsule is inaccessible to the visitor in the real museum and this is the only way a member of the public can see the instrumentation close up. This sequence also gives a good impression of the cramped conditions experienced by the astronauts.

4 Remote audiences

In the real world museums already have remote audiences. Outreach programmes usually involve paper publications, open days and site visits, teaching programmes of one kind or another or visits by museum staff to talk to groups of people about the work of the museum. All of these outreach activities are designed with a specific audience in mind. Whether it is academics, school children, community groups or groups with a common interest.

A museum World Wide Web site offers the possibility of attracting remote visitors from all of these groups plus a new, mass audience many of whom do not have any particular interest in museums. This new audience is potentially global, may not speak the same language as you and its attention span is likely to be measured in seconds rather than minutes.

A survey in December 1996 (note 7), one of an on-going series by the Georgia Institute of Technology in the US, revealed that the most popular activity on the Web is browsing, followed by entertainment. In other words most of the visitors to your Web site are most likely not looking for any specific information or outcome from your pages -- just the mental stimulation provided by a constant parade of nice images, clever animations and perhaps a little interesting text. This perhaps sounds a little harsh -- why bother to take the time to create a Virtual Museum on the Web at all? The answer is that even if only a small percentage of visitors to your Museum Web site stop long enough to gain something lasting from their visit this still represents a very large number of actual people. For example in April 1997 there were over 25,000 visits to the Science Museum Web site. This figure is not the number of 'hits' or pages downloaded (which is much greater) but an estimate of the number of individuals visiting the site. This is about a quarter of the number of 'real' visitors to the 'real' Science Museum and, as such, is not an insignificant audience.

5 Educational visitors

What can educational groups get out of the "virtual museum"? Last year about a quarter of a million school children visited the Science Museum. Some of those children are lucky enough to have access to the World Wide Web either at school or at home. According to the National Council for Education Technology 5,500 schools were reported as being connected to the Internet in November 1996, although many of these will have just one PC connected via a modem. Given government support, and that of businesses such as BT, most schools and colleges are likely to get connections over the next few years.

One way Museums can help and encourage this process is to provide well thought out resources and appropriate material that are aimed specifically at teachers and students. A project called Science Resources for Teachers and Educators in Museums (STEM) has been established on the Science Museum's Web site which aims to create one such resource (note 8). This project encourages schools who have visited the real museum to create their own Web pages and to link these to a search facility on the Museum's pages. Teachers from other schools can then search across a range of material produced by many different schools on topics related to exhibits in the Science Museum. This project and a similar one called COMO have both attracted considerable interest from sponsors. The Science Museum has also participated in the MUSENET project, which has enabled the museum Education Department set up video-conferencing facilities and run events with schools and other museums using the equipment. The Museum has also run several e-mail conferences (note 9) where students exchange e-mail messages with a range of experts in universities and research centres in the UK and further afield.

Looking forward to the future, the Science Museum's Education department is keen to set up a web based Multi-user object oriented virtual environment (a MOO) for schools to help build and to use for collaborative work with the museum. This, if it happens, will be a real 'virtual' museum if that is not a contradiction. A small beginning has been made with the creation of a virtual reality environment which represents the Science Museum's Education services (Fig. 3). The 3D world (note 10) is populated with objects such as tables, notice boards and imaginative sculptures. Each object leads to one of the Museum's conventional Web pages. More virtual rooms are planned together with the introduction of avatars (icons that represent real people) and chat facilities to allow the participants to talk to each other.

6 New environments and interfaces

Three dimensional virtual environments have some advantages over the simple text and image Web site. The visitor can move around the hypermedia space using familiar metaphors such as doors, rooms and everyday objects rather than hypertext links. Applied to the virtual museum, 3D virtual environments may make access possible or at least easier for certain groups. For example, those whose first language is not English (currently the most predominant language on the Internet) or whose reading skills are minimal including very young children. The 3D virtual environment is already familiar territory to children who play computer games. Some adults on the other hand have problems with interfaces that do not present clear instructions and limited choices. They may give up before they worked out what it is they are supposed to do rather than explore on a trial and error basis.

7 Conclusion

What of the future? National or even local on-line catalogues or inventories on anything but a small scale are still some way off. In fact they may prove too costly for some time to come.

Museums have always been about communicating with audiences and about giving and receiving information about the objects in their collections. If museums are to compete with other leisure activities they will have to make sure that they capitalise on the physical experience provided by seeing, touching and smelling real objects and on the opportunities that they provide for real social interaction.

In comparison with a real visit to a real museum a virtual visit to a 'virtual museum' is a poor experience. On the other hand, today's technology offers museums the opportunity to communicate with new audiences on an unprecedented scale. It also offers the opportunity to extend the quantity and depth of information presented in a way, which may not be possible in the real gallery. However, we must face the fact that the technological novelty and passive stimulation provided by the computer display, whether 3D or not, will be all that many virtual visitors will be looking for. How to take people beyond this entertainment threshold and into a deeper more rewarding world where they can begin to learn about the past is a real challenge to museums.

Notes

1. http://www.comlab.ox.ac.uk/archive/other/museums/uk.html

2. http://www.hants.gov.uk/museums/index.html

3. http://www.scran.ac.uk

4. http://www.nmsi.ac.uk/

5. http://www.nhm.ac.uk/sc/sc_front.htm

6. http://www.nmsi.ac.uk/on-line/apollo10/

7. http://www.gvu.gatech.edu/user_surveys/survey-10-1996/

8. http://www.nmsi.ac.uk/education/stem/index.html

9. http://www.nmsi.ac.uk/education/paper.htm

10. http://www.nmsi.ac.uk/education/

Bibliography

Delouis, D, 1993 Telecommunications in Museums, in Museums & Interactive Multimedia: Proceedings of the Sixth International Conference of the MDA, 1993 and the Second International Conference on Hypermedia & Interactivity in *Museums* (ed D Lees), 118

Gill, T, and Dawson, D, 1996 *The MDA Survey of Information Technology in Museums* 1995-1996

Gordon, S, 1995 Is Anybody Out There?, in *Hands on Hypermedia and Interactivity in Museums* (ed D Bearman), 115-122

Gordon, S, 1996 Museums and the information superhighway, in *Online Information Proceedings* (eds D I Raitt and B Jeapes), 305-310

Jackson, R, 1996 Science Centres and Museums in the Electronic Age: are we doomed?, in *The Informal Science Review*, September-October 1996

Museums Association Briefing, Number 15, March 1997

Platnauer, H M, and Howarth, E (eds), 1890 *Report of Proceedings, Museums Association*. First Annual Report, 1-10

Roberts, D A, 1985 *Planning the Documentation of Museum Collections*, 16-17

Roberts, D A and Light, R B, 1986 The cooperative development of documentation in United Kingdom museums, *in Museum Documentation Systems* (eds R B Light, D A Roberts and J D Stewart)

Contact details

Sue Gordon
Head of Information Systems
Science Museum
Exhibition Road
London SW7 2DD
UK

CIMEC - A Web Site for Romanian Archaeology: Dissemination by Integration

Irina Oberländer-Târnoveanu

Abstract

Communication on the Internet is a turning point for any cultural heritage information resource. In theory, the users can get direct access to information, from anywhere, at any time, for as long as they need. Electronic publication of scientific information does not exclude the traditional printing but can be quicker, cheaper, larger and more comprehensive. Browsing, reading, querying the information, linking it with other sources and updating when needed it is obviously a better way of handling the scientific material. It is stimulating. Communication on the Internet is global. That means a better co-operation across present administrative boundaries. Especially for a country where only a small part of the archaeological research has been published, where the main archaeological journals are already fully booked until 1999, the Internet is a chance for better dissemination of archaeological information. Are the Romanian archaeologists aware of that? Most of them have no Internet access yet. CIMEC opened an Internet server in May 1996 and offers hundreds of brief archaeological excavation reports from Romania and Moldavia, plus information on archaeological museums, archaeological terminology and sites. We believe in the significant impact of the Internet in the near future, on the Romanian professional circles. Moreover, we hope that the internetisation of Romanian archaeology will be an important factor in the acceleration of the growth in the number of Net connections in Romania.

1 Once upon a time...

...There was a CAA conference in Leiden (1995), where the organisers had the generous idea to offer the participants free access to the Internet. I happened to be there and to enjoy my first direct contact with the Web, at a time when that sounded like science fiction for many of us. I spent many hours in the Leiden computer room surfing the Internet, visiting archaeological web sites and thus discovering a rich world of information and global communication. It was so easy to use an Internet browser! Everybody can learn that in ten minutes. It was so fascinating to click and go to Internet pages in many countries, to navigate from one place to another following the hyperlinks! The very principle of hypertext proved to be intuitive and easy to understand. The possibility to see good images was a very useful and attractive feature. Getting access to the latest browsers from the beginning, I can hardly imagine how things must have been at a time when only plain text circulated on the Net. Still, the information dissemination facilities and the global character of communication are by far the most significant features, even for novices. I was amazed by the novelty of many texts, accessible very soon after they have been written. The participants at the conference in Leiden commented on an important French discovery of a cave with prehistoric paintings, presented on the Internet, with very beautiful images, soon after the event had happened (http://www.culture.fr/culture/arcnat/chauvet/fr/gvpda-d.htm).

My first Internet experience showed me also the role of indexes and directories to help people find their way to pages of interest. The Dutch ArchWeb site (http://archweb.Leidenuniv.nl/archweb_gb.html) and its pointers to other archaeological resources helped us find our way through an otherwise jungle-like wealth of information.

I suppose that many archaeologists had similar feelings on their first Internet day. If I write about mine, it is only to testify once more how important international meetings are for spreading new ideas. My direct contact with the Internet was more convincing than any written papers, handbooks and recommendations. I understood the real value of an Internet connection for better communication and dissemination of information. Back home, I proposed as a priority for CIMEC (the Romanian Information Centre for Culture and Heritage) to get an Internet connection before the end of 1995. I am grateful to the organisers of the Leiden CAA conference for their friendly kickstart.

2 The beginnings of the CIMEC web server

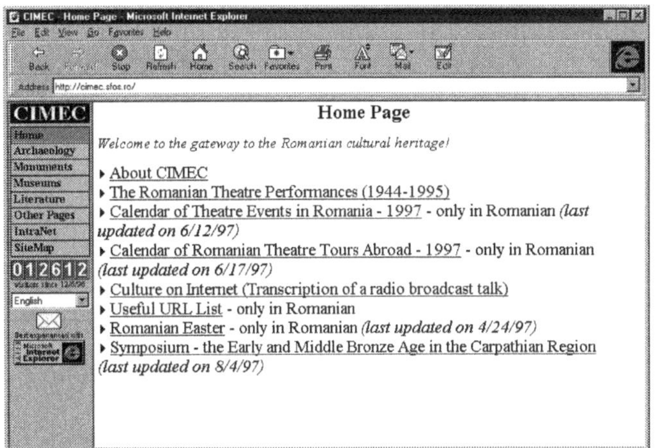

Figure 1.

In fact it was not before the end of 1995, but in spring 1996 when CIMEC got an Internet connection, established an Internet server and developed its first home page (see Fig. 1 and URL http://cimec.sfos.ro). It took us one year because the Internet was at its very beginnings in Romania at that time. Only a couple of institutions of technical profile, and computer research centres in the country had network connections and e-mail addresses. Romania is still suffering both in terms of telecommunications infrastructure (old telephone lines which need significant investments over many years), and in terms of the number of computers and computer networks. Above all, a lack of government strategy for adjustment to the information society made any initiative a costly and risky adventure that we had to embark on on our own.

The Internet wave started to rise in our country in the summer of 1996 and CIMEC had some of the first Romanian Internet servers. The connection by telephone line proving to be impossible, we discovered a much better alternative: the coaxial cable of a CATV company, KappaNet (http://www.kappa.ro), which developed a metropolitan network in Bucharest. The speed is six to ten times better than on telephone lines. The alternative of TV cable use is very promising taking into consideration that Romania is second in Europe in cable TV development with two millions users. As to the costs, we got and still benefit from a sponsorship program by the Soros Foundation for an Open Society, dedicated to connecting to the Internet schools, public libraries, museums and other non-profit Romanian institutions. The foundation played an important role in promoting the Internet in Romania (http://www.soros.ro). As to content, the Ministry of Culture finances the development of web pages for the Romanian cultural heritage at CIMEC.

We opened our web site in May 1996 and started our Internet adventure. Our server is a Dual Pentium with Windows NT 4.0. Being the main electronic gateway for the Romanian cultural heritage, we began to systematically fill in the blank space Romania has been until recently in cyberspace.

3 Why has the Internet been such a high priority for us ?

An Internet server is an investment sometimes difficult to defend when financial resources of an institution are scarce. Several reasons prompted us to consider it a priority for CIMEC:

3.1 Better public access to CIMEC databases and other electronic resources

There are institutions, organisations and services like CIMEC, that maintain national records, cultural heritage databases and other information resources in electronic format (Oberländer-Târnoveanu 1996). Without Internet, public access to these records was limited. The information systems were not friendly enough. Requests for information were frequently met with delays. Results of searches using these databases were traditionally provided either as hard copy or on diskettes. Users were mainly administrative bodies, museums or researchers. Access was slow and the textual information boring to anyone but a very specialised client. The information dissemination was poor even when brochures were printed. For example, CIMEC annually produced an Archaeological Chronicle of the past year's archaeological campaign (brief reports) for the National Archaeological Commission, in no more than 300 copies, distributed to the participants at the Annual Archaeological Reports Meeting. The archaeological excavations database behind the brochure, and the facilities of querying by period, place, institution, archaeologist, site type remained unused.

With the Internet, for the first time we can benefit from an authentic tool for information dissemination. It came just in time for us. We began to design web versions of archaeological reports and other databases: museums, museum collections, monuments and sites, cultural and scientific events, as well as image archives.

Following the general trend to better serve the public, to improve the communication and educational function of cultural heritage institutions, organisations from Canada to England and from Norway to Romania are changing their policy and taking advantage of the new technologies to offer their information to a larger public. "More" for the public, means more democratic access to scientific data, more stories, more images and an interactive way to communicate. Now we have the means to join this trend.

3.2 Electronic publication

Internet is a good publishing medium for scientific information as well. Especially for a country where only a small part of the archaeological research has been published and where the main archaeological journals (*Dacia* and *SCIVA*) are already committed until 1999, the Internet is a chance for better and more timely dissemination of archaeological research. We want to encourage the electronic publishing of archaeological materials as an alternative or parallel route to traditional journals and books. We expect only a limited audience until sufficient Romanian archaeologists get computers and Internet connections, to truly benefit as readers and authors of electronic papers, catalogues and news. The medium of the electronic paper should eventually be acknowledged for both personal bibliography and citation in the academic world. In the meantime, we are considering producing a limited paper version of Web publications. Young researchers, authors rejected by editors because of either too narrow topics or the quantity of text and illustrations offered for publication, scientists looking for international recognition, should be our first clients for electronic publication on the Internet.

Internet is also a good medium to publish the archaeological collections and archives, either as catalogues, inventories or as scientific papers. It is cheaper than paper. The information can be refreshed as often as one wishes, can be queried interactively by the user, and may develop over time without having to wait for new editions.

3.3 Information exchange and world-wide communication

Communication on the Internet is a turning point for any cultural heritage information resource. Users can, in theory at least, get direct access to information from anywhere, at any time, for as long as they need. Electronic publication of scientific information does not exclude the traditional printing press but can be faster, cheaper, larger and more comprehensive. Browsing, reading, querying the information, linking it with other sources and updating it when needed is obviously a better way of handling scientific material.

Secondly, communication on the Internet is global and stimulating too. That means a better co-operation across present administrative boundaries, a wish to contribute, to write, to answer. For people working in our organisation, the Internet is a source of learning, of professional contacts, of news, never experienced before. Joining news groups and e-mail discussion lists, visiting sites and reading electronic papers, downloading programs and searching for information related to our work, we become part of a global community, save time for documentation, and enjoy great opportunities of personal progress. In general, the quality and motivation of our work have improved.

4 What does CIMEC's offer on the Internet?

Our main goal is to provide wider access to information regarding museums and their collections, monuments and sites, archaeological excavations, and scientific events; to offer Romanian versions of international documentation standards and glossaries, to publish scientific papers, reports and recent discoveries which could otherwise wait for years to be published. In short, we plan:

1. to disseminate information gathered at CIMEC during the past twenty years, with contributions by Romanian museums, libraries and National Cultural Heritage County Offices;
2. to facilitate access to other cultural resources (Romanian and foreign) by integrating their URLs in our pages, in special indexes and directories;
3. to improve cultural heritage documentation, in theory and practice;
4. to encourage the development of Internet-based communication in the cultural heritage field;
5. to facilitate communication among people and institutions.

We have a web resource of 40 MB at present, half of it downloaded and home made software useful for our users. Archaeology is well represented with the following main topics:

Archaeological excavations and sites:

1. 298 brief descriptions of sites, excavated during 1983 - 1992 in Romania and the Republic of Moldavia (in Romanian, with introduction and search indexes on counties and periods in English as well) (see Fig. 2 or http://cimec.sfos.ro/arh/situri/siturien.htm)
2. 154 descriptions and images of monuments and sites in restoration, in Romanian and English (http://cimec.sfos.ro/scripts/her/monument/moe.idc)
3. industrial heritage: old iron-built factories in danger of being demolished (text in Romanian and English)
4. 160 brief excavation reports for the 1995 campaign, in Romania and the Republic of Moldavia (in Romanian, with introduction menu in English) (http://cimec.sfos.ro/arh/arh95.asp)

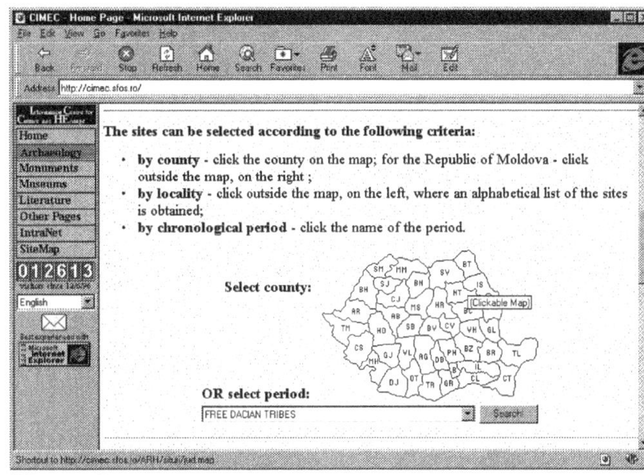

Figure 2.

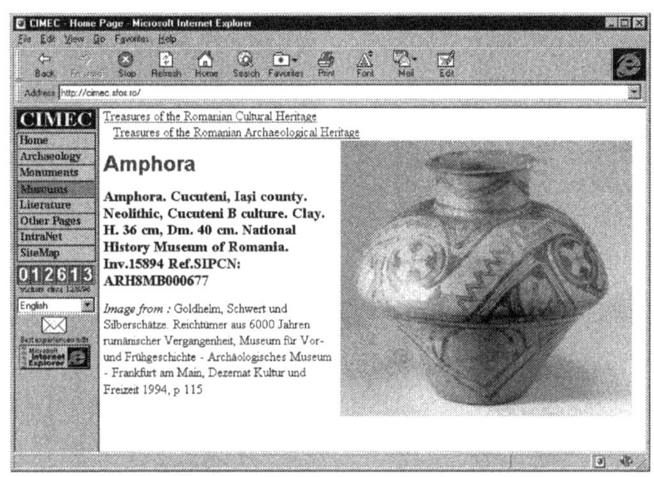

Figure 3

Collections, museums and persons:

1. museums with archaeological collections - more than 100 museums and collections (in Romanian and English): address, contact persons, short descriptions (http://cimec.sfos.ro/vlmp/muzee/muzeee.htm)
2. treasures from our archaeological heritage (22 images and descriptions of important archaeological pieces from various periods, in Romanian and English) (see Fig. 3 or http://cimec.sfos.ro/her/PCNMobil.asp)
3. Romanian Archaeology page: an introduction to archaeology in our country, institutions, publications and the site of Histria (in English and French) (http://cimec.sfos.ro/arh/mircea/arhe.htm)

4. a database of more than 180 archaeologists working in museums
5. special pages of archaeological museums

Conferences:

1. the CAA'96 conference in Iasi, Romania: 55 abstracts in English, a database of 102 participants with their addresses and e-mail addresses, event information and contributions included (in English), the program of the conference and other links (see Fig. 4 or http://cimec.sfos.ro/arh/caa96/caa96.asp)

Terminology:

1. Glossary (a project of the Council of Europe): 113 Romanian terms and definitions for European Bronze Age monuments, in English and French, with their Romanian equivalents and definitions (see Fig. 5 or http://cimec.sfos.ro/scripts/arh/bronz/bronze.idc)

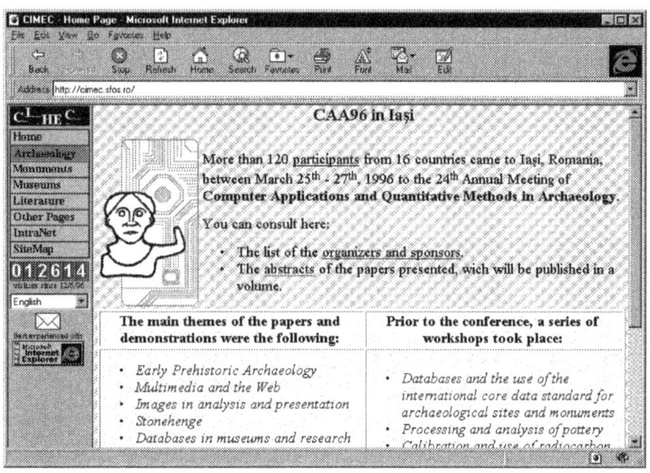

Figure 4.

We have focused on page content, and on access facilities in both Romanian and English. The interface design is simple and clear. We plan to give access to more and more information resources: archaeological papers, perhaps an electronic archaeological journal, maps and images of the most important archaeological sites, presentations of archaeological events and projects.

5 Who are our Internet readers?

What is seen as a revolution from the outside – Romania is not a blank page any more – has apparently had little impact inside the country. For the moment, we have a larger audience from abroad than from our own country: of around 1000 visitors per month, 60% come from abroad (USA, England, Norway, and Italy, many for the archaeological pages or following the ICOM Virtual Library Museums Pages web links) and 40% from Romania (school students, cultural institutions, newspapers and media). Only six Romanian museums have an Internet connection (in Bucharest, Sibiu, Cluj, and Braila) and e-mail communication with CIMEC, but we hope to convince more institutions about the benefits of the Internet.

Are Romanian archaeologists aware of the potential of the Internet? In general there is little interest, computer illiteracy being still widespread among archaeologists, beyond text editing. There is also a fear of losing control over information, and of language barriers (you must know English pretty well to become familiar with the Internet). The younger generation is more interested, but lack the means to influence decision making in their organisations; most of them have no Internet access yet. The senior generation, with few remarkable exceptions, is sceptical or even rejects the idea of using the Net. We therefore face not only the bad communication infrastructure, but also the conservative mentality of the decision makers - a fear of the democratisation of access to information. Apart from fear of improper use of the Internet, this is obviously a conflict between generations. The younger archaeologists are more familiar with computers and would undoubtedly make more use of the Internet, thus getting an independence hardly acceptable to the older generation. The recent refusal by the Institute of Archaeology in Bucharest of an offer for a free Internet connection is only one example of this.

The need for access to hardware and network connections is coupled with an even greater need for access to training. There are not enough courses and trainers.

Time works for us, and the general trend in using information technology will in the end convince reluctant institutions. We publish Internet pages in Romanian for an increasing number of Romanian users, who will find the resources already on the web when they need them. We believe the Internet will have a significant impact in Romanian professional circles in the near future. Moreover, we hope that the internetisation of Romanian archaeology will be an important factor for the acceleration of the growth of the number of Net connections in Romania. Besides, integrating a number of separate archaeological resources — as, for instance, the regional archaeological inventories — in one accessible environment will improve the dissemination of the archaeological data. In this technological context the importance of the indexes and — by extension — of the authority files is growing.

6 Internet - a moving target: old problems in a new environment

The Internet has a serious impact on both people and institutions. One must expect to reconsider, as we did, all current projects. Although the Internet tools are not yet entirely satisfactory and need further development, all documentation projects must be Internet oriented in view of being accessible with an Internet browser sooner or later. That implies changes in the record structure, in image processing, in programming and applications design, in terminology control etc. The organisational structure of the institution may need to be revised to accomplish new tasks and jobs in connection with the Internet, such as Web mastering, Internet page design and programming. Our staff had to learn a lot of new things in a short time. New relations are developing among those responsible for the content of the projects - historians, archaeologists, art historians - and the technical staff. With using the Internet, a range of new problems arise and old ones must be solved in a new environment: How to organise the information? How to promote it? Updating regularly, advertising, planning the development of the web site, browsing the Net for new links may become critical in terms of time and costs.

6.1 Organising

When you have more than five entries on your web page, you already face an organisation problem. Pointers to information are not enough. A short introduction is needed to explain the value of the resource pointed at. The need for proper organisation of web pages in order to facilitate the route to the actual information drove us to try out various solutions, from thematical folders and frames to a site map. We still are not fully satisfied and changes are being made while the site continues to grow. The problem is made more difficult by the large variation in both computer types and Internet browser versions used by the visitors.

6.2 Updating

Refreshing page content regularly is one of the great challenges of the global network. Most of the activity on the Internet is based on voluntary work of many enthusiasts. Few institutions with web pages seem to have understood the need to regularly maintain their web pages and to allocate the required financial resources for that purpose. It is so frustrating to visit obsolete pages, last updated a year or more ago! If we want to make use of the Internet, news must be presented quickly, that being one of the basic principles of network communication. Another problem is: once you have made web pages, how do you let people know that you exist and have something new to offer? Publicity becomes more important - you can't just wait to be discovered. We saw the positive effect of announcing by e-mail our pages to administrators of specialised networks such as ARGE (Archaeological Resource Guide for Europe, http://www.bham.ac.uk/ARGE), on discussion lists such as CIDOC-L, and to web masters of large organisations.

6.3 Retrospective work

The Internet electronic library is in its early stages. Browsing through, or looking for a specific topic, the general feeling is mixed. Following indexes you meet a variety of good and poor links, "poor" not necessarily in terms of quality of information, but in terms of its scarcity. Firstly, it is frustrating to find, lumped together on the same page, primary, secondary and tertiary sources, archaeological reports and short notices - the last ones prevailing. Moreover, the URL addresses of these sources change quite often and without proper notice.

Secondly, most of the bibliography remains outside the Net. So do the great names in various humanistic fields. Why do the best scientists in humanistic disciplines remain mostly outside the Internet? Maybe they have neither the skills nor the time to produce electronic papers (or web versions of their printed works). The lions' share of important contributions to archaeology have of course occurred prior to 1994, the year of the rapid expansion of the Internet, and as a consequence also remain outside the Internet. This very fact diminishes the complexity and the integrity of the virtual library on the Internet. Who should do something about it? Are the most recent papers also the most important? Usually in humanistic fields changes in concepts take time. The presence of scientific authorities is stimulating for other scientists to contribute too. The Internet needs that aura of quality in order not to remain like a newspaper one browses through once and then throws away. One of the potential solutions are projects of retrospective electronic publishing of important works in each country and discipline. We are considering such a project named 'Golden Pages of Romanian Archaeology'.

6.4 Indexes

As web resources are expanding in number, it is more and more difficult to find your way through the Net. Search engines like Alta Vista, Lycos, and Yahoo return thousands of links for a single search. Who should catalogue these web pages and sites, just as classic publications are catalogued? The large traditional libraries are concerned with their own collections and have not yet developed a professional interest in cataloguing web pages. An important role is played by thematic and regional indexes and directories: ARGE, the WWW World of Archaeology (http://www.he.net/~archaeol/wwwarky/wwwarky.html) and many others maintained in large universities, research centres, cultural administrative bodies and organisations. They are useful places to check for both beginners and experienced Internet users. Not only do you get the links you need, but also they are trustworthy places to visit. Should those responsible for the specialised pages and directories become censors? Should they make a selection? The balance between freedom of information and the need to prevent valuable information from mixing with less valuable information is delicate.

7 ... And they lived happily on the Internet many years after

We believe in the future of electronic publishing. The Internet has changed our life in only one year. The life of many other institutions and of archaeology in Romania and also world-wide will certainly change in the near future. The CIMEC team has many plans and wants to play an active role in those changes.

Bibliography

Oberländer-Târnoveanu, I, 1996 Statistical View of the Archaeological Sites Database, in *Interfacing the Past. Computer Applications and Quantitative Methods in Archaeology, CAA95* Vol. I 1996 (Analecta Praehistorica Leidensia 28, eds. H Kamermans, and K Fennema), 47-50.

Contact details

Irina Oberländer-Tarnoveanu
CIMEC - Centrul de Informaticã si Memorie Culturalã
(Information Centre for Culture and Heritage)
Piata Presei Libere 1
CP. 33-90
71 341 Bucharest
ROMANIA
email: irina@cimec.sfos.ro

EARP - European Archaeological Research Projects: A Fieldwork Opportunities Database on the Internet.

CAA 97

Nuccia Negroni Catacchio, Monica Miari, Barbara Setti, Giovanni Meloni, Emilia Groppo

Abstract

EARP (European Archaeological Researches Project) is a fieldwork opportunities database on the Internet. It is part of the European Project ARCHEONET - ARCHAEOLOGY TOWARDS THE THIRD MILLENNIUM, one of the key Socrates SIGMA projects, in close collaboration with the European Association of Archaeologists and headed by the University of Bristol. One of the major task of the Archeonet project is to help and increase reciprocal field training. EARP major aim is to link together European students with Universities and Institutions promoting archaeological researches in Europe. In this way EARP will facilitate student mobility and promote educational training and archaeological information exchanges in Europe. This database is an Object Oriented Relational Data Base, and its technology handles not only alphanumerical but even complex data as images, sounds, videos etc. The authors of this project are the Istituto di Archeologia - Universita' degli Studi di Milano and the CILEA (Consorzio Interuniversitario Lombardo per l'Elaborazione Automatica).

1 Introduction

The Istituto di Archeologia of the Università degli Studi di Milano and the CILEA (Consorzio Interuniversitario Lombardo per l'Elaborazione Automatica, Segrate) are participants in the ARCHEONET project (http://archweb.LeidenUniv.nl/archeonet/), one of the only 28 thematic networks funded by DG XXII of the European Community. This network is the result of a study made by a group of European Universities developed in close collaboration with the European Association of Archaeologists. Its aim is to increase the education and training of common professional standards within the European Union while retaining cultural diversity, and to solve the problem of students' mobility through the use of distance teaching modules, videoconferences, and general information exchanges on line.

CILEA attends to the implementation, the Istituto di Archeologia to the contents, following a scheme well tested in the past with excellent results.

In the Archeonet first phase the activity of these two institutions is divided into different development lines:

1. creation and management of an European Database (*EARP*) on fieldwork opportunities;
2. creation and management of a HyperMail system for the community of archaeologists;
3. creation of ARGE[1] mirror site;
4. participation in thematic videoconferences.

The second phase of Archeonet will start this autumn: all these actions will be put into operation and new projects will start, including the participation of new European projects.

2 The Web Site

The Internet site *European Archaeological Research Project* (*EARP* - http://archeonet.cilea.it/archeosite) is part of the European project Archeonet - Archaeology towards the third millennium. One of the major tasks of the network is to help students and researchers to take part in archaeological projects in Europe. A major aim of EARP is therefore to put students and researchers directly in contact with Universities and Institutions promoting fieldwork and surveys.

We thought that a database would be the best tool to see on-line details of research projects looking for foreign students, and to manage the participation forms sent by the students. To simplify access to the database, this Internet site is simple and user friendly; that's how the browsing speed has been minimised.

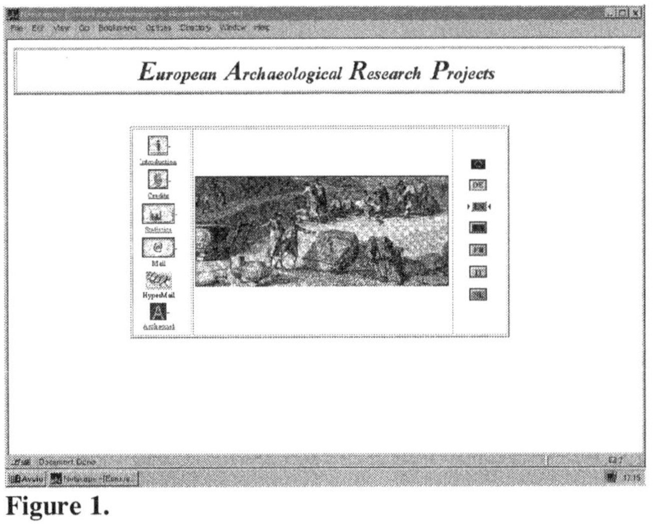

Figure 1.

From the Homepage (see Fig. 1), before starting the research, you can select some icons:

1. *Information*, to obtain more information about the project;
2. *Credits*, to know the authors;
3. *Statistics*, to see the number of contacts[2] and the joining forms sent by the students;
4. select the language;
5. the link to the *Archeonet*.

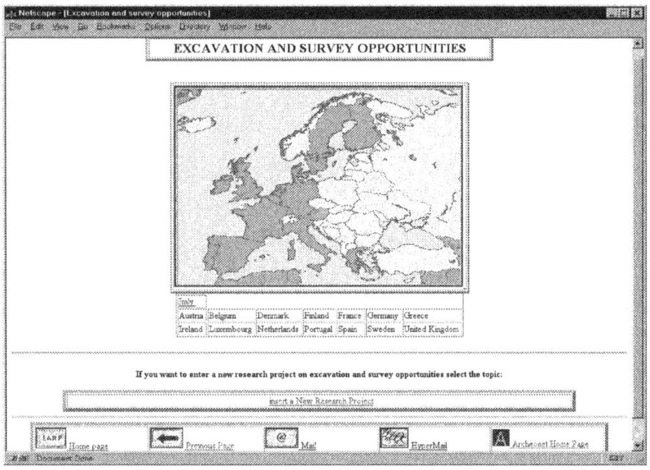

Figure 2.

Starting the research, firstly you see an image of a map of Europe (see Fig. 2); from here you can reach the pages of the countries (see Fig. 2). Now you have two choices: you can make a direct search to reach the *Site Form* and to fill in *Participation Forms*; you can also select a region on the Nation image map.

In the first case the direct search is divided into:

1. Chronology, divided into:
    1.1. Prehistory and Protohistory
    1.2. Preroman and Greek age
    1.3. Roman age
    1.4. Late antiquity and Medieval
2. Type of excavation, such as:
    2.1. settlement
    2.2. cemetery
    2.3. sanctuary
    2.4. cave excavation
    2.5. urban excavation
    2.6. underwater excavation
    2.7. survey
    2.8. pluristratified excavation
3. Site
4. Institution promoting the research
5. Degree of training: this is aimed at students; in this way they can choose between:
6. field school
7. academic research with educational training
8. academic research

If you select a region on the nation image map, you see its enlarged image with all the excavation sites, showed by a number and explained by a legend (see Fig. 3).

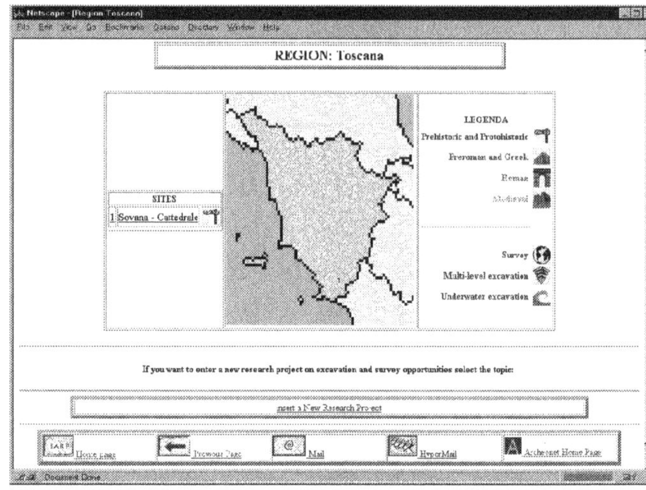

Figure 3.

The sites have been chronologically subdivided into the classification explained before (Prehistory and Protohistory, Preroman and Greek age, Roman age, Late antiquity and Medieval). Each one of them is related to a specific icon and a colour, to immediately identify the site. Near the chronological division there is also the classification into project type with a huge chronological extension (survey, multi-level excavation) and underwater excavation. If you select one of those, you reach a list of the sites; from here you can enter the *Site Form*.

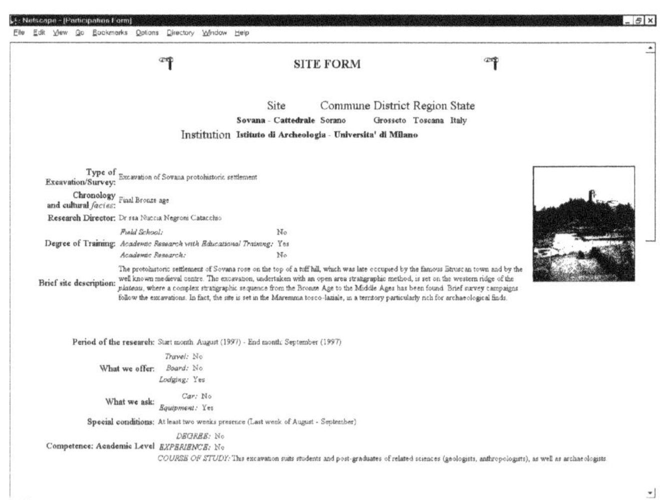

Figure 4.

The *Site Form* is organised into three parts (see Fig. 4). The first one has the "registry data" - such as the name of the Site, the institution and the research director - the degree of training and the specific information about the type of excavation, the chronology and the cultural facies, and a brief description of the site. The second part of the form has all the information necessary to the students, such as length and period of the research, what is supplied, and the competence/ academic level request. The third part contains the *Participation Form* (see Fig. 5), that can be sent directly by E-mail. The student will then be personally contacted by the research director.

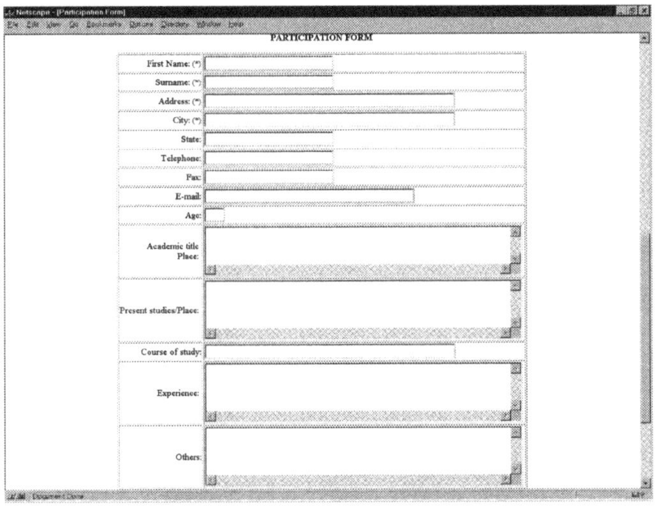

Figure 5.

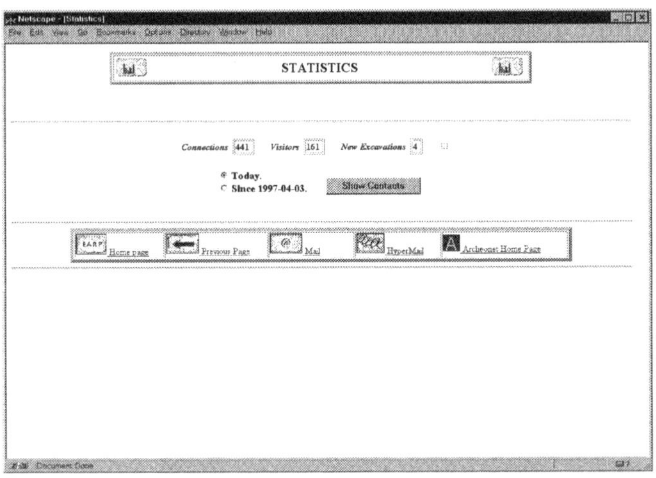

Figure 6.

Another guide to choosing the site is offered by consultation of the statistics (see Fig. 6), on the participation form sent by the students. You can reach them by selecting the topic *Statistics* in the Homepage. In order to reconstruct the general information about this Internet site it is also possible to see the general statistics, about the type of excavation/survey, the chronology and the region, the number of connections, visitors and new excavations and so on.

Institutions wanting to advertise a new research project can select the topic *Insert a new research project* (see Fig. 7) and can directly E-mail to the *EARP* the form with all the data necessary for the creation of a new site form.

3 Technical Notes

The *European Archaeological Research Project* is an application that builds and manages dynamic Internet pages. That means that this project has a database with all the necessary information that can be queried, managed and updated by processes activated from Internet pages.

This database consists of two main archives, linked together and with other index tables.

The two main archives are:

1. Excavation projects;
2. Participation in the excavation project.

The index tables are:

1. Chronological legends
2. Type of excavation legends
3. Nations
4. Regions.

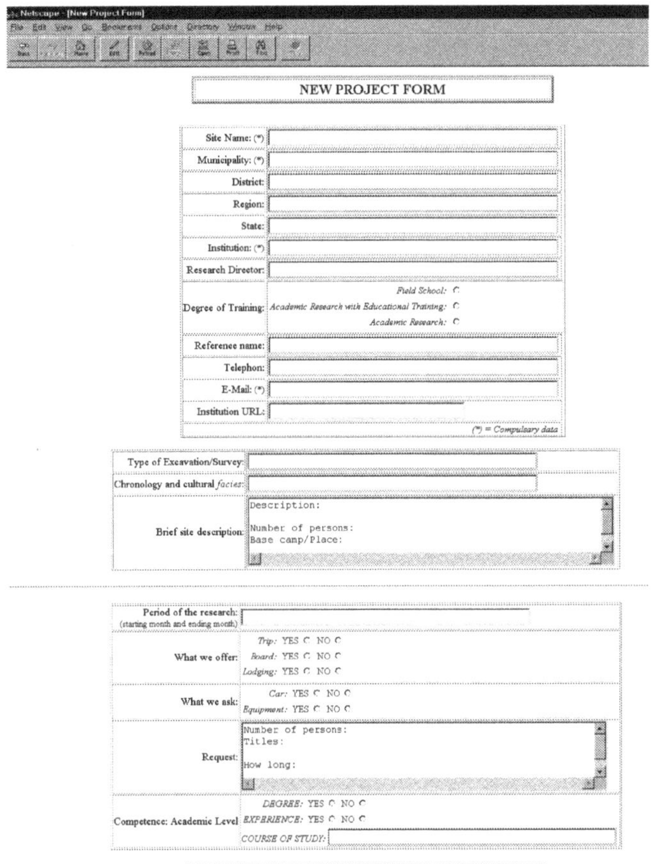

Figure 7.

For the implementation of the *EARP*, the Informix software ILLUSTRA has been chosen, set up on a Unix HP-UX 9000/735 platform. ILLUSTRA is an object DBMS linking the potential of a relational database with the possibility of defining new types of data stored inside an archive and managed in the same way as classical data (numerical and alphanumerical). We have defined image data in order to store the excavation site images (gif or jpg files) into a special archive or to store all the icons or the maps used to enrich the appearance of the pages. ILLUSTRA databases are managed by SQL language, now a standard in this sector.

The main characteristic of ILLUSTRA is the availability of a high number of DataBlades, which can interact and manage data in a new way. Web Datablade has been used to realise the *EARP* Internet site. With this module the system Web server can have dialogue with the ILLUSTRA archives. The Web Datablade gives some instructions (TAG) to the Internet pages (in the now classic HTML language); in this way it is possible to execute the SQL directions on the database tables, the variable managing and other programming operations.

The source code of an EARP Internet page contains either classical HTML statements or an ILLUSTRA Web Datablade. The Web Datablade receives this page, reads the tags, makes the operations, produces and restores a new page converting its tags into HTML instruction, that can be read by all the browsers on sale (e.g. Netscape, Internet Explorer).

With ILLUSTRA and its Web Database it is possible to store any kind of information in all the different archives composing the database. In this way we have realised tables containing the subject data of the applications (excavation site, Participation form, legends etc.). These tables store images; in this way the procedure is not bound to read an external file with the expected image residing in some directories of the system hosting the application. The image is extracted from the proper archive with a select operation (SQL), in the same way of any other classical data.

The HTML Internet pages too are stored within the Web Datablade proprietary tags into a proper table asked every time to extract the page requested by the user. In this way the whole application identifies itself with the database; in fact it finds in the database all the elements needed for its working: from the data to the images and the Internet pages providing the browsing, the insertion, the research and the visualisation of the needed information.

Notes

1 See M. van Leusen, this volume.

2 To verify site visibility and utility we provided for registration not only of the contacts, but also of the visitors, in the sense of people who started the research on the database.

Contact Details

N. Catacchio, M Miari, B. Setti
Istituto di Archeologia
Università degli Studi di Milano
via Festa del Perdono 7
20122 Milano
ITALIA
email: negroni@cilea.it

G. Meloni, R. Ferrari, E. Groppo
CILEA
via R.Sanzio 4
20090 Segrate (MI)
ITALIA
email: meloni@cilea.it

Museums, Education and the Internet
Abstracts of papers held on CD-ROM

CAA 97

The Homer Project
Phil Perkins

The Homer Project is research into the viability of multimedia as a distance teaching medium for undergraduate courses. The project has taken part of the Open University A295 'Homer: Poetry and Society' course and converted it into multimedia on a CD-ROM and will be assessing it's effectiveness in 1998.

Digging the Web: German Archaeology on the Internet
Andreas Brunn

This paper gives a brief summary of the kind of archaeological information available on the internet in the German language (and who is offering it), how museums, institutions and individuals represent themselves and their work on the web, and what is done to make these sometimes almost hidden parts of the web more easily accessible to everybody interested in German archaeology. Furthermore the acceptance of this electronic medium by German archaeologists is discussed.

ARCHAEOLOGY IN THE AGE OF THE INTERNET

CAA 97

Section 8
Making History

Making History: the Once and Future Roles of the Royal Commissions

Jennifer Stewart

Introduction

1. The Royal Commissions (of England, Scotland, and Wales) were established by Royal Warrant in 1908 with the stated aim of the preservation of antiquities by inventory. Since that time the Commissions have continued making significant contributions in heritage information through the collection, curation and management of archaeological information, as well as expanding their dissemination and access facilities and roles. The following short notes, which form this section, will look at how the Commissions are addressing the challenges of the electronic age. This is not intended to be a comprehensive review of the totality of the work of the three Commissions, but to describe work in progress germane to the theme of archaeological computing.

2. This is the first time that all three Commissions have organised a joint session at the Computer Applications in Archaeology conference. Next year, the ninetieth anniversary of the founding of all three Commissions, an Anniversary CD will be launched to illustrate the current work of the three Commissions as well as looking to future challenges.

3. During this century the role of the three Commissions has gradually changed and evolved into the following three main activities.

3.1 Data collection: either by acquiring physical collections of records and images or via survey work. Robert Bewley of the Royal Commission on the Historical Monuments of England (RCHME) describes the work of the National Mapping Programme, which since its inception in 1988, includes all archaeological features seen on aerial photographs. As he notes the NMP is not just about creating maps and images, but to aid the understanding of the archaeological sites in their landscape context.

Hazel Riley in her article describes recent work utilising Global Positioning System (GPS)

to survey and record the archaeological sites within the Exmoor National Park. This landscape-based approach has ensured integration not only into the RCHME's text-based database but also into the National Park's GIS.

3.2 Information management: all three separate National Monuments Records carry out this activity. Chris Watkins in his paper describes the processes whereby the English Commission prepared a new strategy to guide its future use and development of information systems and information technology, to support the changing business needs of the organisation and to develop the business benefits which will accrue from an IS Strategy. Bryne in her article describes current and planned developments to increase public access facilities into the National Monuments Records of Scotland. The underlying aim is this work as she notes is to present the user with logically connected pieces of information while making the underlying 'mechanics' invisible. An innovative pilot is mentioned which will look at ways of managing queries across multiple distributed databases using metadata as an intermediary across the Web.

Loretta Nicolic describes the situation in Wales, where the Royal Commission on the Ancient and Historical Monuments of Wales is gathering and exchanging data with the Welsh SMRs, CADW and the National Parks to set up a national index of every known site in Wales, called ENDEX. ENDEX is part of the Extended National Database (END) of Wales, which also provides a forum to establish core data standards and database structures. She also sets out the Welsh Commission's plans in imaging and GIS – while such plans will greatly facilitate their public access, she rightly underlines the need for long term management strategies for the future preservation of digital data.

3.3 Dissemination of this information can be facilitated through the Commissions' public search facilities, by conventional publications and increasingly, by electronic means. Robin Taylor in his paper describes the English Commission's experience in setting up its Web site (www.rchme.gov.uk), where electronic access is seen as an active response to the challenge of the information society. RCHME's Web site was launched in October 1995 and acts as an electronic brochure for the Commission's work and information services. He notes the interesting statistic that the resource required to set up the Web site and provide it for one year is equivalent to the cost of producing one printed book, this making more information available for less cost.

4 Within these three main activities, the main challenges for the three Commissions in archaeological computing include the following:

increasing digital access (and especially meeting the demand for digital products);

balancing a complex plural funding arena based on central government funding, partnerships, Lottery bids and income generation from the selling of services and informational assets while still maintaining free access at point of access;

maintaining technical innovation and integration with existing systems;

managing complex copyright issues.

Neil Beagrie carried out for the RCHME a wide-ranging review of its rights management procedures and the implications of current and proposed changes to copyright legislation. This survey was viewed as critical underpinning to RCHME's plans for developing its 'Electronic Commission' by increasing electronic access. As he notes in his paper, all archaeologists now have to address copyright as part of a project bid and when drawing up contracts, and he reinforces that copyright needs to be addressed right at the beginning of a project rather than at the end.

5. This summary of the work in progress within the three Commissions shows their commitment not only to archaeological computing but also to one of their main roles, of reaching a wider, national and global audience through the means of electronic access.

Contact details

Jennifer Stewart
Director of Information Services and Development
RCHME
National Monuments Record Centre
Great Western Village
Kemble Drive
Swindon SN2 2GZ
UK
email: swncsd@rchme.gov.uk

Understanding England's Landscapes: An Aerial Survey Approach To A National Mapping Programme For England

Robert H. Bewley

Abstract

The purpose of this paper is to present the challenges and problems we face at a national level in utilising the existing aerial photographic resource and the roles that computer applications play in maximising the potential for aerial survey. This includes the collections of aerial photographs, approaches to mapping, interpretation, as well as the presentation and dissemination of results.

1 Introduction

Aerial photography for archaeology is a cyclical process. The process involves taking aerial photographs, curating and making them accessible in libraries as well as interpreting them for mapping projects. Ultimately their use can lead to a better understanding of past human behaviour as well as assisting in the development of preservation strategies. The purpose of this paper is to present a brief résumé of the RCHME's National Mapping Programme which began as a cropmark classification project in 1988 (Edis *et al* 1989) and broadened its scope to include all archaeological features seen on aerial photographs (Bewley 1995).

The National Mapping Programme is now at a cross-roads in terms of new technologies and new approaches to record dissemination and creation within the National Monuments Record (NMR). The methodology which has developed since 1988 has to be evaluated in the light of these developments and in particular in the use of computer applications, especially new software development and GIS.

2 The background

Aerial photography for archaeology is approaching its ninetieth birthday, and archaeological aerial photographs have been accumulating in a number of libraries throughout England. The two major sources, National Monuments Record (NMR), the public archive of the RCHME, and the Cambridge University Committee for Aerial Photography's library hold over 900,000 photographs taken for archaeological purposes (Bewley 1993). Each year more aerial reconnaissance takes place adding new information to this enormous resource (Featherstone *et al* 1995, Featherstone 1994; Griffith 1990). See also Figure 1.

The majority of the twentieth century has been one of data gathering (i.e. reconnaissance surveys and taking photographs). The exception in the early years was the work of OGS Crawford (Crawford 1924, 1929 and 1955) whose approach was to use aerial photographs as a means of creating maps which depicted an archaeological site or landscape, with an interpretation of its meaning. This approach was further developed by the RCHME (RCHME 1960) and by others (Bewley 1984a and b, Palmer 1984, Whimster 1989) in the early 1980s.

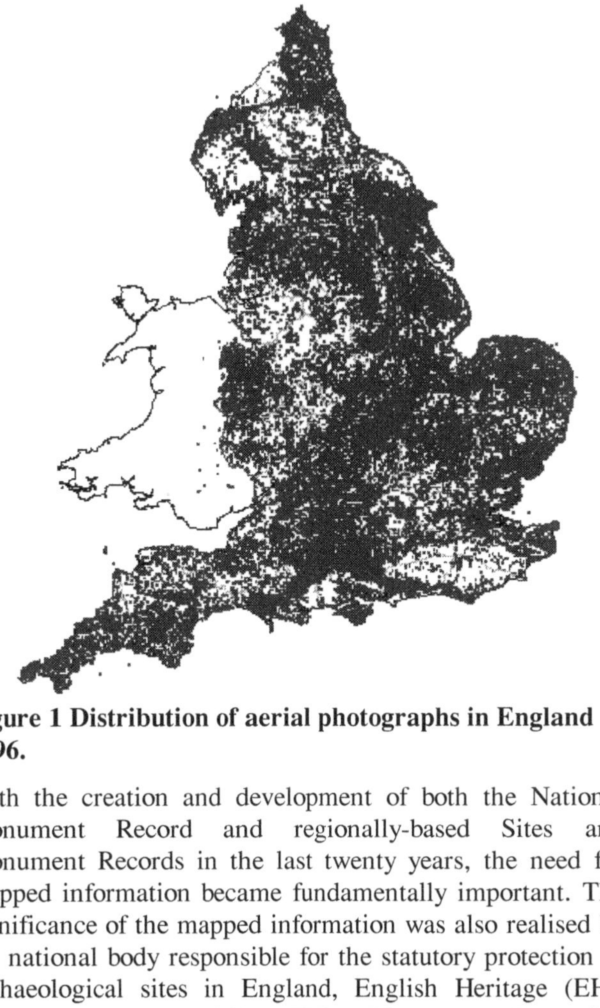

Figure 1 Distribution of aerial photographs in England 1996.

With the creation and development of both the National Monument Record and regionally-based Sites and Monument Records in the last twenty years, the need for mapped information became fundamentally important. The significance of the mapped information was also realised by the national body responsible for the statutory protection of archaeological sites in England, English Heritage (EH). During the late 1980s EH's Monument Protection Programme (MPP) was established to increase the number of protected sites within England (Fairclough 1996). Research projects working on the classification of archaeological sites seen on aerial photographs (especially cropmarks and soilmarks) had begun in the 1980s (Bewley 1984a and b, Whimster 1989). Classification was taken further in a project designed specifically to solve the problem of describing sites in a systematic way, for use in the MPP when the MORPH and MORPH2 computerised recording systems were developed (Edis *et al* 1989, Bewley 1995). Four pilot projects were jointly funded by the RCHME and English Heritage (Hertfordshire, Kent, Thames Valley and Yorkshire Dales) see Figure 2.

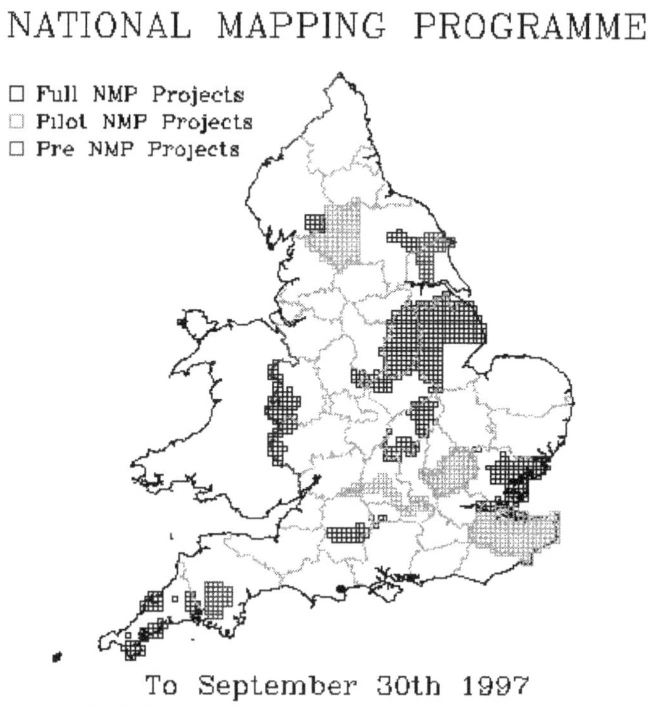

Figure 2 NMP progress.

Since then all NMP projects, which includes those mapping projects which preceded the pilots but had similar aims, e.g. the Yorkshire Wolds (Stoertz 1997) and Dartmoor, as well as new projects, have mapped 1187 maps. This represents 22% of the total of 5,444 maps at 1:10,000 scale. During 1995 an internal review of NMP was completed and with the changes to the organisation of the RCHME it was an appropriate period to evaluate possible new approaches to the methodology of NMP.

3 Current position and future directions

The evaluation falls into three areas: methodology of mapping, approaches to recording, and analysis of results.

3.1 Methodology of mapping

The approach to date has been a mixture of manual transcription onto translucent film overlays and computer-aided rectification using the AERIAL 4.2 programme (Haigh 1991). The one exception to this has been the project, funded by the RCHME and run by Northamptonshire Heritage, to map Northamptonshire using digital methods. This project is still ongoing and has been a research and development opportunity to examine the feasibility of working in a totally digital environment. So far the products have been highly successful and digital maps are used every day for planning purposes on the local GIS network using Mapinfo. The digital plot files from AERIAL are enhanced using Adobe Photoshop package and can then be linked to the MORPH2 records and cross-referenced to the SMR.

Within the RCHME there is a commitment to move to digital mapping, and trials using digital Ordnance Survey (OS) maps have begun (late 1997). For one project, to map the archaeological sites in the Avebury World Heritage Site area, the OS have supplied digital maps (Bewley *et al* 1996). The AERIAL program will still be used (including the newer versions 4.3 and 5.0) as will AutoCad 14 for preparing the final digital plans. The move to digital mapping for all the NMP projects (which are based in two RCHME locations, Swindon and York, as well as in the other two external locations, in the Cornwall Archaeological Unit and Essex County Council; the Northamptonshire Heritage project has already been mentioned) will take a number of years. The resources required are not yet available to purchase the required hardware and software and the training of staff in the new methodologies, which has now begun, is also a considerable commitment of time.

3.2 Approaches to recording

Since the early pilot projects began and with subsequent developments in the requirements at a national level, the current recording system, MORPH2, has to be replaced. The basic approach and philosophy behind the recording system, as published (Edis *et al* 1989) will not change. The need for morphological descriptions of sites whose date or function are unknown is an agreed, fundamental principle, though it is more likely to be useful for prehistoric, Roman and Romano-British periods than later ones. There are four morphological tables on the international database - one for Enclosures, Linear Features, Linear Systems and Macula, (see Edis *et al* 1989). For the Yorkshire Dales project, which was the first to use MORPH2 and included the systematic recording of earthworks and stoneworks as well as cropmarks, an input screen to include industrial sites on a presence-absence basis was devised (Horne and MacLeod 1994). MORPH2 is a suite of programs that manage a number of related databases providing a closely structured method of describing archaeological features. The database conforms to the dBase3 standard, the programs are run using FOXR (the runtime version of FoxPro) and the indexes are of the FoxPro type.

The need for a recording system which produces a database which can be analysed within the project areas, or by combining project areas is also fundamentally important. However, the development of the MONARCH system for the National Monument Record and the requirement for all new archaeological sites recorded by the survey staff to be input to MONARCH meant that a more streamlined flow of information was necessary. The transfer of data from MORPH2 to MONARCH is too costly in time and a replacement was necessary. The review of NMP and the requirements of a national monument recording system, currently MONARCH, has allowed for some of the anomalies and problems of using MORPH2 to be ironed out.

A proposal for a new recording system has been drawn up and is currently being evaluated in terms of its feasibility and costs. The approach has been to allow the core fields, required by MONARCH, to be input as an opening screen and then to allow further, more detailed morphological recording to take place, if necessary, on subsequent screens. The current system of recording (MORPH2) uses PCs, and transfer its data, via a tag loader to the MONARCH system.

MONARCH is a three-tier client server application which comprises an Oracle 7.3 database on a SUN SPARC server. Part of the evaluation will be to consider the best approach in terms of hardware for rapid input, easy analysis facilities and rapid transfer of records to the national monument recording system.

3.3 Analysis of results

The National Mapping Programme is not just about creating maps and records. Its approach has been to aid understanding landscapes using one particular strand of evidence, aerial photographs. The databases created (MORPH2 using FoxPro) are amenable to analysis in many ways (Fenner and Dyer 1994, Horne and MacLeod 1994) but the main focus is to examine the possibility of creating new classes of sites. Known site types (e.g. henges, Roman Forts etc.) can be easily classified but the numerous enclosures of various sizes and shapes, which are discovered in large quantities in all NMP projects (e.g. 3,318 in the Thames Valley, 1,394 in SPTA, 5,233 in Lincolnshire, 4,525 in the Yorkshire Dales) can be broken down by size and shape and then are available for further research (Bewley 1994).

However this approach does not provide an understanding of the archaeological sites in a landscape context which is important if the association of sites and site types is to be appreciated. The future approach has to include the use of GIS to allow for analyses on spatial variables such as soil and locational preferences. One of the fundamental questions relating to the use of information derived from aerial photographs is whether it is representative of past human behaviour or is a reflection of our own abilities to discover sites. The analytical capabilities of GIS will allow these questions to be answered more efficiently (Bewley 1994).

4 Conclusion

As the national body of survey and record the RCHME not only has to adopt and adapt to new developments but also to decide when is the best time to do it. An analogy is the way in which a river, following an oxbow will cut through the neck of the oxbow and re-create a straight line of flow. If technology is the river where are we on the oxbow? Over the past five years we have been going with the flow, turning the bend of the oxbow but the time is now right to join the mainsteam and accept the developments in technology and implement the new approaches to digital mapping, recording and GIS analytical tools which are available to us.

Bibliography

Bewley, R H, 1993 Aerial Photography for Archaeology, in *Archaeological Resource management in the UK* (eds J Hunter and I Ralston), 197-204, IFA/Alan Sutton

Bewley, R H, 1984a *Prehistoric and Romano-British Settlement in the Solway Plain, Cumbria*, PhD. University Library, Cambridge

Bewley, R H, 1984b An approach to the Classification of Aerial Photographs, *Scottish Archaeological Review*, 3.2, 141-145

Bewley, R H, 1994 *Prehistoric Romano-British settlement in the Solway Plain, Cumbria*, Oxbow Monograph, 36

Bewley, R H, 1995 A National Mapping Programme for England, *in Luftbildarchäologie in Ost - und Mitteleuropa, Forschungen zur Archäologie im Land Brandendurg3*, Potsdam

Bewley, R, Cole, M, David, A, Featherstone, R, Payne, A and Small, F, 1996 New features within the henge at Avebury, Wiltshire: aerial and geophysical evidence, *Antiquity*, 70, 639-46

Crawford, O G S, 1924 *Air Survey and Archaeology*, Ordnance Survey Professional Papers, new series 7

Crawford, O G S, 1929 *Air Photography for archaeologists*, Ordnance Survey Professional papers, new series 12

Crawford, O G S, 1955 *Said and Done*. The autobiography of an archaeologist, London

Edis, J, MacLeod, D and Bewley, R H, 1989 An archaeologist's guide to the classification of cropmarks and soilmarks, *Antiquity*, 63, 112-26

Fairclough, G, 1996 *The Monuments Protection Programme 1986-1996 in retrospect*, English Heritage Leaflet, XH 20033

Featherstone, R, 1994 Aerial reconnaisance in England 1994, *Antiquity* 68, 812-15

Featherstone, R, Horne, P, Macleod, D and Bewley, R, 1995 Aerial reconnaissance in England, summer 1995, *Antiquity*, 69, 981-8

Fenner, V E P and Dyer, C, 1994 *The Thames Valley Project*, A Report for the National Mapping Programme, RCHME internal report

Griffith, F M, 1990 Aerial Reconnaissance in mainland Britain in the summer of 1989, *Antiquity*, 64, No. 242, 14-33

Haigh, J G B, 1991 The AERIAL program, Version 4.1, *Aargnews* No. 3.

Horne, P and MacLeod, D, 1994 *The Yorkshire Dales Mapping Project*, A Report for the National Mapping Programme, RCHME internal report

Hunter, J and Ralston, I, 1993 *Archaeological Resource management in the UK*, IFA/Alan Sutton

Palmer, R, 1984 *Danebury: an Aerial Photographic Interpretation of its Environs*, RCHME Supplementary Series No. 6

RCHME, 1960 *A Matter of Time*, HMSO

Stoertz, C, 1997 *The Ancient Landscapes of the Yorkshire Wolds*, RCHME, Swindon

Whimster, R P, 1989 *The Emerging Past*, RCHME

Contact details

Robert H. Bewley
RCHME
Kemble Drive
Swindon SN2 2GZ
UK
email: swindon@rchme.gov.uk

The Use of Global Positioning System Technology to Record and Interpret Archaeological Sites and Landscapes

CAA 97

Hazel Riley

Abstract

This paper describes and discusses the use of differential Global Positioning System (GPS) equipment for the survey and recording of archaeological sites and landscapes within the Exmoor National Park, an upland area in southwest England. The technique facilitates the production of earthwork plans, site management information, contour maps and digital terrain models (DTM), all surveyed to the Ordnance Survey (OS) National Grid. The digital data obtained can then be used in the GIS (Geographic Information System) operated by Exmoor National Park Authority (ENPA).

1 Introduction

1.1 The Exmoor archaeological survey project

The Exeter Office of the Royal Commission on the Historical Monuments of England (RCHME) instigated two major upland archaeological survey projects in 1993. The aim of these projects was to record the archaeology contained within the former Royal Forest of Dartmoor and the Exmoor National Park. This paper is concerned with the development of a survey methodology designed to cope with the rigours of the complex topographic and archaeological landscapes of Exmoor.

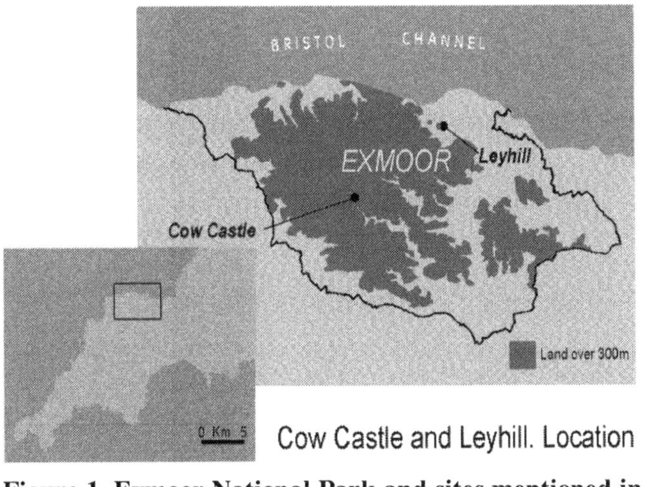

Figure 1. Exmoor National Park and sites mentioned in text

The Exmoor National Park covers approximately 700 km^2 of diverse landscape type in the southwest of England (see Fig. 1). The landscape ranges from bleak high moorland such as the Chains, which rise to over 400m OD, to the deep wooded valleys of the Barle and Exe rivers. The Exmoor coast offers high cliffs, coastal heath and a foreshore environment, whilst the Brendon Hills to the east are mainly enclosed and improved (Binding 1995).

1.2 Exmoor's archaeology

The range of archaeology encountered is similarly diverse (Grinsell 1970). Prehistoric sites are largely confined to the unenclosed moorland. The earliest field remains consist of stone monuments: stone settings and stone circles, which tend to be elusive and vulnerable to damage. These monuments are undated, but probably belong to the later Neolithic and earlier Bronze Age periods. Bronze Age burial cairns are often substantial monuments, situated in prominent positions on the ridge tops of the dissected upland plateaux. On the coastal fringes, these cairns command splendid views over the Bristol Channel to the Welsh coast. Smaller cairns are often associated with fragmentary field systems and house platforms. The later prehistoric period is represented by earthwork enclosures and hillforts (see Fig. 2). Castle earthworks and several deserted medieval settlement sites with associated field systems are some of the earliest documented sites. Post medieval sites encompass a wide range of industrial, agricultural and recreational activities.

Figure 2. Cow Castle: Iron Age hillfort in Barle Valley, Exmoor.

Previous archaeological surveys of the Exmoor landscape have either been monument based (Grinsell 1969; Quinnell and Dunn 1992), or have focused on a specific area for management purposes (McDonnell 1985). The

RCHME Exmoor survey project is designed to consider the archaeology of all periods for the whole of the Exmoor National Park, both to improve the locational and textual record for known sites, and to reconnoitre for new sites. This targeted reconnaissance is based on air photograph inspection, map work, local knowledge and experience (Wilson-North and Sainsbury 1994; Exmoor National Park Authority 1995).

2 GPS and its use in archaeological survey

2.1 Principles of GPS survey

Only the basic principles of GPS survey are set out here, further details are given in Hern 1989. The method of working will, to some extent, depend on the type of equipment and software being used. The RCHME Exeter Office has had access to differential GPS survey equipment since 1995. The equipment in use is Leica single frequency System 200 (SR 261 GPS sensor and CR 233 controller). This equipment utilises the American Department of Defence navigational satellites. These are 24 NAVSTAR satellites, which orbit the earth at an altitude of 10,900 nautical miles, constantly transmitting radio signals. Triangulation from these satellites is the basis of the system. To triangulate, GPS measures distance using the travel time of a radio message. Readings from a minimum of four satellites are required to give a position. Depending on the type of equipment used, the position given can be accurate to within, say 50-100m (*navigation solution*), this is the type of solution given by hand held equipment for walkers. Working in differential mode, as described below, allows measurements to be taken on a feature centimetres apart.

2.2 Differential GPS survey

Differential GPS equipment is required for precise land survey. Two sets of equipment are used. One GPS receiver (the *reference* station) is set up over a point with known GPS coordinates (WGS 84). This records radio signals transmitted from the satellites throughout a survey session. On East Exmoor, two permanent reference stations have been established, both in secure sites owned by the ENPA. The second set of equipment (the *rover*) is taken to the survey area, which can be up to 10km from the reference station. The rover is set up for a specified amount of time to *initialise*, then the operator is free to walk where he chooses to record either fixed survey points, or the archaeological detail (see Fig. 3). A set of data thus recorded is known as a *kinematic chain* (see Fig. 4). OS triangulation pillars or other co-ordinated points also need to be incorporated into the survey data set if the survey is to be related to the OS National Grid.

The survey data is processed using Leica's SKI GPS processing software. The data collected from the rover is processed in relation to the reference station, a known, fixed point. The survey data is now in the form of WGS84 co-ordinates, expressed as either latitude/longitude or Cartesian co-ordinates (see Fig. 4). A further transformation program allows the conversion of this data to the OS National Grid (OSGB36). The resulting ASCII file is then processed using Trimmap integrated survey-processing software, to resolve feature codes, and plotted or further enhanced in AutoCAD and CorelDraw.

Figure 3. GPS survey on Exmoor

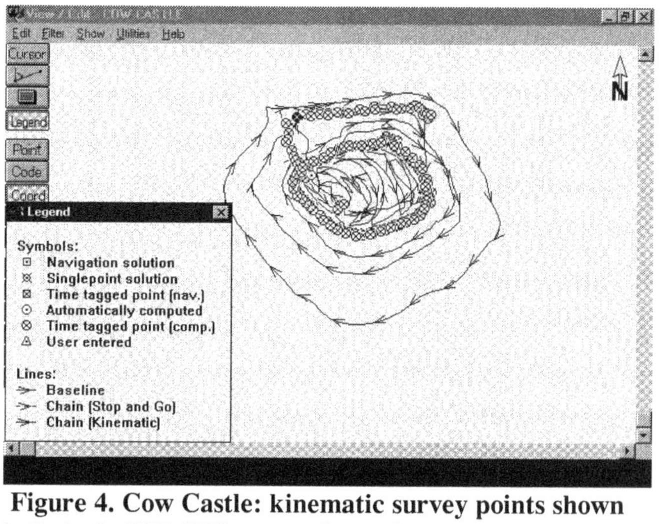

Figure 4. Cow Castle: kinematic survey points shown in Leica's SKI GPS processing software

2.3 Advantages and problems of GPS survey

This method of working has several advantages over traditional EDM survey. The most obvious is that it allows the operator to walk wherever he needs, there is no longer any need for intervisibility between survey stations. A team of two people can thus concentrate on finding and recording the archaeological features. A second major advance is that the co-ordinates obtained are absolute, there is no need for laborious traversing to obtain OS control. This is particularly beneficial in upland areas, where OS map detail is sparse. GPS thus allows sites and landscapes to be tackled in a way that was hitherto prohibitive in terms of fieldwork time. The whole of the archaeological landscape including, for example, extensive areas of extractive industrial remains, can be recorded in some detail. The continuous recording of 3-D kinematic points facilitates the production of DTMs and contour plans, either of individual sites or detailed topographic features.

GPS receivers will not function properly close to trees or buildings, where the satellite constellation is blocked. The kinematic technique has proved to be particularly suited to areas with unrestricted, open horizons, such as moorlands and inter-tidal or coastal landscapes (Riley 1995). The reference station must be in a secure position, as it will be left unattended for the duration of the survey session.

3 Archaeological sites and landscapes

3.1 Introduction

One of the key aims of the RCHME's Exmoor archaeological survey project is to provide a record of Exmoor's archaeology at 1:2500 scale. Within the project there is scope for the larger scale survey of discrete sites or areas of particular regional or national importance. The project also allows the archaeology of Exmoor to be considered in a wider, landscape-based context. The use of GPS technology has aided all types of survey work undertaken within the project.

3.2 Large scale survey of archaeological sites using GPS

A large-scale survey of the univallate hillfort known as Cow Castle was undertaken early in 1997, at the request of the ENPA. The survey was part funded by the ENPA within their Monument Management Scheme, which is itself jointly funded with English Heritage. The site also comes under the remit of the RCHME's Exmoor archaeological survey project. Cow Castle lies on an isolated, conical hill in the Barle Valley (see Fig. 2). The aim of the survey was to record the earthworks in detail, and to produce information to aid the management, presentation and interpretation of the site, which is close to a popular riverside footpath.

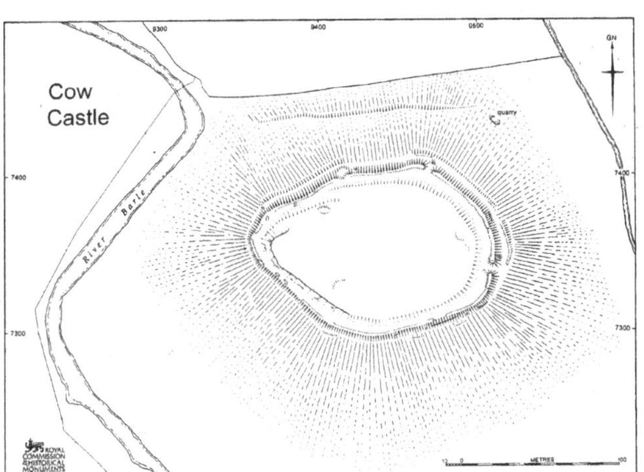

Figure 5. Cow Castle: 1:1000 earthwork survey, RCHME, 1997

The site was surveyed entirely by GPS equipment. An established reference station *c* 6 km from Cow Castle was used. The first stage of the survey was to record the earthworks in detail (see Fig. 5). The position of footpaths, areas of damage and erosion were also surveyed, and the positions of two survey pegs were determined. The second stage was to record enough data to produce a contour plan and DTM of the whole of the hill (see Figs. 6 & 7). This was achieved by walking over the interior of the site, collecting data at a 10 second time interval, on a 10m grid. The hill itself was surveyed by walking a spiral route down and around the hill (see Fig 4). Approximately 2000 points were collected and the fieldwork took two days.

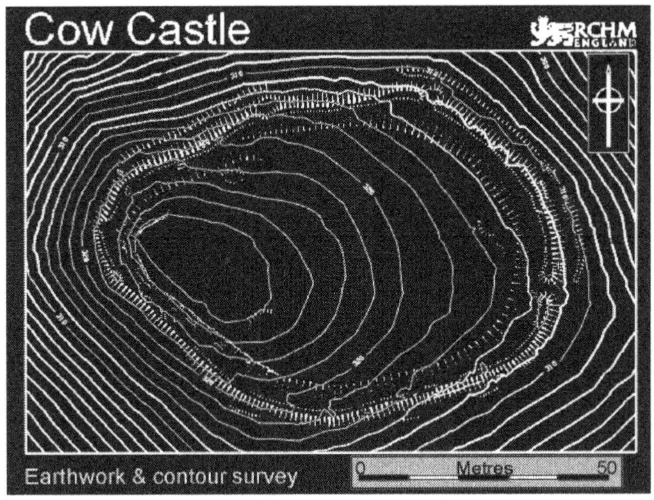

Figure 6. Cow Castle: contour plan

GPS survey is a time effective way of surveying earthwork sites at large scale, particularly if, like Cow Castle, the site is remote. The resolution is accurate enough to take points centimetres apart. The survey of the archaeological detail provides a base for the work required to produce a contour map and DTM (see Figs. 6 & 7). The contour map is particularly effective when the earthworks of the hillfort are superimposed on it (see Fig. 6; earthworks shown on CD-ROM version). The DTM can be observed from different viewpoints, and has proved to be an important tool in the interpretation and visualisation of the site. The CD-ROM version of Figure 7 contains a selection of viewpoints of the DTM. Those from the northwest and east are viewed from a higher altitude, giving an aerial perspective. That from the south has an exaggerated vertical scale and shows the position of the hillfort on the hill in profile. The view from the southwest shows the way the interior of the site falls to the east in a series of terraces which have been utilised for prehistoric habitation sites (Fig. 7).

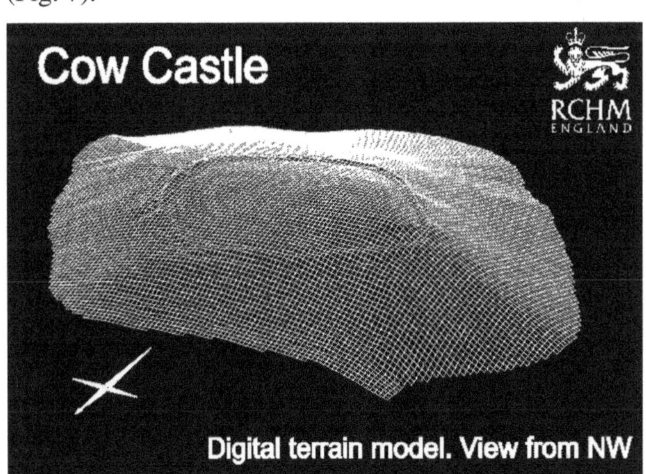

Figure 7. Cow Castle: digital terrain model

This method of digital survey is also an efficient way of dealing with the preparation of drawings for reports. The data is managed in AutoCAD. A number of layers are set up, enabling the production of overlays for the main earthwork drawing, showing the areas of erosion and footpaths, and contours, which are used for the ENPA's ongoing management initiative (Riley 1997).

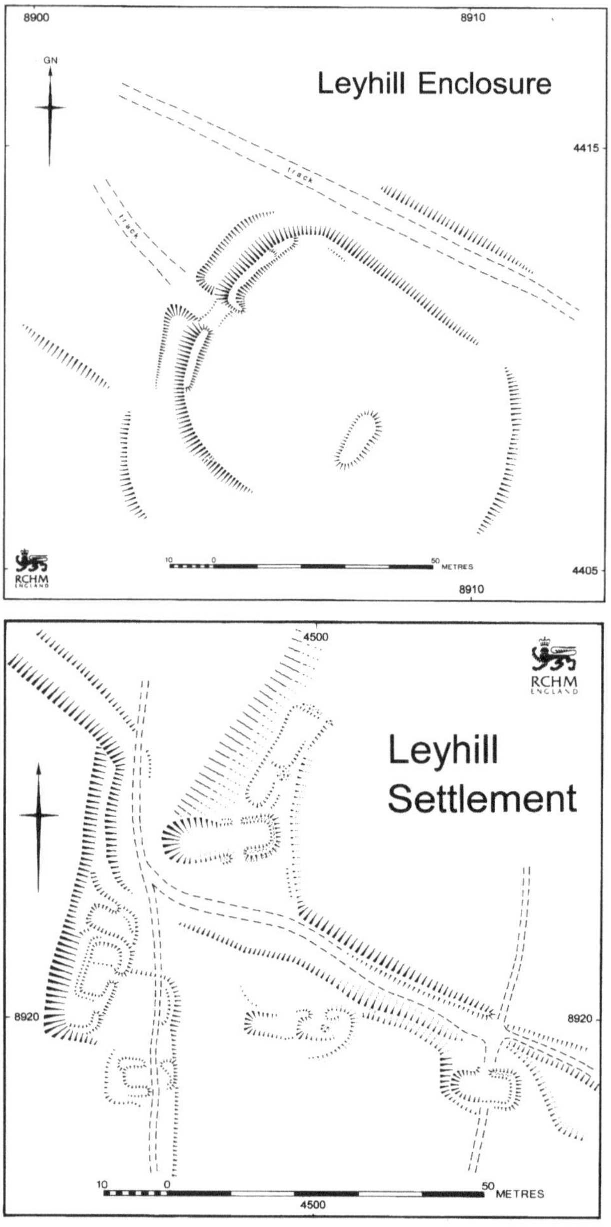

Figure 8. Ley Hill: prehistoric enclosure and deserted medieval field system, 1:500 earthwork plans, RCHME, 1997

3.3 A landscape based approach

At the beginning of the project, the area was divided into two, West Exmoor and East Exmoor. GPS has been available since the start of the East Exmoor area. This has allowed the recording of all the archaeological features on the unenclosed parts of East Exmoor digitally. So far some 50kms^2 have been surveyed in this way, including the block of land surrounding Dunkery Beacon, the highest point on Exmoor. The data is again managed on AutoCAD, in a series of simple layers that relate to the date of the archaeological features. The descriptions of these features are contained in MONARCH at the National Monuments Record Centre; RCHME's text based record.

The margins of the unenclosed land have proved to be some of the most fruitful areas for the discovery of previously unrecorded sites. One such area is on Ley Hill, above Horner Wood (see Fig. 1). The National Trust commissioned a survey of Horner Wood as part of a management plan, and two important earthwork sites were discovered (McDonnell 1994). These sites are an Iron Age enclosure and a deserted medieval settlement. Both sites are located on the edge of woodland and unenclosed moorland. Because of this, locating the sites on the National Grid and surveying the detail is both difficult and time consuming using traditional survey methods. There is very little local OS control, and the nearest OS triangulation pillar is over 3km away, across very difficult terrain.

GPS was used to locate survey pegs on the edge of the prehistoric enclosure, where a clearing in the wood allowed a reasonable array of satellites. The enclosure was then surveyed using an EDM, and the plot was transformed to the National Grid using a conventional program in the Trimmap software. A detailed earthwork plan of the settlement site was then produced (see Fig. 8). The medieval settlement was more complex. Seven buildings survive on the woodland edge, and an associated field system lies both on open, unenclosed land and within the wood itself (see Fig. 9). The settlement was located and surveyed in a similar manner to the enclosure, with survey pegs fixed by GPS, and detail recorded by an EDM to produce a large scale plan of the earthworks (see Fig. 8). The field system was recorded using GPS on open ground. In the wood, the field system was surveyed by traversing with the EDM and pegs were left on the edge of the wood. The pegs were located with GPS in order to relate this survey to the National Grid. This method of working again proved very time efficient. This was particularly important, as there was only a short time window available for survey when both the bracken on the open moorland had died back and the broad-leaved trees had shed their leaves. This survey located two previously unrecorded sites to the National Grid, and enabled them to be placed in their landscape context for the first time (see Fig. 10) (Wilson-North 1997).

Figure 9. Ley Hill: EDM survey of deserted medieval settlement

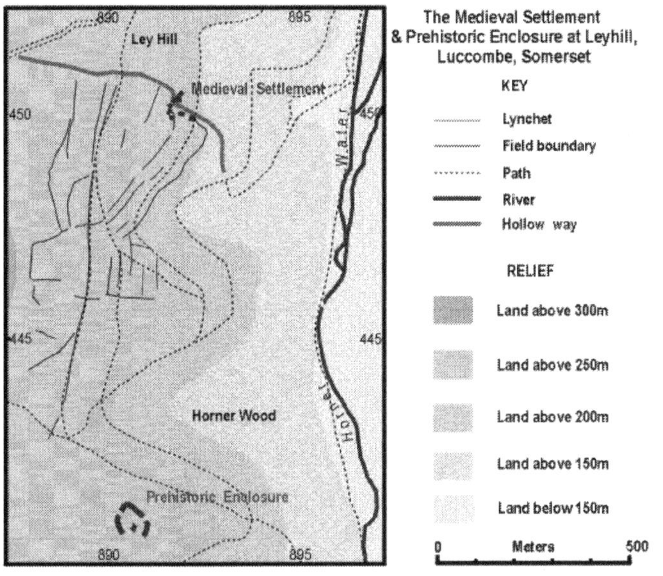

Figure 10. Ley Hill: archaeological landscape

4 The future

The ENPA have a GIS that is used throughout the Authority. MapInfo V4.1 and the Planning System, PACs, are both used. The OS data comprises Landline, OSCAR, 1: 10000 Raster and Address Point. The ENPA have about 200 layers of data on this system, including aerial photographs for the whole of the National Park, taken in 1995, which have been scanned and rectified. Historic maps are currently being input to the system. The RCHME's digital survey data will provide a further layer of information. Digital survey information has been incorporated for two pilot areas from the RCHME survey project. The ability to look at the survey data in conjunction with the aerial photographs aids fieldwork preparation, survey, interpretation and presentation of the survey work. The GIS will be an essential tool in the preparation of the publication of the results of the Exmoor project as a synthetic and interpretative report.

A DTM for the Exmoor National Park is currently being purchased, and the superimposition of 3-D survey data, such as that from Cow Castle, over the DTM, then draped with an aerial photographic image, is planned.

A further site for the raw survey data may be on the Internet, where users could download and manipulate the 3-D co-ordinates for the Cow Castle site in their own Virtual Reality programs.

Acknowledgements

The survey work was carried out by Rob Wilson-North and Hazel Riley. Phil Newman prepared the illustrations. Veryan Heal and Donna Wright from the ENPA provided help and advice. Thanks are given to all the landowners and tenants who allowed access to their land, and to the ENPA for their co-operation in providing safe sites for the GPS equipment.

Archive arrangements

Site accounts and plans produced for the project area completed to date are available for public consultation through the archive of the RCHME, at the National Monuments Record Centre, Kemble Drive, Swindon.

Bibliography

Binding, H, (ed.) 1995 The changing face of Exmoor. Exmoor Books, Dulverton.

Exmoor National Park Authority, 1995 Annual Report 1994/95. Exmoor National Park Authority, Dulverton.

Grinsell, LV, 1969 Somerset barrows part 1: west and south. Proceedings of the Somerset Archaeological and Natural History Society (supplement) 113, 1-43.

Grinsell, L V, 1970 The Archaeology of Exmoor. David and Charles, Newton Abbot.

Hern, J, 1989 GPS: a guide to the next utility. Trimble Navigation, Sunnyvale CA

Mcdonnell, R, 1985 Recommendations for the management of archaeological sites in the Exmoor National Park. Western Archaeological Trust, project report.

Mcdonnell, R, 1994 Horner Wood: report on the preliminary archaeological field assessment of two sample areas. The National Trust, project report

Osborn, B, 1983 Parish Surveys in Somerset 5: Minehead Without. Somerset Archaeological and Natural History Society, Taunton.

Quinnell, N.V.Q. and Dunn, C.J. 1992 Lithic monuments within the Exmoor National Park. Royal Commission on the Historical Monuments of England, project report.

Riley, H, 1995 Brean Down, Somerset: interim report on a new survey by the Royal Commission on the Historical Monuments of England, Archaeology in the Severn Estuary 6, 13-21.

Riley, H, 1997. Cow Castle, Exmoor, Somerset. Royal Commission on the Historical Monuments of England, project report.

Wilson-North, R, 1997 A medieval settlement and prehistoric enclosure on Ley Hill, Luccombe, Somerset. Royal Commission on the Historical Monuments of England, project report.

Wilson-North, R, and Sainsbury, I, 1994 Exmoor National Park, Proceedings of the Somerset Archaeology and Natural History Society 138, 166.

Contact details

Hazel Riley
RCHME
5 Marlborough Court
Manaton Close
Exeter EX2 8PF
UK

Any Time, Any Place, Anywhere

Chris Watkins

CAA 97

Abstract

Last year, the Royal Commission on the Historical Monuments of England carried out a review of its Information Systems Strategy. After consultation, it prepared a new strategy which it hopes will guide the future use and development of its Information Systems and Information Technology to support the changing business needs of the organisation. The first section sets out to describe the processes which were used to conduct the review and it also presents a few of the review's key findings. The second paper represent the new strategic statement itsel

1.1 "A lust for"... information

The clichéd title of this paper was chosen somewhat arbitrarily several months ago to serve as a way of expressing a perception held by some people of the world we live in today. According to this particular perception we appear to possess an insatiable lust for information, similar to the "lust for life" which Irvine Stone attributed to Vincent Van Gogh in his book of the same title. Another way of expressing this ravenous desire might be to say that collectively we have a need for information at any time, from any place, held anywhere, which is not constrained by such things as differences in: time zone, language or technology.

I strongly suspect that this perception - of people not being able to go about their daily lives without continual reference to information - is one that is held more passionately by the companies that sell information services and equipment than by the people who use and pay for them.

There is, however, a ring of truth to this perception. For instance, how many of us have found that networks, such as the Internet, have provided us with access to information we might have found hard or even impossible to obtain by other means?

The title, "Any time, any place, anywhere", is also meant to act as a reflection on the findings of a review which the Royal Commission conducted recently of its IS strategy. The rest of this paper describes the processes which led up to the preparation of a new statement of IS strategy and the following paper represents the Statement itself.

2 A recent IS Strategy Study

During the winter months of 1997, the Royal Commission carried out a review of its current IS Strategy and, after consultation with staff, it prepared a new strategy to guide the future use .and development of Information Systems and Information Technology to support the changing business needs of the organisation.

In essence, the study tried to address three simple questions:

Where are we now with our IS?

Where do we want it to be in the future?

How do we get there?

The first two questions were addressed by the Statement of IS Strategy in the following paper and the third was answered by a separate IS Implementation Plan.

The work of the review was controlled internally by three management teams: an in-house Study Team was appointed to plan and carry out the review; a Strategy Board of senior staff watched over the Team and picked up on the wider issues as they emerged; and a User Group acted to assure the quality and accuracy of review findings.

Consultants were used sparingly during the process - mainly to help increase staff awareness of new and emerging technologies and to assist in the production of a set of technical scenarios which would serve as a guide to identifying the alternative ways in which the Commission might develop its technical infrastructure in the future.

2.1 Conducting the IS Strategy Study

During the course of the review, the Study Team conducted a series of 35 interviews as a means of understanding what people actually did at the Royal Commission - as opposed to what the organisation thought they were doing - and to find out how they were using their Information Systems, what improvements they wanted and what new facilities they required.

The information gathered from these interviews went through a number of analytical stages before it began to provide answers to the above questions. During the course of these stages, the study threw up a number of observations about how the organisation worked and two examples of these may be of interest to others engaged in similar studies. The first is an example of the duplication of effort to get things done and the second an example of not enough effort being applied.

2.2 An example of the duplication of effort

Following a recent major structural reorganisation, which took place just before the study commenced, the Commission was keen to eliminate any areas of duplication which might still exist where, for instance, staff were still carrying out some of their former duties as well as their new ones. A series of business models, which were constructed as part of the study, were particularly good at highlighting where duplication was still occurring and so, using the interview results, a table showing business teams mapped against business functions was set up to show the areas of overlapping activity, so that they could be eliminated.

Some duplication is necessary, even in the most streamlined of organisations. The banking institutes, for example, have to duplicate certain elements of their business in each of their high street branches in order to provide a nation-wide service. The Commission does the same in its regional offices.

2.3 An example of not applying enough effort

When the Study looked at which parts of the organisation were responsible for dealing directly with the outside world a surprising picture emerged. Out of the 35 people who were interviewed, 19 of them said that their staff dealt with enquiries from members of the public but only 6 of them kept a formal record of the enquiries. So the indicators that the Commission was using at the time to measure its public enquiry service were based upon incomplete data. This has since been put right.

2.4 Conclusions

Returning to the title of this paper, maybe another way of stating this need for access to electronic information "any time, any place, anywhere" is to rephrase it in terms of the underlying technology and state it as a need to access "any data, through any application, using any interface". With its new IS Strategy in place, the Commission is now turning to the task of developing a new technical infrastructure which will be flexible enough to support the many needs of the organisation, both now and in the future.

The Commission believes that if it is to survive in the modern business world it must change the way it works and the way in which it promotes itself, and it must turn its Information Systems outwards to help it to reach a wider audience.

3 Information Systems Strategy Statement

"In recent years we have seen an enormous interest and enthusiasm for the documentation and protection of our historic environment. The Royal Commission on the Historical Monuments of England (RCHME) has a central role to play in making information available to the public, satisfying the demand for knowledge as well as creating a climate of understanding in which historic monuments can continue to flourish for future generations". Lord Faringdon, Chairman (RCHME 1996, 2)

3.1 Introduction

RCHME collects, manages and disseminates information on the archaeological landscape and built heritage of England. It collects information through programmes of research and survey; it manages information through the administration of the inventory and collections of the National Monuments Record; and it makes information available through the provision of publications and public search facilities, through personal contact and through the exchange of digital information.

Over the years the Royal Commission has invested heavily in Information Systems (IS), primarily to help it collect and manage records, and in the future it aims to realise that investment by directing its IS focus towards the better provision of information resources to a wider audience.

3.1.1 Purpose of the IS Strategy

The purpose of the Commission's IS Strategy is to direct the use and development of Information Systems in support of the current and future business needs of the organisation and the purpose of the IS Strategy Statement is to inform people what the strategy is and how it can be achieved. The Statement was prepared as part of a recent IS Strategy Study conducted between September 1996 and March 1997 (RCHME 1997a), using, where appropriate, the CCTA guidelines described in *Strategic Planning for Information Systems* (CCTA 1989).

3.1.2 Scope of the Strategy

The scope of the Strategy covers the Information Systems used in all RCHME business areas. The Statement is intended to remain in effect for the Strategic Plan period 1996-2001.

3.2 The Statement

3.2.1 The business environment and its future direction

The business of the Royal Commission as defined in its Royal Warrant "is to compile and assess, curate and make available the national record of England's ancient monuments and historic buildings for the use of individuals and bodies concerned with understanding, interpreting and managing the historic environment" (RCHME 1996, 1).

In 1995 Virginia Bottomley, the Secretary of State for National Heritage, confirmed that the primary function of the Commission is to make available the record of the historic environment which "must serve those involved directly in preservation and management as well as those who simply want access to the record for education or pleasure, both now and in the future" (RCHME 1996, 24).

The Commission considers that, in order to satisfy the requirements of the Royal Warrant and the wishes of the Secretary of State, its core activities must be:

1. to ensure the maintenance of, and public access to, the dispersed national index of the historic environment on a national basis;
2. to coordinate national policy for heritage archives and to curate core NMR collections of national importance;
3. to coordinate the definition of the national research agenda for the historic environment.

RCHME is a major supplier of heritage information and is unique in the national coverage it provides. It is committed to delivering a service which is of benefit to the community and it has recognised that in order to survive, it is having to face up to the rigours of the modern business world. Demand from customers is forcing it to broaden its range of products and to raise its standards of service, while pressure from Treasury to reduce public spending is forcing it to examine new sources of funding, including: tapping into revenue streams, bidding for lottery money, and exploring the benefits of joint ventures, partnerships and Private Finance Initiatives (Newchurch 1996).

3.2.2 Current status and contribution of IS

RCHME believes that IS has a major role to play in helping it to achieve its primary business objective of providing heritage information.

In the past, provision of IS within the Commission has tended to focus on the management of records. Several single-function databases were developed in the 1980s to support a variety of tasks including the emergency recording of listed buildings, the processing of orders for photographic work and the rectification of aerial photographs. In 1990, when an IS Strategy Study found that "the data held by RCHME is not unified in the way that the Commission's current and future clients would wish" (ORACLE 1990,1-3), the Commission responded by developing the MONARCH system to provide a means of sharing information across internal business areas and to replace many of the smaller databases. Some local authorities adopted MONARCH to manage their own Sites and Monuments Records.

National and international data standards for the management of heritage information have been developed from the MONARCH data model, and reference data from MONARCH word-lists and thesauri have formed the basis of recommendations for vocabulary control within electronic records.

In 1993 Peter Brooke, then Secretary of State for the DNH, introduced the Heritage Management Programme and as a result of this RCHME computerised the statutory lists of historic buildings in collaboration with English Heritage and DNH.

Over the years the Commission has automated the way in which it captures data in the field and it currently makes extensive use of modern technology, including electronic distance measuring (EDM), global positioning (GPS) and computer aided design (CAD) to help speed up the work of surveying and preparing maps and drawings.

The Commission is aware that while the above systems serve collectively the needs of records collection and management there is an urgent need to build and integrate these systems so that they can better support the sharing of information with professional colleagues.

The Internet is already being used to increase awareness of the work of the Commission and a major area for future development will be the provision of remote public access to the Commission's information resources.

3.2.3 Vision of the future use of IS

The RCHME Strategic Plan recognises that our knowledge and understanding of the archaeological landscape and built heritage will advance only through survey and the curation, interpretation and dissemination of recorded information by RCHME and others.

RCHME will ensure that, through this strategy, its information systems will:

1. support the creation, management and dissemination of NMR record resources
2. support the capture, analysis and interpretation of information on structures and landscapes in England and its territorial waters
3. assist in the dissemination of information to aid the understanding of those directly involved in preservation and management as well as those who need access to the record for education or pleasure
4. interface with the survey and recording activities of others for the mutual good of our understanding of archaeology and buildings
5. underpin the exemplary role of RCHME in survey techniques and in setting standards for the records of others, including text, drawings, spatial data and images
6. improve the efficiency of the business, particularly in the areas of: improving the flow of information within RCHME and between it and other bodies, increasing staff productivity and reducing administration costs

3.2.4 The way forward to achieve the 'vision'

The way forward to achieve the vision is set out in detail in the IS Implementation Plan (RCHME 1997b), but the broad areas in which the Commission will improve its IS are listed below:

management of information: the development of better systems to help it to manage the inventory and to clean and make consistent its records; and to catalogue and manage the growing collections of both conventional and digital materials;

information gathering: making improvements in the range of software currently used to help identify, interpret, survey and record the sites, buildings and landscapes of England;

information dissemination: the provision of better access to information for people both for visitors to the public search rooms and for people using remote access; automation of the production of publications and reports; and making use of visitor information to help provide a better response to customer demand;

supporting technology: the enhancement of the technical infrastructure to provide for a more unified approach to management of information; the development of a common user interface for the use of everybody wishing to access systems and multimedia information; the setting up of the data communications networks needed to support remote public access, electronic mail and electronic data exchange facilities;

information standards: joining with others to set standards for the collection, management, exchange and dissemination of information;

RCHME Strategic aims (RCHME 1996)	IS Strategic aims (RCHME 1997a)	IS objectives (RCHME 1997a and Amtec 1997)
To fulfill the terms of its Royal Warrant, RCHME will:	RCHME will ensure that its Information Systems will:	The broad areas in which RCHME will improve its IS are:
compile, maintain and curate the inventory and collections of the NMR as the national record the historic environment	support the creation, management and dissemination of the record resources of the NMR	information management: development of better systems to manage the inventory, to clean and make consistent its records, to catalogue and manage collections of conventional and digital materials
identify, interpret, survey and record sites and buildings of archaeological and architectural interest in England and its territorial waters, including the statutory recording of threatened buildings	support the capture, analysis and interpretation of information on structures and landscapes in England and its territorial waters	information gathering: making improvements in the range of software tools currently used to help identify, interpret, survey and record the sites, buildings and landscapes
promote the use of the Commission's work and the contents of the NMR through public access, information remote	assist the dissemination of information to aid the understanding of those directly involved in preservation	information dissemination: provision of better access to information both for visitors to the public search rooms and for people using
services, research and publication, anticipating and responding to the need for expert information, synthesis and advice on all aspects of the archaeological and architectural heritage	and management as well as those who need access to the record for education or pleasure	access; automation of the production of publications and reports; and making use of visitor information to provide a better response to customer demand
develop the technologies necessary for the recording, management, retrieval and dissemination of heritage information at a national level and beyond		supporting technology: enhancement of the technical infrastructure to provide for a more unified approach to the management of data; development of a common user interface for the use of everybody wishing to access the systems and multimedia information; setting up of the data networks to support remote access, electronic mail and data exchange
collaborate with others in all appropriate ways to enhance the understanding of the archaeological sites and historic buildings of England, for the purposes of education, planning and protection	interface with the survey and recording activities of others for the mutual good of our understanding of archaeology and buildings	
cooperate with others in establishing, maintaining and encouraging national and international standards in investigation and interpretation, and in documentation of the heritage	underpin the exemplary role of RCHME in survey techniques and in setting standards for the records of others, including text, drawings, spatial data and images	information standards: joining with others to set standards for the collection, management, exchange and dissemination of information
	improve the efficiency of the business, particularly the areas of: improving the flow of information within RCHME and between it and other bodies, increasing staff productivity and reducing administration costs	management support: development of systems to provide executive information for managers to help them control and deploy resources more effectively; and establishment of a library of business information to help the Commission to recognise and exploit business opportunities

Figure 1. IS objectives set against the business and IS strategic aims of the Commission

management support: the development of systems which provide executive information for managers to help them control and deploy resources more effectively; and the establishment of a library of business information to help the Commission in the task of recognising and exploiting business opportunities. (RCHME 1997a and Amtec 1997).

These improvements to IS can be seen in context, set against the business and the IS strategic aims of the Commission, in Figure 1 at the end of the this paper.

For the Commission to achieve the aims of its IS Strategy it will:

1. provide a management structure to control, plan and implement the strategy
2. set the policy, standards and procedures needed to develop, manage and use IS
3. identify the resources needed to build, operate and maintain the systems
4. harness the technologies needed to construct them

The Commission is committed to taking on new challenges and in particular to the delivery of information systems which will serve the needs of the heritage community of the future.

3.2.5 Business Benefits expected to accrue from IS

The Commission considers that by aligning the provision of IS to the needs of the business it can improve the services and products it offers to its customers and professional colleagues and it can also make efficiency savings in the way it conducts its business. The likely benefits from doing this can be seen as improvements in the following areas:

services to the public: the provision of better quality information, the faster processing of orders, and the quicker delivery of products and remote access to services;

collaboration with others: the sharing and exchange of information with professional colleagues and their willing participation in joint ventures which are of mutual benefit;

revenue generation: the use of electronic methods to help in the promotion of goods and services, in responding better to customer demand and in exploiting business opportunities;

operational effectiveness: the harnessing of IS to help improve internal flows of information, the delivery of executive information and the management of resources.

By making all of these improvements the Commission believes that it can increase its potential of generating the funds needed to carry out its programmes of work and so increase its chances of succeeding in achieving strategic business objectives.

3.3 Management of the Strategy

3.3.1 Responsibility for strategy progression

The management structure needed to set and progress the strategy consists of three management groups:

1. an IS/IT Strategy Board to act as controlling authority for the strategy and IS planning cycles, to initiate strategic studies and reviews as appropriate to provide the overall direction for IS;
2. an IS Committee to set policy, standards and practice, to manage the execution of the IS Implementation Plan and to manage the resources allocated to it by the Strategy Board;
3. an IS User Management Committee to provide quality assurance for new initiatives, to administer user acceptance testing, to control the applications change process and to act as a forum for users.

Responsibility for executing the implementation plan of the strategy lies with the Information Services and Development Division.

Bibliography

Amtec, 1997 Technical Consultancy Report.
CCTA, 1989 A2 Strategic Planning for Information Systems, The Information Systems Guides, CCTA, John Wiley and Sons
Newchurch, 1996 Funding Consultancy
ORACLE, 1990 Information Systems Strategy Study
RCHME, 1996 Strategic Plan, RCHME
RCHME, 1997a Deliverables of the IS Strategy Study
RCHME, 1997b IS Strategy Implementation Plan (forthcoming)

Contact details

Chris Watkins
Operations Manager
Information Services and Development Division
RCHME
National Monuments Record Centre
Kemble Drive
Swindon, SN2 2GZ
UK
email: swncsd@rchme.gov.uk

Providing Access to the National Monuments Record of Scotland

Kate F. Byrne

CAA 97

Abstract

For more than a decade, RCAHMS has been using computer databases to manage its data holdings, in particular the National Monuments Record of Scotland (NMRS). In the past the computer applications have been designed principally for staff use, with the emphasis on ease of data capture and management. Flexible retrieval functions have always been important, but it was not always possible, with earlier software tools, to combine flexibility with ease of use; so visitors to the NMRS usually required staff help to get useful information from the database. Technology has moved on, and this is no longer the case. This article looks at the public access facilities already available in the NMRS, and those planned for future development.

1 Introduction

The Royal Commission on the Ancient and Historical Monuments of Scotland (RCAHMS) has three central aims:

1. to *survey and record* the man-made environment of Scotland;
2. to *compile and maintain* in the National Monuments Record of Scotland a record of the archaeological and historical environment; and
3. to *promote an understanding* of this information by all appropriate means.

This article is concerned with the third of these: promoting understanding of the National Monuments Record of Scotland (NMRS) by making access to it more straightforward. It is based on a presentation made at the CAA97 Conference, as part of the session entitled 'Making History: the once and future role of the Royal Commissions'.

The NMRS database developed over a period of years, as computer technology improved and made new functions possible. It is still developing continuously, as we move towards the goal of integrating related datasets which exist in different formats, and making the total repository as accessible as possible. As well as the core textual data, which has been held in computer format since the 1980s, there are, for example, digital maps and plans, field and aerial survey work, and various other spatial datasets - all of which can now be interrogated from a single point of entry. The large collections of photographs, plans and manuscripts in the NMRS are indexed in the database, and the next step is to start making them available electronically, alongside the related textual and spatial information.

The focus of this paper is on methods rather than content. The datasets are considered primarily according to their type: textual, spatial or image, since these are handled differently, irrespective of what the data is about. The aim of course is to present the user with logically connected pieces of information and make the underlying mechanics invisible. But the mechanics are interesting when considering the problems and opportunities for data access.

2 Database development

Computerisation of the NMRS database started in the late 1980s, with the scanning of the Ordnance Survey card index to archaeological sites in Scotland. The text management system first used did not provide sufficiently flexible management and updating facilities, and the data was later transferred into a specially developed Oracle database application, completed in 1990. Part of the development project was to examine overlaps with the data holdings of Historic Scotland, for Scheduled Ancient Monuments and Listed Buildings. Rather than trying to merge separate datasets, it was decided to build links between them, and this has led to the present set of inter-related databases. This arrangement has proved very satisfactory: each organisation maintains its own data but the records are linked so that users of, for example, the NMRS database, can look up the statutory Scheduling or Listing details, where applicable, at the press of a button.

The next significant change was in 1994, when the Oracle databases were moved from the Scottish Office's IBM mainframe to local machines, and upgraded to use graphical interfaces. Although the data management techniques were unchanged, the new interfaces made a big difference to the ease of use of the systems, and the change of platform (to Unix) made links to other types of application feasible. The first major project undertaken after the move from the mainframe was to link the NMRS database to a GIS application based on the Genamap package. By 1995 a bridge was in place to allow data insertion and updating from either end, i.e. records in the textual database can be added or amended via digital maps in the GIS, and vice versa. Using a GIS makes integration of other spatial datasets simple, so the NMRS database has now effectively expanded to include spatial data such as aerial photograph transcriptions and survey maps produced by RCAHMS field teams.

Also in 1995, the database structure was altered to incorporate maritime archaeology. The following year a major extension of the NMRS textual database was completed, to allow architectural data to be integrated seamlessly alongside the archaeological material. Data capture on the architectural side is still on-going, and of course cataloguing of new material is a continuous process, but the NMRS database now integrates both textual and spatial material across its main subject areas. The next obvious step is to incorporate image data, by digitising the collections of photographs, plans and drawings.

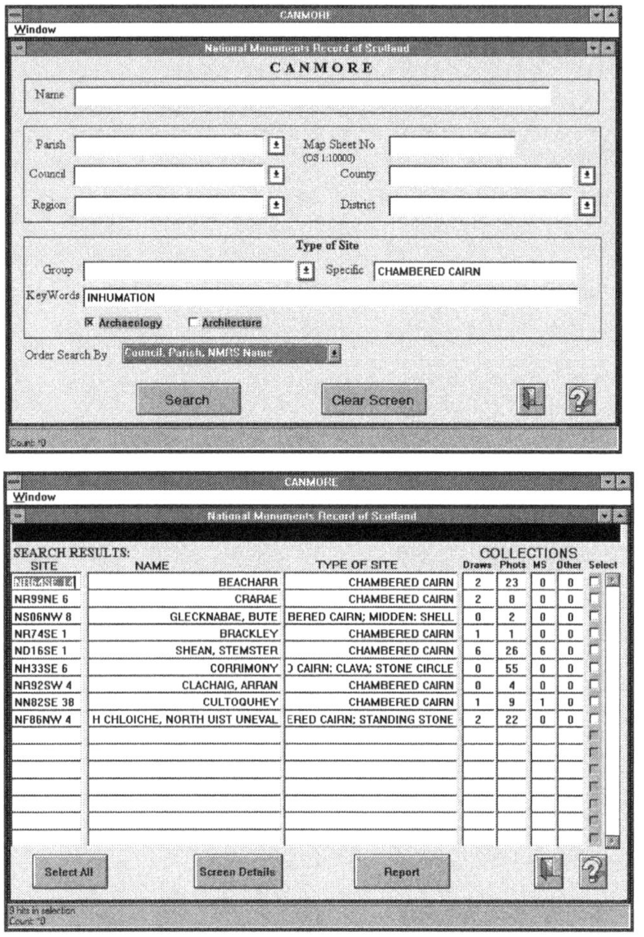

Figure 1. Two of the CANMORE screens, showing a simple query and the summary of search results.

3 Text-based enquiries - CANMORE

Once the major task of integrating the Archaeological and Architectural Records was finished, development effort was directed towards making access to the NMRS database more straightforward for the general user. Querying of the central database was very flexible, but required some knowledge of the software and of NMRS cataloguing procedures. A major drawback was that a significant amount of information is contained in text notes and commentaries, which cannot be searched using the standard tools. Part of the requirement for the new query application was to remove this limitation. This has been achieved using Oracle's TextServer software, and the system now permits searching both within formatted fields and across free text. To keep things simple, the number of query fields is limited, but each of them searches a selected group of relevant database fields. The question of what should be returned from a web of interrelated data in response to, for example, a single keyword query, is a very interesting one; so far we are only scratching the surface of what is theoretically possible with tools like TextServer.

The user enters his or her query on the first screen, using as many of the query fields as required. A summary list of hits is returned, showing basic identifying information for each record found: site name, location, classification, and a summary of the holdings in the NMRS for the site. From this list the user can go on to see details either on screen forms or in a formatted report, for all sites of interest on the list. They can be picked one at a time by double-clicking on the name, or a group can be selected by checking a box against each record wanted in the set (see Fig. 1).

The new application was christened CANMORE (*C*omputer *A*pplication for *N*ational *MO*nument *R*ecord *E*nquiries) - one of our more successful attempts at a snappy acronym, and particularly appropriate for the Scottish national record because Malcolm Canmore (crowned King of Scots in 1058) was so significant a figure in Scotland's history. The development of CANMORE has been described elsewhere (Collison Owen Forthcoming). CANMORE is available for use by visitors to the NMRS at John Sinclair House in Edinburgh.

A sister application, CANMORE-Web, is currently under development. This is being written using Oracle's Web Server, and will allow queries of the NMRS database from WWW pages. It will provide very similar functionality; the same set of query fields search the database in the same way, but the formatting of the response is necessarily slightly different. This application is being developed as part of a project with the Archaeology Data Service (http://ads.ahds.ac.uk/ahds/) and the SCRAN (Scottish Cultural Resources Access Network) Millennium Project (http://www.scran.ac.uk/), called 'Accessing Scotland's Past'. This pilot project will also be looking at ways of managing distributed queries across multiple databases, over the WWW, using metadata as an intermediary.

4 Spatial queries

Over the last few years RCAHMS has developed a suite of GIS applications, which are used by staff throughout the organisation for a range of data management and research functions. Details of the GIS development are available (Murray and Dixon 1995). The four main applications are:

1. *Artemis,* for general purpose analysis and querying of spatial and textual data;
2. *Icarus,* which is an index to the collections of air photographs of Scotland;
3. *Pandora,* for maintaining the two-way link to the Oracle text database; and
4. *Midas,* for importing spatial data from a range of sources.

As users of GIS applications will be aware, the benefits include greater clarity of presentation, faster access to information and new functions that only become possible when data is analysed spatially. The NMRS database is essentially a site-based record and so lends itself naturally to spatial interpretation. The single most significant advantage we have derived from using GIS applications is the automatic correlation of varied datasets. For example, when the work of the Scottish Office Air Photographs Unit was transferred to RCAHMS in 1993, we acquired an enormous collection of material, and had to develop the *Icarus* application to deal with it. The very fact of the index being held in the GIS now makes it possible to cross-reference NMRS sites with aerial photographs dating from 1941 to the present day. This correlation was never a specific objective, and would certainly not have been attempted when the two databases were in text form only, but it is a very useful by-product. There are similar examples for the range of spatial datasets we now hold, in particular land cover data, and of course the field survey material produced in-house.

As yet, the GIS applications have been designed for use primarily by trained staff. They include functions for combining spatial and textual queries and deriving plots accompanied by formatted text reports, and these can be produced by staff to answer enquiries. But the mechanisms for achieving a useful result are not straightforward enough to be used directly by the average visitor. This is one of our goals for the future.

5 Next steps

We hope to be able to develop the GIS as the primary entry point for NMRS database queries. This would involve designing an interface for the casual user, trying to achieve that difficult balance between high flexibility and low apparent complexity, which is the target for all successful computer systems. The interface would be linked to CANMORE for combining spatial and textual queries. The logical next step would be to make a GIS query interface available over the WWW, which is already theoretically possible using the Genamap Web Broker linked to our applications.

The third significant type of data RCAHMS holds, alongside the textual and the spatial, is image-based. The NMRS database currently incorporates an index to around 270,000 items of archive material, well over half of which is photographic. At the present rate of data capture and new accession, this figure will be approaching one million by the end of the century. The dream of having this material available on screen automatically has been with us for several years, but the cost is prohibitive. However, as a founding partner in the SCRAN project, RCAHMS is now starting to digitise selected items from its collections to contribute to the SCRAN resource base, and it is hoped that this will provide a seed for gradually building up a digital image collection.

RCAHMS is privileged to maintain a wonderful resource. One of our core aims is to make it more accessible to the interested public, and each new generation of technology provides new tools to do this. It is traditional at this point to say we are limited only by our imaginations, but I think, alas, the more significant limitations are likely to be time and money.

Bibliography

Collison Owen, V, Forthcoming Introducing CANMORE, *Monuments on Record 1996-7*
ADS, http://ads.ahds.ac.uk/ahds/
SCRAN, http://www.scran.ac.uk/
Murray, D M, and Dixon, P J, 1995 Geographic Information Systems for RCAHMS, *Monuments on Record 1994-5*, 32-4

Contact details

Kate F Byrne
Information Systems Manager
RCAHMS
John Sinclair House
16 Bernard Terrace
Edinburgh EH8 9NX
SCOTLAND
email: rcahms.jsh@gtnet.gov.uk

New Developments at the RCAHMW

Loretta P. Nikolic

CAA 97

Abstract

The Royal Commission on the Ancient and Historic Monuments of Wales has been applying Information Technology to develop new means of enhancing our archaeological and historical records and improving the services we provide. We are exchanging data with other record holders, such as the Archaeological Trusts with the aim to eventually produce an index of every known site in Wales. Geographic Information Systems (GIS) would bring considerable advantages for working with site data and though lack of an effective map base has limited development into this area, work is underway in the Air Photo Mapping Programme using GIS technology. Our records could be enhanced by holding archive images in digital format in order to link them with database records or to view them easily. We are considering the long term consequences of holding our archive data in digital format and the complexity of preserving such data.

1 Introduction

The application of Information Technology to Heritage Management is long established. Almost constant developments in technology increase the range of applications and improve existing uses. At the Royal Commission in Wales, we have been looking at ways in which IT can enhance our records and improve our services.

Among the projects which are under development and research are those involving digital image technology to assist in building survey and to enhance our database records, improving the accessibility of certain collections.

By exchanging data with other major heritage bodies in Wales, the Extended National Database (END) will improve database record coverage of sites for all those involved. CAD and GIS technology are being used to survey for existing sites and create new site records. They will eventually provide a means for those working with the database to access site and related data more intuitively and effectively by bringing spatial data into the equation of record location and creation. (See Fig. 1)

The Royal Commission in Wales is a much smaller than its sister organisations in England and Scotland. It is made up of only 37 staff, two of whom work within and manage Information Systems. The RCAHMW is also a relative latecomer to Information Technology; it began computerising its systems only five years ago. The question of resources, both financial and human is always a limiting factor when embarking on new projects in Information Technology.

2 The Extended National Database of Wales

A number of bodies in Wales gather and hold information on the archaeological, architectural and historical heritage. The Extended National Database (END) represents the coordination of efforts between these heritage bodies to develop a national index of sites and monuments. By gathering together the data from the National Monuments Record (NMR), Regional Sites and Monument Records (SMRs) and other bodies such as Cadw listed buildings and scheduled monuments, its aim is to set up a national index of every known site in Wales (ENDEX). The results will provide an integrated information service which could be subscribed to by other institutions such as museums, universities and the new unitary authorities.

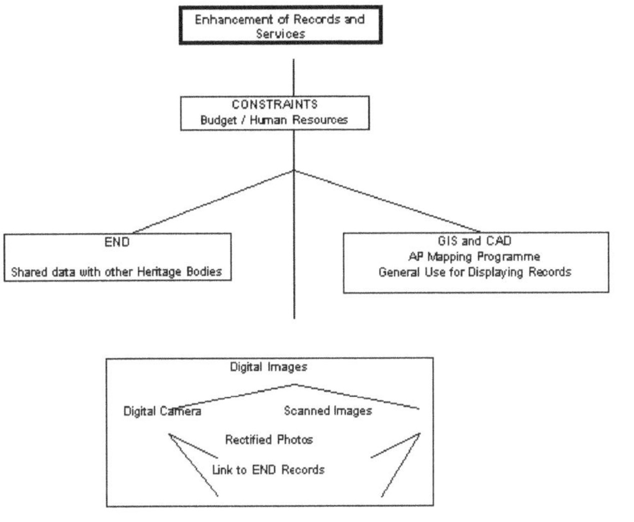

Figure 1: Latest Developments in Information Technology at the RCAHMW

In 1992, the new Royal Warrant directed the Royal Commission to "...provide for the survey and recording of ancient and historical monuments...of the life and people in Wales...from the earliest times...by collecting and exchanging data with other record holders and providing an index to data from other sources;...and by exercising responsibility for the oversight of local Sites and Monuments Records." Through the forum of END the Royal Commission is exchanging data with other record holders, and by providing funding and guidance it is fulfilling its responsibility for overseeing the Regional Sites and Monument Records (SMRs).

Those involved in the END are the RCAHMW, the Archaeological Trusts and Cadw. The National Trust in Wales is currently computerising its records and is also seeking to become an associate of END. There are four regional SMRs in Wales which are held by the corresponding Archaeological Trust. They have existed as computerised records for nearly twenty years though their principle focus has been principally on archaeological sites. The Royal Commission has maintained a card index of sites in the National Monuments Record (NMR) since the 1960's which principally provides access to its collections, including material on archaeological, architectural and industrial monuments. It started its own programme of computerisation in 1992.

The information to be exchanged between the organisations are the fields common to each database, making up the Core data about a site. That is the minimum level of information and recording, for example, site location, type, and condition. Those organisations involved have agreed to move towards a common glossary and data dictionary, to standardise terminology. END is a forum for the discussion to establish Core data standards and database structures.

The work of END has been facilitated by such key factors as the close funding relationship of certain heritage bodies and the small number of organisations involved. Interaction between these organisations in the past has created many similarities between recording methods and data structures, and in the software used, thus facilitating the exchange of data. The long term goal is to have the records on-line and networked between the organisations with the paper map base replaced by digital maps.

Organisation	*Current Figures*
RCAHM(W)	**46,000**
Cadw Listed Buildings	**17,500**
Cadw Scheduled Monuments	**3,000**
DAT	**29,000**
GAT	**7,000**
CPAT	**29,000**
GGAT	**20,000**
Total	**151,500**

Organisation	*Expected Figures*
Royal Commission including Cadw Listed Buildings and SAM's	**60,000**
The Four Welsh Trusts	**120,000**
Total	**200,000**

Figure 2: Current and Expected Record Numbers in END

END has raised issues regarding the ownership, copyright and stewardship of electronic data, which is currently being debated between the main participants. Procedures for maintaining and creating records are under consideration, a difficult task given the numbers of records involved (see Fig. 2). Access to, and the use of the data is still being negotiated to safeguard the varied interests of source organisations.

3 Enhancing the electronic data

The Commission could greatly enhance its database records if it were able to *show* archive material along side its records and not just the references to that material. Photographs and plans could be on-line and available to users. This would greatly assist in identifying a record as relating to a site. Also, an image can convey so much more information and more immediately than any text record.

Developments in IT have made it possible for the above scenario to become a reality, at least in theory. Digitising large collections of images has been undertaken by many libraries and museums. If the resources are available there are many advantages in having digital collections: the need to handle the originals is kept to a minimum thus reducing the likelihood of loss or damage, producing copies is simple, and access is greatly facilitated. Other advantages of digital images are that they can be manipulated for publication or for other purposes.

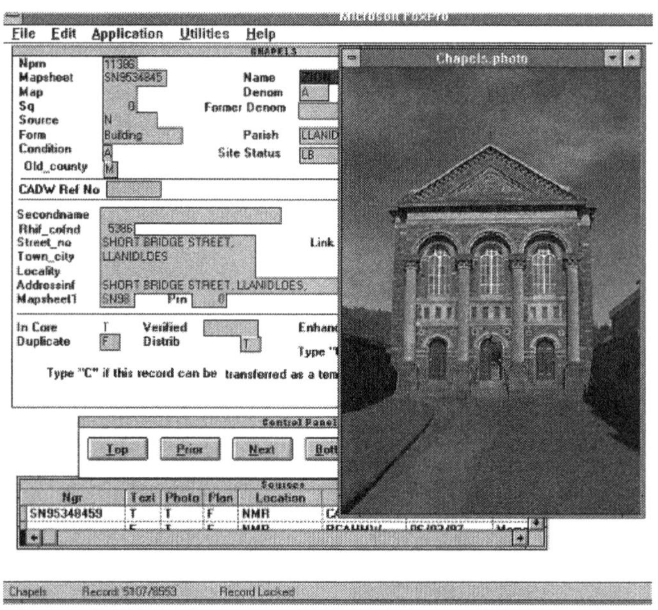

Figure 3: Digital camera image linked to Zion Chapel, Llanidloes in the Chapels Database, viewed on-screen in FoxPro 2.6.

The advantages of having site photographs on line is such that the Royal Commission has invested in a digital camera. It will capture images in the field and bypass the wet processing and scanning stages normally needed to produce digital photographs. The Kodak digital camera has a resolution of 756x504 pixels (approximately 180 dpi). The images being collected with the camera are not yet publishable quality. It is currently being used in a pilot study in the Chapels project to test its possible application to fieldwork. The Chapels project is recording information about 6000 non conformist Chapels and other religious buildings in Wales, including their architectural styles. A photograph of a chapel related to a database entry and displayed on screen is very useful (see Fig. 3). There is also interest in the work of rectifying scanned photographs of buildings to produce elevation drawings, by surveying control points in the field and rectifying the photograph in Aerial (the Bradford rectification program) in much the same way as aerial photographs are handled. This allows a very rapid survey of buildings, particularly since the digital camera will also speed up the process of producing digital images for rectification.

At the moment, the small image files produced in the pilot study are managed easily. However, if large numbers of image files were to be held digitally then we should need to consider the most appropriate means of handling them. The solution may be thumbnail copies for on line use, with the high resolution scans held off line on such a medium as CD-ROM.

The creation of image data directly into digital format has consequences in the long term for the handling and preservation of the files. There are many other pictures and photographs in the Royal Commission which could be scanned for use in projects or by researchers. Materials in the archive could benefit from becoming digitised if their current medium is not stable and this would provide another form of conservation. The preservation and accessibility of this material must therefore be carefully considered.

The colour slides held in the Royal Commission are numbered in their thousand. They are a set of images which would be ideal to hold in digital format if resources allow. They are a working collection, frequently taken away and used to give lectures. Some of them hold unique site information, not recorded elsewhere. It was felt that these slides should enter the archive, particularly as they could suffer loss or damage whilst being used in lectures.

Currently, the slides are in storage and are being catalogued. If they are required for use in lectures they are copied. The life span of slides is only 30 years so the original medium of the slide is not ideally suited to the archive. Duplicating the slides is not the best means of preservation, and is extremely expensive. Creating digital images from the slides may be a possible solution. Once the slides have been scanned, further copying of the image will not cause the image to be degraded. Though the task would be initially expensive, creating digital images would allow the pictures to be accessed easily, related to the database record and duplicated quickly and cheaply. The question of preserving the files would remain of some concern given the current uncertainty over the long term preservation of digital data. This last point is particularly important since the Royal Commission is producing a lot of digital data of its own and is also receiving information in digital format for its collections, such as CAD drawings and database material.

4 Considerations for preserving digital data

The problem with archiving digital material is complex and relates to not just the life span of the physical medium but also the life span of the software and hardware platforms which are required to read the data and give it meaning.

Emigration and emulation are two possible solutions to hardware and software obsolescence. The first relates to transferring data to new platforms as they evolve, the latter refers to software which will emulate the environments of old operating systems on the new platforms. It may be preferable to keep the data that is archived in a basic format that is easily read such as comma delimited text for database tables, and .tif files for images, though this is not always possible and can be problematic. Archiving of digital data requires a large amount of investment in terms of management and maintenance. One advantage of digital data is that copying is easy and does not degrade the quality of the original, it is relatively fast and allows the data to be copied onto almost any medium, thus increasing its chances of survival.

It is not clear what the life spans of digital storage mediums are. Magnetic media can have a life span of a few decades though this will vary according to how well they are managed. It is possible however to delete data from them, accidentally or intentionally, and are they more at risk from damage caused by heat, dust, or mishandling.

CD-ROM's and re-writable CD's are more robust than magnetic media and the data on them can not be altered or erased. Their expected life spans can vary between a hundred years plus or ten years. Not all CD's are designed for longevity and the quality of manufacture is very important in determining life span, particularly in the new generation of re-writable CD's. (Kodak's Photo CD is claimed to have a life expectancy of 200 years if kept in dark conditions, at 25 degrees centigrade and at 40% relative humidity). However, the claims are made from the results of accelerated ageing tests which have been carried out by the manufacturers themselves, and not an independent body. Early problems with CD's due to oxidation and delamination have been addressed by manufacturers. However many of those involved in preserving digital data are wary. A more conservative view of the average life of CD-ROM estimates 5 to 15 years before a physical problem could be encountered. Write-once-read-many (WORM) disks have an expected life-span of 30-40 years, they are more expensive but are considered more reliable by those concerned with preserving digital data. Both manufacturers and archivists would advise that the best security for data is in keeping copies on many different formats including analogue, and in different locations. The actual life span of a CD will in no doubt be foreshortened by changes in technology and the rapid obsolescence of hardware and software. It may be that questions relating to the longevity of the medium are redundant in some cases since the most important aspect of preservation may be the management of files and maintaining a viable path for migration to new platforms.

5 GIS and digital mapping

Information Technology can help to improve the way we handle our data and make the services we provide more efficient. Since our record data is spatially based it would seem fundamental that Geographic Information Systems (GIS) should be applied to the work we do, most obviously for placing record data in its spatial context and alongside other spatial information such as survey results. Retrieving and manipulating data would be more efficient within a GIS. Developments in this area have been delayed by the lack of an Ordnance Survey (OS) map base because of high costs. As yet there is no service level agreement between the Welsh Office and the Ordnance Survey. We have purchased a 1:250 000 vector map of Wales from Bartholomew's, and a 1:50 000 raster map from the Ordnance Survey. The scale and functionality of these resources do not allow full development of digital mapping facilities. A number of OS Landline map squares are also purchased annually for specific projects. The Air Photo Mapping programme uses CAD and GIS to carry out a rapid survey of archaeological sites. A first level graphic record of all archaeology is made from a variety of air photo resources, working to quarter map sheet areas selected on the grounds of threat or conservation. Database records are also created from these at the same time (see Fig. 4). On average 60 to 70 new sites are found on a map sheet. At Sennybridge MOD range in Powys, the number of known sites increased by 80%. Eventually the plots will constitute an air photo layer in a GIS for use in combination with survey data, GPS plots and record data.

Changes are under way at the RCAHMW which will enhance our services and our records by facilitating access and management of them. Through the forum of END we may one day be sharing data with other heritage organisations across a network, probably over the Internet. GIS will allow us to map our information on sites along side graphical representations from aerial photographs and from survey work. Photographic and drawing material could be held digitally making it possible to view records and the collection material from a PC. With the growth in applications we must look carefully at how to handle the digital material and develop long term management strategies for their future preservation.

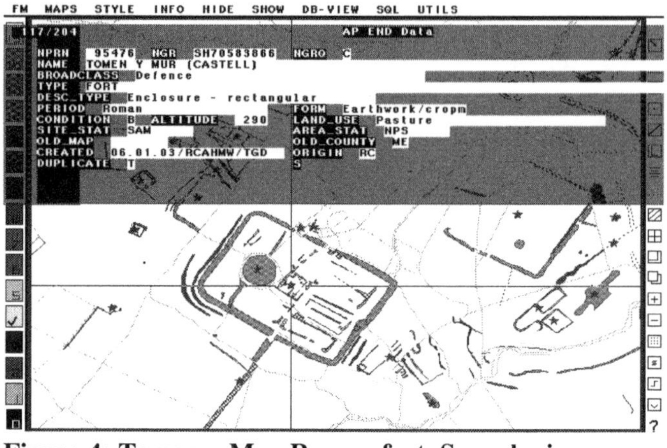

Figure 4: Tomen y Mur Roman fort, Snowdonia. Detailed site plot showing archaeology mapped from air photographs, viewed on-screen in FastMAP GIS.

Acknowledgements

I gratefully acknowledge the help of my colleagues in writing this paper, particularly Toby Driver for his assistance with information regarding the Air Photo Mapping Project and my manager Terry James for his guidance. I would also like to thank both Dr. Vanessa Marshall and Michael Alexander at the British Library for discussing with me the issues surrounding archiving digital data.

Bibliography

Eastman Kodak Company, 1995 Kodak Digital Science: Permanence, Care, and Handling of CDs, www.Kodak.com.

Hedstrom, M, 1996 Preserving Digital Information, in Long Term Preservation of Electronic Materials, JISC/British Library Workshop, British Library R&D Report, 6238, 1996

Foot, M, 1996 A Preservation Policy for Digital Material: A Librarian's Point of View, in Long Term Preservation of Electronic Materials, JISC/British Library Workshop, British Library R&D Report, 6238, 1996

Contact details

Loretta P. Nikolic
The Royal Commission on the Ancient and Historic Monuments of Wales
Crown Building, Plas Crug
Aberystwyth
Ceredigion SY23 1NJ
WALES

Reaching the World

Robin J. Taylor

Abstract

The RCHME has a long tradition of supplying heritage information: we are seeking to maintain that tradition into the developing information society to ensure that we remain relevant to our users. Communication is a critical part of this process and the Web has been identified as a powerful route for this communication. The setting up of www.rchme.gov.uk and the response of users are briefly described. This is set within the context of changing from the passive supply of information to the active response which will meet the challenge and opportunity of the information society. The aim is to reach the world - now and into the next millennium and beyond!

The Royal Commission (RCHME) has defined its main aim as "to compile and assess, curate and make available the national record of England's ancient monuments and historic buildings for the use of individuals and bodies concerned with understanding, interpreting and managing the historic environment"[1]. We make information available to all enquirers, as part of our remit as a public body, through the unique resource of the National Monuments Record (NMR).

In recent years much of the record has become accessible in digital form through:

1. MONARCH, the Commission's database of heritage information
2. the Listed Buildings System, a repository of statutory information which is being linked with digital images in the Images of England project
3. and the RCHME Web site.

As part of a process of change, in common with many public bodies, the RCHME has been restructured and reorganised and is now aiming to reach out to a wider audience. This should increase opportunities for income generation and enable us to respond to an expectation from users for the remote delivery of information.

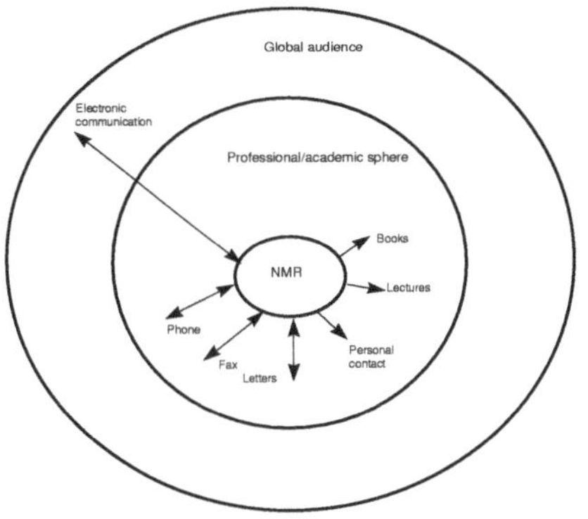

Figure 1: Communication is the key

Communication is the key to this process (Fig 1). The NMR has traditionally dealt with a professional and academic sphere, communicating by conventional means such as telephone, fax, books and lectures. Electronic communication can break this boundary and help us to reach out to the wider world, sharing information easily with other organisations and bringing greater awareness of our work. Electronic information can have added depth for those that need it and thus greater value, while rapid feedback helps us to improve our responsiveness.

During 1995, we became increasingly aware of the potential that a Web site could bring to our work and how it could place us in the global information society. It took six weeks to carry out background research, develop the framework or storyboard, learn how to code in HTML, procure the necessary software and equipment and get connected to the Internet. A further six weeks were then spent in creating the pages, using simple design principles and adding a selection of images which were scanned to be of low resolution and of small file size to deliver rapidly over telephone connections.

The Web site was launched in October 1995 and, in essence, forms an electronic brochure of our work and information sources[2] with the navigational links taking the user to discrete areas of information. The resource required to set up the Web site and provide it for one year is the equivalent of that required to produce one printed book, making more information available for less resource. We have continued to develop the Web site with regular updates and the addition of new features from time to time.

The Web site has generated a good response among users and we track the user figures on a weekly basis. We have seen an increase in the number of visitors from around 200 per week to around 500 with a strong emphasis initially from the academic user community. These visitors are largely from the United Kingdom, as would be expected for an organisation promoting information on England's heritage, but there has been a growing trend of users from across the world. Simple analysis has shown that around half of the UK users come from the academic sector, ie one of our traditional user bases, while the other half come to our site from commercial domains, representing company accesses and individuals connecting through information service providers.

Despite the limitations of bandwidth and download times, we have found that images are popular and a key part of our product. Hotlinks to other organisations are also useful to the user and help to reinforce the connections between heritage organisations, developing the sense of community that is growing around heritage Web sites. The provision of information about the diverse nature of our work has helped to reinforce those activities and further raise awareness, while feedback from users (both in user figures and analysis of them and in comments sent in about the site) helps us to develop the site and adds to our responsiveness.

We now need to build further on the expectation that the Web site has brought. We will work towards linking our databases through a Web interface, so that users can interrogate our information systems easily and retrieve digital images files: such activities are likely to be accessed by some form of on-line charging, perhaps based on the depth of information retrieved, for example. To help us in providing more up-to-date information on the Web site and to enhance our response systems, we are working towards an internal Web site, or Intranet, with e-mail connections for all staff. We believe that this will truly help us to turn our data into information.

By taking part in the information society, we have raised our profile and also the expectations of our users, and by responding to that expectation we will further increase expectation. Our internal systems, both human and technological, have to be able to respond to these demands, and this may require further organisational adjustment to ensure that we can truly deliver what people want, when they want it. This activity should also make us ready for the next millennium, when we believe that heritage information will be shared on a global basis via seamless links, although we are conscious of the danger of outstripping the individual requirement when too much information can lead to overload.

The RCHME has a long tradition of supplying heritage information: we are seeking to maintain that tradition into the information society to ensure that we remain relevant to our users. Society is undergoing radical change and the RCHME is responding to this change by fundamentally altering the way in which we work and respond to user demand. The Web offers a powerful route for communication which is a critical part of this process. We are seeking to change from the passive supply of information to the active response which will meet the challenge and opportunity of the information society. We are truly reaching the world - now and into the next millennium and beyond!

Notes

1 RCHME 1996. Strategic Plan. Royal Commission on the Historical Monuments of England

2 www.rchme.gov.uk

Contact details

Robin J Taylor BA PhD FSA
Publications Manager
Royal Commission on the Historical Monuments of England
National Monuments Record Centre
Kemble Drive
Swindon SN2 2GZ
UK
email: pubs@rchme.gov.uk

Making History: Copyright and Rights Management

Neil Beagrie

Abstract

Copyright is central to any policy of access to archaeological work, particularly if that work is in a digital format, and access can occur on many different levels from academic research to commercial exploitation. Copyright is therefore increasingly a major issue for electronic records and all organisations involved in archaeological fieldwork or disseminating research. The RCHME is no exception to this. Like many other public sector bodies the RCHME wishes to expand access to its collections by all appropriate means and to generate revenue to supplement its core funding. It is also conscious of current and impending changes to copyright law and their potential impact on the Commission's activities, and has recently completed a wide-ranging internal review of copyright and licensing. This paper presents an overview of the main copyright issues in the UK and their relevance to archaeologists working with electronic or traditional records and uses the current dispute over the Chauvet Cave paintings as an example of copyright issues in archaeological material.

1 Introduction

Copyright is increasingly a major issue for electronic records and all organisations involved in archaeological fieldwork or disseminating research. The RCHME is no exception to this. A review of its rights management procedures and the implications of current and proposed changes to copyright legislation was considered to be critical to underpinning its plans for providing extensive access through the WWW to its national database and associated records in digital form. This paper sets out the importance of copyright to archaeology using the discovery of the famous Chauvet Cave in France as an illustration of some of the issues which can arise. It also presents a selection of the findings and issues identified in RCHME's own review of copyright and implications for its work. The paper is therefore concerned primarily with the operation of copyright law in the UK and Europe but many of the issues will be recognisable to a wider international audience.

This paper can only indicate some of the areas that archaeologists should consider in addressing copyright. Copyright law and its application is complex and in many cases there will be exceptions and qualifications to the outline statements given here. Copyright law will also vary according to national legislation. More detailed sources of advice and guidance are therefore given at the end of the paper. Please note that specific legal advice must always be taken by individuals and institutions and this paper does not constitute legal advice by the author, his employer or RCHME.

2 The Chauvet Cave

The discovery of the paintings in the Chauvet Cave at Pont-d'Arc in France is one of the most important palaeolithic finds made this century. They were found by Jean-Marie Chauvet, an amateur speleologist employed by the French government as a warden whilst potholing with two volunteers in December 1994. The three potholers made a short video film and took photographs of the stunning cave paintings they had discovered. There was intense world-wide interest in the discovery and many archaeologists and others will have seen the digital images of the paintings hosted on the French Ministry of Culture's website (http://www.culture.fr/culture/arcnat/chauvet/). There was extensive press coverage of the find in national newspapers and on television networks.

However how many archaeologists are aware of the sequel to this discovery? Two years later there is a bitter dispute over the copyright in the film and photographs of the cave paintings, which is attracting some press coverage in the UK (Lowry 1997, Macintyre 1996). This press coverage has reported that the French Ministry of Culture had laid claim to the copyright and sold on the film rights to television stations at Fr3,000 a minute, and reproduction rights for the collection of photographs at Fr14,000, making some £1 million to date. Its claim to the copyright is based on Chauvet discovering the cave whilst on official duty and in the employment of the French government. However Chauvet has claimed that the discovery was made on Christmas Day, in his and the volunteers own time as part of their hobby and as such had nothing to do with the Government. He has sued the Government for forgery alleging that officials deliberately ante-dated documents to 15 December to suggest he had made the discovery whilst on official duty. Judgement in the case is awaited, but it illustrates in sharp relief many of the issues of copyright ownership, employment contracts, use of volunteers, and commercial exploitation of archaeological work which are explored further below.

3 What is copyright ?

Copyright is an intellectual property right, which can be sold, transferred or licensed. It exists automatically and there is no need for registration. It can therefore be difficult or impossible to find out who is the current copyright owner of a particular item. It is also possible for several different forms of copyright to exist in a single object, eg a book can have separate copyrights in the text and photographs as well as the copyright in the arrangement held by the publisher.

Copyright exists in original works and copies will only have a secondary copyright if skill and judgement is used in their creation. This is important in archaeology in two areas. Within museums photographing an out of copyright object can create a new copyright. This copyrighted image can then be used for reproduction and additional revenue. Secondly in an electronic context a separate copyright from the original can exist in a digital image if skill and judgement are involved in its creation. Awareness of this potential additional copyright in any digital image is important in granting permission or awarding contracts for imaging projects to ensure this copyright is not inadvertently given away to others.

4 Ownership of copyright

Ownership of copyright is usually vested in the author of a work. There are two principal exceptions:

1. Where an employee in the course of their employment creates a "work", their employer holds copyright.
2. Where an agreement exists transferring copyright from the author to someone else.

Authorship is defined by the type of copyright and can be the person who creates the work or makes the necessary arrangements (e.g. a publisher).

It is also important to recognise that if work is not undertaken by an employee but by a contractor then the contractor has the copyright unless the contract specifically assigns the copyright to you. Similarly you should note that ownership of the material is separate from any copyright associated with it. Hence possession and ownership of a physical item, eg an archive or manuscript, does not itself mean you have the copyright and rights to use it.

The ownership issue is central to the dispute over the Chauvet Cave discussed above. It is important for individual archaeologists to be aware of the rights of their employer in any work they create during their employment and equally for employers to be aware of the copyright implications of voluntary work or of unpaid and unofficial overtime!

If legal ownership of any archaeological work is unclear or is excessively fragmented, it may be impossible for anyone to actively disseminate or use that work in the future. It is vital therefore for anyone involved in an archaeological project who has a potential copyright ownership or part ownership of datasets and other works created by that project to agree at the outset as to how the rights are to be held and any benefits shared.

5 Crown copyright in the UK

A unique feature of copyright in the UK compared to other countries is the existence of Crown copyright.

Under the 1988 Copyright, Designs and Patents Act (HMSO 1988) all works made by Her Majesty or by an officer or servant of the Crown in the course of his or her duties are governed by Crown copyright.

Prior to the 1988 Act the definition of Crown copyright was much wider. The 1911 Copyright Act gave copyright to the Crown in any work prepared or published by, or under the direction or control of the Crown, and also covered any "Crown" works created before the Act came into force. The 1956 Act replaced this with slightly more elaborate provisions. Essentially it established Crown copyright in: all works made by or under the direction or control of the Crown; and all works first published by or under the direction of the Crown (hence all works published by HMSO became Crown copyright even if the authors had no connection with the Crown in any other way).

Crown copyright is of considerable importance for archaeologists in the UK as most archaeological work prior to the 1980's was funded by the government, or is now undertaken by government bodies covered by Crown copyright such as RCHME. The provisions of Crown copyright therefore cover many archaeological archives and publications. It is worth noting however that the 1983 Act establishing English Heritage specifically states its employees are not to be considered as Crown servants and for this reason Crown copyright does not apply to EH's work.

An interesting anomaly has arisen because of the uniqueness of Crown copyright. EEC copyright directives could not accommodate it and therefore the duration of Crown copyright has been unaffected by the EEC Copyright Term Directive. Crown copyright therefore still remains valid for 50 years in published material and 125 years in unpublished material.

6 Moral rights

The 1988 Act introduced a series of "moral rights" usually exercisable by the author or his/her heirs. These are as follows:

1. Paternity- the right to be identified as the author or director of a work
2. Integrity- the right to object to the derogatory treatment of the author's work or its false attribution
3. Privacy- the right to privacy in relation to photographs and films commissioned for private and domestic purposes

All archaeologists need to be aware of these rights and ensure they are respected or ensure that contracts include the necessary waiver of these rights.

7 "Fair Dealing" and permitted acts

There are a number of "fair dealing" and other provisions within the 1988 UK Copyright Act for individuals, libraries, and archives. Providing the use of copyright material falls within these provisions no permission from the copyright holder or payment of a royalty is required. Examples include:

1. "Fair Dealing"- a single copy of a work for the purposes of research or private study, criticism or review
2. Preservation copying by a library or archive.

These provisions are important for both users and information providers accessing archaeological data in traditional formats.

8 Recent or proposed changes to copyright legislation

8.1 Publication right

A new intellectual property right known as "Publication Right" has been introduced as a result of a Directive (EEC 1993) to harmonise copyright terms and related rights in member states by the European Commission.

A Statutory Instrument giving legal force in the UK to this Right came into force in December 1996. The Right applies to all works covered by copyright including literary works (eg manuscripts, computer programmes) or artistic works (eg photographs and maps).

A Publication right will come into existence in works where copyright existed at some point but has since expired, when the work is first "made available to the public" either by:

1. issuing copies
2. publication
3. exhibition
4. broadcast (eg TV, cable or online access)
5. Making it "available for inspection" at an establishment open to the public

The publication right will not automatically be held by the owner or curator of the work but by the person/organisation who first makes the work available to the public. The Right will exist for 25 years from the end of the calendar year in which the work is first made available to the public. The Right can be assigned, or licensed in return for a royalty.

The Publication Right is potentially important to the RCHME and other public repositories and may provide new intellectual property rights in some out of copyright and unpublished collections for archaeological organisations (or for others if it is overlooked).

8.2 EEC directive on copyright term

The copyright term provisions of this directive (EEC 1993) was implemented in UK law from 1st January 1996 and has changed the term of copyright protection from the norm of "life plus 50 years" to "life plus 70 years". It extends by 20 years the copyright protection in works still in copyright and revives copyright in works where copyright has expired during the last 20 years. The duration of Crown copyright is unaffected by this change.

8.3 EEC directive on database copyright

In March 1996 a new directive (EEC 1996) was announced by the EEC which will need to be enacted in UK law within 2 years.

The directive aims to give a degree of copyright protection to databases which might otherwise be excluded from copyright law. Current copyright law is designed to protect creativity and facts in themselves cannot be copyrighted: hence most databases have limited protection in law except where appropriate as compilations/ literary works.

The directive defines a database as a collection of independent items accessed by electronic or other means. It confers rights for a period of 15 years to prevent certain actions eg extraction and re-utilisation of work. However others can take an "insubstantial" part. For protection under the directive to apply an organisation must demonstrate investment in a database in any of the following ways: verification of data, obtaining data, or its presentation.

If any of these processes are continuous then effectively the database will never be out of copyright as the protection rolls forward.

9 Electronic media

It is important to recognise that there is no separate copyright for electronic media and that copyright in an electronic work is a sum of the parts, which are covered by existing categories of copyright material (photos, sound, etc) in analogue form. The EEC Directive on Database Copyright, when it is implemented in the UK, will therefore represent an important departure: the first time that an electronic medium is covered by separate legislation (although the term database will cover items in a collection accessed by electronic or other means).

Many of the difficulties in obtaining or drafting licences for electronic materials arise because of the particular challenges they represent in protecting the owner's rights. Electronic material can have very high resolution and be copied repeatedly with little or no degradation. Electronic images are therefore frequently only made available in low resolutions unsuitable for traditional publications, protected by encryption or watermarking, and/or are available with stringent licensing conditions.

The fact that electronic media are more easily manipulated and altered also means that maintaining the integrity of the information is a major issue. Most licences for electronic media even from archaeological projects need to consider the limits to alteration and manipulation permitted to prevent potential abuse. The authenticity and validation of electronic materials is also of far greater importance and increasingly problematic.

Another area of difficulty is that there is considerable uncertainty as to the legitimacy of fair dealing in electronic materials under current legislation. This is because a single copy of a work is permitted but the process of transmitting over a digital network or caching within a PC will always create additional, often transient, but potentially infringing copies. There is therefore potentially no "fair dealing" defence in using digital materials and you must acquire specific rights to make information available in digital formats.

The recent World Intellectual Property Organisation treaty negotiations have concluded and the treaty is open for signature by governments until December 1997. The treaty recognises that the principal of fair dealing should apply to electronic materials but there is considerable debate over its interpretation and it will be interesting to see how the governments who are signatories to the agreement implement the treaty (for further information see http://www.wipo.int/).

10 Conclusion

Archaeological research is demanding and it is easy for copyright issues to be looked upon as of little interest or of too great a complexity for professionals in the field to consider. However copyright is central to developing computerised records in archaeology and ensuring access to them: the implications are now too great for copyright to be overlooked. The partnerships and licences needed for widespread distributed access to digital collections to develop further will raise many issues including ensuring due acknowledgement of an author's work if it is re-used, developing agreements for educational use, and controlling commercial exploitation.

Although copyright can be daunting for individuals alone to consider, there are many organisations within the archaeological community or in related areas that have combined or can combine, to develop frameworks and licences for archaeological use, or to lobby for the copyright changes needed in an age of digital information. A good example of this is the guidance and model transfer of title and copyright, or copyright licences for archaeological archives developed by the Society of Museum Archaeologists on behalf of its members with funding from the Museums and Galleries Commission (Owen 1995, 14-19 and 61-67). Another is the common Rights Management Framework and licences being developed for digital collections held by the five Services (Archaeology, History, The Oxford Text Archive, Performing Arts, and Visual Arts) forming The Arts and Humanities Data Service, which has been established within the UK Higher Education sector (full details of this Framework and licences will be available from the AHDS web pages at http://ahds.ac.uk later in 1997).

Archaeologists must now always address copyright as part of any funding bid or in drawing up contracts, and consider copyright at the outset of a project rather than the end. In doing so they can draw on experience in a wide range of institutions from libraries, or museums to photo archives. A selection of these resources is given below.

11 Further Reading and Sources of Information

11.1 Web Resources

For information on Crown copyright see HMSO Crown Copyright Unit (http://www.hmso.gov.uk/copy.htm)

For information on copyright in archives see the Public Record Office copyright pages (http://www.open.gov.uk/pro/copy1.htm)

For information on copyright in libraries see the International Federation of Library Associations copyright and intellectual property bibliography pages (http://www.nlc-bnc.ca/ifla/II/copyright.htm)

For information on international copyright treaties see World Intellectual Property Organisation pages (http://www.wipo.int/)

11.2 Printed Publications

Oppenheim, C, Phillips, C, and Wall, R A, 1996 *The Aslib Guide to Copyright,* Release 4. This Guide published by The Association for Information Management is updated annually and provides an authoritative and accessible guide to copyright matters. The inclusion of the texts of relevant EEC Directives and UK legislation is particularly valuable.

11.3 Organisations

BAPLA- British Association of Picture Libraries and Agencies
18 Vine Hill
London EC1R 5DX

The Copyright Licensing Agency
90 Tottenham Court Road
London W1P 0LP

Design and Artists Copyright Society
Parchment House
13 Northburgh Street
London EC1V 0AH

Bibliography

EEC 1993 Directive 93/98/EEC of 29 October 1993 harmonizing the term of protection of copyright and certain related rights. *Official Journal of the European Union* L290, 24.11.93, 93ff

EEC 1996 Directive 96/9/EC of 11 March 1996 on the legal protection of databases. *Official Journal of the European Union* L77, 27.3.96, 20ff

HMSO 1988. *The Copyright, Designs and Patents Act*. HMSO London

Lowry, S. 1997 The oldest art gallery, *The Sunday Telegraph* 15 July 1997, 7

Macintyre, B, 1996 Potholers lay claim to cave art, *The Times* 15 December 1996

Owen, J, (ed.) 1995 *Towards An Accessible Archaeological Archive*. Society of Museum Archaeologists (ISBN 1 871855 09 8)

Contact details

Neil Beagrie
The Executive
Arts and Humanities Data Service
King's College London
Strand
London WC2R 2LS
UK
email: neil.beagrie@ahds.ac.uk

ARCHAEOLOGY
IN THE
AGE OF THE INTERNET

CAA 97

Section 9
The Strategic Management of Information Systems

The Strategic Management of Information Systems: Innovation and Vision

Ben Booth

CAA 97

Foreword

Having first attended CAA in Birmingham in the early 1980's and having seen how the conference has prospered in the intervening years, it was a great pleasure to return to Birmingham for this 25th anniversary meeting. It is no less pleasing to see that contributions in the "Strategic Management" session match the maturity and confidence which now characterises this conference. Indeed I can report that my keynote paper at CAA 1994 has proved to be over-pessimistic and that there are now information strategies in place in many areas.

Papers in this section show how the UK's major archaeological bodies have individually developed strategic plans for information use, and there are refreshing signs of co-operation between major bodies and interest groups both in England and Scotland. As would be expected for a discipline so heavily dependent on mapped data there are several initiatives in the GIS field, all of which involve collaboration between different interests, and between both private and public sectors. The European and Global dimensions are also referred to. The interrelation with museums provides a channel through which archaeological knowledge may be disseminated out of the professional sphere to the general public.

In the past much information has remained unused because it could not be accessed. Today as more information comes on-line users of archaeological information are becoming empowered through having a choice in what to use and what to reject. In the future I believe that this will drive a customer focused approach which we may well see as a developing theme at future conferences.

Ben Booth
ICIS-LOR Group Ltd.
Quadrant House
Sutton
Surrey
SM2 5AS
ben.booth@icislor.com

Have we Failed to Provide a Strategic Vision for Information Systems in Archaeology?

Nigel D. Clubb

Abstract

During the celebrations of the last twenty-five years of the Computer Applications in Archaeology (CAA) Conference in 1997, it is timely to look back over the papers presented on the innovative use of computing in many individual projects in archaeology. The concept of 'computer applications' in the conference title has, perhaps, encouraged the submission of case studies to conferences, rather than strategic and corporate analysis. It may be argued that there are omissions in the body of CAA literature concerning the potential of information systems to improve communications within the discipline and dissemination to the new mass market opened up by new technology. Elsewhere, there is a continuing concern at the contemporary state of British archaeology, including the lack of a broad intellectual and political framework and a sense of isolation and fragmentation in the discipline (for example, see Olivier 1996). It is surprising that there are few CAA papers which have attempted to review the strategic direction of the use of information systems in archaeology across its various sectors, including academics, national and local government, archaeological fieldworkers, museums and education and the voluntary sector. There does not appear to have been a serious analysis of how the discipline might use the technology to communicate its vision and knowledge to society. This will be particularly important as initiatives on access to information impact on organisations sponsored by Government (see Cabinet Office 1997) and increasing numbers of individuals develop high expectations of access to international networks. This paper attempts to:

1. revisit the key papers delivered over the last twenty-five years which surveyed and/or classified computer applications in archaeology or sought to address the management of information systems to achieve strategic objectives
2. summarise current initiatives relating to the management of heritage records in England and the UK. It suggests a significant change has occurred during 1996 and 1997, giving rise to some optimism for the future direction of information systems. It also suggests that some new frameworks may be needed to plan, develop and implement such a programme.
3. signpost the potential role of the Council for British Archaeology (CBA) as the most inclusive organisation in the UK in facilitating a strategic programme for information systems in archaeology.

1 The purpose of strategic planning for information systems

Information systems have long been required by virtually all organisations, including archaeological organisations. The initial purpose of strategic planning for information systems in the public sector was the rather prosaic, but critical objective of ensuring benefits in return for the investment in information systems for the business objective (CCTA 1989), which is often considerable. This approach assumes that the goals of the business are known and understood and may force organisations to clarify or further refine goals, if they are not sufficiently clear. Information systems should support their achievement of objectives. The administrative benefits which might be expected, therefore, are as follows:

1. Achievement of business and policy objectives
2. Development of new business opportunities
3. Communication, internally and externally
4. Effective allocation and use of resources
5. Increased efficiency and effectiveness at lower cost
6. Integrated use of systems
7. Reduced risks of abortive expenditure

Of equal, or even greater importance, corporate organisations should, and normally do, develop information systems strategies as part of the articulation of their overall business vision. This should be one of the vehicles of ensuring effective organisational management. Within the UK and elsewhere, most heritage organisations of any size, including the national public-sector heritage bodies, such as English Heritage (EH) and the Royal Commission on the Historical Monuments of England (RCHME), have developed strategies and attempted to update them to reflect their changing business environments. Without such strategies, information systems risk developing as islands of technology. Over the course of the history of archaeological computing there have been clear indications of this link (Clubb and Startin 1995). Information strategies depend on analysis and understanding of requirements, followed by the analysis of data and processes to meet those requirements. They should always be driven by the users of information systems. It follows that the compilation, curation and dissemination of information should be properly analysed and understood, with the strategy being driven by the requirements of the users and that technical solutions should be based on a business case and an appraisal of available options (for example Clubb 1989).

Information systems are also concerned with flows of information, both within an organisation and in relation to the outside world. There seems to be no intrinsic reason why common strategic benefits of information systems could not be provided for a whole discipline such as archaeology, covering all organisations and directly supporting the objectives of archaeology itself.

2 A retrospective on Information Systems Strategy

An information systems strategy for a heritage organisation can only be established if the objectives, activities and uses involved are fully understood. Contributors to CAA and other conferences over the years have often tried to classify the various uses of computing in archaeology. Since the papers have different aims, they may only serve as crude, although useful, indicators of changing perceptions of the relationship between information systems and archaeology over the last 25 years. Three examples have been chosen to illustrate thinking at different points in time. The papers chosen are:

1. Wilcock 1973
2. Cooper 1984
3. Ryan 1988

2.1 The Wilcock classification of 1973

In 1973, Wilcock attempted a classification of the use of information technology in archaeology as part of a wider survey of computing (Wilcock 1973), and are summarised in Figure 1.

Data banks and information retrieval
Specialist data
Museum records
Excavation records
Statistics
Seriation
Multi-dimensional scaling
Trend surface analysis
Clustering
Routine reduction of instrument survey readings
Graphics

Figure 1: Wilcock's 1973 functional grouping of archaeological computing

Wilcock's classification was a commendable start, reflecting many of the perceptions of the time. However, in retrospect, his paper illustrates that the relationships and flows between the different types of applications were not fully understood at this date and there was little analysis of the objectives of computing. Wilcock reflected the early interest in computing in higher education with areas such as museums and excavations grouped generically as 'databanks and information retrieval'. The use of information systems in Sites and Monuments Records (SMRs) was largely absent. This is, perhaps, unsurprising, since early SMRs did not, in the main, have access to computers. Many archaeologists in local government shared a suspicion that they would be more of a hindrance than a help (see Burrow 1985b).

2.2 The Cooper classification of 1984

Over ten years later in 1984, Cooper produced one of the few papers published on the need for a national strategy for computing. It is arguably one of the most important papers on archaeological computing published in the UK (Cooper 1985). His attempt to classify computer systems in archaeology is set out in Figure 2.

Field archaeology
Excavation
Post-excavation
Research
Statistical and multi-variate analysis
Simulation and spatial analysis
Cultural resource management

Figure 2: Cooper's 1985 grouping of archaeological computing

Cooper demonstrated an understanding of the cycles and relationships between different types of computer application and of computers as part of the business infrastructure for archaeology. He recognised that the future of computers in archaeology should be based on an explicit and long-term strategy, rather than implicit and random developments. While he criticised the failure of the national archaeological organisations to take a lead, he also recognised that none of them had the full range of responsibilities necessary to make such a strategy work for the discipline. He advocated that a single national body should be given the responsibility of establishing goals for archaeological computing, both short and long term, as well as the prioritisation of those goals. He also identified the need for a policy statement and the establishment of mechanisms to bring together discordant interests. His paper reflected some of the changes in practice brought about during the 1980s, with an emphasis on the need for archaeology to become more business-like. Cooper suggested that archaeologists should become more familiar with management theory. At the time, this may have seemed quite radical to his contemporaries, but this view has now gained increased support.

The use of computing to support the management of archaeology was still new in 1984. At that time, the Department of the Environment's record of scheduled monuments was a relative pioneer of heritage management records. This was established in 1980 (Chadburn 1988), while in 1983, optical coincidence retrieval systems were still the major mechanism in the retrieval of SMR information, with limited use of machine-based retrieval (Fraser 1985).

2.3 The Ryan classification of 1988

A classification of computer applications in archaeology was made in conjunction with Nick Ryan's important bibliography of qualitative applications and quantitative methods in archaeology (Ryan 1988). The principal findings of this classification are summarised in Figure 3.

Quantitative methods and simulation
Finds analysis
Survey and excavation recording and stratigraphical analysis
Sites and Monuments Records
Graphics
Expert systems and knowledge representation
Education
Publication
Scientific techniques
Museums
General

Figure 3: Ryan's 1988 grouping of archaeological computing

Ryan's list reflected a more detailed understanding of the cycles of activity linking different applications. By the late 1980s, management training for archaeologists was more common and within the 'General' category, papers on the specific use of computing for strategic and management purposes were starting to appear (recognising that computing has a part to play in the organisation of archaeology as a holistic discipline, not just in discrete projects). His bibliography contained a significant body of literature on both national and local organisations, (for example the papers referenced from Burrow, 1985a). Above all, Ryan's categories provided a basis for the understanding of a cycle of activity in archaeological computing from investigation to analysis, interpretation to curation, and dissemination together with the requirement for further investigation.

3 The CAA 93 session on strategic planning issues

The classifications summarised above are interesting as historical snapshots, but they do not provide any serious analysis of the ultimate aims of computing in archaeology. During the early to mid 1990s, there was a debate about the use of information systems in the management of archaeological organisations. By 1993, some archaeologists had expressed a concern that even those who had a specific interest in archaeological computing were not taking its use for the management and communication of archaeology seriously. In response, Booth organised a session on strategic planning issues at CAA 93 (Wilcock and Lockyear 1995). In his preface to the session (Booth 1995a), he suggested that the identification of the importance of information as a key resource within organisations had caused many institutions to treat information systems and information technology in a strategic manner. He argued that archaeology, as an 'information-rich' discipline, should also adopt this pattern. He went on to suggest that if information technology were to justify its costs, it must be closely aligned to the business aims of the organisation it purported to serve.

The session on strategic planning at CAA 93 resulted in five published articles. Three of these were concerned with the development of information strategies and systems by organisations responsible for recording, protecting and managing the archaeological and built heritage, one with local government and one with a large national museum. The contributions from the larger organisations stressed that information is a key corporate resource within an organisation and, as with other resources, such as finance, staff and property, it must be managed effectively in order to help achieve the objectives of the organisation.

One paper dealt with the development of information systems strategies within English Heritage (Clubb and Startin 1995). This explored the relationship between business goals and information systems as well as the requirement to manage internal and external flows of data to serve the business. Another paper (Cooper and Dinn 1995) showed how even in a relatively small body concerned with a local administrative area (the archaeological service within Hereford and Worcester County Council), the effects and importance of information systems and technologies can be much greater than might be anticipated. The purpose of their paper was to investigate the relationship between archaeological organisations and computer technology from a management perspective. Technological change is likely to have significant influence on both archaeological organisations and their structures and also on the roles of archaeological professionals. Hence, discussions between organisations should be of great value to the discipline as a whole.

Another paper (Booth 1995b) reviewed the development of an information systems strategy for a large national museum (the National Science Museum) and showed how such an initiative had established, as a central objective, the encouragement of communications throughout the organisation. Booth identified the highest priorities which information technology can address as being improvement of the management of the museum, information resources and their use, delivery of service to the public and the generation of revenue and cost effectiveness.

The papers delivered in the session of 1993 were an important contribution, but in the main, they dealt with the role of strategy within organisations, not between them.

4 The Booth key-note address of 1994

In a provocative key-note paper delivered to the CAA conference in 1994, Booth continued his campaign, focusing on the discipline as a whole, rather than individual organisations (Booth 1995c). He identified the hallmarks of the 'Information Age' as being substantial increases in computer processing power, and the convergence of computing and telecommunications, (and latterly, with mass entertainment). Booth identified the potential for the dissemination of information via high-speed networks and easily distributed media such as CD-ROM as one of the major benefits of these developments. The use of such techniques as multi-media, hyper-media and virtual reality have made information more accessible to its users.

Booth concluded that the performance of archaeology in terms of the 'Information Age' has been disappointing. In his review of relevant literature, he acknowledged that there have been papers discussing strategic issues for individual organisations and there has been guidance on the development of Inventory records at national and local levels. However, in terms of excavation records, he argued there have been no moves towards the adoption of a national system. Moreover, there has been little discussion of the relationship between archaeological fieldwork and museum collections. His assessment of archaeological fieldworkers who have the responsibility to recover, analyse and disseminate the results of their work was particularly harsh, suggesting that for the most part, they have not taken advantage of available technology. Overall, Booth's thesis suggested that the lack of dissemination through digital techniques would make archaeology - and, by implication, the built heritage - more marginal in the public consciousness. He considered this general failure to embrace contemporary electronic means of presenting information, whether as text, images or sound would reduce the enthusiasm for public participation in the heritage.

5 A response to Booth in 1995

At the following CAA conference in 1995, there was an attempt at a strategic appraisal of the past, present and future of information systems for archaeology and architecture in England. In part, this was aimed to provide a response to Booth's presentation of the previous year (Clubb and Lang 1996). This analysis concentrated on monument record systems, which limited its scope. It presented a model of the information relationships between the various heritage bodies and their related functions in terms of policy and data. Clubb and Lang then looked in detail at the historical inter-relationships of the systems created, assessed progress towards an idealised model and the extent to which those heritage information systems have transcended Booth's thesis. They concluded that there is some truth in Booth's suggestion that heritage data is still not being disseminated effectively to the wider heritage community and beyond. Nevertheless, they also argued that significant steps have been taken towards establishing compatible information systems within archaeology and architecture, notably in the development of data standards, controlled vocabulary and reference data, both at national and international levels. They noted that progress and developments in geographical and spatial information systems, imaging and multi-media have often only been feasible at a local rather than national level.

Clubb and Lang concluded that, at least for monument recording systems, significant progress was being made towards a co-ordinated approach which would, in time, lead to a coherent information network, embracing not only national interests, but with the rapid potential to operate within a truly national framework, although the precise nature of this framework was not described.

6 Darvill's critique of 1995

Also in 1995, a critique was presented by Tim Darvill of the difficulties for users in gaining consistent access to the various discrete information systems in England. His comments were based on his experience in using national and local records in connection with the English Heritage-funded Monuments at Risk Survey (Darvill 1995). While advocating geographical information systems (GIS) as part of the solution, he warned that "before the powerful new engine of GIS is hitched to a rickety old cart", there would be a need for more strategic thinking by the national bodies, greater co-operation between the creators, curators and users and further research and development.

Darvill has long been an advocate of the view that archaeological information must be seen as part of a much wider environmental dataset in a global context.

7 Recent developments

In spite of the development of sophisticated information systems strategies in the national organisations and a number of local authorities as well as national museums, the lack of strategic direction in computing for archaeology across the whole discipline as a whole is not very encouraging to date. However, there have been a number of initiatives during 1996-7 which give hope for a better future. These include the following:

1. a contribution to the establishment of a research framework for archaeology in England which should help set objectives for the conservation sector of the discipline
2. increased partnerships between organisations and sectors of the discipline within the UK, notably initiated by the higher-education sector, and between museums and Inventory records in Europe, including research into metadata as a mechanism for retrieval across data-sets
3. the proposed quantification of the resources required to provide the necessary infra-structure for the development of a strategic approach for records of sites and monuments records for the profession and for society at large
4. renewed interest by the Council for British Archaeology
5. improved mechanisms for the development of data standards.

These initiatives are dealt with in more detail below:

7.1 English Heritage research frameworks

In 1996, English Heritage published Frameworks for our past (Olivier 1996) as a review of research frameworks, strategies and perceptions of current concerns over a general lack of academic focus and content in areas of archaeology, especially those driven by PPG-16 on Archaeology and Planning (DoE 1990). The review suggested that there is a vacuum at the heart of conservation policies. Olivier recognised that the discipline required a general framework within which to consider curatorial concerns and make recommendations for the protection and recording of archaeological sites. He argued for an integrated approach that combines expertise and information, academic processes and public appreciation, national and local organisations and professionals and local societies. Many of the perceived problems result from practical and structural difficulties which hinder effective communication, mainly due to a lack of technical infrastructure, especially information systems. The main elements of infrastructure required all imply computing capability. Olivier's framework is summarised in Figure 4, below.

Publication, where new mechanisms should be put in place for:

- Technical reports
- Developer-funded work
- Access to local Sites and Monuments Records
- Digital publication
- Dissemination

Communication, through:

- Multi-disciplinary fora
- Organisational links
- Digital communication
- UK-wide information forum

Education and training

Figure 4: Olivier's infra-structure for research frameworks

Olivier's analysis suggests that, in order to make longer-term objectives sustainable, frameworks are needed in which all those active in curatorial decisions can participate and on which curatorial decisions can be firmly based and firmly judged. These should involve all sections of the archaeological discipline. In analysing the frameworks required, it is clear that these all need to be supported by information systems.

7.2 The establishment of the Archaeology Data Service

At a launch in London in January 1997, the Archaeology Data Service (ADS) which began operations in October 1996, became a major force in UK archaeology, originating in the higher-education sector, but building interfaces across the discipline. The ADS was established to collect, describe, preserve and provide user support for digital resources that are created as a result of archaeological research (see Richards, this volume). It has a responsibility for promoting standards and guidelines for best practice in the creation, description, preservation and use of spatial information across its host body, the Arts and Humanities Data Service. ADS is run by a consortium of eight British Universities and the Council for British Archaeology; initial funding being provided by the British Academy. Like the Aquarelle project (section 7.5. below), it has provided a research and development function for the profession in areas such as the use of metadata and the preservation of digital archives.

7.3 A networked multi-media resource for Scotland (SCRAN)

The National Museum of Scotland, the Scottish Museums Council and the Royal Commission on the Ancient and Historical Monuments of Scotland have been successful in obtaining funding from the Millennium Commission for a networked multi-media resource of the historical and material culture of Scotland (see Murray, this volume). This is a splendid example of co-operation across the Inventory and museums sectors.

7.4 The forthcoming RCHME/EH/ALGAO co-operation statement

RCHME, English Heritage and the Association of Local Government Archaeological Officers (ALGAO) have been working with representatives of users of SMRs on a new statement of co-operation designed to secure the future of local SMRs. This is due to be signed early in 1998. All three organisations place an overriding priority on establishing a network of well resourced SMRs providing an information service covering the whole of England. This statement will promulgate agreed principles governing SMRs, the national Inventory maintained by RCHME and the statutory records maintained by English Heritage, covering areas such as those set out in Figure 5.

Definition of SMRs

Content

Management

Functionality, including software

Integration and networking

Coverage

Standards

Training

Tourism, leisure, education and research

Figure 5: Agreed principles governing Sites and Monuments Records

The initiative is intended to develop and apply criteria for assessment to all existing SMRs in England to help determine the scale of the resource needed to bring them to the required standard. The statement recognises the need for a national network of SMRs to be co-ordinated at a national level, and that new capital will be required as well as adequate resources within local authorities themselves. The authors of the statement hope that as the National Heritage Lottery fund develops its policy for archaeology, there may be a place for funding the enhancement of SMRs as a phased programme.

7.5 The European Community Aquarelle project

Co-operation at national level is one encouraging sign, but it is also taking place on a European level. The European Community Aquarelle project is being funded under the Telematics, Information Market and Exploitation of

Research programme (information engineering). It aims to share cultural heritage through multimedia telematics. Several categories of users are anticipated. These include professionals, publishers, cultural mediators, museums and historical monument curators, art galleries and art traders, architects and town planners, researchers and students in art, art history, archaeology and the humanities. The programme is market and technically-driven. Of particular interest is the co-operation between Inventories of monuments, such as the RCHME National Monuments Record and similar organisations in France, Italy and Greece, as well as major museums in Europe. The participation of both RCHME and the Museums Documentation Association (MDA) as cultural resource partners should also assist with co-operation in the UK and build on the tradition of working together by the two bodies on data standards.

7.6 The establishment of an RCHME data standards unit

Progress in data standards is largely based on the key role of RCHME in close partnership with many others, including English Heritage, local government, the British Archaeology Bibliography hosted by the CBA and the MDA. Activity has been in progress since 1984 in the development of national and international standards for the recording of information about archaeology and the built heritage (for examples see RCHME 1993, RCHME/English Heritage 1993, RCHME/English Heritage 1995, Council of Europe 1995 and CIDOC 1995). In 1996, the RCHME established its own dedicated Data Standards Unit within the National Monuments Record, recognising the importance of data standards and the need to apply them vigorously internally, as well as the value of outreach and continuing involvement in national and international initiatives. Quine (this volume) sets out progress achieved by the Unit, current initiatives and concludes that the advantages of standards in terms of consistency, retrievability and compatibility, as well as in terms of facilitating access to and the sharing of heritage information, continue to outweigh any potential disadvantages, such as the additional overhead.

RCHME has also been active in sponsoring new SMR software to be provided by the private sector and incorporating agreed data standards and models to assist compatibility between national and local record systems.

8 Conclusion

The development of the concept of partnership in archaeology in recent years has lead to a recognition that one organisation is often not large enough to achieve all that is needed, but that, in a national framework, all organisations and sectors have a part to play. While the initiatives mentioned above give some hope for the future, it may be questioned whether it is sufficient for new partnerships and initiatives to develop in a relatively uncoordinated way. Perhaps, the most significant initiative yet is likely to come from the CBA, which has long recognised the problems of the lack of a strategy which unites the information systems of all elements of the discipline of archaeology. It has supported the development of the British Archaeological Bibliography and the Defence of Britain recording project, the latter funded by the Heritage Lottery Fund, both with significant information systems components. This seems a propitious time for the launch of a new programme, due to the increasing potential of information technology in combination with:

1. the possibility of funding from the Heritage Lottery Fund for information technology projects which support archaeology
2. the current spirit of co-operation between the national bodies in England and the archaeologists in local government
3. the establishment of the Archaeology Data Service, bringing in the sector of higher education and access to research and development
4. the co-operation of monument records and museums in a UK and European context and the probable requirement for monument records and museums to co-operate in England and Wales on the recording of portable antiquities.

The CBA Research and Conservation Committee has begun investigating the requirement and feasibility of an information infra-structure covering the UK as a whole. This is a development which all members of the profession, particularly those who are users of archaeological information, should watch with interest and seek to support, particularly as its objectives become more closely defined. However, the CBA cannot act alone. All organisations, national, local, professional, academic and voluntary must pull together to assess the current situation, define the future vision and plan a migration strategy with appropriate resources sought with great creativity. Underlining this is the requirement for a research and development resource for the development of computer applications in archaeology. Areas requiring exploration include the modelling of the past, including spatial and geographical information systems, networks both for the profession and the public and the preservation of digital archives.

There are opportunities and pitfalls in the growing potential of the technology to disseminate information when there are backlogs in data capture and interpretation and badly-curated digital archives which are not readily accessible. There are, however, new sources of funding in the UK, such as the Heritage Lottery Fund which have strengthened the scope of the voluntary recording sector in areas such as the recording of historic defensive works, heritage ponds and public monuments and sculptures and there may also be an opportunity to help deal with the technical infrastructure required. A new strategic vision now seems to be possible which articulates how the several sectors in archaeology could work in partnership to develop a vision for the discipline as a whole. The potential of the technology should be harnessed to assess the archaeological resource, to inform the agenda for research, to end the relative isolation of archaeology by linking to databases serving the environment and leisure and 'cascading the fruits' of knowledge to inspire the imagination of society. This will require more proactive shaping by the archaeological profession as a whole than has been demonstrated to date and there is an urgent need for a debate on how to achieve this.

Archaeology tends to proceed on the basis of a cycle of increasing knowledge whereby interventions are followed by the analysis and curation of data for dissemination which in turn informs further intervention. This cycle should take place in the context of agreed standards and accessible networks. It needs to embrace text, spatial information, images and scientific analysis. The stage is a large one; it transcends England to include the home countries of the UK. Beyond lie Europe and the rest of the world. The vision of information systems for archaeology is a worthy and inspiring one and if we fail to develop it then archaeology will fail all those who, increasingly, will expect direct and easy access to information.

Bibliography

Booth, B K W, 1995a Strategic Planning Issues: Preface In: J Wilcock and K. Lockyear (eds.),*Computer Applications and Quantitative Methods in Archaeology 1993*, BAR International Series 598, Oxford: Tempus Reparatum, 65

Booth, B K W, 1995b Developing an information strategy for the National Museum of Science and Industry. In: J Wilcock and K. Lockyear (eds.),*Computer Applications and Quantitative Methods in Archaeology 1993*, BAR International Series 598, Oxford: Tempus Reparatum , 95-99

Booth, B K W, 1995c Has archaeology remained aloof from the information age? In: J Huggett and N.Ryan (eds.), *Computer Applications and Quantitative Methods in Archaeology 1994*, BAR International Series 600, Oxford: Tempus Reparatum, 1-12

Burrow, I, 1985a *County Archaeological Records: Progress and Potential.* London: Association of County Archaeological Officers

Burrow, I, 1985b The history of the sites and monuments records system. In: I Burrow (ed.), *County Archaeological Records: Progress and Potential*, London: Association of County Archaeological Officers, 6-15.

Cabinet Office 1997 *Open Government: Code of Practice on Access to Government Information.* Second Edition, Stationery Office.

Central Computer and 1989 *Strategic Planning for Information Systems.* Information System Guides A2. Chichester: Telecommunications Wiley. Agency (CCTA)

CIDOC 1995 *Draft International Core Data Standard for Archaeological Sites and Monuments Records.* International Documentation Committee, International Council of Museums, Paris : ICOM.

Clubb, N D, 1989 Investment appraisal for information technology. In S P Q Rahtz and J D Richards(eds.), *Computer Applications and Quantitative Methods in Archaeology 1988*, BAR International Series 446, Oxford: British Archaeological Reports, 399-408.

Clubb, N D, and Lang N A R, 1996 A strategic appraisal of information systems for archaeology and architecture in England-Past, Present and Future. In H. Kammerman and K Fennema (eds.), *Computer Applications and Quantitative Methods in Archaeology 1995*. Publication of the Institute of Prehistory, University of Leiden 28, 51-72.

Clubb, N D, and Startin W D, 1995 Information systems strategies in national organisations and the identification, legal protection and management of the most important sites in England. In J. Wilcock and K. Lockyear (eds.), *Computer Applications and Quantitative Methods in Archaeology 1993*, BAR International Series 598, Oxford: Tempus Reparatum , 67-73.

Cooper, M A, 1985 Computers in British Archaeology: the need for a national strategy. In :M. A Cooper and J D RICHards (eds.) *Current Issues in Archaeological Computing*, BAR International Series 271, Oxford: British Archaeological Reports, 79-92.

Cooper, M A, 1995 Computers and the evaluation of archaeological organisations. In : J Wilcock and K. Lockyear and J L Dinn. (eds.),*Computer Applications and Quantitative Methods in Archaeology 1993*, BAR International Series 598, Oxford: Tempus Reparatum , 89-93.

Council of Europe 1995 *European Bronze Age Monuments. A Multi-Lingual Glossary of Architectural Terminology. A draft covering Denmark, France, The Netherlands, the Republic of Ireland and the United Kingdom.* Amersfoot: Council of Europe Glossary SS7, May 4th 1995.

Department of 1990 *Policy Guidance Note 16: Archaeology and Planning.* London: HMSO. Environment

Darvill, T, 1995 Researching Archaeology? That's tough. In : *British Archaeology 9*, York. CBA, 6.

Fraser, D, 1985 Sites and Monuments Records: the state of the art. In I. Burrow (ed.), *County Archaeological Records: Progress and Potential*, London: Association of County Archaeological Officers, 47-55.

Oliver, A, 1996 *Frameworks for our past : A review of research frameworks, strategies and perceptions.* London : English Heritage.

Royal Commission on the Historical Monuments of England 1993 *Recording England's Past : A data standard for the extended national archaeological* of England *record.* London : Royal Commission on the Historical Monuments of England.

Royal Commission on Historical Monuments Monuments of England of England and English Heritage 1989 *Revised Thesaurus of Architectural Terms.* London: London: Royal Commission on the Historical Monuments of England.

Royal Commission on Historical Monuments of England and English Heritage 1992 *Thesaurus of Archaeological Site Types* (2nd edition). London: Royal Commission on the Historical Monuments of England.

Royal Commission on Historical Monuments Monuments of England of England and English Heritage 1995 *Thesaurus of Monument Types: A Standard for Use in Archaeological and Architectural Records.* Swindon: Royal Commission on the Historical Monuments of England.

Ryan, N, 1988 A Bibliography of computer applications and quantitative methods in archaeology. In S P Q R Rahtz (ed.), *Computer Applications and Quantitative Methods in Archaeology* 1988, International Series 446(i), Oxford : BAR, 1-27.

Wilcock, J D, 1973 A general Survey of Computer applications in archaeology. In : J .D Wilcock (ed), *Computer Applications in Archaeology 1*, Science and Archaeology 9, Stamford: George Street Press,17-21.

Contact details

Nigel D. Clubb
RCHME
National Monuments Record Centre
Great Western Village
Swindon SN2 2GZ
UK

CAA 97

Public Heritage in an Age of Decline.

Neil Lang

Abstract

Government policy during the 1980s attempted to re-appraise the role of the Public Sector in the UK. The result, from successive Administrations, has been a general 'down-sizing' of Public Sector functions, a trend which seems set to continue. Most heritage activities now produce records of some sort or could benefit from their efficient exploitation. Despite the growth in resources and influence of heritage activities during this period, the development of heritage records will be increasingly affected by a declining resource base. This paper suggests that managers of heritage records will need to explore similar 'end-game' strategies to those employed by declining private sector industries to thrive during a period of substantial change. It explores the role of management in securing policy support and resources for the heritage within the Public Sector and the importance of expanding public interest as we approach the new Millennium.

1 Background

1.1 The public sector as an industry in decline

"Every major industry was once a growth industry. But some that are now riding a wave of growth enthusiasm are very much in the shadow of decline. Others which are thought of as seasoned growth industries have actually stopped growing. In every case the reason growth is threatened, slowed, or stopped is not because the market is saturated. It is because there has been a failure of management."

(Levitt 1975)

The Public Sector in Britain is in decline. The paper will develop an explicitly economic framework to examine, on the one-hand, implications for the information strategies of the heritage sector in general, and to examine issues which will be relevant to those bodies involved in the use, generation and curation of records of the historic environment. Most heritage activities involve the creation of records of one sort or another. In the last fifteen or so years, there has been massive growth in the creation of 'heritage information' as a result of the application of information technology.

The application of analytical business models and techniques to heritage management may be unfamiliar territory for CAA, and their relevance to information systems and technology may not be at first apparent. However, it is argued that without a proper appreciation of trends influencing public sector policy, the functions under-pinned by information strategies will find difficulty in maintaining or expanding their resource base.

The starting point for this paper suggests that public administration is as susceptible as the private sector to cyclical changes. The cycles tend to be longer term, without the more volatile changes characteristic of many private sector industries nonetheless there are discernible trends which are largely being ignored by the heritage community, a service industry still predominantly funded through the public purse.

As archaeologists studying the past, it is common to warn against viewing human evolution as a form of linear progression, with each successive society in some way improving on its predecessor. However, recently, there seems to be an assumption that support for archaeology (and the historic environment in general) will continue to increase, building on the platform of government heritage policy founded during the 1980s.

By contrast, the overall level of investment in the public sector is reducing and has been doing so for some time. Public Sector financing has steadily declined over the last two decades (e.g. utilities, transport, creation of executive agencies) while assets of the remaining Public Sector have also been sold (council housing, MoD property). The rising cost of welfare on demand is already forcing rationing of access to areas which were once given to all as of right (for example, certain types of medical care). In consequence, many of the social objectives of governments of all political persuasions are having to be re-considered. Since 1979, the total number of jobs within the Public Sector has been cut by a quarter (figure 1).

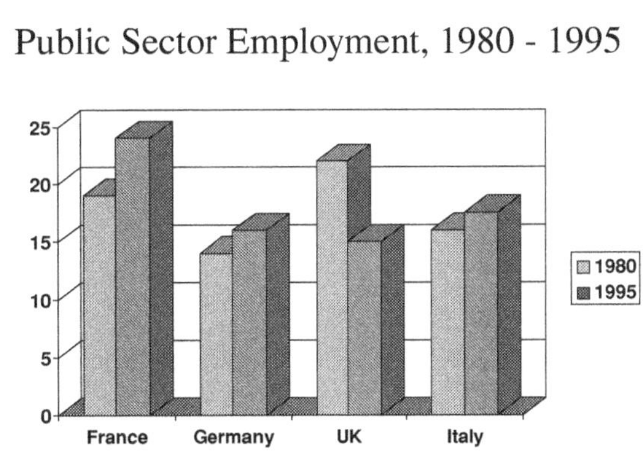

Figure 1 - Source: OECD Finance Ministry, 1997

It is an axiom of the public sector that there are never enough resources to go around. Whereas the private sector is in general concerned with maximising demand for products, the public sector is often engaged in regulating demand, so that scarce resources can be 'stretched' as far as possible. Perhaps this is in part responsible for the inward-looking attitude of the profession.

It has become fashionable to describe our current era as an 'information age'. The quest for ever increasing access to information is a major driver within many industries while the process of providing information has spawned several industries in itself. And yet, for the vast majority of the public, access to heritage information is quite limited and is frequently 'packaged' as a manipulated image of a past few professionals would acknowledge ever existed. While 'heritage attractions' have risen to great prominence in the last fifteen years, the actual work of those involved in the heritage still remains in most areas quite obscure. It is argued that well managed information strategies can assist in offsetting this trend, by making the heritage more accessible, interesting and relevant to justify continued public investment.

The first major attempt to quantify the archaeological resource - David Fraser's seminal paper 'England's Archaeological Resource' (Inspectorate of Ancient Monuments 1984) presaged the importance of quantified information on the heritage in the development of policy. It formed a significant part of the argument for English Heritage's Monument Protection Programme (Darvill *et al* 1987), a long term re-evaluation of statutory protection for archaeological monuments. Previously, many heritage policy initiatives had been undertaken in something of an information vacuum. This paper suggests that information is a vital resource not only for the preservation of the historic environment, but also for its full enjoyment.

The implications of these trends may be analysed through reference to the political, economic, social and technological (PEST) developments in the sector.

2 The PEST environment

2.1 Political

Although the membership of CAA has been innovative and explored a wide range of approaches to the exploitation of computer technology, as this celebration of 25 years admirably shows, it is all too frequently inward looking. While members enjoy the latest Baysean statistic or marvel at the elegance of a database design, there is rarely a look outwards at the sorts of influences which structure and guide our profession. This myopia is symptomatic of the wider heritage community.

Political influences in the heritage sector have had a major impact on the character of archaeological work in particular since the 1980s, and the conservation movement in general. New Public Sector capital projects are encouraging investment from the private sector (for example, through the Private Finance Initiative, introduced in 1994). Both of the major political parties are committed to reducing the cost of public spending.

By contrast, there is also a greatly enhanced environmental awareness, with conservation (of both ecology and the built heritage), with 'Green Issues' and sustainability seen as key elements of environment policy. The 1980s saw a major change in thinking on approaches to historic conservation, culminating in the issue of Policy Planning Guidance Notes 16 covering archaeology (DoE 1990) and 15 (DoE 1994) covering the built heritage. These formalised the principle of developer-funded archaeological recording, generating large volumes of new fieldwork and information.

Local government has emerged as a key focus for the implementation of conservation policy. With the support of English Heritage during the 1980s and the Royal Commission on the Historical Monuments of England (RCHME) during the 1990s, the combination of local Sites and Monuments Records and curatorial advice provides the core framework for the local management of the historic environment.

Recent Government policy has stressed public access to information held by public bodies (e.g. the Code of Practice on Open Government, Cabinet Office 1996). The Department of National Heritage (now the Department of Culture, Media and Sport, DCMS) have placed considerable importance on increasing quality and wider access to the RCHME's records and archive. This has also emerged as a key theme in a statement of co-operation on Sites and Monuments Records jointly signed by the RCHME, EH and the Association of Local Government Archaeological Officers (forthcoming, 1997). An overview of the political environment governing the strategic development of heritage records in the last fifteen years is provided in Clubb and Lang, 1996.

The number of organisations exerting influence on heritage records from within the sector is tending to increase and the 'internal' political landscape is becoming increasingly complex. They include national bodies such as English Heritage, CADW and Historic Scotland, the Royal Commissions, national and local museums, local government Sites and Monuments Records, curatorial heritage managers and more recently the Archaeology Data Service (ADS).

Professional organisations have developed an increasingly strong membership and voice (e.g. the emergence of the Institute of Field Archaeologists (IFA) as a general professional body for archaeology alongside specific professional bodies such as the Association of Conservation Officers (ACO) and Association of Local Government Archaeological Officers (ALGAO)). The number of Private Sector archaeological units and individual consultancies has grown appreciably, and an increasingly vocal voluntary sector, including the Council for British Archaeology (CBA) and a significant body of projects supported through the Heritage Lottery Fund such as the Defence of Britain project, recording Second World War defensive structures, the Public Monuments and Sculptures project, a proposed project to record churches and related projects covering biological and ecological records.

Taken overall, the heritage sector is quite decentralised. There are considerable overlaps of function and, in some areas, a lack of clarity of roles.

2.2 Economic

Economic cycles have an effect on heritage records. The growth in the leisure and tourism industries (estimated to be worth £26 billion) has been fuelled by the maintenance of a vibrant historic environment. Foreign visitors frequently cite this as a major reason for visiting Britain. Affluence has tended to increase demand for heritage activities, fuelling the growth of heritage attractions during the 1980s (Hewison 1987). There is now a significant commercial market for aspects of the past, ranging from living history 'experiences' such as Jorvik to merchandising based on period items, such as the Past Times stores[1].

Economic influences also include the impact of cyclical patterns within the construction industry, which in turn affect the discovery of new information and impact on the units undertaking fieldwork and the curatorial staff processing applications for development.

Since the 1980s, the Public Sector has been encouraged to adopt the practises of the Private Sector. In parallel, it has been an axiom of Government that profitable Public Sector functions should be privatised. Hence there has been a trend towards the identification of potential Public Sector functions which can be hived off to the Private Sector and pressure for Public Sector bodies to become more efficient through progressive reduction (in real terms) of public funding (though public expenditure on the heritage has increased substantially over the last 15 years and has received a further boost in the last two through the operation of Lottery funded projects.

Organisations are increasingly needing to be "flexible systems" which can respond effectively to rapid changes in the external environment. In the last ten years, the heritage world has become much more volatile. For example, the development of the voluntary sector and the influence of capital projects funded via the Lottery is creating a significant number of new national databases [2]. These in turn have implications for other organisations, both local and national, in accessioning and using the information. The onset of the 'flexible organisation' is presenting new challenges in most areas of the workplace.

The general trend towards realising year on year efficiency savings is placing increased reliance on information technology to support functions, and requiring multi-skilling from staff.

2.3 Social

In the last fifteen years, there is evidence to suggest that public consciousness of the heritage has increased substantially. Reporting of heritage stories has increased within the broad sheet press, including a number of high profile planning cases (e.g. the Rose Theatre), and a number of television programmes covering heritage themes capture increasingly large audiences (for example, the Time Team programme now regularly reaches audiences of over 3 million)[3].

There is a widespread acceptance of the philosophy of continuous education, (the "learning society"), which has lead to increased demand for heritage/conservation-based education. The activities of learning and education are now widely acknowledged to be worthwhile pursuits in their own right. The changing demographic profile with earlier retirement and increased leisure time provides a receptive market for consumption of heritage products.

The 'Millennium factor' will change public perceptions of the past. The growth of 'heritage as nostalgia' in the 1980s may be more pronounced than the Fin de Siècle phenomena experienced in the late nineteenth century[4]. If heritage is to continue to appeal, it will need to recast itself to emphasise new discovery and to harness exciting information technology to promote new ways of seeing the past. In 2001, the majority will be looking forward to a new age of discovery and of new information. Unless the presentation of the past is adjusted to take this into account, it may fail to continue to appeal.

Although the longer term interest in funding heritage projects through the Lottery is difficult to judge, it has the potential to provide a major re-vitalisation of participation in the heritage through the voluntary sector.

2.4 Technological

Increased public familiarity with information technology has raised expectations for the delivery of heritage information[5]. Looking back, the early years of computing in archaeology scarcely look like the 'white heat of technology' famously forecast by Harold Wilson, more closely resembling an amber glow. But we are moving towards a point in time when a combination of technology convergence and greatly improved price performance can be harnessed together within a coherent information strategy rather than through the *ad hoc* investment of individual organisations to provide information to a mass market. In terms of heritage records, the technological trends which are likely to be most influential will include telecommunications and increased emphasis on wireless transmission, the progressive and seamless merging of text, spatial, visual and audio media into applications, improved data searching and processing of data and increasingly 'natural' forms of interaction with computers (e.g. through voice activation).

The rise in usage of the Internet has opened up a significant opportunity for delivery of on-line heritage information via public access points and home computers. The Internet seems set to become a commonplace technology in the home. National initiatives such as the National Land Information Service (NLIS) are under development to exploit the integration of spatial, text and imaging datasets[6].

3 Analysis

In the light of this background, it is possible to start to explore the potential strategies open to organisations in order to maintain stasis in an increasingly complex and difficult world. A useful framework for analysis is the SWOT Matrix, which sets out an internal and external model of the environment within which an organisation or sector exists (see figure 2). For the individual organisation, this suggests that those who succeed in using their internal strengths in exploiting environmental opportunities and neutralising environmental threats, while avoiding internal weaknesses, are more likely to gain competitive advantages than other kinds of organisation. In applying this to the broad area of heritage records, this is of course a generalised model, and does not necessarily equate to the specific condition of any particular organisation.

FRAMEWORK

INTERNAL	**Strengths** • Innovation • Expertise • Growing Professionalism • Motivation	**Weaknesses** • Introspection • Fragmentation • Lack of IS Investment • Lack of Strategic Planning
EXTERNAL	**Opportunities** •Public interest •Accessibility •Information integration •Harnessing management expertise	**Threats** •Changing public support •Government Policy shifts •Economic priorities •Marginalisation

Figure 2

The grid suggests that the principal strengths of the discipline are an ability to be innovative, (for example, in the use of new technology, in the re-definition of the subject matter, such as the recent growth in industrial, military and maritime records); expertise (an ability to record, explain and interpret the past), the development of a professional approach (though an area where considerable further development is necessary) and possibly one of its strongest assets, the dedication, enthusiasm, intelligence and motivation of the vast majority of those involved.

Its weaknesses, as noted above, are a tendency towards introspection. The sanction of the professional peer group is commonly viewed as far more important than reaching a public audience. It lacks a unity of purpose (logical connections between organisations and activities are often limiting or missing, resulting in much duplication and waste); partly as a result of this, there has been limited investment, particularly in IS infrastructure and data quality for heritage records, to secure a wider information base and there is often a poor awareness of how or why planning for the longer term is desirable. This is exacerbated by the largely short term nature of funding. In turn, this fosters transient employment contracts, and is rarely conducive to investment in professional development.

There are a number of opportunities which may be harnessed towards securing future funding. The key issue is maintaining public focus and interest. It is not sufficient to state that the recording, understanding and conservation of the past is a facet of civilised society, contributing to a greater good. There must be direct popular engagement and a demonstrable, and ideally quantifiable, interest. Related to this is the opportunity to make the past accessible, particularly through providing information This has major implications for the way in which records are compiled and in the facilities which are provided to make use of them. There is also a major opportunity in integrating heritage information with other data. For example, the inclusion of heritage attractions as part of a tourism information service, or providing information on historic buildings as part of an estate agent's or solicitor's conveyancing system. Realising these opportunities will require high quality management.

The threats quadrant is made up of external adverse factors affecting the sector. Perhaps the most damaging would be changing government policy towards the heritage, not only in terms of direct resources provided to public sector bodies, but also in terms of the framework of conservation. Some commentators already perceive a shift in policy in the new Labour Administration (e.g. Morris 1997). Swings in the economy, and economic policy will have an impact on the rate of discovery and potentially, attitudes towards conservation. Finally, there is the possibility that the very idea of conservation will become marginalised, with the onset of a forward looking vision in the new Millennium.

For the strategic development of the individual organisation, the Ansoff Matrix provides an analytical framework for business outputs (whether products or services) (See figure 3). This presents a matrix based on products/services and markets. The first quadrant offers options for current products in present markets: do nothing (stay exactly as you are), partial or total withdrawal, consolidation through taking positive steps to retain the organisation's position, and market penetration, aimed to actively increase market share. The second quadrant examines new markets for present products, through market development (for example, bringing an existing product to a new market segment). The third quadrant explores product development for existing markets, through product or process innovation and the fourth, diversification. This may be in a related industry (e.g. a field excavation unit developing an educational CD ROM series about archaeology) or an unrelated industry (a field unit marketing project management services to the construction industry). Both are high-risk strategies

The Organisational Perspective

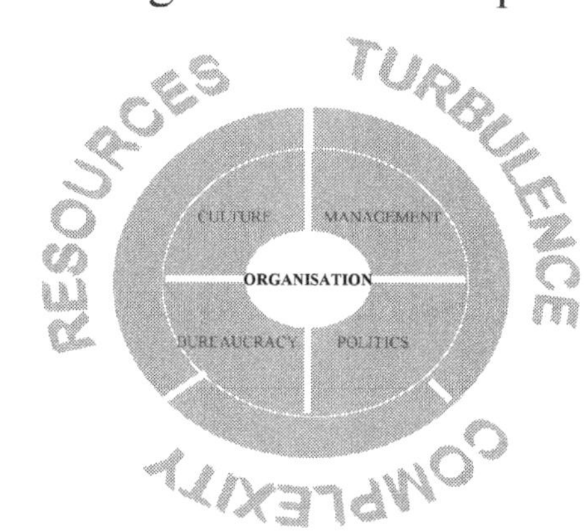

Figure 3 The Organisational Perspective

In addressing the organisational decisions represented by the Ansoff and SWOT Matrices, heritage organisations will need to avail themselves of management expertise. Having successfully broadened and integrated the discipline into new areas (such as the planning system), professionals within the heritage arena are having to explain what they do and why it is valuable in terms which government and society will countenance (for example, the concepts of accountability, performance indicators, value-for-money and marketing). As Cooper has noted (1995), archaeologists now face a choice between leaving management to external professionals (as experienced in the Health Service) or to bring management techniques explicitly within the profession.

In tandem, the profession as a whole will need to mature and become far more co-operative, for its greater good. Part of this process is about learning to understand what the public and professional market actually wants from it (rather than the current set of 'products', assumed to satisfy public needs and wants), who are the stakeholders and what influences they will bring to bear. Additional to the understanding of the market, the management process can help to identify and understand the unique contributions and strengths individual organisations may make towards it.

Core competency analysis is designed to explore the key things an organisation does well, to ensure it can continue to survive. Core competencies of an organisation are the activities, skills and linkages or combination of these which provide the key to a company's performance and which others would find difficult to replicate. Core competencies do not reflect market or product variables but are vested in an organisation's resources such that these can be employed effectively in the market place. Although these are generally applied in a commercial context, there are useful lessons to be drawn in their application within the public sector (whether within individual organisations, or in examining the heritage sector as a whole).

The concept of core competency may seem obvious, but it is often misunderstood. It is often taken to refer to activities which companies perform. In fact, core competencies are those areas which *significantly differentiate* the company from its competitors (either through the application of particular expertise, cost efficiency, or exploitation of unique assets). For example, an archaeological unit's core competency is unlikely to be based in an ability to excavate *per se*, since this is something numerous organisations can do. However, a unique understanding of the archaeology of a particular region, an acknowledged specialism in particular types of site or capacity to handle very large projects *may* all be core competencies of archaeological units. Cooper (1995, p.83) presents a five-tier model of the environments within which an archaeological section of a county council operates, each with different needs of customers and stakeholders requiring specific competencies.

Information systems can play a crucial role in supporting these. As pressure to achieve gains in efficiency intensify, it is ever more necessary to be critical of their balance and health. A useful model for examining information systems represents these from the perspective of an organisation. Figure 4 illustrates the forces affecting information systems within an organisation, and suggests these are broadly in balance (symmetrical quadrants within a circle).

The model represents the internal and external forces on information systems from an organisational perspective. The central (light grey) quadrants of the circle represents the internal forces of the organisation. These are the organisational culture, its management, bureaucracy and politics. All influence the information systems. From a technological perspective, these might be considered as hardware, software, telecommunications and databases. The external ring (dark grey) represents the external influences on information systems, some of which may act as drivers for change. These are the complexity of the world within which the organisation operates; the resources which are available to the organisation; and turbulence, the volatility of the environment within which the organisation operates. Current trends are towards increasing complexity and more sophisticated demands, pressure on resources (though taken overall, expenditure on the heritage has significantly increased in the last fifteen years) and greatly increased volatility. The recent local government review provides a good example, affecting not only local government organisations, but also the efficacy of national heritage policies.

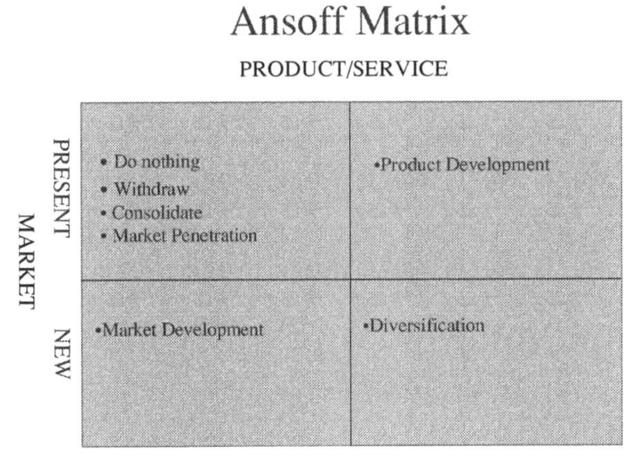

Figure 4 Ansoff Matrix

From a technological perspective, the equivalent external influences might be capacity, compatibility and change (i.e. whether the systems are still meeting organisational needs). In the idealised model, the organisation is in balance (represented by the symmetry of the concentric circles). In practice, many of the organisations responsible for compiling heritage information have failed to harmonise their IS with the organisation, or its corporate objectives. In a recent survey of IT managers (Daniels 1994), the two main long-term concerns were stated to be achieving effective integration of IT with corporate objectives and meeting project deadlines in terms of cost and time. The commitment and involvement of senior management continues to be the critical factor in building strategic information systems.

4 Future opportunities

In developing the future market for heritage information, it is not only the direct consumers (i.e. the interested public and those professionally engaged with the heritage) that must be considered. Much of the value in heritage information is not inherent in the raw data, but in its combination with other data sets in 'value-added' products. For the planning profession, this might be the inclusion of statutory information as part of an environmental planning service. In a tourism context, it might be the ability to include heritage attractions, and supporting information as part of a service to potentially high-spending consumers.

An important recent development in this respect is the National Geospatial Data Framework (NGDF). The National Geospatial Database is, at present, largely a theoretical construct, developed by a consortium of bodies in which the most prominent are the Ordnance Survey and the Association for Geographical Information. It is attempting to provide a common framework for the integration of data sets from different suppliers to enable exploitation of spatial data for different purposes, on the assumption that collectively, data will be far more valuable than the sum of the individual sets. It should provide a framework to encourage the growth of applications based on an increasingly information-rich society.

The National Geospatial Data Framework is not a physical database nor is it ever likely to be. It is best described as a virtual database or framework enabling all those involved - government bodies, data brokers, software vendors, service providers and many potential customers - to benefit in a future where the needs for data in often novel combinations will grow, but the developments are likely to be unpredictable in detail. It will therefore require data standards, data access, collaboration and creating an environment for business opportunity. Integration implies a high-level framework to facilitate the linking, combining and widespread use of the many geospatial data sets collected, maintained and held by different organisations.

There are a number of existing examples of NGDF-type applications including the Bristol Land Registry Pilot, NLIS lead by Her Majesty's Land Registry (HMLR) and the equivalent in Scotland, SCOTLIS, the Intergraph GeoMedia Service (a consortium of data providers using Intergraph GIS technology on the World-wide Web). Similar developments are underway by most of the leading GIS vendors.

There is currently a considerable gulf between the realisation of such potential applications and the reality of the current state of heritage information. One of the most ambitious attempts to link related data sets from different information suppliers, the Monuments at Risk Survey (MARS) project, experienced considerable difficulties in dealing with variable data structures, units of record and data quality (Darvill 1995a).

Thus far, discussion has focused on professional curatorial concerns. A thorough analysis of the response of heritage practice within academic institutions is beyond the scope of this paper, though it is worth noting the general success of many academic institutions in adjusting to the changing environment of the 80s and early 90s (in a wide range of disciplines, both related and unrelated to heritage). In this respect, it is worth noting that the organisation selected to undertake the MARS project on behalf of English Heritage was a University institution.

Despite demonstrating an aptitude for managing change, as Cooper (1995) has noted, there is comparatively little discussion on the application of management models and techniques to the heritage sector from the academics than the professional camps[7]. Discussion of their relevance to the Public Sector and information strategies is an even more rarefied category. The areas explored in this paper have attempted to stimulate debate on the role of management within the discipline, with examples of techniques which can be applied to assess the position of organisations in relation to one another and in terms of the sector as a whole. Effective control of information, both in terms of systems and content is a key area for the continued survival and success of their core functions.

The relative success of organisations performing similar functions (whether cultural resource management within local authorities, field units or national organisations is not entirely a matter of serendipity. In many cases, it is a reflection of managerial competence. While the growth of what is perceived to be a 'management culture' in archaeology, (notably thorough the incipient rise of project management in relation to field archaeology) is sometimes seen as detrimental to the profession, it is surprising that there has not been more discussion of the nature and quality of management skills and techniques required. In a discipline so heavily reliant on educational and knowledge-based skills, the paucity of managerial training within the heritage sector is a cause for serious concern. While many future archaeologists may only require passing familiarity with business management, (Darvill 1995b), if this skills gap remains, senior managers operating in the public sector will increasingly be brought in from outside the profession.

5 Conclusion

" ....many businesses today face problems in their use of our wonderful technology so serious that they threaten to jeopardise [their] bright future...key to [the] solution is the foundation of comprehensive strategy for the development of information resources....."

Allan, B 1982

"We are in danger of drowning in our own data ..... continuous enhancement .... is splendid but it will not work unless we also have continuous enhancement of indexing ..... professionalism in archaeology is hardly in doubt ..... what I am asking for is professionalism in information retrieval ....."

Lavell, C 1985

These two quotations, (both from papers nearly fifteen years old) crystallise two of the major challenges faced in exploiting information technology for heritage records. On the one hand, is the question of persuading heritage organisations, both individually and collectively that strategic planning for information systems is essential to their individual well being and to the long term survival of heritage concerns. On the other, that the ability to retrieve information in a manner usable and useful to the end user assumes knowledge of customer needs, data quality and an infrastructure capable of serving them. This requires a sufficient degree of vision and willingness to rise above short term considerations.

There is a analogy drawn by Peter Senge in The Fifth Discipline [Senge 1990] in which he discusses the impact of dropping a live frog into a pan of boiling water. Senge suggest that, in this instance, the frog will hop out immediately. But if the frog is dropped into its more familiar environment of cold water and then the temperature is gradually raised, the frog is cooked without it even noticing. This is because a frog only responds to rapid changes in his environment. This process is precisely what is happening in the heritage sector, through a lack of strategic direction and a general failure to harness information to maximum effect. Many in the heritage community behave in this way, not recognising the changes in their environment until they are undone by them.

For most IS professionals, the 'Millennium Time Bomb' is the prospect of information systems failing in the year 2000 due to the formatting of date functions. For those engaged in the information strategies for the heritage sector, the Millennium Time Bomb may be quite different. It will be the realisation that we have failed to keep the public in touch with and interested in their past or secured the confidence for continued public investment towards its exploration and enhancement.

Notes

1 A single product - the Country Diary of an Edwardian Lady sold over 2.6 million copies in thirteen languages, with £75 million worth of merchandised products based on the book.

2 (e.g. the Council for British Archaeology Defence of Britain Project, recording monuments associated with the First and Second World War).

3 The programme explains archaeological discovery and issues faced by professional archaeologists in an accessible format. It attracts an audience of over 3 million viewers.

4 For example, the growth of Romanticism in art, design and literature, the Gothic Revival in architecture, the Pre-Raphaelite Art movement.

5 This includes remote access via Internet, multi-media and modern graphical user interfaces for end-users of heritage databases.

6 e.g. the National Land Information Service pilot as an application of the National Geospatial Data Framework. Such initiatives enable information to be made available to other bodies. Listed buildings could be made available to estate agents, on-line conveyancing facilitated between solicitors and HM Land Registry.

7 Although there was a brief vogue for 'Public Archaeology' sessions in the early to mid 80s, there was little consideration of the management expertise required to achieve some of the high-minded ambitions discussed.

Bibliography

Allan, B, 1982 An unmanaged computer system can stop you dead, *Harvard Business Review,* 60, 77-87

Ansoff, I, 1965 *Corporate Strategy,* McGraw Hill

Booth, B K W, 1995b Has archaeology remained aloof from the information age?, in Huggett, J and Ryan N (eds), *Computer Applications and Quantitative Methods in Archaeology 1994*, International Series 600, Tempus Reparatum, Oxford, British Archaeological Reports, 1-12

Burrow, I (ed) 1985 *County Archaeological Records: Progress and Potential*, Association of County Archaeological Officers, London

Cabinet Office, 1996 *Open Government, Code of Practice on Access to Government Information,* London

Clubb, N D and Lang, N A R, 1996 A Strategic Appraisal of Information Systems for Archaeology and Architecture in England - Past, Present and Future', in Kamermans, H and Fennema, K (eds), *Interfacing the Past: Computer Applications and Quantitative Methods in Archaeology CAA 1995,* Analecta Praehistorica Leidensia University of Leiden, 51-72

Cooper, M A, 1985 Computers in British Archaeology: the need for a national strategy, in Cooper, M A and Richards, J D (eds.) *Current Issues in Archaeological Computing*, International Series 271, Oxford, British Archaeological Reports, 79-92

Cooper, M A, 1995 The archaeological manager: applying management models to archaeology, in Cooper, M, Firth, A, Carman, J and Wheatley, D (eds.) 1995 *Managing Archaeology,* 71 - 88, Routledge, London

Cooper, M, Firth, A, Carman, J and Wheatley, D (eds.), 1995 *Managing Archaeology, Routledge,* London

Daniels, C N, 1994 *Information Technology. The Management Challenge,* The Economist Intelligence Unit, Cambridge

Darvill, T,1995a Researching Archaeology? That's tough, *British Archaeology, 9*, CBA, York

Darvill, T, 1995b Preparing archaeologists for management, in Cooper, M, Firth, A, Carman, J and Wheatley D (eds), 1995 *Managing Archaeology,* Routledge, London, 175-187

Darvill, T, Startin, W D and Saunders, A, 1987 A question of national importance: approaches to the evaluation of ancient monuments for the monuments protection programme in England, *Antiquity, 61(233),* 393-408

Department Of The Environment, 1990 *Planning Policy Guidance Note 16: Archaeology and Planning,* HMSO, London.

Department Of The Environment and Department Of National Heritage, 1994 *Planning Policy Guidance Note 15: Planning and the Historic Environment*, HMSO, London

Hansen, J H, 1993 European archaeological databases: problems and prospects, in Andresen, J, Madsen, T and Scollar I (eds), *Computing the past. CAA 92 Computer Applications and Quantitative Methods in Archaeology 1992,* Aarhus, 229-237

Hewison, 1987 The Heritage Industry, Methuen, London

Inspectorate of Ancient Monuments, 1984 *England's Archaeological Resource. A rapid Quantification of the National Archaeological Resource and a Comparison with the Schedule of Ancient Monuments,* Department of the Environment, London

Kvamme, K, 1992 Geographic Information Systems and Archaeology, in Lock, G and Moffett, J (eds), *Computer Applications and Quantitative Methods in Archaeology 1991*, International Series 577, Tempus Reparatum, Oxford, British Archaeological Reports, 77-84

Lavell, C, 1985 Information: Are we retrieving it?, in Burrow, I (ed), *County Archaeological Records: Progress and Potential,* Association of County Archaeological Officers, London, 42-45

Leech, R, 1986 Computerisation of the National Archaeological Record, in Laflin, S (ed), *Computer Applications in Archaeology 1986*, University of Birmingham Centre for Computing and Computer Science, Birmingham, 29-37

Levitt, T, 1975 Marketing Myopia, *Harvard Business Review*, September-October 1975, No. 75507

Morris, R, 1997 Let culture and conservation co-reside, *British Archaeology*, July 1997, 26, CBA, York

Porter, M E, 1985 *Competitive Advantage: Creating and Sustaining Superior Performance,* The Free Press, New York

Royal Commission On The Historical Monuments Of England, English Heritage and Association Of Local Government Archaeological Officers, (forthcoming), *Unlocking the Past for the new Millennium. A New Statement of Co-operation on Sites and Monuments Records between the Royal Commission on the Historical Monuments of England, English Heritage and the Association of Local Government Archaeological Officers,* RCHME, Swindon

Senge, P M, 1990 *The Fifth Discipline: The Art and Practice of the Learning Organisation,* Century Business, London

Wheatley, D, 1995 The impact of Information Technology on the Practice of archaeological management, in Cooper, M, Firth, A, Carman, J and Wheatley, D, 1995 *Managing Archaeology,* Routledge, London

Contact details

Neil Lang
RCHME
NMRC
Kemble Drive
Swindon
UK
smrgis@rchme.gov.uk

Ordnance Survey and the Depiction of Antiquities on Maps: Past, Present and Future. The Current and Future Role of the Royal Commissions as Suppliers of Heritage Data to the Ordnance Survey

Diana Murray

Abstract

The background and history of the mapping of archaeological sites is described, followed by an account of the method used to transfer information on 'antiquities' to the Ordnance Survey today. The impact of digitisation on the appearance of archaeology on OS maps has been of concern but the use of digital technology by the Royal Commissions, in particular GIS, opens up many opportunities for future mapping of the archaeological landscape.

1 Background

From the earliest stages of the development of modern mapping, 'antiquities' have been depicted as integral and important visual elements of the landscape. Antiquities appear on maps as early as the 17th century but it was only when, in the mid-18th century the systematic mapping of Scotland was undertaken for military purposes in response to the 1745 rebellion, that surveyed mapping of archaeological sites began. The man responsible was General William Roy who was a surveyor, engineer and archaeologist and sometimes called the 'father' of the Ordnance Survey (OS). He set the standard for the detailed and accurate mapping which has been the trademark of the Ordnance Survey for over 200 years and it was his example that led to the inclusion of archaeological monuments in the specifications for the National Survey started in 1791.

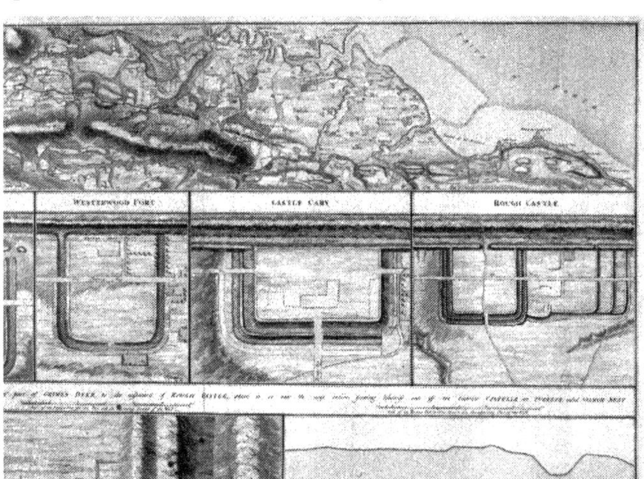

Figure 1. The Antonine Wall showing the section around Falkirk and plans of the forts at Westerwood, Castlecary and Rough Castle. Reproduced from the *Military Antiquities of the Romans in Britain* W Roy 1793 with the kind permission of the Society of Antiquaries of London

The Societies of Antiquaries also played a part. The Society of Antiquaries of Scotland in 1855 wrote to Government, 'The Society, having had its attention recently directed to the fact that many of the primitive monuments of our national history, partly from the progress of agricultural improvements, and in part from neglect and spoilation, were in the course of being removed, was of the opinion, that it would be of great consequence to have all such historical monuments laid down on the Ordnance Survey of Scotland in the course of preparation'. Reply from the War Department: 'I have much pleasure in complying with the society's wishes in this matter, so far as may be practicable, and that instructions will immediately be given to the Engineer department; but I must rely upon the Society of Antiquaries of Scotland endeavouring to assist the surveyors with local information.'(PSAS 2 1854-7,129).

In 1882, the Ancient Monuments Protection Act was passed, and it was not long before it was realised that more information was required about the monuments to be protected, including their location. In 1896, David Murray FSA. called for an archaeological survey of the United Kingdom to be carried out at Government expense. He considered that this would best be achieved by using the OS, but now giving the engineers more detailed specifications rather than relying upon the somewhat variable information previously gained from local landowners.

The Commissions were established in 1908 to make an inventory of monuments and indicate those most worthy of preservation, and from that time, the OS and the Commissions recorded archaeological information in parallel, maintaining discrete roles until 1983.

In 1920, O G S Crawford was appointed as the first OS Archaeology Officer. 'The primary purpose of my appointment' recorded Crawford,' was to reduce to order the chaotic mixture of antiquarianism and speculation that disfigured the Ordnance maps, and to bring it into conformity with existing knowledge.' Crawford undertook field investigation throughout Britain and made his notes in pencil directly on the 6-inch (County Series) mapsheets and was responsible for starting the systematic process of archaeological revision of OS maps which continues today.

In 1947, these maps were used by his successor, C W Phillips, in the expanding Archaeology Branch, to introduce a system of Record Sheet numbers in which each site was given a unique number on that particular mapsheet marked either at its exact location or listed in the margin if the location was uncertain.

Phillips also introduced the card index on which information about each site was recorded. These cards were designed to give information to assist with the publication of the site on the map and to list the authorities for that information. The Division assembled an unsurpassed card index and set of annotated 1:10,000 maps relating to monuments covering the whole of Great Britain and were responsible for the validation and publication of all the 'antiquities' on the OS map series. This index reached its zenith following the OS resurvey of Britain completed in the late 1970's, as every site had been assessed during that work for depiction (or not) on the map. It was extensively copied in the 1970's to form the nucleus of many local Sites and Monuments Records set up in the newly reorganised local authorities and it forms the basis of the National Monuments Records databases in England, Wales and Scotland.

This background and history serves to emphasise how the archaeological community has always been responsible for encouraging the depiction of antiquities on maps and for monitoring the standard and accuracy with which they are portrayed. This has not been without its struggles (Crawford 1955; Phillips 1980; Seymour 1980).

2 Serpell review

In 1979, a major reassessment of the role and procedures of the OS was conducted by the OS review committee under the chairmanship of Lord Serpell in 1979. It was recommended that the responsibilities for recording and surveying of antiquities should be transferred to the three Royal Commissions in England, Scotland and Wales, while responsibility for publishing remained with OS. This was put into effect in 1983 and the Royal Commissions have been carrying out their role in supplying information to OS for mapping purposes ever since, while encouraging the OS to continue their role as publishers of this information.

The Royal Commissions regard the supply of information to OS as essential to ensure that information published on maps does not deteriorate in quality and relevance to map-users. This responsibility is now enshrined by Government in the Royal Warrants that govern the activities of the Commissions.

In 1992, the OS requested a review of the relationship between the OS and the Commissions, the result of which was the establishment of a Service Level Agreement recognising the continuation of a special relationship between OS and the three Royal Commissions for the publication of Antiquities on OS regular map series. The Commissions still have a special and specific role in supplying information to OS for publication which is unlike that of other organisations with whom OS has regular contact.

3 Method

Information about sites of archaeological or historical significance is transferred to the OS in a rigorously standardised format, known as an 'Antiquity Model'. An 'Antiquity Model' may take the form of a generalised plan designed to show the archaeological site in a style suitable for publication on a map, or an instruction to revise the descriptions of published monuments or to delete those which have been destroyed or which no longer fall within the publication policy of OS, such as find spots.

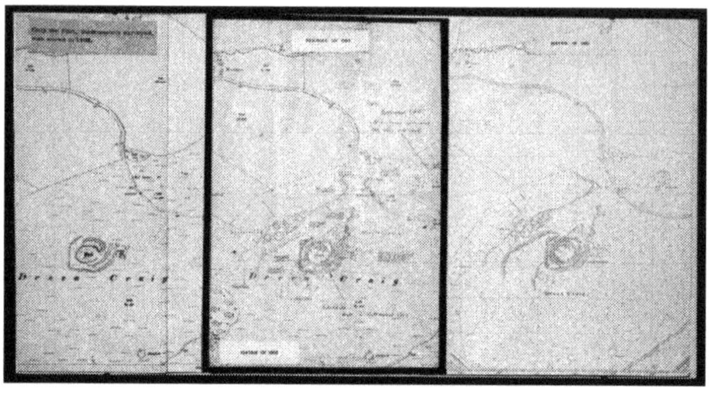

Figure 2. The three panels (originally prepared by the OS Scottish Archaeology Branch) show the revision of the depiction of the fort at Dreva Craig in Peeblesshire from the rather crude plan of 1908, through the meticulously penned antiquity model, to the 1965 published map which also shows the surrounding settlement first recorded in 1958 by the Royal Commission.

The necessity for the Commissions to map archaeology at the 'basic scale' (i.e., the same scales of survey as the OS), combined with technological advances in surveying techniques led to a reappraisal of the recording of archaeological landscapes and has had a major impact on the way the Commissions now carry out field survey.

At RCAHMS, EDM equipment is used in the field for data capture and, most recently 'Penmap' has been adopted, a system which allows digital maps or other relevant data to be taken out and updated on site. Antiquity Models are now only one of a series of plans derived from the detailed survey data using AUTOCAD. Antiquity Models are produced in the same style as the OS Superplan and are therefore presented to the OS in the way the Commissions expect to see it depicted on the plotted map. Means of transferring this data directly to OS in digital form are being actively pursued. After the information has been transferred to the digital archive an edit plot is sent by OS to the Commissions to check that the depiction has been correctly incorporated.

Field survey for OS is routinely undertaken in areas which are part of the Commissions survey programme, although specific areas are also surveyed on request by OS on occasion. In Scotland, antiquities are illustrated on some 16,000 of the kilometre squares, of which about 3% are updated annually. About 40% of the sites within the archaeology database of NMRS are depicted on OS standard series maps and must conform to OS criteria for depiction which have been agreed in consultation with the Commissions. The sites must be of archaeological significance as defined by the Commissions, so that this can include sites of importance to our industrial heritage or rural settlement of the eighteenth and nineteenth centuries as well as prehistoric, Roman and medieval monuments. All scheduled sites and all grade 1 and selected grade 2 listed buildings are included. Otherwise the site has to be a topographic feature of at least 0.3m high. The Commissions also play a role in checking over information relating to antiquities on maps at smaller scales and have continued to publish thematic maps with OS including *Roman Britain* and *Ancient Britain*.

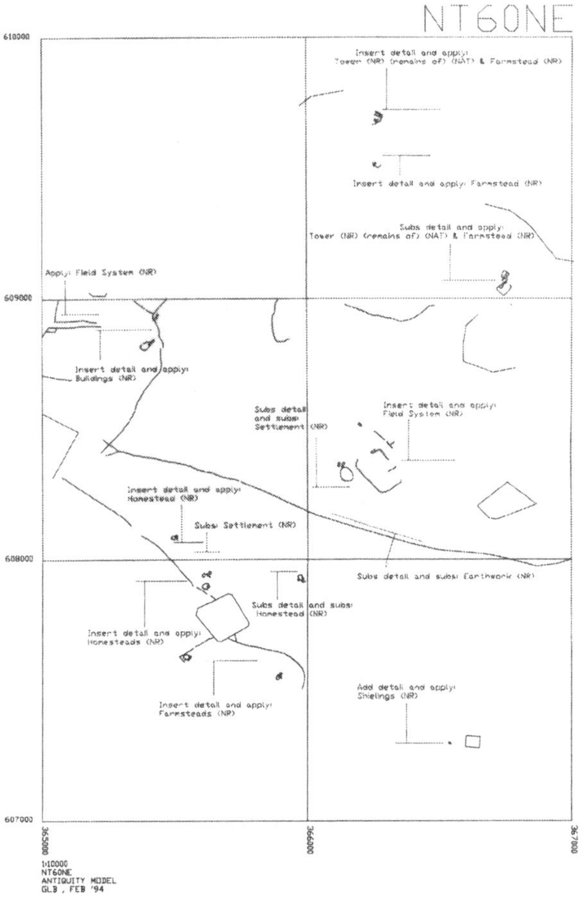

Figure 3. Digitised Antiquity Model

Although originally surveyed by the OS archaeology branch or the Commission staff, the vast majority of the depictions of antiquities in the OS digital data archive are the result of desk-based digitising from the original master survey documents by OS or their contractors. Some of the digitised depiction is quite difficult to interpret for those familiar with hachures, ornament and line detail, all of which have been heavily used on conventional maps to illustrate archaeological remains and manmade features in the landscape. Neither is the digital data in Landline particularly well conceived in the rural areas as the driving force for completion of the programme came from a powerful lobby most interested in the urban areas. The digitised data, however, has the potential to offer major advantages in terms of speed and efficiency, flexibility and analysis as well as transfer to other media, copying, converting and selecting and enhancing specific features.

RCAHMS now uses digital data as an integral part of survey, analysis, publication and NMRS record work. Data from survey is brought directly in digital form from the field and translated into AUTOCAD for manipulation into Antiquity Models or detailed survey drawings. Data is digitised from aerial transcriptions or from other sources such as first edition OS maps. All this digitised data is transferred into the GIS where it can be combined with other data such as land use, OS height data and OS mapping, as well as data held in the NMRS Oracle database.

There can be no doubt, from the experience of all the heritage agencies in the UK, that the illustration of monuments on the OS maps has been and remains a very important influence working towards their public understanding, enjoyment and preservation. Under the Agriculture Acts of 1986 and the Ancient Monuments Acts of 1979, it is incumbent on the landowner to inform himself of the presence of a monument on his land and OS maps are one of the primary sources of information in this regard. Depiction on the OS map also provides a significant stimulus to the consideration of archaeological and historical sites at an early stage in the planning process and the accurate location and extent of sites is important in the determination and indication of constraint areas.

The landscape is a cumulative expression of many influences, human and natural, that have taken place, and maps are a powerful tool in its analysis and explanation. The depiction of archaeological and historical sites adds a chronological dimension essential to the use of maps in universities and schools, especially with the inclusion of 'environmental studies ' in the National Curriculum. Archaeological monuments are also of interest to general users - tourists, ramblers or local study groups for whom the OS maps can be the key to a life-long love of countryside and townscape.

It is in the OS interest to continue to ensure that topographic detail, in which extant monuments make up a significant component, is both accurately portrayed and correctly interpreted otherwise the credibility of other data on the map is brought into question. Also, it is in the national interest that this information is disseminated in a number of ways, but by far the most economical, wide-reaching and publicly available means is through OS mapping. The Commissions intend to continue to work closely with OS to improve the depiction of monuments on the OS digital data and their annotation as an essential part of the topography and landscape of Britain. The opportunity to do this may occur during the restructuring of OS data though the National Topographic Database (NTD) initiative. The National Topographic Database will address the issues of structured data, increasing the amount of layering and themes in the data, and one of those data sets is related to the 'heritage'. At present, the labels on the map have no intelligent relationship with the depiction on the digital map and there is no separate coding for the antiquities. The archaeological sites on a map cannot therefore be selected as a dataset in the same way that all the roads or all the rivers can be selected. This is a drawback which inhibits the use of this data in GIS systems used by those needing heritage data e.g., for heritage management, planning or those concerned with landuse, and it also limits the OS scope for adding value in the new NTD.

Other OS initiatives such as the National Geospatial Data Framework which is examining ways of relating and integrating geospatial data held by different bodies is also a potential mechanism for the future dissemination of antiquity information.

While there continues to be a major role for the depiction of antiquities on OS maps, there are a number of opportunities opening up which provide a more flexible approach for the dissemination of geospatial historical and archaeological information to the archaeological community, researchers and other users. The exciting use of technology such as GIS is that the map becomes an element in a whole spectrum of data and can provide a signpost to data held elsewhere. The Commissions' role will be to maintain the national records in the NMRS through detailed field and aerial survey and the collection of archive information and through the exchange or harmonisation of information with local records.

The archaeological database becomes a satellite of the GIS along with all the other accessible datasets, both visual and textual, and puts the map back into the centre as the key to distributed data. For NMRS this has cut down considerably on accessioning and cataloguing time and revolutionised the presentation of the information.

Data preparation time can be saved in pre- and post-survey as data is available on line in a format which is ready for manipulation and analysis. Predictive modelling can inform field strategies and draw attention to locations where field visits might be productive.

Any data, providing that it has spatial attributes such as National Grid Reference, Latitude and Longitude or Postal address, can be displayed. Boundaries and place-names, including historical and alternative names, as well as imprecise locational information (such as North of) can be managed by the GIS and analysed through it. It has proved particularly valuable for managing boundary changes in relationship to other data, especially that held in the database.

Distribution maps and presentational data can be easily produced. Some of the data which is now being held in the GIS, was previously transferred to the NMRS to be catalogued and made available on paper, e.g.. air photograph transcriptions, field surveys. This information is now transferred directly to the GIS where it is maintained and is available not only for display, but also for interrogation and for analysis against other data layers.

External data can be imported where appropriate and a project to test the import of contractor's data from an archaeological coastal survey will soon be undertaken by RCAHMS. This not only provides information in relation to other data but has the potential to address the serious problem of preserving the archive of work carried out using digital technology and to test the standards which will need to be put in place to ensure that this information is available for the future.

Procedures of this kind have enabled the integration of data relating to the historic landscape which was becoming increasingly difficult to do using conventional methods and which is now so crucial to heritage management and archaeological research.

In Scotland, as a joint development with Historic Scotland the GIS is now being made available on line to HS staff to access all the data available in RCAHMS and to provide interfaces which will allow the use of GIS in the scheduling and listing programmes. Maps can be created to HS specifications and survey, aerial transcriptions or information derived from the archive catalogue will be available on-line to inform decision making.

Using GIS as the focus, RCAHMS will be developing the concept of 'heritage layers' by undertaking a programme to transfer as much depicted data as possible into digital form. In parallel to this, the attribute data relating to this digital data is being further developed so that the depictions themselves derived from transcriptions or from field surveys or other data capture projects can be interrogated, as well as linking to the main NMRS and Historic Scotland databases which themselves will be linked to scanned images.

The power of this data integration cannot be underestimated, but is important to make this available not only to staff but more publicly. Firstly, the GIS itself is being developed to produce outputs tailored to meet users requirements. Although the presentation still requires some development, it is already possible to provide data on all the sites within 50km of the coastline, or all sites on wetland areas. Details relating to other government department initiatives such as Environmentally Sensitive Areas, and the Countryside Premium Scheme are already being supplied on demand.

Secondly, RCAHMS is also exploring the provision of access to the NMRS database through the WWW in a project which is jointly sponsored by RCAHMS, ORACLE, ADS (Archaeology Data Service) and SCRAN (Scottish Cultural Resources Access Network) and while this will not include access to maps in the first instance, it is only a matter of time.

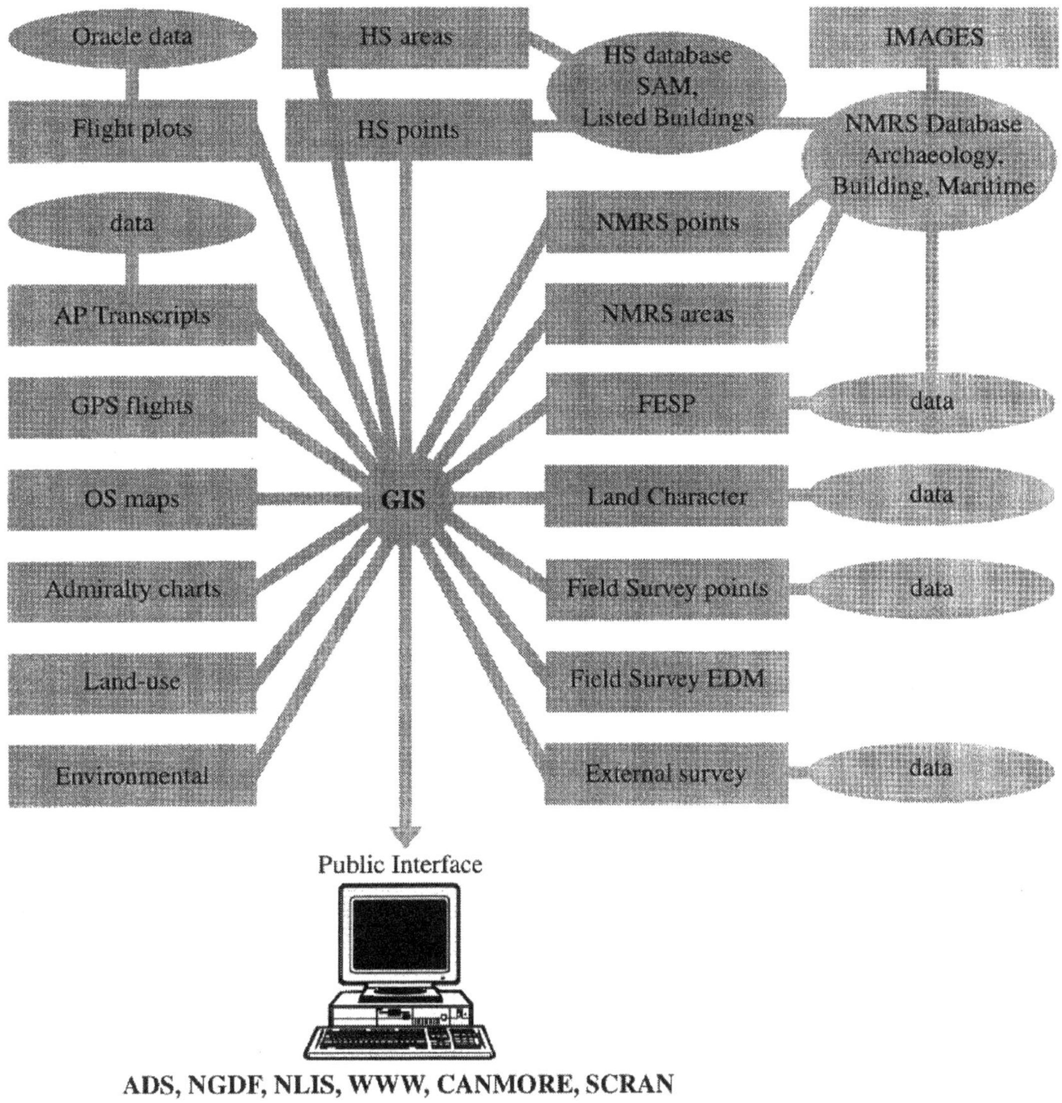

Figure 4. Diagram of relationships between data sets and RCAHMS GIS

Bibliography:

Crawford, O G S, 1955 Said and Done, The Autobiography of an archaeologist

Murray, D M, and Dixon, P J, 1995 Geographic Information System for RCAHMS, Monuments on Record, RCAHMS Annual Review 1994-5, 32-34

Murray, D M, 1994 Changing Relationships with the Ordnance Survey, Monuments on Record, RCAHMS Annual Review 1993-4, 28-29

Phillips, C W, 1980 Archaeology in the Ordnance Survey, 1791 - 1965, Council For British Archaeology

Phillips, C W, My Life in Archaeology

Proceedings of the Society of Antiquaries for Scotland 2, 1854-7, 129

Seymour, W A (ed), 1980 A History of the Ordnance Survey

Diana Murray
RCAHMS
John Sinclair House
16 Bernard Terrace
Edinburgh
SCOTLAND
email: rcahms.jsh@gtnet.gov.uk

Electronic Commerce and Geomarketing

Alan A. Wild

CAA 97

Abstract

This paper details how the latest developments in technology, coupled with the imerging capabilities of the Internet are providing opportunities to allow large geographically related datasets to be made more freely available. These opportunities will change forever how data is provided, accessed and used. The paper discusses the sense in data being made freely available but not necessarily for free. In addition these new technologies will provide for the merging of different datasets to allow analysis which was previously very difficult and sometimes plainly impossible in an easy and low cost environment.

1 Introduction

"GeoMarketing" has traditionally focused on the use of Geographic Information Systems techniques to assist in the tasks of marketing - specifically in the area of market location and segmentation. Thus we have seen increasingly sophisticated use of demographic data to find clusters of attractive prospects, use of complex spatial analysis to assist in the location of facilities, focused promotion to finely controlled areas, and so on.

This paper examines a different marketing problem, that is confronting the owners of many datasets with a geographic dimension; how to gain access to the potential market for the data, and create greater value for their data - thus leading to enhanced business.

2 Changing requirements and opportunities

It has been widely quoted that 80% of all events have a location associated with them, and this is often recorded within computer systems, in the form of an address or other description - or even as a formal spatial co-ordinate set. There are in fact many more geographically based datasets than may be first imagined - for example the UK Government and its agencies have over 580 such datasets, which are potentially available to the public. If one includes the many commercial data providers, the extent and variety of the potentially available data is vast indeed.

However, the use of these datasets is usually limited to small communities of users, and the market is at best static. The potential benefits are not realised. It is essential to examine why this is.

There are a number of reasons that can be readily identified. For example, the very existence of many datasets is unknown outside their small community of specialist users. Potential users who may be interested are not able to identify the benefits. Equally, many datasets are virtually "locked away" in remote locations, thus discouraging casual or exploratory use. In the UK, for example, information on geology is located in Nottingham, information on environmentally sensitive sites is located in Peterborough, a company in Exeter has data on contaminated land, many government statistics are kept in London. Equally, much data is still stored in paper records - some estimates put the proportion of all data still in paper form as high as 90% - although many data owners have undertaken the long (and expensive) task of conversion to digital form.

Today there are many pressures for change. The former UK government created an initiative known as *Government.direct* in order to facilitate public access to government datasets. These were to be freely available (which does not equate to available for free!). Funding changes are forcing the need for cost recovery on investments made in conversion of the paper records into digital form. Data providers are investigating a number of proposed strategies that will expose their product range to a wider client base, accelerate the provision of data and ultimately create greater revenue streams. Many organisations in the private sector see changing market conditions, with new competitors enjoying significant advantages. For example, the banks have seen large retailers begin to offer banking services, and small real estate companies see the banks and retailers as strong new competitors.

However, the biggest change of all is in the earliest stages of its effects. The Internet offers the ability to provide access to the market in the most direct and pervasive manner ever imagined. As the Internet matures in to Electronic Commerce, with associated secure payment mechanisms, it offers owners of products - especially information products - a new marketing model of how to do business. The potential markets are enormous, potentially world-wide, and the channel to access these markets is cheap, direct and common across markets. The downsides of Internet use include the way that it runs counter to many other current marketing strategies, which focus on finer segmentation and carefully targeted offers. The Internet, by its very nature, is a largely undifferentiated medium, dominated by customer "pull", although the emergence of "push" technologies provides an interesting counterweight. It is also difficult to use when large amounts of data are to be transferred, as there is a perennial problem of bandwidth which makes transfers slow.

Equally, it is only recently that products offering the ability to access, use and display spatial data have become commercially available. Even today, many such products use raster technology which implies greater data volumes to be transferred, and offer limited interaction with the map.

Finally, for the Internet to be an electronic commerce medium, the ability to conduct secure transactions without compromising sensitive data such as credit card numbers is absolutely essential. Already, there have been sufficient scare stories to make most organisations and individuals wary.

3 Some recent developments

Intergraph(UK) has been at the forefront of working with our customers to assist them in exploiting the changes outlined above. There are a number of developments, some of a prototype nature, and some already being used as a commercial venture.

3.1 Satellite delivery

One of the first projects in which we became involved was directed at the problem of the transfer and use of large amounts of data. Under the Multimedia Programme of the Department of Trade and Industry (a government department), and in conjunction with ESYS, a specialist satellite communication company, a successful pilot project was created to show the potential for the delivery of spatial data via a satellite. Information delivery today has well understood cost/speed trade-offs, with an ISDN line offering up to 50 times the performance of a modem link, but at 10-20 times the cost to deliver a 100 KB file. However, the bandwidth is only required in one direction, as sending requests and queries consumes little bandwidth, but large file downloads take much bandwidth. The pilot system was asymmetric in the sense that requests for information are sent via normal means over the Internet. During the project, modem connections up to 33.6 Kbps were tried, but the system performance was not overly sensitive to changes in this link. However, responses from the server are sent via a satellite uplink to a communications satellite and then down to the user via a 60 cm receiving dish. The speed of transfer possible is very high - to the point at which data is delivered at comparable rates to transfers from a local hard disk drive. This type of service is becoming more economically viable as equipment costs fall.

3.2 Information broking

We have also established a commercial Internet service to market geographically based datasets. Here Intergraph manages the system, and acts as an information broker. Owners of datasets can use this service to broaden their market access, and users can identify, browse, correlate and purchase relevant data. Intergraph makes money from the data sold, rather than from traditional product sales.

The first service established was to provide data on borehole samples which the British Geological Survey have taken throughout the UK. A borehole record is an item of text or graphics describing the subsurface material recovered at a site as a result of drilling a borehole. This service will supply copies of original borehole records held by BGS within its National Geological Records Centre.

BGS holds records in excess of 500,000 boreholes which have been drilled for a wide range of purposes and include: shallow drilling for site investigations; mineral exploration; water extraction; hydrocarbon exploration; geothermal energy and monitoring. The records have been deposited as a result of active collecting, statutory legislation, exchange agreements and voluntary donations. They range in length from site investigation boreholes of around 2 m for civil engineering purposes to stratigraphic boreholes of over 3 km. This information can be of critical importance in land use development decisions and has assumed greater importance in recent years as changing weather patterns have effects on land stability.

This service will allow selection of a geographic area and the viewing of metadata details about specific boreholes from a database of over 500,000 records. You may select the boreholes you have identified and place those items into your shopping basket, confirm your selection and complete the order form. Prices for each record selected will be displayed on checkout. In the initial release, information is despatched and payment made by traditional methods, but the second release extends this on-line data provision and secure electronic transaction for payment via credit card.

The second service has now been added, which provides access to environmentally sensitive site information - SSSIs (Sites of Special Scientific Interest), which is owned by English Nature. These sites carry development restrictions, which vary depending on the reasons the site was listed - for example, rare wildlife or archaeological interest. Customers can see the location of sites, but need to purchase the precise boundary definition and information on the restrictions.

Users of the service will be able to buy a full background map of their area of interest, and correlate different datasets, thus extra levels of added value.

More datasets will be brought into the service over time. Already interest has been expressed by municipalities who could provide local land use planning information, economic development data, and tourism data, as well as commercial firms who can see the marketing advantage provided by this service.

Of particular interest is the signing of a contract between Intergraph (UK) and the National Association of Estate Agents, who represent the great majority of real estate agents. The intention is to create a national Internet based service to sell properties, which will use geography as a key factor, with the intention that this would be extended to show details of local schools and shopping, local medical facilities, etc.

This allows the typical small real estate agent to compete effectively against national chains and new large entrants in their market, such as retailers or banks through the use of technology based geomarketing.

4 The impact of geomarketing

It is worth examining the impact these geomarketing developments have already had on the marketing strategy of the organisations with which we are working. In terms of classic marketing theory, we have already seen effects on all four "P's" - Product, Price, Place, Promotion.

There have already been *Product* changes, in that the deliverable has become smaller in terms of extent. For example one of our partners used to sell their data only as a national dataset. This has been progressively broken down, first to Counties, and now to single items. We are beginning to see datasets and services bundled together as added value is created by the new marketing model.

Pricing has been moved from a model based on low volume sales with high administrative overheads, to a model based on much higher sales and much simpler administration. This in itself reinforces the willingness of users to explore data and buy speculatively. However, for the great majority of users, price is not the key barrier, as the value of the information is very high if its use prevents mistaken investment decisions.

Place or channel is the key change. Previously it was very difficult to access these datasets, as noted earlier. By making access direct and simple, and adding value in the channel, the use of the data becomes a much more attractive business proposition.

These services offer immediate access to the data from the customers office or home.

Promotion is changed in that the existence of the data is much more widely recognised, as it is advertised in Internet search engines and through hot links from related Web sites. It is also in the strong self interest of the information broker (Intergraph) to promote the service, as our revenues depend on use of the services.

5 Conclusion

Geographically based information is an important resource which has been of limited use historically, for a variety of reasons. With the advent of cheap, pervasive distribution channels exemplified by the Internet, and the associated technology to exploit the information in these channels, such as Intergraph's GeoMedia Web Map, the entire business model has been revolutionised for the owners of the data. They are now seeing new markets opening for their product, and greater revenues flowing from their products, which in turn can be invested in developing their products for this new market, thus creating further growth.

Truly, a virtuous circle!

Contact details

Alan A. Wild
Major Accounts Manager
Central Government
Intergraph (UK) Ltd

ARCHAEOLOGY
IN THE
AGE OF THE INTERNET

CAA 97

Section10
Moving Through Space

CAA 97

Engaging Place: a Framework for the Integration and Realisation of Virtual-Reality Approaches in Archaeology

Mark Gillings

"The resulting 3-D experience has to be seen to be believed: *that* is what virtual reality is all about"
Renfrew 1996, 7 (emphasis added)

Abstract

As archaeologists have embraced and welcomed developments in information technology and visualisation, they have found themselves working increasingly under the auspices of Virtual-Reality. Despite this enthusiastic uptake, it can be argued that as of yet, archaeology has failed to realise that as a defining term, Virtual-Reality is far from unproblematic. As a direct result, questions as to what we *mean* by Virtual-Reality, and what our expensively assembled models *represent* have been left largely unexplored.The present discussion aims to address precisely these questions, by taking a critical look at the term Virtual-Reality. Current dominant conceptualisations and definitions of Virtual-Reality will be characterised, along with the frameworks and attitudes they foster, and the notional Virtual-archaeology they imply. Following on from this, an alternative developmental trajectory will be suggested that better exploits the unique capabilities of such systems in helping to facilitate archaeological interpretation. Issues such as authenticity, the representation as fake and role of Virtual-model as static end-product will be investigated, and an alternative definition will be offered and explored which has enormous significance for the future realisation of the technology within the broad context of archaeological research.

1 Introduction

1.1 Preamble

As a term, 'Virtual-Reality' has become ubiquitous within all aspects of contemporary Western society, synonymous with a developing generation of photo-realistic and fully interactive computer-generated environments. As a discipline, archaeology has been quick to begin to explore the potential of such developments through a number of initiatives and innovative case-studies. These have involved the generation of highly complex, and it should be added *costly*, models such as Virtual-Stonehenge, and continued research into more egalitarian technologies such as the Virtual Reality Modelling Language (VRML) extensions to the World Wide Web (WWW). The result has been a steady flow of innovative research papers and the recent appearance of more weighty mainstream tomes, such as "Virtual Archaeology" (Forte 1996).

As archaeologists have embraced and welcomed such developments in information technology and visualisation, they have found themselves working increasingly under the explicit auspices of Virtual-Reality. Yet despite this enthusiastic uptake, it can be argued that as of yet, archaeology has failed to face up to the fact that as a defining term, Virtual-Reality is far from unproblematic. As a direct result of this uncritical acceptance, fundamental questions relating to issues such as what we actually *mean* by Virtual-Reality, and what our expensively assembled models truly *represent* have been left largely unexplored.

The present discussion aims to address precisely these questions, by taking a critical look at the term Virtual-Reality. This conceptual investigation will be framed and contextualised with reference to a case-study involving research into potentially the most exciting and accessible of all of the current wave of developments in Virtual-Reality, VRML. Through an explicit discussion outlining the issues which prompted and directed this study, an attempt will be made to characterise current dominant conceptualisations and definitions of Virtual-Reality, along with the frameworks and attitudes they foster, and the notional Virtual-archaeology they imply. Following directly on from this, the conceptual underpinnings of existing archaeological applications will be shown to be lacking, and an alternative developmental trajectory will be suggested, that better exploits the unique capabilities of such systems in helping to facilitate archaeological interpretation. During the course of this discussion issues such as authenticity, the representation as a fake and role of VR model as desired end-product will be investigated. Building upon this, an alternative definition of Virtual-Reality will be offered and explored which has enormous significance for the future realisation of the technology within the broad context of archaeological research.

1.2 A brief background

This attempt to outline a developmental framework for archaeological Virtual-Reality is embedded within a wider exploration of the role that can be played by virtual-modelling applications, in close association with GIS-based approaches, in bridging developments in archaeological theory and practice. By way of general clarification, in the context of the present discussion, the term Virtual-Reality is used as a generic 'blanket' descriptor to refer to the growing range of dynamic-interactive visualisation approaches currently finding increasing application within archaeological research. A number of introductory case-studies, including the Peel Gap study that will feature here, have already been published in detail along with an explicit, worked methodology (Gillings and Goodrick 1996). In the context of this discussion the emphasis will not be on replicating this information but instead building upon it, by addressing more directly a number of background issues. These are namely *what drove the study* and *what the resulting models represent and, more importantly, do not represent*. Each of these issues will be discussed in turn.

2 Putting theory into practice

2.1 What drove the study - why virtual reality?

Let us begin by looking at the factors that prompted the original decision to explore the potential of Virtual-Reality based approaches, in effect addressing the question: *why attempt to expand the GIS-approach through the avenue of virtual modelling?* The principal motivation derived from a growing interest in issues relating to embodiment, process and the social nature of space and time, as fore-grounded in a number of recent theoretical debates by researchers such as Barrett and Tilley (Barrett 1994; Tilley 1994). This interest was itself driven by the growing realisation that a number of clear theoretical shortcomings existed in my own ongoing research into person-environment relations in the complex prehistoric flood-plain landscapes of north-eastern Hungary. Here, the traditional functionalist and deterministic interpretive frameworks offered by the generic-GIS proved increasingly sterile as more experiential and embedded notions of Being and Dwelling, such as those discussed by Thomas and Ingold, came increasingly to the fore (Thomas 1996; Ingold 1995).

In wanting to accommodate such conceptual approaches into my GIS-based analytical framework, I became deeply dissatisfied with existing attempts within the field of archaeological-GIS to identify, challenge and overcome a perceived theoretical inertia. This sense of stasis has been discussed exhaustively over the last three years and I do not want to repeat debates in any detail here, suffice to say that the inertia manifested itself most clearly as an environmental bias, whether in the guise of hard determinism or soft possibilism. As I have argued elsewhere, arguments in defence or support of an environmental primacy in GIS-based work, appeared to be caught up with the symptoms rather than the cause, failing to address or acknowledge the existence of much more fundamental underlying dualisms such as that enforced between culture and nature (Gillings, forthcoming). The dominant alternative to determinism, championed by those calling for a more "humanised" GIS, took the form of viewshed analysis. As an approach this also seemed far from unproblematic, being dominated by an uncritical visualism and enforcing an implicit dichotomy between a static, privileged observer and that to be observed. Following on from the work of the psychologist Gibson, and the elaboration of his ecological approach to perception within the spheres of anthropology and geography, I wanted to structure my ongoing investigations into people and landscape from the perspective of people as active exploring animals situated in an environment (for a useful summary of Gibson's approaches see: Ingold 1992, 45-8; Rodaway 1994, 19-22).

This not only entailed a re-questioning of dualisms such as culture : nature, but also stressed the active and mobile nature of multi-sensual perception and the necessity of fore-grounding embodiment. In an attempt to move beyond the see-saw arguments regarding Determinism, and the limited and far from unproblematic platform of viewshed based analyses, the decision was made to move in a different direction. This comprised an attempt to incorporate the notion of an active, mobile, situated observer into my GIS analytical environment. In an attempt to achieve this, research was initiated with the aim of exploring the potential synergy that could be harnessed from integrating developments in affordable visualisation and virtual-reality technologies and GIS.

The key point to highlight is that the investigations into the potential of Virtual-Reality were driven by an explicit problem and constituted from the outset, a clear attempt to bridge developments in theory and practice. In addition, in developing and exploring methodologies a number of criteria were brought to the fore: the approaches developed had to be flexible and affordable, the latter being partly contingent but also inexorably tied up with the fact that they also had to be reproducible by, and communicable to, the wider community of archaeologists and interested parties.

2.2 The Hadrian's Wall tower at Peel Gap

To illustrate how these aims and objectives were realised in practice I will take a brief look at one of the first case-studies undertaken, focusing upon the enigmatic Roman tower of Peel Gap. As mentioned earlier, the precise methodologies employed in the generation of the various models and visualisations to be discussed, have been published in detail elsewhere and I will only attempt to briefly summarise them here. The Tower at Peel Gap comprises a small, rectangular structure which was added to the back face of Hadrian's Wall shortly after its construction in the early second century AD. For a simple account of the feature itself and general locational and structural details concerning the broader context of Hadrian's Wall see Johnson (1989:61-2). In its size and ground plan, the structure resembles most closely the regular series of turrets that characterise the length of the wall. These turret features have traditionally been interpreted as observation posts, functionally located so as to maximise the views out beyond the frontier and to either side along the line of the Wall. The location of the Peel Gap tower however, appears to directly contradict this received notion of optimum defensive location, as it is nestled neatly at the base of a narrow pass through the dramatic crags which dominate the central sector of the wall. This choice of location appears to be deliberate and is in preference to more defensibly suitable high ground situated immediately to either side. The location of this tower feature has long proved a source of curiosity to Hadrian's Wall scholars and the question as to its defensive utility comprised the subject of the case-study, a visibility analysis of the tower feature.

In practice a detailed micro-topographical survey of the immediate landscape of the tower was undertaken and a detailed record was made of the footprint of the Wall and related features, such as the course of the contemporary road - the Military way, as they crossed the study area. The survey derived data was then imported into the Arc/Info GIS where a 1m resolution digital elevation model (DEM) was constructed and a viewshed calculated from the top of the tower, assuming a combined tower and look-out height of 11m. The resulting viewshed served to confirm earlier reservations as to the strategic significance of locating an observation post in this position, as the identified zone of visible ground was heavily restricted, focusing not upon the lands beyond the frontier but instead upon the immediate surroundings of the pass itself and the area to the rear of the Wall.

Although undoubtedly highly useful, the viewshed as generated had a number of shortcomings, particularly given the overall aims of the research exercise. The analysis failed to incorporate the notion of the observer as mobile and situated, instead the viewshed was static, serving to abstract a dynamic and uncertain perceptual act into a simple, well-defined projected zone, located unambiguously upon a flat projected map. Taking the GIS-based viewshed not as an end-product but as a first step, attempts were then made to enhance and complement it through the application of visualisation and Virtual-Reality based approaches. In practice, the line of the wall and tower foundations were used as a template from which a basic structural re-construction was undertaken in CAD. This was simply rendered and a number of animation sequences were generated. These served to re-create the view yielded by a gentle 360 degree rotation by a hypothetical observer located atop the reconstructed tower. As well as exploring the 'view-from', the effects of 'viewing-to' were explored by moving an observer past the structure along the course of the Military Way. The results were fascinating. In the former case, although the view out to the area beyond Hadrian's Wall was indeed seen to be blocked, as indicated by the GIS-based study, what was not at all obvious was the way in which the course of the Military Way dominated the view to the rear, often tracking the visible sky-line. In the case of the 'view-to' what was most striking was the suddenness with which the tower first appeared out from behind the looming bulk of the crags.

These re-constructions and animation sequences served to situate the observer and incorporated a degree of mobility, but they were still prescriptive. The final, and critical stage was to generate a representation whereby the observer was able to freely engage with the re-creation, choosing their own paths through, and their own viewing points within, the landscape. In addition, an important proviso was that observers should not only be able to freely engage with the representation, but they also had to be able to obtain, view, modify and alter it, treating it not as a definitive end-product but as a manipulable medium that could be incorporated into their own analytical environments. This would enable our tendered interpretation to be scrutinised and new interpretations to be formulated. As a result the decision was taken to implement the re-creation using Virtual-Reality based techniques, specifically VRML, with the resulting model being freely distributed via the WWW. The landscape could now be viewed from anywhere within it. Observers could explore the views from the tower or approach the wall from within the landscape actively seeking a position on the crags where you could see over the wall to the mysteries beyond. Functional factors such as the possibility of a Wall-top walkway could be assessed and the effects of altering the reconstructed tower height explored dynamically.

In each case the visualisations and Virtual-Reality model added further dimensions to the Boolean viewshed yielded by the traditional GIS-based study. These are best viewed not as steps in a procedure, nor as evolutionary 'stages' - in effect progressively more useful replacements for one another. Instead they should be regarded as a group of complementary approaches which as a whole offer a unique methodology for looking in a more flexible and situated way at the functional status of Hadrian's Wall with respect to its direct landscape context.

Having generated our Virtual models how do we, and the wider public perceive them?	Having generated our virtual models what do we then do with them?
Are they realistic? Are they faithful? - Here we encounter issues relating to the status of reality, authenticity and the potentially problematic status of the representation as fake.	The VR representation as end-product, an ingenious picture to be viewed and studied, as opposed to the VR representation as interpretive device, open to negotiation, exploration and the principles of montage and collage.

Figure 1: The underlying Issues.

2.3 What the resulting VRML model *is* and what it *is not*

Having looked briefly at the factors that prompted an original investigation into the utility of Virtual-Reality and how this was realised in practice, it is important to move on to consider the principal topic of the current discussion, and attempt to clarify what precisely the results of the Virtual-reality modelling component of the exercise represent and, I would argue more importantly, what they do not represent. My contention here will be that whatever they do represent it is not reality, nor is it in any way an end-product.

To explore this proposition I intend to pose a number of fundamental questions and examine a number of important concepts. For the purposes of structuring discussion these can be grouped under two broad thematic headings (see Fig. 1).

3 The dominant perception

3.1 What is virtual reality?

One of the principal questions asked of any computer-based representation, by archaeologists and the general public alike, is a variation of '*How realistic is it*' [1]. Implicit in this question is a degree of suspicion, and the notion that the model is in some way trying to deceive, fool or seduce the viewer. To be able to adequately explore this phenomenon, we must take fundamental issue with the term Virtual-Reality itself. As mentioned in the introduction, the term is ubiquitous within all aspects of contemporary Western culture, yet as a term it is far from unproblematic. It finds itself being used increasingly in a host of disparate contexts, yet rarely is it explicitly theorised. I would argue that the uncertainties arising from this state of affairs are particularly acute in the context of archaeological applications. As a result, in discussing how we and others actually perceive our carefully generated representations, we must first establish what we actually *mean* when we define a given re-creation or model as Virtually-Real. In effect pose the question: *what is virtual-reality?*

In his discussions as to the mathematisation of experience, the historian of Science, Gray, proposed two definitions. The first, and dominant definition, positions Virtual-Reality as a *manufactured deficiency*. This suggests that a Virtual-Reality represents a reality that is lacking, in Grays words 'almost but not quite real'. The second definition positions it instead as a *manufactured intensity*. Here the suggestion is that a Virtual-Reality represents a reality that 'is more intense and concentrated than so-called everyday nature' (Gray 1995, 343-6). A statement that we could perhaps simplify to read *more* real than real.

Looking more directly to the field of archaeological research, the most clear and influential definition has been that provided by Reilly in his seminal paper "Towards a Virtual Archaeology" (Reilly 1991). Here Virtual-Reality and the virtual-archaeology it implied were defined in terms of the notion of a surrogate. The Virtual-Reality model serves to act as a replacement for an original. The closeness or "faithfulness" of the approximation of any given model to its original referent is dictated by the quality and volume of data that has gone into its generation. This is implicit in the pioneering work of the Furness Abbey project published in the same volume, where ground-plans and traditional 2-D archaeological drawings were used to re-construct and model portions of the abbey on a meticulous stone-by-stone basis (Delooze and Wood 1991). This approach has been refined more recently by Bayliss in his stunning re-construction of the Basilica church of the Alacami in southern Turkey. Here a detailed combination of texture mapping and architectural reconstruction have been used to model the entire structure of the building (Bayliss forthcoming). In each case the re-creation is achieved through the painstaking manipulation and re-assembly of the basic units of architectural detail. The issues of faithfulness, realism and authenticity are addressed through ever closer attention to recording, the optimisation of data collection techniques, and the fine-detail of model construction[2]. In both examples the Virtual reconstruction is seen to stand in an inferior position to an original referent, with the degree of closeness related directly to the quantity and quality of information put into it. Simply put, the better and more optimised the data used in its construction, the more faithful the Virtual model is, and the closer it comes to the reality it seeks, or purports, to represent. In addition, as a result of this notion of the Virtual-Reality model as a painstakingly sophisticated surrogate, the reconstructions run the risk of being reified, becoming in effect end-products, finished, completed, free-standing and there to be visually devoured. As suggested in the introductory quote, ingenious pictures but pictures nevertheless. This is in opposition to the reconstructions as flexible components in a much wider, on-going process, open to negotiation and manipulation.

As such, this dominant archaeological interpretation of Virtual-Reality parallels closely Gray's notion of a manufactured deficiency, with the Virtual-model taking the form of a doppelganger, or surrogate, which is as faithful a replica as possible but somehow, somewhere, lacking. Underlying the definition offered by Reilly and the examples cited, is the idea of an attainable, tangible reality to which the virtual representation, or surrogate, aspires and therefore against which it invites comparison and can in some way be tested and compared. On this point it is interesting to note that in studying 'Virtual-Stonehenge' it could be argued that the observer-explorer becomes aware of the painstaking attention to detail and accuracy that has gone into its production not when moving amongst the stones themselves, but instead when they encounter the everyday familiarity of the underpass, information boards, turnstiles and post-box of the visitors centre, which they have already repeatedly encountered at Stonehenge and in a host of other routine daily contexts [3].

Assuming that this proposition is valid, in the case of an extant structure, whether the Alacami or Stonehenge turnstile, you could argue that a tangible original does in fact exist. With the majority of archaeological representations, however, whether of built structures or the very landscape itself, there is no tangible referent.

Looking to the Peel Gap case-study, beyond some neatly re-pointed foundation stones, there is no reality against which the representation can be tested or to which it can aspire. We could argue that what reality there is resides wholly within the confines of the representation itself. We have generated a wall and a tower rather than offered up a faithful copy. Nor does it represent an end-product, a completed and free-standing entity presented to the observer for interpretation. The re-creation is flexible and shifting and observers are actively encouraged to manipulate and re-negotiate our tendered representation. This is a point that will be returned to later when we begin to discuss the status of a given Virtual model not as an end-product but as an ongoing dialogue.

What is clear is that there are a number of fundamental problems associated with the acceptance of, and adherence to a dominant definition of Virtual-Reality as manufactured deficiency. In what sense are our archaeological representations and re-constructions lacking and how are we to evaluate them? In addition, by enforcing the notion that a given Virtual-model aspires to the 'real' we focus attention not on the Virtual-representation as a flexible interpretive device, but instead run the risk of exhausting ourselves on issues intimately bound up with faithfulness and authenticity, such as suspicion, deception and the problematic status of a given representation as fake.

What I intend to argue here is that in the context of archaeological Virtual-Reality models and dynamic-interactive visualisations, whether highly complex and reified such as the Alacami or simple and negotiable such as the Peel Gap tower, the term Virtual-Reality as traditionally understood and applied is misplaced and misleading. Far from providing archaeology with a valid and all-encompassing framework within which to develop and explore approaches, the uncritical adoption of the term Virtual-Reality could instead serve to marginalise such approaches, by restricting the extent of their application and clouding and muddling their true utility. As the Phenomenologist Dovey has argued in a broad discussion as to the nature of authenticity and the replication of environmental meaning, approaches such as the archaeological tendency to characterise Virtual-representations as surrogates, i.e. manufactured deficiencies, engenders an investigative operation on the part of the observer. There is an active search for clues indicating authenticity, which itself leads to a sense of empirical testing rather than an openness to disclosure of the represented place. This attitude of mistrust in turn feeds a growing sense that the Virtual-representations have to become increasingly sophisticated in order to, in Dovey's words, "thwart investigations and capture real meanings" (Dovey 1985, 38-9). As a result we will rapidly find ourselves caught up in an increasingly sophisticated, but ultimately circular, dead-end, that runs the risk of relegating Virtual-Reality research to the marginal fringes of archaeological investigation.

Assuming then that the term Virtual-Reality, with its dominant connotation of manufactured deficiency is of limited value to archaeology what is the alternative? Here I would like to build upon and adapt Gray's notion of Virtual-Reality as manufactured intensity. Looking to the work of critical theorists such as Baudrillard and Eco, rather than adopting Virtual-Reality as a blanket descriptor within the field of computer-based archaeological re-creation, a particular reading of the term 'hyperreality' may be more appropriate.

3.2 Hyperreality

"Hyper-reality is a slippery term."

(Rodaway 1995:244)

At this point it would be sensible to provide a clear definition of hyperreality, however, the first thing to realise about the term is that it is highly provisional, continually metamorphosing and thus works tirelessly to elude concise definition (Rodaway 1995:244). The term was fore-grounded by Baudrillard in the context of discussions relating to modes of signification and a perceived breakdown in the relationship between signs and original referents. The notion of the hyperreal developed in his claims that within modern society the existence of reality was no longer guaranteed by the signs it emitted, instead signs were now seen to construct the real, as simulations. To Baudrillard a simulation did not provide an equivalent for a given reality nor reproduce it, instead the simulation generated it. To quote Baudrillard, "Abstraction today is no longer that of the map, the double, the mirror...Simulation is no longer that of territory, a referential being or substance. It is the generation of models of a real without origin or reality: a hyperreal. The territory no longer precedes the map, nor survives it. Henceforth, it is the map that precedes the territory.... it is the map that engenders the territory" (Baudrillard 1983: 2)

In discussing formulations of hyperreality, to Baudrillard the 'real' became nothing more than that it is possible to reproduce and is always *already* reproduced. The hyperreal became simply the *more* real than real (Baudrillard 1983: 146; Horrocks and Jevtic 1996:109). Commentators disagree as to whether hyperreality is best treated as a concept or a tool, and more significantly for archaeology, whether it represents a tangible thing that resides in specific places, for example Disneyland, Jorvik and Virtual- Stonehenge, or a process that exists in the relationship between subjects (for example archaeologists) and objects (re-evocations such as Jorvik and Virtual-Stonehenge) [4].

The former is best illustrated by studies such as Eco's observations of contemporary America, and in the archaeological context, Diamond's fascinating study of the Lascaux II cave re-creation (Eco 1986; Diamond 1996, 30-41). Hyperreality as process has been most fully explored by Rodaway in his detailed examination of the mapping of the subject in the context of 'living' heritage museums, such as Beamish, and theme parks (Rodaway 1995, 256-63).

Such a distinction is perhaps illusory. In the context of the present discussion hyperreality is best thought of as both, being embodied within particular locations and situations, which are themselves part of a broader on-going process of experiencing the world.

Far from suggesting a wholesale replacement within the context of archaeological research of the term Virtual-Reality with that of hyperreality, for reasons which will become clear when we begin to discuss the issue of authenticity, the central theme I wish to extract from the above discussion concerns the recurring characterisation of the hyperreal in terms of simulations which are generated *of* the real without origin or reality, the only reality being that generated by the simulation.

Returning to the example of the Furness Abbey project, in discussing why the model had been created, one of the clear benefits of a virtual model over a traditional set of abstracted plans, elevations and reconstruction drawings was identified by the authors as the facility to actually get inside and walk around the reconstructed buildings. This would give the observer a greater sense of "being there" (Delooze and Wood 1991, 144). In light of the preceding discussions into Virtual-Reality as manufactured intensity and the role of the status of a given re-creation as hyperreal the question we must now ask is being precisely *where*?

The simulations are more real than real in that they provide a vision which, quite literally, gives you more (Rodaway 1995, 246). This, I feel, is the key to a re-definition of Virtual-Reality that will enable us to overcome current tendencies towards increasing methodological refinement and reification, and more fully realise the potential of such techniques and approaches within mainstream archaeological research.

3.3 The issues of authenticity and faithfulness.

If then, a definition of Virtual-Reality is taken which emphasises the status of any given model not as a manufactured deficiency but as an intensity, what becomes of the issue of authenticity and the investigative operation this encourages in the observer, that I have claimed is inexorably tied up with the former conceptualisation?

Taking the discussion of hyperreality to its logical and extreme conclusion we could argue that the issue simply does not exist, or that it is a non-issue. Questions relating to authenticity and faithfulness no longer have meaning as, to quote Baudrillard, "...illusion is no longer possible because the real is no longer possible" (ibid. 246). I do not, however, intend to side-step the issue of authenticity by hiding behind a veneer of postmodern rhetoric. The issue is critically important to an interpretive archaeology. As Shanks has argued in his recent discussion of photography and archaeology, uncertainty and doubt are the roots of interpretation. Meaning can only come through embracing both certainty *and* doubt, making connections and exploring contexts (Shanks 1996,79-80). However, in discussing the authenticity of a given model, rather than stressing the issue of visual approximation, intimately bound up in ideas of manufactured deficiency, I intend to follow Dovey in asserting that authenticity is not a property of form, but instead is a property of process and a relationship or connectedness between people and their world. Dovey asserts that authentic meaning cannot be created through any manipulation of form, as authenticity is the very source from which form gains meaning, a position echoed by a number of recent archaeological investigations into agency, practice and monumentality, for example Barrett's study of Avebury (Dovey 1985, 33; Barrett 1994).

Returning to the examples mentioned earlier, however architecturally faithful the Virtual re-creations of Furness abbey or the basilica church of Alacami are, the virtual-stones do not carry mason's marks, the virtual-floor the shine of a thousand footfalls nor is the virtual-interior cluttered with the bricolage of everyday social practice. And the vital point is that painstakingly adding them is *not* the answer as it will make *no* difference to the issue of authenticity. What Dovey argues is that the critical difference between an original and its representation is not in the detail of form but in the richness of environmental, or experiential, depth. He illustrates this with reference to a "fake" beach recently constructed in the Arizona desert. The beach has waves and sand but no crabs, sharks, undertow, driftwood, shells to be found, rockpools to explore, sea breezes or salt air (Dovey 1985, 39-40). Whereas the original is a learning environment that fully embodies a sense of encounter, experience and process, the representation lacks spatial and historical depth, diversity and variation. This echoes Shank's distinction in the realm of archaeological photography between Naturalism and Realism. Here Naturalism refers solely to the replication of external features whereas Realism is more concerned with extended metaphors, patterns of association and allegory. To quote Shanks "A realistic representation is not only, or necessarily naturalistic" (Shanks 1996, 78).

The point here is that any given Virtual-representation can *never* be authentic. The considerable efforts currently being expended in incorporating ever more detail into models, whether through the use of individual bricks and stones rather than simplified macro-entities, or the application of highly complex textures, achieve little more than the generation of an even more fastidious investigative attitude on the part of the observer. This is summarised neatly by Dovey in his assertion that "..authenticity has the indigenous quality of being inborn. The problem lies not in the searching, which is genuine, but in the misplaced belief that authenticity can be generated by the manipulation of appearance" (Dovey 1985, 47). Saying that a given re-creation is inauthentic is not, however, to say that it is either actively deceiving us or that it is not useful. A beach located in the middle of a desert is not in a position to fool anybody but it does not stop it being a nice place to spend an afternoon. Neither is it to be seen as advocating and endorsing some naive form of judgemental relativism (for a useful discussion on the issue of relativism see Shanks and Hodder 1995, 19). This brings us onto the last of the issues that need to be addressed, having generated a Virtual archaeological model what do we then do with it?

3.4 The role of virtual-reality in archaeological research.

If we accept that far from directly reflecting or aspiring to an original referent or "reality", the only reality is that generated by the models themselves, and in addition acknowledge that the issue of authenticity is concerned not with direct comparison and evaluation of form, but with engagement and process, we are in a strong position to move forward. If we regard our representations, however fine the detail that has gone in, as always critically lacking depth, we can begin to move beyond attitudes of suspicion and the rampant and fastidious empiricism they foster.

The dominant characterisation of Virtual-Reality as a deficient surrogate prompts an investigative procedure on the part of the observer which in turn leads to ever more refined attempts to thwart it. And so the cycle goes on. We must realise that the negative connotation of deception arises directly from the notion that our carefully constructed representations *should* and faithfully *do* represent the past, which is in turn a legacy of our dominant characterisation of Virtual-Reality as a manufactured deficiency. Our Virtual-representations are fakes but they are not trying to deceive us into thinking anything otherwise, and this in no way diminishes their utility to us as archaeologists as catalysts for exploration and interpretation. Looking to the Peel gap case-study, the Virtual model and related visualisations were driven by a problem. This was simply, '*if a tower, connected to a continuous stretch of walling was located here, what could be seen from it*', and they contributed greatly to the exploration of this problem area. The exercises were not driven, or structured around a desire to '*re-create a stretch of Hadrian's Wall*' which they fail, and will always fail to do comprehensively.

When we come to exploring arguably the most fundamental issues of all, what are the models for, and how do they help us in the process of interpretation, we often find that far from embracing the Virtual-models as a new means of exploring ideas, we have exhausted ourselves in addressing and maintaining this cycle of suspicion. As a result the models are left as little more than ingenious images to be viewed and consumed. To quote Renfrew from his introduction to the recent volume 'Virtual Archaeology' "As he (the editor) puts it, the aim is 'to make archaeological information... visually real': the great quantities of data now available must actually be made to inform us, not just sit in a data bank" (Renfrew 1996, 7). They become a closed end-product, something passive to be gazed at, whether from without, within, a fixed viewing point or a flexible one. In effect they become the passive images rather than objects of analysis highlighted by researchers such as Molyneaux (Molyneaux 1996). Building on the recent work of Shanks, and his translation of the passive photograph into the active Photowork, Virtual-representations can instead serve to facilitate new modes of engagement and interpretation. The emphasis must be on process rather than the critical appraisal of mere form. In this sense, in the case of the Peel Gap re-creation the sense of frustration in not being able to see over a section of wall to the other side becomes as important as the attention that has gone into 'realistically' weathering the texture of the stones blocking our view. The Virtual-models are there to be worked with and on rather than consumed, and can and must be negotiated, modified and engaged in the exploration of connections and context inherent in the twin processes of collage and montage that Shanks sees as central to a developing mode of archaeological practice (Shanks 1996, 83-4).

4 Conclusions

Virtual-Reality applications within archaeology represent a growing and highly fertile field of study. At present however, applications are under-theorised, dominated by a received notion of Virtual-Reality that emphasises the role of Virtual models as deficient surrogates. It has been argued that whilst such an interpretation remains in place the true utility and potential of such developments to the wide field of archaeological research will not be realised, as time and effort is expended not on analysis and interpretation but on ever increasing visual sophistication.

The suggestion here is that far from treating our models as deficient surrogates a more productive approach is to characterise them as manufactured intensities, emphasising their hyperreality and inauthenticity and encouraging archaeologists to explore their true potential in the study of issues bound intimately with engagement and process. Developments in Virtual-reality have the potential to radically re-orient how we approach, negotiate and interpret our carefully recorded archaeological information and it is crucially important that such approaches are not relegated to the creation of ingenious but esoteric galleries. Rather than a programmatic statement for the development of a Virtual archaeology, the aim of the present discussion has been to highlight a number of limitations and suggest a platform from which applications can more freely develop. The rest is up to us.

Notes

1. This assumption was reinforced, in an entirely qualitative way, during a gruelling open-day held at the School of Archaeological studies in the University of Leicester on a chilly day in February 1997. During the course of the day a number of VR models and visualisations, ranging from the most basic to the most sophisticated were exhibited to a seemingly endless stream of field archaeologists, academics and members of the public alike.

2. Contra to Daniel, in his recent discussion as to the importance of solid-modelling, I would argue that this is regardless of whether initial efforts are directed towards the accurate texture-mapping of a simple geometric structure, or the more Lego-based approach advocating the use of solid representations of the original component building blocks (Daniel 1997).

3. As an aside it is worth noting that one of the most striking things about archaeological Virtual-models is the lack of people in them. As a result, wandering around re-creations such as Virtual-Stonehenge can be a very ghostly and unsettling experience.

4. It is interesting to note that authors cannot even decide whether the term should be hyphenated or not. In the present discussion I have followed Baudrillard and Eco in not hyphenating, excepting when directly quoting from other authors.

Bibliography

Barrett, J C, 1994 *Fragments from Antiquity,* Blackwell, Oxford

Baudrillard, J, 1983 *Simulations*, Semiotext(e), New York

Bayliss, R, forthcoming The Alacami in Kadirli: Transformations of a Sacred Monument, *Anatolian Studies,* Vol. XLVII

Daniel, R, 1997 The need for the solid modelling of structure in the archaeology of buildings, *Internet Archaeology,* 2, 2.3, (http://intarch.ac.uk/journal/issue2/daniels_index.html)

Delooze, K, and Wood, J, 1991 Furness Abbey Survey project: the applications of computer graphics and data visualisation to reconstruction modelling of an historic monument, in *Computer Applications and Quantitative Methods in Archaeology 1990* (eds K Lockyear and S Rahtz), British Archaeological Reports, Supp. Series 565, 141-148, Oxford

Diamond, S J, 1996 *Replicating Rock Art: the European Appropriation of a Palaeolithic Past at Lascaux II,* Unpld MA Dissertation: University of Southampton
Dovey, K, 1985 The quest for authenticity and the replication of environmental meaning, in *Dwelling, place and environment: towards a phenomenology of person and world* (eds D Seamon and R Mugerauer), 33-49, Martinus Nijhoff Publishers, Dordrecht
Eco, U, 1986 *Faith in Fakes: Travels in Hyperreality,* Minerva, London
Forte, M (ed),1996 *Virtual Archaeology: Great Discoveries Brought to Life Through Virtual Reality,* Thames and Hudson, London
Gillings, M, forthcoming Embracing uncertainty and challenging dualism in the GIS-based study of a palaeo-flood plain, *Journal of European Archaeology,* 7(1)
Gillings, M, and Goodrick, G T, 1996 Sensuous and Reflexive GIS: exploring visualisation and VRML, *Internet Archaeology,* 1, http://intarch.ac.uk/ journal/issue1/gillings_index.html
Gray, N, 1995 Seeing Nature, *History of European Ideas,* vol.20, No.s 1-3, 341-48
Horrocks, C, and Jevtic, Z, 1996 *Baudrillard for Beginners,* Icon Books, Cambridge
Ingold, T, 1992 Culture and the perception of the environment, in *Bush Base: Forest Farm* (eds E Croll and D Parkin), 39-56, Routledge, London
Ingold, T, 1995 Building, dwelling, living: how animals and people make themselves at home in the world, in *Shifting Contexts: transformations in anthropological knowledge* (ed M Strathern), 57-80, Routledge, London
Johnson, S, 1989 *Hadrian's Wall,* Batsford, London
Molyneaux, B L, 1996 Introduction: The cultural life of images, in *The Cultural Life of Images* (ed B L Molyneaux), 1-10, Routledge, London
Reilly, P, 1991 Towards a Virtual Archaeology, in *Computer Applications and Quantitative Methods in Archaeology 1990* (eds K Lockyear and S Rahtz), British Archaeological Reports, Supp. Series 565, 133-40, Oxford
Renfrew, C, 1996 Foreword, in *Virtual Archaeology: Great Discoveries Brought to Life Through Virtual Reality* (ed M Forte), Thames and Hudson, London
Rodaway, P, 1994 *Sensuous Geographies: Body, sense and place,* Routledge, London
Rodaway, P, 1995 Exploring the Subject in Hyper-Reality, in *Mapping the Subject: geographies of cultural transformation* (eds S Pile and N Thrift), 241-266, Routledge, London
Shanks, M, and Hodder, I, 1995 Processual, postprocessual and interpretive archaeologies, in *Interpreting Archaeology: Finding Meaning in the Past* (eds I Hodder, M Shanks, A Alexandri, V Buchli and J Carmen), 3-29, Routledge, London
Shanks, M, 1996 Photography and Archaeology, in *The Cultural Life of Images* (ed B L Molyneaux), 73-107, Routledge, London
Thomas, J, 1996 *Time, Culture and Identity,* Routledge, London
Tilley, C, 1994 *A Phenomenology of Landscape: Places, paths and Monuments,* Berg, Oxford

Contact details

Mark Gillings
School of Archaeological Studies
University of Leicester
University Road
Leicester, LE1 7RH
UK
email: mg41@le.ac.uk

Presenting Archaeological Information with Java Applets

R. M. Yorston

CAA 97

Abstract

In this paper I look at the use of Java applets in presenting archaeological information. I start by describing the Java language environment, and some of the reasons why it has been the subject of much excitement and hype over the past eighteen months. I then discuss some of the applets which were developed as part of a project, funded by the Nuffield Trust, to perform an integrated analysis of known monuments from the early Neolithic through to the Late Bronze Age in the area around Stonehenge. A discussion of some of the advantages of the technique is followed by mention of some of the problems encountered, and thoughts for the future.

1 Java

One of the more exciting developments in computing in recent years has been the invention of the Java programming language by Sun Microsystems. What has caught the attention of many people is Java's ability to generate applets, small programs, which can be downloaded over the Internet and run on Web browsers. This can be used to add dynamic features to Web pages which would be quite impossible to achieve with previous technologies.

Although caught up in the hype associated with the Internet, Java has many features which make it useful in other contexts. In "The Java Language Environment: A White Paper", Gosling and McGilton characterise Java in terms of a list of buzzwords: they claim it is a simple, object-oriented, distributed, interpreted, robust, secure, architecture neutral, portable, high-performance, multithreaded and dynamic language. Any subset of these could, in the right circumstances, be a powerful argument for using Java. I shall expand on just a few of them.

Java is a language of the C/C++ family. The syntax for expressions and control structures will be familiar to C programmers. In adding object-oriented features, though, Java takes a more radical approach than C++: everything in Java (apart from the basic numeric and character types) is an object. There are no standalone functions, only object methods. It has also avoided some of the more obscure and little-used features of C++, like multiple inheritance.

Although one of the buzzwords was 'interpreted', Java is still a compiled language. Once a program has been written it has to be run through a compiler. Instead of assembler or machine code for a particular processor the compiler generates class files containing Java byte codes. These byte codes are the instruction set for an imaginary processor, the Java Virtual Machine, or JVM. To run Java applications you need an implementation of the JVM for your computer. This implementation interprets the byte codes.

Security is an important consideration where code of unknown provenance is to be downloaded across the Internet and executed on the local machine. The possibility for abuse is obvious. Before execution the code is subject to a verification stage to ensure that no invalid operations can be performed. There are also run-time checks on array bounds which prevent programmers from accessing memory which doesn't belong to them.

One departure from the C/C++ programming model is in the way memory is managed. Java has no concept of a pointer to memory and allocated memory is managed by an automatic garbage collector. This avoids a whole class of difficult-to-find bugs involving dynamic memory allocation, although it does tend to have a cost in reduced performance.

2 Applet Technology

One of the major uses of Java is in the development of applets to run in Web browsers. An applet is a small program which can be incorporated into a Web page in much the same way as graphics. A tag in the HTML of the Web page references the main class file of the applet. The executable code of the applet is downloaded along with the text of the page. Once the code arrives from the server it is executed by the browser on the local machine. This allows the programmer to do many things which would be impossible in a normal Web page. Among other things the applet can display dynamic graphics on the Web page, it can allow the user to interact with it and it can connect back to the server from which it came to download further information or query a database there. Some of these capabilities are illustrated in the present work.

The infrastructure required to support the applet is built into the latest versions of Web browsers like Microsoft Internet Explorer and Netscape Navigator. This has a number of consequences. Firstly, the applet will run on any platform on which a Java-enabled browser is available: the environment provided by the browser insulates the applet from the underlying operating system. This is obviously a key feature in allowing use over the Internet, where users may have machines with widely different processors and operating systems. Secondly, the applet code is compact. All of the standard libraries for such things as the graphical user interface and network access are provided on the client platform. The only code which needs to be transferred across the Internet is that which is unique to the applet.

3 The Stonehenge Applets

There are undoubtedly many ways in which applets can be used to present archaeological information. The approach taken here is essentially an extension of the map-based illustration which is a common feature of the literature. This has the advantage of being familiar and easily interpreted. The dynamic nature of the applets provides the opportunity to add new features to a familiar medium. Very similar techniques could be used for graphs and scatter diagrams.

As has been mentioned the applets described here were developed as part of a larger project to re-examine the relationship between the landscape and monuments of the Stonehenge region. They have been used in a number of capacities during this project. Initially they were developed as a means of exploring the data set. The greater part of the data processing was performed on a GIS at the Birmingham University Field Archaeology Unit. The author did not have ready access to these facilities and wrote the applets as a means of visualising data generated in Birmingham. Secondly, applets provided a means of communicating results between the geographically separated members of the multi-disciplinary team working on the project. As well as making the applets available on the Internet they have also been distributed on floppy disks to standalone machines. Finally, the applets provide a means of publishing some of the results of the project. They have already been used in two different ways: as part of a Web site describing the work (http://www.pobox.com/~rmy) and as an adjunct to more traditional visual aids during a presentation at the Liverpool TAG conference. In future it is also conceivable that they may be published on CD-ROM.

The first applet was developed to gain familiarity with the study area and to illustrate the intervisibility of the monuments (See Fig. 1). The display consists of a map of the region around Stonehenge with all of the monuments plotted. Positioning the mouse pointer close to a monument causes the monument name to be displayed in the browser status bar and all the other monuments visible from that point to be highlighted. A separate control panel allows the user to customise the appearance of the display. There are controls to change the backdrop, to turn the highlighting of visible monuments on or off, to enable different forms of highlighting based on barrow type and richness, and to turn the display of different types of monument on or off.

This way of presenting information has a number of advantages over the use of static diagrams.

1. To associate a descriptive legend with each of several hundred points would add considerable clutter to a map. This would typically be addressed by having a number beside each of the points and a separate table associating text with the numbers. Putting the identifying text in the browser status bar is an efficient use of space. One possible enhancement would be to add a text entry field to let the user type in the name of a monument and have that point highlighted.

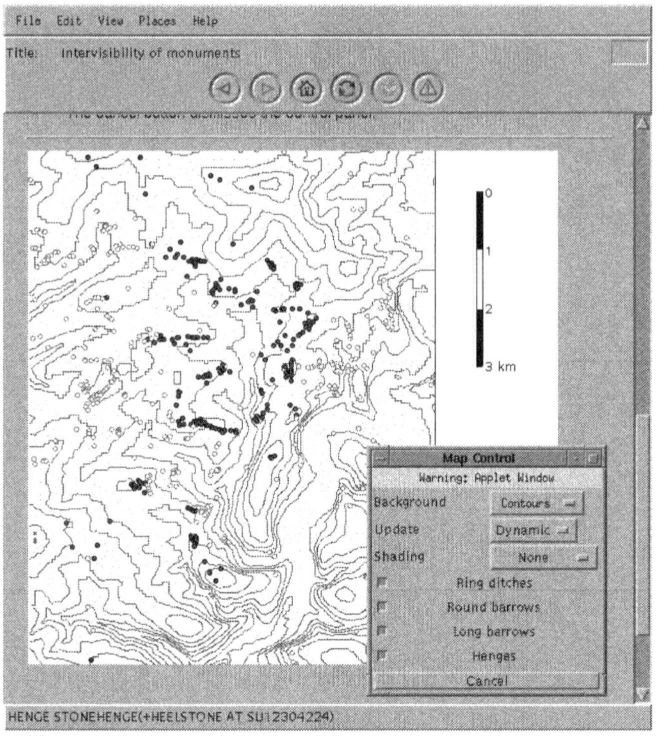

Figure 1. The basic intervisibility applet, showing the control panel. The highlighted monuments are those visible from Stonehenge.

2. To display intervisibility information for all of the monuments would require as many maps as monuments, which is clearly impractical. This would normally be dealt with by publishing intervisibility maps only for those monuments considered by the authors to be significant. Publishing intervisibility data for all the monuments in this way clearly avoids any preconceptions on the part of the authors and empowers the viewer.

3. Allowing the user to customise the appearance of the display lets them concentrate on aspects of the data which interest them.

The second applet (See Fig. 2) retains many of the features of the first (hardly surprising since it is based on the same code) but has backdrops showing the viewsheds of each of the henges in the Stonehenge region. This applet was written to investigate the relationship between the visible monuments and the viewshed edges. Monuments within the viewshed are highlighted differently depending on their distance from the viewshed edge. A text box in the control panel lets the user change the relevant distance.

This illustrates a further advantage of the dynamic nature of applets: the viewer can be provided with the means to interrogate the data set. In selecting values for the viewshed distance parameter they are not restricted to pre-computed values selected by the author: arbitrary values can be used. All the code necessary to calculate statistics based on the downloaded data is present in the applet.

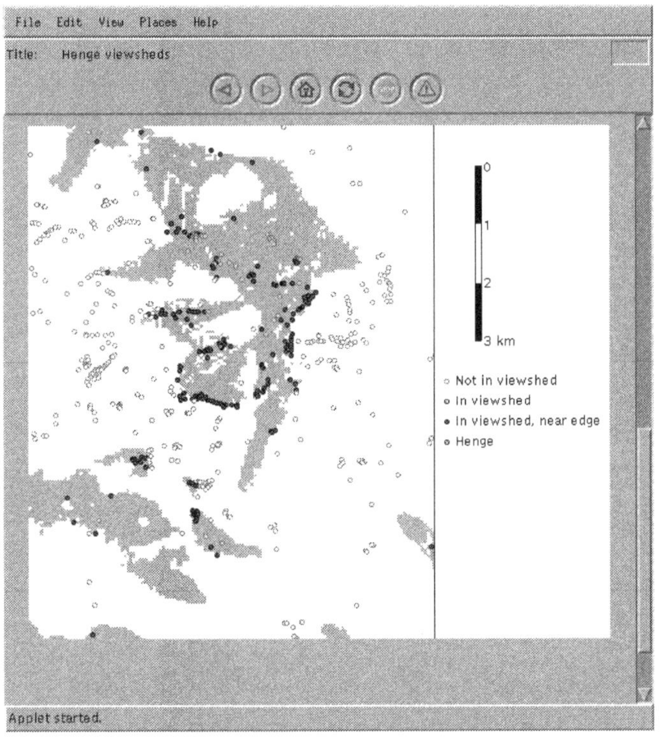

Figure 2. The henge viewshed applet. The grey area represents the viewshed of Stonehenge. The highlighted monuments are those within 100 metres of the edge of the viewshed.

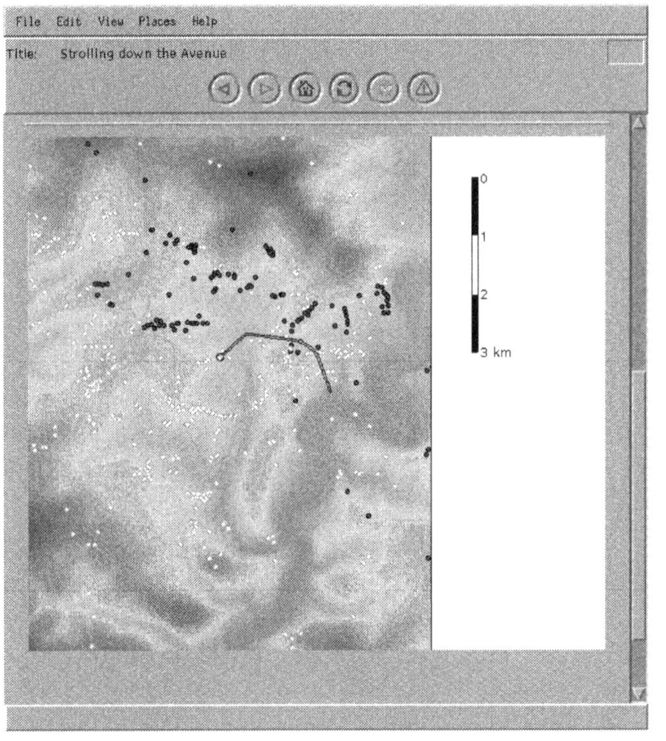

Figure 3. A snapshot of the animation of a walk along the Avenue. The viewpoint is close to the crest of the King Barrow ridge. The backdrop represents the topography.

The third applet (See Fig. 3) displays animations of the monuments visible from a number of points along extended features like the Stonehenge Avenue and the Greater Cursus. Again there is a control panel, this time to allow the user to select the backdrop, the path to be animated and the speed of motion.

The use of animation allows the viewer to see how vistas open and close as the viewpoint moves across the landscape. This style of display is well suited to extended monuments which can be considered to delineate processional routes. Similar animation techniques could be used to illustrate temporal development as well a spatial motion.

There are other advantages to the dynamic display of results. The type of display used here is a middle route between static maps and publication of the full data set. Most readers of a paper do not require access to the original data: they will have neither the time nor the inclination to perform a complete reinterpretation. The sort of applets described here allow authors to increase the amount of information they make available without the need for any additional interpretative effort on the part of their readers.

Moreover, there may be sound reasons, such as copyright or commercial confidentiality, why it is not possible for the original data to be published. Often it would be permissible to print a static map of such data because the resolution of the diagram would limit the precision of the information which could be gleaned from it. Where such sensitive data is to be downloaded into an applet for interactive manipulation a similar technique can be applied: the data points can be provided at a precision sufficient for the final display but without revealing the full detail of the original data set.

4 Problems

The technology used here is still relatively immature. There are bugs and inconsistencies in the implementation of the Java Virtual Machine and Abstract Windowing Toolkit on different platforms. These manifest themselves in inexplicable failures: sometimes the animation fails to start in Microsoft's Internet Explorer; some of the components of the control panel fail to appear in Sun's HotJava; and attempting to run the applets in early versions of Netscape Navigator cause a fatal crash.

As well as being immature the technology is in a state of flux. At the time of writing version 1.1 of Java had recently been introduced, with version 1.2 on the horizon. When new systems are introduced it takes some time for ports to become available on all platforms, and for all browsers to support them. In addition, there is intense competition between suppliers such as Netscape and Microsoft to develop foundation classes which can be used to build applications. Anyone choosing to develop in Java is currently faced with difficult decisions as to which technologies to learn and use, with the danger that an investment in an unsuccessful technology will be wasted.

Another problem is the speed of the Internet. The applets consist of a number of class files, graphical images and data files. It can take some time for all of these to be downloaded. There are ways of mitigating this limitation of current technology.

Connection setup is often the slowest part of downloading a file from a Web server. The class files can all be combined into one archive file, so avoiding the need to make a number of separate connections to the server. A drawback of archive files is that there are currently three different technologies in use: uncompressed zip files, Microsoft's cabinet files and Sun's JAR files.

The backdrop images of the henge viewsheds have been combined into one large graphics file, with the appropriate section being displayed for the henge selected by the user. This again avoids the overhead of making connections to transmit multiple graphics files.

Another work around for the slow speed of the Internet is to use the multi-threading capabilities of Java to permit some limited operation of the applet while the required data is being downloaded. Thus data which is vital to the operation of the applet can be fetched first with less significant files, such as the different backdrops, being fetched later. As data arrives the different features of the applet are progressively enabled.

A third technique is to minimise the amount of information which needs to be transmitted.

For example, the positions of the monuments are encoded, not as full grid references, but in terms of their pixel positions within the final display.

In the animation, for each point along the path there is a single bit of data for each monument, to indicate whether it is visible from the point. These arrays of bits have been encoded into a GIF file. Such files are normally used for graphical images, but are used here to transmit raw data because the GIF standard includes compression which considerably reduces the file size. (Version 1.0 of Java includes support for GIFs. Version 1.1 has support for compressed data streams, which provide a more natural and more general solution.)

Downloading the code is not the only limiting factor. Because Java is interpreted it suffers a performance penalty relative to a language which is compiled into native code. This was found to result in the applets having a somewhat sluggish response. Performance was improved by using some of the usual optimisation techniques, such as pre-computing values in advance rather than working them out on the fly. The main improvement in the response of the first applet was obtained by performing the minimum amount of redraw. When highlighting the monuments as the cursor was moved around the display only the monuments whose state changed are now redrawn. This is much faster than trying to redraw everything.

Even with these improvements the response is still inadequate on slow hardware. The situation will improve in future:

1. Java compiler technology will increasingly make use of optimisation techniques.
2. New versions of the Java Virtual Machine are becoming available which employ 'just-in-time' compiler technology to convert Java byte codes into native machine instructions.
3. Hardware is constantly becoming faster.

5 Conclusion

The above considerations suggest that the generation of efficient and effective applets currently requires careful design and cunning programming. In future, as these techniques are developed, it may become possible to package the technology so that non-technical users can publish information with applets as easily as they can now produce tables and charts from a spreadsheet.

Acknowledgements

The work described here forms part of a project sponsored by The Nuffield Trust. The other members of the project team are Sally Exon, Vince Gaffney and Ann Woodward, all of Birmingham University Field Archaeology Unit.

Bibliography

Flanagan, D, 1996 *Java in a Nutshell* Sebastopol, O'Reilly & Associates
Gosling, J and McGilton, H, 1995 *The Java Language Environment: A White Paper*, Mountain View, Sun Microsystems
Arnold, K and Gosling, J, 1996 *The Java Programming Language*, Reading,Addison-Wesley

Contact details
R. M. Yorston
1 Church Terrace
Lower Field Road
Reading RG1 6AS
UK
Email: rmy@pobox.com

Visualising Danebury: Modelled Approaches to Spatial Theory

Graeme P. Earl

CAA 97

Abstract

Danebury Iron Age hillfort is examined via spatial modelling in an attempt to answer explicit theoretical questions surrounding the function of altered spaces. Within the confines of a small-scale research project, interpretation is placed as the driving force behind methodology, with high-order theoretical arguments approached via modelled spaces constructed in 3d Studio, animation packages, VRML, bubble worlds and Grass, linked via AutoCAD. Military and defensive interpretations in Iron Age work are challenged by the identification of spatial orders, via modelling, which lack defensive function, and seem to conform to ideas of 'liminality' discussed in detail in the Neolithic. These conclusions are then used to assess the role computer models play in 'archaeological fictions' at Danebury, and the extent to which limited technology can pursue experiential goals.

1 The site

The Iron Age hillfort of Danebury lies on chalk downland south of Andover in the county of Hampshire. Its hilltop landscape is at a maximum elevation of 143m, with steep slopes in all directions, apart from at the eastern approach (Cunliffe 1984, 1). The site was excavated to a high standard and presents us with a well-documented, complex Iron Age resource. It is defined by three sets of earthworks, enclosing a total of 16 hectares and excavation of these has revealed a series of major developments, characterised by significant alterations to the landscape (Lock 1989). The focus of the changes to the site, and indeed of the site itself, is the elaborate eastern entrance. The research described thus concentrates on this entrance and attempts to look at it from the standpoint of recent Iron Age work, and proceeds from questions regarding the role of computer modelling in archaeological theory.

2 Space in the Iron Age

The current Iron Age hypotheses considered have examined in particular the use of landscape for the development, attribution, conveyance and embodiment of symbolic meaning. Entrance spaces, defining movement through manufactured landscapes, are frequently seen as powerful means of both demonstrating and orchestrating social behaviour (Hillier and Hanson 1984; Parker-Pearson and Richards 1994a and b; Thomas 1993; Tuan 1977). More general theories of spatial function have been augmented in the computing literature by Gillings and Goodrick (1996), who offer a view of the potential for landscape modelling to approach this engagement.

In this study models were produced which could be navigated around, in an attempt to identify the role both of defining features such as banks and ditches at different stages in their use, and the areas thus defined. Localised Iron Age 'landscapes' were to be examined interactively via models rather than assessed in plan or in surviving states. Here concepts of liminality were placed alongside the 'warrior Iron Age' (Sharples 1991) hypothesis of the 1980s, allowing parallel consideration of the two approaches. This was particularly important given the broad spectrum of opinion regarding entrance function present in the literature.

3 The defensive function debate

The traditional interpretation of the Danebury earthworks views the impressive east entrance as a defensive barrier, defining an approach which makes attack very difficult and dangerous. This is a familiar, readily accessible view and can be substantiated on military grounds. However, the Iron Age debate surrounding the concept of a 'different' Iron Age - that is to say, one in which pre-suppositions are deliberately confronted - may suggest such defensive utility to be a byproduct of other aims (Cunliffe 1995 cf. Hill 1993; 1995). Bowden and McOmish (1987) and others have suggested that sites such as Danebury, Maiden Castle and Kerr's Knowe may indicate continuity of social practice, with ritual or other significance attached to places and occasions via manufactured divisions such as ramparts.

4 Modelling processes

In the completed stage of the project the construction of Danebury's past and present landscape was approached via the derivation of a DEM surface, VRML modelling used interpretatively to define areas for concentrated study and interpretation, and the development, rendering and animation of multiple solid elements through AutoCAD, 3d Studio and, most recently, 'bubble worlds'. The computing literature has identified the considerable power exercised by rendered surfaces and the variety of approaches was intended to offer differing perspectives, highlighting both the more obvious subjective factors and robust conclusions and approaching the "non-linear access" to data discussed by Lock (1995, 16). In addition, at every stage an attempt was made to consider the significance of different data types (Miller and Richards 1995). Thus, initial impressions of the site were gained by a number of visits. Photographs and sketches were produced and notes written, prior to the detailed examination of any descriptive texts. These notes were intended to act as a link between the computer modeller, with component biases regarding the arrangement and 'function' of the site, and the excavated data. Since all data, models, views and animations used in the project followed a set of naming conventions it was possible to link any piece of recorded data, any note written during the initial visits and during the modelling process, to every related part in the final models. This has lead to a cyclical process of modelling and adaptation identifying a considerable subjective element to the appearance of 'final' products.

4.1 Terrain surfaces

The basis of the study was a set of AutoCAD digitised plans, sections, sketches, maps, and textual descriptions. The final dataset incorporated over 30 digitised drawings, in addition to a large textual database. These were combined via external links and embedding into a single AutoCAD file. The first modelling exercise involved the production of a series of DEM surfaces in the Grass geographic information system. The final version, created via an algorithm using weighted flood fills between digitised spot heights and isolines, was then sampled by piping output direct from Grass into a separate text file, providing a mesh of point data. Finally, this mesh was used to define a point surface (Autodesk 1992) by writing a DXF file from the ASCII Grass output. This was imported into AutoCAD for the interpretation of topographic variation and viewpoints around the east entrance. Unfortunately, following topographic meshes proved difficult in AutoCAD and as a result only portions of the models produced are snapped to the appropriate topographic positions. However, where terrain surfaces *were* used, different models were produced to compare the defined spaces produced with differing DEM algorithm surfaces and also with a flat platform. In the comparison of viewpoints the topographic variation was found to effect results at the extremes of modelling — i.e. where the conceptual distance between data and extrapolated spaces was greatest. It was clear that even at this micro scale DEM algorithm choice could play a significant role in conclusions. This echoes Gillings and Goodrick's emphasis on micro as well as macro scale variation in modelled landscapes of any scale (1996).

4.2 Spatial feature models

The next process involved the building of AutoCAD spatial feature models. These were based on composite mesh primitives defined by the digitised data and comparative datasets (see Fig. 1). Surface modelling was used rather than solids for reasons of speed and it was felt that the complex surfaces to be modelled made a surface approach more appropriate. The surfaces themselves were defined by constructing regular rectangular meshes which corresponded to the measurements available. Points within these were then used to define extrapolated surfaces via the AutoCAD edgesurf and rulesurf commands. Different parameters for these commands were compared for particular modelled areas. This identified considerable variation in the final modelled surfaces, dependent upon choices such as the number of ruled lines, which filtered through to the appreciation of the spaces produced in the final analyses. Without this comparison conclusions produced would have seemed far more robust.

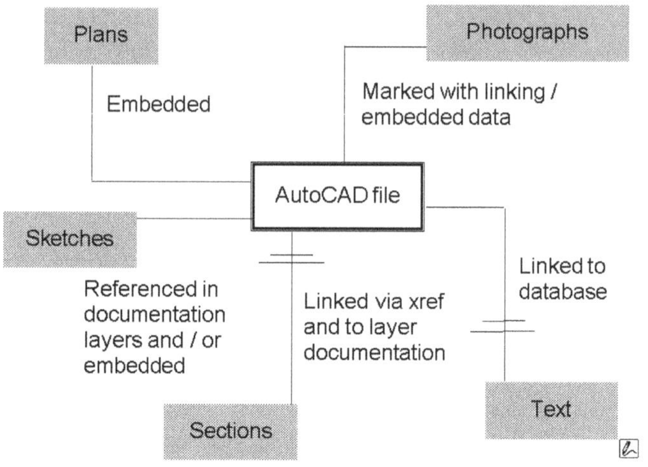

Figure 1. Data types and links to the final AutoCAD surfaces

The visual sparcity of the models produced was a consequence of the background motivations of the project - namely the maintenance of total data integrity, the qualification of extrapolation and the production of readily updatable *different* constructs. Given the limited time and technological resources available, the choice was made to concentrate on producing a number of models which could offer the range of spatial interpretations required by the complexity and ambiguity present in the excavated data. This proved to be at the expense of the 'photorealistic' results defined by Chalmers (Chalmers *et al* 1995) as an enhancing factor in the experience provided by navigable archaeological models.

4.3 Simple VRML

In the third modelling stage Virtual Reality Modelling Language (VRML) was applied to generate a very simple modelled landscape which could be interpreted on an intuitive level (see Fig. 2). The models were engaged with under differing conditions of light and rendered colour. It was this approach which allowed a set of apparent discrete spaces within the Danebury landscape to be viewed. However, it was noted that Hill (pers. comm.) had identified an alignment at the east entrance consistent with the direction of motion *prior* to the construction of any models and it was therefore necessary to subject the models to fairly rigorous testing. Ideally this interrogation should have involved a number of re-interpretations by other parties and more extensive use of the range of different models available. However, the time restraints only allowed for assessment at a mechanical level, with reference to 'objectivity' in comparison. Thus, VRML models derived from variations in the interpretation of excavation data and in the methods of extrapolation were compared.

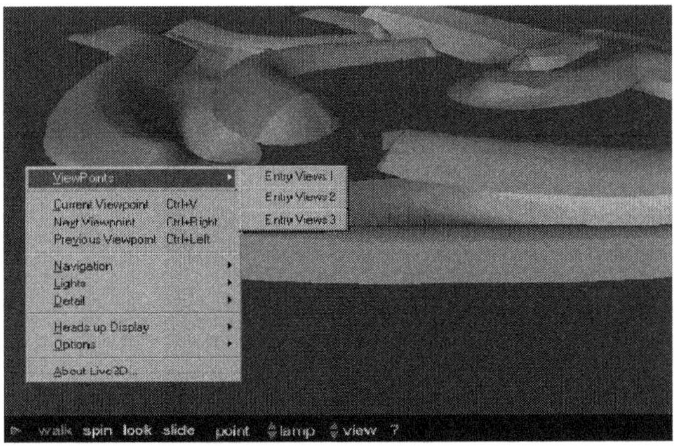

Figure 2. One of the VRML models produced for the east entrance in phase 6

4.4 Rendered views and animation

In the final stage the viewpoints and associated spaces were examined in greater detail via simply rendered and lit models. Viewpoints were set up to correspond with spaces apparently visible in the VRML models, and comparisons between the extrapolated models and the surviving earthworks was made possible using bubble worlds. The defined viewpoints could be adjusted more 'empirically' via the AutoCAD vpoint and dview commands. It was felt that this combination of reactive VRML navigation and controlled AutoCAD viewpoint definition offered a clearer impression of the range of potential viewpoints. Again, the rendered views created followed the naming conventions employed in the digitised and constructed data and could therefore be linked throughout the process from data to model.

To begin with it was hoped to render views with the conventional aim of approaching a modern aesthetic 'realism' . However, given the project's technological limitations and, more significantly the desire to escape a past-as-same, auto-interpretative approach, the views produced are now intended to define simple viewpoints alone. Any absorption will proceed from the imagination of the viewer rather than from definition by the modeller. The viewpoints may therefore be considered analogous to viewshed coverages, with colour serving only as a mental key. In this way it was possible to produce lots of spatial scenarios in a comparatively short time. However, the incorporation of more detailed elements such as variations in rampart construction and illumination to create different Iron Age pasts at Danebury must rely on technology with the potential described by Chalmers and others (Chalmers *et al* 1993, Chalmers and Stoddart 1994, Chalmers *et al* 1994; Chalmers *et al* 1996).

5 Conclusions

Interrogation of the models suggests that discrete spaces seem to be defined within and around the east entrance landscape, with an emphasis on liminal zones of some form (see Fig. 3). Some kind of symbolic emphasis is suggested by a continuity in arrangement and interconnectivity of space which is clearly visible in the models of different phases of the entrance, and much less obviously in plan. This contradicts other work which has emphasised the alterations to the entrance. For example, additions to the earthworks made towards the end of the fourth century would seem, on the basis of plan, to have altered the east entrance completely. However, the three dimensional model reveals consisitencies in the landscape's arrangement - particularly regarding the direction of movement and views.

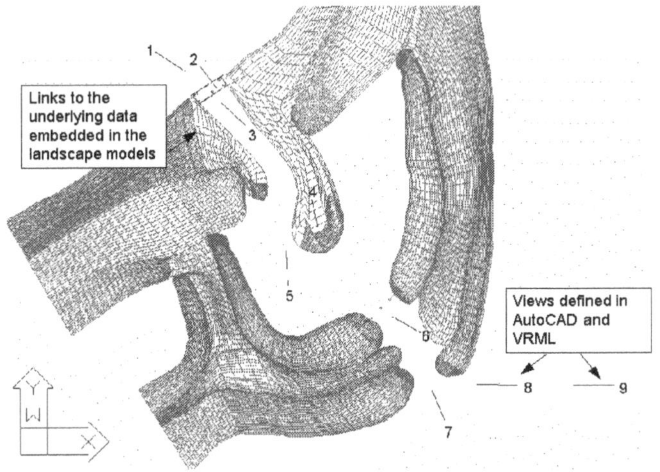

Figure 3. The different spaces - identified in an HTML imagemap, with hotspots to simple animations, VRML files, rendered AutoCAD views and bubble worlds

5.1 Defensive roles

The spaces do not appear to offer any defensive benefits in their early stages and it may be hypothesised that their later embellishment and continuity were similarly a product of symbolic as opposed to defensive requirements. This hypothesis fits with a body of research limiting the bellicose nature of Iron Age societies and with other spatial arrangements noted elsewhere at Danebury and at other 'hillfort' sites. Movement through the spaces, perhaps mediated by social circumscription, leads to the opening of new vistas with access to views of the hypothesised central shrine area closely defined by the earthworks (cf. Chalmers *et al* 1994). The viewpoint analyses identify some defensive utility in the later (phase 6) development of the entrance but modelling of the gateway itself suggests it to serve very little role as a lookout point. Here the models, defined by the views of Cunliffe and others (Avery 1993; Cunliffe 1984) regarding earthwork construction, contradict to a certain extent the impression gained by viewing the surviving earthworks via bubble worlds or in reality.

5.2 Recursive data integration

The modelling itself has supported the emphasis placed by other work on integration of all data types in intuitive ways. This allows for a better critique both of methodology and interpretation. It is also clear that the integration of these different datasets in simple models which allow for rapid *change* has helped an understanding of Danebury's complexity and suggested both problems and solutions at every modelling stage. For example, the period 5 and period 6 entrance alignments are extremely complex but alternating between layers and re-exporting dxf. files allowed for multiple virtual access to the data, and a better understanding of the possible spatial arrangements. Future research is intended to maximise this potential for integrated, reactive archaeological landscape data.

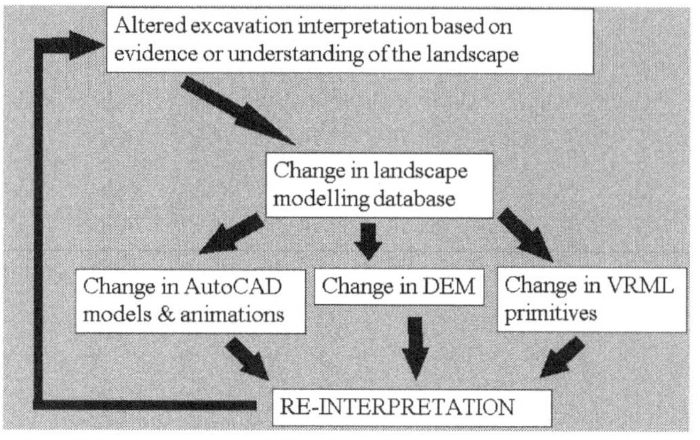

Figure 4: The proposed reactive system of integrated data types for further research at Danebury.

An awareness of the role of the computer modeller in the construction, rather than the reconstruction, of the past at Danebury and elsewhere has identified a need for recursive approaches to modelling, where each alteration to interpretation of excavated material, explicit application of sketches and personal perspectives, choice of 'correlates' and use of technology would define new spaces to be engaged with (see fig. 4). Such an approach would offer a great deal to current theory. The work to date at Danebury suggests that where data such as GIS coverages, models, animations and text are combined they provide a useful platform upon which to construct multiple representations of a physical past, whilst retaining some kind of data dependence. In this case, a certain lack of absorption need not be problematic. Indeed, an explicit detachment from Danebury as modelled may allow a great breadth in our recognition of Danebury as excavated and as theorised.

Acknowledgements

The research described here is formed in part by a dissertation submitted for the MSc in Archaeological Science at the University of Southampton. Its completion would have been impossible without the support and advice of my supervisors Dr. J.D. Hill and Dr. David Wheatley, and the technical expertise of Mr. Tim Sly and Dr. Keith Westcott. I am also grateful to my colleagues in the Department of Archaeology for advice during and subsequent to the masters course. In particular thanks are due to Sarah Poppy. The research continues to be funded by the States of Guernsey Education Council.

Bibliography

Autodesk, 1992 *AutoCAD Release 12 Reference Manual,* Autodesk BV, Neuchatel

Avery, M, 1993 *Hillfort defences of Southern Britain - volume one* (British Archaeological Reports, 231), Oxford, British Archaeological Reports

Bowden, M and McOmish, D, 1987 The required barrier, *Scottish Archaeological Review,* 4, 84-97

Chalmers, A G, Pattanaik, S N, Biriukov, A and Sharpe, P, 1993 Parallel processing for interactive photo-realistic building walkthroughs, in Strasser, W and Wahl, F (eds.), *Graphics and Robotics,* Schloss Dagstuhl

Chalmers, A and Stoddart, S, 1994 Photo-realistic graphics for visualising archaeological site reconstructions, Unpublished paper from the International Conference on Imaging the Past, British Museum

Chalmers, A, Martin, T, Stoddart, S and Wahl, B, 1994 The INSITE project, in Wilcock, J and Lockyear, K (eds.), *Computer Applications and Quantitative Methods in Archaeology 1993* (British Archaeological Reports, International Series 598) Oxford, Tempus Reparatum

Chalmers, A, Stoddart, S, Tidmus, J and Miles, R, 1995 INSITE: an interactive visualisation system for archaeological sites, in Huggett, J and Ryan, N (eds.), *Computer Applications and Quantitative Methods in Archaeology 1994* (British Archaeological Reports, International Series 600), 225–228, Oxford, Tempus Reparatum

Chalmers, A, Martin, T, Stoddart, S and Wahl, B, 1996 Investigating southern African archaeology, Unpublished paper from the University of Bristol

Cunliffe, B, 1984 *Danebury: an Iron Age hillfort in Hampshire - Volume 1, The Excavations, 1969-1978: the site,* Council for British Archaeology Research Report, 52

Cunliffe, B, 1995 *Danebury: an Iron Age hillfort in Hampshire - Volume 6: A hillfort community in perspective,* Council for British Archaeology Research Report, 102

Gillings, M, and Goodrick, G T, 1996 Sensuous and Reflexive GIS: exploring visualisation and VRML, *Internet Archaeology,* 1

Hill, J D, 1993 Can we recognise a different European past ?: a contrastive archaeology of later prehistoric settlements in southern England, *Journal of European Archaeology,* 1, 57–75

Hill, J D, 1995 How should we understand Iron Age societies and hillforts ? A contextual study from southern Britain, in Hill, J D and Cumberpatch, C G (eds.), *Different Iron Ages: studies on the Iron Age of Temperate Europe* (British Archaeological Reports, International Series 602) Oxford, Tempus Reparatum

Hillier, B and Hanson, J, 1984 *The social logic of space.* Cambridge, Cambridge University press

Lock, G, 1989 Comments on an alternative Danebury, *Scottish Archaeological Review,* 6, 3–5

Lock, G, 1995 Archaeological computing, archaeological theory and moves towards contextualism, in Huggett, J and Ryan, N (eds.), *Computer Applications and Quantitative Methods in Archaeology 1994* (British Archaeological Reports, International Series 600), 13–18, Oxford, Tempus Reparatum

Miller, P and Richards 1995 The good, the bad, and the downright misleading: archaeological adoption of computer visualization, in Huggett, J and Ryan, N (eds.), *Computer Applications and Quantitative Methods in Archaeology 1994* (British Archaeological Reports, International Series 600), 19–22, Oxford, Tempus Reparatum

Parker-Pearson, M and Richards, C, 1994a Ordering the world: perceptions of architecture, space and time', in Parker-Pearson, M. & Richards, C. (eds.). *Architecture and Order: approaches to social space* 1–37 London, Routledge

Parker-Pearson, M and Richards, C, 1994b Architecture and Order: spatial representation and archaeology, in Parker-Pearson, M and Richards, C (eds.), *Architecture and Order: approaches to social space,* 38–72 London, Routledge

Sharples, N, 1991 Warfare in the Iron Age of Wessex, *Scottish Archaeological Review,* 8, 79–89

Thomas, J, 1993 The politics of vision and the archaeologies of landscape, in Bender, B (ed.), *Landscape: politics and perspectives,* 19–48, Providence, R.I., Berg

Tuan, Y-F, 1977 *Space and Place: the perspective of experience,* London, Edward Arnold

Contact details

Graeme P. Earl
Department of Archaeology
University of Southampton
Southampton SO17 1BJ
UK
email: gpe195@soton.ac.uk

Moving Through Space
Abstracts of papers held on CD-ROM

CAA 97

From The Ground Up: Visualising Ligurian Archaeological Sites
Michael McCullagh, Roberto Maggi, Mark Pearce and Jerry Ratcliffe

Three archaeological sites in Liguria were surveyed by a University student party in April 1997, in cooperation with the Italian state archaeological Service, to provide the basis for building computer views to enhance interpretation of the sites, and to provide educational material for use in University and other student courses. The survey methods used were chosen to enable rapid and cheap generation of results and were combined with some pre-existing survey data. A major constraint on the whole project was that the process of data collection, modelling, visualisation, and final video presentation of the results had to be completed in a three week time frame: one week preparation, one week in the field, and a final week preparing and presenting the results and the digital video at the CAA97 meeting. An assessment of the results from this exploratory project indicates that the methods used, together with additional recently available approaches, can be employed successfully to generate useful model, visual, and animated interpretations of complex sites in a relatively short period of time.

Using Visualization in the Archaeological Excavations of a Pre-Inca Temple in Peru
Alan D. Kalvin, Alfredo Remy, Luis Jaime Castillo, Kim Morla, Eduardo Nolazco, Jorge Prado, Victor Fernandez, Regulo Franco and Guillermo Wiese

We describe an on-going project that is using visualization as an indispensable tool for the restoration of the disintegrated ceiling of a ritual precinct that was recently discovered during archaeological excavations of a group of pre-Inca temples in Peru. This ceiling is unique - it is the only one ever found that has pictures painted on it, rather than being simply white-washed. The restoration of the ceiling, and the recovery of these iconographic figures will provide an unprecedented opportunity to study the culture of the Moche people who built and used these temples.

Virtual Stonehenge: a Fall from Disgrace?
N. R. Burton, M. E. Hitchen and P. G. Bryan

In October 1995 English Heritage, with sponsorship from Intel (UK), began a project to use Virtual Reality to create a model of Stonehenge and the surrounding landscape. Two products were created and premiered on the eve of the 1996 summer solstice: one designed for the internet where browsers can download, explore and interact with the 3D world in a variety of time periods; and another which contains much more detail, utilising three dimensional data produced from a recently completed comprehensive photogrammetric survey of the monument. The following text discusses the construction and specific features of these two developments which include the accurate positioning of stars in the night sky, the use of draping photographs in an attempt at photorealism, as well as the first 'virtual sunrise'.

Virtual Worlds for Archaeological Research and Education
Donald H. Sanders

The use of virtual reality for archaeology has only recently begun to take full advantage of the technology's abilities to create near firsthand experiences of ancient buildings, sites, and environments. Virtual worlds can be much more than sets of fancy pictures; objects throughout the worlds can be linked to text, image, and sound databases permitting self-guided educational or research virtual tours of ancient sites in which users can learn about history, construction details, or daily life with a click of the mouse. Worlds programmed in VRML can be sent over the Internet or run off CDs providing an interactive and exciting research experience. Alternative publications can supplement or supplant traditional paper-based source material; for instance, a 3D computer model can be a visual index to an excavation report. The same models and virtual worlds can also be used for up-to-date instructional materials for public schools or museums directly engaging students or the general public in a participatory learning experience utilizing the very latest archaeological evidence. We can create a globally integrated and interactive system of linked virtual worlds for teaching, research, archaeological fieldwork, museum exhibitions, and on-site interpretation centers. Utilizing virtual reality as the container to which all other data and image types are linked offers unprecedented access to information. Whether computers help to change the questions we ask of the past may depend on the techniques chosen to visualize the answers.

PAROS. Close Range Photogrammetry and Architectural Models
Michel Florenzano, Jean-Yves Blaise and Pierre Drap

The main purpose of the PAROS survey process will be integrating architectural knowledge and a photogrammetrical survey tool. In other words, PAROS is concerned with the implementation of a tool connecting the fields of architectural photogrammetry, knowledge representation and imagery together. We focus our activity on three research guidelines:

1. Knowledge representation (architecture and geometry) using object oriented programming.
2. Computational models of the comparisons between the theoretical predefined architectural models and their counterpart: the actual survey.
3. Deductive mechanisms using predefined typo-morphological definitions and rules in order to re-create virtual "could have been" buildings illustrating archaeological hypothesis.

This paper presents an experimental part of the PAROS research carried out on the remains of the north portico of the roman forum at Arles. Key words: Architecture, Cultural_heritage, Modelling, Imagery, Knowledge_base, Close_range, Object_oriented programming.

"Data-In" or "Lets Try it with the Horse in Front". 3D modelling Automated but put in its Place
Steve Nickerson

The computer systems we have at our disposal today offer many amazing tools to sort, analyze, display and present our data. However, much less progress has been made at the other end of this process, that of data acquisition and its accurate input into the computer formats that will do the processing and prepare the reports and graphics. One problem has been that the graphic "cart" has somehow been placed in front of the data "horse" and a lot of information has found its way into a variety of proprietary CAD formats where it is difficult to search and which may not even be accessible to the next generation of software. This data may also be available in field sketches and notes (even harder to search) but often its only computerized manifestation is as a CAD file painstakingly developed from a combination of survey and hand measurements and enhanced with a great deal of assumption and generalization into a "drawing" that looks right and presents the hypothesis in the best possible light. What is needed is a data acquisition strategy that acknowledges that our primary purpose is to create a database accommodating, or at least pointing to, all the available information. One which can be easily searched.

VisTA: An Interactive Visualization Tool for Archaeological Data
Rieko Kadobayashi, Eduardo Neeter, Kenji Mase and Ryohei Nakatsu

VisTA is an interactive visualization and simulation tool for archaeological and geographical data. The goal of the system is to support archaeologists in their work of forming and discovering knowledge on the evolution of ancient villages. Users of the system can visualize ancient villages, using 3D Computer Graphics, simulate the transition of a village over time, as well as the lifespan of each house. VisTA also allows users to walk through villages, greatly helping archaeologists study the spatial and geographical layouts of the villages. For museum exhibitions, we developed VisTA-walk which allows users to walk-through reconstructed villages and get information through gesture interaction.

VRML, Virtual Reality and Visualisation: The best tool for the job?
Glynn Goodrick

No Abstract Supplied

ARCHAEOLOGY
IN THE
AGE OF THE INTERNET

CAA 97

Section 11
Finds Analysis and Curation

Enhanced Reality Fieldwork: the Context Aware Archaeological Assistant

Nick Ryan, Jason Pascoe and David Morse

CAA 97

Abstract

Portable and laptop computers enable most of the capabilities of a desktop machine to be taken into the field. However, their limited battery life and not insignificant weight limit them to stationary, if not sedentary use. On the other hand, Personal Digital Assistants (PDAs) lack the processing power and range of software of more general purpose portables. Despite being designed as electronic equivalents of the paper based 'personal organiser', many PDAs are programmable and offer a clear potential for use as a highly portable adjunct to desktop and portable systems. This potential extends far beyond the simple data-logging tasks for which they have often been used. This paper describes a JISC funded project in which we are investigating the potential for extending computer learning and research tools into the field. A central theme of the project is 'context awareness', a term that describes the ability of the computer to sense and act upon information about its environment, such as location, time, temperature or user identity. This information can be used not only to tag information collected in the field, but also to enable selective responses such as triggering alarms or retrieving information relevant to the task at hand. Further details of this and related projects can be found at http://www.ukc.ac.uk/computer_science/Html/MobiComp/

1 Introduction

The Mobile Computing in a Fieldwork Environment (MCFE) project aims to develop 'context-aware' tools for hand-held computers that will support the authoring, presentation and management of field notes[1]. The project deliverables will be designed to support student fieldwork exercises and our initial targets are fieldwork training in archaeology and the environmental sciences. Despite this specialised orientation, we anticipate that many features of these tools will prove to be equally well suited to use in research data collection in these and other disciplines.

An important theme of the project is 'context awareness', a term that describes the ability of the computer to sense and act upon information about its environment, such as location, time, temperature or user identity. This information can be used not only to tag information as it is collected in the field, but also to enable selective responses such as triggering alarms or retrieving information relevant to the task at hand. Because of the importance of location in fieldwork applications, the hand-held computers used in the project are normally connected to a GPS receiver. Other environmental sensors could, of course, be added if required.

Approaches to the provision of on-line teaching and learning aids have, understandably, concentrated on classroom or laboratory based provision using desktop computers or terminals. Similarly, the concerns of many of those who are addressing the provision of distance learning materials have been focused on replicating or replacing such provision on individual, remote machines. In some cases, the material presented in such learning packages has been used to prepare students for fieldwork by developing skills such as map reading or the recognition of landscape features, flora or fauna (see, for example, earlier reports on the various TLTP projects, including Martlew and Cheetham 1995). There has, however, been less work on the role of portable computers and nomadic computing during the conduct of the fieldwork exercise itself.

Several disciplines have shown a growing interest in 'virtual fieldwork laboratories', in some cases using virtual reality techniques to simulate fieldwork experiences (see, for example, Williams 1997). In contrast to these, our approach can be termed 'Enhanced Reality'. Here, the real fieldwork experience is enhanced by providing timely and appropriate information that can be tailored to the needs of the individual user. Simple example applications include data collection forms, the control of sampling during fieldwalking, and locating features on remotely sensed images for a field survey team on the ground. A more complex system might provide a multimedia guide to the archaeological, geological or environmental features of a region. In each case the central requirement is for a continuous knowledge of location that provides a means of tagging collected data as well as a primary route for information retrieval.

2 The MCFE 'field notes' model

The term 'field notes' is used here to cover a wide range of types of information that might be taken into the field, created or modified in the field, or consulted and analysed after returning from the field. In their simplest form, these notes might be plain text such as instructions to students or recorded descriptions. For many applications the 'notes' will need to be more complex. A typical requirement would be for data entry forms with text boxes, buttons, pick- lists and other interface objects commonly found in familiar graphical user interfaces. In many cases, raster and vector graphics should also be supported so that location maps or images can be included in the notes. At a somewhat more complex level, other possible note types include multimedia presentations and active, or executable, objects such as Java applets. As with text, the graphics requirements apply to both presentation and authoring of notes. It should, for example, be possible to record sketches and, perhaps, images from a digital camera whilst in the field. Indeed, a field authoring facility is a general requirement for all types of notes. Data entry forms will normally be designed in advance, but few researchers can have escaped the need to modify their forms once data collection is in progress. Individual notes rarely stand alone; they will often be interrelated and arranged in sequences, hierarchies, or more general networks. Cross-referencing between notes is therefore an essential requirement that can be provided by hypertext-style links. As witnessed by the increasing number of Web oriented submissions to this and other conferences, students and researchers are becoming practised users of the World Wide Web. Web browsers and HTML documents now provide the most widely known and familiar interface for accessing and navigating related information. This in itself is a strong argument for basing the look and feel of MCFE notes on that of WWW documents.

The overall management of collections of field notes is a task better suited to a conventional desktop machine. A 'notes database' will be required to serve as a repository for instructions and field exercises as well as for data collected in the field. This should provide straightforward means of data exchange with other database, GIS and analytical tools. Packages of tasks tailored to suit particular groups of students or research projects will then be selected for downloading to the mobile machines. In a pure research context, these field resources might often include information recorded during previous visits to the field site. On return from the field, exercise results and other recorded data will be uploaded to the desktop system where it will then be available for analysis and re-use.

For longer stays in the field it will be more appropriate to use a laptop as a surrogate for the desktop machine and to provide regular backup facilities for the hand-held devices. In principal, there is no reason to limit the mobile machines to autonomous operation. Given suitable data links, such as a radio modem or GSM mobile phone, forms might be used as remote database access tools or as a remote 'window' on a Geographical Information System hosted on a remote server. Indeed, the possibility arises of using the mobile hand-held computers as nodes in a 'field network', perhaps with a laptop acting as a local 'field server' to provide bulk storage and to buffer communications with the main system back at base.

3 Stick-e notes

One of the main inspirations behind this project has been Peter Brown's Stick-e note metaphor (Brown 1997). This defines a means of delivery for context-aware information that is particularly suited to mobile applications. Notes are associated with an environmental context and become active when the user enters that context. They are an electronic equivalent of the 'Post-it' note. Examples of the elements of a stick-e note context include location, states of external sensors or of the computer itself, imaginary companions or temporal events. Thus context is understood to have both physical and logical domains. Brown has successfully completed a general implementation of stick-e notes. One of its strengths is that it allows authors to produce and publish materials without any need for programming skills. Notes are prepared in SGML form and look similar to WWW pages, but with extra fields specifying context (at some location, during some time-period, etc.). This work, together with a prototype implementation by Jason Pascoe, has provided the initial architectural model for context-aware applications used in the current project (Pascoe 1997). However, we have adopted a different encoding format for our field notes.

4 Field notes in HTML

Despite the relative ease with which notes can be prepared in SGML format, we are aware that many of our potential user groups might not be familiar with this format. Although appropriate editing and viewing tools exist, they are virtually unknown outside of the highly specialised electronic publishing and text processing communities. Even though the two languages are closely related – HTML is defined in terms of SGML – we decided to examine the possibility of a mobile context-aware note system based on the now well known format of World Wide Web pages written in HTML.

Current HTML browsers running on desktop machines and extended where necessary by helper applications can support all of the different types of note envisaged above. There are limitations in the current browser implementations for hand-held devices. Most are very basic and do not support many of the more recently developed features of HTML. However, we anticipate rapid developments in this area, at least for the more powerful PDAs such as those running Windows CE or the new generation of Apple MessagePads. In the meantime, several of the less powerful devices should still be able to support simple browsers with limited graphical capabilities.

There are clearly a number of benefits to our project that arise from using HTML as the language for implementing field notes. The most immediately significant are the widespread familiarity with HTML amongst our target user community and a reduced need for software development. Reliance on an existing standard should ease the adoption of unfamiliar tools, and existing authoring programs and browsers can be used wherever possible. A desktop note authoring and editing system was originally seen as a major development effort, one that can be largely avoided by adopting this approach.

5 Context as metadata

There was, of course, one fundamental problem that needed to be solved if we were to develop an HTML based note system. Brown's SGML form provides special purpose fields to hold the contextual information needed to trigger a note. How could we represent this information in HTML? The solution came from the realisation that there is a close correspondence between context-awareness and resource discovery, and that context can be seen as a form of resource discovery metadata.

Resource discovery is a topic more normally associated with library catalogues and Internet search engines. Users of mobile context-aware applications are also engaging in a resource discovery activity. Firstly, they would register a set of contexts in which they were interested, for example, location and temporal period. This corresponds to the entry of keywords or other terms in a search engine. Then, as they move about their environment, the system tracks their location and retrieves information appropriate to their current location. For example, when returning to the site of a DMV visited the previous summer, one user might apply the following constraints:

Subject: earthwork, building Temporal coverage: medieval Created by: Nick Ryan Date created: 1996-06-01 ~ 1996-09-30 A similarly equipped companion might apply a different set of constraints: Subject: flora, fauna Temporal coverage: 1996 Created by: David Morse Date created: 1996-06-01 ~ 1996-09-30

Then, when walking over the same ground, the two users would be presented with quite different sets of notes corresponding to their different interests.

With a conventional search engine, one might restrict the required location to a comparatively large area and the search result might contain a very large number of hits. Alternatively, many separate queries could be submitted, each referencing only a very small area. The context-aware system can be thought of as taking the second approach, but with the repetitive querying being handled automatically.

The huge volume of resources available on the Internet is a major factor in the recent growth in interest in cataloguing and resource discovery metadata. Amongst the more promising of these developments is the Dublin Core[3]. This comprises fifteen basic elements suitable for describing a wide range of resources. Although not intended to be limited to describing Web resources, much of the early work on the Dublin Core has used metadata examples embedded in HTML META tags and there has been agreement on a suitable syntax. We have taken this syntax as a starting point for defining our own set of contextual elements to form an MCFE field note metadata schema that closely follows the pattern of the basic Dublin Core elements. An extended discussion of this aspect of the project and the definition of the MCFE field note metadata elements is available on the project web site (note 1).

6 Prototype applications

In the early stages of the project we have concentrated on evaluating earlier work, gathering requirements, evaluating possible hardware platforms and developing simple prototypes. The requirements gathering stage benefited from collaboration with a number of colleagues in archaeology and other fieldwork oriented disciplines. During this time we were also able to carry out a field evaluation of a simple stick-e note system developed by Jason Pascoe as part of his doctoral research. This ran on a Hewlett Packard HP200LX, essentially a miniature MS-DOS based computer, and provided much of the basic functionality that we would expect to see in a context-aware system. Starting from this prototype we were able to concentrate rapidly on application requirements. Amongst those identified were a need to handle many types of input, including free text, forms and sketches. Field notes are not always associated with simple point locations; for many applications the ability to record the route taken along a linear earthwork, or the boundary of an enclosure are equally important. Also immediately apparent was a need for a background map on which sketch detail could be superimposed, with the capability of indicating the locations of available notes in the area of interest.

7 Hardware

In addition to application requirements, this early system also pointed to a number of hardware issues. It became clear that, for many purposes, a keyboard was not the most appropriate input device for use in the field, particularly for graphical input. Indeed, the conventional 'clam shell' design of the HP200LX and similar machines made it difficult to hold in one hand, and it is most easy to operate when seated. Although it was easily pocketable, had a far greater battery life and was far lighter than a laptop computer, it shared several disadvantages with the larger machines. These considerations led us to an evaluation of hand-held machines capable of pen rather than keyboard input. Although we concluded that the ideal hand-held field computer does not yet exist, at least at an affordable price, the Apple Newton MessagePad and the US Robotics Pilot both offered a reasonable approximation to our requirements. We are continuing to watch the hand-held market with interest, while using both of these machines for application development. Both machines have distinct benefits and disadvantages. The Newton is quite large and relatively heavy, but this is offset by a large clear screen and, in the more recent MP2000 model by a very powerful processor. The Pilot has a very small screen but is also inexpensive, light and able to fit in a shirt pocket.

Apple handwriting recognition has improved significantly in recent years while the Pilot uses the 'Graffiti' method of recognising simplified character shapes. The Graffiti software is also available for the Newton. Both machines also provide straightforward means of recording sketches as graphical shapes.

8 GPS equipment

Many archaeologists will probably associate the use of GPS with high precision survey work. However, whilst expensive survey quality equipment is appropriate for tasks such as locating grids for excavation or geophysical survey, there are many circumstances in which lower precision is acceptable. Whilst we anticipate applications of context awareness in precision survey applications, the remit of this project is to investigate the use of relatively low-cost devices, so we have chosen two quite different types of 'navigational quality' devices, manufactured by Garmin and Trimble.

The main limitation in the positional accuracy of these devices comes from the deliberate introduction of errors in the satellite signals by the US Department of Defense. This error component, known as Selective Availability, ensures that 95% of computed locations are within 100 metres of the true location. Accuracy can be improved by long term averaging of readings, typically over several hours, or by differential correction using a second receiver at a known location. Averaging methods typically give an accuracy better than 30 metres and differential correction can achieve 10-15 metres, or better. For a basic introduction to GPS, see

Trimble 1997, and for detailed coverage of GPS navigation and survey techniques, see Leick 1995.

The Garmin GPS45XL is one of several inexpensive hand-held receivers readily available from marine and outdoor equipment shops. It is capable of tracking up to eight satellites and generates machine-readable output in NMEA form[2]. This format is intended for communication between marine and aircraft navigation systems, but includes generally useful information such as current time and position.

The precision of these devices is limited by Selective Availability, but they are capable of accepting differential correction input from an RTCM-104 beacon transmitter (RTCM 1994). Most of these beacons are on or near coasts to serve the marine navigation community, and in some countries a fee is charged for their use. Accuracy is typically better than 15 metres, but the added costs of receivers and reception licences would represent a two to three times increase in the cost of our equipment, and add significantly to its bulk.

The Trimble 'SVeeSix-CM3' and 'Lassen-SK8' are both bare printed circuit board devices intended for use in a variety of applications including vehicle navigation systems. The cost of the board is similar to that of the complete Garmin hand-held system, and it must be built into a box with an appropriate power supply and interface electronics. Details of the electrical interface can be found on the project web site (note 1).

Command input and data output is in Trimble Serial Interface Protocol (TSIP), a proprietary format employing binary command and report packets. Both accept RTCM-104 correction data input on a second serial port. On the SVeeSix-CM3, the second port is used for input only whereas the Lassen-SK8 outputs NMEA format on this port.

The main benefit gained from using TSIP is in the range of data that it makes available. Access is provided not only to computed position, but also to all satellite data including orbital parameters and the raw 'pseudorange' data from which position can be computed. When this information is recorded, it is possible to apply differential corrections by post- processing techniques. If the corrected locations are required whilst in the field, a second receiver located at a known fixed location at or near the field site can supply the necessary corrections. However, high precision observations are also made at many sites around the world and are readily available via the Internet. In either case the method is not dependent on the availability of differential beacon transmitters.

9 Software applications

Prototype applications have been developed for both the Newton and Pilot machines. The development of these has been largely independent, but to a common basic specification. This approach has enabled the two developers to concentrate on different aspects of context aware applications, with the intention that the experience gained from the two prototypes can later be combined in a single design for the second generation tools. The Pilot application builds on the earlier HP200LX software and has been designed to help investigation of note triggering and rapid data entry using simple forms (figure 1). It is particularly suited to recording multiple similar observations at a single point, or whilst walking along a transect. This approach should make it equally suited to a range of tasks from wildlife censuses to archaeological fieldwalking. Notes are stored in a compact internal format on the Pilot and converted to and from HTML when they are exchanged with the desktop machine.

Figure 1. Prototype context aware application running on a US Robotics Pilot computer.

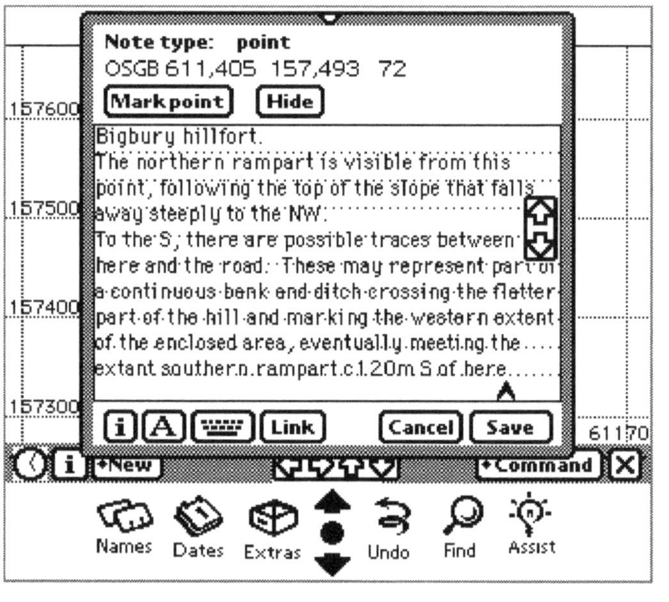

Figure 2. Creating a text note with the Newton field note application.

At present, the Pilot application can only be used with the NMEA format navigational messages from the GPS units. This makes it best suited to use as a low-cost device in combination with a simple hand-held device such as the Garmin GPS45. However, accuracy is limited by Selective Availability unless position averaging at a fixed location or a live feed from a differential beacon receiver can be used.

The main tasks addressed in the Newton prototype are the use of native HTML notes, an active map display, co-ordinate transformation to UTM or Ordnance Survey grid, and improved locational accuracy. The system is currently limited to storing text notes, but these are automatically generated in HTML form, together with all associated metadata (figure 2). Notes and their metadata can be retrieved by clicking on icons displayed on the map, which also indicates the users track and current position (figure 3). The notes are stored using the built-in 'notepad' application and can be edited in this (figure 4), or within the application. For read access, notes can be opened using a shareware HTML browser, Newt's Cape (Weyer 1997) (figure5).

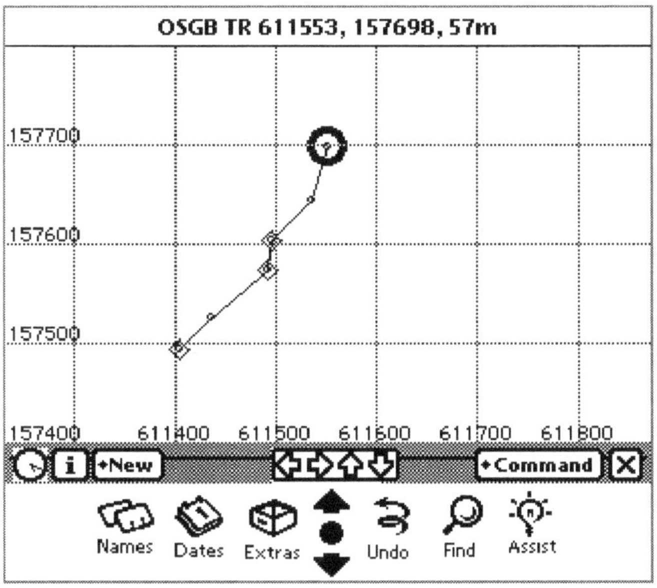

Figure 3. Newton map display showing track, current position (heavy circle) and the location of nearby field notes (diamonds).

The Newton application has been designed to work with the Trimble GPS units and so can record computed positions as well as the raw 'pseudorange' measurements from each satellite. Although a live differential feed can be used with these units, we can achieve higher accuracy at much lower cost by post-processing the raw measurements.

10 The next stage of the project

After further development of the prototype software described above, the next steps will involve extensive field trials in a variety of different areas. Members of the project team will be working with colleagues from a range of disciplines to test the prototypes in several graduate training and research situations.

With colleagues in the environmental sciences we will be taking part in graduate training and research programmes including bird censuses on the Isle of Mull and giraffe feeding behaviour in Kenya. Archaeological and historical fieldwork will include taking part in research surveys of a roman town in Andalusia and 17-19th century seasonal pastoral settlements in the mountains of southern Corsica. We also plan to produce several collections of field notes covering the natural and archaeological environment around our base at Canterbury. These and other field trials will be reported at future conferences and interim reports will also appear on the project Web pages.

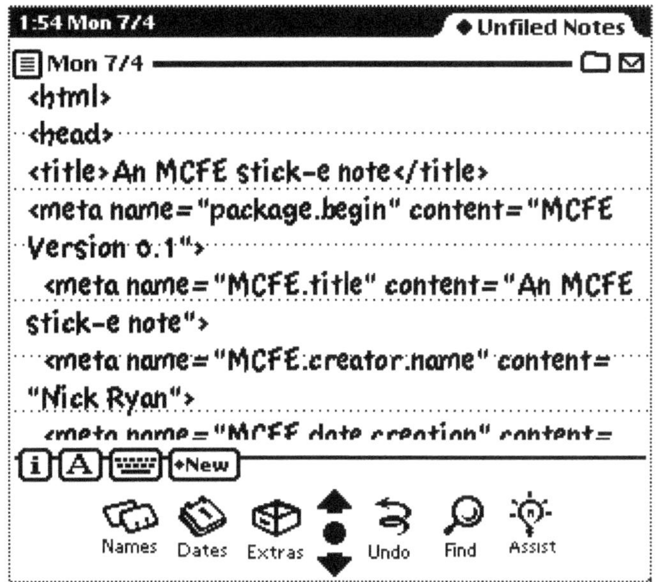

Figure 4. HTML source for a field note stored in the built-in notepad application on the Newton.

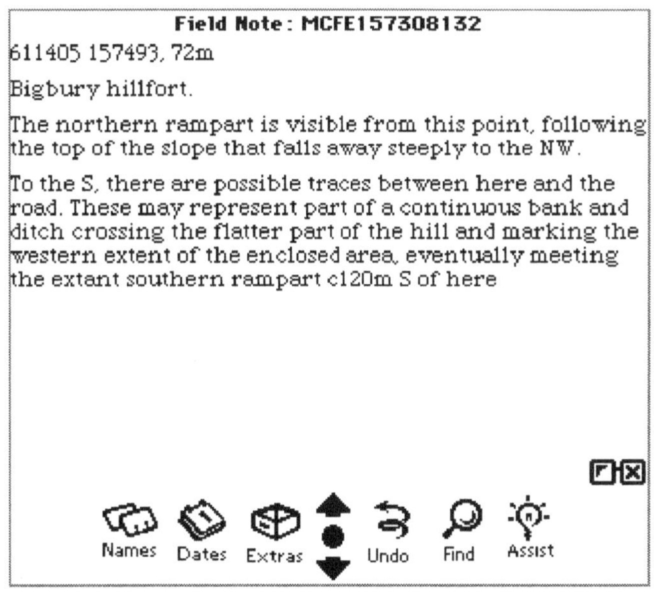

Figure 5. Viewing a field note in the NewtsCape HTML browser.

Following this period of field testing, the second year of the project will concentrate on three main areas:

1. Refinement of field software in the light of lessons learned in the field.
2. Development of desktop facilities including the storage and manipulation of large collections of spatially referenced field notes.
3. Examining the suitability of tools developed primarily in a research and graduate training context for undergraduate field training.

11 Conclusions

Context-awareness is a widely applicable concept. Many users of desktop and mobile computer systems are familiar with diary and 'personal organiser' software that is able to provide reminders of meetings and other events through a limited temporal awareness. With a computer that is also able to determine location such systems could be extended to provide only those reminders that are appropriate to a location. For example, a reminder to go to a particular shop or library when the user next visits London.

By generalising this view of context to cover a range of physical and logical attributes of the user's environment, such as particular subjects, authorship of information or temporal coverage, we are able to produce a powerful and flexible platform for field applications. The nature of mobile computing is changing very rapidly. With the increasing capabilities of hand-held computers and the equally rapid development of mobile communications and small, low power consumption GPS units, we anticipate greater integration of these components in mass-produced units. We believe that context awareness can make a significant contribution to the application of such equipment and offer an ideal basis for the development of fieldwork applications.

Acknowledgments

We are indebted to the following for their helpful collaboration and the opportunity to participate in their various fieldwork activities:

Julian Richards, Department of Archaeology, University of York.

David Wheatley and Simon Keay, Department of Archaeology, Southampton University.

Alan Fielding, Dept of Biological Sciences, Manchester Metropolitan University.

Janet Bagg, Department of Social Anthropology, University of Kent at Canterbury.

Notes

1 'Mobile Computing in a Fieldwork Environment' (MCFE) is a two-year project funded by the JISC Technology Application Program (JTAP), grant number JTAP-3/217. The MCFE project web pages are at http://www.cs.ukc.ac.uk/research/infosys/mobicomp/

2 The National Maritime Electronics Association home page is at: http://www4.coastalnet.com/nmea/default.html

3 The Dublin Core Metadata Element Set home page is at http://purl.org/metadata/dublin_core/

Bibliography

Brown, P, Bovey, J D, and Chen, X, 1997 Context-aware Applications: from the Laboratory to the Marketplace, *IEEE Personal Communications*, 4(5)

Martlew, R D, and Cheetham, P N, 1995 The development and implementation of a computer-based learning package in archaeology, in J. Huggett and N. S. Ryan (eds.), *Computer Applications and Quantitative Methods in Archaeology 1994*. BAR International Series 600, Tempvs Reparatvm, Oxford, 1995

Pascoe, J, 1997 The Stick-e Note Architecture: Extending the Interface Beyond the User, *International Conference on Intelligent User Interfaces*, 261-264, Orlando, Florida, USA

RTCM 1994 *Recommended Standards for Differential Navstar GPS Service*, Version 2.1,
Radio Technical Commission for Maritime Services, Washington, USA

Trimble 1997: *All About GPS*, http://www.trimble.com/gps/

Leick, A, 1995 *GPS Satellite Surveying*, Wiley, New York, USA.

Weyer, S, 1997 *Newt's Cape web browser*, http://www.netaxs.com/~weyer/newton/releases.html

Williams, N, 1997 *The Virtual Field Course*, http://www.geog.le.ac.uk/vfc/

Contact details

Nick Ryan, Jason Pascoe, David Morse
Computing Laboratory
University of Kent at Canterbury
Canterbury
Kent, CT2 7NF
UK
email: N.S.Ryan@ukc.ac.uk, J.Pascoe@ukc.ac.uk,
D.R.Morse@ukc.ac.uk

IT-based Documentation of Large Scale Excavations - Drengsted: A Case Study

Lars Christian Nørbach

CAA 97

Abstract

Managing the amount of data from large scale excavations with conventional methods is often a cumbersome job and leads frequently to backlog problems - an increasing number of Danish excavations are left unpublished. A new IT-based approach on the data from the Drengsted site, excavated during the 1960s and 1970s has been shown to be an appropriate method for handling data from a large scale excavation. The methods and applications used are discussed, and the paper also focuses on how future backlog problems can be avoided.

1 Introduction

The project presented here: *A settlement analysis of sites with iron production from 200 AD to 600 AD in Denmark* is a part of the research programme: *Settlement and Cultural Landscape*, funded by the Danish Research Council of Humanities. The main goals of the project are to analyse the distribution of iron production within a number of sites and across the landscape. The research area is present day Denmark.

Several sites dating to the Late Roman and Early Germanic Iron Age form the basis of the analysis. So far five sites with excavated areas ranging from 50.000 sq. m. to a few thousand sq. m. have been IT-documented and thereby made ready for a more carefull analysis at site-level. IT-based documentation was considered to be less time consuming than traditional methods, and the opportunity to present the results rapidly was a major reason for the choice. The use of IT-based documentation of large excavations has little precedence in Danish archaeology, consequently much experience was gained during the procedure.

Analysis and visualiation was carried out within the userfriendly MapInfo. This was chosen initially because of its accessibility along with its capability to manage both graphical data and databases saimultaneously. The main aim of this article is to describe the software and methods used in the process. The recording of the Drengsted-site situated in the south-western part of Jutland is an appropriate example to demonstrate this.

Drengsted is a well known and important site in Danish archaeology. An Iron Age hamlet; the site has structures dating from the Early Pre-Roman Iron Age (c. 4th to c. 3rd century BC) as well as occupation in the second half of the Late Roman and Early Germanic Iron Age (late 4th century to late 6th century AD) (Nørbach 1997). The site is only partially published. The latter period is of primary interest to this project. Approximately 50.000 sq. m. were excavated in a series of campaighns between 1957 and 1973 initially under the supervision of Dr. Olfert Voss, operating from the University of Aarhus and later from the National Museum of Denmark. More recent excavations were carried out by the author in 1996 and were intended to find the limits of the hamlet.

2 Data entry

The data sources related to the Drengsted-site are generally representative of a Danish large scale excavation and are as follows:

1. Excavation plans and related finds databases.
2. Graphical documentation of selected finds e.g. pottery important for dating.
3. Archaeomagnetic survey.
4. The central SMR records held by the National Museum of Denmark
5. Soil maps made by the Geological Survey of Denmark (GEUS).
6. Historic cadastral maps.

It is difficult to think of an IT-project without considering the labour and problems associated with data entry, and the Dregsted project is no exception to this. The excavation plans represented a number of levels of documentation therefore different methods for IT-documentation were used. The aim was, of course, always to produce vector plans in order to make use of MapInfo´s capability of combining objects like postholes within, for example, a house-structure and attach information to the structures. Some excavation plans were manually digitised and others (most of the plans from the Drengsted) could be scanned first, and then vectorised in a application like R2V (Raster to Vector) from Able Software and imported into MapInfo as DXF-files.

R2V can produce closed objects in DXF which are interpreted as regions when imported into MapInfo. Unfortunately, one cannot take full advantage of this because of the frequency of closely lying objects on site. Groups of adjacent features, e.g. postholes, are often percived as a single object by the scannersoftware and they are then given common lines. This is a problem if the aim is to get distinct objects. This problem can only be solved by time consuming manual editing.

The finds database (with a flat hierachy) was Microsoft Access; chosen because the National Museum of Denmark is using also Microsoft Access as a common interface to the

Danish Central SMR (Hansen 1992; 1994). Using identical tools always helps to integrate data from different archives.

Beside the textual information of the finds, approximately 150 finds from Drengsted are recorded in PhotoDraw, a software product combining photography and digital halftoning techniques. The advantages of this method are primarily a document of the object produced approximately 4 times quicker than with conventional methods. Secondly it produces faster files compared to conventional photos. Besides this it is relatively easy to display the object in the requested size (Holm 1997). By using this technique it is possible to reach a high level of documentation. The number of artefacts thus recorded are beyond the limits of conventional manual drawing methods (Fig. 1).

Figure 1: Pottery from Drengsted displayed in PhotoDraw. ACC cup with ornaments. Created by Jørgen Holm.

Historical cadastral maps contain important information about the historic and prehistoric landscape. They are an exellent source for demonstrating the exploitation of the landscape before the agricultural reforms in Denmark at the end of the 18th century AD, and before the introduction of modern farming. The maps are scanned and displayed as bitmaps, then registered together with the excavation plans of the same area. The historical maps can with advantages be used at the site level to demonstrate the very local settlement pattern. Unfortunately, MapInfo only displays one bitmap at a time. A composite picture containing several bitmaps must be composed in a picture processing application like Adope Illustrator before integration within MapInfo.

The central SMR is supplied with my own documentation at local museus to ensure that the data are up to date, and modern maps displaying the soil types provide the data source at the regional level. MapInfo provides good tools for simply displaying maps including site distribution across different soil types. Simple analystical operations such as buffer, cluster, classify etc. can also be carrried out using MaoInfo, but when it comes to more complex analytical operations such as analytical operations on elevation models you are left with no possibility other than to turn to an application like ArcView.

When considering the disadvantages of MapInfo the lack of an ability to work in 3-D is important. However the problems of working in 2-D can in some way be "solved" by working in different layers and attaching the levels to the finds database.

Getting a composite plan can be a cumbersome job when working with large scale excavations and MapInfo allows little flexibility when you want to display several different coordinate systems within one overall system. This problem can of course be solved by using another application with such a capability, this would, however, probably result in loss of data attached to the objects (e.g. information of finds in postholes). Despite this, there is a way of carrying out this operation within MapInfo - with a little help from Microsoft Excel. The displacement coordinates and rotation angle can be calculated in Excel and then entered in the MapBasic Programme: Rotator (note1).

3 Conclusion

MapInfo with its low learning curve and potential for integration with Microsoft Access provides a good platform for a usefull GIS which will fulfil the demands of most archaeologists. As the case study of Drengsted showed, the application can handle the most common data sources from a large scale excavation. Beside this, the IT-based documentation saved time during post-excavation analysis, and with this in mind it is clear that the IT-based documentation of excavations probably will help avoiding future back log problems in Danish archaeology.

The methods and applications used also clearly demonstrated that the basic demands of the IT-based documentation of data sources is a tight interrelationship between graphical objects and databases (Madsen 1997). It is therefore important that one does not stop with the ordinary CAD drawings, a common practise in Danish archaeology, in the mistaken believe this will pass for a GIS. This is, in my opinion, a waste of time and good money.

Notes

1 To calculate the angle V between two coordinate systems A and B the following equation can be used. The coordinate system A is an overall coordinate system where two coordinates are known (x_1; y_1), (x_2; y_2). The coordinate system B is a local coordinate system with two known coordinates (u_1; v_1), (u_2; v_2) equal to the two known coordinates from A. If $x_1 / x_2 = 0$ then transverse x_1 with y_1 and x_2 with y_2 and u_1 with u_2 and v_1 with v_2. The equation used in Excel is; $V = \tan^{-1} ((((v_2 - v_1) / (u_2 - u_1) - (y_2 - y_1) / (x_2 - x_1)) / (1 + (y_2 - y_1) \times (v_2 - v_1) / ((x_2 - x_1) \times (u_2 - u_1))))$ For help with the equation and Excel, I thank Mads Kæhler Holst.

Bibliography

Hansen, H J, 1992 Content, Use and Perspectives of DKC, the National Record of Sites and Monuments. In C. U. Larsen (ed.) *Sites and Monuments. National Archaeological Records,* 23-42.

Hansen, H J, 1994: Den elektroniske sognebeskrivelse - landsdækkende arkæologi på computer. Mark og Montre. *Museerne i Ribe Amt 1994,* 54-58.

Holm, J, 1997 G5.1. PhotoDraw. *Arkæologisk Felthåndbog.* Det Arkæologiske Nævn.

Madsen, T, 1997 GIS and Scandinavian Archaeology - A tale from the real world. In Johnson and North (eds.) *GIS Applications in Archaeology at Forli: Proceedings of Colloquium II, UISPP XIIIth, Forli, Italy, September 1996.* Sydney University Archaeological Methods Series 5.

Nørbach, L, 1997 Drengsted - Backlog Problems in Danish Archaeology. In Johnson & North (eds.) *GIS Applications in Archaeology at Forli: Proceedings of Colloquium II, UISPP XIIIth, Forli, Italy, September 1996.* Sydney University Archaeological Methods Series 5.

Contact details

Lars Christian Nørbach
Settlement and Cultural Landscape
Department of Prehistoric Archaeology
University of Aarhus
DK-8270 Højbjerg
DENMARK
email: Farkln@moes.hum.aau.dk
http://www.hum.aau.dk/dk/forhisto/fark/farkln/home.htm

CAA 97

Finds Analysis and Curation
Abstracts of papers held on CD-ROM

Mobile Computing for Real Time Support in Archaeological Excavations

Massimo Ancona, Gabriella Dodero, Vittoria Gianuzzi, Carlotta Fierro, Vincenzo Tiné and Antonella Traverso

The paper presents a joint ongoing project between archaeologists and computer scientists at the University of Genova. The goal of the cooperation is the development of a hardware/software integrated system to be applied to stratigraphic excavation; such a system is based on two new technologies: wireless mobile computing and pen-based man-machine interfaces.

Theoretical Foundations and Enabling Technologies for Cultural Resources Management Systems

César A. González Pérez

Cultural Resource Management (CRM) involves many activities, objects, relationships, and people, and a number of tasks, procedures, and conventions. All this work has been done until now manually, although many initiatives have been carried out to computerize, automate, or otherwise facilitate the everyday work. This paper presents the information technologies that have been adopted within the CRISys Project, funded by the Spanish Telematic Programme (project code TEL96-1386). This project is still in its first year, so the technologies described here are likely to change during the project's estimated life of three to five years. A sound theoretical basement is essential for any information system; we have chosen an approach to the archaeological record called the Valorative Sequence, and the object-oriented paradigm from the computer realm. Object-oriented modelling allows us to model the perceived world as a set of classes and relationships. In particular, the Fusion method by Coleman et al. offers a full lifecycle methodology for object-oriented software development. Also, an object-oriented database is required to store information in a convenient way. Almost every single object in CRM can be geographically located, so GIS (Geographic Information Systems) technology must be used to provide a geographic frame for everyday work. Two- and three-dimensional terrain models, capable of offering a number of views such as contours, sections, or human-eye perspectives are considered, and data geovisualization is used to gather information from computerized landscapes. Documents play a very important role in CRM, and a documental management system is crucial. Time-aware document versioning, intra- and inter-team workflow, and collaborative authoring are required functionality, and ISO-standard SGML (Standard Generalized Markup Language) has been adopted as a foundation. From a more technical viewpoint, the client/server architecture is necessary to achieve concurrent access and high performance. A flexible four-tiered schema, the WRAP model, has been adopted, decomposing the system into World, Representation, Application, and Presentation layers, which can be balanced between client and server endpoints as desired.

A GIS and Hypertext-based System for Excavation Documentation

Margarita Dekoli and Thanasis Hadzilacos

The time-honoured method of recording an excavation, namely writing on a hardbound notebook has several advantages: robustness, ease of use and uniform recording of all elements that constitute the description of the excavation in progress. It also has some drawbacks but the lack of any reasonable alternative so far has made them seem natural : looking for anything specific requires a full sequential scan, statistical processing or querying requires re-inputting the information in a database and publishing requires a whole new reset. Recent advantages in computational technology, mainly the power of personal computers reasonably priced, may offer an alternative system of excavation documentation that will alter the present situation dramatically. In this paper we present a PC-based system for the documentation of an excavation which allows direct storing of text, organised data, maps and pictures. The excavation log is recorded as hypertext and the navigation across the information is richer, through hyperlinks. The data from the excavation are stored and can be queried spatially or based on their description and are presented in different ways. So, the system is a composition of a GIS system, a database and a web browser for viewing the information and with the help of a web server, questions can be submitted to the database and the results can be viewed.

Quantifying shape: African Red Slip Ware and eating habits
Peter Durham and J. J. Hawthorne

African Red Slip Ware (ARS) is a particularly common late Roman fineware and has been extensively studied. However few previous studies have examined the artefacts' shapes for any purpose other than the generation of typologies. In addition, such studies have tended to concentrate on particular diagnostic parts of the shape rather than the shape as a whole. The problem with using shape as a whole is that it is difficult to quantify. In the past, this difficulty has been tackled by quantifying aspects of a shape and comparing those rather than the shapes themselves. The current work uses a methodology developed by Durham, based on well-known pattern matching algorithms to quantify shape, to enable artefacts' shapes to be compared directly. We have analysed the shapes of the entire ARS form range in relation to economic trends, and this has highlighted a hitherto unsuspected relationship between these factors. Specifically, it has been found that the vessels of the third century cluster strongly together, all having a flat bottomed profile which is different to both earlier and later vessels. These third century pots are also of substantially greater capacity then the others, and these features together suggest that the comparative dearth of pots in the third century is more related to size and shape than economics.

A Computerized Data Base for Lithic Use-Wear Analysis
E. S. Lohse and D. Sammons

Recent advances in digital imaging and construction of computerized data bases have great potential for the development of more sophisticated lithic use-wear analyses. We have applied commercially available image analysis packages to the study of stone tool assemblages. Use of high resolution digital imaging techniques greatly aids in the identification and recording of distinctive attributes and patterns of stone tool manufacture and wear. Importing images and selected measurements to standardized data bases and statistical packages, as well as automeasurement routines, greatly facilitates information transfer and analysis. This paper describes the system we have developed, identifies problems, and suggests future directions. To date, many problems have been practical, solvable technical ones focused on usable memory, transfer rates, and file sizes. More compelling problems are definition of data base structure and development of explicit terminology and standardized measurements indicative of current research. We have constructed an analytical framework in Visual dBASE. We are now developing a presentation that will train student analysts in use of our analytical system through simulations run on a highly interactive CD-ROM. This paper summarizes construction of that CD-ROM and outlines avenues for future work.

The Effect of Computerisation on Pottery Recording
P. D. Rauxloh and R. P. Symonds

This paper discusses the effect which the implementation of a new relational database system has had on the way Roman pottery is recorded, analysed and interpreted. Instead of a technical description, it considers some of the issues which the implementation has raised, and in particular the improvement it provided for the validation of ceramic data. The paper further differentiates itself from a straight technical discussion by being the joint product of the system's developer, and a Roman ceramic specialist who uses it.

Computer Useage in Post-Excavation: what do we really, really want?
Jane C. Evans

No abstract supplied

www.ingramcontent.com/pod-product-compliance
Lightning Source LLC
LaVergne TN
LVHW072250300926
849160LV00018B/1631